HUMAN RIGHTS
IN AUSTRALIAN LAW

Life is nothing without expectation.
Peter Carey, *Peeling*.

HUMAN RIGHTS IN AUSTRALIAN LAW

Principles, Practice and Potential

Editor
David Kinley

Foreword
The Hon Justice Michael Kirby AC CMG

The Federation Press
1998

Published in Sydney in 1998 by

The Federation Press
71 John St, Leichhardt, NSW, 2040
PO Box 45, Annandale, NSW, 2038
Ph: (02) 9552 2200 Fax: (02) 9552 1681

National Library of Australia Cataloguing-in-Publication data:
 Human rights in Australia law: principles, practice and potential

Includes index.
ISBN 1 86287 306 2

1. Human rights – Australia. 2. Civil rights – Australia. 1. Kinley, David.

342.94085

Typeset by The Federation Press, Leichhardt, NSW.
 Printed by Ligare Pty Ltd, Riverwood, NSW.

FOREWORD

The Hon Justice Michael Kirby AC CMG

This book chronicles nothing less than a legal revolution. Every chapter records the growing impact of international human rights law on Australian law.

In busy lives it is easy to overlook or forget particular developments: whether in statutory or judicial law. This book pulls the threads together. It demonstrates, in a way that even sceptics cannot ignore, that international human rights law is now permeating the nooks and crannies of Australian substantive and procedural law.

One might perhaps expect these developments to occur in areas of Federal public law: constitutional, administrative, migration, environmental and criminal law. There are found the actions of the Executive Government which, in its international aspect, is involved in, and increasingly committed to, the world-wide movement for the protection of human rights. But the development is now affecting public law in the States and areas of private law: family law, the protection of individual privacy and equal opportunity decisions. No corner of Australian law, it seems, is now exempt from the influence of international human rights law.

The special value of this book is that it demonstrates this fact in a multitude of practical instances where courts and tribunals, faced with difficult decisions, have looked beyond the hitherto orthodox sources of legal reasoning to a new realm of intellectual discourse which is growing beyond Australia but which has relevance to the way in which we order our society.

The gradual reconciliation of Australian municipal law with the expanding notions of international human rights law has actually been going on for more than 50 years. However, it has gathered pace in recent decades. It received a notable impetus from the reasoning of the justices of the High Court of Australia in *Mabo v Queensland (No 2)*[1] and in *Minister for Immigration and Ethnic Affairs v Teoh*.[2] To those brought up in the comfortable days of the British Empire and in the often cloistered, technologically resistant, world of the legal profession, the new notions were confronting, and sometimes uncongenial. They required something of a leap of the imagination – a feat unpleasant for many minds. But once it is appreciated that the legal, political and technological world in which Australian law must operate has changed forever, the accommodation between that world and the international law of human rights became both desirable and inevitable.

Scarcely a week goes by in a sittings of the High Court of Australia that a case does not involve, in some way or other, an international treaty to which Australia is a party or values that find reflection in the principles of international law. The ultimate boundaries of the impact of the new sources of jurisprudence are not yet known. For example, in the *Hindmarsh Island Bridge* case[3] I suggested that, in

---

1   (1992) 175 CLR 1 at 42.

2   (1995) 183 CLR 273 at 288-92.

3   *Kartinyeri v Commonwealth* (1998) 72 ALJR 722 at 765-66.

construing an ambiguous provision of the Australian Constitution (such as the race power), regard might be had to universal human rights. Not only does the Australian Constitution speak to the people of this nation who gave it birth. It speaks to the international community of which Australia is a part. Some have questioned this approach. But no one can doubt that, in the coming century, the basic laws of every nation will go through a process of *rapprochement* with the extraordinary developments of international law affecting nation states and their peoples. This is an outcome of globalisation and regionalisation; and also of the technology that links us together and of the common problems that demand multi-national solutions.

It is important to see the legal developments, in the interstices of the detail of Australian law recounted in this book, in the context of the broad changes in the world about us. Fifty years after the adoption of the *Universal Declaration of Human Rights*, the changes increasingly concern the protection of fundamental human rights and the removal of derogations from those rights. The Parliaments of Australia, Federal and State, have the primary responsibility to give effect to such standards. But the judges of Australia, aided by an informed legal profession, have functions that cannot be disclaimed. The central lesson of this book is that Australian courts and tribunals are accepting their new obligations in a way that would have seemed astonishing even 20 years ago.

The most striking feature of these essays is that they demonstrate beyond argument what a practical subject the study of human rights jurisprudence is now becoming for the judge and lawyer in Australia. In keeping with this practical approach, this book is not only a helpful anthology of pertinent law. It contains, at the end, a most useful collection of the references to the Internet sites where the relevant texts and jurisprudence can be found.

Australians, who have been blessed with a stable Constitution, independent judges and adaptive statute and common law have never been a backwater of antipodean legal isolation. For two centuries we have had the stimulus of legal principles from England and other countries of the common law. We still have these. But in time for a new millennium we can now add to our treasury of ideas an additional source of legal principle to guide us and to help us. This book shows that an irreversible process has been set in train. It is natural. It is timely. It is happening.

Michael Kirby
High Court of Australia
Canberra
1 October 1998

CONTENTS

Foreword *Justice Michael Kirby*   v
Preface   ix
List of Contributors   xi
Table of Cases   xvii
Table of Legislation   xxiv
Table of main international human rights instruments relevant to Australia
   (*Kate Eastman*)   xxxii

Part One
Human Rights and the Legal Framework

1   The legal dimension of human rights   2
    David Kinley

2   The role of the judiciary in the development of human rights in
    Australian law   26
    Sir Anthony Mason

3   Constitutional law and human rights   47
    Stephen Gageler and Arthur Glass

4   Administrative law and human rights   63
    John McMillan and Neil Williams

Part Two
Human Rights and Substantive Law

5   Indigenous Australian peoples and human rights   92
    Jennifer Neilsen and Gary Martin

6   Criminal law and human rights   120
    Simon Bronitt and Maree Ayers

7   Immigration law and human rights   141
    Mary Crock and Penelope Mathew

8   Family law and human rights   169
    Juliet Behrens and Phillip Tahmindjis

9   Labour law and human rights   194
    Therese MacDermott

10   Environmental law and human rights   221
    Nicholas Brunton

CONTENTS

11 Information technology law and human rights   243
   Chris Arup and Greg Tucker

12 Health law and human rights   267
   Ian Freckelton and Bebe Loff

Part Three
Human Rights and Legal Practice and Procedure

13 The operation of anti-discrimination laws in Australia   292
   Peter Bailey and Annemarie Devereux

14 Using human rights laws in litigation: the practitioner's perspective   319
   Kate Eastman and Chris Ronalds

15 Human rights research and electronic resources   343
   Michael Bliss and Shahyar Roushan

Index   363

PREFACE

Human rights are not a prominent part of Australian legal tradition; still less are they endemic to our legal culture. Yet, it cannot be said that the enjoyment of human rights in general in Australia is appreciably inferior to that in comparable countries in which such rights are recognised in more explicit legal terms and where rights discourse is more surely rooted in the legal heritage. Australia's legal protection of human rights is not complete; indeed, in certain respects, it is embarrassingly deficient. The absence of a Bill of Rights or a history of rights jurisprudence, however, does not mean that Australian law, and more especially Australian lawyers, are hamstrung in seeking to enhance human rights protection. Rather, lawyers and law-makers must be more inquisitive and enterprising in the methods they employ in their efforts to understand, apply and extend existing legal rights. The potential of pursuing such an innovative course lies in the use that can be made of international human rights law by which Australia is bound and relevant human rights jurisprudence of other domestic jurisdictions. Human rights may not readily be identified as such in Australian law, but they exist nonetheless. In addition to their express provision, they lie implicit in restrictions on action, and in duties, powers and procedures which are specifically provided for by law; importantly, also, they may be inferred from the absence of legal regulation or prohibition. What remains to be done is for these legal provisions to be revealed, recognised and promoted *as* human rights.

Together, the 15 chapters in the book are concerned to reverse the tendency to view "human rights law" as another category of law (if recognised as a category at all) separate or separable from other legal categories. The chapters are not arranged according to particular human rights, as is common practice in human rights law texts, but according to particular subject areas of law and legal practice. Approached singly and collectively, the chapters first expose and then analyse the human rights laws that exist within these other categories of "Law School law" and legal practice. Such an alternative conception and presentation of the relationship between law and human rights is not only new, it reflects a perspective that has to be adopted if the object of the protection and promotion of human rights through law is to be fully appreciated and more effectively pursued.

The book is divided into three parts. Part One, on the legal framework, comprises chapters that cover human rights in domestic law from a structural or generic point of view; each chapter deals with an issue that affects the overall relationship between human rights, the law and legal system in Australia. The chapters in Part Two on the substantive law focus on the coverage of human rights in specific areas of domestic law. The issues discussed generally under Part One are drawn out in the particular contexts of the subject areas addressed in the Part Two chapters. Part Three, on legal practice and procedure, covers a number of important aspects of the practice, preparation and presentation of legal arguments based on, or involving, human rights matters.

The book is intended primarily for use by legal practitioners, law students and legal scholars, as well others involved in the protection of human rights through various means, including law. It seeks to provide in an integrated form both practical guidance as to how the law and the legal system is, and can be, used to protect and promote human rights, and conceptual analysis of their location, status and opportunities for development in Australian law. The blending of legal academics and practitioners in the authorships of the chapters in the book reflects the intention to deliver on these two fronts.

Acknowledgments

The germ of the idea for this book arose out of the improbable circumstance of banter with Simon Bronitt over a burnt breakfast saved by dangerously strong coffee. The idea appealed; as, it must be said, is normally the case with Bronitt's cooking.

The mulling over the idea in the ensuing months would never have developed beyond that had I not benefitted from the support, skills and acquiescence of many others. To these folk and institutions I owe a great debt of gratitude that I am happy here to record: to my colleagues and friends at the Australian Law Reform Commission and the Human Rights and Equal Opportunity Commission at which institutions I was working (on leave from the ANU Law School) during the book's conception, and especially to Joanna Longley (of the ALRC) for her bibliopolistic beneficence; to Chris Holt and Kathy Fitzhenry of Federation Press for their advice and encouragement and for seeing worth in the idea; to Shahyar Roushan without whose critical eye, intellectual rigour, generous nature and warped wit the editorial process would have foundered; to the Law Foundation of New South Wales for providing funding for the editing process; to His Honour Justice Michael Kirby for agreeing to write the Foreword at a time when not a word of the book had been committed to paper; and, above all, to the authors of the chapters herein whose sustained enthusiasm for the theme of the book and whose ability to articulate its application to their areas of expertise was inspiring. And to Kati.

David Kinley
Sydney
8 September 1998

LIST OF CONTRIBUTORS

Christopher Arup is an Associate Professor in the School of Law and Legal studies, La Trobe University and Head of School. He researches in the areas of intellectual property, trade practices and international trade. His writing includes the monograph *Innovation, Policy and Law* which was published by Cambridge University Press in 1993. He is a former editor of *Law In Context* and presently co-editor of the Cambridge University Press international series, Studies in Law and Society.

Maree Ayers BSc LLB (Hons) (ANU) has been employed as a solicitor at the Commonwealth Director of Public Prosecutions since 1991 after stints in private practice and at the ACT Director of Public Prosecutions. Between 1990 and 1997 she tutored in Criminal Law and Procedure at the Australian National University. She is the author of *The Laws of Australia* sub-title "Consequences of Conviction" and is co-author of the loose leaf service *Watson and Watson Federal Offences*.

Peter Bailey has been a Visiting Fellow with teaching duties at the Faculty of Law in the Australian National University since 1987. Before that he was Deputy Chair and chief executive officer of the Commonwealth's Human Rights Commission and assisted the Attorney-General and his Department to negotiate with the States the acceptance of the relevant legislation and ratification of the International Covenant on Civil and Political Rights and then the passage of the legislation through the Commonwealth Parliament. He is author of *Human Rights: Australia in an International Context* (1990) and *Bringing Human Rights to Life* (1993), and has recently completed the Civil and Political Rights title (350 pages, including 125 pages on equality and discrimination) in *Halsbury's Laws of Australia*. He is also Title Editor for, and a contributor to, the Human Rights title in *The Laws of Australia*.

Juliet Behrens graduated with an Arts/Law degree from University in Tasmania in 1988. In 1988 she was an inaugural Lionel Murphy Bicentennial Post-graduate Scholar, and graduated with a PhD from the University of Tasmania in 1991. In 1991 she was appointed a lecturer in the Faculty of Law, Australian National University. She is now a Senior Lecturer in Law. Her recent work has been largely in the area of Family Law, adopting feminist and critical approaches and focusing particularly on the issue of the relevance of domestic violence to family law disputes. She is a co-author of one of the major teaching books in the area: Parker, S, Parkinson, P and Behrens, J, *Australian Family Law in Context* (1994), the second edition of which is currently in preparation. She is a member of the editorial board of the *Australian Journal of Family Law*, and the Violence Sub-Committee of the Family Law Council. In addition to her academic work, she is a part-time member of the Social Security Appeals Tribunal. She is partner-in-life to Christopher and mum to two young children.

Michael Bliss LLB (UNSW), LLM (Columbia) is currently studying for admission to the New York Bar. Between 1997 and 1998 he was a Fulbright Scholar and Bretzfelder Fellow in International Law at Columbia University. Formally, he was the Associate to the Principal Member at the Refugee Review Tribunal (1994-95) and a Legal Officer at the Refugee Review Tribunal (1995-97). He has published a number of articles in the areas of refugee law, administrative law and environmental law.

Simon Bronitt LLB (Bristol), LLM (Cambridge) is a Senior Lecturer at the Australian National University, Canberra. He teaches Criminal Law and Procedure, Criminal Justice and Criminology. His research interests range across these fields, focusing specifically on human rights issues. Recent publications include articles on HIV/AIDS, consent, rape law reform, complicity, covert policing, electronic surveillance, drugs and public order. He is a State Editor of the *Criminal Law Journal* and was recently appointed an Associate of the Australian Institute of Criminology

Nicholas Brunton is a solicitor in the environment law group of the Sydney office of Freehill, Hollingdale and Page. His practice involves acting for industry and a variety of State and Commonwealth departments and authorities in the areas of environmental, planning, local government and international law. He has been a lecturer in environmental law at the University of Melbourne for three years and in 1992-93 was the President of the Victorian Division of the National Environmental Law Association. He has written numerous articles on pollution law and policy and is the New South Wales Editor of the Butterworths Digest and the environmental law sub-editor of the *Environmental and Planning Law Journal*. He has acted in a wide range of matters including infrastructure projects, major acquisitions, contaminated sites, pollution prosecutions and planning disputes. He has spoken widely in Australia on planning and environmental law, risk management, and issues for major projects. He has recently completed a PhD thesis on coastal water pollution.

Mary Crock is a Lecturer in Law at the University of Sydney where she teaches administrative law, migration law and a variety of other public law subjects. Mary has written extensively on the subjects of migration and refugee law, and administrative law. Her text, *Immigration and Refugee Law in Australia* was published by the Federation Press in July 1998. Her interest in human rights reflects her past involvement in direct advocacy work. Mary Crock helped to establish and run the Victorian Immigration Advice and Rights Centre Inc in Melbourne, recently renamed the Refugee and Immigration Law Centre (Vic). She is Chair of the Nationality and Residence Committee, International Law Section, Law Council of Australia; Principal examiner, migration law, Specialist Accreditation programs (Victoria and New South Wales); and editor of the *Immigration Review Tribunal Digest* (Butterworths). She is also a trustee of the Australian Sanctuary and Settlement Fund, a charitable trust founded to aid in the settlement of refugees in Australia. Mary is married to Ron McCallum and has two sons and one daughter.

Annemarie Devereux is currently pursuing doctoral studies in international Human rights law at the Centre for International and Public Law, ANU. Since 1996, she has also been lecturing at the ANU in the graduate and undergraduate constitutional and human rights law courses. Her practice has mainly been in the area of public law – having worked for several years in the Office of International Law and the Office of General Counsel of the federal Attorney-General's Department, though she has spent periods working in private practice and with community legal centres. Her specialist interest in human rights has developed out of her community work, in particular with persons with mental illness, addictions and intellectual disabilities and her previous studies at the ANU and Columbia University, New York.

Kate Eastman BA LLB (UNSW) LLM (Lond) LLM (UTS) is a Sydney barrister who practises and writes in the areas of anti-discrimination, human rights and public law. She has previously worked at the Human Rights and Equal Opportunity Commission as a Senior Legal Officer, where she has participated in several High Court and Federal Court proceedings involving human rights. She is a part-time lecturer at the University of Technology, Sydney, teaching human rights law. She is also President of Australian Lawyers for Human Rights.

Ian Freckelton is a barrister in full-time practice in Victoria doing medico-legal, administrative law and white collar crime work. He is also an Adjunct Professor of Law and Legal Studies at La Trobe University and an Honorary Associate Professor of Forensic Medicine at Monash University. Dr Freckelton is a member of the Victorian Mental Health Review Board and Immediate Past President and Honorary Life Member of the Australian and New Zealand Association of Psychiatry, Psychology and Law. He edits the *Journal of Law and Medicine* and the journal, *Psychiatry, Psychology and Law*. He is also the editor of a five-volume work on *Expert Evidence*, a three-volume work on *Criminal Law, Investigation and Procedure*, and three volumes of *The Laws of Australia*. He is the author of books on health law, policing, indictable offences, evidence and criminal injuries compensation. He is currently completing books on coronial law and principles of medical law.

Stephen Gageler is a barrister practising principally in the fields of Constitutional and Administrative law. He was Associate to Sir Anthony Mason (1983-85), a Senior Legal Officer in the Commonwealth Attorney-General's Department (1985-87) and Assistant to the Commonwealth Solicitor-General (1981-89). He has published a number of articles on contract, federal jurisdiction and constitutional law and is a joint editor of Butterworth's *Practice and Procedure of the High Court and Federal Courts*.

Arthur Glass teaches law at University of New South Wales Law School. He has written in the fields of legal theory, especially on the topic of legal interpretation, and public law. He is the co-author of *Federal Constitutional Law: An Introduction* and has published articles in *Rechtstheorie, Ratio Juris*, the *Sydney Law Review* and *Law/Text/Culture*.

David Kinley is currently working as a consultant to the Human Rights and Equal Opportunity Commission writing an Internet community guide and annotated bibliography on human rights and is teaching international and domestic human rights law part-time at Sydney University and the University of New South Wales. Formally, between 1995 and mid-1998, he worked at the Australian Law Reform Commission as legal specialist in human rights, international and constitutional law. He lectured in law at the Australian National University from 1990 to mid-1998, and before that taught law, whilst completing his doctorate, at Cambridge University, 1988-89. He writes and researches mainly in the areas of human rights and public law, and is author of *The European Convention on Human Rights: Compliance without Incorporation* (Dartmouth, 1993) and co-author of *Principles of European Community Law* (Law Book Co, 1995). He is a member of the Human Rights Council of Australia.

Bebe Loff is a lawyer currently undertaking her PhD in the Department of Epidemiology and Preventive Medicine, Monash University. Ms Loff holds a Masters degree in Medical Law and Ethics from London University. She previously held the position of Manager, Policy and Legislation Review in the Health Department, Victoria and was a consultant to the Office of the Health Services Commissioner and the Mental Health Review Board. She has provided legal advice on public health law to governments of other Australian states and other countries. She was recently appointed a temporary United Nations Adviser on the topic of the ethics of HIV vaccine research. Ms Loff co-ordinates a subject entitled Health, Ethics and Human Rights in the Master of Public Health program at Monash University. She was responsible for the formation of Feminist Lawyers and the Prostitutes Collective of Victoria. She is an honorary associate to the Macfarlane Burnet Centre for Medical Research and the Department of Forensic Medicine, Monash University.

Therese MacDermott holds degrees from the University of Queensland and Oxford University. She is a Senior Lecturer in the Faculty of Law, University of Sydney, where she has taught since 1992. Her major research and teaching interests lie in the area of labour law and anti-discrimination law, with particular reference to the intersection of these two areas.

John McMillan is a Reader in the Law Faculty of the Australian National University, specialising in administrative law and constitutional law. He was formerly an Associate to Justice Mason of the High Court of Australia; a solicitor in private practice; a Principal Investigation Officer with the Common-wealth Ombudsman; and was self-employed in public interest advocacy. He is presently the administrative law consultant to the Government Services Group of national law firm, Clayton Utz. He is a founding member and currently Vice-President of the Australian Institute of Administrative Law, for which he has been the research director for a number of national conferences on administrative law. He has written widely in the public law field on topics such as freedom of information, administrative law, whistle-blowing, broadcasting, standing, and constitutional reform. His publications include, *Administrative Law: Does the Public Benefit?* (ed,

1993); *Administrative Law under the Coalition Government* (ed, 1997); *The AAT – Twenty Years Forward* (ed, 1998); and (with Senator Gareth Evans and Haddon Storey), *Australia's Constitution: Time for Change?* (1983).

Gary Martin is a Lecturer with the College of Indigenous Australian peoples, Southern Cross University. He has taught courses in Indigenous legal issues from an Indigenous Australian perspective for the past five years. He has also worked in several Indigenous Australian community organisations and enterprises, and is Public Officer to the Bundjalung Elders Council Aboriginal Corporation. He is a co-editor, along with Jennifer Nielsen and Associate Professor Greta Bird, of *Majah: Indigenous Peoples and the Law* (1996).

The Honourable Sir Anthony Mason AC KBE presently holds the positions of Chancellor of the University of New South Wales and National Fellow Research School of Social Sciences, Australian National University He is a Judge of the Supreme Court of Fiji, President of the Court of Appeal of the Solomon Islands and a non-permanent Judge of the Hong Kong Court of Final Appeal. Sir Anthony's former positions include Commonwealth Solicitor-General, Justice of the Supreme Court of New South Wales, Chief Justice of the High Court of Australia and Arthur Goodhart Professor in Legal Science, Cambridge University. Sir Anthony holds Honorary Doctorates from the Australian National University, Sydney, Melbourne, Monash, Griffith and Deakin Universities, and is an Honorary Doctor of Civil Law, Oxford University.

Penelope Mathew is a Senior Lecturer in Law at the University of Melbourne. Her key area of research is human rights, particularly the rights of refugees, and she has published a number of articles and papers in these areas. She has also worked with non-governmental human rights organisations, in Australia and elsewhere, that are concerned with the rights of refugees and asylum-seekers.

Jennifer Nielsen is a Lecturer with the School of Law and Justice, Southern Cross University. She is admitted to practise in Victoria and in New South Wales, and has worked in private practice, as well as with the Victorian Aboriginal Legal Service Inc. She has contributed to the writing of teaching materials for several units related to Indigenous legal issues, and is currently working on her Masters of Laws (Thesis) in the area of discrimination against Indigenous Australians. She is a co-editor of *Majah: Indigenous Peoples and the Law* (1996).

Chris Ronalds AM is a Sydney barrister specialising in discrimination, employment and administrative law. She has written a number of books and government reports in the areas of discrimination and redress for disadvantaged people. Her latest book is *Discrimination Law and Practice* (Federation Press, 1998).

Shahyar Roushan is a solicitor and barrister of the Supreme Court of the ACT. He studied law at the Australian National University and was awarded the Bailey Prize for Human Rights in 1995. He graduated with First Class Honours in 1996. He is also a graduate of Flinders University where he studied philosophy. From 1997 until August 1998 he worked as a government lawyer with the Human Rights Branch, in the Commonwealth Attorney General's Department. Shahyar is currently working at the South African Human Rights Commission in Cape Town. He researches and writes in the areas of human rights and critical theory, and Islamic law and human rights.

Dr Phillip Tahmindjis is the Associate Dean of the Faculty of Law at the Queensland University of Technology and is the author of numerous articles on human rights, discrimination law and family law. He has been a legal consultant to the Queensland office of the federal Human Rights and Equal Opportunity Commission and to the Queensland Anti-Discrimination Commission, as well as serving as acting Registrar of the Queensland Anti-Discrimination Tribunal and appearing as counsel before the Tribunal. He is the Chairperson of the Discrimination and Gender Equality Committee of the International Bar Association, in which capacity his current projects are a world survey of women judges and world benchmark guidelines on the non-discriminatory running of legal practices. He is the Consulting Editor for CCH Australia for the *Australian and New Zealand Equal Opportunity Law and Practice Reporter* and is currently writing a commentary on Discrimination Law for Oxford University Press and editing a book on comparative sexual harassment law for Kluwer.

Greg Tucker BA LLM is an Associate Professor in the Faculty of Business and Economics. He is the author of *Information Privacy Law in Australia* (Longman Cheshire, 1992) and two OECD reports on data protection across the OECD member countries. He has written extensively on banking law, privacy and electronic commerce. He was also a member of both federal (1995) and State (1996) government taskforces reviewing the laws relating to privacy in the context of an emerging electronic commerce environment.

Neil Williams BEc (Syd), LLB (UNSW), MPubLaw (ANU) is a Sydney barrister who practises principally in administrative law. Before commencing practice at the Bar, he held the positions of Senior Adviser to the Attorney-General, Senior Legal Officer in the Office of Legislative Drafting in the Commonwealth Attorney-General's Department and Principal Legal Officer in the Office of the Commonwealth Director of Public Prosecutions. He has taught administrative law and industrial relations, and has written extensively in administrative law, especially on the *Administrative Decisions (Judicial Review) Act* 1977 (Cth). He is co-author of *Commonwealth Criminal Law* (Federation Press, 1990) and the Butterworths *Federal Criminal Law* Service.

TABLE OF CASES

A v Australia (1997): 159, 162
A v Hayden (1984): 79
A v MIEA (1997): 345
Adelaide Company of Jehovah's Witnesses v Commonwealth (1943): 49, 333
Air Caledonie International v Commonwealth (1988): 57, 145
Airedale NHS Trust v Bland (1993): 268
AIS v Banovic (1989): 197-98
Al Saeed and Secretary, Department of Social Security, Re (1991): 65
Albert Reynolds v Times Newspapers (1998): 41
Aldridge v Booth (1988): 334, 339
Alister v R (1983): 131
AMC v Siddiqui (1996): 307
Amodu Tijani v Sec of Southern Nigeria (1921): 95
Anasson v Koziol (1996): 276
Annetts v McCann (1990): 82
Ansett Transport Industries Ltd v Minister for Aviation (1987): 82
Anthony Lagoon Station Pty Ltd v Maurice (1987): 79
Applicant A v Minister for Immigration and Ethnic Affairs (1997): 44, 81, 156, 167, 321
Arthur Yates & Co Pty Ltd v Vegetable Seeds Committee (1945): 80
Associated Provincial Picture Houses Ltd v Wednesbury Corporation (1948): 76
Astill (1992): 129
Ates v Minister of State for Immigration and Ethnic Affairs (1983): 76
Attorney-General (Cth) v Schmidt (1961): 34
Attorney-General (Cth) v The Queen (1957): 31
Attorney-General (Cth); ex rel McKinlay (1975): 32, 51
Attorney-General (NSW) v Milat (1995): 342
Attorney-General (NSW) v Quin (1990): 46, 89
Attorney-General (NSW) v Stuart (1994): 131
Attorney-General (UK) v Guardian Newspapers (No 2) (1988): 252
Attorney-General (UK) v Heinemann Publishers Pty Ltd (1987): 69
Attorney-General (Vic); ex rel Black v Commonwealth (1981): 34, 49
Atyeo v Aboriginal Lands Trust (1996): 271-72
Australasian Meat Industries Employees Union v Meat & Allied Trades Federation of Australia (1991): 219
Australian Broadcasting Authority v Project Blue Sky (1996): 251
Australian Broadcasting Tribunal v Bond: 65

Australian Capital Television Pty Ltd v Commonwealth (ACTTV) (1992): 11, 29, 37, 49, 51, 69, 251, 333
Australian Iron and Steel Pty Ltd v Banovic (1989): 45, 310-11, 315, 338
Australian Iron and Steel Pty Ltd v Najdovska (1985): 311
Australian Manufacturing Union v Alcoa of Australia Ltd (1996): 212
Australian Medical Council v Wilson (1996): 325
Australian National Airways Pty Ltd v Commonwealth (1945): 36
Australian National Industries Ltd v Spedley Securities Ltd (in liq) (1992): 330
Australian Postal Commission v Dao (1986): 306, 309
Australian Postal Commission v Dao (1987): 334
Australian Railways Union v Victorian Railways Commission (1930): 339
Automotive, Food, Metals, Engineering, Printing and Kindred Industries Union v HPM Industries Pty Ltd (1998): 205
B and R and the Separate Representative (1995): 116, 186, 191
B v B (1997): 176, 181-82, 184, 187, 326, 330, 339
Balaquer v Spain: 172
Ballina Shire Council v Ringland (1994): 80, 329
Bank of New South Wales v Commonwealth (Bank Nationalization Case) (1948): 34, 67
Barker v City of Hobart and Barratt, Gentile and Stacey (1993): 202, 316
Barley Marketing Board (NSW) v Norman (1990): 34
Barton v The Queen (1980): 122, 329
Bath v Alston Holdings Pty Ltd (1988): 34
Bear v Norwood Private Nursing Home (1984): 105
Bengescue v Minister for Immigration and Ethnic Affairs (1994): 152
Best and Best (1993): 187
Binse v Governor of HM Prison Barwon (1997): 80
Birmingham City Council v Equal Opportunities Commission (1989): 315
Blom v Sweden (1988): 295
Bolam v Friern Hospital Management Committee: 276
Bollag v Attorney-General (Cth) (1997): 72
Bolton, Re; ex p Beane (1987): 324
Botany Bay Instrumentation & Control Pty Ltd v Stewart (1984): 128
Bradley v Commonwealth (1973): 320
Brandy v HREOC (1995): 24, 28, 31, 306, 309
Braswell v US (1988): 127

Breen v Williams (1996): 277, 284-85

Brennan v Comcare (1994): 76

Briginshaw v Briginshaw (1938): 314

Bropho v Western Australia (1990): 79, 324

Brown v Members of Classification Review Board of the Office of Film and Literature (1997): 324, 335

Brown v R (1986): 33, 56

Broyles (1991): 129

Buck v Bavone (1976): 57, 72

Bugden v State Rail Authority of New South Wales (1991): 313

Builders Labourers Federation of NSW v Minister for Industrial Relations (1986): 56

Builders Licensing Board v Sperway Constructions (Sydney) Pty Ltd (1976): 65

Buksh v Minister for Immigration, Local Government and Ethnic Affairs (1991): 70

Bunning v Cross (1978): 129, 132-33, 135

C and D, In marriage of (1979): 189

Cachia v Hanes (1991): 330

Cadette (1995): 128

Cambell v Minister for Environmental Planning (1987): 239

Cameron v HREOC (1993): 301

Canadian National Railway v Canadian Human Rights Commission (1987): 315

Capital Duplicators v Australian Capital Territory (1992): 58

Carroll v Mijovich (1992): 330

Cartwright and Cartwright (1977): 188

Casimel v Insurance Corporation of British Columbia (1993): 95-96, 118

Castlemaine Tooheys Ltd v South Australia (1990): 34, 101

CEPU v Woodside Heating and Airconditioning Pty Ltd (1997): 207

Chan v Minister for Immigration and Ethnic Affairs (1989): 44, 155-56, 324

Chappel v Hart (1996): 278

Chaudhary v Minister for Immigration and Ethnic Affairs (1993): 75

Cheatle v R (1993): 32-33, 56

Chen v Minister for Immigration and Ethnic Affairs (1994): 81, 149

Chief Constable of the North Wales Police v Evans (1982): 70

Chow Hung Ching v The King (1948): 320

Christie v Qantas Airways Ltd (1995): 323-34

Chu Kheng Lim v Minister for Immigration and Ethnic Affairs (1992): 29, 54-55, 149, 159, 167, 320, 325, 335, 341

Church of New Faith v Commissioner for Pay-Roll Tax (1983): 35, 49

Clunies-Ross v Commonwealth (1984): 34

Coco v The Queen (1994): 30, 43, 45, 78, 324

Coe v Commonwealth (1993): 98, 320, 336

Coe v Commonwealth (Wiradjuri Claim) (1979): 98

Cole v Cunningham (1983): 82

Cole v Whitfield (1988): 34, 57

Commissioner for Railways v Small (1938): 127

Commissioner of Police v Tanos (1958): 79

Commissioner of Taxation (Cth) v Citibank Ltd (1989): 324

Commonwealth v Human Rights and Equal Opportunity Commission and X (1998): 200, 325

Commonwealth v John Fairfax & Sons Ltd (1980): 69, 252

Commonwealth v Tasmania (Tasmanian Dam case) (1983): 28-29, 323

Comptroller-General of Customs v Kawasaki Motors Pty Ltd (1991): 67

Connelly v Director of Public Prosecution (1964): 123

Consolidated Press Holdings Ltd v Federal Commissioner of Taxation (1995): 82

Controlled Consultants Pty Ltd v Commissioner for Corporate Affairs (1985): 125, 127

Cooper v Wandsworth Board of Works (1863): 82

Corbett v Corbett (otherwise Ashley) (1970): 189

Cossey v United Kingdom (1990): 172, 189

Costello-Roberts v UK (1995): 8

CP, In (1997): 186

Croome v Tasmania (1996): 339, 341

Cunliffe v Commonwealth (1994): 38, 167

Daemar v Industrial Commission of New South Wales (1988): 330

Damouni v Minister for Immigration, Local Government and Ethnic Affairs (1989): 77

Dampier Salt (Operations) Pty Ltd v Collector of Customs (1995): 76

Darling Casino Ltd v New South Wales Casino Control Authority (1997): 79

Davis v Commonwealth (1988): 333

Davies and Davies, In marriage of (1995): 180

De L v Director General, NSW Department of Community Services (1996): 44, 321-22, 324

Delgamuukw v British Columbia (1993): 95

Delgamuukw v Queen in Right of British Columbia (1997): 95-96, 110

Department of Immigration and Ethnic Affairs v Ram (1996): 84, 86, 151

Derbyshire County Council v Times Newspapers (1993): 41

Derschaw v The Queen (1996): 109

Devenish v Jewel Food Stores (1991): 219

Dhayakpa v Minister for Immigration and Ethnic Affairs (1995): 152

Dhillon v Minister for Immigration and Ethnic Affairs (1989): 150

Dietrich v R (1992): 30, 43, 45-46, 54, 89, 121, 121-24, 181, 323-24, 329, 340, 345

Director of Public Prosecutions v Saxon (1992): 330

Director of Public Prosecutions v Serratore (1995): 80, 324, 326

Dixon v Attorney-General (British Columbia) (1989): 33
DM v TD (1994): 307
Doyle and Doyle (1992): 188
DPP *see* Director of Public Prosecutions
Drake v Minister for Immigration and Ethnic Affairs (1979): 65
Dugan v Mirror Newspapers Ltd (1978): 328
East African Asians v United Kingdom (1973): 143
Eaton v Yanner (1998): 109
Enterprise Flexibility Test Case (1995): 213
Environment Protection Authority v Caltex (1993): 54, 125, 236
Erbs v Overseas Corporation Pty Ltd (1986): 314
Eshetu v Minister for Immigration and Multicultural Affairs (1997): 76-78
Evans v Staunton (1958): 127
Eve, Re (1986): 192
F & M1 & M2 (1994): 339
F and F (1989): 184
F v R (1983): 276
Fang v Minister for Immigration and Ethnic Affairs (1996): 84, 88
Farah and Secretary, Department of Social Security, Re (1992): 332
Ferguson and Secretary, Department of Employment, Education, Training and Youth Affairs, Re (1996): 79
Foley v Padley (1984): 79
Foster v Mountford (1977): 106
Francis and Minister for Immigration and Ethnic Affairs, Re (1996): 151
Friends of Hinchinbrook Society Inc v Minister for Environment (1996): 334
Fuduche v Minister for Immigration, Local Government and Ethnic Affairs (1993): 76
Fuller and Cummings v DPP (Cth) (1994): 122
Fuller v Field (1994): 122
General Manager, Department of Health v Arumugam (1987): 310
General Practitioners Society in Australia v Commonwealth (1980): 36
Georgiadis v Australian and Overseas Telecommunications Corporation (1994): 52
Gerhardy v Brown (1985): 10, 44, 101, 104, 323
Gill v Walton (1991): 330
Gillick v West Norfolk and Wisbech Area Health Authority (1986): 182-83
Goertz v Gordon (1995): 187
Goudge (1984): 190
Grace Bible Church v Reedman (1984): 49
Gradidge v Grace Bros Pty Limited (1988): 330
Gratwick v Johnson (1945): 57
Green (1996): 131
Griggs v Duke Power Co (1971): 311
Grinham, Ex p; Re Sneddon (1961): 79

Grollo v Commissioner of Australian Federal Police (1995): 31, 323
Guerin v The Queen (1984): 95
Gunaleela v Minister for Immigration (1987): 324
Guo Wei Rong v Minister for Immigration and Ethnic Affairs (1996): 338
H and W (1995): 181, 183-84
Hall v Sheiban (1989): 310
Hamer v UK: 190
Hanbury-Brown, In Marriage of; Director-General of Community Services (1997): 324
Hannan (F) Pty Ltd v Electricity Commission (NSW) (No 3) (1985): 239
Harrison v Department of TAFE (1978): 105
Heard v De Laine (1996): 177
Hebert (1990): 129
Heidt and Heidt (1976): 176
Henry v Boehm (1973): 35
Herron v McGregor (1986): 330
Hewer v Bryant (1970): 182
Hilton v Wells (1985): 31
Hindi v Minister for Immigration and Ethnic Affairs (1988): 74
Hodak, Re (1993): 185
Hopper v Mount Isa Mines Ltd (1997): 201
Horne v Press Clough Joint Venture (1994): 201-02, 301
Horta v Commonwealth (1994): 31, 44, 320, 332
Huang v Minister for Immigration and Ethnic Affairs (1996): 149
Human Rights and Equal Opportunity Commission v Secretary of Department of Immigration and Multicultural Affairs (1996): 162, 325
Hunter v Southam (1984): 11
HV McKay, Ex p (1907): 203
Irwin Toy Ltd v Quebec (Attorney-General) (1989): 11
IW v City of Perth (1997): 325
J v Lieschke (1987): 327
J, Re (A Minor): 274
Jacobsen v Rogers (1995): 79
Jago v District Court of New South Wales (1988): 121-23, 330
James v Commonwealth (1939): 42
Jane, Re (1988): 282, 331, 339
JM v QFG (1997): 189
Jong Kim Koe v Minister for Immigration and Multicultural Affairs (1997): 166
Jumbunna Coal Mine NL v Victorian Coal Miners' Association (1908): 209, 324
K, Re: 179, 183
Kable v Director of Public Prosecutions (NSW) (1995): 324, 337
Kable v Director of Public Prosecutions (NSW) (1996): 23, 46, 56, 124, 337-38
Kartinyeri v Commonwealth (1998): 44, 101, 105, 334, 339

Kennedy and Cahill, In marriage of (1995): 180

Khan (Sultan) (1996): 132

King v Jones (1972): 32

King v R (1986): 126

Kingswell v R (1985): 33, 56

Kinkri Devi v State of Himachal Pradesh (1988): 223

Kioa v West (1985): 46, 73-74, 82, 320

Kitok v Sweden: 104

Klass v Federal Republic of Germany (1978): 135

Koowarta v Bjelke-Petersen (1982): 28-29, 296, 323, 330, 334

Koppen v Commissioner of Community Relations (1986): 313-14

Kress and Kress, In marriage of (1976): 176

Kruger v Commonwealth (1997): 42, 51, 54, 58, 115, 334, 337

Kruslin v France (1990): 135

Kwong Leung Lam v Minister for Immigration and Multicultural Affairs (1997): 85

L and L (1983): 188

Lam v Minister for Immigration and Multicultural Affairs: 85

Lamb v Cotogno (1987): 108

Lamshed v Lake (1945): 36

Lange (1997): 40

Lange v Atkinson (1998): 41

Lange v Australian Broadcasting Commission (1997): 29, 38-40, 46, 50, 333

Langer v Australian Electoral Commission (No 2) (1996): 339

Langer v Commonwealth (1966): 33, 333

Lansman v Finland: 104

Latoudis v Casey (1990): 239-40

Lawless v The Queen (1979): 131

Le Geng Jia and Minister for Immigration and Multicultural Affairs, Re: 152

Leask v Commonwealth (1996): 323, 335

Lee v Darwin City Council (1993): 320

Leeth v Commonwealth (1992): 36, 42-43, 53-55, 333

Lek v Minister for Immigration, Local Government and Ethnic Affairs (1993): 82, 324, 338

Levy v Victoria (1997): 41, 50, 333

Lichtenstein v Guatemala (1955): 143

Lim v Minister for Immigration, Local Government and Ethnic Affairs (1992): 80

Limbo, Re (1989): 336

Linden v Commonwealth (No 2): 336

Lingens v Austria (1986): 41

Liverpool City Council v Roads and Traffic Authority (No 2) (1992): 239

LK Koolwal v State of Rajastan (1988): 223

Lovelace v Canada (1977): 104

Luu v Renevier (1989): 74, 82

M v R Pty Ltd (1988): 202

Mabo v Queensland (No 1) (1988): 102

Mabo v Queensland (No 2) (1992): 20, 24, 29-30, 43, 45, 80, 89, 94-95, 98, 106, 108, 110, 122, 181, 193, 323, 328, 345

McAuliffe v Puplick (1996): 313

McGinty v Western Australia (1996): 32-33, 37, 38, 51

McInerney v MacDonald (1992): 285

McInnis v The Queen: 137

McKellar v Smith (1982): 330

McKinney v The Queen (1991): 127

Macksville & District Hospital v Mayze (1987): 67

McL (1991): 191

McLean v Airlines of Tasmania Pty Ltd (1997): 201

McMillan v Jackson (1995): 180

Madhavi v Tilakan (1988): 223

Magno (1992): 324

Malone v United Kingdom (1984): 135

Manning v Hill (1995): 41

Marion (No 2), Re (1994): 281, 332, 339

Marion, Re (1991): 181, 191

Marion's case (HC) see Secretary, Department of Health and Community Services and JWB and SMB

Maritime Union of Australia v Patrick Stevedores No 1 Pty Ltd (1998): 208

Marks v Beyfus (1890): 131

Mason v Tritton (1994): 96, 109

Metwally v University of Wollongong (1984): 27

Michael (No 2), Re (1994): 339

Mikmaq Tribal Society v Canada: 99

Milirrpum v Nabalco Pty Ltd (1971): 93

Miller v TCN (1986): 57

Milpurrurru v Indofurn (1994): 106-08, 250

Minister for Aboriginal Affairs v Peko-Wallsend Ltd (1986): 71

Minister for Foreign Affairs and Trade v Magno (1992): 69, 181, 321

Minister for Immigration v Mayer (1985): 324

Minister for Immigration and Ethnic Affairs v Conyngham (1986): 66

Minister for Immigration and Ethnic Affairs v Guo Wei Rong (1997): 89

Minister for Immigration and Ethnic Affairs v Maitan (1988): 72

Minister for Immigration and Ethnic Affairs v Pochi (1980): 74, 82

Minister for Immigration and Ethnic Affairs v Teo (1995): 76

Minister for Immigration and Ethnic Affairs v Teoh (1995): 20, 30, 43, 45-46, 74, 77, 80, 83-88, 119, 137-38, 147, 150-52, 167, 171, 324, 333

Minister for Immigration and Ethnic Affairs v Wu Shan Liang (1996): 44, 72, 87, 89, 147

Minister for Immigration and Multicultural Affairs v Thiyagarajah (1997): 164

Minister for Immigration, Local Government and Ethnic Affairs v Mok Gek Bouy (1994): 82, 328

Minister for Immigration, Local Government and Ethnic Affairs v Pashmforoosh (1989): 82

Mitchell and Mitchell (1995): 187

Mohazab v Dick Smith Electronics Pty Ltd (No 2) (1996): 322

Morato v Minister for Immigration, Local Government and Ethnic Affairs (1992): 324

Mudginberri Station v Australasian Meat Industries Employees Union (1985): 219

Muldowney v South Australia (1996): 333

Murray v Director, Family Services, ACT (1993): 180, 325

Murray v Director-General, Health and Community Services Victoria (1995): 287

Murray v United Kingdom (1996): 126

Myers v DPP (1965): 130

N and N (1977): 188

N and S (1996): 181, 184

Najdovska v Australian Iron and Steel Pty Ltd (1985): 301, 311

Namibia Case (1971): 295-96

Nationwide News Pty Ltd v Wills (1992): 11, 29, 37, 39, 49, 333

Nem and Director-General of Social Security, Re (1984): 81

Nettheim v Minister for Planning and Local Government (1988): 239

New South Wales Corporal Punishments in Schools: Determination on preliminary matters, Re (1986): 301-02, 314

New York Times Co v Sullivan (1964): 11, 39

Newcrest Mining (WA) Ltd v Commonwealth (1997): 34, 43, 48, 52, 58, 324, 334

NIB Health Fund Ltd v Hope (1996): 189

Nicholas v Western Australia (1972): 56

Nintendo Co Ltd v Centronics Systems Pty Ltd (1994): 52

Nintendo v Centronics (1991): 34

Nolan, Re; ex p young (1991): 32

North Coast Environment Council Inc v Minister for Resources (1995): 342

Northern Territory v Mengel (1995): 67

Nottebohm Case: 143

Observer and Guardian v United Kingdom (1991): 12

Ominayak and the Lubicon Lake Band v Canada: 104

O'Neill (1995): 128

Orkem v European Commission (1989): 127

Oshlack v Richmond River Council (1998): 239-40

O'Sullivan v Farrer (1989): 71

O'Toole v Charles David Pty Ltd (1991): 67

P v P (1994): 339

P and P, In the Matter of (1995): 187, 192, 282

Park Oh Ho v Minister for Immigration and Ethnic Affairs (1989): 66

Parker (1995): 128

Patrick Stevedores Operation No 2 Pty Ltd v Maritime Union of Australia (1998): 208

Pavic v R (1998): 128

Petty v The Queen (1991): 125

Phillips v Disciplinary Appeal Committee of the Merit Protection Review Agency (1994): 82

Piper v Corrective Services (1986): 324

Pitjantjatjara Council Inc and Peter Nguaningu v Lowe and Bender (1982): 106

PJE v The Queen (1996): 337

Polites v Commonwealth (1945): 44, 80, 324

Polyukhovich v Commonwealth (1991): 21, 23, 31, 55, 323, 331

Pont Data v ASX Operations (1990): 257

Potter v Minahan (1908): 79, 324

Prasad v Minister for Immigration and Ethnic Affairs (1985): 74

Premelal v Minister for Immigration, Local Government and Ethnic Affairs (1993): 73

Prineas v Forestry Commission for New South Wales (1983): 239

Proceedings Commissioner v McCulloch (1996): 313

Project Blue Sky v Australian Broadcasting Authority (1998): 81, 251

Proudfoot (1991): 302

Public Service Association (SA) v Federated Clerks Union of Australia (SA Branch) (1991): 79

Pyneboard v TPC (1983): 125

Qantas Airlines Ltd v Christie (1995): 324

Qantas Airways Ltd v Cameron (1996): 338

Qantas Airways Ltd v Christie (1998): 200, 323, 325, 339

R (A Minor), Re (1991): 182

R v Anunga (1976): 111

R v Archdall and Roskruge; ex p Carrigan and Brown (1928): 33, 56

R v Astill (1992): 330

R v Australian Broadcasting Tribunal; ex p 2HD Pty Ltd (1979): 71

R v Bernthalr (1993): 123

R v Bon Jon (1841): 93

R v Brown (1993): 129

R v Catalano (1992): 329

R v Chief Immigration Officer; ex p Bibi (1976): 138

R v Coldham; ex p Australian Workers' Union (1983): 67

R v Craigie (1979): 110

R v Davidson and Moyle; ex p Attorney-General (1996): 128

R v Equal Opportunity Board; ex p Burns (1984): 301, 314

R v Federal Court of Bankruptcy; ex p Lowenstein (1938): 33

R v Gayne (1991): 131

R v Hollingshed and Rodgers (1993): 326

R v Home Secretary; ex p Asif Khan (1984): 46

R v Horseferry Road Magistrates Court; ex p Bennett (1994): 123

R v Jean Denise Izumi (1996): 112

R v Kina (1993): 112
R v Kirby; ex p Boilermakers' Society of Australia (1956): 31
R v Latif & Shahzad (1996): 123
R v Ludeke; ex p Customs Officers' Association of Australia (1985): 339
R v Metropolitan Police Commissioner; ex p Blackburn (1968): 137
R v Metropolitan Police Commissioner; ex p Blackburn (No 3) (1973): 137
R v Ministry of Agriculture, Fisheries and Food; ex p Hamble Fisheries (1995): 46
R v Morgan (1993): 123
R v Pearson; ex p Sipka (1983): 32
R v Phillips and Pringle (1973): 326
R v PJE (1995): 123
R v Preston (1993): 131
R v Richards; ex p Fitzpatrick and Brown (1955): 32
R v Saleam (1989): 131
R v Seaboyer (1991): 131
R v Secretary of State for the Home Department; ex p Brind (1991): 74-75, 122
R v Secretary of State for the Home Department; ex p Ruddock (1987): 46
R v Shrestha (1991): 329
R v Smithers (1912): 57
R v Sparrow (1990): 95, 109
R v Swaffield; Pavic v The Queen (1998): 128, 328
R v Truong (1996): 133-34, 327
R v Walker (1993): 111
R v Ward (1993): 131
Rajan v Minister of Immigration (1996): 75
Ram v Minister for Immigration and Ethnic Affairs (1995): 156
Rees v United Kingdom (1987): 172
Reibl v Hughes (1980): 276
Reno v American Civil Liberties Union (1997): 250
Rice and Miller (1993): 185
Richmond River Shire Council v Oshlack (1996): 239
Ridgeway v The Queen (1995): 79, 123, 128, 135
Robertson v Canadian Imperial Bank of Commerce (1995): 260
Rogers v Whitaker (1992): 276-78
RTZ v The Netherlands (1987): 295
Rundle v Tweed Shire Council (No 2) (1989): 239
S & M Motor Repairs Pty Ltd v Caltex (Oil) Pty Ltd (1988): 80, 320, 330
Sajdak and Sajdak, In marriage of (1993): 180
Salameh v Minister for Immigration and Multicultural Affairs (1997): 152
Sang (1980): 132
Saunders v United Kingdom (1996): 125, 127-28
Schaik v Neuhaus (1996): 320, 326
Schlieske v Minister for Immigration and Ethnic Affairs (1988): 70

Schloendorff v Society of New York Hospital (1914): 280
Scott v Telstra Corporation Ltd (1995): 338
Sean Investments Pty Ltd v MacKellar (1981): 72
Secretary, Department of Health and Community Services and JWB and SMB (Marion's Case): 30, 182, 191-92, 279-80, 283, 339
Secretary, Department of Social Security and Clemson, Re (1991): 81
Secretary, Department of Social Security and Knight, Re (1996): 76
Secretary, Department of Social Security and Kumar, Re (1992): 332
Secretary, Department of Social Security and Underwood, Re (1991): 332
Secretary, Department of Social Security v SRA (1993): 189
Secretary of the Department of Foreign Affairs and Trade v Styles (1989): 312, 316
Shipping Corp of India v Gamlen Chemical Co A/Asia Pty Ltd (1980): 322
Shortland v Northland Health (1997): 274, 290
Sidaway v Bethlem Royal Hospital Governors: 276
Sillery v R (1981): 55, 326
Simpson v Attorney-General (Baigent's Case) (1994): 42
Simsek v McPhee (1982): 320, 324
Sinnapan v Victoria (1994): 317
Sinnathamby v Minister for Immigration and Ethnic Affairs (1986): 77
Smith v The Queen (1991): 330
Smith, Turner and Altinas (1994): 129
Sobh (1993): 131
Somaghi v Minister for Immigration, Local Government and Ethnic Affairs (1991): 83, 324, 3345
Soobramoney v Minister of Health (Kwazulu-Natal): 274
Sorby v Commonwealth (1983): 54, 125
South Australia v Tanner (1989): 79
South West Africa (Second Phase) (1966): 12, 296
Sparks v R (1964): 130
Spry and Spry (1977): 188
Stephens v West Australian Newspapers (1994): 39-40, 50-51, 333
Stinchcombe v The Queen (1991): 130
Street v Queensland Bar Association (1989): 35, 53, 101, 323, 333
Sui and Minister for Immigration and Ethnic Affairs, Re (1996): 81
Sun Zhan Qui v Minister for Immigration and Ethnic Affairs (1997): 74, 77, 82
Sunday Times v United Kingdom (No 1) (1979): 12
Sunday Times v United Kingdom (No 2) (1991): 12
Surinakova v Minister for Immigration, Local Government and Ethnic Affairs (1991): 77

Sutton v Derschaw (1995): 109
Svikart v Stewart (1994): 57
Swan Hill Corporation v Bradbury (1937): 71
Sykes v Cleary (1992): 323
T Damodar Rao v Special Officer, Municipal Corporation of Hyderadad (1987): 223
T v Attorney-General (1988): 260
Taciak v Commissioner of the Australian Federal Police (1995): 324
Tasmanian Conservation Trust Inc v Minister for Resources (1995): 342
Tasmanian Dam case see Commonwealth v Tasmania
Tavita v Minister for Immigration (1994): 75, 325
Te Weehi v Regional Fisheries Officer (1986): 109
Teenager, In re a (1988): 339
Telstra Corporation Ltd v Scott (1995): 201
Teoh's case see Minister for Immigration and Ethnic Affairs v Teoh
Teper v R (1952): 129
Theophanous v Herald & Weekly Times Ltd (1994): 29, 39-40, 48, 50 333
Thomas v Brown (1997): 250
Thorpe v Commonwealth (1997): 94, 98, 336
Tickner v Bropho (1993): 76
Tillmanns Butcheries v Australasian Meat Industries Employees Union (1979): 219
Todea v Minister for Immigration and Ethnic Affairs (1994): 81, 152
Toonen v Australia (1994): 29, 139, 189, 269-71, 340
Tournier v National Provincial and Union Bank of England Ltd (1924): 260
Tracey, Re; ex p Ryan (1989): 32, 54
Trade Practices Commission v Tooth & Co Ltd (1979): 34
Tucker v News Media Ownership Ltd (1986): 260
Tweed Valley Fruit Processors Pty Ltd v Ross (1996): 213
Tyler, Re (1994): 32
United States Tobacco Co v Minister of Consumer Affairs (1988): 339
United States v Eichman (1990): 355
University of Wollongong v Metwally (1984): 55, 299, 334
Vabaza v Minister for Immigration and Multicultural Affairs (1997): 152
Vaitaiki v Minister for Immigration and Ethnic Affairs (1998): 74, 85, 152, 333
Vaitaiki v Minister for Immigration and Multicultural Affairs (1997): 152
Vaitaiki and the Minister for Immigration and Ethnic Affairs, Re (1995): 152
Vazquez and Minister for Immigration, Local Government and Ethnic Affairs, Re: 65

Victoria Park Racing and Recreation Grounds Co. Ltd v Taylor (1937): 260
Victoria v Commonwealth (1995): 299
Victoria v Commonwealth (1996): 216, 330
Victoria v Commonwealth (1997): 358
Victoria v Sinnapan (1995): 317
Victrawl Pty Ltd v Telstra Corp Ltd (1995): 322
Viskauskas v Niland (1983): 27, 299, 334
W (A Minor), Re (1993): 182
W v G (1996): 189
Waanyi People's Native Title Application, Re (1995): 96
Wackerow (1997): 128
"WAG" and Minister for Immigration and Multicultural Affairs, Re (1996): 151
Walden v Hensler (1987): 110
Walker v NSW (1994): 96, 110
Walsh v Department of Social Security (196): 325
Walton v The Queen (1989): 129
Warne v Genex Corporation Pty Ltd (1996): 252
Water Conservation and Irrigation Commission (NSW) v Browning (1947): 72
Waterhouse v Bell (1991): 105
Waters v Public Transport Corporation (1991): 45, 53, 197-98, 311-12, 325
Waters v Rizkalla (1990): 311
Weissensteiner v The Queen: 126
Western Australia v Commonwealth (1995): 101
Whiteman v Secretary, Department of Veterans' Affairs (1996): 76
Wik Peoples v Queensland (1996): 29, 94, 96, 104
Williams v South Australia (1990): 104
Williams v Spautz (1992): 122
Wright v McQualter (1970): 137
Wu Shan Liang v Minister for Immigration and Ethnic Affairs (1994): 338
Wu Yu Fang v Minister for Immigration and Ethnic Affairs (1996): 162, 339
X v Australia: 193
X v Dr McHugh (1994): 197
XY, In the Matter of: 287
Yad Ram and Department of Immigration and Ethnic Affairs, Re (1995): 152
Yarmirr v Northern Territory (1998): 94
Young v Registrar, Court of Appeal (No 3) (1992): 81
Young v Registrar, Court of Appeal (No 3) (1993): 325
Yumbulul v Reserve Bank of Australia (1991): 107
Zarb v Kennedy (1968): 33
ZP v PS (1994): 339

TABLE OF LEGISLATION

Constitution: 26ff, 47ff
s 7: 38, 50
s 24: 32, 38, 50, 51
s 41: 32
s 51(ii): 53
s 51(XXIIIA): 36, 334
s 51(xxvi): 44, 101-102
s 51(xxix): 33
s 51(xxxi): 33, 36, 52, 53, 100
s 62: 50
s 64: 50
s 71: 54
s 75: 155
s 75(v): 66
s 92: 34, 57
s 99: 53
s 109: 299
s 116: 34-35, 49, 58, 338
s 117: 35, 36, 52
s 122: 57, 334
s 128: 38, 50
Ch III: 28-29, 31, 37, 46, 54-58, 307

Commonwealth
Aboriginal and Torres Strait Islander Heritage Protection Act 1985: 101
Acts Interpretation Act 1901: 21
s 15AB: 21, 321
s 15AB(2): 80
Administrative Appeals Tribunal Act 1975
s 27A: 68
s 44: 151
Administrative Decisions (Judicial Review) Act 1977: 64, 155, 316
s 5: 66
s 13: 66, 68
s 16: 66
Administrative Decisions (Effect of International Instruments) Bill 1997
s 5: 30-31
s 7: 31
Affirmative Action (Equal Employment Opportunity for Women) Act 1986: 199
Archives Act 1983: 68
Australian Citizenship Act 1948: 21, 178
s 10: 44
s 21: 144
s 23D: 144
Broadcasting Act 1942
Pt IIID: 37-38
Broadcasting Services Act 1992
s 122: 251
Copyright Act 1968: 247, 249
ss 41-43: 253

s 115(4)(b): 108
Pt V Div 4: 248
Pt VA: 255
Pt VB: 255
Copyright Amendment Bill 1997
Sch 1: 249
Copyright (World Trade Organisations Amendments) Act 1994: 247
Crimes Act 1914
s 16A(2)(p): 325
ss 23A-23W: 127
s 23H: 111
Crimes (Torture) Act 1988: 147
s 3(1)(b): 321
Customs (Prohibited Exports) Regulations 1958: 264
Disability Discrimination Act 1992: 27, 196, 199-200, 358
s 4: 200
ss 5-9: 180
s 31: 200
s 32: 200
s 34: 200
s 29: 180
s 69: 313
s 71(2): 300
s 76: 300
Evidence Act 1995: 129, 135
s 20: 125
s 65 92)(c): 129
s 83: 327
s 89:125
s 128: 125
s 130: 131
s 130(5): 131
s 138: 321
s 138(1): 133, 136
s 138(3): 134
s 138(3)(g): 136
s 165(1)(f): 127
s 174(1): 321
Family Law Act 1975: 116, 169, 175
s 43(ca): 176
s 55A: 177
s 60B: 177, 193
s 60B(2): 116
s 60D(3): 116
s 61aff: 176
s 61C: 116
s 64(1): 176
s 65E: 176
s 65G: 170
s 67L: 176
s 67V: 176
s 67ZC(2): 176

s 68E(3): 170
s 68F: 176, 179
s 68F(2): 170
s 68L(1): 179
s 68F(2)(f): 116
s 68F(3): 170
s 68(2)(f)(i): 176
s 111B: 322
s 114: 180
Part VII: 176-177
Family Law Reform Act 1995: 176, 326
Family Law (Child Abduction Convention)
    Regulations: 322
reg 16(3): 322
Federal Court of Australia Act 1976: 301,
    338
Freedom of Information Act 1982: 68, 230
s 48: 244
Hindmarsh Island Bridge Act 1997: 101
Human Rights Commission Act 1981: 73
Human Rights and Equal Opportunity
    Commission Act 1986: 27, 100, 104,
    146, 181, 196, 199, 280, 297, 303, 306-
    307, 358
s 3(1): 105
s 4: 105
s 7: 192
s 11(1)(f): 162
s 11(1)(o): 331, 339
s 15: 192
s 31(j): 339
s 47: 147
Human Rights Legislation Amendment Bill
    1997: 306-307
Human Rights Legislation Amendment Bill
    1998: 331
Human Rights (Sexual Conduct) Act 1994:
    321, 340, 358
s 4: 139
Industrial Relations Act 1988: 37, 209
    see also Workplace Relations Act 1996
Industrial Relations Reform Act 1993: 204,
    217-19
Judiciary Act 1903: 56, 61
s 40A: 61
Marriage Act 1961: 175
ss 45: 175
s 46: 175, 189
Migration Act 1958: 21, 76, 147, 322, 341
s 6A: 44
s 22A: 147
s 36(2): 155
s 85-91: 149
ss 91A-91F: 163
s 166: 145
s 189: 159
ss 193-196: 161
s 198: 159, 161

ss 200-204: 151
s 256: 161
s 420: 77
s 500: 151
s 501: 151-152
s 502: 151
Migration Legislation Amendment Act
    (No 4) 1994: 163
Migration Legislation Amendment (Streng-
    thening of Character and Conduct Pro-
    visions) Bill 1997: 153, 155, 161-162
Migration (1994) Regulations
reg 1.03: 150
reg 1.15A: 150
Sch 1, 1229: 50
Sch 1, 1220A: 50
Sch 2, subcl 100: 50
Sch 2, subcl 309: 50
Sch 2, subcl 801: 50
Sch 2, subcl 820: 50
Schs 4-5: 148
Native Title Act 1993: 94, 101, 110
s 10: 94
s 223: 94, 108
Native Title Amendment Bill 1993: 101
Native Title Amendment Act 1998: 102
Passports Amendment Act 1984
s 9: 321
s 10: 321
Public Service Act 1922: 316
s 16: 68
Privacy Act 1988: 68, 136, 244, 258, 260,
    · 321, 358
Pt III: 244
Racial Discrimination Act 1975: 27-28, 72,
    100-01, 147, 196, 303, 358
s 8(1): 44
s 9: 180
s 9(2): 104
s 10: 180
s 24(2): 300
s 24(3): 314
s 25: 300
Racial Hatred Act 1995: 148
Sex Discrimination Act 1984: 27, 148, 196,
    198, 201, 215, 303, 316, 358
ss 5-7D: 180
s 6: 358
s 8: 315
s 26: 180
s 50A: 215
s 52(2): 300
s 58: 300
s 83A: 306
Sex Discrimination Amendment Act 1991
s 11: 175
Social Security Act 1991: 325, 332

Telecommunications Act 1997 (Cth)
    Pt 7 Div 6: 256
Telecommunications (Interception) Act
    1979: 131
    s 7: 131
    s 62: 131
    ss 74-77: 131
    ss 107A(1)-107F: 136
Trade Practices Act 1974, 216, 218
    ss 52-53: 106
    s 45D: 219
Trade Practices Amendment (Telecom-
    munications) Act 1997: 257
Workplace Relations Act 1996 (formerly
    Industrial Relations Act 1988): 196,
    205, 208-209, 212-213, 217-219
    s 43(2): 215
    s 89A: 213
    s 113(2A): 215
    s 118A(1B): 210
    s 127: 218
    s 127AA: 211
    s 170BD: 204
    s 170BE: 204
    s 179BI: 204
    s 170LU(2A): 207
    s 170MI: 218
    s 170MI(2): 218
    s 170MI(3): 218
    s 170MT: 218
    s 170PA(1)(e): 330
    s 170VG: 213
    s 170VPB: 213-214
    s 170VPE: 214
    s 170VPG: 214
    s 187AA: 218
    s 187AB: 218
    s 187AC: 218
    s 187AD: 218
    s 188(1)(c): 209
    s 267: 208
    s 280A: 209
    s 280B: 209
    s 285G: 211
    s 298K(1)(d): 207
    s 298L: 207
    ss 298P-298S: 207
    s 298V: 208
    s 298Z: 207
    s 312: 217
    s 334A: 217
    Part XA: 207
Workplace Relations and other Legislation
    Amendment Act 1997: 207

New South Wales
Anti-Discrimination Act 1977
    s 7(2): 105
    s 24(3): 45

Births Deaths and Marriages Registration
    Act 1995: 178
    s 21: 178
Children (Care and Protection) Act 1987:
    118
Community Protection Act 1994: 337
Constitution Act 1902: 56
Contaminated Land Management Act 1997:
    231
Crimes Act 1900
    s 405A: 126
Defamation Act 1974
    s 22: 40
Environmental Offences and Penalties Act
    1989: 237
Environmental Planning and Assessment
    Act 1979: 232
    s 5(c): 228
    s 123: 235
Evidence Act 1995: 129,135
    s 20: 125
    s 65 92)(c): 129
    s 89: 125
    s 128: 125
    s 130: 131
    s 130(5): 131
    s 138(1): 133, 136
    s 138(3)(g): 136
    s 165(1)(f): 127
Freedom of Information Act 1989: 230
Heritage Act 1997
    s 153: 235
Land and Environment Court Act 1979: 240
Land Rights Act 1983: 108
Local Government Act 1993
    s 674: 235
Mental Health Act 1990
    s 4(1): 288
    s 4(2): 288
    s 6: 287
National Parks and Wildlife Act 1974
    s 176A: 235
Ombudsman Act 1974
    s 26(1)(a): 66
    s 26(1)(b): 66
Pollution Control Act 1970: 232
Privacy Committee Act 1975: 261
Protected Disclosures Act 1994: 68
Protection of the Environment Adminis-
    tration Act 1991
    s 10: 231
    s 24: 229
Protection of the Environment Operations
    Act 1997 228, 235
    s 3(b): 228
    s 3(c): 228
    s 17: 229
    s 203(1): 236

s 212: 236
s 212(3): 236
s 252: 237
s 252(5): 242
s 253: 237
ss 308-309: 230
Threatened Species Conservation Act 1995
s 3: 227
Transgender (Anti-Discrimination and Other Acts Amendment) Act 1996: 178
Wilderness Act 1987: s 27

Queensland

Environmental Protection Act 1994: 231-232
s 4(b): 228
s 4(4)(b): 228
s 5: 229
s 5(b): 228
s 6: 228-229
s 26: 229, 230
s 28: 229
s 45: 232
s 85: 233
s 87: 233
s 194: 238
s 194(2): 238
s 202: 233
s 202(7): 233
ss 213-214: 230
s 218: 213
Sch 1: 233
Invasion of Privacy Act 1971: 78
Fauna Conservation Act 1974: 110
Judicial Review Act 1991: 64
s 32: 68
Queensland Heritage Act 1992
s 3: 227
Registration of Births Deaths and Marriages Act 1962: 178
s 27A: 178
Whistleblowers Protection Act 1994: 68

South Australia

Administrative Decisions (Effect of International Instruments) Act 1995: 333
Adoption Act 1993: 118
Births Deaths and Marriages Registration Act 1996: 178
s 21: 178
Children's Protection Act 1993: 118
Criminal Law Consolidation Act 1935
s 285c: 126
Environmental Protection Act 1993
s 10: 227
s 10(b)(ix): 228
s 10(1)(ix): 228
s 28: 229
s 28(6)(d): 230

s 39(1): 232
s 104: 237
s 104(7)(b): 238
s 104(7)(c): 238
s 109: 230
Div 2: 229
Pitjantjatjara Land Rights Act 1981: 44
Prohibition of Discrimination Act 1966: 296
Whistleblowers Protection Act 1993: 68
Youth Court Act 1993: 118
Youth Offenders Act 1993: 118

Tasmania

Criminal Code
s 122(a): 270, 340
s 122(c): 270, 340
s 123: 270, 340
Environmental Management and Pollution Control Act 1994
s 22: 230
Land Use Planning and Approvals Act 1993: 232
s 57: 232
s 61(5): 235
s 64: 237
cl 1(c) Sch 1: 228
Sch 1: 227
Registration of Births Deaths and Marriages Act 1895: 178
s 20: 178
State Policies and Projects Act 1993: 229, 231-232
s 23: 232

Victoria

Administrative Law Act 1978: 64
s 8: 68
Adoption Act 1984: 118
Births Deaths and Marriages Registration Act 1996: 178
s 23: 178
Children and Young Persons Act 1989: 118
Coastal Management Act 1994
s 4(e): 228
Constitution Act 1975: 41
Crimes (Criminal Trials) Act 1993
s 8: 131
s 11: 131
s 15(1): 126
s 15(2): 126
Environmental Protection Act 1970: 239
s 16: 229
ss 18A-18D: 229
s 19B(3)(b)(iv): 232
s 33B: 234
Equal Opportunity Act 1984
s 29: 45

Equal Opportunity Act 1995 (Vic): 313
  Pt 7 Div 2: 317
Mental Health Act 1986
  s 4(1)(a): 288
  s 4(1)(c): 288
  s 4(1)(e): 288
  s 4(2)(a): 288
  s 4(2)(b): 288
  s 6A(a): 289
  s 6A(b): 289
  s 6A(c): 289
  s 6A(d): 289
  s 6A(e): 289
  s 6A(g): 289
  s 6A(i): 289
  s 6A(j): 289
Mental Health (Amendment) Act 1995: 288
Wildlife (Game) (Hunting Season) Regulations 1994
  reg 5: 41

Western Australia

Acts Amendment (Abortion) Act 1998: 269
Environmental Protection Act 1986: 239
  s 54(3): 232
  s 100: 235
  s 102(3): 234
  s 107: 235
  Pt IV: 235
Health Act 1911
  s 99: 271
Mental Health Act 1996
  s 5: 288
Registration of Births Deaths and Marriages Act 1961: 178
  s 21A: 178

Australian Capital Territory

Administrative Decisions (Judicial Review) Act 1989: 64
  s 13: 68
Adoption Act 1993: 118
Discrimination Act 1991: 312
Domestic Relations Act 1994: 189
Environmental Protection Act 1997
  s 3(1)(f): 228
  ss 19-20: 230
  s 48: 232
  s 49(1): 232
  s 92(2)(b): 234
  s 127: 238
  s 135: 234
  s 135(5): 234
Public Sector Management Act 1994
  Pt XII: 68
Registration of Births Deaths and Marriages Ordinance 1963: 178
  s 18: 178

Northern Territory

Aboriginals Ordinance 1918: 42, 337
Adoption of Children Act 1994: 118
Community Welfare Act 1983: 118
Northern Territory Aboriginal Sacred Sites Act 1989: 105
Registration of Births Deaths and Marriages Act 1980: 178
  s 17: 178

Canada

Canadian Bill of Rights 1960: 354
Canadian Charter of Rights and Freedoms 1982: 354
Charter of Rights and Fundamental Freedoms 1982: 8, 11, 121
  s 11: 45
Environmental Bill of Rights 1994: 224
Indian Act: 104

New Zealand

Bill of Rights Act 1990: 8, 27, 75, 352
  s 21: 42
Employment Contracts Act 1991: 212
Health and Disability Act 1993: 274
Privacy Act 1993: 260

Portugal

Constitution: 223

South Africa

Bill of Rights 1996: 9, 356
  s 24: 9
  s 25: 11
  ss 26-29: 9
Constitution: 223
  Art 24: 223

United Kingdom

Criminal Evidence (Northern Ireland) Order 1988
Criminal Justice and Public Order Act 1994: 126
  ss 34-37: 126
Criminal Procedure and Investigations Act 1996: 131
Human Rights Act 1998: 356
Police and Criminal Evidence Act 1984
  s 78: 132

United States

Bill of Rights 1789: 8, 355
Constitution 1789: 36
  Art 1 s 2: 32
  Art 4 s 2: 35

International

African Charter on Human and People's Rights: 10

Berne Convention for the Protection of Literary and Artistic Works: 247, 249
Art 15(4): 106

Code of Conduct for Law Enforcement Officials
Art 2: 111, 113
Art 5: 113
Art 9(2): 255
Art 10: 255
Art 13: 255

Convention on Biological Diversity 1992: 225

Convention concerning Discrimination in respect of Employment and Occupation: 204

Convention on the Elimination of All Forms of Discrimination Against Women 1979 (CEDAW): 147, 173, 201, 204, 272, 282, 294, 348, 350
Art 2: 14
Art 3: 13
Art 4: 13
Art 9: 143
Art 9(1): 173
Art 11(f): 201
Art 11(1)(d): 203
Art 11(1)(f): 272
Art 11(2): 195   art 12: 282
Art 16: 174
Arts 16(1)(a)-(h): 174
Art 16(2): 174
Art 24: 174

Convention on the Nationality of Married Women 1957: 143

Convention for the Protection of Individuals with Regard to Automatic Processing of Personal Data 1981: 259
Art 25: 259
Art 26: 259

Convention for the Protection of the Marine Environment of the North-East Atlantic 1993: 225

Convention on the Rights of the Child (CROC): 83, 86, 116, 146, 148, 170, 174-179, 183-185, 189, 191, 200, 272, 348, 350
Art 2: 188
Art 3: 151, 174
Art 3(1): 30, 176
Art 3(2): 177
Art 4: 174
Art 5: 177
Art 5(e)(iv): 272
Art 5(3): 176
Art 7: 185

Art 7(1): 174, 177
Art 8: 176
Art 8(1): 174
Art 9: 176, 183, 185
Art 9(1): 174
Art 9(3): 177, 184
Art 12: 174, 183
Art 12(1): 179
Art 12(2): 179
Art 14(2): 174
Art 18: 176-177
Art 18(1): 174-175, 185
Art 19: 176, 179, 185
Art 27: 185, 332
Art 30: 114, 117-118, 190
Art 34: 185
Art 37(a): 175

Convention Relating to the Status of Refugees 1951: 44, 81, 154-155, 157, 163
Art 1A: 147
Art 1A(2): 165
Art 31: 157, 164
Art 31(2): 164
Art 32: 153, 164
Art 33: 154, 163
Art 33(2): 153
Art 43: 145
1967 Protocol: 145

Convention Relating to the Status of Stateless Persons: 81

Convention Against Torture & Other Cruel, Inhuman or Degrading Treatment or Punishment (CAT): 113, 146, 340
Art 3: 163

Declaration on the Elimination of All Forms of Intolerance and Dis-crimination Based on Religion or Belief: 104

Declaration on the Rights of the Child, 73, 81, 148, 326

Declaration on the Rights of Disabled Persons 1971: 200

Declaration on the Rights of Mentally Retarded Persons: 200
Clause 1: 191
Clause 7: 191

Declaration on the Rights of Persons Belonging to National or Ethnic, Religions and Linguistic Minorities: 103

Declaration on Social and Legal Principles relating to the Protection and Welfare of Children, with Special Reference to Foster Placement and Adoption Nationally and Internationally
Art 2: 117
Art 4: 117

Discrimination in Employment and Equal Opportunity Convention 1958: 199
Draft Declaration on the Rights of Indigenous Peoples 1994: 97-98, 103
  Art 2: 144
  Art 3: 98
  Art 6: 114
  Art 12: 144
  Art 12(4): 144
  Art 13: 144-145
  Art 14: 145
  Art 21: 100, 108
  Art 22 100
  Art 26: 108, 144
  Art 27: 100
  Art 29: 100
  Preamble: 114
Equal Remuneration Convention: 204
  Art 1: 205
  Art 2: 204
European Convention for the Protection of Human Rights and Fundamental Freedoms 1950 (ECHR): 8, 13, 64, 74, 121, 172, 323, 352
  Art 3: 143
  Art 6: 45, 126
  Art 10: 335
  Art 10(1): 67
  Art 34: 12
  Protocol No 11: 353
Hague Convention on the Civil Aspects of International Child Abduction: 322, 325
International Covenant on Civil and Political Rights 1966 (ICCPR): 12-13, 27-28, 45, 73, 87, 89, 102-103, 105, 108, 113, 116, 118, 120-21, 124-25, 130, 134, 136, 139, 144-46, 159, 163, 170, 172, 175, 184, 187, 189, 194, 206, 236, 260, 270, 272, 282, 294-96, 319, 326, 340, 348, 350-51
  Art 1: 98
  Art 2(1): 294
  Art 2(2): 14, 172
  Art 2(3): 159, 341
  Art 3: 294
  Art 4.1: 294
  Art 5.2(b): 136
  Art 7: 163, 175
  Art 9: 146, 159
  Art 9(1): 158-59, 341
  Art 9(4): 159, 161, 162, 341
  Art 10: 114, 146, 158, 162
  Art 12: 265
  Art 12(1): 175
  Art 14: 120, 121, 161-62, 251
  Art 14(1): 130, 193
  Art 14(3): 121, 124

Art 14(3)(b): 130, 138, 251
Art 14(3)(e): 130
Art 14(3)(g): 124, 236
art 17: 258, 270, 275, 340
Art 17(1): 172
Art 18(1): 175, 193
Art 19: 250, 335
Art 19(3)(a): 251
Art 22: 265
Art 23: 148, 170, 193
Art 24: 148, 189
Art 26: 172, 294
Art 27: 193
Art 28: 172
Art 34(3): 143
Art 19(2): 67
Art 25: 146, 231
Art 26: 100
Art 27: 103-104
Art 40: 158
First Optional Protocol: 28, 99, 136
International Convention for the Elimination of All Forms of Racial Discrimination 1965 (CERD): 27-28, 100-102, 104, 114, 173, 272, 294, 340, 348, 350
  Art 1(4): 13
  Art 4: 147
  Art 2: 294
  Art 2(2): 13
  Art 5: 104
  Art 5(d): 100
  Art 5(d)(iv): 173
  Art 5(e)(iv): 272
International Covenant on Economic, Social and Cultural Rights (ICESCR): 12-13, 103, 108, 146, 173, 195, 199, 206, 272, 294, 348
  Art 1: 98
  Art 2: 100, 173
  Art 2(3): 294
  Art 3: 103, 204
  Art 4: 14
  Art 6: 195
  Art 7: 113, 195, 201, 203-204, 332
  Art 8(1)(d): 216
  Art 9: 332
  Art 10: 114, 173
  Art 10(2): 282
  Art 12: 272, 282
  Art 15: 103, 106
International Labour Organisation Convention No 154 (Collective Bargaining Convention): 211
International Labour Organisation Convention No 87 (Freedom of Association and Protection of the Right to Organise): 195, 206, 209

Art 2: 206
Art 11: 208, 210
International Labour Organisation Convention No 169 (Indigenous and Tribal Peoples in Independent States): 97
Art 4: 100
Art 15: 100
Art 23: 106
International Labour Organisation Convention No 98 (Right to Organise and Collective Bargaining): 195, 206, 209, 212
Art 4: 211
International Labour Organisation Convention No 107 (Tribal and Indigenous Populations): 97
International Labour Organisation Convention No 156 (Workers with Family Responsibilities): 174
Arts 3-5: 174
Art 7: 174
Art 8: 174
International Labour Organisation Convention No 135 (Workers' Representatives Convention) 1971: 210
Performances and Phonograms Treaty
Art 18: 248
Rio Declaration on Environment and Development: 225
Trade-Related Aspects of Intellectual Property Rights Agreement
Arts 1-8: 106
Art 22: 106
Art 27: 106
UNESCO Convention on Cultural Property: 106
United Nations Framework Convention on Climate Change 1992: 225

Universal Declaration of Human Rights 1948 (UDHR): 4, 12, 14, 101-102, 203, 258, 294, 327, 331, 348
Art 1(3): 100
Art 2: 100
Art 7: 100
Art 8: 235
Art 12: 327
Art 13: 144
Art 13(b): 100
Art 13(1): 144
Art 13(2): 144
Art 15(1): 143
Art 15(2): 143
Art 16: 114, 171-72, 327
Art 17: 246
Art 18: 104
Art 21: 231
Arts 22-23: 195
Art 23(2): 203
Art 24(2): 148
Art 25: 229
art 25(2): 327
art 26(3): 327
Art 55(c): 100
Vienna Convention on the Law of Treaties 1969: 322
Art 31: 322
Vienna Declaration and Programme & Action 1993: 9
Washington Declaration of Protection of the Marine Environment from Land-Based Activities: 225
World Intellectual Property Organization Copyright Treaty 1996: 247-48, 254
Art 11: 248
Art 14: 247

Main international human rights instruments relevant to Australia

Convention/ Declaration	Date of entry into force internationally	Date of entry into force for Australia	International monitoring body	International reporting requirements	Individual remedies and enforcement procedures	Express recognition in federal Australian law
Universal Declaration of Human Rights	10.12.1948	10.12.1948				
Convention relating to the Status of Refugees *and*	22.04.1954	22.01.1954	UNHCR			*Migration Act* 1958 (Cth) – adopts the Convention definition of refugee in section 5
Protocol relating to the Status of Refugees	04.10.1967	13.12.1973				
Declaration on the Rights of the Child	20.11.1959	20.11.1959				*Human Rights and Equal Opportunity Commission Act* 1986 (Cth) – Schedule 3
Discrimination (Employment and Occupation) ILO – 111	15.06.1960	15.06.1974	ILO			*Human Rights and Equal Opportunity Commission Act* 1986 (Cth) – Schedule 1
International Convention on the Elimination of all Forms of Racial Discrimination	04.01.1969	30.10.1975	CERD Committee	Article 9	Article 14 (28.01.1993)	*Racial Discrimination Act* 1975 (Cth)
Declaration on the Rights of Mentally Retarded Persons	20.11.1971	20.11.1971				*Human Rights and Equal Opportunity Commission Act* 1986 (Cth) – Schedule 4
						Disability Discrimination Act 1992 (Cth)
Declaration on the Rights of Disabled Persons	09.12.1975	09.12.1975				*Human Rights and Equal Opportunity Commission Act* 1986 (Cth) – Schedule 5
						Disability Discrimination Act 1992 (Cth)

Convention	Date	Date	Committee	Article	Article	Relevant legislation
International Covenant on Economic Social and Cultural Rights	03.01.1976	10.03.1976	Committee on Economic, Social and Cultural Rights	Article 16		*Disability Discrimination Act 1992* (Cth)
International Covenant on Civil and Political Rights (ICCPR)	23.03.1976	13.11.1980	Human Rights Committee	Article 40		*Human Rights and Equal Opportunity Commission Act 1986* (Cth) – Schedule 2; *Disability Discrimination Act 1992* (Cth); *Human Rights (Sexual Conduct) Act 1994* (Cth) and *Privacy Act 1988* (Cth) – article 17
First Optional Protocol to the ICCPR	23.03.1976	25.12.1991	Human Rights Committee			
Convention on the Elimination of Discrimination Against Women	03.09.1981	28.08.1983	CEDAW Committee	Article 18		*Sex Discrimination Act 1984* (Cth)
Declaration on the Elimination of All Forms of Religious Intolerance	25.11.1981	25.11.1981				*Human Rights and Equal Opportunity Commission Act 1986* (Cth)
Convention against Torture and other Cruel Inhumane and Degrading Treatment or Punishment	26.06.1987	07.09.1989	CAT Committee	Article 19	Article 22 (28.01.1993)	*Crimes (Torture) Act 1998* (Cth)
Convention on the Rights of the Child	02.09.1990	16.01.1991	CROC Committee	Article 44		*Human Rights and Equal Opportunity Commission Act 1986* (Cth); *Disability Discrimination Act 1992* (Cth)

Table compiled by Kate Eastman

Part One

Human Rights and the Legal Framework

1

THE LEGAL DIMENSION OF HUMAN RIGHTS

David Kinley

THE SIGNIFICANCE OF LEGAL AND NON-LEGAL DIMENSIONS OF HUMAN RIGHTS

To a lawyer the title of this chapter might seem odd, implying as it does the existence of other dimensions of human rights. He or she might protest initially that it is surely difficult to conceive of rights, including human rights, in any dimension other than that of legal; and that in any case such non-legal dimensions as might exist are surely of marginal significance to lawyers. More particularly they might suggest that as this book is explicitly concerned with human rights *in* Australian law there is little or no need for any consideration of dimensions of human rights other than that of the legal.

On the face of it these are fair questions, even if rhetorical, as they point to issues that lie at the heart of the debate on law and human rights. It is supposed, what is more, that the concerns upon which these questions are based are not uncommonly raised in one form or another.[1] Such concerns, however, are at best ill-conceived and at worst deceptive. It is the object of this chapter to explain why this is so in the process of analysing what constitutes the legal dimension of human rights, both in terms of concept and practice. In short, my aim is to stress the importance of the context in which the law embraces human rights.[2]

Human rights do possess non-legal dimensions and they are amenable to expression in non-legal terms. They may be expressed in moral or ethical terms and the obligations they impose are often claimed to operate at the moral level; they have an impact upon and, constitute essential elements of, most social and cultural orders; and the questions as to their nature form the basis for much that is pursued in political and philosophical endeavour. It is, of course, clear that these dimensions

---

1 One might, for instance, fairly suspect that Greg Craven's dubbing of the High Court's contextual analysis of implied constitutional rights in Australia as "an exercise in metaphysics", is not to be found without support (even if largely silent) in the legal community; Craven, G, "The High Court of Australia: a Study in the Abuse of Power", Alfred Deakin Lecture (unpublished paper, 1997), p 35.

2 Such contextual analysis of law is not, of course, novel. Most strikingly perhaps, critical theorists like Stanley Fish attack the notion that law has a formal autonomous existence within a social order by exposing the fallacy of such a stance and by insisting upon law's necessarily contingent or contextual existence. Fish, S, *There's No Such Think as Free Speech … and it's a Good Thing Too* (Oxford University Press, New York, 1994), especially Chs 11 and 12.

together with the legal dimension of human rights overlap at the conceptual level, as well as at the level of their practical implementation; though equally it is clear that the degree and significance of such overlap may differ markedly depending on the perspective of the observer.

Within the confines of this book – seeking as it does, to analyse the place and operation of human rights in the existing Australian legal system – there is no need to establish precisely the boundaries of the various dimensions of human rights, their distinctiveness and the areas in which they intermingle. It is sufficient for the present purpose to accept that the legal dimension of human rights with which this chapter is concerned comprises the two basic elements of (i) legal expression – that is in the form of legislative statement or judicial pronouncement, and (ii) the backing of legal sanction – that is, the provision of means by which human rights are or can be enforced and redress provided for any breaches.

Whilst accepting the multi-dimensional nature of human rights, it must be conceded that the most readily apparent expression of human rights is, to lawyers and non-lawyers alike, in legal form; much of their promotion is by way of legal terms and the bulk of their implementation through legal means. Indeed, consideration of the law's relationship with any purported human right is necessary, though not alone sufficient, to obtaining an understanding of the nature of human rights:

> [T]he issue of whether something is a human right, whether such rights exist or whether people have them, cannot be decided without consideration of the whole range of practices, which include recognition in law and governmental maintenance of the claimed ways of acting or being treated. Such practices are ingredient to the very notion of what it is for something to be a human right. ... [t]here is a deep parallelism – or, better, a convergence at a deep level – between legal rights and human rights.[3]

Human rights expressed in law do not exist in a societal vacuum. Their formulation, enunciation, interpretation, determination, application, enforcement and reform are factors that affect, and are affected by, the wide variety of forces that together constitute any social order. It is then, only through an appreciation of the existence, relative impact and interrelationship of the many dimensions of human rights that one is able to place the legal dimension in perspective and to comprehend its significance for both society at large and the law and legal system in particular.

This chapter's contextual analysis of the legal dimension of human rights proceeds by way of three steps. First, the question of the various definitions of human rights is addressed and some conclusions reached as to which of these best explain that part of human rights associated with "the legal". That is followed by an assessment of legally oriented theories of rights and an attempt made to frame human rights in a legal perspective that best suits the form in which human rights are perceived in Australian law and the manner in which they are and might be implemented through the Australian legal system. The third and final step moves away from the theoretical or conceptual level to the practical by focusing on what is, and what can be, the role of the law and the legal system in the "operation" of human rights within the Australian legal order – that is, from their conception, through implementation, to their promotion and enforcement.

---

3   Martin, R, *A System of Rights* (Clarendon Press, Oxford, 1993), p 87. In addition to legal recognition Martin includes social convention and moral recognition as other "relevant practices".

The existence as well as the significance of the interrelations between the legal and non-legal dimensions of human rights is apparent throughout the discussions under each of the three substantive sections (relating to the issues of definition, legal perspective, and the role of law and the legal system, respectively) into which the remainder of the chapter is divided.

DEFINING HUMAN RIGHTS

The theoretical conception of human rights is intimately associated with the enormous body of rights discourse. The salient feature that distinguishes human rights theories from "general" rights theories (or serves to qualify them), is that of their apparent necessary connection with the human condition. What is it that constitutes, or at any rate, is essential to, the state of being human and what social consequences and expectations necessarily flow therefrom are questions the answers to which are beyond the parameters of this chapter. However, it is possible to set out the most important factors that mark out the conceptual boundaries of human rights. It is accepted that there is no agreement over the weight that is to be accorded to each, but it can be said that the very depth of the debate and controversy they attract indicates the significance each has played in the perpetual quest to define human rights.[4]

Universality of human rights

The meaning of the universality of human rights is not a settled issue. Indeed, the meaning of universality itself is not a settled issue,[5] despite the fact that its resolution is logically antecedent to addressing the questions of whether the principle of universality applies to basic human rights, and if so to which ones. The discussion in this section provides only the briefest overview of the debate and no settlement, or even a set of options for settlement, is offered.

The assertion that human rights apply universally to all human beings flows directly from the notion that as a human being one is automatically entitled to respect for one's human dignity. On this basis the object of preserving and promoting the dignity of individual human beings constitutes the central concern of human rights. The coalition of human dignity and the universality of human rights constitutes the bedrock upon which the *Universal Declaration of Human Rights* (UDHR) was established in 1948. The first words of the Preamble read:

> *Whereas* recognition of the inherent dignity and of the equal and inalienable rights of all members of the human family is the foundation of freedom, justice and peace in the world, ...

Maurice Cranston, in one of the seminal texts in the area, encapsulates this universality by declaring that human rights to be "a form of moral right, [though] they differ from other moral rights in being the rights of all people, at all times and in all situations".[6]

---

4   See generally, Shestack, J, "The Jurisprudence of Human Rights" in Meron, T (ed), *Human Rights in International Law: Legal and Policy Issues* (Clarendon Press, Oxford, 1984), pp 69-105, and, more recently, by the same author, "The Philosophic Foundations of Human Rights" (1998) 20 *Human Rights Quarterly* 201.

5   A matter discussed further under "Substantive and Structural Limitations" below.

6   Cranston, M, *What are Human Rights?* (Bodley Head, London, 2nd ed, 1973), p 21.

Such claims as to the universality of human rights, however, do not go unchallenged. There are forceful arguments that such rights do not inhere in the natural condition of being human (as natural law theorists would have it),[7] nor are they part of a transcendental moral code that is necessary to maintain a base stratum of human dignity (as Kantian rights theorists would have it).[8] Rather, the existence, or potential existence, of human rights is in general terms culturally dependent, and specifically, their expression and form contingent on the relevant legal order. In other words, prevailing cultural norms will determine what human rights can and do exist, and the legal order will articulate their terms and conditions. The human rights that emerge are bestowed upon individuals as a result of the operation of the overlaying social and legal orders, rather than as expressions of innate human characteristics.[9] As one commentator puts it:

> In its simplest form the cultural relativist criticism asserts that human rights are a Western concept of limited applicability to non-western cultures. Human rights are said to be "Western", not only as a matter of contingent historical fact, but also in their individualistic, ontological implications. ... There seems little point in disputing that the modern concept of human rights has a peculiarly European inheritance. To reach such a conclusion is, of course, not to deny the existence of respect for human values in philosophical and political systems outside Europe, at present or past.[10]

The argument over the cultural relativism of human rights is well illustrated in the continuing debate about the relationship of so-called Asian values with purported universal human rights. It is claimed by some, for instance, that the importance attached to the maintenance of social order and respect for cultural traditions over that of protection of the rights of individuals within Asian value systems is crucially significant.[11]

---

7   See, for example, Finnis, J, *Natural Law and Natural Rights* (Clarendon Press, Oxford, 1980), Ch 8.

8   See, for example, Dworkin, R, *Taking Rights Seriously* (Duckworth, London, 1977), pp 198-99, and, generally, Gerwirth, A, *Human Rights: Essays on Justification and Applications* (University of Chicago Press, Chicago, 1982).

9   See Pollis, A, "Cultural Relativism Revisited: Through a State Prism" [1996] *Human Rights Quarterly* 316.

10   Pritchard, S, "The Jurisprudence of Human Rights: Some Critical Thought and Development in Practice" (1995) 2 *Australian Journal of Human Rights* 3 at 9. For a general account of human rights and cultural relativism, in respect, inter alia, of Islamic and Asian cultural traditions, see Steiner, HJ and Alston, P, *International Human Rights in Context* (Clarendon Press, Oxford, 1996), pp 166-255. See also Lee, E, "Human Rights and Non-Western Values" in Davis, M (ed), *Human Rights and Chinese Values* (Oxford University Press, Hong Kong, 1995), p 72.

11   The impact that such a concern can have on the twin notions of the universality and invisibility of human rights depends on the degree of its emphasis. According to the *Bangkok Declaration on Human Rights* (signed by 40 Asian Governments on 2 April 1993), for instance, such concern justifies the elevation of the sovereignty of the state above human rights protection (paras 4 & 5). Whereas to the contrary, both the *Bangkok NGO Declaration on Human Rights* (adopted on 29 March 1993) and the *Asian Charter on Human Rights* (also an NGO-sponsored document; declared on 17 May 1998) insist that state sovereignty must be subordinate to the aim of human rights protection (paras 1, 2 & 4; and 2.5, respectively). For further general discussion, see Ghai, Y, "Human Rights and Governance: The Asia Debate" (1994) 15 *Australian Yearbook of International Law* 1, and Joint Standing Committee on Foreign Affairs, Defence and Trade, *Improving but ... Australia's Regional Dialogue on Human Rights* (AGPS, June 1998), Ch 2.

An equivalent argument is also raised in developing nations throughout the world, in respect of their concern to advance the process of economic development ahead of guaranteeing individual human rights.[12]

An additional dimension to the challenge to the notion of the universality of human rights posed by differing cultural perspectives stems from the form in which human rights are recognised in any given society and the extent to which they are protected. Thus, in effect, the very existence of a human right or groups of human rights will depend on the nature of a society's governance and the legal order through which it is prosecuted. It is argued that:

> Rights have no separate ontological status; they are a by-product of a particular kind of society, one in which the "state" operates constitutionally under the rule of law, is separated from civil society and the "family", and in which private and public realms are, in principle, clearly demarcated. [In consequence] ... the international regime which attempts on a global scale to promote decontextualised human rights is engaging in a near impossible task.[13]

This public/private dichotomy points to yet another critical perspective of universality – namely, that provided by feminist analysis. Feminist scholars argue that the jurisprudence of international law, including and especially international human rights law, assumes the universal and neutral application to all states and individuals. "It is not recognized, however, that such principles may impinge differently on men and women; consequently, women's experiences of the operation of these laws tend to be silenced or discounted."[14] There are gendered disparities in power such that men and women are not usually equal in relation to the human rights they have or can use.[15] There are two particular systemic reasons for this. First, the fact of the public sphere orientation of international human rights guarantees women are disadvantaged women as this is not the arena in which customarily they have authoritative presence.[16] And second, the fact that many principal human rights are "negative rights", in that they are couched in the form of freedoms – that is, freedoms from state interference – which has the effect of perpetuating rather than challenging existing power imbalances between men and

---

12 For a critical assessment of this argument, see Donnelly, J, *Universal Human Rights in Theory and Practice* (Cornell University Press, Ithaca, 1989), Chs 9 and 10. Note that the United Nations Declaration to Development (adopted by the UN General Assembly, under Resolution 41/28, on 4 December 1986), whilst proclaiming the right to development to be a universal and inalienable right, nonetheless stresses the fact that it is also an integral part of fundamental human rights which are interrelated and interdependent (arts 1(2) & 6(2)).

13 Brown, C, "Universal Human Rights: A Critique" (1997) 1 *International Journal of Human Rights* 41 at 58-59; see also, Ng, M, "Are Rights Culture Bound?" in Davis, above, n 10, p 59. Some scholars aligned with the so-called Critical Legal Studies movement venture even further claiming that a State's provision for legal mechanisms by which rights may be asserted is contingent on the maintenance of whatever form of societal order that States takes. Rights, in other words, operate as a means by which truly radical political or social change is deflected and deflated. See further, Tushnet, M, "An Essay on Rights" (1984) 62 *Texas University Law Review* 1363.

14 Charlesworth, H, Chinkin, C and Wright, S, "Feminist Approaches to International Law" (1991) 85 *American Journal of International Law* 595 at 625.

15 Charlesworth, H, "What are 'Women's International Human Rights?'", in Cook, RJ, (ed), *Human Rights of Women* (University of Pennsylvania Press, Philadelphia, 1994), pp 60-62.

16 See, ibid, pp 68-71.

women.[17] The freedoms from interference in respect of one's speech, one's religion and religious practice, one's founding of a family, and one's privacy are especially important in this regard.

Evidently then, the philosophical debate that surrounds the conceptual framing of human rights as universal is, and will likely always be, contentious. Yet, to proceed along the path charted for this chapter, it is necessary to reach some sort of determination of the issue; to provide, as it were, a working understanding of the principle of human rights' universality. In this respect, one can draw upon the work of Jack Donnelly who, as an advocate of the universality of human rights, maintains that to advance the notion of universality does "not ... argue that human rights are timeless, unchanging, or absolute; any list or conception of human rights – and the idea of human rights itself – is historically specific and contingent".[18] It is upon such a qualified basis as this that much of the philosophical and jurisprudential debates on human rights can be best understood.

Rights and duties

The matter of the relationship between rights and duties is crucial to the understanding of the nature and functioning of all rights, including human rights.[19] It is often considered that duties are the "flip side" to rights, in that for every right there is a corresponding duty or obligation – namely, to protect, or at least, not to transgress, the right.[20] As a statement of general principle this can be readily accepted. What, however, it does not tell us is at what point in the existence or exercise of a right does a duty come into play; nor does it indicate upon whom the duty falls. For those of us who are interested in the promotion of human rights through legal means which, especially if by way of litigation, is so reliant upon the identification of obligation and responsibility, such questions cannot be left unanswered.

One's duty not to infringe upon another's human right is not established on account merely of the existence of the right; nor is it necessarily established as a consequence of the right being exercised. It is only at the point where action, inaction or desisting to act is required (whether before, during or after the right-holder's invoking of a right) in order that the right not be infringed upon or curtailed, that the duty becomes apparent.[21] Thus an individual's right to privacy

---

17 See Romany, C, "State Responsibility goes Private: A Feminist Critique of the Public/Private Distinction in International Human Rights Law" in Cook, above, n 15, pp 92-94.

18 Donnelly, above, n 12, p 1. See also Dianne Otto's argument that universality can be seen in a "transformative paradigm", in which the notion is "understood as dialogue, in the sense of struggle, rather than as a disciplinary civilizing mission of Europe": Otto, D "Rethinking the 'Universality' of Human Rights Law" (1997) 29 *Columbia Human Rights Law Review* 1 at 5.

19 The issue of the legal implications of this relationship are discussed below, under "Legal Perspectives of Human Rights".

20 The jurisprudential basis of this notion is discussed below, under "Legal Perspectives of Human Rights".

21 Whilst a right does not of itself necessarily attract a corresponding duty, it would appear that such a necessary correlation does apply to the obverse. Joseph Raz , for example, proclaims that "[a] duty is towards a certain person if and only if it is derived from his right"; Raz, J, *Ethics in the Public Domain* (Clarendon Press, Oxford, 1994), p 243 (n 11).

need not *necessarily* attract corresponding duties owed by the state, institutions and other individuals if they all conducted themselves in ways that did not impinge upon the right-holder's enjoyment of that right. It is accepted, however, that in reality those who are able to invade the right to privacy are not so benign. The right places various duties on them to establish prior safeguards against violation of the right (protection of records, and protection of one's personal space and bodily integrity; restrictions on covert surveillance, and on the collection of information) and to seek to ensure that they are observed at all times (by way of accountability and sanctioning mechanisms), whether or not so requested by the right-holder.

Another important aspect to the right/duty dichotomy relates to the question of upon whom do duties fall. There is, in this regard, a fundamental difference between the obligations imposed by international human rights instruments and those imposed by domestic laws. International instruments expressly bind the signatory states – that is, the organs through which the states function. Domestic human rights laws, on the other hand, may place obligations of observance on private individuals as well as state organs. This may be the case with certain issue-specific laws – for example, employment and anti-discrimination laws in Australia.[22] Generic human rights statutes (such as Charters or Bills of Rights), however, are typically not so broad in their scope, binding only public bodies.[23]

An area of potential development of states' obligation under international law has been opened up in respect of the *European Convention on Human Rights* 1950 (ECHR). It has been suggested that individuals who under international law have a right of action against the state for its *direct* actions, may also be able to hold the state *indirectly* responsible for the activities of others (namely private individuals and other legal persons) within its jurisdiction. In the case of *Costello-Roberts v UK*, the European Court of Human Rights declared that as a matter of principle "the State cannot absolve itself from responsibility by delegating its obligations to private bodies or individuals".[24]

Structural and substantive boundaries of human rights

There are certain features of human rights – or at least of their legal expression – that limit the extent of their application. This is so in three principal respects – namely (i) the subject matters covered by human rights, (ii) the nature or status of those who claim human rights; and (iii) the conditions imposed on their protection.

---

22   See Ch 9 (by MacDermott) and Ch 13 (by Bailey and Devereux) in this volume.

23   This is typically so whether the domestic statute in question is "home-grown" (for example, the United States' *Bill of Rights* (1791), the *Canadian Charter of Rights and Fundamental Freedoms* (1982) or the *New Zealand Bill of Rights Act* 1990), or takes the form of an incorporation of an international instrument (as is the case with the United Kingdom's Human Rights Bill, currently before Parliament, which incorporates the ECHR. The South African Bill of Rights, on the other hand, expressly declares that in addition to all organs of the state it binds any natural or juristic person: s 8 of the Constitution; see further, n 30 below.

24   (1995) Series A, No 247-C; (1995) 19 EHRR 112, para 27. For further discussion of this case see Clapham, A "The Privatization of Human Rights" (1995) *European Human Rights Law Review* 20.

(i)   Subject matters covered

The question of the extent of legal coverage of human rights is not easily answered. At the level of international law, the answer appears to be straightforward: the coverage extends so far as rights are provided for under all international human rights instruments in force. At the broadest level of human rights categorisation, furthermore, economic, social and cultural rights, and civil and political rights, have equal recognition under the two principal human rights covenants that have flowed from the UDHR and that bear their respective names.[25] Indeed, recently the equal status of all human rights, and of these two sets of rights in particular, were expressly acknowledged by the *Vienna Declaration's* reiteration of their "universal, indivisible, interrelated and interdependent" nature.[26]

In practice, civil and political rights have almost always been given precedence at both international and domestic levels. Indeed, the neglect[27] of the protection and promotion of economic and social rights in particular (cultural rights, as we see below, have gained some purchase within traditional human rights ideology and practice) has been such that their claims to the status of rights is fundamentally challenged. It has been argued, for instance, that the fact of their relative unenforce-ability at international and domestic levels means that they cannot "be considered as 'real' legal rights".[28] They are conceived, in this view, as matters that are essentially contingent – their determination being little more than the product of variable policy deliberation, rather than that of moral necessity or legal principle.

In fact, governments have demonstrated a manifest ambivalence towards such rights. In the international arena they actively promote the equal status of economic, social and cultural rights with civil and political rights, while at home they "fail to take particular steps to entrench those rights constitutionally, to adopt any legislative provisions based explicitly on the recognition of specific economic and social rights as human rights or to provide effective means of redress to individuals or groups alleging violations of those rights".[29]

The express provision for rights to a safe environment, housing, health care, food, water and social security, children's welfare, and education in the South African Bill of Rights[30] is the glaring exception that proves this rule among western democratic states. It is, as yet, too early to assess the justiciability of these rights in South African domestic law. The growing body of academic opinion and speculation is divided on the issue of whether they will be instrumental in delivery

---

25   The *International Covenant on Economic, Social and Cultural Rights* 1966 (ICESCR) and the *International Covenant on Civil and Political Rights* 1966 (ICCPR).

26   The United Nations World Conference on Human Rights, *Vienna Declaration and Programme of Action* (adopted 25 June 1993), Preamble and para 5.

27   This is the term used by Philip Alston, "Economic and Social Rights" in Henkin, L and Hargrove, JL (eds), *Human Rights: An Agenda for the Next Century* (American Society of International Law, Washington DC, 1994), especially pp 151-54.

28   Vierdag, EW, "The Legal Nature of the Rights Granted by the International Covenant on Economic, Social and Cultural Rights" (1978) 9 *Netherlands Yearbook of International Law* 69 at 77; see also, pp 83-94.

29   Steiner and Alston, above, n 10, pp 256-57.

30   The "Bill of Rights" comprises Ch 2 of the *Constitution of the Republic of South Africa* 1996. The rights indicated are provided by ss 24 and 26-29 of the Constitution.

of greater social justice or whether they will prove to be merely "constitutional ropes of sand".[31] What, however, transpires from the South African experience over the next decade or so is likely to have a profound effect on the future of economic, social and cultural rights in the legal arena, both inside and outside South Africa.

In Australia, substantive economic, social and cultural rights are provided for. Even though such rights terminology may not be readily employed in legislation or public policies, "rights" are provided for through programs and initiatives covering housing and welfare, education, public health care, and a clean environment.[32] Fundamentally, however, these rights are seldom directly enforceable.[33] Rather, they rely on indirect enforcement through the exercise of the procedural rights bestowed upon individuals by administrative law.[34]

(ii)   By whom are human rights exercisable?

On the face of it, this question ought to be easily answered: "by human beings, of course". But there are at least two separate perspectives that complicate the issue. The first, and more obvious, is whether all human beings in all circumstances possess human rights and are capable of exercising them. Aside from the continuing debate as to whether and to what extents the unborn, the dead and the insane have human rights,[35] there is the question of whether groups of persons as well as individuals can claims rights guarantees.

In one sense, it is clear that group rights are provided for in international and domestic guarantees ascribed to individuals against discrimination on group-distinctive grounds such as gender, race, political or philosophical conviction, disability, age or union membership. There are also specific group rights commonly provided for in international human rights instruments and domestic law, relating to cultural activities, minority languages, religious belief and self-determination. These group rights may be exercisable by the group *qua* group, as well as by its individual members.[36] The *African Charter on Human and Peoples' Rights* (1986)[37] contains

---

31   See, for example, Craig, S and Macklem, P, "Constitutional Ropes of Sand or Justiciable Guarantees? Social Rights in the New South African Constitution" (1992) 141 *University of Pennsylvania Law Review* 1.

32   See generally, Bailey, P, "The Right to an Adequate Standard of Living: New Issues for Australian Law" (1997) 4 *Australian Journal of Human Rights* 25. See also the third periodic report of the Australian Government on the ICESCR, which is Australia's first comprehensive (if uncritical) report to the UN Committee on Economic, Social and Cultural Rights on the conformity of all Australian laws with the Covenant. At the time of writing the submission of the report was imminent.

33   An obvious exception to this rule in Australian law is that group of rights provided under employment law which accord with art 7 of the ICESCR; see further, Ch 9 by MacDermott in this volume.

34   See Ch 4 by McMillan and Williams in this volume.

35   For discussion see White, AR, *Rights* (Clarendon Press, Oxford, 1984), pp 75-92.

36   For a discussion of the conceptual and practical differences between the two usages see Jones, P, *Rights* (Macmillan, London, 1994), pp 182-87. See also, Triggs, G, "The Rights of Peoples and Individual Rights: Conflict or Harmony?", in Crawford, J (ed), *The Rights of Peoples* (Oxford University Press, Oxford, 1988), p 141, especially her analysis (on pp 148-50) of *Gerhardy v Brown* (1985) 159 CLR 70.

37   Articles 19-24 (which cover rights to equality; self-determination; property; development; security and a safe environment) refer to "all peoples", rather than "everyone" or "all individuals", and declare that the rights are exercisable "individually or collectively".

such group rights, and the South African *Bill of Rights* (1996) protects the rights to property of "a person or community".[38]

The second complicating perspective is singularly legal in that it raises the prospect of redefining the nature of those in whom rights inhere by replacing "human" with the notion of "legal person". The significance of this, of course, lies in the fact that the category of legal persons comprises more than just human beings; it includes, inter alia, corporations, trades unions and many other unincorporated bodies. Legal entities, as distinct from the human beings that comprise them or through whose agency they act, are peculiarly situated in this regard. By their very nature non-human legal persons are unable to exercise, claim or be protected by certain human rights. This is the case, for example, in respect of rights to life, equality, religious and cultural practice, to found a family, to education, health, food and housing, and to be free from torture. On the other hand, there are other rights that are not necessarily beyond the reach of corporate entities. It is possible to conceive of public and private bodies invoking rights to freedom of expression and movement, and to privacy and fair trial. Out of these, most conspicuously, the right to freedom of expression has been claimed by corporate bodies and been readily condoned by the European Court of Human Rights,[39] and courts in Canada,[40] the USA[41] and Australia.[42]

Interestingly, there has been relatively little attention paid to the conceptual and practical problems that such claims have on the objects and operation of the legal protection of human rights. The anthropomorphism involved in the extending of human rights to non-human legal bodies can lead to absurdity and inconsistency. In relation to the reasoning employed in the Supreme Court of Canada's decision in *Irwin Toy Limited*[43] protecting a corporation's freedom of expression under the Canadian Charter of Rights, Allan Hutchinson observes:

> Repeating at length that the law's solicitude for free speech centres upon "individual self-fulfillment and human flourishing" [at 979], whether as an end in itself or as a means to truth-finding and democratic participation, the Court managed to overlook the fact that the Irwin Toy company is not human, but only a human creation.[44]

Hutchinson is also critical of the fact that the protection afforded by Charter rights to the actions of corporations is not extended to trades unions in the same way;[45] this he claims to be a sign of the inconsistent application of reasoning to analogous circumstances.

---

38   Section 25; see above, n 30, on the constitutional status of the Bill of Rights.

39   See below, ns 47 and 48.

40   See *Hunter v Southam* [1984] 2 SCR 145.

41   See *New York Times Co v Sullivan* 376 US 254 (1964).

42   See *Australian Capital Television Pty Ltd v Commonwealth* (1992) 177 CLR 106 and *Nationwide News Pty Ltd v Wills* (1992) 177 CLR 1; for discussion; see Ch 3 by Gageler and Glass in this volume.

43   *Irwin Toy Ltd v Quebec (Attorney-General)* [1989] 1 SCR 927.

44   Hutchinson, AC, *Waiting for Coraf: A Critique of Law and Rights* (University of Toronto Press, Toronto, 1995), p 32.

45   Hutchinson points to the fact that the Supreme Court has insisted that the rights of assembly and association are individual rights not collective rights to be exercised by associations; see, for example, *Re Public Service Employees Relations Act* [1987] 1 SCR 313.

At the international law level, this matter is variously treated. The terms of the right to individual petition under art 25(1) of the ECHR[42] refer explicitly to the competence of persons, groups of individuals and non-governmental organisations to lodge petitions alleging violation of Convention-protected rights. Under the last mentioned category, the European Commission on Human Rights has accepted petitions from a variety of non-incorporated bodies (such as trades unions and private associations) as well as corporations.[43] Indeed, some of the most celebrated freedom of expression cases within ECHR jurisprudence concern the violation of the rights of newspaper companies.[44]

On the other hand, under the terms of the right to individual petition under art 1 of the First Optional Protocol to the ICCPR the right is bestowed only on individuals. As such, corporations, trades unions and other like bodies have had petitions declared inadmissible by the Human Rights Committee.[45] There appears, however, to be some scope for such bodies to be heard indirectly through petitions lodged by the people "behind" them in their individual capacities as owners or shareholders.[46]

(iii)   Conditions on protection

As is clear from the discussion earlier in this section, there are, in terms of the ontology of human rights, widely divergent views as to their universality. However, at the level of their practical implementation or potential, the urgency of the universality debate is less pressing. This is due to a number of factors, among the most important of which are those that relate to the substance of international human rights instruments and the conditions attached to their application.[47]

As regards substance, in the UDHR, the ICCPR and, especially, in the ICESCR, there is express provision for many culturally, philosophically and religiously contingent rights relating, for example, to freedoms of speech; of religion, thought and cultural practices; to found a family; to self-determination; to culturally distinct education; to property rights; and, language rights. Indeed, the very right to equality has to be interpreted in a way that permits differential treatment where appropriate. As Judge Tanaka of the International Court of Justice made clear in his seminal (dissenting) judgment in the *South West Africa Case (Second Phase)*:

> The principle of equality before the law does not mean absolute equality, namely the equal treatment of men without regard to individual, concrete circumstances, but it

---

42   Renumbered art 34 upon the coming into effect of Protocol 11 to the ECHR on 1 November 1998.

43   For lists of examples and further discussion, see Zwart, T, *The Admissibility of Human Rights Petitions* (Martinus Nijhoff, Dordrecht, 1994), pp 46-47.

44   *Sunday Times v United Kingdom (No 1)* Series A No 30 (26 April 1979); *Observer and Guardian v United Kingdom* Series A No 216 (26 November 1991); and, *Sunday Times v United Kingdom (No 2)* Series A No 217 (26 November 1991).

45   See Communications Nos 360/1989 and 361/1989, HRC 1989 Report, pp 308 and 310, respectively.

46   Zwart, above, n 47, p 42.

47   There is, in addition, the ultimate qualification of a state avoiding altogether application of a right or rights within its jurisdiction by way of entering a reservation to, or derogation from, the relevant treaty. For a survey and analysis of the use of these devices, see Gardner JP (ed), *Human Rights as General Norms and a State's Right to Opt Out* (British Institute of International and Comparative Law, London, 1997).

means the relative equality, namely the principle to treat equally what are equal and unequally what are unequal ...

To treat unequal matters differently according to their inequality is not only permitted but required.[48]

There is even greater potential for differentiation in interpretation and application of the same human rights, either by domestic courts in the context of their own legal order or by an international body having regard to the legal order of a particular state, provided by the so-called "margin of appreciation" that commonly forms part of the conditions under which rights are protected. For example, allowance is made under the ICCPR for the limitation of rights "where necessary in a democratic society" or for "the protection of national security or of public order or of public health or morals".[49] Similarly, a discretion akin to that of a margin of appreciation is also extended to states in respect of the "special measures" provisions in the International Convention for the Elimination of All Forms of Racial Discrimination 1965 (CERD) and the Convention on the Elimination of All Forms of Discrimination Against Women 1979 (CEDAW),[50] in that they permit "appropriate" conditions or qualifications to be placed on the right of formal equality or non-discrimination, in an effort to advance the notion of substantive equality.

The notion of "margin of appreciation" was designed to enable states to implement rights differently, in deference to pressing and/or peculiar domestic circumstances, without betraying the essence of the right in question.[51] Yet, clearly, there is a fine line between claiming a "legitimate" cultural, social or other distinction and the disingenuous use of such a distinction in order to dilute or even avoid the obligation to protect a given human right; especially, that is, when so many of these qualifications to rights are permissible so long as they are considered necessary according to such an ill-defined notion as "a democratic society". It is significant that the judicial and scholastic consideration of such "margin of appreciation" conditions is now sufficiently well developed in respect of the ECHR that the matter has spawned what is fast becoming a distinct sub-category of European rights jurisprudence. This development has important implications in jurisdictions beyond the reach of the ECHR.[52]

---

48 [1966] ICJ Rep 6, 303-04 and 305. The same rationale is used in the UN's Human Rights Committee's General Comment on Article 26 of the ICCPR: General Comment 18 (1989), paras 7-13.

49 See arts 21 and 22, and arts 18 and 19 (as well as art 3), respectively. See also art 4 of ICESCR.

50 See arts 1(4) and 2(2) of CERD and arts 3 and 4 of CEDAW. For a review of the nature and use of special measure provisions under CERD and the corresponding provisions in the *Racial Discrimination Act* 1975 (Cth), see Pritchard. S, "Special Measures" in Office Commonwealth Race Discrimination Commissioner, *The Racial Discrimination Act 1975: A Review* (AGPS, Canberra, 1995), especially, pp 190-95.

51 It has been defined in the context of the ECHR as "the freedom to act; manoeuvering, breathing or 'elbow' room; or the latitude of deference or error which the Strasbourg organs will allow to national legislative, executive, administrative and judicial bodies, before they are prepared to declare a national derogation from the Convention, or restriction or limitation upon a right guaranteed by the Convention, to constitute a violation of one of the Convention's substantive guarantees"; Yourow, HC, *The Margin of Appreciation Doctrine in the Dynamic of European Human Rights Jurisprudence* (Martinus Nijhoff, The Hague, 1996), p 13.

52 See ibid, generally.

The open-endedness of so many fundamental human rights is more generally catered for by the common use of generic "margin of appreciation" statements in the Preambles or opening articles of international human rights instruments;[53] by the availability of derogation provisions in such instruments;[54] and also by the 1993 *Vienna Declaration*.[55]

The fact that such limitations and conditions exist is not, it must be emphasised, being challenged. It is likely, in any event, that if they were not expressly provided for in human rights instruments, they would be established in practice by those responsible for implementation and be acknowledged and effectively implied by courts through rules of interpretation. Rather, the concern of the present discussion is simply to establish the fact that human rights cannot be, and, as expressed in legal form are not monolithic or absolute.[56]

It has been evident throughout this general assessment of the defining features of human rights how dependent the concept of human rights is on factors antecedent to law, or determinative of it – for example, moral or philosophical principles or cultural mores. The same is true of those factors that operate at the same level as law or contemporaneously to it – as is the case, for example, with political, social or economic demands and expectations. In the following section, the discussion moves from this fundamental conceptual perspective to consider the specifically legal perspectives of human rights.

LEGAL PERSPECTIVES OF HUMAN RIGHTS

In the introduction it was stated that the two base elements of the legal dimension of human rights are their expression in legal terms and the fact that they are backed by legal sanction. A discussion of the mechanisms by which these legal features are bestowed upon human rights is the direct concern of the next section. There remains, however, the preliminary question of at what point in the conceptual formulation of human rights do they become clothed in this legal garb? Or, to put it another way, at what point in the exercise of identifying and articulating human rights is the (or a) legal perspective employed? It is with the issues raised by such questions that this section is concerned.

Rights, including human rights, come in many different forms; or at least, they are *said* to come in many different forms. From a legal perspective, this is an

---

53 See, for example, the UDHR, Preamble, which refers to the rights it guarantees as "common standard[s] of achievement", which are to be striven towards "by progressive measures"; the ICESCR which obliges States to recognise the rights in the Covenant "to the maximum of its available resources ..." (art 2) and permits limitations to rights protection provided they are solely for the purpose of promoting the general welfare in a democratic community" (art 4); and, the use of the essentially subjectively determined command to protect and promote human rights by "appropriates means" throughout art 2 of CEDAW. See also, ICCPR, art 2(2).

54 See, for example, ICCPR, art 4 (allowing derogation in respect of specified rights in the Covenant in "time of a public emergency"), and ICESCR, art 4 (see previous footnote).

55 See above, n 26. While laying stress on the universality and indivisibility of human rights, the Declaration accepts that "the significance of national and regional particularities and various historical, cultural and religious backgrounds must be borne in mind ..." (para 5).

56 See further, Australian Law Reform Commission, *Multiculturalism and the Law*, Report No 57, (AGPS, 1992), especially paras 1.15-18 and 1.25-32.

important distinction as it is only those that conform to certain criteria that are capable of being recognised by, or translated into, law. Rights are variously styled as interests, goods, powers, immunities, liberties, claims, demands, "trumps", and entitlements (moral or otherwise); the generic term, it seems, encompasses many categories.[57] In addressing these categories, what is at issue is the degree to which they are capable of legal recognition. Each of them, it can be argued, plays, or can play, some role in the legal determination of rights *per se*. Rights as interests or goods or even demands may operate at the level of persuasion in, for example, the policy debate that constitutes part of the process of law-making, rather than by force of their necessary legitimacy.[58] Rights as powers, immunities and even liberties may also operate at the level of persuasion; more usually, however, they constitute the outcome of such policy deliberations, in that they take the form of legal powers and prerogatives. Yet, even in this latter form, it is argued, they differ crucially from rights proper.

Hohfeld distinguishes these particular rights manifestations from "true" rights (which are, for him, rights as "claims")[59] by labelling them as "privileges" – that is, they are contingently extended to the holder. The contingency in this case is that the body (usually the state) that extends the privilege is under no express *legal* obligation or duty to honour or respect the privilege; or to put it another way, the privilege-holder cannot mount any legal demand, nor does he or she possess any legal entitlement, to have the privilege honoured. "A right" according to Hohfeldian reasoning, "is one's affirmative claim against another, and a privilege is one's freedom from the right of claim of another".[60] The freedom afforded by such a privilege under this formulation, lasts only as long as no "affirmative claim" is made against it or in contradiction to it. Upon such a claim being made the privilege immediately evaporates and is replaced by a duty to meet the claim.

The value of Hohfeld's analysis in the present context lies in his exposition of the relationship between rights and duties. Within the matrix of legal concepts that constitutes the basis for his primary work, Hohfeld characterises this relationship as one of a "jural correlative" such that as the imposition of a duty necessarily follows a claimed right, so a right respected is the necessary result of a duty fulfilled.[61]

Many rights theorists agree with this basic line of reasoning that associates rights with duties; indeed, it is fair to say that among legal theorists the principal area of dispute in rights discourse surrounds the questions of the nature of the duty (*why* is it obligatory?) and its form (*what* is required to meet it?), rather than the existence of the duty itself.[62] It is widely accepted that as the correlation of rights with obligations gives rights conceptual authority, so it is the nomination and

---

57   For an overview and analysis of the great variety of rights forms, see Jones, above, n 36, Ch 1.

58   For a discussion of the relationship between rights (proper) and right-holders' interests, see Raz, above, n 21, Ch 2.

59   Hohfeld, WN, *Fundamental Legal Conceptions* (Greenwood Press, Westport, 1964), pp 37-38.

60   Ibid, "Introduction", by Wheeler Cook, W, p 9.

61   Ibid, pp 35-40.

62   For discussion of these points and a survey of relevant literature see Jones, above, n 36, Ch 2. For a thorough and incisive study of the relationship between legal rights and legal duties see Beatty, D, "Human Rights and Rules of Law" in Beatty, D, (ed), *Human Rights and Judicial Review* (Martinus Nijhoff, Dordrecht, 1994), 1.

imposition of obligations within a legal framework that provides rights with practical authority .

The formulation of rights in this manner serves to elevate what might otherwise be merely particular interests, whether individual or group oriented, to a higher plane. It is the case that this result flows primarily from the fact of the transformative effect of legal prescription;[63] a prescription which itself depends on the putative rights taking the form of claims to which duties are or can be necessarily attached.[64] From a legal perspective, the significance of this elevation of rights lies in the effect it has on the outcomes in various other social discourses when rights are at issue. It is in this context that Ronald Dworkin's singular characterisation of rights as "trumps" is of particular relevance. "Individual rights" according to Dworkin, "are political trumps held by individuals".[65] It is, for Dworkin, through the medium of the legislative, administrative and judicial lawmaking processes of the legal system at large,[66] that such rights are accorded a superior status to that of mere interests or policy goals (that is, they trump them) on account of their pre-established claims to higher "political morality".[67]

. The matter of the legal recognition of certain pre-eminent interests or claims as rights, thereby providing a crude order of merit for use within the legal system, is an important feature of the legal prescription of rights. The same matter, however, raises a further problem for rights enforcement. That is, how does one settle disputes arising out of apparent rights conflicts? In respect of some rights regimes, this question can be relatively simply addressed through the establishment by law of priorities between rights, as is the case, for example, in express rights over implied rights in either contract or constitutional law, and in the principle of the paramountcy of children's' rights or interests over those of parents, in family law. But in terms of basic human rights the provision of such a hierarchy is not only invidious it is also extremely difficult to establish with any degree of precision. Thus, an additional feature of the legal perspective of *human* rights, in particular, is that of a conceptual framework within which such rights conflicts can be addressed. It was with this object in mind that Dworkin constructed his so-called Herculean judge model, in which the judge settles such "hard cases" through the application of the cardinal principles that underpin the law, as opposed to the application of politically or socially contingent policies.[68]

---

63   On which effect see the following section.

64   The apparent circularity of this reasoning is a matter of considerable importance and cannot be separated from the instant discussion. The fundamental questions surrounding the process by which one can distinguish the primacy or legitimacy of some claims over that of others – upon which answer the key to unlock this conundrum depends – were, in respect to *human* rights, discussed under "Defining Human Rights" above.

65   Dworkin, above, n 7, p xi.

66   Ibid, pp 105-10.

67   Ibid, p 90. See MacCormick, N, *Legal Right and Social Democracy* (Clarendon Press, Oxford, 1982), Ch 7, for a critical analysis of Dworkin's failure properly to explain this process of the justification of rights as trumps; a failure which leads MacCormick to conclude that Dworkin's definition of right is "viciously circular", p 143.

68   Dworkin, above, n 8, Ch 4. By insisting that the judge appeal to inherent, transcendental legal principles Dworkin maintains that the judge's objectivity is sustained, where it would be lost if he or she was instead to rely upon the social, economic or political policies that prevailed at the relevant time.

Legal positivists, in contrast, argue that such appeals to transcendental legal norms – no matter, as with Dworkin, how subtly styled to avoid direct reliance on the necessity of moral justification – are neither prescriptive nor descriptive of how the law deals with conflicting rights. The arguments that mount a denial of the *necessary* correlation of law with morality, like those of HLA Hart and Joseph Raz,[69] provide an alternative conceptual approach to human rights conflict. Following this reasoning, there is no necessary (moral) hierarchy of rights, nor are there immutable legal principles that one can depend upon to settle conflict between rights. Rather, there is the proffered assurance that the mode by which the conflict can be settled (by legislative provision, court order or administrative direction) is legally or ethically[70] valid according to the norms of justice that prevail in the relevant society.

Legal theorists like Hart have developed rules for recognising whether a purported law or legal process is legally valid.[71] Such formulae are generic and apply equally to the legal embracing of human rights as to any other form of rights. What, however, is fundamental to the determination of legally recognised human rights from the perspective of legal positivists is the nature of the underlying theory of justice; it is upon that base that choices are made as to which rights are to be protected, at what level and under what conditions, *vis a vis* other rights. It is in this respect that Neil MacCormick cogently argues that:

> Men are not born free; yet they are not everywhere wholly in chains; and thus a capital question for the philosophy of law in its critical, if not analytical, modes, is that of attempting to settle what are the forms of social organization which deserve approval as just and well fitted to the human condition and the human situation. To answer the question is to advance a theory of justice.[72]

There is, of course, no articulated theory of justice being advanced in this chapter; but it is clear from those who have worked to that end that justice, at both conceptual and practical levels, is not absolute, but rather is always subject to conitions and qualifications. The elemental object of justice for John Rawls, for example, is that "all social primary goals – liberty and opportunity, income and wealth, and the bases of self-respect – are to be distributed equally". The realisation of this object, however, requires in practice that utilitarian choices be made between competing claims upon these "social primary goals".[73] It is for this reason that Rawls adds the crucial qualification to the above statement, that such an object may be waived without forsaking justice where "an unequal distribution of any or all of these goods is to the advantage of the least favored".[74] In this case the challenge for

---

69 Whilst both accept that there often is, as there ought to be, a high correlation between legal validity and morality, the two concepts can and do depart from each other. Both theorists talk of morally good laws and morally bad laws, but laws nonetheless: Hart, HLA, *The Concept of Law* (Clarendon Press, Oxford, 1961), pp 195-207, and Raz, J, "The Rule of Law and its Virtue" (1977) 93 *Law Quarterly Review* 195 at 198.

70 See Campbell, below, n 76.

71 Hart, ibid, Ch 5.

72 MacCormick, above, n 71, p 85. It is this need legitimise, or at least to distinguish between just and unjust social orders, that forms the basis for Tom Campbell's thesis that there is an ethical dimension to legal positivist theory; Campbell, TD, *The Legal Theory of Ethical Positivism* (Dartmouth, Aldershot, 1996), pp 2-5, 63-73 and 97-101.

73 Rawls, J, *A Theory of Justice* (Clarendon Press, Oxford, 1972), p 303.

74 Ibid. Together – the base statement and this qualification – are what Rawls refers to as the "general conception" of his "two principles of justice"; see pp 54-114.

the legal order is, in essence, to provide the rules by which such determinations can be made.

The purpose of this discussion in the context of the aspirations of the present chapter is to demonstrate the necessary dependence of the legal perspective of human rights on more fundamental philosophical questions. In result, it is clear that not all rights manifestations are amenable to the particular conceptual demands of form that facilitate their investment with what may be termed the "force of law". But for those rights that are so amenable, the questions remain as to how such legalisation occurs and with what consequences. It is upon these concerns that the following section is focused.

THE ROLE OF LAW AND LEGAL SYSTEM

That there is an almost unqualified expectation that human rights are to be protected and promoted through law is unsurprising. Evidently this was the assumption of the drafters of the base international human rights instruments. The Preamble to the UDHR, for example, proclaims "that human rights should be protected by the rule of law".[75] Indeed, one eminent human rights scholar goes so far as to assert that "giving legal effective force to these rights is the ultimate aim of the struggle for human rights".[76] The concern of this section is to investigate what this requirement of legal effectiveness means in terms of the operation of the law and legal system in Australia.

For human rights to be protected through the rule of law, the twin elements of their being expressed in legal terms *and* that mechanisms exist for their enforcement, must be present. The legal expression of human rights is not by itself sufficient; enforcement – and, in particular, enforcement by those directly, adversely affected by a breach – must be provided for. Broadly speaking the two factors together represent the combined roles of substantive law and legal process in the explication of human rights.

That having been said, the answers to the questions of what precisely constitutes the legal expression and enforcement of human rights, and by what agents these ends are achieved, uncover a more complex picture than might be assumed. The practical (as opposed to conceptual) mechanics of the legal dimension of human rights operate, in reality, in a continuum of interrelated and overlapping processes, sequences and manifestations of human rights propagation. There are, what is more, a number of institutions, both public and private, and sets of sub-systems (Australia's nine jurisdictions and the more or less distinct spheres of the legislature, the executive, the bureaucracy, and the judiciary in each) that all have an impact on the precise form in which the law deals with human rights. Crucially, also, all are open, to greater of lesser extents, to influences that may be related to neither legal nor human rights concerns. It is upon reaching this point that the broad context in which human rights operate becomes most apparent.

It is possible to identify five features of what might be referred to as the "legal expression and enforcement continuum" as it relates to human rights:

---

75   Third paragraph.
76   Donnelly (1989), above, n 12, p 14.

- the formulation of human rights
- the articulation and definition of human rights
- the implementation and application of human rights
- the protection and promotion human rights
- the determination of breaches and provision of means for obtaining redress.

The full ambit of the legal system's incorporation of human rights is covered by these features. To provide a comprehensive analysis of what each comprises, of their collective interrelationships, and of the relative and combined impacts of institutions and social forces on their operation is an enormous task. It would require, in effect, the development of a complete sociology of law as it applies to human rights. Such an undertaking is beyond the reach of this chapter. It is sufficient for present purposes to provide an overview of how this matrix of forces and factors operates in practice.

These features or stages of legal process are essentially sequential and their impact upon human rights cumulative, in that the broad objects of the legal expression and enforcement of rights are progressively met as the rights pass through each stage. That having been said, however, it is equally clear that the process is not necessarily linear, nor always proceeding in the one direction – "stages" may be skipped; they may merge into one another; or, the developing law may double-back to an earlier stage. These characteristics of the legal process are apparent in the following discussion.

Formulation

The identification and conception of human rights within the law is essentially an exercise in policy analysis, philosophical conviction and, inevitably, political expediency. As such, the functions and operation of the core institutions and processes of government are the most important factors. All three organs of government as well as the bureaucracy (if one chooses not to view it as subsumed under the executive) may be involved in the process, in different ways and to different extents, according to the particular policy at issue.

The impetus for public policy formulation or re-formulation may arise out of the parliamentary or parliamentary committee inquiries, scrutiny, debates or resolutions,[77] or from judicial developments in the common law or statutory

---

[77] Perhaps the most enduring of these processes is that of the pre-legislative scrutiny committees that exist in every Australian Parliament, part of whose function is to scrutinise legislative proposals for compliance with broad human rights standards and whose operation regularly involves the committees in discussion (usually informal) with Ministers and departmental policy-makers. For a tabulated survey of the powers and coverage of these scrutiny committees see The Working Party of Chairs of Scrutiny of Legislation Committees throughout Australia, *Scrutiny of National Schemes of Legislation*, Discussion Paper No 1 (AGPS, Canberra, July 1995), para 3.4. For a critique of their operation and an assessment of their potential, see Kinley, D, "Parliamentary Scrutiny of Human Rights: A Duty Neglected?" in Alston, P, (ed), *Promoting Human Rights Through Bills of Rights: Comparative Perspectives* (Oxford University Press, Oxford, 1998, forthcoming). In respect of the Commonwealth Parliament the Senate's Legal and Constitutional Legislation Committee and its Legal and Constitutional References Committee, and the Human Rights Sub-Committee of the Joint Standing Committee on Foreign Affairs, Defence and Trade, in particular, regularly undertake public inquires into policies and prospective legislative initiatives that impact upon human rights standards in Australia. The Annual Reports of each committee identify and provide brief overviews of the matters they have covered.

interpretation,[78] as well as by way of the more usual and structured channels of executive and "bureaucratic brain-storming". A determination by the executive to sign or ratify a particular international human rights covenant, or to accede to the process of individual petitioning under such a covenant, or to act on a covenant's reporting requirements,[79] is not only the consequence of policies already in place but these acts themselves contribute to new or further policy initiatives. They might also provide the impetus for general policy statements on human rights issues,[80] as well as the opportunity for wider public influence to be brought to bear on the policy-making process through consultations with, and the independent actions of, interest groups, lobby groups, other non-government organisations, and individuals.[81]

In terms of the concern to secure effective, long-lasting human rights protection and promotion, the single most important stage in the legal process upon which to focus is that of policy formulation. So important is it, ultimately, to win or maintain policy support, that it can fairly be said that all the other stages or features of the legal dimension of human rights are essentially subordinate to this aim. If a supportive policy is in place and its pursuit is being undertaken in earnest then the rest – the legal definition, protection, implementation and curial determination of human rights – will follow. If it is not, in contrast, human rights standards will be diminished or extinguished by the very operation of the law and legal system that reflects such an absent or detrimental policy. The histories of the various anti-discrimination laws in Australian jurisdictions bear out this general point.[82]

Articulation and definition

The legal articulation of human rights occurs in three principal forms: in statutes; in judgments; and, in administrative rules or regulations. The same human rights may

---

78 The landmark "human rights cases" in various areas of the law discussed in the chapters that comprise this book are testimony to the effect that judicial decisions can have on policy thinking. Reference, in particular, to the two cases of *Mabo v Queensland (No 2)* (1992) 175 CLR 1 (in respect of common law development – see Ch 5 by Neilsen and Martin in this volume) and *Minister for Immigration and Ethnic Affairs v Teoh* (1995) 183 CLR 273 (in respect of statutory interpretation – see Ch 4, by McMillan and Williams and Ch 7, by Crock and Mathew, in this volume) is sufficient to demonstrate how profound that effect can be. For a discussion of the phenomenon in the Canadian context, see Hogg, P and Bushell, AA, "The *Charter* Dialogue Between Courts and Legislatures" (1997) 35 *Osgoode Hall Law Journal* 75.

79 For a survey (in tabular form) of Australia's reporting obligations to the UN's human rights treaty bodies, see *National Action Plan on Human Rights*, below, n 82, Appendix D (pp 105-06)

80 See, for example, the *National Action Plan on Human Rights* 1994 (and subsequent annual Updates), drawn up by the Department of Foreign Affairs and Trade (DFAT) pursuant to a recommendation of the 1993 *Vienna Declaration* that National Action Plans be formulated by each state party to the *Declaration*. The Australian document proclaims that "[t]he universal enjoyment of human rights remains a matter of fundamental importance for Australia. As such, Australia accords a high priority to the promotion and protection of human rights, both internationally and domestically" (p 3). See also the current Commonwealth Government's *In the National Interest* 1997 policy statement (also drawn up by DFAT) which emphasises the importance to Australia of promoting human rights protection, both within and without its borders, paras 26-31.

81 The Commonwealth Department of Foreign Affairs and Trade and the Commonwealth Attorney-General's Department both run one or two day human rights policy consultations, two or three times per year, with invited human rights NGOs.

82 See Ch 13 by Bailey and Devereux in this volume.

be subject to expression in all three mediums; indeed, almost invariably this is the case as, by the very gravity of their nature, they demand the collective attention of legislators, the judiciary and administrators. The concern for each, in this respect, is to define human rights in some way, whether in terms of their basic nature, scope or application.

A feature of Australia's common law tradition is that there is an onus placed on parliament especially, but also the executive, to endeavour to define legal rights in legislation as fully as possible. This is as true of human rights as of any other form of right. In so doing, legislators may seek directly to define the essence of the right and the legal components of its protection and exercise and the limits of its application. The *Privacy Act* 1986 (Cth) exemplifies this approach. Additionally, or in the alternative, the right may be indirectly defined by the operation of legislative provisions which, though not mentioning the right itself, effectively delimit it. The boundries of the rights to freedom of speech and movement are established in this manner.[83]

This is not to say, of course, that as a result of the heavily prescriptive form of Australian statutes, rights are in fact exhaustively defined. It remains the case that the judiciary plays a vital part in the articulation and definition of legal rights, not just in respect of common law rights not covered by statute, but also, more importantly, in respect of those rights incompletely addressed in legislation. Without exception, legislatively expressed rights fail to anticipate or provide for every circumstance in every detail that might arise in respect of their use or abuse. When such situations lead to litigation, the judiciary may be compelled, or feel itself to be compelled, to determine the rights in question through refinement, augmentation or even reformulation of their legislatively provided details.[84] That is, whether on the pretext of seeking to divine the general or specific legislative intention of the provision at issue,[85] or, where such an intention is unclear or non-existent, to fill the lacuna that would otherwise lead to a perceived injustice.

In respect of human rights law this is apparent from the judiciary's impact upon the meaning and extent of anti-discrimination laws[86] and immigration law[87] which are in the main detailed in legislation, as much as its role in the development of the constitutional right to free political speech[88] and the right to a fair trial[89] which are

---

83   By way, for example, of the various state and territory defamation laws, the proscription of racial vilification under the *Anti-Discrimination Act* 1977 (NSW) and the *Discrimination Act* 1991 (ACT) and pertinent, implied constitutional limitations on legislative power, in respect of freedom of speech, and the *Migration Act* 1958 (Cth) and the *Australian Citizenship Act* 1948 (Cth), in respect of freedom of movement.

84   It is widely accepted that the power to determine existing legal rights constitutes an integral part of the judicial function which falls within the province of judicial power as provided under Ch III of the Australian Constitution; see, for example, discussion of the matter in the judgments in *Polyukhovich v Commonwealth* (1991) 172 CLR 501. See further, Ch 2, by Sir Anthony Mason and Ch 3, by Gageler and Glass, in this volume.

85   By consulting such sources as the second reading speeches of the legislation in question, and relevant reports of parliamentary inquiries and law reform commissions under s 15AB of the *Acts Interpretation Act* 1901 (Cth).

86   See Ch 13 by Bailey and Devereux in this volume.

87   See Ch 7 by Crock and Mathew in this volume.

88   See Ch 3 by Gageler and Glass in this volume.

89   See Ch 6 by Bronitt and Ayers in this volume.

hardly detailed at all in legislation. It is also evident in respect of legislation the principal purpose of which though not centered on human rights, nonetheless incidentally affects the meaning of human rights standards.[90]

Certainly, then, the primary, or at least initial, responsibility for the legal articulation and definition of human rights lies with the parliament and executive; inevitably, however, further definition is provided by the judiciary.

Implementation and application

Once human rights have been identified and defined in law, it is incumbent upon the state to ensure that their terms are implemented generally and as specific instances demand. It is principally through the administrative departments under the policy and political direction of ministers individually and the executive collectively, on the one hand, and the courts on the other, that these functions are fulfilled. The rights to privacy, to vote, to own property, to a healthy and safe environment, to education, to welfare benefits, and the rights to be free from discrimination, unwarranted detention, restrictions in speech or political conviction or religious belief, as well as all the legitimate qualifications to these rights, require a substantial administrative and dispute settlement structure if they are to be delivered to individuals in a complex society like Australia.

The fulfillment of these functions is intimately associated with the objects of the protection and promotion of human rights through legal means.

Protection and promotion

The very processes of the policy formulation, legal definition, implementation and application of human rights establish the basis for their protection and promotion. Thereby, the means are provided by which human rights breaches may be prevented or at least limited, and where infringements do occur, the process for the imposition of sanctions is set in place and mechanisms are made available to individuals to seek redress before courts and tribunals. The obligation to ensure human rights guarantees in law are honoured in promise as well as practice falls, in the main, on the state. This is clearly the case where the relevant legal obligations expressly bind the state alone − as is the case in the areas of immigration, administrative, privacy and criminal laws. The burden, however, also rests with the state, albeit indirectly, where legal strictures bind private legal actors − as is the case with family law and anti-discrimination laws in Australia. The state, by operation of its organs of government, in other words, is always, ultimately responsible for the protection and promotion of human rights.

The responsibilities of the parliament, the executive, and to a limited extent the judiciary, are, as we have seen, largely strategic in kind; those of the bureaucracy (including such agencies as the police and tribunals) and the judiciary are more particular on account of being more situation-specific. In addition, the duties of protection and promotion are discharged by way of a number of "satellite" public

---

90   As, for example, with nascent information technology legislation; see Ch 11 by Arup and Tucker in this volume.

bodies such as the Commonwealth's Human Rights and Equal Opportunity Commission and the States' Anti-discrimination Boards and Equal Opportunity Commissions under their respective empowering statutes.[91] For not only do these bodies typically possess dispute settlement powers, they also invariably have more general preventive roles.[92] Inquiries into particular human rights issues; community wide and group-specific education programs; scrutiny and analyses of government policies, and ongoing communication with interested and affected parties are all essential parts of human rights protection and promotion. Ombudsman offices, law reform bodies and legal aid commissions are also important to the fulfillment of these ends, through the indirect, but essential, concerns of their respective functions.

Outside the realm of government, some NGOs, including and especially Community Legal Centres, play a significant and direct role in the promotion of human rights laws throughout the community. Some also, more indirectly, assist in the protection of human rights, by way of exerting pressure on governments to amend policies or laws by extending their protective or enabling reach, or by removing impediments to the enjoyment of rights.

Determination of breaches and redress

The process of determining whether there has been an infringement of a legally protected human right in particular instances, as with all legal rights, is essentially judicial in character. In the Australian context, this means that courts at all levels address disputes concerning laws affecting human rights, in respect of all matters within and without federal jurisdiction,[93] although the High Court has *ultimate* authority to make such determinations under the terms of Ch III of the Constitution.[94]

The redress that a successful litigant may obtain from the courts accords with what remedies are available to the court as regards the right in question. Such a statement may seem obvious and somewhat simplistic, but the importance within common law jurisdictions of the existence of a cause of action and a concomitant remedy cannot be overestimated. Together they comprise the essential elements of enforcement by way of litigation of all rights, including human rights. Indeed, in a comparative analysis of the differing common law and civil law perspectives on this issue, Pierre Legrand proclaims that in the common law world "one has no 'rights' unless one is protected by a cause of action", and that, in consequence, "the point of departure for any legal action is the existence of a wrong, not that of a right".[95]

---

91 For details and discussion see Ch 13 by Bailey and Devereux in this volume.

92 The HREOC is guided in this respect by the inclusion of major international anti-discrimination and human rights instruments (including the ICCPR) that relate to the Commission's functions in the Schedules to the *Human Rights and Equal Opportunity Commission Act* 1986 (Cth).

93 Which, following *Kable v Director of Public Prosecutions (NSW)* (1996) 189 CLR 51, may encompass much more of what was once thought to be the preserve of state jurisdiction; see further Ch 2, by Sir Anthony Mason and Ch 3, by Gageler and Glass, in this volume.

94 See *Polyukhovich v Commonwealth* (1991) 172 CLR 501.

95 Legrand, P, "European Legal Systems are not Converging" (1996) 45 *International and Comparative Law Quarterly* 52 at 70-71. He notes that, in contrast, "[t]he focus of the national civil codes is … on rights with the law of actions having been confined to 'technical' (and in the legal community's mind, secondary) codes of procedure": ibid.

Tribunals, and similar administrative or quasi-judicial bodies, may also have determinative and remedial powers. The extent of these powers varies from jurisdiction to jurisdiction, with the tribunals in the federal sphere being barred from making final determinations under the separation of powers doctrine,[96] while those in the States suffer no such barriers.[97] Notwithstanding the fact that the decisions of all such bodies, irrespective of jurisdiction, are subject to judicial review, the decisions made by tribunals are clearly significant in terms both of numbers of disputes settled and the effective setting of standards of human rights observance.[98]

In fulfilling these functions tribunals and, more especially, courts operate at a number of levels within the broad ambit of the practical legal dimension of human rights that is the concern of this section of the chapter. At the most immediate level, the determination of a dispute concerning legally protected human rights constitutes the basis for settlement of the dispute. In addition, however, it may represent the culmination of all the above stages or features of identification; definition, application and protection,[99] or a lesser combination of those stages.[100]

It is only after a review, such as that undertaken in this section, that of all the nominated stages in the legal system's dealing with human rights, that the system's fully integrated nature in this regard becomes most apparent, its form better understood, and the significance of both these perspectives best appreciated.

CONCLUSIONS – THE SIGNIFICANCE OF CONTEXT

Two themes run through this chapter. The first reiterates the importance of the legal dimension of human rights – that is, the legal expression and enforcement of human rights – to the object of securing their observance and advancement. The second is built around the phenomenological point that such legal protection of human rights necessarily exists within, and is vitally affected by, a broader, non-legal context. The whole process of the law's interaction with human rights is contextually situated – from the manner in which human rights are conceived in legal terms to the consequences of an arbitral determination that there has been a breach of their terms.

Patently, the legal dimension of human rights is but one dimension. For anyone to focus on it, to the willful or unconscious neglect of all else, is to fail fully or even adequately to appreciate the nature of human rights and their role in our social order. For lawyers to do so is to diminish their practice of the law and to squander potential. A fuller appreciation of the place of human rights within a legal system, their origins and the factors that continue to influence them, not only permits their

---

96 As made clear in *Brandy v Human Rights and Equal Opportunity Commission* (1995) 183 CLR 245; see, for further discussion, Ch 2 by Sir Anthony Mason, Ch 13 by Bailey and Devereux, and Ch 14 by Eastman and Ronalds in this volume.

97 For a comparative analysis in the context of anti-discrimination bodies in Australia, see Ch 13, by Bailey and Devereux in this volume.

98 See Ch 4 by McMillan and Williams in this volume.

99 The common law right of native title, as established in the *Mabo (No 2)* (1992) 175 CLR 1, is emblematic in this regard.

100 The tentative steps taken by the judiciary in identifying and articulating human rights in the areas of information technology (see Ch 11 by Arup and Tucker in this volume) and health law (see Ch 12 by Freckelton and Loff in this volume) provide examples of such combination.

more effective pursuit through the means provided by that legal system, it also inspires debate and change within broader social and political spheres.[101] The part then, that can be played by those who seek to advance the cause of human rights through law is significant indeed.

---

101 See Charlesworth, H, "The Australian Reluctance about Rights", in P Alston (ed), *Towards an Australian Bill of Rights* (Centre for International and Public Law, Canberra, 1994), pp 49-51, and Sarkin, J, "The Role of the Legal Profession in the Promotion and Advancement of Human Rights Culture" (1995) 21 *Commonwealth Law Bulletin* 1306.

2

THE ROLE OF THE JUDICIARY IN DEVELOPING HUMAN RIGHTS IN AUSTRALIAN LAW

The Hon Sir Anthony Mason AC KBE

INTRODUCTION

"Human rights" is an expression which is not merely evocative; it is also amorphous in the sense that it conjures up a concept with constantly moving boundaries. Sometimes it is used as a synonym for individual rights; it can also refer to collective rights, such as the collective rights of an aboriginal people. The collective rights of an aboriginal people or group to land ownership or possession, individual ownership not being a significant element in aboriginal custom, is an example. Another example is the right of a people to autonomy or self-determination, that being widely regarded as a fundamental right.

An important aspect of human rights is the very strong emphasis given to democratic rights. Democratic rights, considered as individual rights, are the counterpart of the collective rights of a people to autonomy. Much of the human rights based criticism of the People's Republic of China is directed to the perceived lack of democratic institutions and processes in the Republic. Likewise, the criticism of democratic arrangements in Hong Kong has a strong human rights flavour.

So, in discussing the role of the judiciary in relation to human rights in Australia, it is necessary to take account of an expansive international conception of human rights, one which threatens to devour all other legal titles which exist in close proximity to it. That said, it must be acknowledged that human rights jurisprudence has not had as strong an impact in Australia as it has had elsewhere. Indeed, as will appear, there are grounds for apprehension that Australia is not as deeply committed to *judicial* protection of human rights as a number of Western nations, including the United States, the United Kingdom, Canada and New Zealand.[1]

---

1   The reader might wish to read this chapter in parallel with Ch 3 by Gageler and Glass in this volume, entitled: "Constitutional Law and Human Rights". The distinguishing feature of the treatment of constitutional human rights issues in the present chapter is that of the judicial perspective adopted. The central question sought to be answered in this chapter, therefore, is to what extent Australian judges can and have employed human rights arguments in their deliberations.

THE AUSTRALIAN FRAMEWORK
OF HUMAN RIGHTS PROTECTION

One reason for the absence of such a deep commitment to human rights jurisprudence is the absence in Australia of comprehensive guarantees of human rights in the Australian Constitution and the Constitutions of the States. Australia does not even have a statute-based Bill of Rights, such as the *New Zealand Bill of Rights Act* 1990. Constitutional protection of human rights is a significant factor in generating a climate of acceptance of human rights protection and human rights jurisprudence. Hence the absence of constitutional protection is a matter of significance.

The protection of human rights in Australia therefore rests largely on statutory foundations. The relevant statutes, whether Commonwealth or State, deal with particular aspects of human rights. The *Racial Discrimination Act* 1975 (Cth) (RDA) is an example. It gives effect to the *International Convention on the Elimination of All Forms of Racial Discrimination* which has been ratified by Australia. The RDA has counterparts in State legislation. A notable instance is Pt II of the *Anti-Discrimination Act* 1977 (NSW) dealing with racial discrimination. In *Viskauskas v Niland*,[2] the High Court held that s 19 of the State Act making racial discrimination in relation to the provision of goods and services unlawful and other provisions to the extent that they related to s 19 and to complaints for breaches of that section were inconsistent with the RDA and were invalid by reason of s 109 of the Constitution. The basis of the decision was that the RDA manifested an intention to occupy the relevant field to the exclusion of any other law. Subsequently the High Court in *Metwally v University of Wollongong*[3] held that the enactment of a Commonwealth statute, with retrospective effect, to exclude from the 1975 Act any intention to occupy the relevant field to the exclusion of State law, did not eliminate the inconsistency between Commonwealth and State law which existed before the enactment of the retrospective law.

The most comprehensive legislative protection of human rights in Australia is that given by the *Human Rights and Equal Opportunity Commission Act* 1986 (Cth) (HREOC Act). That Act established the Human Rights and Equal Opportunity Commission and entrusted it with the responsibility of promoting and protecting human rights in Australia under the RDA, *the Sex Discrimination Act* 1984 (Cth), the HREOC Act and the *Disability Discrimination Act* 1991 (Cth). The Commission also has the responsibility of monitoring compliance with the *International Covenant on Civil and Political Rights* 1966 (ICCPR), Australia having ratified the ICCPR and the First Optional Protocol thereto, though it has not implemented the ICCPR by enacting it as part of our domestic law.

In entrusting the enforcement of human rights under these statutes to an administrative tribunal rather than to the orthodox courts, the HREOC Act follows a model that has become a standard model in both Commonwealth and State legislation providing for human rights protection. Administrative determination is thought to be less formal, less expensive and more expeditious than judicial

---

2   (1983) 153 CLR 280.

3   (1984) 158 CLR 447.

determination. The consequence of reposing jurisdiction in administrative tribunals is that judicial protection of human rights under Commonwealth and State statutes is generally exercised by way of judicial review of the decisions of the tribunal in which jurisdiction is vested by the relevant statute.

The separation of powers effected by the Australian Constitution and, more importantly, the vesting by Ch III of the Constitution of the judicial power of the Commonwealth in the courts for which Ch III provides, present an insurmountable obstacle to the complete enforcement by a Commonwealth administrative tribunal of a right arising under a Commonwealth law. In *Brandy v Human Rights and Equal Opportunity Commission*,[4] the High Court held that ss 25ZAA, 25ZAB and 25ZAC of the RDA, which required registration of the Commission's determinations, on a complaint of discrimination in breach of that Act, with the Federal Court and made registered determinations enforceable as orders of that court, were invalid. That was because the sections combined to make a determination of the Commission binding, authoritative and enforceable and therefore invalidly vested judicial power in the Commission. In order to overcome the defect in the Commission's jurisdiction exposed by the decision in *Brandy*, jurisdiction is to be vested in the Federal Court.[5]

The Commonwealth Parliament has no general legislative power with respect to human rights under the Constitution. The parliament can legislate for human rights protection to the extent that such protection falls within specific heads of Commonwealth legislative power conferred by the Constitution. The specific heads of legislative power fall far short of enabling the Commonwealth to enact a statute providing for general human rights protection. However, according to the interpretation given by the High Court to the power to make laws with respect to external affairs, conferred by s 51(xxix) of the Constitution, that power enables parliament to enact laws giving effect to and implementing treaties and international conventions ratified by the Australian Government.[6]

That is why human rights protection in Australia rests to a not insignificant extent on the existence of international conventions which Australia has ratified. Ratification of a convention providing for human rights protection enables parliament to enact legislation giving effect to that convention, notwithstanding that the law would not otherwise fall within the legislative powers conferred upon the parliament by the Constitution.[7] Reference has already been made to the *International Covenant on the Elimination of All Forms of Racial Discrimination* on which the RDA is based. The ICCPR, though not enacted as part of our domestic law, may be invoked by means of a complaint by an individual pursuant to the First Optional Protocol (which Australia has ratified) that Australia has violated the ICCPR. Such a complaint gives jurisdiction to the UN Human Rights Committee, whose decision may result in a change in Australian domestic law, as it did in the

---

4   (1995) 183 CLR 245.

5   Pending implementation of the decision to vest jurisdiction in the Federal Court, the Commission is exercising jurisdiction, though its determination is not enforceable as a decision of the Federal Court. The exercise of jurisdiction by the Federal Court currently requires a hearing de novo.

6   *Koowarta v Bjelke-Petersen* (1982) 153 CLR 168; *Commonwealth v Tasmania* ("*Tasmanian Dam Case*") (1983) 158 CLR 1.

7   *Koowarta* (1982) 153 CLR 168.

Toonen Case.[8] More importantly, ratification of an international convention by Australia enables the Commonwealth Parliament to legislate, under s 51(xxix) of the Constitution, to give effect to the provisions of the convention.[9] It was in the exercise of that power that the Commonwealth Parliament validly enacted the RDA.[10]

Although the Australian Constitution does not contain guarantees which amount to a general Bill of Rights, it does contain some specific provisions which are capable of being construed as guarantees of human rights. The Constitution also provides for a separation of powers and the exercise of federal judicial power by an independent judiciary, these being constitutional elements which in combination are regarded as an indispensable protection of human rights. Apart from what is explicit, there are implicit elements in the Constitution. One issue which has commanded attention in recent times is whether it is possible, by means of implication, to distil from the Constitution protection of human rights and, if so, to what extent. The High Court has held that, based on the constitutional provisions setting up a system of representative government, there is to be implied a freedom of communication as to matters of government and politics.[11] And Ch III of the Constitution has generated implications in relation to curial due process which are significant for the protection of human rights, notably the constitutional principle that no person can be detained in custody by Commonwealth authority except pursuant to a court order made in the exercise of the judicial power of the Commonwealth, subject to certain exceptions such as contempt of Parliament, breach of military law and deportation of aliens.[12]

The final, and perhaps the most important, element in the legal framework of human rights protection in Australia, at least from the perspective of the role of the judiciary, is the common law. There is much to be said for the view that the judiciary's principal contribution to the protection of human rights in Australia has been in formulating the principles of the common law. First, there has been the statement of principle governing the land rights of indigenous people with respect to the unalienated waste lands of the Crown in the well-known case of *Mabo v Queensland (No 2)*[13] and its successor *Wik Peoples v Queensland*,[14] where the court acknowledged the possibility that indigenous rights to the use of land might not be extinguished under a pastoral "lease" which confers a right to depasture stock rather than a right to exclusive possession.

Apart from the rights of indigenous people, there have been important common law decisions affecting human rights. One decision concerned the sterilisation of a

---

8   See the *Toonen* Case, Communication of the UN Human Rights Committee (Com 488/1992); (1994) 5 *Public Law Review* 72 at 156.

9   *Tasmanian Dam* Case (1984) 158 CLR 1.

10 *Koowarta* (1982) 153 CLR 168, upheld the RDA as a valid exercise of the power conferred by s 51(xxix).

11 *Nationwide News Pty Ltd v Wills* (1992) 177 CLR 1; *Australian Capital Television Pty Ltd v Commonwealth (ACTTV)* (1992) 177 CLR 106; *Theophanous v Herald and Weekly Times Ltd* (1994) 182 CLR 104; *Lange v Australian Broadcasting Commission* (1997) 145 ALR 96.

12 *Chu Kheng Lim v Minister for Immigration* (1992) 176 CLR 1 at 28-29.

13 (1992) 175 CLR 1.

14 (1996) 187 CLR 1.

mentally handicapped young female. In that decision, the court recognised the individual's right to physical integrity and autonomy.[15] In the interpretation of statutes, the High Court adopted in *Coco v The Queen*[16] rules of construction which are designed to ensure that rights traditionally protected by the common law and fundamental rights are not abrogated or curtailed otherwise than by express words or by an unambiguous and unmistakable manifestation of statutory intention so to do.

Of great importance has been the interaction between international law and the common law. In formulating the principles of the common law relating to human rights, the High Court has emphasised the importance of international law and the provisions of international conventions, at least to the extent that they have been ratified by Australia. In a series of cases, most notably *Mabo (No 2)*, the High Court has affirmed the proposition that international law is a legitimate and important influence on the development of the common law, especially when international law declares the existence of universal human rights.[17] In the context in which the proposition has been affirmed in the cases, it is clear that it applies to the provisions of an international convention which has been ratified by Australia but not implemented by legislation so as to make it part of our domestic law.

In *Minister for Immigration and Ethnic Affairs v Teoh*,[18] the third of the series of cases just mentioned, the majority of the court, after adopting the proposition stated above, held that art 3(1) of the *Convention on the Rights of the Child*, a convention ratified but not implemented by Australia, generated a legitimate expectation that the rights of the child would be dealt with by the decision-maker in accordance with the provisions of the article. It provided that "the best interests of the child shall be a primary consideration".

The decision in *Teoh* excited considerable controversy.[19] Successive Ministers for Foreign Affairs and Attorneys-General issued joint statements to the effect that entering into an international instrument should not give rise to legitimate expectations and that legislation would be introduced to set aside any such expectations. These statements were based on an observation in the joint judgment of Mason CJ and Deane J that a legitimate expectation would not arise if there is an executive or legislative statement to the contrary. In 1997 the Administrative Decisions (Effect of International Instruments) Bill 1997 was introduced. Section 5 of the Bill provides:

> The fact that:
> (a) Australia is bound by, or a party to, a particular international instrument; or
> (b) an enactment reproduces or refers to a particular international instrument;

---

15   *Re Marion* (1992) 175 CLR 218.

16   (1994) 179 CLR 429.

17   *Mabo v Queensland (No 2)* (1992) 175 CLR 1 at 42 per Brennan J; *Dietrich v The Queen* (1992) 177 CLR 292 at 306-07, 319-21 per Mason CJ and McHugh JJ; *Minister for Immigration and Ethnic Affairs v Teoh* (1995) 183 CLR 273 at 288-89 per Mason CJ and Deane J.

18   *Minister for Immigration and Ethnic Affairs v Teoh* (1995) 183 CLR 273 at 288-89 per Mason CJ and Deane J.

19   See discussion in Ch 4 by McMillan and Williams in this volume. For an illuminating discussion of *Teoh* and its relationship with the law as it has developed in the United Kingdom, see Hunt, M, *Using Human Rights Law in English Courts* (Hart Publishing, Oxford, 1997), pp 242-59.

does not give rise to a legitimate expectation of a kind that might provide a basis at law for invalidating or in any way changing the effect of an administrative decision.

As the Senate Legal and Constitution Legislation Committee has recommended that the Bill be enacted without amendment, it now seems unlikely that the Bill will be enacted during the life of the present government.

Section 7 of the Bill is important. It provides that, to avoid doubt, s 5 does not affect any other operation or effect, or use that may be made, of an international instrument in Australian law. The effect of s 5 is to enable the courts to continue to draw upon the provisions of an international convention as source material for developing the common law.

Australian courts, however, do not exercise a jurisdiction to compel the Australian Government to comply with obligations arising under international conventions or obligations not recognised by Australian law.[20]

THE CONSTITUTIONAL DIMENSION

Express provisions

Separation of powers and the exercise of judicial power

The High Court has given strong emphasis to the separation of powers and the vesting of judicial power by Ch III in courts constituted by an independent judiciary as central elements in the rule of law as provided in the Constitution. As *Brandy's Case*[21] shows, the court has refused to countenance attempts to allow administrative tribunals to exercise the judicial power of the Commonwealth. Correspondingly, the court has refused to allow the parliament to confer upon the Federal courts administrative functions which are not incidental to the exercise of judicial power.[22]

At the same time, the court has allowed non-judicial functions to be exercised on a voluntary basis by a judge as a *persona designata* provided that those functions are compatible with the discharge by the judge of the duties of his judicial office and with the proper discharge by the judiciary of its responsibilities as an institution exercising judicial power.[23] Hence the power to issue telephonic interception warrants, exercisable by a federal judge as a designated person, not being an exercise of judicial power, was held not to be incompatible with the discharge by a judge of his judicial duties or with the discharge by the judiciary of its responsibilities.[24]

The constitutional separation of powers precludes parliament from legislatively declaring a person guilty of an offence and imposing punishment. That function is vested in the Ch III courts.[25] An exception is parliament's power to punish for

---

20   *Horta v Commonwealth* (1994) 181 CLR 183; and see Perry JW, "At the Intersection of Australian and International Law" (1997) 71 *Australian Law Journal* 841.

21   *Brandy* (1995) 183 CLR 245.

22   *R v Kirby; ex p Boilermakers' Society of Australia* (1956) 94 CLR 254; affd *Attorney-General (Cth) v The Queen* (1957) 95 CLR 529.

23   *Hilton v Wells* (1985) 157 CLR 57; *Grollo v Commissioner of Australian Federal Police* (1995) 184 CLR 348.

24   Ibid.

25   *Polyukovich v Commonwealth* (1991) 172 CLR 501.

contempt of parliament, a power arising under s 49 of the Constitution.[26] Another apparent exception is the limited capacity of defence force tribunals to adjudge and punish breaches of service discipline.[27]

Democratic rights

In its interpretation of s 41 of the Constitution, the High Court has adopted a conservative approach. The section provides that no adult person who has or acquires a right to vote at elections for the numerous Houses of the parliament of a State, shall be prevented by any law of the Commonwealth from voting at elections for either House in the Commonwealth Parliament. The court applied to the expression "adult person" the principle that the meaning to be given to a term is that which it had at the date of enactment of the Constitution, namely 1900, and concluded that only a person who attained the age of 21 years was such a person.[28] Subsequently, the court held that the section preserved only voting rights which existed when the federal franchise was established.[29] That interpretation rested, however, on the text and policy of the section rather than upon any rule of construction.

It is questionable whether the rule of construction applied to s 41 is appropriate to a constitution and, even more so, to a provision which deals with voting rights. There is a cogent case for construing liberally provisions relating to democratic rights. Moreover, the rule of construction applied to s 41 contrasts sharply with the modern statements favouring a progressive or dynamic interpretation of constitutional terms adopted in other cases.[30]

In *McGinty v Western Australia*,[31] the High Court affirmed its earlier decision, *Attorney-General (Cth); ex rel McKinlay v Commonwealth*,[32] to the effect that the language of s 24 of the Constitution requiring members of the House of Representatives to be chosen by the people of the several States does not mandate "one vote one value", that is, electoral divisions with, as far as practicable, an equal number of electors. In reaching that conclusion, the majority of the court[33] distinguished the United States decisions on a similarly worded provision (art 1 s 2) in the United States Constitution, largely on the basis that Australia had inherited and adopted the British parliamentary tradition whereby the franchise and the electoral system were a matter for parliament to determine. The circumstance that the Australian Constitution provided for a system of representative government was not an obstacle to this conclusion because representative government is an evolving concept. Hence, though in 1900 the franchise did not extend to females and many

---

26   *R v Richards; ex p Fitzpatrick and Brown* (1955) 92 CLR 157.
27   See *Re Tracey; ex p Ryan* (1989) 166 CLR 518; *Re Nolan; ex p young* (1991) 172 CLR; *Re Tyler* (1994) 181 CLR 18.
28   *King v Jones* (1972) 128 CLR 221.
29   *R v Pearson; ex p Sipka* (1983) 152 CLR 254.
30   See *Cheatle v The Queen* (1993) 177 CLR 541 at 560-61; *McGinty v Western Australia* (1996) 186 CLR 140 at 166-67, 200-01, 216, 286-87.
31   (1996) 186 CLR 140 at 166-67, 200-01, 216, 286-87.
32   (1975) 135 CLR 1.
33   (1966) 186 CLR 140.

males in 1900, they could not now be excluded from the vote.[34] The evolving or dynamic interpretation of both representative government and s 24 adopted by the court, though inherently at odds with the view that the Constitution leaves the franchise to be determined by parliament, appears to be based on an evolution brought about by parliament's extension of the franchise to an expanded class of voters. In rejecting the American interpretation, the court was influenced by the approach developed by the Canadian courts.[35]

Trial by jury

Much the same approach was adopted in the interpretation of s 80 of the Constitution in *Cheatle v The Queen*.[36] That section provides "[t]he trial on an indictment of any offence against any law of the Commonwealth shall be by jury".

A South Australian statute provided for majority jury verdicts in criminal cases. In *Cheatle*, the High Court held unanimously that s 80 requires a unanimous verdict of guilty in respect of indictable offences against a Commonwealth law. This was because unanimity was an essential element of trial by jury in 1900. In order to overcome the argument that this would mean that juries would consist only of men who satisfied a property qualification, this being a requirement for jury service in 1900, the court stated that the essential feature of trial by jury at that time was that jurors should be representative of the community. Relaxation of jury qualifications had the effect of making the jury more representative. A return to a male property qualification would no longer be seen as providing the requisite representative character of the jury.

In another and important respect, s 80 has not been interpreted in a manner appropriate to a guarantee of a fundamental right to trial by jury of an indictable offence. Despite powerful dissents, the court has treated the provision as procedural, not substantive, so that there is no obligation to compel procedure by indictment, leaving the parliament free to legislate for summary trial when it thinks it appropriate to do so.[37] The section has therefore been denied a substantive operation as a fundamental guarantee.

Acquisition of property on just terms

Section 51(xxxi) confers power on the parliament to make laws with respect to the acquisition of property on just terms. Although expressed as a power, the provision has been accorded the status of a constitutional guarantee which was designed to protect citizens from being deprived of their property except on just terms. As a

---

34   *McGinty* (1996) 186 CLR 140 at 166-67, 200-01, 216, 286-87; *Langer v Commonwealth* (1966) 186 CLR 302 at 342.

35   See *Reference re Electoral Boundaries Commission Act (Alberta)* (1991) 81 DLR (4th) 16; *Dixon v Attorney-General (British Columbia)* (1989) 59 DLR (4th) 247.

36   (1993) 177 CLR 541. For further discussion, see Ch 6 by Bronitt and Ayres in this volume.

37   *R v Archdall and Roskruge; ex p Carrigan and Brown* (1928) 41 CLR 128; *R v Federal Court of Bankruptcy; ex p Lowenstein* (1938) 59 CLR 556 but cf at 580-82 per Dixon and Evatt JJ; *Zarb v Kennedy* (1968) 121 CLR 283; *Kingswell v The Queen* (1985) 159 CLR 264, but cf at 308-14 per Deane J; *Brown v The Queen* (1986) 160 CLR 171.

constitutional guarantee it is to be given a liberal construction.[38] It fetters the legislative power by forbidding laws with respect to acquisition on any terms that are not just,[39] except such acquisitions as may be made under a power which contemplates acquisition on terms that may not be just; for example, the power under s 51(xviii) with respect to copyright, patents, designs and trade marks.[40] The requirement of just terms applies to acquisitions in a Commonwealth territory pursuant to s 122 of the Constitution.[41]

Freedom of interstate trade, commerce and intercourse

Section 92 provides that "trade commerce and intercourse among the States ... shall be absolutely free".

The deceptively simple words of s 92 lend themselves to a variety of possible interpretations with which the High Court flirted for almost a century. In 1988, in *Cole v Whitfield*,[42] the court decided that the section provides for freedom of interstate trade and commerce from discriminatory burdens of a protectionist kind.[43] That interpretation recognises the right of the individual to immunity from discriminatory legislative (and executive) treatment in respect of interstate trade. It falls short, however, of affirming an individual right to engage in interstate trade. Indeed, one of the grounds for rejecting an earlier interpretation favoured by the court was that it treated s 92 as creating such an individual right. To that extent, *Cole v Whitfield* is not an instance of fundamental rights interpretation. The decision is based largely on a view of the Australian federal movement which saw as one of its goals the abolition of discriminatory treatment of interstate trade of a protectionist kind.

Freedom of religion

Section 116 of the Constitution provides that the Commonwealth Parliament shall not make any law of establishing any religion, or for imposing any religious observance or for prohibiting the free exercise of any religion. The High Court has interpreted the section as prohibiting a law which has the effect or purpose of constituting or recognising a particular religion as a national institution, like the Church of England in the United Kingdom, but not as forbidding State aid to church schools.[44] In the latter respect, the High Court has not followed the interpretation given to a counterpart provision in the United States Constitution, the First Amendment. The difference between the interpretations adopted by the High Court

---

38   *Clunies-Ross v Commonwealth* (1984) 155 CLR 193 at 202.

39   *Bank of New South Wales v Commonwealth (Bank Nationalization Case)* (1948) 76 CLR 1 at 349-50; *Attorney-General (Cth) v Schmidt* (1961) 105 CLR 361; *Trade Practices Commission v Tooth & Co Ltd* (1979) 142 CLR 397.

40   *Nintendo v Centronics* (1991) 184 CLR 134 at 160-61.

41   *Newcrest v Commonwealth* (1997) 147 ALR 42.

42   (1988) 165 CLR 360.

43   See also *Bath v Alston Holdings Pty Ltd* (1988) 165 CLR 411; *Castlemaine Tooheys Ltd v South Australia* (1990) 169 CLR 436; *Barley Marketing Board (NSW) v Norman* (1990) 171 CLR 182.

44   *Attorney-General (Vic); ex rel Black v Commonwealth* (1981) 146 CLR 321.

and the Supreme Court of the United States is due in part to the difference in the relevant history of the two countries.

The first limb of s 116 is expressed as a prohibition on legislative power rather than as a fundamental right. On the other hand, though expressed as a prohibition on legislative power, the last limb of s 116 dealing with the "free exercise of any religion", does involve a fundamental right and might require a broader construction.[45] Consistently with that approach, in a statutory context, a broad meaning was given to the expression "religious institution" for the purpose of statutory exemption from pay-roll tax.[46]

Equal rights of out-of-State residents

Section 117 provides:

> A subject of the Queen, resident in any State, shall not be subject in any other State to any disability or discrimination which would not be equally applicable to him if he were a subject of the Queen resident in such other State.

On its face, s 117 appears to be a constitutional guarantee of equal rights to all residents in all States, like its model, art IV s 2 of the United States Constitution. But that was not the accepted view until *Street v Queensland Bar Association*[47] was decided in 1989. The case concerned the entitlement of a barrister resident in New South Wales to practise in Queensland. The Queensland rules required, initially, that an applicant for admission to practise be a resident of Queensland and cease to practise in other States and, subsequently, that an applicant have an intention to practise principally in Queensland.

In an earlier decision, *Henry v Boehm*,[48] the court had distinguished between permanent and temporary residence, holding that s 117 provided protection only against discrimination or disability based on permanent residence. In *Street*, the court unanimously overruled *Henry v Boehm* and held that s 117 requires a comparison to be made between the out-of-State citizens' actual position under the relevant State law and the position in which that person would be if that person were a resident of the State. Subject to some possible qualifications which need not be mentioned, that is how s 117 is to be read. In the result the Queensland rules did not apply to the New South Wales applicant.

Two points should be made about s 117. First, the object of the section, one of fundamental importance, is to promote national unity by ensuring that persons resident in one State are treated in another State as citizens of one nation, not as foreigners.[49] Secondly, the section is explicitly directed to the protection of the rights of the individual. In this respect, it is to be contrasted with other provisions which are primarily directed at limiting the powers of the Commonwealth. Hence the decisions on art IV s 2 of the United States Constitution provide some useful elucidation.

---

45   Ibid at 603 per Gibbs J.

46   *Church of New Faith v Commissioner for Pay-Roll Tax* (1983) 154 CLR 120.

47   (1989) 168 CLR 461.

48   (1973) 128 CLR 482.

49   *Street* (1989) 168 CLR 461 at 485, 522, 541.

Civil conscription

Section 51(xxiiiA) confers legislative power with respect to medical and dental services (but not so as to authorise any form of civil conscription). Practical as distinct from legal compulsion is enough to give rise to civil conscription but civil conscription does not refer to compulsion to do, in a particular way, some act in the course of carrying on practice or performing a service when there is no compulsion to carry on the practice or perform the service.[50]

Comment on the express provisions

The express provisions in the Constitution to which reference has been made are a motley and disconnected array. Some, for example, s 51(xxxi), s 117, the civil conscription prohibition in s 51(xxiiiA) and the final limb of s 116 dealing with the free exercise of any religion, can be regarded as guarantees of fundamental rights and should therefore be construed liberally. Other provisions have a more ambiguous character either because they are primarily a limitation on power rather than the protection of an individual right or because their history reveals that they are intended to serve a particular and limited purpose. Section 92 falls into both categories. Section 80 may fall into the second category. Section 41 has not been given the dynamic interpretation appropriate to a provision dealing with a fundamental democratic right.

The ambiguous character of some provisions reflects the origins of the Constitution. It was designed to define the structure and powers of government rather than to define individual rights and freedoms of individuals. The framers of the Constitution "refused to adopt any part of the Bill of Rights Act of 1791 and ... the Fourteenth Amendment"[51] because individual rights were thought to be sufficiently protected by the common law and parliament. There is little, if anything, to support the view that the delegates to the Convention considered that a Bill of Rights was to be implied in the Constitution. It would indeed be a strange way in which to entrench such rights in the Constitution.

Implied rights

The making of implications in the Constitution has been the subject of continuing controversy, notably in recent times. Implication is a natural and necessary incident of the process of interpretation, whether it is a constitution, a statute or a contract that is being interpreted. Sir Owen Dixon, who was noted for his adherence to legalism, said "I do not see why we should be fearful about making implications".[52]

That is not to say that implications are freely made. On the contrary, courts are cautious about making implications. They are only made when they give expression to the intention of the relevant instrument as that intention is revealed by reference

---

50   *General Practitioners Society in Australia v Commonwealth* (1980) 145 CLR 532.

51   Sir Owen Dixon, *Jesting Pilate* (Law Book Co, Sydney, 1965), p 102; but cf *Leeth v Commonwealth* (1992) 174 CLR 455 at 485 fn 57 per Deane and Toohey J.

52   *Australian National Airways Pty Ltd v Commonwealth* (1945) 71 CLR 29 at 85; see also *Lamshed v Lake* (1945) 99 CLR 132 at 144.

to its language considered in the light of context (including history) and the nature and purpose of the instrument.

That is why reference is made to "necessary implications", indicating that an implication is not made unless it is necessary. Here, however, a distinction must be drawn between the making of an implication based simply on a manifestation of intention to be gathered from the provisions of the Constitution, in which event one is concerned only to ascertain whether that intention is manifested, and an implication based on the structure of the Constitution. In the latter case the implication must be logically or practically necessary for the preservation of the integrity of that structure.[53]

Chapter III of the Constitution apart, little has been achieved by the High Court in implying human rights protection in the Constitution. In the ultimate analysis, this is because the Australian Constitution is an instrument which defines the structure of government and distributes the power of government rather than one which defines individual rights and freedoms in conformity with the British parliamentary tradition and the doctrine of parliamentary supremacy.

Freedom of communication on matters of government and politics

The most notable implication of a right or freedom in the Australian Constitution is the implication of freedom of communication on matters of government and politics. The existence of that implied freedom was first upheld in *Nationwide News Pty Ltd v Wills*[54] and *Australian Capital Television Pty Ltd v Commonwealth (ACTTV)*.[55] The existence of the implication was based on two propositions, first, that the structure and the provisions of the Constitution, notably ss 7 and 24, provided for a system of representative government; secondly, that freedom of communication was indispensable to the efficacious working of that system of representative government. In other words, the implication was made on the footing that it was practically necessary to ensure the efficacious working of the system of government mandated by the Constitution.

In *Nationwide News*, the High Court held that s 299(1)(d)(ii) of the *Industrial Relations Act* 1988 (Cth) provided that a person shall not by writing or speech use words calculated to bring a member of the Industrial Relations Commission or the Commission itself into disrepute. A majority[56] considered that the provision violated the freedom of communication because it penalised criticism of the Commission and its members which could be reasonable, fair and justifiable. The provision went further than was necessary for the protection of courts pursuant to the principles of contempt of court.

In *ACTTV*, Pt IIID of the *Broadcasting Act* 1942 (Cth) was held invalid. Part IIID was designed, subject to certain exceptions, to prohibit the use of radio and television during election periods for political advertisements and even for political

---

53   *Australian Capital Television Pty Ltd* (1992) 177 CLR 106 at 135; *McGinty* (1996) 186 CLR 140 at 168-69.
54   (1992) 177 CLR 1.
55   (1992) 177 CLR 106.
56   Brennan, Deane, Toohey and Gaudron JJ.

information, comment, argument and discussion. The exceptions related to the broadcasting of news, current affairs and talk-back radio programs, party political launches and political broadcasting under a régime of free election broadcasts. A majority[57] held that Pt IIID was wholly invalid on the ground that infringed the implied freedom in that it discriminated in favour of those political parties and politicians who were represented in the parliament leading up to the election and against other parties, candidates as well as interest groups, who might wish to disseminate their views on radio and television. The discrimination was manifested in the provisions governing entitlements to participate in the régime of free election broadcasts.

The Pt IIID prohibitions applied not only to Federal elections but also to State, Territory and local government elections. The declaration that Pt IIID was invalid extended the freedom to matters of State and local authority government and politics. This extension was the subject of differing views in *McGinty v Western Australia*,[58] notably in the judgments of McHugh and Gummow JJ.[59] This question was ultimately resolved in the unanimous judgment of the court in *Lange v Australian Broadcasting Commission*,[60] where the court held that the freedom protects only communications relevant to the system of responsible and representative government for which the Constitution provides, that is Federal and Territory government. Insistence on this proposition may involve the High Court in the difficult task of distinguishing between information and comments relevant only to Federal and Territory government and politics and those that are not.

The unanimous judgment in *Lange* tied the freedom more closely to the express provisions of the Constitution, particularly ss 7, 24 and 128, and emphasised that the freedom enables the people to exercise a free and informed choice as electors to cast informed votes in a referendum. Nonetheless the freedom is not confined to an election period and it extends to communications concerning the affairs of statutory authorities and public authorities required to report to the legislature or a responsible Minister.[61]

The court stated that a law will be invalid as infringing the freedom if:

(a) it effectively burdens the freedom in its terms, operation or effect; and

(b) the law is not reasonably appropriate and adapted to serve a legitimate end, the fulfilment of which is compatible with the maintenance of the constitutionally prescribed system of government and the procedure prescribed by s 128.[62]

Lange was a case in which a former Prime Minister of New Zealand sued the ABC for defamation and the ABC pleaded, first, a defence that the defamatory material was published pursuant to the freedom of communication guaranteed by the

---

57   Mason CJ, Deane, Toohey and Gaudron JJ.

58   (1996) 186 CLR 140. In *Cunliffe v Commonwealth* (1994) 182 CLR 272, though a majority held that restrictions imposed on the giving of assistance to aliens and the making of representations on their behalf was not protected by the implied freedom, a majority held that the making of representations to a Minister was a communication on a matter of government and politics.

59   *McGinty* (1996) 186 CLR 140 at 250-51, 291.

60   (1997) 145 ALR 96.

61   Ibid at 107.

62   Ibid at 108, 112.

Constitution and, secondly, a defence of qualified privilege. The court held that the constitutional defence was bad in law and should be struck out. The court found that the second defence was not supported by the particulars given but did not strike it out and allowed the defendant to provide further particulars.

In order to appreciate the *Lange* decision, it is necessary to mention two decisions which followed hard on the heels of *Nationwide News* and *ACTTV*. The two decisions are *Theophanous v Herald & Weekly Times Ltd*[63] and *Stephens v Western Australian Newspapers Ltd*.[64] In *Theophanous*, the defendant published of the plaintiff, who was a member of the House of Representatives in the Federal Parliament and chairman of the Parliamentary Standing Committee on Migration, a letter written by Mr Bruce Ruxton which was critical of the plaintiff. According to the imputations pleaded, the letter accused the plaintiff of bias, of standing for things that most Australians were against and of being an idiot.

By majority,[65] the court held that the implied freedom of communication gave rise to a constitutional defence to an action for defamation. The defence applied to the publication of material (a) discussing government and political matters, (b) concerning Federal members of parliament which relates to the performance of their duties, and (c) in relation to the suitability of persons for office as members of parliament.

According to the majority, the effect of the constitutional defence was that a publication is not actionable in defamation if the defendant establishes that (a) it was unaware of the falsity of the material published; (b) it did not publish the material recklessly, that is, not caring whether the material was true or false; and (c) the publication was reasonable in the circumstances. The constitutional defence was based on the proposition that the constitutional freedom of communication required that the law of defamation did not inhibit freedom to criticise the institutions of government. The majority accepted that the existing laws of defamation had a tendency to suppress criticism. The constitutional defence endeavoured to arrive at an appropriate balance between the need to protect the public interest in maintaining freedom of communication about government and political matters and the preservation of personal reputation. In achieving that balance, the majority modified the test that was applied by the Supreme Court of the United States in the famous case *New York Times Co v Sullivan*.[66] There, the Supreme Court held that the guarantee of free speech contained in the First Amendment protected even false defamatory speech unless the plaintiff could prove actual malice or reckless disregard for truth or falsity on the part of the defendant. This test, in the view of the majority in *ACTTV*, tilted the balance too far against the protection of individual reputation.

The test formulated in *ACTTV* was applied in *Stephens v Western Australian Newspapers Ltd* where members of a State Legislative Council sued the defendant in relation to publications which alleged misconduct on the part of the plaintiffs in

---

63   (1994) 182 CLR 104.

64   (1994) 182 CLR 211.

65   Mason CJ, Toohey and Gaudron JJ to whom Deane J, who favoured a more radical approach unsupported by any other member of the court, gave his support.

66   376 US 254 (1964).

their official capacity. The constitutional defence failed because the defendant failed to plead that it was unaware of the falsity of the material published and did not publish the material recklessly. Nonetheless a majority of the court[67] held that the freedom of communication as to government and political matters implied in the Australian Constitution extends to the public discussion of the performance, conduct and fitness for office of members of a State legislature.

In both *Theophanous* and *Stephens*, the majority decided that a defence of qualified privilege at common law was available on the basis that the common law defence must be viewed in the light of the implied constitutional freedom.[68] This aspect of the two decisions became important in the reconsideration of them in *Lange*. The absence of what was thought to be a true majority in the two cases opened the way to that reconsideration.

In *Lange*, the court held that the implied freedom of communication was not a foundation for a constitutional defence as such in an action of defamation on the ground that the Constitution, being an instrument that defines the powers of government, does not attempt to formulate the principles of private law applicable to individuals in their relationships with each other. This conclusion was consistent with the proposition that the implied freedom is a negative restriction on the exercise of legislative and executive power, not the grant of an individual right.[69] Although the court unequivocally accepted that there was under the Constitution a freedom of communication as to government and political matters, the court confined those matters to matters relevant to Federal and Territory government and political matters,[70] rejecting the view expressed in *Theophanous* and *Stephens* that freedom extended to matters of State significance.

At the same time, the court accepted that statute law and the common law, even when regulating private rights, must conform to constitutional requirements. That led to the question whether the common law of defamation and the statute law of defamation were reasonably adapted to serving the legitimate end of protecting personal reputation without unnecessarily or unreasonably impairing the constitutional freedom.[71] In the ultimate analysis, the constitutional freedom was satisfied by a defence of qualified privilege which protects matter published to any person where the recipient had an interest or apparent interest in having information on a subject, the matter was published in the course of giving information on that subject to the recipient, and the conduct of the publisher in publishing the matter was reasonable in the circumstances.[72] On this footing, s 22 of the *Defamation Act* 1974 (NSW) was valid in that it provided for a defence of qualified privilege that satisfied these requirements. The common law defence of qualified privilege, expanded by the court to conform to the constitutional freedom by protecting a communication made to the public on a government or political matter, including

---

67   Mason CJ, Deane, Toohey and Gaudron JJ.

68   See, in particular, *Theophanous* (1994) 182 CLR 104 at 140.

69   *Lange* (1997) 145 ALR 96 at 106-07.

70   Ibid at 108, 112.

71   Ibid at 113.

72   Ibid at 118.

matters concerning the United Nations or other countries and government or politics at State, Territory or local government level, was not at odds with the freedom.

Despite the elimination of the constitutional defence practically all that it offered is protected by the defence of qualified privilege affirmed by the court. One qualification is that defence will be defeated if the plaintiff proves that the publication, though otherwise reasonable, was actuated by malice or improper purpose.

For the future, much will depend on how the courts apply the "reasonably appropriate and adapted to the fulfilment of a legitimate purpose" test.[73] The most recent example of the application of that test is *Levy v Victoria*[74] where the validity of reg 5 of the Wildlife (Game) (Hunting Season) Regulations 1994 (Vic) was upheld. That regulation made it an offence to enter into a permitted hunting area during prohibited times without an authority to do so. The plaintiff, who had entered such an area in breach of reg 5 in order to protest against Victorian laws which permitted licence holders to shoot game birds and also to protest against the illegal killing of protected species, contended that reg 5 violated the freedom of communication under the Australian Constitution or, alternatively, a like freedom said to be implied in the Victorian Constitution. The regulation was upheld on the ground that it was appropriate and adapted to protect the safety of persons in hunting areas. The constitutional freedom was not curtailed to an extent greater than was reasonably necessary to serve the public interest in the personal safety of persons and that curtailment was appropriate and adapted to the aims pursued in the regulations.

A feature of the judgments in the cases on freedom of communication is the extent to which they draw upon the jurisprudence of other jurisdictions. The impact of freedom of expression on the law of defamation is a matter of contemporary concern not only in the United States but also in the United Kingdom,[75] the European Court of Human Rights[76] and Canada.[77] In this and other areas of human comparative jurisprudence is an international resource drawn upon by various national courts.

Implication of other substantive rights and freedoms

The singular nature of the foundation for the implication of freedom of communication distinguishes it from other human rights and freedoms. Freedom of communication is representation-reinforcing, necessitated by the system of representative (and responsible) government for which the Constitution by its very provisions and structure provides. There are, in addition, other considerations which tell against "rights" implication, some of which have been mentioned. The Constitution is concerned with the powers of government rather than with individual

---

73 (1997) 146 ALR 248 at 253.

74 Ibid.

75 *Derbyshire County Council v Times Newspapers* [1993] AC 534; see also *Albert Reynolds v Times Newspapers* (unreported, Court of Appeal, 8 July 1998) not following *Lange v Atkinson* (unreported, NZ Court of Appeal, 25 May 1998).

76 *Lingens v Austria* (1986) 8 EHHR 407.

77 *Manning v Hill* (1995) 126 DLR (4th) 129.

rights;[78] the Anglo-Australian tradition, shared by the framers of the Constitution, has been opposed to a jurisprudence of constitutionally guaranteed rights. Last, but certainly not least, is the proposition, long accepted in Australia, that the Constitution does not create a private right of action for damages for an attempt to exceed the powers it confers or to ignore the restraints it imposes.[79] That proposition is consistent with, but not mandated by, the principle that constitutional freedoms and prohibitions operate only as restrictions on legislative and executive power. Note, however, that an action for damages, though not specifically provided for, lies for violation of s 21 of the *New Zealand Bill of Rights Act* 1990,[80] a provision which confers "the right to be secure against unreasonable search and seizure".

The high water mark reached in the effort to imply human rights in the Australian Constitution is to be found in the judgment of Deane and Toohey JJ in *Leeth v Commonwealth*.[81] Their Honours considered that the Constitution incorporated every fundamental constitutional common law doctrine fully recognised when the Constitution was enacted and that the doctrine of legal equality was one such doctrine.[82] That doctrine was said to have two aspects: (i) the subjection of all persons to the law and (ii) the equality of all persons under the law and before the courts. The second aspect was equated with a principle that prohibited the exercise of Commonwealth legislative (and executive) power in such a way as to discriminate between people unless it does so on grounds which are reasonably capable of being seen as providing a rational and relevant basis for the discriminatory treatment.[83] However, this principle was not accepted by other members of the court.[84] In the result, the court held valid a Commonwealth law which empowered State courts to fix minimum terms of imprisonment for offences against Commonwealth law by reference to State laws fixing minimum terms. The relevant State laws differed as to the length of such terms. The view of the majority in *Leeth* has been recently confirmed by a majority of the court in *Kruger v Commonwealth*.[85] There Dawson, Gaudron, McHugh and Gummow JJ held that apart from equality before the courts, the Constitution does not require equality or uniformity in the operation of laws made by parliament.

In *Kruger* each of the plaintiffs save one was, when a child, removed into, detained and kept in the care, custody and control of the Chief Protector under the *Aboriginals Ordinance* 1918 (NT) in institutions or reserves away from his or her mother and family. The first detention occurred in 1925 and the last detention ended in 1960. The plaintiffs argued that the Ordinance violated a number of rights and

---

78   This view is contested by Detmold, M, "The New Constitutional Law" (1994) 16 *Sydney Law Review* 228 at 230.

79   *James v Commonwealth* (1939) 62 CLR 339; *Kruger v Commonwealth* (1997) 146 ALR 126.

80   *Simpson v Attorney-General (Baigent's Case)* [1994] 3 NZLR 667. See the discussion of this decision in Campbell E, "The Citizen and the State in the Courts", in Finn, PD (ed), *Essays on Law and Government*, Vol 2 (Law Book Co, Sydney, 1996), pp 20-24; Rishworth, P (ed), *The Struggle for Simplicity in the Law* (Butterworths Wellington, 1997), pp 319-20.

81   (1992) 174 CLR 455.

82   Ibid at 485.

83   Ibid at 488.

84   Mason CJ, Dawson and McHugh JJ; Brennan and Gaudron JJ.

85   (1997) 146 ALR 126.

freedoms to be implied in the Constitution and the Genocide Convention (ratified by Australia) and sought damages. The plaintiffs' case failed both as to the grounds relied upon and as to the availability of damages. Sir Maurice Byers QC, a former Solicitor-General for Australia, has described *Kruger* as "an extraordinary, indeed a shocking, decision".[86]

What the decision reveals is that Australian law provides no remedy for what in many jurisdictions would be regarded as a fundamental violation of human rights. To that extent, the decision demonstrates a glaring inadequacy in Australian human rights protection.

Applicable interpretive principles

Although the High Court has accepted that a guarantee of a fundamental right should be liberally construed, for reasons already stated very few constitutional provisions have been characterised as guarantees. Endeavours to interpret the Constitution as a manifestation of underlying principles embedded in the common law or as charter of unexpressed citizens' rights and freedoms, reflected in the approach adopted by Deane and Toohey JJ in *Leeth*, have not prevailed in the face of a constitutional history which gives scant comfort to the existence of such an intention on the part of the framers. To accord a modern human rights interpretation to the Constitution, such as the European Court of Justice has given to the Treaty of Rome,[87] runs counter to that constitutional history. So far the resort to dynamic or evolving interpretation has not surmounted that hurdle.[88]

The result, in the words of Kirby J, is that "Australian law, including its constitutional law, may sometimes fall short of giving effect to fundamental rights".[89] This led to his Honour to say:

> Where the Constitution is ambiguous, this court should adopt that meaning which conforms to the principles of fundamental rights rather than an interpretation which would involve a departure from such rights.[90]

That approach is entirely consistent with the principle of statutory construction adopted in *Coco v The Queen*[91] and it shares something in common with the use of international law and conventions as a source for the development of the common law as expounded by Brennan J in *Mabo (No 2)*[92] and subsequently by other justices in *Dietrich v The Queen*[93] and *Teoh*.[94]

---

86 "The Kruger Case" (1997) 8 *Public Law Review* 224 at 227.

87 See Hartley, TC, *The Foundations of European Community Law* (Clarendon Press, Oxford, 3rd ed, 1994), pp 139-49.

88 *Newcrest v Commonwealth* (1997) 147 ALR 42 at 147.

89 Ibid.

90 Ibid.

91 (1994) 179 CLR 427; see discussion above at n 16 and accompanying text.

92 (1992) 175 CLR 1 at 42.

93 (1992) 177 CLR 292.

94 (1995) 183 CLR 273; for discussion of the principle, see Walker, K, "Treaties and the Internationalisation of Australian Law", in Saunders, C (ed), *Courts of Final Jurisdiction* (Federation Press, Sydney, 1996), p 204, and Ch 4 by McMillan and Williams in this volume.

Subsequently, in *Kartinyeri v Commonwealth* (the *Hindmarsh Island* Case),[95] Kirby J dissenting adopted this approach to the interpretation of the race power in s 51(xxvi) of the Constitution in concluding that the power does not extend to the enactment of laws detrimental to, or discriminatory against, the people of any race by reference to their race.[96] On the other hand, Gummow and Hayne JJ rejected that construction of the power. In so doing, they concluded,[97] in reliance on the decisions in *Polites v Commonwealth*[98] and *Horta v Commonwealth*[99] that, although the interpretive principle applies to legislation enacted pursuant to the constitutional power, it has no application to the interpretation of the constitutional power itself. Whether this limitation on the interpretive principle will be accepted remains to be seen. If, however, the principle is capable of applying to ambiguous constitutional powers, the question in each case is essentially particular: is there an ambiguity? And, if the ambiguity can be resolved by recourse to history, tradition and Convention Debates, are they to be overridden by the presumptive rule of construction?

Statutory protection of human rights

Some statutes give effect to Australia's human rights obligations. Section 6A of the *Migration Act* 1958 (Cth) enables an entry permit to be granted to a person who, among other things, is determined by the Minister to have the status of refugee within the meaning of the 1951 *Convention relating to the Status of Refugees* and the 1967 Protocol relating to the Status of Refugees. In *Chan v Minister for Immigration and Ethnic Affairs*,[100] the High Court held that an applicant for refugee status would satisfy the Convention definition of "refugee" if he showed a genuine fear founded on a real chance that he would be persecuted for one of the stipulated reasons if he returned to the country of his nationality. The court, in reaching its conclusion, took into account international opinions in the Convention and held that the decision of the Minister's delegate that the applicant was not a refugee was unreasonable.[101]

Gerhardy v Brown[102] upheld the *Pitjantjatjara Land Rights Act* 1981 (SA) as a special measure taken for the sole purpose of securing adequate advancement of certain groups of Aboriginal peoples requiring such protection as may be necessary to ensure to those peoples equal enjoyment or exercise of human rights and fundamental freedoms, within the meaning of s 8(1) of the RDA. The State Act

---

95 (1997) 152 ALR 140.

96 Ibid at 593.

97 Ibid at 571-573.

98 (1945) 70 CLR 60.

99 (1994) 181 CLR 183.

100 (1989) 169 CLR 379. See further, Ch 7 by Crock and Mathew in this volume.

101 Other High Court decisions on the Convention are *Minister for Immigration and Ethnic Affairs v Wu Shan Liang* (1996) 185 CLR 259; *Applicant A v Minister for Immigration and Ethnic Affairs* (1997) 71 ALJR 381. As to the *Convention on the Civil Aspects of International Child Abduction* and its impact on the interpretation of the Family Law (Child Abduction Convention) Regulations, see *De L v Director-General, NSW Department of Community Services* (1996) 71 ALJR 588.

102 (1985) 159 CLR 70.

vested an area of land, being more than one-tenth of the area of the State in a body corporate representing the Aboriginal peoples giving those peoples unrestricted rights of access to the lands and prohibiting others from entering without permission.

In *Australian Iron & Steel Pty Ltd v Banovic*[103] the High Court held that under s 24(3) of the *Anti-Discrimination Act* 1977 (NSW) it was open to the Tribunal to hold that the employer discriminated against retrenched female ironworkers by terminating their services on the "last on, first off" principle on the basis that it exacerbated the effects of past discriminatory practices by the employer. The judgments made extensive use of anti-discrimination decisions in other jurisdictions, as did the judgments.

In *Waters v Public Transport Corporation*,[104] people with disabilities complained that the corporation had discriminated against them by removing conductors from some trams and introducing "scratch tickets". The court in applying s 29 of the *Equal Opportunity Act* 1984 (Vic) made use of authorities in other jurisdictions and found that the disabilities of the complainants made it impossible or exceedingly difficult for them to use scratch tickets.

COMMON LAW PROTECTION OF HUMAN RIGHTS

Mabo (No 2), *Coco*, *Dietrich*[105] and *Teoh* provide eloquent evidence of the role of the judiciary in protecting human rights in the common law sphere. *Dietrich* acknowledged that the Australian common law does not recognise the right of an accused to be provided with counsel at public expense. However, *Dietrich* decided by majority[106] that the courts have power to stay proceedings that will result in an unfair trial. That power extends to a case in which representation is essential to a fair trial as when the accused is charged with a serious offence. Then, in the absence of special circumstances, on application by the accused who, through no fault of his own is unable to obtain legal representation, the judge should adjourn or stay the trial until legal representation is available. The reasoning to this conclusion stemmed from the accused's common law right to a fair trial and the inherent jurisdiction of the courts to stay proceedings in order to prevent an abuse of process. That jurisdiction extends to a case in which lack of representation may mean that an accused is unable to receive a fair trial.

Although the reasoning to that conclusion was based on the common law right to a fair trial, the judgments considered the relevant law in Canada, the United States, Ireland and India and the provisions of art 6 of the *European Convention for the Protection of Human Rights and Fundamental Freedoms*, art 14 of the ICCPR and s 11 of the *Canadian Charter of Rights and Freedoms* conferring minimum rights on an accused with respect to adequate time and facilities for his defence.[107]

---

103 (1989) 168 CLR 165. See further, Ch 13 by Bailey and Devereux in this volume.

104 (1991) 173 CLR 349. See further, Ch 13 by Bailey and Devereux in this volume.

105 (1996) 177 CLR 292.

106 Mason CJ and McHugh J, Deane, Toohey and Gaudron JJ.

107 (1996) 177 CLR 292 at 304-09 per Mason CJ and McHugh J, 328-37 per Deane J, 351, 357, 360-61 per Toohey J, 370-73 per Gaudron J.

The majority judgments made the point that under the instruments just mentioned, as with the common law, accused persons did not have an absolute right to legal representations. A significant element in the reasoning was that the court elevated the traditional right of an accused to have a conviction set aside if the trial was unfair into something that resembled a positive right to fair trial. In this respect *Dietrich* may be seen as an outgrowth of the rules of natural and procedural fairness which has been an important element in judicial development of the common law in recent years, notably in immigration and deportation cases where the court has insisted on standards of procedural fairness and objective scrutiny.[108]

CONCLUDING COMMENTS

The strong development by Australian judges of the rules of procedural fairness is to be contrasted with the absence of a corresponding development of rules of substantive fairness. The concept of legitimate expectations is presently confined in Australia to procedure,[109] though, in conformity with European law, it extends to matters of substance in England.[110] The same contrast can be drawn between a willingness to make curial implications from Ch III of the Constitution and the separation of powers, of which *Kable v Director of Public Prosecutions (NSW)*[111] is a particularly striking example, and an unwillingness to make substantive implications for which, again, in most cases, there are justifiable reasons.

These contrasts may well have significance for future human rights jurisprudence in Australia. It is possible that Australian judges are not comfortable with "rights jurisprudence" which is more policy based in the sense that it calls for a weighing and balancing of competing policy considerations; for example, the tension between private reputation and freedom of expression resolved by *Lange*.

On the other hand, rights jurisprudence occupies a dominant position in international law and in other national systems of jurisprudence. More and more judges in Australia and elsewhere are making use of comparative law. It would be very surprising if protection of human rights proves to be the exception to the general rule.

Finally, as I noted in the discussion of *Teoh*, the proposed legislation directed at that decision leaves the judges at liberty to use international conventions as source material for developing the common law. That is a matter of significance now that it is accepted that international law, using that expression to include conventions, is a legitimate and important influence on the development of the common law.

---

108 See, for example, *Kioa v West* (1985) 159 CLR 550. See further, Ch 4 by McMillan and Williams in this volume.

109 *Attorney-General (NSW) v Quin* (1990) 170 CLR 1. For a discussion of its potential development in Australian administrative law, see Ch 4 by McMillan and Williams in this volume.

110 *R v Home Secretary; ex p Asif Khan* [1984] 1 WLR 1337; *R v Secretary of State for the Home Department; ex p Ruddock* [1987] 1 WLR 1482; *R v Ministry of Agriculture, Fisheries and Food; ex p Hamble Fisheries* [1995] 2 All ER 714.

111 (1996) 138 ALR 577.

3

CONSTITUTIONAL LAW AND HUMAN RIGHTS

Stephen Gageler and Arthur Glass

INTRODUCTION

In this chapter we do not ask ourselves such general questions as – what are human rights? why the popularity these days of "rights talk" within constitutional law? are rights in fact promoted or inhibited by constitutional review? We assume on the one hand an understanding of the basic interests and needs which are presently understood as human rights. We assume on the other hand that Australia is not in the position of choosing whether or not to take up judicial review of constitutional rights. We already have this practice. This is not to say that the judicial review of rights could not be expanded (if we adopted a Bill of Rights) or restricted (if judges came to see their role in all of this differently).

Human rights become constitutional rights when they can be said plausibly to be *in* the Commonwealth Constitution or a State Constitution. This is how we distinguish between constitutional norms and everyday legal rules.

For the most part the constitutional rights recognised in Australia arise out of a lack of governmental power rather than from a "positive right" placed in the hands of the legal subject.[1] One consequence of this is that these rights may operate against one law-maker but not another. As we move from right to right we need to distinguish between Commonwealth and State constitutional rights. The Territories are different again.

A serious impediment to the development of State constitutional rights should be mentioned at the outset. State Constitutions are ordinary Acts of Parliament not "higher law". Consequently, unless a State "right-giving" provision can be regarded as entrenched in some way, "rights issues" will remain here in the realm of statutory interpretation rather than constitutional law.

The terminology of "negative" and "positive" rights may be further clarified, for there are in fact three classes which can be identified. First, there is the right not to be prohibited by governmental action from doing something. In Australian constitutional law this permissive right is the most common right encountered. It is simply the other side of the limits which operate at times upon governmental power. But this right would become a different type of right (the second class of rights) if the individual was guaranteed freedom from hindrance by both governmental and

---

1   For analysis of the jurisprudential basis for human rights expressed in legal form, see Ch 1 by Kinley in this volume.

non-governmental restrictions. The novelty of *Theophanous v Herald & Weekly Times Ltd*,[2] which we discuss below, was that it had the appearance of bringing about this kind of transformation. Third, there are enabling rights. These are rights whereby individuals must be provided by a government with a particular capacity or material good. Examples are where a government is obliged to provide litigants with legal aid or counsel or interpreters. This type of right is not to be expected under the present constitutional arrangements in Australia.

It is not uncommon to describe constitutional rights under the headings express rights and implied rights distinguishing again between implied rights arising out of specific provisions from those derived more generally from the basic structure of the constitution. We have not adopted this framework. Our concern is not with how constitutional rights are presently grounded but rather with describing the scope of the various rights and the practical use to which they can now be put.

Implications play a role here as elsewhere in law for it is simply not possible to restrict the meaning of the right under discussion to the express words of the Constitution. More context will always be needed, if only the context of the English language. This context may well be given by more general legal norms (such as the rule of law, separation of powers or representative government) or by the common law. But the distinction must be kept between constitutional text and interpretive context. Basic legal or moral notions are not binding until they have been brought in to our legal system.[3] And while the common law is obviously part of our legal system it remains below the Constitution. The common law is not on its own a source of constitutional norms.

The same point applies to international law. International law forms part of the context within which the Constitution falls to be interpreted. It has recently been described by one justice of the High Court as "a legitimate and important influence on the development of ... constitutional law".[4] Nevertheless, international law is not a direct source of constitutional norms in Australia. Its real significance for constitutional interpretation lies in its influence on modes of judicial thought. The relatively recent nature of that influence is the subject of discussion in Sir Anthony Mason's chapter earlier in this book.[5]

What follows is first an outline of the present position with regard to nine Commonwealth constitutional rights including reference (where appropriate) to their application to the States. We then discuss separately the position of the Territories, the application of constitutional rights and a number of procedural matters.

---

2   (1994) 182 CLR 104.

3   For a different approach see Bailey, P, "Righting" the Constitution without a Bill of Rights" (1995) 23 *Federal Law Review* 1 and Doyle, J, "Common Law Rights and Democratic Rights" in Finn, PD, (ed), *Essays on Law and Government* Vol 1 (Law Book Co, Sydney, 1995).

4   *Newcrest Mining (WA) Ltd v Commonwealth* (1997) 147 ALR 42 at 148 per Kirby J.

5   See Sir Anthony Mason, "The Role of the Judiciary in the Development of Human Rights in Australian Law", Ch 2 above. Sir Anthony's chapter focuses primarily on the judicial perspective adopted towards human rights in Australian law.

CONSTITUTIONAL RIGHTS

Religious freedom

Section 116 of the Constitution provides that no Commonwealth law may establish any religion, impose any religious observance or prohibit the free expression of any religion and that no religious test shall be required of any office under the Commonwealth. The learning associated with this section can be reduced to four points. First, while the Commonwealth cannot establish a particular religion as the national religion it is free to assist the practice of religion, for example, by providing financial assistance to religious schools.[6]

Second, s 116 stands for the idea that people should be left alone to practise their religion free from interference from Commonwealth law. But this right may be legitimately qualified in two ways – in the interests of national security and to maintain observance of the "ordinary laws" of the community.[7] The issues raised by these formulations include whether a law is reasonably necessary for national security and whether what appears to be an ordinary law is unreasonably discriminatory when applied to certain religious practices.

Third, although a broad approach has been taken to the question of what constitutes religion[8] just which beliefs are religious beliefs so as to be protected by s 116 is a matter which may vary with context. For example, the need to define religion is less pressing if the free exercise principle is under consideration. Here it can be said without absurdity that the freedom of religion extends to the freedom of irreligion.[9]

Fourth, s 116 does not apply to State law,[10] although one State, Tasmania, has its own constitutional guarantee of religious freedom.[11]

Freedom of political communication

In *Australian Capital Television Pty Ltd v Commonwealth*[12] and *Nationwide News Pty Ltd v Wills*[13] the High Court recognised for the first time that the Commonwealth Constitution requires the existence of some degree of freedom of political communication. In the first of those cases, the High Court held invalid provisions of a Commonwealth law which purported to restrict the broadcasting of political advertisements during Commonwealth, State and Territory election campaigns. In the second, the court held invalid a Commonwealth law which purported to restrict criticism of the Industrial Relations Commission.

The principles enunciated in *Australian Capital Television* and *Nationwide News* cases were further considered by the High Court and their reach extended in

---

6   *Attorney-General (Vic); ex rel Black v Commonwealth* (1981) 146 CLR 559.

7   *Adelaide Company of Jehovah's Witnesses v Commonwealth* (1943) 67 CLR 116.

8   *Church of the New Faith v Commissioner for Pay-roll Tax (Vic)* (1983) 154 CLR 120.

9   *Adelaide Company of Jehovah's Witnesses v Commonwealth* (1943) 67 CLR 116 at 123.

10 *Grace Bible Church v Reedman* (1984) 54 ALR 511.

11 *Constitution Act* 1934 (Tas) s 46.

12 (1992) 177 CLR 106.

13 (1992) 177 CLR 1.

Theophanous v Herald & Weekly Times Ltd[14] and *Stephens v West Australian Newspapers Ltd.*[15] In those cases the court held there to be a defence to a defamation action based on the constitutional freedom. The effect of the decisions was to treat the Constitution as effecting an alteration of the rights between individuals. While this gave the constitutional freedom the appearance of a personal right, the majority in *Theophanous* made it clear that they were not deciding the issue of whether this was a positive or negative right.[16] Their reasoning was that political discussion in Australia was inhibited by the laws which established a cause of action for defamation. In these circumstances the Constitution prevailed over private rights, whether common law based or statute law based. This approach raised the prospect of similar reasoning being applied in other areas where common law or State statute law attempted to strike some balance between free speech and other social interests – for example, the present law relating to contempt of court, sedition, obscenity, blasphemy, racial vilification, confidentiality, and privileges of Parliament.

Whatever may be in store for us in these other areas the approach adopted in *Theophanous* has been significantly reconsidered in *Lange v Australian Broadcasting Commission*[17] and *Levy v Victoria*[18]. The judges in *Lange* connected the right of political communication specifically to the sections in the Constitution which deal with representative and responsible government – ss 7, 24, 62, 64 and 128 in particular. There is nothing new in this when stated in general terms (except perhaps for the addition now of responsible government) but what is made clear is that the starting point is not the needs of representative government in general terms but more specifically the question – what are the needs of the system of representative government authorised by the Constitution?

Lange provides the following framework for thinking about this right:

- Does the law effectively burden freedom of communication about government matters either in its terms or effect?

- If it does, is the object of the law compatible with the maintenance of the constitutionally prescribed system of representative and responsible government?

- If it is, is the law reasonably appropriate and adapted to serve that legitimate object?[19]

The various judgments in *Levy* show that the degree of fit between means and ends required by the third part of this framework may vary according to the nature of the law and the nature of the burden it places on freedom of communication. A greater degree of scrutiny may be required of a law which targets political communication than is required of a law regulating a field of general activity which merely has an incidental effect on political communication.

---

14 (1994) 182 CLR 104.

15 (1994) 182 CLR 211.

16 (1994) 182 CLR 104 at 125.

17 (1997) 145 ALR 96.

18 (1997) 146 ALR 248.

19 (1997) 145 ALR 96 at 112.

There is an issue as to the extension of the right into the State sphere. In *Australian Capital Television* a majority of the judges described the right of free political discourse as extending to all tiers of government in Australia – State, Territory and local (because of the practical interrelationship). The case clearly assumes that the right could prevent a Commonwealth law interfering with State elections. *Theophanous* for its part brought down State law which interfered with the freedom, while *Stephens* applied the freedom directly to State political affairs.

It is possible to see these three cases as examples based on the need properly to protect the freedom in relation to Commonwealth affairs in which case their approach is in line with the original derivation of the freedom in *Australian Capital Television*. A different approach was also considered in *Stephens*, namely, that an implied freedom similar to the one inferred from the federal Constitution could be drawn out of the Western Australian Constitution. Four of the judges in that case accepted this argument.[20]

The right to vote and equality of voting power

Stating the present constitutional position is a matter of summarising the variety of opinion to be found in *McGinty v Western Australia*.[21] Basically (according to the majority)[22] s 24 of the Commonwealth Constitution does not demand "one vote one value".[23] But there is majority support for a lack of governmental power to take away a general right of enfranchisement for adult citizens in Commonwealth elections. Three judges in *McGinty* (Toohey, Gaudron and Gummow JJ) went further and treated equality of voting power as an important constitutional principle. Only two judges (Toohey and Gaudron JJ), however, were willing to find these two principles within the Western Australian Constitution.[24]

Freedom of association, freedom of assembly

If freedom of political communication is required in order to sustain a system of representative government, then the same could be said plausibly about freedom of association or freedom of assembly, for these freedoms are just as important for a system of representative government as freedom of speech on political matters. The discussion of representative government in *McGinty* and *Kruger v Commonwealth*[25] would appear to support this type of argument. The extent to which the right of freedom of association is protected under Australian labour laws is discussed later in this volume.[26]

---

20 Mason CJ, Deane Toohey and Gaudron JJ (1994) 182 CLR 211 at 231.

21 (1996) 186 CLR 140.

22 (1996) 186 CLR 140 at 167, 173ff, 184, 263ff.

23 In other words, the result in *Attorney-General (Cth); ex rel McKinlay* (1975) 135 CLR 1 is still the law; see *McGinty* (1996) 186 CLR 140 at 167, 180, 227.

24 See generally Carne, G, "Representing Democracy or Reinforcing Inequality?: Electoral Distribution and *McGinty v Western Australia* " (1997) 25 *Federal Law Review* 351.

25 (1997) 146 ALR 126.

26 Chapter 9 by MacDermott.

Right to property

The specific conferral on the Commonwealth Parliament by s 51(xxxi) of the Constitution of legislative power to acquire property from any State or person subject to the requirement of "just terms" has long been interpreted as a constitutional guarantee having the effect of preventing the Commonwealth from exercising that or other powers to acquire property otherwise than on "just terms". The result is that a Commonwealth law purporting to acquire the property of a person without providing reasonable compensation will ordinarily be invalid provided that the law is capable of being characterised as a law with respect to the "acquisition" of "property".

The section has been liberally interpreted. The "property" to which it refers extends "to every species of valuable right including real and personal property". While the extinguishment or modification of a property right does not itself constitute an "acquisition", an acquisition within the meaning of the section may occur where the extinguishment or modification results in the Commonwealth or another person obtaining some identifiable and measurable countervailing benefit or advantage. Thus, the extinguishment by Commonwealth legislation of an existing cause of action without compensation has been held to be invalid.[27] So too has the inclusion of mining leases within a national park.[28]

On the other hand, it has been recognised that there are some exercises of legislative power necessarily involving the acquisition of property otherwise than on just terms which lie beyond the scope of the guarantee afforded by the section. These include the enactment of laws providing for the imposition of taxation, for the imposition of penalties and for the forfeiture of the property of enemy aliens. It has also been accepted that a law which is "not directed towards the acquisition of property as such but which is concerned with the adjustment of competing rights or claims or obligations of persons in a particular relationship or area of activity is unlikely to be susceptible of legitimate characterisation as a law with respect to the acquisition of property" for the purposes of the section even if it has the incidental effect of enhancing the proprietary interests of one person at the expense of another.[29]

Non-discrimination on the basis of State residence

As s 117 of the Commonwealth Constitution quaintly puts it, "a subject of the Queen, resident in any State, shall not be subject in any other State to any disability or discrimination which would not be equally applicable to him if he were a subject of the Queen resident in such other State". The section confers a right or immunity from discriminatory State legislative or executive action. This right is expressed as an individual right. If it comes into play it protects the disadvantaged out of State resident but leaves the law otherwise valid.

---

27   *Georgiadis v Australian and Overseas Telecommunications Corporation* (1994) 179 CLR 297.

28   *Newcrest Mining (WA) Ltd v Commonwealth* (1997) 147 ALR 42.

29   *Nintendo Co Ltd v Centronics Systems Pty Ltd* (1994) 181 CLR 134 at 161.

The application of this right calls for a comparison between residents in the legislating State and the circumstances of the out-of-State complainant. This comparison is to take account of the practical effect of the law and not just the legal rights as these appear on the face of the Act.[30] The crucial question here, of course, is not whether there is a difference in the treatment of residents and non residents but whether different treatment can be justified.[31]

The scope of s 117 is limited in three ways. First, it is unclear whether the words "subject of the Queen" operate to keep this right from non-citizens or from legal subjects not persons, such as corporations. Second, the case law acknowledges that there are some restrictions which a State may impose upon non-residents (without offending s 117) in the interests of fostering its "State community". For instance, it may impose residential restrictions on voting or upon appointment to public office. Whether a State can favour its own residents over others with regard to welfare benefits (for example, access to schools and hospitals) is less clear.[32] Third, whether the section extends to Commonwealth legislative or execution action is still an open question.

Right of equality

Section 117, as we have seen, provides protection against a particular type of discrimination. Other provisions of the Commonwealth Constitution restrict the power of the Commonwealth to discriminate geographically. An example is the qualification contained in s 51(ii), against a Commonwealth law with respect to taxation discrimination between States or parts of States. Another is s 99 which prevents the Commonwealth by a law or regulation of trade or commerce giving preference to one State over another. But as the aim here is to shore up the federal system, the use which may be made of these provisions (or doctrine) by individuals is greatly restricted.[33]

In *Leeth v Commonwealth*[34] it is clear that two judges (Deane and Toohey JJ) found the doctrine of legal equality to be a necessary implication of the Commonwealth Constitution. According to this doctrine courts should treat persons subject to the law fairly and impartially as equals before the law and refrain from discrimination on irrelevant or irrational grounds.[35] What is meant by equality is the idea that the similarly situated should be treated the same and those differently situated, treated differently. It is the second part of this formulation which makes it such a potent weapon for a review court. For, it is argued, equal treatment demands that differences should not lead to disadvantages.

---

30   *Street v Queensland Bar Association* (1989) 168 CLR 461.

31   *Waters v Public Transport Corporation* (1991) 173 CLR 349 at 364.

32   *Street v Queensland Bar Association* (1989) 168 CLR 461 at 492, 512ff, 548, 560 and 583.

33   See Saunders, C, "Concepts of Equality in the Australian Constitution" in Lindell, G, (ed), *Future Directions in Australian Constitutional Law* (Federation Press in association with the Centre for International and Public Law and the Law Faculty, Australian National University, Sydney, 1994), p 209.

34   (1992) 174 CLR 455.

35   (1992) 174 CLR 455 at 488.

In *Kruger v Commonwealth* only one judge endorsed the approach of Deane and Toohey JJ in *Leeth*. This was (not surprisingly) Toohey J.[36] All the other judges in *Kruger* specifically reject the idea that there is an implied right of equality in the Commonwealth Constitution.

Due process rights

There is no shortage of relatively recent statements in the High Court that s 71 and more generally Ch III of the Constitution provide a guarantee of procedural due process.[37] In this respect, the separation of judicial power – traditionally seen as essential to the maintenance of the federal structure of the Constitution – has come to be seen also as a guarantee of individual freedom.

There are a number of issues to discuss. First, in so far as the doctrine imposes an inability on the Commonwealth Parliament or the Commonwealth executive to interfere with the judicial process just which aspects of judicial proceedings are protected from legislative or executive intrusion? It would appear that it is only the core aspects of the traditional judicial process which are protected by Ch III. Obviously a court cannot be directed to ignore the rules of natural justice or to decide cases otherwise than in accordance with the law. The right to a counsel was linked by two of the judges in *Dietrich v R*[38] to Ch III. But going in the other direction is the ruling in *Sorby v Commonwealth*[39] (as confirmed in *Environment Protection Authority v Caltex Refining Pty Ltd*[40]) that the right against self-incrimination is not protected by Ch III.

So what of legislation which, say, alters the standard or burden of proof or restricts the circumstances in which the court may adjourn or stay a trial or which greatly increases the penalties for lesser offences? Or perhaps legislation which modifies common law adjudication along the lines of the civilian inquisitorial system, as may be recommended by the Australian Law Reform Commission at the conclusion of its current "adversarial litigation system" reference? Clearly not much can be said in general terms about these examples. It will come down to the question of whether in the particular circumstances of the case the legislative intrusion affects the fairness of the trial.[41] Related problems are whether Ch III extends its protection to all trials or only to trials for serious crimes? Or, to what extent the requirement of a fair trial extends to procedures which are linked with the trial but which occur earlier or later; police investigations, say, or punishment?[42]

---

36   (1997) 146 ALR 126 at 179ff.

37   For example, *Re Tracey; ex p Ryan* (1989) 166 CLR 518 at 580; *Leeth v Commonwealth* (1992) 174 CLR 455 at 470; *Chu Kheng Lim v Minister for Immigration* (1992) 176 CLR 1 at 27.

38   (1992) 177 CLR 292 at 326 and 362.

39   (1983) 152 CLR 281.

40   (1993) 178 CLR 477.

41   *Dietrich v R* (1992) 177 CLR 292 at 328, 364. This is well discussed by Hope, JA, "Constitutional Right to a fair Trial? Implications for the Reform of the Australian Criminal Justice System" (1996) 24 *Federal Law Review* 17. See also Wheeler, F, "The Doctrine of Separation of Powers and Constitutionally Entrenched Due Process in Australia" (1997) 23(2) *Monash University Law Review* 248; and Winterton, G, in Lindell (ed), above, n 33, p 185.

42   Again issues discussed by Hope, JA, ibid. See also Ch 6 by Bronnit and Ayers in this volume.

Three specific examples can be mentioned if only briefly – these are acts of attainder, retrospective laws and the norm of equal treatment.[43] An act of attainder declares that a person is guilty, and leaves the court with the reduced role of simply finding as a fact whether X is that person. Such acts it has been said violate the separation of powers doctrine embodied in the Australian Constitution[44].

Retrospective criminal laws have been said by two judges in *Polyukhovich v Commonwealth*[45] (Deane and Gaudron JJ) to offend against Ch III. But this was not the view of the majority in that case. At present the only scope for arguing against retrospectivity is (in the appropriate circumstances) to rely upon an implication drawn out of s 109 of the Constitution. The Commonwealth it is said is prevented from reviving (or for that matter rendering inoperative) State law by retrospectively declaring its intention not to cover (or to cover) the relevant field[46].

One judge (Gaudron J) has linked the norm of equal treatment under the law to Ch III. In *Leeth* she accepted the argument that a Commonwealth Act could not require a court exercising federal jurisdiction to treat offenders differently depending on the law of the State in which they were convicted.[47] Chapter III in her view prevented the law maker from calling upon Ch III courts to apply laws which were discriminatory; or, rather, laws which in the view of the court were unreasonably discriminatory. This approach to Ch III is not shared at present by the other members of the court.

Complimentary to the rules which are designed to preserve the integrity of the judicial process in the interests of a fair trial are rules which require the adjudgment and punishment of criminal guilt to be committed exclusively to the courts. In *Chu Kheng Lim v Minister for Immigration*[48] Brennan, Deane and Dawson JJ stated that by reason of Ch III it would be "beyond the legislative power of the Parliament to invest the Executive with an arbitrary power to detain citizens in custody notwithstanding that the power was conferred in terms which sought to divorce such detention in custody from both punishment and criminal guilt".[49] The reason given was that under the Commonwealth Constitution any form of involuntary detention having a penal or punitive character is entrusted by Ch III exclusively to the judiciary.

It is unclear at this stage whether other due process rights familiar in other jurisdictions will be drawn out of Ch III. We have in mind such rights as freedom from unreasonable search and seizure, freedom from excessive bail or double jeopardy, the right to be tried within a reasonable time, the right to not be subject to cruel or unusual punishment, the right to an interpreter, etc.[50] But what can be said is that this is an area where the usual constraints upon judicial activism – the lack of

---

43 These examples are more extensively discussed by Zines, L, *The High Court and the Constitution* (Butterworths, Sydney, 4th ed, 1996), pp 204ff.

44 *Polyukhovich v Commonwealth* (1991) 172 CLR 501.

45 (1991) 172 CLR 501.

46 *University of Wollongong v Metwally* (1984) 158 CLR 447.

47 (1992) 174 CLR 455 at 501ff.

48 (1992) 176 CLR 1.

49 (1992) 176 CLR 1 at 27.

50 Murphy J discusses cruel and unusual punishment in *Sillery v Queen* (1981) 35 ALR 227 at 233.

democratic warrant, the lack of institutional competence – have less force. For the rights associated with fair treatment by the courts is an aspect of the state-subject relationship which judges have traditionally supervised.

Last there is the issue of the reach of Ch III into State law. This is a question of some importance given that criminal law is primarily a State matter. Of course it is possible to argue that the doctrine of separation of powers is *in* a particular State Constitution. But this claim has frequently been denied.[51] Further, only the New South Wales Constitution at present entrenches some notion of judicial independence in a way which makes this a constitutional argument rather than merely an argument about statutory interpretation.[52] More decisively, comments made in *Kable v Director of Public Prosecutions*[53] would appear to block this line of argument.

However, a way of linking State courts with the Commonwealth Constitution was made available by *Kable*. Because the Commonwealth Constitution authorises the investing of Commonwealth judicial power in State courts, these bodies, it was said, must be kept fit to receive this power. State courts are not suitable repositories if State law confers upon them powers incompatible with Ch III. *Kable* also gave consideration to another type of argument. It was said that once the *Judiciary Act* 1903 (Cth) confers federal jurisdiction upon a State court, a State law which imposes functions on that court inconsistent with Ch III is rendered invalid. It would seem that a State court is seized of Federal jurisdiction whenever a party raises just this Ch III point. The extent to which this form of constitutional bootstrapping may be employed to enlarge the reach of Ch III into State judicial proceedings remains to be seen.

Right to a jury trial

This right, expressly granted by s 80 of the Commonwealth Constitution, at present extends only to offences against laws of the Commonwealth (that is, not to State or Territory laws). Its application is restricted to offences for which Commonwealth law requires prosecution by indictment.[54]

If the guarantee of a jury trial applies, then this right cannot be waived by the accused.[55] And it is not open to the law maker – Commonwealth, State or Territory – to change the basic common law requirements of a jury trial. One such requirement is the need for a unanimous verdict of guilt.[56]

---

51 See, among other discussions, *Builders Labourers Federation of NSW v Minister for Industrial Relations* (1986) 7 NSWR 372; *Nicholas v Western Australia* [1972] WAR 168.

52 *Constitution Act* 1902 (NSW) s 53.

53 (1996) 138 ALR 577 at 582, 591, 617 and 639.

54 *R v Archdall* (1928) 41 CLR 128, confirmed not without vigorous dissent in *Kingswell v R* (1985) 159 CLR 264.

55 *Brown v R* (1986) 160 CLR 171.

56 *Cheatle v R* (1993) 177 CLR 541.

Freedom of movement

There have been suggestions that this freedom can be grounded more generally in the Commonwealth Constitution[57] but s 92 is the more obvious source of a freedom "to pass to and fro among the States without burden, hindrance or restriction".[58]

Section 92 provides in provocatively categorical terms that "trade, commerce and intercourse among the States ... shall be absolutely free". *Cole v Whitfield*[59] fashioned an understanding of s 92 based on the discrimination between inter and intra state trade. In doing this it rejected an earlier approach; a view that relied upon an individual right to take part in interstate trade. Less famously, *Cole v Whitfield* also established that the intercourse part of s 92 should be applied differently, more absolutely, than the better known trade and commerce part.[60] Whatever this amounts to, it is hard to envisage that the reasonableness of the interference would not be considered at some stage of the court's inquiry.

Air Caledonie International v Commonwealth[61] should also be noted. In this matter the court spoke of the right of citizens (unlike non-citizens) to re-enter Australia without the need of executive authorisation.[62]

The position of the Territories

As already noted, the position of the Territories in relation to constitutional rights is different from both the Commonwealth and the States. Just how different is difficult precisely to say.

The legislative power of the Commonwealth under s 122 of the Constitution to make laws for the government of any Territory has traditionally been treated as a power of a plenary nature which is unconstrained by ordinary limitations on Commonwealth powers such as those drawn from federalism or those contained in Ch III of the Constitution requiring trial by jury and the observance of due process. As late as 1994, it was described in the judgment of the majority in *Svikart v Stewart*[63] as "a largely unfettered as well as an exclusive power to legislate with respect to the government of a territory".

However, since the grant of self-government to the Northern Territory in 1978 and to the Australian Capital Territory in 1988 there has been an increasing tendency on the part of the High Court to equate the constitutional rights of Australians resident in Territories with the constitutional position of Australians resident in States. This was first shown in *Capital Duplicators v Australian Capital*

---

57 As a right of every free citizen to participate in the affairs of the nation or a right arising from the union of the people in a Commonwealth: Griffith CJ and Barton J in *R v Smithers* (1912) 16 CLR 99; Murphy J in *Buck v Bavone* (1976) 135 CLR 110; cf four judges in *Miller v TCN* (1986) 161 CLR 556 (Gibbs CJ, Mason, Brennan, Dawson JJ).

58 *Gratwick v Johnson* (1945) 70 CLR 1 at 17.

59 (1988) 165 CLR 360.

60 (1988) 165 CLR 360 at 388.

61 (1988) 165 CLR 462.

62 (1988) 165 CLR 462 at 469.

63 (1994) 181 CLR 548 at 563.

Territory[64] where the powers of a Territory legislature were held to be constrained by the same inhibition on raising duties of excise as applies to the States. More recently, in *Newcrest Mining (WA) Ltd v Commonwealth*,[65] a majority of the court took the view that a Commonwealth law acquiring the property of a person in a Territory may be invalid if it fails to provide just terms.

The High Court looked closely at the question of constitutional rights of Australians in a Territory in *Kruger v Commonwealth*.[66] In that case a number of Aboriginal people of the "stolen generation" claimed that their constitutional rights had been breached by action taken under Northern Territory legislation in place between 1918 and 1957 which authorised their removal from their families and detention in institutions. The claim was rejected by most members of the court principally on the basis that the legislation in question was properly characterised as welfare legislation, however misguided that might seem by modern standards, so that the legislation was not invalidated even if the constitutional rights claimed by the plaintiffs existed. The court split on the question whether the due process guaranteed by Ch III of the Constitutions extends to the Territories, with three justices maintaining the traditional view that it does not[67] and three justices entertaining at least the possibility that it does.[68] There was also a split on the question whether the Territories power is limited by s 116 of the Constitution: two justices deciding that it was,[69] two justices deciding that it was not[70] with two not deciding.[71]

Although the issue has perhaps not been finally determined, there seems little doubt that the implied freedom of political communication which applies elsewhere throughout Australia applies also within the Territories.

THE APPLICATION OF CONSTITUTIONAL RIGHTS

We have stated in outline the basic constitutional rights presently at work in the Australian legal system. At the level of application of these rights, as elsewhere in law, everything turns on the detail of the legislation, and upon the content of the subject matter under discussion. However, something further can be added in general terms.

The application of the right will almost always involve evaluative concepts. It is possible that the question might be something like: is this a prosecution by indictment? – but there is unlikely to be an argument over this type of issue. And even with the right to a jury trial some evaluation of just what are the basic requirements of trial by jury may be called for. In as much as this evaluation

---

64   (1992) 177 CLR 248.

65   (1997) 147 ALR 42.

66   (1997) 146 ALR 126.

67   Brennan CJ, Dawson and McHugh JJ.

68   Toohey, Gaudron and Gummow JJ.

69   Gaudron and Gummow JJ.

70   Dawson and McHugh JJ.

71   Brennan CJ and Toohey J. For further discussion of this case, see Ch 14 by Eastman and Ronalds in this volume.

concerns notions drawn out of the constitutional text – the requirements of a fair trial, say, or the elements of representative and responsible government – we cannot speak here to these large questions. In any case, so much of this depends on the approach adopted by the judge.[72]

What we will address here is a number of legal concepts which operate below the abstract concepts set out in the constitutional text yet above the particularly of each case. We have in mind such middle-order notions as "direct interference", "proportionably", "reasonable necessity" and "appropriate and adapted".

Cases involving constitutional rights will at times generate such questions as – does the law interfere with religious freedom or the freedom of political communication? does the law discriminate on the basis of religion, State residence or interstate movement? The answer that there is interference with a freedom or that there is discriminatory treatment will not dispose of the case. For, as it is often said, constitutional rights are qualified, not absolute, rights. An apparent infringement may turn out to be a legitimate (that is, constitutional). In these circumstances, the question is not whether the constitutional right has been infringed, but whether it has been *unduly* infringed. This is where such notions as "proportionality", "appropriate and adapted" come into play. They help to structure the inquiry into the character of the infringement.

What is involved in the application of these notions is an evaluation by the review court of means, ends and (unintended) consequences. For in the application of the constitutional right the court cannot avoid such questions as – how legitimate are the lawmaker's goals? How effective are the means chosen to achieve these goals? What are the intended (and unintended) consequences of these means? What is the fit between the chosen means and ends? Answering these questions involves at some stage some weighing or balancing of the relevant interests. And this is to be done, of course, in a context in which it is not the court's task to chose the appropriate goals or to rule upon the best means available.

In dealing with these ever present issues the High Court has lately resorted to such concepts as "proportionality" and "appropriate and adapted".[73] One point to note is that this supervision by the court of ends and means can always be done with more or less scrutiny (or from the other direction with more or less deference to the lawmaker). Here is where talk of the "margin of appreciation" fits in.[74] Some judges are happier to embrace this idea than others. But even those judges who reject the concept of a "margin of appreciation" when questions of constitutional rights are involved must implicitly acknowledge its force in the form of the questions which the court takes up. The question is never – is this legislative goal worthy or are these legislative means the best means available? Rather, the questions are – is the goal constitutionally permissible? or are the means chosen within the range of available means?

---

72   See Ch 2 by Sir Anthony Mason in this volume.

73   For discussion of these notions, clarifying the different ways in which they are used see Kirk, J, "Constitutional Guarantees, Characterisation and the Concept of Proportionality" (1997) 22 *Melbourne University Law Review* 1 and Selway, B, "The Rise and Rise of the Reasonable Proportionality Test: Public Law" (1996) 7 *Public Law Review* 212.

74   For a discussion of this concept within the context of international human rights law, see Ch 1 by Kinley in this volume.

At times the adoption of notions such as "proportionality" may involve an implicit shift in the persuasive onus. There is in Australian constitutional law and practice a presumption of validity. The onus of establishing constitutional invalidity is on the person asserting it. That person must show at least a prima facie infringement of a constitutional right. In a practical sense, once a prima facie infringement of a constitutional right is established the onus then shifts to the government in question to persuade the court that, for instance, there are no better (that is, less restrictive) means available to attain the stated ends or that the law will not produce undesirable consequences (that is, an unacceptable interference with constitutional law rights). Of course, once these issues come into play it is as much open to the non-government party to raise uncertainty about them as it is for the government to show that its law is, all relevant things considered, appropriate.

The extent to which questions of fact come into play in the resolution of these questions and the means by which the court is to ascertain the relevant facts are largely unresolved issues. In general, a fairly broad-brush approach has been taken to the ascertainment of facts in constitutional cases. The High Court has never insisted on the standard of strict proof required in ordinary non-constitutional litigation. General conclusions have been drawn from publicly available material (such as government reports and historical treatises) and these have usually been seen to be sufficient for the purposes at hand. It remains to be seen whether other more formal methods of proof may be required in some cases involving an examination of the justification for an alleged infringement of a constitutional right and (if so) who is to bear the formal onus of proof.

TAKING A CONSTITUTIONAL POINT [75]

No special procedures for raising an issue concerning the application of constitutional rights exist in Australia. A claim that a constitutional right has been infringed falls to be dealt with in the same way as any other constitutional point which may be raised in litigation.

The High Court has original jurisdiction in all matters arising under the Constitution or involving its interpretation. The High Court is also the final court of appeal on all questions arising in legal proceedings in Australian courts.

In practice, major constitutional litigation is generally heard and determined in proceedings commenced in the original jurisdiction of the High Court. The practice is generally for a person seeking to challenge the validity of Commonwealth or State legislation to commence proceedings by writ and statement of claim filed in the High Court and served on the appropriate Commonwealth, State or Territory government seeking a declaration that the legislation in question is invalid. If there is no dispute of fact, the proceedings will be referred to the Full Court of the High Court for hearing either on a demurrer or on a case stated or question reserved by a single justice. The Full Court of the High Court is almost invariably constituted by all seven justices when hearing a constitutional case. If there is a dispute of fact, the normal practice is for the proceedings – or at least the factual issues – to be remitted

---

75   See also Ch 14 by Eastman and Ronalds in this volume.

to the Federal Court or the Supreme Court of a State for hearing and determination before being considered by the High Court.

An alternative way of commencing constitutional litigation in the original jurisdiction of the High Court is to seek a writ of prohibition or mandamus. This is appropriate where the challenge is to the jurisdiction of a Commonwealth tribunal or administrative official. This type of proceeding is commenced by filing an affidavit and draft order nisi in the registry of the High Court. The proceedings are then brought before a single justice who determines whether the case is sufficiently arguable to justify an order nisi being granted. An order nisi is an order calling on the tribunal or official concerned to show cause why final relief should not be granted. If an order nisi is made, it will be made returnable before a Full Court for final argument.

However, constitutional litigation is by no means restricted to the High Court. This was not always the position. Until its repeal in 1976, s 40A of the *Judiciary Act* had the effect of automatically removing into the High Court most constitutional questions arising in proceedings in a court other than the High Court. It was therefore extremely rare for a case raising a constitutional issue to be heard in any court other than the High Court.

As a result of amendments to the *Judiciary Act* introduced in 1976 and progressively since then, the Supreme Courts of the States and other State courts as well as the Federal Court all now have both jurisdiction in matters arising under the Constitution or involving its interpretation and the ability to hear and determine all constitutional questions as might properly arise in proceedings before them. There is no reason why proceedings seeking a declaration to the effect that some governmental activity is unconstitutional should not now be commenced in the Federal Court or the Supreme Court of a State.

It has also become increasingly common for less important constitutional cases commenced in the original jurisdiction of the High Court to be remitted in their entirety to the Federal Court or to the Supreme Court of a State by order made in the discretion of a justice of the High Court. However, it is important to recognise that a constitutional point can be taken in any proceedings in any court where the point properly arises for determination. It is possible, for example, in criminal proceedings before a magistrate in a court of summary jurisdiction to raise by way of defence the constitutional invalidity of the legislation pursuant to which the charge has been brought.

Where a constitutional issue arises in a case, it is the duty of the court not to proceed with the matter unless the court is satisfied that reasonable notice of the constitutional issue has been given to the Attorneys-General of the Commonwealth and of the States and Territories. The Attorneys-General each have a right to intervene in the hearing of the case in the court where the issue arises. They also have a right to have the case or the constitutional issue removed directly into the High Court for hearing. The right to intervene is frequently exercised by Attorneys-General. The right to remove proceedings to the High Court is almost never exercised.

Appeals from judgments in proceedings involving constitutional issues are dealt with in much the same way as most other appeals. For practical purposes, all appeals to the High Court are now only by way of special leave to appeal.[76] This gives the High Court a discretion as to whether or not to hear an appeal. If the High Court grants special leave to appeal it will go on usually in a separate hearing to hear and determine the appeal. If the High Court refuses special leave to appeal, the judgment of the lower court remains. Although it is possible to seek special leave to appeal from any decision of any court or judge of a State involving a constitutional issue, the usual course is for an appeal to be taken first to the intermediate appellate court of the State concerned (usually the Court of Appeal, Court of Criminal Appeal or Full Court of the Supreme Court) and then to seek special leave to appeal to the High Court.

CONCLUSION

The Commonwealth Constitution and the Constitutions of the Australian States are not specifically addressed to the preservation of human rights. To attempt to spell out of them a series of positive constitutional rights or to construct a coherent and unified theory of the constitutional protection of human rights in Australia would be misleading. It has nevertheless been possible to discern in the language and structure of the Commonwealth Constitution a number of limitations on the exercise of governmental power which are consistent with the protection of human rights. Those limitations apply differently in relation to the Commonwealth, the States and the Territories. It has also been possible to identify a number of general evaluative concepts which have come to be employed in the application of constitutional limitations.

By and large, the most significant constitutional limitations on the exercise of governmental power which we have outlined have been the product of judicial interpretation and development only in the last decade. The trend of judicial interpretation in that period has generally but by no means uniformly favoured the recognition of limitations on governmental power where questions of the liberty of the individual are involved.

---

76   On which see generally, O'Brien, D, *Special Leave to Appeal: the Law and Practice of Applications for Special Leave to Appeal to the High Court of Australia* (Law Book Co, Sydney, 1996).

4

ADMINISTRATIVE LAW AND HUMAN RIGHTS

John McMillan and Neil Williams

INTRODUCTION

The capacity of the administrative arm of government to affect the human rights of individuals is great. The coercive powers exercised by government law enforcers and investigators can result in the involuntary detention of people, the confiscation of private property and papers, and intrusion into the privacy of residential and business premises. Reports published by government can damage the reputation and standing of those who are mentioned in them. In the distribution of grants, licences, benefits and other concessions, government policies can exhibit discriminatory tendencies that favour one social group over another. Routine decisions by government – to provide income support, grant a visa to enter or remain in Australia, issue a business licence, or approve enrolment in an educational course – will often shape the fortunes of those to whom they apply.

Administrative law is one of the chief methods adopted in a liberal democratic society to check the exercise of governmental powers. The issue addressed in this chapter is the extent to which human rights considerations play an explicit role in administrative law. In this respect Australia is distinguished from most other countries in that executive decision-making in Australia is not subject to a constitutional Bill of Rights or to an equivalent human rights statute with an overarching operation.[1] Without entering into debate on whether that initiative would be desirable, we merely observe that the impact of a Bill of Rights on administrative law can be direct and far-reaching. It can, for example, transform the obligation to observe natural justice from a common law implication to an explicit constitutional duty. A Bill of Rights also provides a foundation for contending that the rights and freedoms enshrined in the document – which can be as varied as freedom of speech, cultural diversity, and the rights of children – are a mandatory consideration in executive decision-making.

---

1   For a discussion of the interrelationship of administrative law and human rights declarations, see Janis M, Kay, R and Bradley, A, *European Human Rights Law* (Clarendon Press, Oxford, 1995); Bradley, AW, "Administrative Justice: A Developing Human Right?" (1995) 1 *European Public Law* 347; Joseph, PA, "The New Zealand Bill of Rights" (1996) 7 *Public Law Review* 162; and Rubenstein, K, "Towards 2001: An Assessment of the Possible Impact of a Bill of Rights on Administrative Law in Australia" (1994) 1 *Australian Journal of Administrative Law* 13 (Pt 1) and 59 (Pt 2).

Absent a Bill of Rights, it is nevertheless the case that human rights considerations have been of growing importance in Australian administrative law in the past decade. Two themes are addressed in this paper: the embodiment of human rights norms in the administrative law framework, and in the criteria for legal validity developed in the context of judicial review.

THE RIGHT TO ADMINISTRATIVE JUSTICE IN THE STRUCTURE OF AUSTRALIAN ADMINISTRATIVE LAW

In a recent analysis of developments under the *European Convention on Human Rights* (ECHR), Professor AW Bradley argued that decisions of the European Court of Human Rights provided "a solid basis for a new human right of immense importance to the study of administrative law", which he coined "the right to administrative justice".[2] In Professor Bradley's account, the right would consist in certain minimum standards of administrative law, of which he highlighted three:

- the right of individuals to seek judicial review of government decisions which adversely affect them;

- a full right of appeal from a first instance decision by an official to a tribunal or other judicial body before the operative decision is made and the need for judicial review arises; and

- that on some issues of great importance to individuals a court should be able to review both the legality and the merits of the decision being challenged.

The core theme in Bradley's definition of a right to administrative justice is the right of an aggrieved individual to seek review of a government administrative action by an independent review body. The same point has been made forcefully by leading civil liberties barrister, Geoffrey Robertson QC: "The most fundamental right of all is the right to challenge the State, under a legal system which allows the possibility, occasionally, of winning".[3]

Administrative justice, as a human right defined in those terms, is already secured in at least four distinct ways in the framework of Australian administrative law. First, in each Australian jurisdiction there is a right to judicial review of the legality of executive decisions in a superior court, being the Supreme Court in the States or Territories, and the Federal Court or High Court for Commonwealth decisions. The right is secured by statute in some jurisdictions,[4] and arises in others from the inherent common law power of a superior court to grant the prerogative writs and equitable remedies to restrain unlawful action.[5] Further remarks are made below about judicial review, and in particular about the Commonwealth review scheme.

---

2   Bradley, op cit, pp 348, 351.

3   Robertson, G, *The Justice Game* (Chatto and Windus, London, 1998), as quoted in the *Weekend Australian,* 21-22 March 1998, p 26 of Review.

4   *Administrative Decisions (Judicial Review) Act* 1977 (Cth), *Administrative Law Act* 1978 (Vic), *Administrative Decisions (Judicial Review) Act* 1989 (ACT), and *Judicial Review Act* 1991 (Qld).

5   See Aronson, M and Dyer, B, *Judicial Review of Administrative Action* (Law Book Co, Sydney, 1996), pp 17-23.

The second important right of review is the right to review the merits of selected administrative decisions in an administrative tribunal. Four jurisdictions have a multi-jurisdiction tribunal – called the Administrative Appeals Tribunal (AAT) in the Commonwealth and the ACT, the Administrative Decisions Tribunal in New South Wales and the Civil and Administrative Tribunal in Victoria. In each jurisdiction there is also a range of specialist tribunals, like the Social Security Appeals Tribunal, Immigration and Refugee Review Tribunals, the Veterans' Review Board, and guardianship, planning and occupational licensing tribunals and boards.[6] Within that framework some decisions can be appealed through a two-tier structure, for instance, from the Social Security Appeals Tribunal to the Administrative Appeals Tribunal. In terms of securing administrative justice, the advantage of a multi-tier system is that formality and adherence to legal principle can be maintained at a higher supervisory level, while the great majority of matters can be resolved quickly, informally and inexpensively at lower tiers.

A further noteworthy feature of merit review is the latitude that exists for incorporation of a human rights perspective in applying the merit review standard that customarily guides administrative review, namely whether the decision under review was the "correct or preferable" decision on the material before the tribunal.[7] A former Deputy President of the Commonwealth AAT, Peter Johnston, has argued that the standards of good management that are part of the Tribunal's role can "be informed by standards adopted by civilised countries", and that "on procedural and systemic grounds the Tribunal ... may take into account considerations of *equity* and *reasonableness* as part of its function".[8] Two examples cited by Johnston are *Re Vazquez and Minister for Immigration, Local Government and Ethnic Affairs,*[9] in which the Tribunal placed emphasis on humanitarian considerations as mitigating the application of ministerial policy; and *Re Al Saeed and Secretary, Department of Social Security,*[10] in which the Tribunal recommended that an *ex gratia* payment be made to a person who did not qualify for special benefit, on the basis that the neglect or refusal by Australia to afford basic assistance to the national of a foreign country could involve a breach of international humanitarian law and the *International Covenant on Civil and Political Rights* (ICCPR). Johnston also notes support for this approach in the observation of Deane J in *Australian Broadcasting Tribunal v Bond,*[11] that the duty of an administrative tribunal to act judicially "excludes the

---

6   For a description of Commonwealth tribunals see Administrative Review Council, *Better Decisions: Review of Commonwealth Merits Tribunals,* Report No 39 (1995). There were proposals under consideration in 1998 for a complete restructure of the Commonwealth tribunal system: see Attorney-General's Department, *Reform of the Merits Review Tribunals: Government Proposal* (1998). For a description of the State administrative law framework, see Access to Justice Advisory Committee, *Access to Justice: An Action Plan* (AGPS, Canberra, 1994), Ch 13.

7   *Drake v Minister for Immigration and Ethnic Affairs* (1979) 24 ALR 577 at 589 per Bowen CJ and Deane J. See also *Builders Licensing Board v Sperway Constructions (Sydney) Pty Ltd* (1976) 135 CLR 616, as to the nature of de novo review.

8   Johnston, P, "The Silence of the Books: The Role of the Administrative Appeals Tribunal in the Protection of Individual Rights" in McMillan, J (ed), *Administrative Law: Does the Public Benefit?* (Australian Institute of Administrative Law, Canberra, 1991), pp 54, 59.

9   (1989) 20 ALD 33.

10   (1991) 22 ALD 675.

11   (1990) 170 CLR 321 at 367.

right to decide arbitrarily, irrationally or unreasonably ... on preconceived prejudice or suspicion ... [and, arguably] requires a minimum degree of 'proportionality'".

The third method of administrative review is via complaints to the Ombudsman or (as they are named in Queensland and Western Australia) the Parliamentary Commissioner. The statutory criteria to be applied by the Ombudsman in deciding whether there has been defective administrative action are framed broadly, and clearly with the intention of encompassing human rights concerns. Examples are that the Ombudsman can examine whether an administrative action was "unreasonable, unjust, oppressive or improperly discriminatory" or was in made in accordance with a legislative or administrative rule that infringed that standard.[12]

Fourthly, the schemes that exist in most Australian jurisdictions for the investigation and adjudication of complaints that infringe human rights and anti-discrimination standards apply to government agencies.[13] To take the Commonwealth scheme as an example, there can be a complaint to one of the Commissioners that comprise the Human Rights and Equal Opportunity Commission (HREOC), complaining about discrimination by a Commonwealth decision-maker on grounds of sex, marital status or pregnancy; race, colour, descent or national or ethnic origin; physical or mental disability; or infringement of human rights standards such as liberty of movement, right to personal liberty and security, and freedom of speech or association. As discussed elsewhere in this book, infringement of the sex, race or disability standards can result in damages being awarded by HREOC against a government agency.[14]

Judicial review

In terms of evaluating whether an opportunity for administrative review can be characterised as the recognition of a right to administrative justice, some aspects of the comprehensive scheme for judicial review of Commonwealth executive action warrant special mention. The first is that the right to judicial review is extensively defined in the *Administrative Decisions (Judicial Review) Act* 1977 (an Act that is copied in the ACT and Queensland). It is significant that the Act defines the grounds for judicial review, listing 18 criteria in all (s 5); it entitles an aggrieved person to seek a written statement of the reasons for a decision before commencing proceedings (s 13); and the powers of the Federal Court to give remedial relief are defined in broad and discretionary terms, and extend to any direction to the parties "which the Court considers necessary to do justice between the parties" (s 16).[15]

Importantly too the Commonwealth judicial review scheme is secured by a constitutional guarantee in s 75(v) of the Commonwealth Constitution, which provides that the High Court has an original jurisdiction to grant mandamus, prohibition and injunction against an "officer of the Commonwealth". This has been

---

12   *Ombudsman Act* 1976 (Cth) s 15(1)(a)(ii) and (iii). Similar wording is used in State and Territory legislation, for example, *Ombudsman Act* 1974 (NSW) s 26(1)(a) and (b).

13   Anti-discrimination and human rights agencies have been established in all jurisdictions except Tasmania; see further, Ch 13 by Bailey and Devereux in this volume.

14   Ibid.

15   As to the scope of s 16, see *Minister for Immigration and Ethnic Affairs v Conyngham* (1986) 68 ALR 441, and *Park Oh Ho v Minister for Immigration and Ethnic Affairs* (1989) 167 CLR 637.

described many times as a constitutional jurisdiction to ensure lawful conduct by officers of the Commonwealth,[16] which cannot be overridden by a privative clause that seeks to insulate executive action from judicial scrutiny.[17]

The major limitation in the review scheme – which some would see as a shortcoming that detracts from its conformity to notions of administrative justice – is that the award of damages is not generally speaking an administrative law remedy. Liability of a public authority to damages is not the natural consequence of invalid action,[18] and the power to award damages is not generally regarded to be a remedy granted by a court in the exercise of its judicial review jurisdiction.[19] Nor as a general rule can administrative tribunals or Ombudsman order the payment of damages for public sector wrong.[20]

Information rights

The role that information plays in defining a democratic relationship between government and citizen is critical.[21] The ability of a government to mould and distort public perception of government policies through propaganda is, at one extreme, the pressing danger that has long been a central concern in democratic theory. In less dramatic ways too the manner in which information is collected, handled and disclosed can have a strong bearing on government accountability and the rights of individuals.

There is a growing recognition of this point in human rights conventions, some of which acknowledge that freedom of information – perceived as a right claimable against the State – is not merely an implied aspect of the more traditional rights to freedom of expression and freedom of the press. Both the ECHR, art 10(1), and the ICCPR, art 19(2), declare that the right to freedom of expression includes the freedom to "receive and impart information and ideas". The reach of this declaration was extended by a "Declaration on the freedom of expression and information" adopted by the Committee of Ministers of the Council of Europe in 1982, asserting that freedom of expression and information are a "fundamental element ... [of the] principles of genuine democracy, the rule of law and respect for human rights", and are "necessary for the social, economic, cultural and political development of every human being". Further, access to government information is important "to enhance

---

16   For example, *Bank of New South Wales v Commonwealth* (1948) 76 CLR 1 at 363 per Dixon J.

17   For example, *R v Coldham; ex p Australian Workers' Union* (1983) 153 CLR 415; and *O'Toole v Charles David Pty Ltd* (1991) 171 CLR 232. For a discussion of the relevance of the Constitutional limits to a current proposal to limit judicial review of migration decisions, see Creyke, R, "Restricting Judicial Review" (1997) 15 *Australian Institute of Administrative Law Forum* 22.

18   *Northern Territory v Mengel* (1995) 129 ALR 1.

19   For example, *Comptroller-General of Customs v Kawasaki Motors Pty Ltd* (1991) 103 ALR 637 at 648, 658; cf *Macksville & District Hospital v Mayze* (1987) 10 NSWLR 708. Damages can be awarded against a public authority in the civil jurisdiction of a court, for instance, for negligence or misfeasance in public office.

20   The power to do so is conferred upon many anti-discrimination and equal opportunity tribunals; for discussion, see Ch 13 by Bailey and Devereux in this volume. The Ombudsman can recommend payment of ex gratia compensation: see, for example, the Commonwealth guidelines, published in *Australian Administrative Law Service* (Butterworths, Sydney), 6049.

21   See Ch 11 by Arup and Tucker in this volume.

the individual's understanding of, and his ability to discuss freely political, social, economic and cultural matters".[22]

Public recognition of the pivotal role that information plays in government accountability spurred a movement in Australia in the 1970s to create a framework for controlling government information practices.[23] The former tradition that government alone will decide what is disclosed has been firmly replaced by legislative recognition and official acceptance of a public "right to know". The major plank of that principle is the *Freedom of Information Acts* that exist in most Australian jurisdictions,[24] to confer a public right of access to government documents. From the perspective of administrative justice, the pertinent features of that scheme are that there is no standing requirement (that is, to obtain access a person does not have to explain or justify why they need a document); the government's right to withhold documents from disclosure is circumscribed by exemptions in the legislation; and a refusal of access can be questioned before an independent court or tribunal, in which the government bears the onus of establishing the correctness of the decision under review.

Information rights have been secured in other ways as well. Privacy laws (such as the federal *Privacy Act* 1988) regulate the collection, storage, use, disclosure and correction of government records. The right to obtain upon request a written statement of the reasons for a decision that would be challengeable before a court or tribunal has been secured by judicial review legislation in four jurisdictions.[25] Statutory obligations are now being imposed upon government agencies to inform people of their review rights.[26] There is also a trend towards the enactment of whistleblower protection laws, that now exist in four Australian jurisdictions.[27] The purport of the whistleblower laws is that in defined situations an individual government employee has the right to engage in an unauthorised disclosure of official information, and be protected against the normal disciplinary or criminal sanctions that might otherwise apply. The significance of this legislative protection, from a human rights perspective, is the recognition that the individual's right of conscience

---

22   Council of Europe, *Yearbook of the European Convention on Human Rights 1982* (1986), Principal Dev 25-27, quoted in Bayne, P, "Freedom of Information and Political Free Speech" in Campbell, T and Sadurski, W (eds), *Freedom of Communication* (Dartmouth, Aldershot, 1994), p 207. See also Malinverni, G, "Freedom of Information in the European Convention on Human Rights and in the International Covenant on Civil and Political Rights" (1983) 4 *Human Rights Law Journal* 443.

23   See Australian Law Reform Commission/Administrative Review Council, *Open Government: A Review of the Federal Freedom of Information Act 1982*, ALRC Report No 77/ARC Report No 40 (1995), Ch 3.

24   For example, *Freedom of Information Act* 1982 (Cth) and *Archives Act* 1983 (Cth). The Northern Territory is the only jurisdiction that has not enacted a Freedom of Information Act.

25   *Administrative Decisions (Judicial Review) Act* 1977 (Cth) s 13; *Administrative Law Act* 1978 (Vic) s 8; *Administrative Decisions (Judicial Review) Act* 1989 (ACT) s 13; and *Judicial Review Act* 1991 (Qld) s 32.

26   For example, the *Administrative Appeals Tribunal Act* 1975 (Cth) s 27A.

27   *Whistleblowers Protection Act* 1993 (SA); *Protected Disclosures Act* 1994 (NSW); *Whistleblowers Protection Act* 1994 (Qld); and *Public Sector Management Act* 1994 (ACT) Pt XII. The proposed new Commonwealth *Public Service Act* s 16 also creates protection for Australian Public Service (APS) employees who report a breach by other officers of the APS Code of Conduct.

can be a superior principle to the obligations of confidentiality and fidelity that are a standard feature of employment in the public and private sector.[28]

There may yet be deeper constitutional support for freedom of information principles in Australia. The implied constitutional guarantee of freedom of political communication that was first recognised in *Australian Capital Television Pty Ltd v Commonwealth (No 2)*[29] sprang from the notion that "sovereign power ... resides in the people".[30] In order that people can exercise their right to comment on and criticise government action, Mason CJ held, "the elected representatives have a responsibility not only to ascertain the views of the electorate but also to explain and account for their decisions and actions in government and to inform the people so that they may make informed judgments on relevant matters".[31] The importance generally of maintaining a free flow of information between citizens and government was a point of emphasis in that case.

Although there is no suggestion at this stage that there is a positive duty upon governments to impart information,[32] the constitutional principles have a clear relevance to administrative law issues. Those principles can properly influence the interpretation of freedom of information and privacy laws,[33] the construction of other statutory powers,[34] and the scope of common law principles like public interest immunity and protection of confidence. For example, in rejecting a breach of confidence claim by the Commonwealth to restrain the unauthorised publication of classified government documents, Mason J in *Commonwealth v John Fairfax & Sons Ltd*[35] held that:

> It is unacceptable in our democratic society that there should be a restraint on the publication of information relating to government when the only vice of that information is that it enables the public to discuss, review and criticise government action.

A similar view was expressed in another case rejecting the attempt by the British Government to restrain the publication of *Spycatcher* in Australia, McHugh J observing that "Information is held, received and imparted by governments, their departments and agencies to further the public interest".[36]

---

28 See McMillan, J, "The Whistleblower Versus the Organisation: Who Should be Protected" in Campbell and Sadurski, above, n 22.

29 (1992) 177 CLR 106.

30 Ibid at 137 per Mason CJ.

31 Ibid at 139 per Mason CJ.

32 See *Final Report of the Constitutional Commission* (1988), Vol 1, para 9.918; and Chadwick, P, "FOI and the Constitution" (1995) 56 *FOI Review* 23.

33 See Bayne, above, n 22, p 199.

34 See, for example, *Minister for Foreign Affairs and Trade v Magno* (1992) 112 ALR 529 per Einfeld J (dissenting), holding that in light of the implied freedom it was beyond power to make subordinate legislation that infringed freedom of political communication.

35 (1980) 147 CLR 39 at 52.

36 *Attorney-General (UK) v Heinemann Publishers Pty Ltd* (1987) 10 NSWLR 86 at 191.

Individual rights protection as an underlying theme of administrative law

The defining feature of Australian administrative law as described above is that the legality and propriety of administrative activity is reviewed at the instigation of the individual who feels aggrieved and initiates an action. In that sense, the *structure* of administrative law is premised more upon the protection of individual rights than it is upon the pursuit of good decision-making. Executive compliance with the standards of legality and propriety is an issue that arises for consideration only at the suit of the aggrieved individual who takes action to assert a right against the State. In the same way the legislative obligations imposed upon government to disclose information to the public are activated by an individual request or claim.

That point pervades other themes in Australian administrative law. It is reflected in the prominence given recently by courts to protection of individual rights as one of the objectives of judicial review. The development of this theme was captured in an evaluation of the first 10 years of the Commonwealth system of administrative law by Brennan J:

> After ten years it may not be possible to say that this society is fairer, or more egalitarian, or more compassionate than it was before. But it is possible to say that this society is one which now accords to the individual an opportunity to meet on more equal terms the institutions of the state. ... The interests of individuals are more fully acknowledged, and the repositories of power are constrained to treat the individual both fairly and according to law. ... [A] society which truly accords that opportunity to the citizen is a free and fair society, and there can be no doubt that the object of the new administrative law was intended to accord that opportunity.[37]

That sentiment, as the remainder of this chapter examines, is reflected in the criteria developed by courts for defining the boundaries of legality for executive decision-making. In a practical sense, an argument to a court or tribunal that is framed in terms of safeguarding individual rights may have added strength. The inconvenience which judicial vigilance can cause for administrative activity has been justified by the Federal Court as "a small price to pay to maintain the primacy that the liberty of the individual should have in our legal system".[38] Courts, it has been said, respond to the "vulnerability of the citizen" facing "the pervasiveness of State power".[39] Likewise, it has been noted that "[t]he purpose of judicial review is to ensure that the individual receives fair treatment".[40]

---

37   The Hon Mr Justice Brennan, "Reflections" (1989) 58 *Canberra Bulletin of Public Administration* 32 at 33.

38   *Schlieske v Minister for Immigration and Ethnic Affairs* (1988) 84 ALR 719 at 730 per Wilcox and French JJ. See also *Buksh v Minister for Immigration, Local Government and Ethnic Affairs* (1991) 102 ALR 647 at 656 per Einfeld J.

39   Justice P Finn, "The Courts and the Vulnerable" in *Law and Policy Papers,* Paper No 5 (Centre for International and Public Law, Australian National University, 1996), p 7.

40   *Chief Constable of the North Wales Police v Evans* [1982] 1 WLR 1155 at 1161 per Lord Hailsham LC. Note, however, the concluding point in this chapter that the courts have no free-standing jurisdiction to protect individual rights, and do so only in the context of defining and enforcing the lawful limits on executive power.

THE HUMAN RIGHTS DIMENSION
IN AUSTRALIAN JUDICIAL REVIEW

Special treatment must be given to the principles of judicial review in any discussion of the human rights dimension in Australian administrative law. It is chiefly in defining the criteria for legality that courts articulate the values of administrative law, and define the duties and obligations (including the protection of human rights) of government agencies in their relations with members of the community. This chapter will look at three areas in which human rights considerations play a direct role.[41]

Controlling executive discretion

At the point at which the business of individuals intersects with the work of government agencies there is frequently a statutory discretion – to grant or refuse a benefit or licence, to waive or recover a debt, to deport a person or regularise their status, to investigate or disregard suspicious activity, or to recognise an interest conditionally or unconditionally. A statute might enumerate exhaustively the considerations or factors to be taken into account, in which case the scope for consideration of human rights issues will usually be a straightforward matter.

In the different situation where the list of relevant factors is inclusive but not exhaustive, or where the discretion is otherwise unconfined or open-textured, whether human rights considerations either can or must be considered can be a vital issue. The starting point is the principle that the boundaries of relevance and irrelevance are to be determined "by implication from the subject matter, scope and purpose of the Act".[42] The conventional view is that that process of statutory construction should be undertaken in a way that concedes a degree of latitude to the administrator in deciding the matters that will be considered in reaching a decision. That is, a court will be cautious in concluding either that an issue taken into account was irrelevant, or that an official was obliged to consider a matter that was not taken into account. The classic statement of the principle was given by Dixon J in *Swan Hill Corporation v Bradbury*:[43]

> [C]ourts of law have no source whence they may ascertain what is the purpose of the discretion except the terms and subject matter of the statutory instrument. They must, therefore, concede to the authority a discretion unlimited by anything but the scope and object of the instrument confirming it. This means that only a negative definition of the grounds governing the discretion may be given. It may be possible to say that this or that consideration is extraneous to the power, but it must always be impracticable in such cases to make more than the most general positive statement of the permissible limits within which the discretion is exercisable and beyond legal control.

---

41 For a broader treatment of judicial review principles, see Aronson and Dyer, above, n 5.

42 *Minister for Aboriginal Affairs v Peko-Wallsend Ltd* (1986) 162 CLR 24 at 39-40 per Mason J.

43 (1937) 56 CLR 746 at 758; approved in *R v Australian Broadcasting Tribunal; ex p 2HD Pty Ltd* (1979) 144 CLR 45, and *O'Sullivan v Farrer* (1989) 168 CLR 210 at 216.

The principle that deference should be accorded to the judgment of the administrator is also captured in two other pronouncements that are frequently quoted. The first is the statement by Deane J in *Sean Investments Pty Ltd v MacKellar*,[44] that:

> [W]here relevant considerations are not specified, it is largely for the decision-maker, in the light of matters placed before him by the parties, to determine which matters he regards as relevant.

The second is the statement by Gibbs J in *Buck v Bavone*,[45] that:

> [W]here the matter of which [an] authority is required to be satisfied is a matter of opinion or policy or taste it may be very difficult to show that it has erred [by considering irrelevant matters or failing to consider relevant matters] or that its decision could not reasonably have been reached. In such cases the authority will be left with a very wide discretion which cannot be effectively reviewed by the courts.

The foremost example of this approach to construction, which illustrates at the same time the obstacle which the approach poses to a human rights claim, is a 1947 decision of the High Court in *Water Conservation and Irrigation Commission (NSW) v Browning*.[46] A power expressed in the statute to be "entirely in the discretion of the Commission" had been exercised to refuse consent to the transfer of an irrigation licence to Italians, for reasons including that leases "should be kept for Australians", that "as a general rule Italians are not good farmers", and that "it is most undesirable that any further aggregation of Italians be built up on an irrigation area". After pointing out that the Commission's discretion was unconfined, and that there was no warrant in the statute for limiting it, the court accepted that the Commission could choose to base its decision on racially discriminatory criteria, adding that "The growth and character and components of the community by which an irrigation area is worked is not a matter altogether foreign to the Commission's responsibilities".[47]

It is unthinkable that the High Court could on those facts reach the same decision nowadays: racial preference would be an irrelevant consideration, not only because of the enactment of the *Racial Discrimination Act* 1975 (Cth), but also because it would be held to fall outside the "subject matter, scope and purpose" of the legislation. The *Browning* principle of unconfined discretion has not been rejected, however, and continues to play an active influence on Australian administrative law, including upon the incorporation of human rights norms. A leading modern illustration is the decision of the Full Federal Court in *Minister for Immigration and Ethnic Affairs v Maitan*,[48] that a Minister, in deciding whether to issue a temporary entry permit, is bound to look only at matters of public or national interest, and though entitled is not bound to look at circumstances personal to an applicant.

---

44   (1981) 38 ALR 363 at 375.

45   (1976) 135 CLR 110 at 119; approved in *Minister for Immigration and Ethnic Affairs v Wu Shan Liang* (1996) 185 CLR 259 at 275-76.

46   (1947) 74 CLR 492 at 505 per Dixon J.

47   Ibid.

48   (1988) 78 ALR 419 at 429. See also *Bollag v Attorney-General (Cth)* (1997) 47 ALD 568.

The principle of unconfined discretion is probably an influential factor too in explaining an aspect of the decision of the High Court in *Kioa v West*,[49] intimating that a decision-maker is entitled to take international and domestic human rights law into account, but is not legally obliged to do so. That case concerned a challenge to the validity of a deportation order made against Mr and Mrs Kioa, who became prohibited immigrants after the expiration of their temporary entry permits. While in Australia the Kioas had given birth to a daughter, who thereby acquired Australian citizenship (a right that no longer arises in that situation). The practical effect of a deportation order would be to deny the daughter, then ten months old, either the fruits of her Australian citizenship or the company of her parents, a result that in either case was said to contravene two international instruments that had been scheduled to the *Human Rights Commission Act* 1981 (Cth), the ICCPR and the *Declaration on the Rights of the Child*. The Preamble to the Act provided that "it is desirable that the laws of the Commonwealth and the conduct of persons administering those laws should conform to" the scheduled conventions.

The submission to the High Court that was premised on the significance of the conventions was dismissed by the court on the basis that a brief acknowledgment by the decision-maker that he was aware that the daughter was an Australian citizen satisfied any legal obligation that might exist to give consideration to her situation.[50] The suggestion that the international conventions might hold a special relevance to the decision-making process was expressly rejected by Gibbs CJ, for the reason that there was no legal obligation upon a decision-maker to ensure that decisions conformed with the international instruments, and by Brennan J for the reason that the decision-maker was entitled but not bound to take those instruments into account.[51]

The view expressed in *Kioa* has not been disapproved by the High Court in any later case,[52] but it has been circumvented by other developments in judicial review described in this chapter that enable human rights considerations to encroach upon statutory discretions, both directly and indirectly. In an indirect way, judicial review can be undertaken in an exacting manner, whereby the failure to give what − in the eyes of the court − is appropriate weight to the interests of an individual or to the human rights dimension of a case is condemned on grounds that have a more orthodox legal ring.[53] This factor probably lies behind the recent judicial disposition

---

49   (1985) 159 CLR 550.

50   Ibid at 570 per Gibbs CJ, at 588 per Mason J, at 604 per Wilson J, at 629 per Brennan J, and at 634 per Deane J.

51   Ibid at 570-71 per Gibbs CJ, at 629 per Brennan J. See also the judgment of the Full Court of the Federal Court: (1984) 55 ALR 669 at 681 per Northrop and Wilcox JJ.

52   Though a single judge of the Federal Court has held that the principle of *Wednesbury* unreasonableness should require a decision-maker to take account of fundamental human rights as recognised in international conventions: *Premelal v Minister for Immigration, Local Government and Ethnic Affairs* (1993) 41 FCR 117 (Einfeld J).

53   See McMillan, J, "Recent Themes in Judicial Review of Federal Executive Action" (1996) 24 *Federal Law Review* 347; Sir Anthony Mason, "The Importance of Judicial Review of Administrative Action as a Safeguard of Individual Rights" (1994) 1 *Australian Journal of Human Rights* 1; Bayne, P, "Administrative Law, Human Rights and International Humanitarian Law" (1990) 64 *Australian Law Journal* 203; Kirby, M, "The Impact of International Human Rights Norms: A 'Law Undergoing Revolution'" (1996) 22 *Commonwealth Law Bulletin* 1181.

to find that "proper, genuine and realistic consideration" was not given to the merits of a case.[54] Or that there had been a failure by a decision-maker to inquire properly into matters of significant relevance to the outcome of a case.[55] The developing support for new legal standards, such as probative evidence to support a decision,[56] and proportionality in the result,[57] are also significant in this regard.

A more direct method for affixing human rights considerations to administrative discretions is the doctrine of natural justice, discussed later in this paper. Perhaps not surprisingly breach of natural justice was the alternative basis of challenge that succeeded in *Kioa*, and its importance to a human rights perspective on administrative law has grown since the decision a decade later in *Teoh*.

Developments in Britain and New Zealand

Similar issues to those arising in *Kioa* and *Teoh* have been examined by superior courts in Britain and New Zealand. The leading British authority is *R v Secretary of State for the Home Department; ex p Brind*,[58] which concerned a challenge to the validity of a discretionary decision by the Home Secretary to issue a directive to the BBC not to broadcast Sinn Fein messages. The House of Lords rejected a submission that the directive was invalid because it contravened art 10 of the ECHR which guarantees the right to freedom of expression, or because it was a disproportionate and unreasonable exercise of power.

The ECHR argument was put in a persuasive fashion, superficially at least. If parliament is presumed to have legislated in conformity with the Convention, it would follow, it was argued, that it was parliament's intention that discretionary powers should be exercised within the limitations that the Convention imposes. The main basis that was given for rejecting this submission is that its acceptance would be tantamount to introducing the Convention into English law by the back door, and overturning the principle that a convention which has not been implemented into domestic law by an Act of Parliament cannot be the source of enforceable rights and obligations. The argument employing a principle of proportionality was also unsuccessful, either because its place in English law was rejected, or because of the high threshhold required for the principle to operate.

Although there was some acknowledgment in *Brind* of the relevance of human rights concerns in the exercise of statutory discretions, the major significance of the case was that the House of Lords declined to impose an obligation upon officials to take the Convention into account in administrative decision-making. Critics of

---

54 For example, *Hindi v Minister for Immigration and Ethnic Affairs* (1988) 91 ALR 586 at 59 and *Vaitaiki v Minister for Immigration and Ethnic Affairs* (1998) 150 ALR 608.

55 For example, *Prasad v Minister for Immigration and Ethnic Affairs* (1985) 65 ALR 549 at 563, *Luu v Renevier* (1989) 91 ALR 39, and *Sun Zhan Qui v Minister for Immigration and Ethnic Affairs* (1997) 151 ALR 505.

56 *Minister for Immigration and Ethnic Affairs v Pochi* (1980) 31 ALR 666 at 690.

57 Selway, B, "The Rise and Rise of the Reasonable Proportionality Test in Public Law" (1996) 7 *Public Law Review* 212.

58 [1991] 1 AC 696.

Brind[59] have argued that in doing so the court failed to acknowledge the legal significance for Britain of the ECHR, which is tied partly to the right of complaint to the European Court of Human Rights against British legislative or executive action that contravenes the ECHR, and partly to the steady integration of British and European Community law. It has been predicted, accordingly, that as *Brind* is gradually undermined its authority will dwindle.

A rather more robust approach was taken in New Zealand, in an oft-cited dictum by Cooke P in *Tavita v Minister of Immigration*.[60] The President of the Court of Appeal commented that an argument that officials could ignore international instruments was "an unattractive argument, apparently implying that New Zealand's adherence to international instruments has been at least partly window dressing". Since then, it has been accepted that a failure by a decision-maker to consider a relevant international instrument can be a ground of invalidity.[61] For practical purposes, however, it is the *New Zealand Bill of Rights Act* 1990 (NZ) that has held centre stage in the development of a human rights jurisprudence in New Zealand administrative law.[62]

Beneficial construction of discretionary language

A major way adopted in Australia for circumventing an unconfined discretion is by transforming the power by reference to Australia's international "moral obligations", or through what is loosely described as "beneficial construction". Human rights considerations can, by this approach, be introduced as an essential element of the discretion.

A leading example is *Chaudhary v Minister for Immigration and Ethnic Affairs*,[63] which concerned an application for permanent residence by the parent of a child with severe intellectual and physical disabilities. The child attended a special school in Australia where she had made significant progress, but equivalent facilities were not available in her country of citizenship, Fiji. The delegate weighed the compassionate grounds against other factors including "the avoidance of an undue burden on Australian public health and other resources". The delegate had before him material showing substantial unmet demand for services for people with disabilities in Australia. While at first instance Beazley J held that the decision was open to the delegate, applying the decision of the Full Court in *Maitan*, on appeal the Full Court overturned the decision, holding that "true national interest has a concern for Australia's name in the world, and may at times involve a measure of generosity".[64] The delegate had failed to take relevant considerations into account, in failing to appreciate that it is in Australia's best interests to be seen as civilised

---

59   For example, Blake, N, "Judicial Review of Discretion in Human Rights Cases" [1997] *European Human Rights Law Review* 391, and Kinley, D, "Legislation, Discretionary Authority and the European Convention on Human Rights" (1992) 13 *Statute Law Review* 63; see also generally, Hunt, M, *Using Human Rights Law in English Courts* (Hart Publishing, Oxford, 1997).

60   [1994] 2 NZLR 257.

61   For example, *Rajan v Minister of Immigration* [1996] 3 NZLR 513.

62   See Joseph, above, n 1.

63   (1993) 44 FCR 510 (Beazley J); (1994) 49 FCR 84 (Wilcox, Burchett and Foster JJ).

64   (1994) 49 FCR 84 at 87-88.

and compassionate, and that an assessment of Australia's interests could not ignore the negative impact in our region of a decision to put material costs so far ahead of human values in relation to a gravely disabled child who would be condemned to regression if thrown back on the limited resources of Fiji. *Maitan*, which Beazley J had regarded as binding in relation to the scope of the national interest discretion, was not referred to at all by the Full Court.

A similar approach has been enunciated in other cases.[65] In *Ates v Minister of State for Immigration and Ethnic Affairs*,[66] Smithers J spoke of the need for decisions to be taken "by reference to a liberal and even compassionate outlook appropriate to a free and confident nation and conscious of its reputation as such". And in *Fuduche v Minister for Immigration, Local Government and Ethnic Affairs*[67] Burchett J preferred to give immigration legislation "a broad and generous construction ... in furtherance of the good name of Australia that its humanity maintains".

While a strongly-constituted Full Court has disapproved of such an approach in *Minister for Immigration and Ethnic Affairs v Teo*,[68] it should not be assumed that that line of authority is no longer influential and has been rejected. The leeways of choice that are open to courts in construing legislation has been shown once again by a line of cases culminating in a controversial decision of the Full Federal Court in *Eshetu v Minister for Immigration and Multicultural Affairs*.[69]

The court in *Eshetu* was undertaking review of a decision of the Refugee Review Tribunal. The scheme for review is defined in the *Migration Act* 1958 (Cth) and substitutes for the judicial review scheme in the ADJR Act. A feature of the *Migration Act* scheme is that the grounds of review are contracted, most notably to exclude natural justice, relevant and irrelevant considerations, and *Wednesbury*[70] unreasonableness. However, the practical consequence of the ruling in *Eshetu* is that those grounds have re-appeared. Section 420 of the *Migration Act* provides that "The Tribunal, in carrying out its functions under this Act ... must act according to substantial justice and the merits of the case". A majority of the court in *Eshetu*[71] held that this requirement imposed obligations upon the Tribunal that could lead to its decision being challenged and set aside under one or more of the grounds of review remaining in the *Migration Act*, in particular that procedures required by law were not observed, or that the decision involved an error of law. Davies J held that

65 The presumption that legislation should be construed beneficially in favour of the citizen has also been noted in respect of legislation dealing with employee compensation (*Brennan v Comcare* (1994) 122 ALR 615 at 621); Aboriginal heritage protection (*Tickner v Bropho* (1993) 114 ALR 409 at 419, 434 and 448); veterans' payments (*Whiteman v Secretary, Department of Veterans' Affairs* (1996) 43 ALD 225 at 232); social security benefits (*Re Secretary, Department of Social Security and Knight* (1996) 42 ALD 765); and diesel fuel rebates (*Dampier Salt (Operations) Pty Ltd v Collector of Customs* (1995) 133 ALR 502).

66 (1983) 67 FLR 449 at 455-56.

67 (1993) 45 FCR 515 at 527.

68 (1995) 57 FCR 194 at 204-07 per Black CJ, Gummow and Beazley JJ.

69 (1997) 145 ALR 621.

70 That is, the ground of review deriving from *Associated Provincial Picture Houses Ltd v Wednesbury Corporation* [1948] 1 KB 223, that a decision can be set aside if the exercise of power is so unreasonable that no reasonable person would have so exercised the power.

71 Davies and Burchett JJ, Whitlam J dissenting.

an element (but not an exhaustive element) of acting according to substantial justice and the merits "is the provision of procedures which are fair and just".[72] The requirement of "substantial justice" also has a substantive as well as a procedural element. Burchett J held that the command in s 420 could not be met by a tribunal that had breached natural justice, ignored relevant evidence, or acted in a way that was *Wednesbury* unreasonable. A reason given by his Honour is that those standards are universally accepted and embody "fundamental rights" that should not be curtailed except by a clear command from parliament.[73]

Leave to appeal to the High Court against the decision in *Eshetu* was given in March 1998. The interest which that appeal holds was captured in a recent comment by North J (in a case affirming *Eshetu*, by majority) that "There have been many decisions on the issue in recent times. There is almost an equal number of decisions on each side of the argument. ... [T]here is an unusually high number of recent single judge decisions which take a different view".[74]

Whatever the outcome of the appeal, *Eshetu* serves to illustrate the point made above that there are leeways of choice in construing legislation, and that this is especially noticeable in situations where a balance has to be struck between protecting individual rights and giving effect to broader social interests. The meaning of "substantial justice" is not the first time that indeterminate statutory language has given rise to differences of opinion, and it will not be the last. In the late 1980s a similar controversy surrounded the meaning of another phrase in the *Migration Act*, "strong compassionate or humanitarian grounds", which was a criterion for granting an entry permit when no other eligibility requirement had been satisfied. The Departmental view was that this was an exceptional category to deal with unforeseen deserving cases,[75] but in a line of cases the Federal Court ruled that the phrase had a far broader operation, extending to any situation in which (from an Australian perspective) a person's situation would excite strong pity or compassion in a reasonable person,[76] even though the person's situation was no different to that of other people – perhaps thousands of other people[77] – in the country from which he or she came.

Looking to the future, there is a seed for circumventing an unconfined discretion sown more recently in the judgment of Gaudron J in *Minister for Immigration and Ethnic Affairs v Teoh*.[78] Her Honour decided the case on a different basis to other members of the court, by detecting a fundamental human right of special value to the Australian community. She held that a decision to deport the parent of an Australian child must be undertaken in full recognition of the principle that:

---

72 (1997) 145 ALR 621 at 624.

73 Ibid at 636-37.

74 *Sun Zhan Qui* (1997) 151 ALR 505 at 564-65. *Eshetu* was affirmed by Wilcox and Burchett JJ, North J dissenting.

75 See Arthur, E, "The Impact of Administrative Law on Humanitarian Decision-Making" (1991) 66 *Canberra Bulletin of Public Administration* 90.

76 For example, see *Surinakova v Minister for Immigration, Local Government and Ethnic Affairs* (1991) 26 ALD 203, and *Damouni v Minister for Immigration, Local Government and Ethnic Affairs* (1989) 87 ALR 97.

77 *Sinnathamby v Minister for Immigration and Ethnic Affairs* (1986) 66 ALR 502.

78 (1995) 183 CLR 273.

[C]itizenship carries with it a common law right on the part of the children and their parents to have a child's best interests taken into account, at least as a primary consideration, in all discretionary decisions by governments and government agencies which directly affect that child's individual welfare.[79]

Interpretation of legislation consistent with human rights protection

The preceding discussion looked at one aspect of statutory interpretation – "beneficial construction" – that can give emphasis to human rights considerations and individual interests. Two other themes in statutory interpretation work the same result, and will be discussed in this section. They are strict construction of legislation to preclude administrative action that is intrusive or detrimental to fundamental common law rights; and interpretation of ambiguous legislative phrases consistently with international human rights instruments and norms. All three approaches are said to illustrate a broader presumption "that the parliament has acted in the public interest".[80]

Strict construction of legislation

The decision of the High Court in *Coco v R*[81] provides the leading contemporary illustration of strict construction of legislation. The Queensland *Invasion of Privacy Act* 1971 provided that it was an offence for a person to use a listening device unless a warrant to do so had been issued by a judge of the Supreme Court. In deciding whether to issue a warrant the judge was to have regard, inter alia, to the gravity of the matters being investigated and the extent to which the privacy of any person would be interfered with. The High Court held that the authority of the judge did not extend to issuing a warrant that would authorise an entry onto private premises to install the listening device, as the legislation did not expressly authorise an invasion of private property rights. This was a rather surprising result, given that the purpose of the legislation was to authorise invasion of the right to privacy, and that the authority to do so had been placed in the hands of a judge. The result was explained on the basis that:

> Every unauthorized entry upon private property is a trespass, the right of a person in possession or entitled to possession of premises to exclude others from those premises being a fundamental common law right. ... [A]n abrogation or curtailment of a fundamental right, freedom or immunity ... must be clearly manifested by unmistakable and unambiguous language.[82]

---

79   Ibid at 304.

80   *Eshetu v Minister for Immigration and Multicultural Affairs* (1997) 145 ALR 621 at 626 per Davies J.

81   (1994) 179 CLR 427. For discussion of basic assumptions affecting the interpretation of legislation, see Pearce, DC, and Geddes, RS, *Statutory Interpretation in Australia* (Butterworths, Sydney, 4th ed, 1996), Ch 5.

82   Ibid at 435, 437 per Mason CJ, Brennan, Gaudron and McHugh JJ.

A similar statement of the principle was adopted by the High Court in *Bropho v Western Australia:*[83]

> [I]t is in the last degree improbable that the legislature would overthrow fundamental principles, infringe rights, or depart from the general system of law, without expressing its intention with irresistible clearness; and to give any such effect to general words, simply because they have that meaning in their widest, or usual, or natural sense, would be to give them a meaning in which they were not really used.

Many other cases could be referred to that illustrate the protection of common law rights and freedoms in this way. It has been held that a power conferred upon an Aboriginal Land Commissioner to do "all things necessary or convenient" for the performance of the function did not authorise entry onto private land.[84] Legislation authorising withdrawal of social security benefits has been classified as quasi-penal, and warranting a strict construction.[85] The right to natural justice in administrative proceedings that lead to a prejudicial result is regarded as "a deep rooted principle of the law", that can only be taken away by "express words of plain intendment".[86] Access to the courts is likewise regarded as an important right that can only be taken away by a privative clause that is clearly worded.[87] The same is true for subordinate legislation that would violate fundamental assumptions of the legal system, like the common law rule against self-incrimination.[88]

The presumption against legislative interference with established rights and freedoms has much in common with other presumptions which, while they do not speak directly to human rights protection, nevertheless advance that aim. This could be said of the principle that government agencies have no inherent right to breach the criminal law.[89] A now famous illustration of that principle is *A v Hayden*[90] (the Sheraton Hotel case) in which the High Court declaimed forcefully that security intelligence authorities had no right to breach the criminal law. This ruling was followed up recently in *Ridgeway v R*,[91] holding that police entrapment activity that connives in a breach of the law is prima facie unlawful and should be restrained by courts, for example, by the exclusion of unlawfully obtained evidence from later criminal prosecution proceedings. The relevance of such cases to the present

---

83 (1990) 171 CLR 1 at 18 per Mason CJ, Deane, Dawson, Toohey, Gaudron and McHugh JJ, approving the statement from *Maxwell on Statutes* (4th ed) cited in *Potter v Minihan* (1908) 7 CLR 277 at 304.

84 *Anthony Lagoon Station Pty Ltd v Maurice* (1987) 74 ALR 77.

85 *Re Ferguson and Secretary, Department of Employment, Education, Training and Youth Affairs* (1996) 42 ALD 742.

86 *Commissioner of Police v Tanos* (1958) 98 CLR 383 at 395 per Dixon CJ and Webb J.

87 For example, *Darling Casino Ltd v New South Wales Casino Control Authority* (1997) 143 ALR 55 at 75; and *Public Service Association (SA) v Federated Clerks Union of Australia (SA Branch)* (1991) 173 CLR 132 at 160.

88 *Ex p Grinham; Re Sneddon* [1961] SR (NSW) 862. Cf *Foley v Padley* (1984) 154 CLR 349, and *South Australia v Tanner* (1989) 166 CLR 161 (Brennan J dissenting in both cases), for a more generous reading of the power to make subordinate legislation.

89 The Crown has a presumptive immunity from legislation, however the scope of that immunity has lessened significantly in recent times, as illustrated by cases like *Bropho v Western Australia* (1990) 171 CLR 1, and *Jacobsen v Rogers* (1995) 182 CLR 572.

90 (1984) 156 CLR 532.

91 (1995) 184 CLR 19.

discussion is that they are an illustration of the broader principle, often coined the rule of law, that governments require legal authority for any action which they take, by contrast with the freedom of individuals to do anything that is not prohibited by law.[92]

Construction of ambiguous legislation by reference to international conventions:

The presumption that "courts should, in a case of ambiguity, favour a construction of a Commonwealth statute which accords with the obligations of Australia under an international treaty"[93] has partly been forged in the context of international conventions that state universal human rights principles. A refinement of the presumption which gives it added importance was explained in *Teoh*:

> [T]here are strong reasons for rejecting a narrow conception of ambiguity. If the language of the legislation is susceptible of a construction which is consistent with the terms of the international instrument and the obligations which it imposes on Australia, then that construction should prevail.[94]

The strong bearing that human rights conventions should have on legislative construction and administrative law generally is captured in an additional remark in *Teoh*:

> [R]atification by Australia of an international convention is not to be dismissed as a merely platitudinous or ineffectual act, particularly when the instrument evidences internationally accepted standards to be applied by courts and administrative authorities in dealing with basic human rights affecting the family and children. Rather, ratification of a convention is a positive statement by the executive government of this country to the world and to the Australian people that the executive government and its agencies will act in accordance with the Convention.[95]

There are a growing number of instances which illustrate the force of that dictum. The ICCPR is frequently raised in litigation,[96] at times successfully – concerning, for example, the construction of legislation relating to telephone interception, so as to safeguard personal privacy,[97] and legislation relating to indefinite imprisonment,

---

92 "It is not the English view of law that whatever is officially done is law ... but, on the contrary, the principle of English law is that what is done officially must be done in accordance with law": *Arthur Yates & Co Pty Ltd v Vegetable Seeds Committee* (1945) 72 CLR 37 at 66 per Latham CJ.

93 *Lim v Minister for Immigration, Local Government and Ethnic Affairs* (1992) 176 CLR 1 at 38 per Brennan, Deane and Dawson JJ. See also *Polites v Commonwealth* (1945) 70 CLR 60 at 68-69, 77, 80-81. Note too that the *Acts Interpretation Act* 1901 (Cth) s 15AB(2) provides that in construing an Act reference can be had "to any treaty or other international agreement that is referred to in the Act". See further, Ch 2 by Sir Anthony Mason in this volume.

94 *Minister for Immigration and Ethnic Affairs v Teoh* (1995) 183 CLR 273 at 287 per Mason CJ and Deane J.

95 Ibid at 291. Note too the similar remark that "international law is a legitimate and important influence on the development of the common law, especially when international law declares the existence of universal human rights": *Mabo v Queensland (No 2)* (1992) 175 CLR 1 at 42 per Brennan J.

96 See, for example, *Ballina Shire Council v Ringland* (1994) 33 NSWLR 680; *S and M Motor Repairs Pty Ltd v Caltex Oil (Australia) Pty Ltd* (1988) 12 NSWLR 358 at 360; and *Binse v Governor of HM Prison Barwon* (unreported, CA (Vic), 19 March 1997).

97 *Director of Public Prosecutions v Serratore* (1995) 132 ALR 461.

so as to safeguard criminal justice rights.[98] The concept of a "special need relative" for migrant entry purposes has been given a broad construction in line with the *Declaration on the Rights of the Child*.[99] It has been said that the discretion to waive recovery of social security overpayments should be exercised with regard to Australia's obligations under the *Convention Relating to the Status of Refugees*.[100] The relevance of the *Convention Relating to the Status of Stateless Persons* to the construction of deportation powers has been accepted.[101] And the AAT has held that the international recognition of a guarantee of freedom of movement meant that social security legislation should be construed in such a way "as to have the least intrusive effect on a person's freedom of movement".[102]

International conventions, like domestic legislation, will frequently offer leeways of choice in construction that will be reflected in an even division of opinion about the relevance of human rights concerns. This is apparent in the reasoning of the High Court in *"Applicant A" v Minister for Immigration and Ethnic Affairs*.[103] The issue before the court was whether a couple who feared forced sterilisation under China's "one child policy" satisfied the definition of "refugee" in accordance with the *Convention Relating to the Status of Refugees*. A minority, Brennan CJ and Kirby J, in holding that the applicants were refugees, took into account a recitation in the Preamble to the Convention stating as a purpose "the principle that human beings shall enjoy fundamental rights and freedoms without discrimination". The majority, Dawson, McHugh and Gummow JJ, in rejecting the claim, pointed out that the Convention protected only a limited category of people and was not framed in a way that fully gave effect to that humanitarian aim.

The importance of international conventions to administrative decision-making is also uncertain following the decision of the High Court in *Project Blue Sky v Australian Broadcasting Authority*.[104] The court was faced with a choice between two statutory provisions that could lead to a contradictory result: one provision conferred power upon the ABA to determine broadcasting standards on Australian content in television programs; and the other provision obliged the ABA to perform its functions consistently with international conventions to which Australia is a party, which in this case meant a trade agreement between Australia and New Zealand. The High Court held that the latter provision, though the more general of the two, set the conceptual framework for the ABA and was accordingly the dominant provision in the case of conflict. On the other hand, the court acknowledged that "many international conventions and agreements are expressed in indeterminate language ... [and] often their provisions are more aptly described as goals to be achieved rather than rules to be obeyed". The consequence, in a case like the

---

98   *Young v Registrar, Court of Appeal (No 3)* (1992) 32 NSWLR 262

99   *Chen v Minister for Immigration and Ethnic Affairs* (1994) 123 ALR 126. See also *Re Sui and Minister for Immigration and Ethnic Affairs* (1996) 42 ALD 163.

100   *Re Nem and Director-General of Social Security* (1984) 7 ALN N37.

101   *Todea v Minister for Immigration and Ethnic Affairs* (1994) 35 ALD 735.

102   *Re Secretary, Department of Social Security and Clemson* (1991) 14 AAR 261 at 277.

103   (1997) 142 ALR 331, discussed in Kneebone, S, "Refugee Test and the One Child Policy" (1997) 4 *Australian Journal of Administrative Law* 173.

104   [1998] HCA 28 (18 April 1998).

present, was that a breach of the legal duty to act consistently with the convention would not necessarily result in invalidity, though in appropriate circumstances the breach could be restrained by a court. This difficult distinction – between actions that are unlawful yet not invalid – will be sure to arise again in relation to the impact of international law on administrative decision-making.

The contribution of natural justice to human rights protection

The doctrine of natural justice is a centrepiece of the common law system for protection of individual rights against arbitrary state power. The requirement that a person be given a fair and unbiased hearing before being deprived of a legal right or interest was described more than a century ago as a principle "founded upon the plainest principles of justice", preserved by "the justice of the common law [supplying] the omission of the legislature".[105] Its enactment as the first of 18 criteria of legal validity in s 5 of the ADJR Act is deservedly symbolic of the importance natural justice plays in Australian administrative law.

The past decade has been marked by a dramatic expansion in the scope of the application of the doctrine.[106] The turning point for this expansion was the High Court decision in *Kioa v West*,[107] applying natural justice to the deportation of prohibited immigrants – a high volume function that did not involve deprivation of rights of the classic sort. The pattern established in *Kioa* has been repeated in numerous other cases, applying natural justice to functions like visa processing,[108] personnel appointment,[109] commercial regulation,[110] administrative investigation,[111] and even outsourcing decisions that affect individuals.[112] The standard of procedural fairness expected in administrative decision-making has also been raised, notably to include a probative evidentiary basis for adverse decisions,[113] a self-initiated inquiry by a decision-maker into unresolved points of relevance and significance,[114] the absence of "institutional bias",[115] and the disclosure of adverse conclusions drawn

---

105 *Cooper v Wandsworth Board of Works* (1863) 14 CB (NS) 180, 143 ER 414 at 418 per Willes J, and 420 per Byles J.

106 See Aronson and Dyer, above, n 5, Ch 8; McMillan, J, "Developments under the ADJR Act: the Grounds of Review" (1991) 20 *Federal Law Review* 50 at 63-70.

107 (1985) 159 CLR 550.

108 For example, *Minister for Immigration, Local Government and Ethnic Affairs v Pashmforoosh* (1989) 18 ALD 77.

109 For example, *Cole v Cunningham* (1983) 49 ALR 123.

110 For example, *Ansett Transport Industries Ltd v Minister for Aviation* (1987) 72 ALR 469.

111 For example, *Annetts v McCann* (1990) 170 CLR 596.

112 *Consolidated Press Holdings Ltd v Federal Commissioner of Taxation* (1995) 129 ALR 443.

113 For example, *Minister for Immigration and Ethnic Affairs v Pochi* (1980) 31 ALR 666.

114 For example, *Luu v Renevier* (1989) 91 ALR 39, *Lek v Minister for Immigration, Local Government and Ethnic Affairs* (1993) 117 ALR 455, and *Sun Zhan Qui v Minister for Immigration and Ethnic Affairs* (1997) 151 ALR 505.

115 For example, *Minister for Immigration, Local Government and Ethnic Affairs v Mok Gek Bouy* (1994) 127 ALR 223, and *Phillips v Disciplinary Appeal Committee of the Merit Protection Review Agency* (1994) 34 ALD 758.

from an applicant's own material if the conclusion "is not an obviously natural response to the circumstances which have evoked it".[116]

Those developments alone attest to the role that natural justice can play in furthering a human rights dimension in government decision-making. The connection was made more explicit, however, by the seminal decision of the High Court in 1995 in *Minister for Immigration and Ethnic Affairs v Teoh*.[117] There it was held that the ratification of an international convention gives rise to a legitimate expectation for Australians that administrative discretionary powers will be exercised in conformity with the terms of the convention. In the result, a deportation decision made against Mr Teoh was set aside on the ground of breach of procedural fairness due to the failure of the decision-maker to direct Mr Teoh's attention to the fact that his forced separation from his children would clash with the *Convention on the Rights of the Child* (CROC). The justification for this result has been referred to earlier in this chapter, and was based principally on the opinion that ratification by Australia of an international convention – particularly a convention concerning human rights – should not be treated "as a merely platitudinous or ineffectual act".

Teoh has sparked two lines of debate that are relevant to the present discussion – how far does the hearing obligation reach, and is the obligation a sensible requirement that is likely to be retained in Australian administrative law?

The reach of the hearing obligation

Important issues were left unresolved by the decision in *Teoh*.[118] Does the principle apply only to human rights conventions, or as well to other treaties on topics like environmental conservation, and labour relations? To date, for reasons discussed below, the issue has arisen only in a similar fact situation to *Teoh* where separation of family members has been in issue. Does a legitimate expectation apply only to action by Commonwealth executive agencies, which are bound in principle to heed executive government policy, or can a convention temper the functions of independent Commonwealth statutory authorities, government corporations, and State and Territory government agencies? The wider operation has been assumed by

---

116 *Somaghi v Minister for Immigration, Local Government and Ethnic Affairs* (1991) 31 FCR 100 at 108 per Jenkinson J.

117 (1995) 183 CLR 273.

118 For discussion generally of the case, see Sir Anthony Mason, "Influence of International and Transnational Law on Australian Domestic Law" (1996) 7 *Public Law Review* 20; Walker, K, "Treaties and the Internationalisation of Australian Law" in Saunders (ed), *Courts of Final Jurisdiction: The Mason Court in Australia* (Federation Press, Sydney, 1996); Evans, G, "The Impact of Internationalisation on Australian Law: A Commentary" in Saunders, op cit; Allars, M, "One Small Step for Legal Doctrine, One Giant Leap Towards Integrity in Government" (1995) 17 *Sydney Law Review* 204; Twomey, A, "*Minister for Immigration and Ethnic Affairs v Teoh*" (1995) 23 *Federal Law Review* 348; Burmester, H, "The Teoh Decision — A Perspective from the Government Service" (1995) 5 *Australian Institute of Administrative Law Forum* 6; McMillan, J, "Teoh, and Invalidity in Administrative Law" (1995) 5 *Australian Institute of Administrative Law Forum* 10; Williams, N, "Legitimate Expectations – Beyond *Teoh*" in Pearson, L (ed), *Administrative Law: Setting the Pace or Being Left Behind* (Australian Institute of Administrative Law, Canberra, 1997); Sheridan, S, "Legitimate Expectation: Where does the Law now Lie?" in McMillan, J, *Administrative Law under the Coalition Government* (Australian Institute of Administrative Law, Canberra (1997); and Senate Legal and Constitutional Legislation Committee, *Report on the Administrative Decisions (Effect of International Instruments) Bill* 1997.

the South Australian Parliament, which has enacted legislation to displace *Teoh*.[119] And what will qualify as "an executive indication to the contrary",[120] sufficient to displace a legitimate expectation? In *Department of Immigration and Ethnic Affairs v Ram*[121] the court was of the view that the High Court was referring to an executive statement made at the time of ratifying a treaty, not to a sweeping declaration applying to all treaties of the kind made by the Commonwealth Attorney-General and Minister for Foreign Affairs soon after the decision in *Teoh*.[122]

Another difficult issue of direct practical importance to decision-making concerns the steps that need to be taken to comply with the ruling in *Teoh*. The obligation to be discharged by the decision-maker in that case was framed in the following terms:

> [I]f a decision-maker proposes to make a decision inconsistent with a legitimate expectation, procedural fairness requires that the persons affected should be given notice and an adequate opportunity of presenting a case against the taking of such a course. So, here, if the delegate proposed to give a decision which did not accord with the principle that the best interests of the children were to be a primary consideration, procedural fairness called for the delegate to take the steps just indicated.[123]

Two interconnected issues face a decision-maker – "Will my decision be consistent with the terms of a relevant convention?" and "How should I frame the invitation to the parties to address me on the convention issue?" As a general rule those questions can only be answered towards the end of the decision-making process. If an announcement was made instead at the *beginning* of the decision-making process – "I intend to decide inconsistently with the convention" – that would surely invite challenge on another ground, such as prejudgment or refusal to consider relevant matters. Even if an early announcement was cast more circumspectly – "It is possible that my decision will be inconsistent with the convention, and I invite submissions accordingly" – the problem does not disappear. A strict reading of *Teoh* suggests that more precise guidance is required, reflecting the fact that a convention expectation is a separate element in the decision-making process which should not be downplayed or conflated with other issues.

Nor do all problems dissolve when the announcement is made at the *conclusion* of the inquiry. On an issue as delicate as "Have I given weight to the children's position as *a primary consideration*", the answer may not emerge until the decision-maker is preparing final reasons for the decision, and even then the answer may be debatable. Should a further hearing then be scheduled to give an airing to the draft

---

119 *Administrative Decisions (Effect Of International Instruments) Act* 1995 (SA). In *Teoh*, Mason CJ and Deane J spoke of the legitimate expectation applying to actions of "the executive government and its agencies" ((1995) 183 CLR 273 at 291), and Toohey J of "the agencies of the executive government of the Commonwealth" (at 302).

120 Ibid at 291 per Mason CJ and Deane J.

121 (1996) 41 ALD 517. See also *Fang v Minister for Immigration and Ethnic Affairs* (1996) 135 ALR 583 at 604.

122 *Joint Statement* by the Minister for Foreign Affairs, Senator Gareth Evans, and the Attorney-General, Michael Lavarch (10 May 1995). A similar statement was made by their successors in office, Alexander Downer and Daryl Williams, QC, respectively, on 25 February 1997.

123 (1995) 183 CLR 273 at 291-91 per Mason CJ and Deane J. See also at 302 per Toohey J and at 305 per Gaudron J.

reasons? Drafting the reasons for the decision will also rouse other perils. For example, if a decision is reached to deport a parent and thereby separate a family, an observer unsympathetic to that conclusion will probably be able to point either to something in the reasons which hints that a criterion other than the children had surreptitiously become the dominant consideration, or to some aspect of the decision-making process which suggests a failure to undertake further inquiries to gauge the full impact of a decision on the children of the deportee.

Three recent cases in which the Federal Court held that the AAT had failed to apply *Teoh* correctly, illustrate that the problems discussed in the previous paragraph are real and not imagined. The facts of *Lam v Minister for Immigration and Multicultural Affairs*[124] were similar to those in *Teoh* – the AAT was reviewing a decision to deport a non-citizen, who had been gaoled for drugs offences in Australia, but who would leave behind a wife and an Australian-born child. The hearing before the AAT lasted for five days, Lam was represented, evidence was led about the impact of deportation upon his son, the Tribunal was addressed on the relevance of *Teoh* and the CROC, and those matters were all discussed by the Tribunal in a 17-page judgment which concluded:

> [T]he Tribunal is faced with the unenviable task of balancing the obligation of the Convention and Mr Lam's family and associated ties to Australia against the other factors which must be taken into account ... Under the established policy guidelines the principal factor which must be considered is the protection of the Australian community. ... In this case the legitimate interests of the Australian community must outweigh the hardship which a decision to refuse permission to take up lawful residence imposes on the family of this illegal immigrant".[125]

On appeal the Federal Court held that the preceding excerpts from the Tribunal's reasons indicated that it was not correctly applying the Convention, in so far as it was treating the protection of the Australian community as the principal factor. That itself was not an error of law, but not so the failure to direct Mr Lam's attention to this outcome:

> According to *Teoh*, the AAT was not obliged to apply art 3 of the *Convention*. However, if it did not intend to apply the *Convention* it was obliged, as a matter of procedural fairness, to inform the applicant and to give him an opportunity to make submissions as to why the proposed course should not be followed. This step was not taken.[126]

The second of the cases, *Vaitaiki v Minister for Immigration and Ethnic Affairs*,[127] also involved a review of an AAT decision to affirm an order for the deportation of a non-citizen who had fathered six children in Australia. The case was heard twice by the AAT, which affirmed the deportation order on both occasions. The first decision of the AAT was made in 1994, shortly before the High Court's decision in *Teoh*, and by consent the parties agreed in a Federal Court action to set the decision aside and to have it re-heard to ensure compliance with *Teoh*. The

---

124 Unreported, Fed Ct, Sackville J, 4 March 1998.

125 *Kwong Leung Lam v Minister for Immigration and Multicultural Affairs* (unreported, AAT, 11 June 1997).

126 Unreported, Fed Ct, Sackville J, 4 March 1998.

127 (1998) 150 CLR 608.

re-hearing was undertaken by the same Deputy President of the AAT, and was principally directed to the receipt of evidence and argument concerning the situation of the children. The reasons of the Tribunal for its second decision canvassed that evidence, noting on a couple of occasions that the interests of the children were being treated by the Tribunal as a primary consideration. The Tribunal's reasons also discussed the linguistic difficulties in treating more than one consideration as "a primary consideration".

In reviewing this second decision of the Tribunal, the Full Federal Court held by majority[128] that a close analysis of the Tribunal's reasons revealed that it had not as it had purported to do given proper and genuine consideration to the interests of the children as a primary factor. As no notice to that effect had been given to the plaintiff as required by *Teoh*, the Tribunal was obliged to decide consistently with the Convention, and it erred in not doing so. (Query whether this conclusion should have been put in a reverse fashion – that the failure of the Tribunal to recognise that its decision was in breach of the Convention and to bring this to the attention of the plaintiff was a breach of natural justice?)

The third decision, *Department of Immigration and Ethnic Affairs v Ram*,[129] had a different twist altogether. The AAT had stated that it was bound to make the interests of the child a primary consideration, and so treated it in concluding that the plaintiff should be permitted to reside in Australia with her child. This time it was the Department which appealed successfully: the Federal Court decided that the Tribunal had erred in considering itself *bound* as a result of *Teoh* to treat the child's future as a primary consideration.

The future of Teoh

Teoh was not well-received in government circles. Legislation was introduced both by the Labor Government in 1995 and by the Coalition Government in 1997 to override the principle that a convention can give rise to a legitimate expectation, while preserving the relevance of conventions to statutory interpretation and as a relevant consideration.[130]

One line of opposition to the decision, cited in the Preamble to the legislation, was that "It is the role of Commonwealth, State and Territory legislatures to pass legislation to give effect to international instruments". In short, *Teoh* was criticised for disturbing the separation of powers by enabling the Executive to create legal rights through the ratification of conventions.

Another line of criticism has been that *Teoh* establishes an uncertain and unsuitable criterion for administrative validity. The cases discussed above show, as *Teoh* itself did,[131] that the standard is not an easy one to apply. It appears to elevate

---

128 Burchett and Branson JJ, Whitlam J dissenting.

129 (1996) 41 ALD 517.

130 Administrative Decisions (Effect of International Instruments) Bill 1997. The latest Bill has not yet been enacted.

131 The CROC was not raised in *Teoh* at the time of the initial decision, before the Immigration Review Panel, during the trial before French J, or in the notice of appeal to the Full Court. As Toohey J commented, "It seems to have surfaced during the hearing of the appeal to the Full Court": (1995) 183 CLR 273 at 298.

form above substance, in the sense that it is the Convention itself and not just the rights that it upholds that must be made an issue in the administrative decision. For example, in the cases discussed above it was not enough for the decision-maker to consider the impact of a decision on children and to weigh this against other factors; this had to be done in the particular way envisaged by the Convention and in a context that acknowledged the authority of the Convention, even though the Convention is not binding.[132] It is difficult to fathom what purpose is being served by this rigid process. The concern of the Convention – the best interests of a child – was in each case addressed as a matter of substance in the decision-making process. A proper compliance with the natural justice premise in *Teoh* would achieve no further result apart from enabling a party to reiterate, "Our submission is that you should honour the Convention".

Those cases have so far dealt with only one phrase in one convention. The difficulty for decision-making is magnified by the potential application of a large number of other principles defined in international conventions that have an arguable relevance to administrative decision-making. The usual retort is along two lines. First, it is said that only a few conventions will end up being relevant – yet a single convention (like the ICCPR) contains many specific standards. Secondly, it is said that the challenge can be met by further education of decision-makers – yet the difficulty encountered already by three highly-respected Deputy Presidents of the AAT indicates that it may not be as straightforward as that.

A declaration of administrative invalidity can also be a serious and complexing matter. In the best of worlds it means that the administrative process has to be undertaken afresh, albeit at some cost. In other situations a finding of invalidity can cause an administrative and political imbroglio, illustrated in cases like the Hindmarsh Bridge case and the prosecution of Mr John Elliott. This suggests that the criteria for administrative validity should be clear, manageable and necessary.

To disagree with the decision in *Teoh* is not to embrace the alternative proposition that Australia's adoption of international conventions is a hollow and platitudinous act. It is merely to contend that the mechanism for ensuring their relevance should not be the troublesome concept of legitimate expectation. This chapter mentions many other ways in which administrative law acknowledges the importance of international human rights norms, through other grounds of judicial review, in statutory interpretation, and through adjudication and investigation by administrative tribunals, Ombudsman and human rights agencies. The concern is surely to ensure that human rights norms are a mandatory consideration in administrative decision-making. That canon can be set in other more suitable ways.

For the moment, however, *Teoh* will continue to be authoritative and to have a strong bearing on the use of human rights conventions in administrative law. It will be interesting in that respect to see whether the principle is extended to fields other

---

132 The decision-maker in *Teoh* had expressly considered the effect of the decision on the children and taken evidence on the point, but not – it was held – in the way envisaged by the Convention. The ruling in *Teoh* is to be contrasted with the later caution by the High Court that "the reasons of an administrative decision-maker are meant to inform and not to be scrutinised upon over-zealous judicial review by seeking to discern whether some inadequacy may be gleaned from the way in which the reasons are expressed": *Minister for Immigration and Ethnic Affairs v Wu Shan Liang* (1996) 185 CLR 259 at 272 per Brennan CJ, Toohey, McHugh and Gummow JJ.

than the separation of parents and children by deportation. To date, for example, there appears to be no attempt to use *Teoh* in the areas foreshadowed by McHugh J in his dissenting judgment – that of a public authority being required to make the best interests of a child a primary consideration in deciding whether to acquire compulsorily the property of a parent, or the Commissioner of Taxation making the best interests of the child a primary consideration in the administration of the tax laws, or a court doing likewise in sentencing adult offenders. One can only speculate that the chief explanation why *Teoh* has not generated the school of imitators that was first suggested is that most litigation practitioners, perhaps in common with public officials, do not have a detailed understanding of the terms of Australia's treaty obligations.[133]

THE LIMITED SCOPE FOR INCORPORATING HUMAN RIGHTS PRINCIPLES INTO ADMINISTRATIVE LAW

This chapter has identified different strands of a trend that predisposes Australian administrative law to a harmonisation with human rights principles. The picture is not altogether clear, but can probably be summarised in the following way. There is no general legal requirement in Australia that a statutory discretion be exercised in accordance with human rights norms, or with an international convention to which Australia is a party. There is an obligation, however, to give consideration to the principles of any international convention which has been ratified by Australia and which has a bearing on the rights affected by the exercise of discretion, and to give notice to a person if the decision to be made will clash with the convention principles. It can also be said that a decision which does not have regard to the human rights dimension will be closely scrutinised on review and is likely to be set aside.

The trend towards consideration of human rights norms is accordingly a strong one, but in the absence of a constitutional Bill of Rights it will be held in check by other principles and trends of equal significance.

Parliamentary supremacy, the pre-eminent principle of Australian law, obliges those administering legislation in either the executive or the judicial branch to apply the legislation according to its terms. International human rights norms must yield to any clear exclusion or contrary intent in the legislation, and will mostly be important when they are incorporated expressly by legislation, or where ambiguity resides in the text. The examples given in this chapter of human rights norms being relied upon by courts and tribunals can be countered by an equal number of cases in which an argument for a similar result was rejected. A good illustration is the recent majority decision of the Full Federal Court in *Fang v Minister for Immigration and Ethnic Affairs*,[134] holding that legislation negated any obligation upon departmental

---

133 Part of the explanation for the limited appearance of *Teoh* in litigation would also be that the large bulk of federal judicial review litigation is of immigration decision-making, for which natural justice – the basis of the *Teoh* ruling – is not an available ground of challenge (see *Migration Act* 1958 (Cth) ss 476(2)(a), 485).

134 (1996) 135 ALR 583, discussed in Lindsay, R, "The Australian Janus: The Face of the Refugee Convention or the Unacceptable Face of the Migration Act?" (1997) 13 *Australian Institute of Administrative Law Forum* 33.

officers to facilitate a refugee application by a recently arrived group of "boat people"; nor, it was held, was there scope within the legislative framework for the operation of international law principles relating to governmental conduct in relation to refugees.

The legislative text is important too in defining the role of judicial review, which provides the context for many of the developments related in this chapter. While protection of individual rights against abuse of state power is an important theme in judicial review, it nevertheless holds secondary importance. As Brennan J cautioned in *Attorney-General (NSW) v Quin*:[135]

> [J]udicial review has undoubtedly been invoked, and invoked beneficially, to set aside administrative acts and decisions which are unjust or otherwise inappropriate, but only when the purported exercise of power is excessive or otherwise unlawful. ... [T]he scope of judicial review must be determined not in terms of the protection of individual interests but in terms of the extent of power and the legality of its exercise. In Australia, the modern development and expansion of the law of judicial review of administrative action have been achieved by an increasingly sophisticated exposition of implied limitations on the extent or the exercise of statutory power, but those limitations are not calculated to secure judicial scrutiny of the merits of a particular case.

The final point made by Brennan J – that judicial review stops short of addressing the merits of administrative action – is also an important part of the backdrop for the debate in Australia about the harmonisation of administrative law rules and human rights norms. Personal liberty and procedural fairness are values which the common law has long protected, and administrative decisions which threaten those values meritably attract more intense scrutiny.[136] But that concern undoubtedly spills over at times into a merits analysis, a point tacitly acknowledged by judges. The High Court has cautioned that a more restrained approach should be adopted by courts in reviewing the reasons for administrative decisions.[137]

The importance of universal human rights norms to Australian administrative law is in an uneasy balance. If parliament is presumed to legislate consistently with those norms, if they can influence the development of the common law,[138] and if there is an individual right of complaint internationally to the Human Rights Committee against Australian legislation and executive practices that contravene the ICCPR and/or other relevant human rights instruments, it is inescapable that human rights norms will continue to play a central if unpredictable role in review of administrative decision-making. The schism between what courts do, and what courts say they are doing, is an important consideration too. In cases which involve personal liberty or human rights, or which for other reasons may attract judicial sympathy for an applicant, an approach which is based purely on legal doctrine may

---

135 (1990) 93 ALR 1 at 24-25. See also Sir Harry Woolf, "Public Law – Private Law: Why the Divide? A Personal View" [1986] *Public Law* 220.

136 Sir Anthony Mason, "Judges, Values and a Bill of Rights" (1997) 9 *Judicial Officers' Bulletin* 67.

137 *Minister for Immigration and Ethnic Affairs v Wu Shan Liang* (1996) 185 CLR 259, and *Minister for Immigration and Ethnic Affairs v Guo Wei Rong* (1997) 144 ALR 567.

138 Human rights principles were influential in *Mabo v Queensland (No 2)* (1992) 175 CLR 1, in defining common law recognition of Aboriginal native title, and in *Dietrich v R* (1992) 177 CLR 292, in defining the common law presumption of adequate legal representation for an accused person.

be an inadequate basis for predicting the outcome. The human rights dimension of the case will always be a potentially significant premise in the decision, even in ways that cannot be foreseen by reference solely to established principle or earlier cases.

Part Two

Human Rights and Substantive Law

5

INDIGENOUS AUSTRALIAN PEOPLES AND HUMAN RIGHTS

Jennifer Nielsen and Gary Martin[*]

We would like to dedicate this chapter to the memory of our friend and colleague Neil Löfgren, who died tragically in May 1998. Neil was an inspirational Indigenous activist and legal academic, and had a particular interest in the issues related to the human rights of Indigenous Australians. We, along with many others, miss him and his very exceptional abilities.

INTRODUCTION

Indigenous peoples have lived on the Australian continent and associated islands since time immemorial. Their culture, laws and societal mores, developed over many millenniums, are unique and diverse at the same time. Within this diversity, these laws and mores are characterised by a strong filial and spiritual connection to land and waters. This connection finds expression in the obligation to protect and respect the land and waters, and the spirits and life-forms contained therein. Societal structures are complex and the interrelationships between and within language and other group structures, are designed to establish lines of responsibility and respect for members of the society, as well as for obligations to law and culture.

These laws and cultural traditions continue to be practised by contemporary Indigenous Australians[1] today, albeit for many, in a fragmented fashion due to the adverse effects of the 210 years of colonisation they have endured. The experience of colonisation and its consequences *in* Australia are unique to Indigenous Australian peoples.[2] No other group in this country has suffered these consequences. That experience is not, however, unique as compared to that of other colonised Indigenous societies.

---

[*] The authors wish to thank Dr Jeannine Purdy and Dr David Kinley for their valuable input and encouragement.

[1] We use the term "Indigenous Australian" to refer to the Aboriginal and Torres Strait Islander peoples of Australia. It is important to understand that Indigenous Australian culture is marked by diversity and is not homogenous, and that Aboriginal peoples are distinct both in culture and laws from Torres Strait Islander peoples. Therefore, care should be taken when investigating and describing law and custom which is relevant to a specific Indigenous Australian group.

[2] See, Royal Commission into Aboriginal Deaths in Custody (RCADIC), *National Report* Vols 1-5 (AGPS, Canberra, 1991); Human Rights and Equal Opportunity Commission (HREOC), *Bringing them home* (1997), <http://www.austlii.edu.au/rsjlibrary/hreoc/stolen/>.

For this reason, it is essential in a work such as this, to address the particular human rights issues relevant to Indigenous Australian peoples. To do so within the legal categories discussed in other chapters of this book would not adequately explain the perspectives of Indigenous Australian peoples in their efforts to assert their human rights, within both the domestic and the international forums.

This chapter does not purport to explain the complete range of human rights issues which are relevant to Indigenous Australian peoples, as this would require a complete work in itself.[3] Instead, this chapter will discuss some issues which are fundamental to the human rights of Indigenous Australians, and will highlight some of the main issues most commonly encountered in legal practice.

Obviously, the broad range of human rights defined in international instruments, and discussed elsewhere in this book, is of significance and relevance to Indigenous Australians, as such rights are to all Australians. However, some of these are of particular relevance to indigenous peoples as a result of their unique status and experience within nation states, or are specifically concerned with indigenous interests.[4] We will examine the most relevant of these.

No enforceable mechanism exists to pursue complaints in some of the areas discussed. In this instance, allegations of breaches in certain areas could be referred to special rapporteurs to the UN Commission on Human Rights, in a way similar to complaining to the Ombudsman at domestic level.[5]

INDIGENOUS COMMON LAW

Indigenous common law[6] is a sophisticated set of laws and beliefs, which provides for the resolution of disputes, determines family and other relationships, and which protects and maintains the belief systems and culture of Indigenous Australian society. While some Indigenous common law has been destroyed by the process of colonisation within Australia, much remains as a living and dynamic feature of contemporary Indigenous Australian society – in urban areas, as well as rural and remote communities. The recognition of Indigenous common law is fundamental to the exercise and enjoyment of human rights by Indigenous Australian peoples.

For some time, the existence of Indigenous common law has been acknowledged by the Australian legal system.[7] A line of cases, starting in 1836[8] and

---

3   See, Hocking, B, (ed), *International Law and Aboriginal Human Rights* (Law Book Co, Sydney, 1998); Anaya, SJ, *Indigenous Peoples in International Law* (Oxford University Press, New York, 1996); and Pritchard, S, (ed), *Indigenous Peoples, the United Nations and Human Rights* (Zed Books/The Federation Press, Sydney, 1998).

4   See Barker, B, *Getting Government to Listen* (Australian Youth Foundation, East Sydney, 1997).

5   Ibid, p 66.

6   Indigenous customary law is being more commonly referred to as "common law", to reflect its equal standing and status to other forms of common law. See *Julayinbul Statement on Indigenous Intellectual Property Rights,* <http://www.cscanada.org/~csc/text/Julayinb.htm>. We would like to acknowledge Dr Jeannine Purdy, who contributed to our development of this discussion.

7   *R v Bon Jon* (unreported, SC (NSW), Willis J, 18 September 1841); *Milirrpum v Nabalco Pty Ltd* (1971) 17 FLR 141; Australian Law Reform Commission (ALRC), *The Recognition of Aboriginal Customary Law* Report No 31 (AGPS, Canberra, 1986).

8   See McRae, H, Nettheim, G, & Beacroft, L, *Indigenous Legal Issues: Cases and Commentary* (LBC Information Services, Sydney, 2nd ed, 1997), pp 157-60.

continuing through until today, have been argued in the Australian courts challenging the application of received English law to Indigenous Australian peoples.[9]

Clearly there is no question of Indigenous common law defining interests in land (native title), being recognised in Australian law. This is subject, of course, to meeting the requirements set out in *Mabo v Queensland (No 2)*[10] (*Mabo (No 2)*) or the *Native Title Act* 1993 (Cth) (NTA),[11] and that those interests have not been *lawfully* extinguished. The NTA, in its current form, also expressly recognises that Indigenous common law may define native title rights over water and waterways, again subject to meeting these requirements.

The full extent of the rights over waterways and coastal areas has not been fully litigated. However, recently Olney J in the Federal Court handed down a decision defining the native title rights applicable to coastal areas.[12] In *Yarmirr v Northern Territory*, a claim was made over coastal areas associated with Croker Island, which is located off the Northern Territory coast. Olney J held that communal native title rights did exist in relation to these sea areas and associated sea-beds. However, the rights associated with these native title rights were, in his view, very limited, and did *not* confer rights of possession, occupation, use and enjoyment of the sea or sea-bed to the exclusion of others. In his view, the interests contained in the native title rights applicable to the area included free access to travel through the area, fishing and hunting performed according to "traditional" purposes, but not commercial ones, access to visit and protect sacred spiritual areas, and in order to safeguard cultural and spiritual knowledge. The rights are also only protected to the extent of, and must yield to, any inconsistency with any valid laws of the Commonwealth or Northern Territory. Whether such rights are extinguished due to the inconsistency "can only be determined by reference to such particular rights and interests as may be asserted and established" (at 128).

Questions will continue to arise[13] about the validity of dealings with land and water subject to native title, both before and after the commencement of the NTA.

Clearly, native title also includes other property rights, such as usufructuary rights: hunting, fishing and gathering rights.[14] These interests can be exercised in much the same way as are profits á prendre or easements. Australian law may recognise native title to include a range of other rights, such as intellectual property rights, though these issues are still being litigated.

What is not clear is to what extent Australian law can and has extinguished Indigenous common law rights, where their existence may not be based on an interest in land or water. This question must be asked both in relation to laws which

---

9 *Thorpe v Commonwealth* (1997) 71 ALJR 767.

10 (1992) 175 CLR 1.

11 Sections 10 and 223. "Native title" interests are those "recognised by the common law of Australia", possessed under the traditional laws and customs observed by Indigenous Australians, in connection with land and water.

12 *Yarmirr v Northern Territory* [1998] 771 FCA (6 July 1998). See also Levy, R, "Croker Seas Native Title Application: Federal Court Hearing" (1997) 4(2)*Indigenous Law Bulletin* 21. See also, Bartlett, R, "Onus of Proof for Native Title" (1995) 3(73) *Aboriginal Law Bulletin* 8.

13 See below, "Equality rights".

14 *Wik Peoples v Queensland* (1996) 187 CLR 1.

define rights which are proprietary in nature, for instance, intellectual property rights, and those which may not be so based, for instance, rights derived by virtue of Indigenous family or criminal laws.

Löfgren[15] points out that in *Mabo (No 2)*, Deane and Gaudron JJ, determined that parts of Indigenous common law were incorporated at "settlement" into the received English common law;[16] the imposition of English common law had the *potential* to override Indigenous common law, but could *only* do so *by authority of statute*, and *not* through the exercise by the Crown of subsequent *prerogative powers*.[17] Brennan J (with whom Mason CJ and McHugh J concurred) expressed the view that Indigenous common law could be extinguished by legislation *or* by executive action, but only if a clear and plain intention to do so was expressed. Legislation or executive action would not be effective to extinguish Indigenous common law if consistent with the continued existence of those laws or if merely regulating the rights given meaning by Indigenous common law.[18]

Thus, Löfgren contends, Indigenous common law was incorporated to some extent into the law received by the colonies and, so, where not extinguished, continues to form part of the common law that exists today. As Dodson observes, "it is an absurd position if our title to land is recognised, but the laws and customs giving meaning to that title are treated as if they do not exist".[19] The content of Indigenous common law is determined by itself.[20]

Nettheim expresses a similar view and argues that, as a result of *Mabo (No 2)* and the introduction of the NTA, two systems of law are now formally recognised to co-exist in Australia. He argues further that there is "no reason why the High Court's approach should not be extended from real property to intellectual property, or into the area of criminal justice, or into the domain of self-government".[21]

Löfgren makes out this argument on the basis that indigenous rights are *sui generis* and that their existence is not dependent upon ownership of land.[22] They are

---

15   Löfgren, N, "Common Law Aboriginal Property Rights" (1995) 3(77) *Aboriginal Law Bulletin* 10.

16   *Mabo* (1992) 175 CLR 1 at 77-94.

17   (1992) 175 CLR 1 at 79-80 (emphasis added). See also *Casimel v Insurance Corporation of British Columbia* (1993) 106 DLR (4th) 720, and *Delgamuukw v British Columbia* (1993) 104 DLR (4th) 470.

18   (1992) 175 CLR 1 at 64-65. See Mulqueeny, KE, "Folk-law or Folklore: When a Law is Not a Law. Or is it?", in Stephenson, MA and Ratnapala, S, (eds), *Mabo: A Judicial Revolution* (University of Queensland Press, St Lucia, 1993), pp 171-72.

19   Dodson, M, "From 'lore' to 'law': Indigenous rights and Australian legal systems" (1995) 20(1) *Alternative Law Journal* 2; 3(72) *Aboriginal Law Bulletin* 2.

20   *Mabo (No 2)* (1992) 175 CLR 1 at 58-63 per Brennan J, at 86-95 per Deane and Gaudron JJ.

21   Nettheim, G, "Mabo and Legal Pluralism: The Australian Aboriginal Justice Experience", in Hazelhurst, K, (ed), *Legal Pluralism and the Colonial Legacy* (Avebury, Aldershot, 1995), p 113.

22   *Mabo (No 2)* (1992) 175 CLR 1 at 89 per Deane and Gaudron JJ, at 133 per Dawson J; *Delgamuukw v Queen in Right of British Columbia* (unreported, SC (Canada), Lamer CJ, La Forest, L'Hereux-Dube, Cory, McLachlin and Major JJ, 11 December 1997, No 23799); *Amodu Tijani v Sec of Southern Nigeria* [1921] 2 AC 399 at 409-10 per Viscount Haldane; *R v Sparrow* (1990) 70 DLR (4th) 385 at 411 per Dickson CJC and La Forrest J; *Guerin v The Queen* (1984) 13 DLR (4th) 321 at 339 per Dickson J; and the dissent in *Delgamuukw v British Columbia* (1993) 104 DLR (4th) 470. For discussion of the *Delgamuukw* case and possible implications for the development of native title law in Australia, see Dick, D "Comprehending the Genius of the Common Law: Native Title in Australia and Canada compared post-*Delgamuukw*" (1998) 5 *Australian Journal of Human Rights* (forthcoming).

"one of a kind", and a "land-based" legal analysis of them is inaccurate and inappropriate. In his view, then, Indigenous common law rights such as hunting, fishing and gathering rights,[23] or customary adoptions,[24] can survive the extinguishment of other land-based rights, such as native title.[25]

Löfgren gleans support from *Mabo (No 2)* (as discussed above), and from Bartlett's argument[26] that Indigenous common law can be extinguished only by statute *or* by abandonment by Indigenous Australian people – that is, by operation of Indigenous common law itself.[27] Thus, unless a statute specifically seeks to extinguish Indigenous common law on a particular area of law, its continued existence can be asserted.

That indigenous rights are *sui generis* forms the basis of the recent decision by the Supreme Court of Canada, in *Delgamuukw v Queen in right of British Colombia.*[28] The Court found that "aboriginal title" (Canada's terminology for "native title") was derived from a unique source, namely native occupation and possession of lands prior to assertions of British sovereignty, and in part from pre-existing systems of "aboriginal law". It also found that the extent of "aboriginal title" was not limited to rights associated with uses of the land, but "presumes a full beneficial interest, including mineral rights".[29]

Thus, it can be forcefully argued that the continued existence of Indigenous common law rights is *not* dependent upon land ownership rights. Nor does the heterogeneous nature of Indigenous common law contradict its existence.[30] Thus, apart from those laws which are *explicitly* overridden by statute, and those which Indigenous Australian peoples have abandoned, Indigenous common law continues with full force.

In relation to criminal laws, at least, the High Court does not currently appear to agree. In *Walker v New South Wales*, Mason CJ, as he then was, held that Indigenous criminal laws had been extinguished "by the passage of criminal statutes

---

23 See *Mason v Tritton* (1994) 34 NSWLR 572 at 580-82, 584 per Kirby P; *Wik Peoples v Queensland* (1996) 187 CLR 1.

24 *Casimel v Insurance Corporation of British Columbia* (1993) 106 DLR (4th) 720.

25 Löfgren, above, n 15, p 11. See also *Re Waanyi People's Native Title Application* (1995) 129 ALR 100.

26 Bartlett, above, n 12.

27 Watson states that the operation of Indigenous common law itself is the *only* way in which Indigenous law can be extinguished: Watson, I, "Indigenous Peoples' Law-Ways: Survival Against the Colonial State" (1997) 8 *Australian Feminist Law Journal* 39.

28 *Delgamuukw v Queen in right of British Colombia* (unreported, SC (Canada), Lamer CJ, La Forest, L'Hereux-Dube, Cory, McLachlin and Major JJ, 11 December 1997, No 23799). For discussion, see Dick, above, n 22.

29 Bartlett, R, "Casenote – *Delgamuukw*" (1998) 4(9) *Indigenous Law Bulletin* 17 at 17. The decision also placed "primary emphasis in the proof of aboriginal claims on the claimants themselves and not on non-aboriginal experts' [usually anthropologists] interpretation and filtering of aboriginal evidence" (at 18). See also Meyers, G, Piper, CM and Rumley, HE, "Asking the minerals question: rights in minerals as an incident of native title" (1997) 2(2) *Australian Indigenous Law Reporter* 203, and Levy, JT, "Reconciliation and resources: mineral rights and Aboriginal land rights as property rights" (1994) 10(1) (Autumn) *Policy* 11.

30 *Casimel* is "consistent with the view that the scope and content of specific common law Aboriginal rights vary from one group of Aboriginal people to another": Löfgren, above, n 15.

of *general* application".[31] Similarly Yeo argues that Indigenous criminal laws have been extinguished by the passage of criminal laws by State parliaments which he characterises as an executive act.[32] Nonetheless, we submit that the matter is not closed and that significant potential remains to argue the continued existence of Indigenous common law.

The importance of recognising Indigenous common law must be emphasised. As Dodson says above, the laws and customs of Indigenous Australian peoples give meaning to their rights. Without the recognition of Indigenous common law, and consequently the ability to exercise *all* aspects of their culture, human rights may become meaningless to Indigenous Australian peoples.

THE BASIC INTERNATIONAL HUMAN RIGHTS INSTRUMENTS SPECIFICALLY RELEVANT TO INDIGENOUS PEOPLES

The Draft Declaration on the Rights of Indigenous Peoples

International law has largely been an instrument used against indigenous peoples, primarily as a means of justifying their dispossession and ill-treatment by colonial and other powers.[33] Nonetheless, international law is developing ways to support and to some degree, meet, indigenous aspirations.

In 1957, the first convention dealing specifically with indigenous peoples – the International Labour Organization (ILO) *Convention on Tribal and Indigenous Populations* (ILO 107)[34] – came into force. Significant criticism of it by indigenous peoples led to its revision in 1989 in the form of the *Convention on Indigenous and Tribal Peoples in Independent States* (ILO 169).[35] Although the latter convention makes a greater contribution to the recognition of the unique rights of indigenous peoples, it still falls short of adequately meeting indigenous rights and aspirations.[36]

In 1985, the Working Group on Indigenous Populations commenced drafting a declaration on the specific rights of indigenous peoples. This was finalised in 1994 and the Draft Declaration on the Rights of Indigenous Peoples (Draft Declaration) was submitted for consideration to the UN Commission on Human Rights. It will likely be several years before the Declaration is considered for adoption by the General Assembly.[37] A significant aspect of the Declaration already, though, is the direct participation of many indigenous groups within the international forum.

---

31   (1994) 182 CLR 45 at 50 (emphasis added).

32   Yeo, S, "Native Title Jurisdiction After Mabo" (1994) 1(9) *Current Issues in Criminal Justice* 6.

33   Watson, above, n 27, p 46; Steiner, H and Alston, P (eds), *International Human Rights in Context: Law, Politics, Morals* (Clarendon Press, Oxford, 1996), p 1007.

34   International Labour Conference, 26 June 1957. Its purpose was to protect indigenous and tribal populations until they were assimilated with the rest of society. See Anaya, above, n 3.

35   International Labour Conference, 27 June 1989. It recognises indigenous peoples' collective rights to self development, cultural and institutional integrity, territory and environmental security. It has not been ratified by Australia. See, Strelein, L, "The Price of Compromise: Should Australia Ratify ILO Convention 169?", in Bird, G, Martin, G and Nielsen, J, (eds), *Majah: Indigenous Peoples and the Law* (Federation Press, Sydney, 1996). On the issue of collective rights, see Sanders, D, "Collective Rights" (1991) 13 *Human Rights Quarterly* 368.

36   See Barsh, RL, "Indigenous Peoples in the 1990s: From Object to Subject of International Law?" (1994) 7 *Harvard Human Rights Journal* 33.

37   Steiner and Alston, above, n 33.

The Draft Declaration[38] is broad ranging and specific provisions are discussed in more detail below. However, the thrust of the Draft Declaration is to secure recognition of the dignity and rights of indigenous peoples as *unique* peoples, including protection of their culture, land and resources, knowledge and traditions, and their rights to participate equally and without discrimination in all facets of their lives.

As it is a Declaration only, it will not establish any enforceable rights in international law,[39] though it may form the basis of Australian domestic laws. If the Declaration is incorporated into any federal law, it will be an extrinsic document to which a court may appropriately refer to interpret the domestic law.[40] The Declaration has been adopted by the United Nations Sub-Commission on Prevention of Discrimination and Protection of Minorities, giving it persuasive value in both international and domestic law.[41]

Two central concerns were raised by indigenous peoples during negotiations on the Draft Declaration: the right to self-determination and the right to protection from all forms of discrimination, including genocide and ethnocide.

Self-determination

The right to self-determination is essential to the enjoyment of all human rights by indigenous peoples, and is recognised in the *International Covenant on Civil and Political Rights* (ICCPR) (art 1),[42] the *International Covenant on Economic Social and Cultural Rights* (ICESCR) (art 1),[43] and the Draft Declaration (art 3). Self-determination is the right of "peoples" to "freely determine their political status and freely pursue their economic, social and cultural development".

A debate has continued between indigenous peoples and nation states of colonial origin, as to whether indigenous people can claim the status of independent nation states.[44] Their claim to do so has been vigorously resisted by "colonial" nation states seeking to protect their territorial integrity. This issue formed a significant part of the debate concerning self-determination in the Draft Declaration.[45] Self-determination can be viewed strictly as describing only the process of decolonisation which is occurring in self-contained territories, or it can be interpreted as a process including a range of outcomes, including self-government or self-management.

---

38 A copy of the Draft Declaration is located at <http://www.halcyon.com/FWDP/un.html/>.

39 Its potential in the international legal forum is discussed in Barsh, above, n 36, pp 75-76.

40 *Acts Interpretation Act* 1901 (Cth) s 15AB(2)(d).

41 See *Mabo (No 2)* (1992) 175 CLR 1 at 41-42, per Brennan J.

42 GA Res, 16 December 1966.

43 GA Res, 10 December 1948.

44 See Barsh, above, n 36, p 35; and Mansell, M, *They Can Keep Their Justice, We'll Keep Our Country: The APG View*, Proceedings of Aboriginal Justice Issues Conference (Australian Institute of Criminology, Cairns, 23-25 June 1992). On the sovereignty of Indigenous Australian peoples, see *Coe v Commonwealth* (*Wiradjuri Claim*) (1979) 53 ALJR 403; *Coe v Commonwealth* (1993) 68 ALJR 110; *Thorpe v Commonwealth* (1997) 71 ALJR 767 (discussed in (1997) 4(7) *Indigenous Law Bulletin* 19).

45 See generally, Barsh, above, n 36.

Nobel Laureate, Rigoberta Menchu, views self-determination as "undeniably the right to full political representation, without intermediaries, or limitations of any kind. This representation must be expressed at the local, regional, and national levels".[46] Thus, indigenous peoples are *at least* entitled to "self-management" of their affairs within a nation state, so that they are full partners in the political process involved in determining and regulating their interests. Significantly, Sibosado notes that the "recognition of native title means that Aboriginal people have a legal basis to be an independent people, both economically and culturally, and not to be marginalised to the fringes of white society".[47]

In *Mikmaq Tribal Society v Canada*[48] the UN Human Rights Committee was asked to consider a complaint by the Mikmaq Tribe against Canada, alleging a breach of their right of self-determination. The Committee acknowledged that the right of self-determination could apply to indigenous peoples, but refused to consider the complaint on the basis that the right is a collective right, and the Committee is only able to consider complaints brought by individuals. This appears to rule out the possibility of a further complaint based on self-determination under the *First Optional Protocol to the ICCPR*.[49] However, the right may still influence litigation domestically.

One way in which self-determination may be expressed by Indigenous Australian peoples is through regional agreements. In Canada, such agreements have been implemented in the form of the self-governing territories of Denendeh and Nunavut, resulting in significant gains for First Nations peoples.[50] Regional agreements are considered to be a viable means by which Indigenous Australians may be able to achieve economic independence and self-government within particular regions.[51]

In Australia, the NTA facilitates the development of regional agreements.[52] It states that native title holders may enter into an agreement with the Commonwealth, a State or Territory, which involves the surrender or extinguishment of their native title rights, or authorising any future act which may affect those rights. Such an agreement can be supported by any form of consideration, including a grant of freehold title, and agreements can be negotiated on a regional or local basis.

---

46   Cited in Barsh, above, n 36, p 40.

47   Sibosado, M, "Native Title and Regional Agreements: Kimberley Region", in Aboriginal and Torres Strait Islander Social Justice Commissioner, *Indigenous Social Justice – Regional Agreements, Submission to the Parliament of the Commonwealth of Australia on the Social Justice Package* (AGPS, Sydney, 1995), p 98.

48   Comm No 205/1986, UN GAOR, Hum Rts Comm, 47th Sess, Supp No 40, at 214, UN Doc A/47/40 (1992).

49   GA Res, 16 December 1966.

50   Byrnes, J, *Aboriginal Economic Independence: A Report on Some Canadian Initiatives* (Rural Development Centre, Armidale, 1990), pp 17-18.

51   Peter Yu, Chairman of the Kimberley Land Council, *The 7:30 Report*, ABC-TV, 23 January 1997. See also Martin, D, "Deal of the Century? A Case Study from the Pasminco Century Project" (1998) 4(11) *Indigenous Law Bulletin* 4.

52   These agreements are described as "indigenous land use agreements", and are governed by Part 2 of the Act (as amended in 1998). See also Jull, P and Craig, D, "Reflections on Regional Agreements: Yesterday, Today and Tomorrow" (1997) 2(4) *Australian Indigenous Law Reporter* 475.

Regional agreements also have the potential to resolve some native title claims to the greater benefit of Indigenous Australian claimants. Sibosado regards the litigious, "claim by claim" approach of the native title process, as far too disadvantageous to claimants. He cites two main reasons for this: first, the cost involved in litigation; and secondly, the time delay involved in the litigation process – claimants must go through mediation, the Tribunal, and the Federal Court, and then perhaps, even the High Court. He contends that Regional Agreements allow an expression of self-determination and that they can ensure Indigenous Australians have "the ability to manage and control land [and the] ... right to practise our culture on our land and the right to pass that culture on to future generations".[53]

Obviously, Indigenous Australian communities being advised on native title claims must be given very clear and comprehensive advice on the full implications of any agreement which includes the extinguishment or surrender of their native title rights.

Equality rights

The right to be equal and to be free from all forms of discrimination is recognised as a fundamental human right and is contained in several international instruments including: the *Universal Declaration of Human Rights* (UDHR) (arts 1(3), 2, 7, 13(b), and 55(c)),[54] the ICCPR (art 26), the ICESCR (art 2), the *Convention on the Elimination of All Forms of Racial Discrimination* (CERD),[55] and the Draft Declaration (arts 2, 16, 18). The Draft Declaration (arts 22, 29), CERD and ILO 169 (art 4) also include the right to "special measures" – affirmative action – to redress past injustices.

Australia's obligations under these instruments have been incorporated into domestic law by several acts, including the *Human Rights and Equal Opportunity Act* 1984 (Cth) (HREOC Act) and the *Racial Discrimination Act* 1975 (Cth) (RDA).

These rights can be usefully explored in the context of Indigenous Australian property rights, given the recent enactment of the *Native Title Amendment Act* 1998 (Cth), which will effect the reduction and/or further extinguishment of native title interests. The changes include: the right of claimants to negotiate is reduced; the threshold for claims is increased; certain acts are validated which reduce or extinguish native title both over land and water which took place after 1 January 1994, and which failed to observe the requirements of the NTA; the range of future acts which will extinguish native title is increased. Although, just terms compensation will be available in limited circumstances, Indigenous Australians would argue that monetary compensation is inadequate to replace their native title interests.

The right to own property without discrimination is guaranteed by art 17 UDHR and art 5(d) of CERD. The land ownership rights of indigenous peoples are recognised in art 15 of ILO 169, and the Draft Declaration (arts 21, 27), and include the right to fair and just compensation. Similarly, s 51(xxxi) of the Commonwealth

---

53 Sibosado, above, n 47.

54 GA Res, 10 December 1948.

55 GA Res, 20 November 1963.

Constitution requires the payment of compensation on just terms, where land is acquired by the Commonwealth.

Pritchard argues that any attempt to override the RDA – which is included in the NTA and the Amendment Act – is contrary to the UDHR and CERD, and would see Australia violate "the peremptory norm of international law [prohibiting racial discrimination] from which no derogation is permitted".[56] Furthermore, the property rights of Indigenous Australians are unique as compared to those of other Australians, due to their cultural connection to their traditional lands. Thus, it can be argued that any violation of their property rights would contravene their cultural rights and their religious beliefs (discussed below), as recognised in international law.

On the other hand, positive action which results in the different treatment of Indigenous Australian rights – such as the protection of native title rights – would not contravene this peremptory norm, as differentiation does not contravene the principle of equality "if the criteria for a differentiation are reasonable and objective and the aim is to achieve a purpose which is legitimate under"[57] international law.

Before its enactment, it was argued that the Native Title Amendment Bill would be a constitutionally valid use of s 51(xxvi) of the Constitution (the race power), despite the fact that the proposed law would adversely affect Indigenous Australian property rights.[58] However, a strong argument can be made that the race power only confers the power to make "special" laws to the *benefit* of a particular race.[59] Reading the race power as also conferring the power to make *detrimental* "special" laws would, again, contravene the international peremptory norm, and produce "negative" discrimination on the basis of race.

This matter was very recently considered by the High Court in *Kartinyeri v Commonwealth*.[60] The matter directly before the court was whether the enactment of the *Hindmarsh Island Bridge Act* 1997 (Cth) (the Bridge Act), which had the purpose of amending the *Aboriginal and Torres Strait Islander Heritage Protection Act* 1985 (Cth) (the principal Act), was a valid exercise of the race power, given that the legislation had a detrimental impact on Indigenous Australian rights, and in

---

56   Pritchard, S, "Native Title in an International Perspective", in Research Institute for Humanities and Social Science, University of Sydney, *Sharing Country – Land Rights, Human Rights and Reconciliation after Wik* (University of Sydney, Sydney, 1997), pp 42-43.

57   Pritchard, above, p 56. In *Gerhardy v Brown* (1985) 159 CLR 70, the High Court interpreted equality in its "formal" sense, holding that any differentiation amounted to discrimination. This is inconsistent with international jurisprudence. More recent pronouncements from the High Court suggest that it may move to a "substantive" view of equality: *Street v Queensland Bar Association* (1989) 168 CLR 461; *Castlemaine Tooheys Ltd v South Australia* (1991) 169 CLR 436; *Western Australia v Commonwealth* (1995) 183 CLR 373. However, see *Kartinyeri v Commonwealth* [1998] HCA 22, 1 April 1998

58   Joint Opinion to the Commonwealth, DF Jackson QC and SJ Gageler, 16 October 1997.

59   See, Aboriginal and Torres Strait Islander Social Justice Commissioner, Dodson, M, *Submission to the Parliamentary Joint Committee on Native Title and the Aboriginal and Torres Strait Islander Land Fund: The Native Title Amendment Bill 1997* (HREOC, Sydney, 3 October 1997); ALRC, *Comments on the Native Title Amendment Bill 1997*, submission to the Senate Legal and Constitutional Legislation Committee (ALRC, Sydney, 24 October 1997) (the text of the submission can be found at <http://uniserve.edu.au/alrc/>); and, Bradson J and Williams J, "The Perils of Inclusion: The Constitution and the Race Power" (1997) 19(1) *Adelaide Law Review* 95.

60   [1998] HCA 22, 1 April 1998. See also, Bourke, J, "Women's Business: Sex, Secrets, and the Hindmarsh Island Bridge Affair" (1997) 20(2) *University of New South Wales Law Journal* 333.

particular the rights of the Ngarrindjeri women seeking to protect their secret/sacred cultural sites and knowledge. The court found, by a majority of 5-1, that the Act was a constitutionally valid exercise of legislative power. Only Kirby and Gaudron JJ took the view that the race power could only be used to support "special laws" to the *benefit* of a particular race.[61] Gummow and Hayne JJ, on the other hand, found that the Bridge Act was a valid exercise of s 51(xxvi), because it could be characterised as a "special law". As such, the Bridge Act is valid. In their view, this characterisation as a "special law" is derived merely from the fact that the law has a "differential operation". That it was disadvantageous to the Ngarrindjeri women did not remove it from this characterisation, as "differential operation of the one law may, upon its obverse and reverse, [validly] withdraw or create benefits".[62] Brennan CJ and McHugh J found that a constitutional head of power which supports an Act also supports enactments which repeal or modify a principal Act's operation, provided there is no constitutional limitation on the power to effect an amendment.[63] Therefore, as s 51(xxvi) supported the principal Act, it also supported the Bridge Act.[64] As a result, they did not see it as necessary to examine the nature of the race power. Nonetheless, they did discuss the matter, and expressed a similar view of its operation to that applied by Gummow and Hayne JJ; in their view, the power authorised laws of a "differential operation", rather than only "beneficial" laws, buts that its use was limited to circumstances which did not amount to a "manifest abuse" of the power.[65]

In our view, this characterisation by Gummow and Hayne JJ, echoed by Brennan CJ and McHugh J, clearly contradicts the international peremptory norm prohibiting racial discrimination. It would also be in breach of Australia's international obligations under the UDHR, ICCPR and CERD. Perhaps of equal concern, the decision appears to lay the ground work for the successful implementation of the Native Title Amendment Act 1998 (Cth), despite the fact that it will act to the detriment of Indigenous Australian peoples, in that it will further reduce and extinguish their property rights.

Furthermore, Kilduff and Kilduff[66] argue that the validating provisions of the original NTA deny procedural fairness to native title holders whose interests have been or will be extinguished, because they were not consulted about the extent or validity of any such extinguishment. This is "a denial of the entitlements to ownership and inheritance of property, including the implicit immunity from arbitrary dispossession, which are the 'rights' [protected by s 10(1) of the RDA]".[67]

---

61 Gaudron J, ultimately, adopted a similar analysis to Brennan CJ and McHugh J (discussed below). In her view, despite the effect of the amendments by the Act, the principal Act retained the quality of being a "special law". This was because it continued to confer benefit upon Indigenous Australians by protecting (albeit in a lesser form) Indigenous Australian cultural heritage.

62 [1998] HCA 22 at 87.

63 [1998] HCA 22 at 15 and 19.

64 [1998] HCA 22 at 17.

65 [1998] HCA 22 at 42.

66 Kilduff, C and Kilduff, P, "Racism And The Native Title Act" (unpublished, 1996) (Peter Kilduff practises at the Melbourne Bar).

67 *Mabo v Queensland (No 1)* (1988) 166 CLR 186 at 231 per Deane J.

The same argument will apply to the further reduction and extinguishment of native title which will be effected by the Amendment Act.

Again, this represents a breach of Australia's international obligations, giving rise to a complaint on the basis of equality rights and/or cultural rights under the UDHR, ICCPR or CERD.

THE RECOGNITION AND PROTECTION OF CULTURAL RIGHTS

Cultural rights

As Nettheim points out, the *Convention on the Prevention and Punishment of the Crime of Genocide*[68] (Genocide Convention) aims to secure the physical survival of peoples throughout the international community. However, for indigenous peoples, their survival cannot be secured *unless* their *culture survives too*.[69] As Puri says so aptly, indigenous culture "is a testimony of the past without which the present would have no future".[70] As is made apparent throughout this chapter, cultural rights are relevant to all facets of the human rights Indigenous Australians may claim.

Almost every provision within the Draft Declaration seeks to recognise and to protect the various cultural rights of indigenous peoples, reflecting the essential nature of culture to the enjoyment of human rights by indigenous peoples. In essence, the Declaration recognises the unique contribution of indigenous peoples to the diversity and richness of the world's common heritage, and to the development and management of a sustainable environment. It seeks to promote respect for and the dignity of indigenous culture, and to secure the right of indigenous people to control, practise, use, develop and teach their culture, and to maintain their spiritual connection to their land.[71]

Cultural rights are given limited recognition in the ICCPR (art 27) and the ICESCR (arts 3, 15). The cultural and linguistic rights of "minorities" are also recognised in the United Nations *Declaration on the Rights of Persons Belonging to National or Ethnic, Religious and Linguistic Minorities*.[72]

The United Nations Human Rights Committee has commented that the cultural rights guaranteed by art 27 of the ICCPR, are rights which are "conferred on individuals belonging to minority groups ... distinct from, and additional to, all the other rights which, as individuals in common with everyone else, they are already entitled".[73]

Article 27 of the ICCPR was invoked by Sandra Lovelace, a First Nations Canadian of the Maliseet band, whose status as an "Indian" ceased after her

---

68   GA Res, 9 December 1948.

69   Nettheim, G, *Indigenous Rights, Human Rights and Australia*, Working Paper No 15 (Australian Studies Centre, Institute of Commonwealth Studies, University of London, London, 1987), p 10.

70   Puri, K, "Copyright Protection for Aborigines in the Light of Mabo", in Stephenson and Ratnapala, above, n 18, p 136.

71   See in particular, arts 3, 4, 9, 12-16, 25, 29.

72   GA Res, 18 December 1992.

73   Human Rights Committee, "General Comment No 23 on art 27 / Minority Rights" (1994) 15 *Human Rights Law Journal* 234 at 235-36.

marriage to a non-Indigenous Canadian.[74] The Canadian Indian Act removed "Indian" status from women upon marrying non-Indigenous Canadians, but not from men who did so. The Canadian government submitted that the Act was drafted in this way to protect the "Indian" patrilineal tradition. However, Lovelace put forward evidence that her band was based on a matrilineal tradition which was denied by and inconsistent with the Act. The Human Rights Committee found that Ms Lovelace's access to her native culture and language, in community with other members of her group, was interfered with by the Indian Act, and thus it breached art 27 of the Covenant.[75] The Canadian Act was subsequently amended.

Other cases brought by indigenous peoples to the Human Rights Committee under art 27 include *Kitok v Sweden* (to protect economic activities), *Lansman v Finland* (to protect livelihood) and *Ominayak and the Lubicon Lake Band v Canada*.[76] The last case is particularly relevant in the context of the so-called *Wik* debate. In *Ominayak's* case, the Lubicon Lake Band complained that art 27 had been breached by the grant of leases for oil and gas exploration to private companies, by the Alberta provincial government (under the auspices of the Canadian nation state). The Human Rights Committee agreed that the action "threatened the way of life and the culture of the Lubicon Lake Band by destroying the Band's economic base and indigenous way of life, thereby making it impossible for the Band to survive as a people".[77]

Many facets of indigenous culture may also be captured, at least in part, within the freedom of belief, thought, conscience and religion, set out in art 18 of the UDHR. Freedom of religion and of belief are also recognised in the ICCPR (art 18) and the *Declaration on the Elimination of All Forms of Intolerance and Discrimination Based on Religion or Belief*.[78] Only the ICCPR raises an actionable complaint in the international forum, though all of these documents may influence the interpretation of Australian common law and federal government policy.

Some protection of Indigenous Australian cultural rights and/or religious beliefs, may be secured within domestic law through the RDA or the HREOC Act. Section 9(2) of the RDA specifically seeks to prevent any interference or impairment of the enjoyment of social and cultural rights referred to in art 5 of CERD. For instance, a failure to acknowledge cultural rights within employment could be argued within the context of a complaint of racial discrimination.[79] The

---

74 *Lovelace v Canada,* Comm No R6/24/1977, Human Rights Committee, July 30 1981, UN Doc A/36/40, Supp No 40, reprinted in (1981) 2 *Human Rights Law Journal* 158.

75 As a result of this finding, the Committee did not consider whether Ms Lovelace's equality rights had also been breached. However, it expressed a view that legislation *could* be passed in the terms set out in the Indian Act, but that there would have to be both reasonable and objective justification of such provisions. This would be consistent with the protection of either a patrilineal or matrilineal tradition, provided these could be proven by reference to the relevant Indigenous common law.

76 Discussed in Annex 13, Barker, above, n 4.

77 Barker, above, n 4, p 149.

78 GA Res, 25 November 1981.

79 A promising, and related, argument was raised in *Williams v South Australia* (1990) EOC ¶92-283, that the complainant had been discriminated against on the ground of race, which she argued included the right of freedom of opinion as set out in CERD which is not specifically included in s 15 (discrimination in employment). HREOC treated s 9 of the RDA as enabling a broader range of rights to be interpreted within the meaning of s 15: at 77,859 per O'Connor. See also Mason J in *Gerhardy v Brown* (1985) 159 CLR 70, and *Convention Concerning Discrimination in Respect of Employment and Occupation,* ILO 111, GA Res, 25 June 1958.

HREOC Act specifically includes any interference with or impairment of religion, within the meaning of discrimination,[80] and may also protect cultural rights as it incorporates within the meaning of "human rights", those rights set out in various international instruments, including the ICCPR.[81]

Relevant State and Territory acts should also be considered for their potential use to protect cultural rights, and the freedom of religion and belief. For instance, s 7(2) of the *Anti-Discrimination Act* 1977 (NSW) states that discrimination on the ground of race may occur if the discriminatory act is based upon "a characteristic that appertains generally to persons of that race". Judicial interpretation of this phrase has not confined such characteristics to physical ones,[82] and so it may be possible to argue that cultural traits or behaviours should be included within its meaning.

Obviously, Commonwealth, State and Territory legislation on cultural heritage protection provides another mechanism for the assertion of cultural rights, and a vehicle for their protection.[83] For instance, the *Northern Territory Aboriginal Sacred Sites Act* 1989 (NT) was enacted, along with the Territory's land rights legislation, to protect sites of spiritual and cultural significance to Indigenous Australian peoples, to provide a means of acquiring the property interest in these sites, and to ensure access by traditional owners and custodians to these sites in accordance with Indigenous common law. The sites which can be claimed for protection are not limited to areas of unalienated crown lands or Aboriginal reserves.

Despite this cultural heritage legislation, the experience of the Ngarrindjeri women who opposed the building of a bridge at Hindmarsh Island belies the efficacy of the legislation – particularly where it is not supported by political will.[84] The situation encountered by the Ngarrindjeri women in the Hindmarsh Island Bridge affair would fall squarely within the proposals mentioned above, to assert cultural and/or religious rights, as the Ngarrindjeri women sought to protect their culture, and their secret, sacred and spiritual beliefs.

---

80   Section 3(1).

81   Section 3(1), (4). The difficulty, of course, is that the HREOC Act does not provide legally enforceable remedies.

82   See *Bear v Norwood Private Nursing Home* (1984) EOC ¶92-019; *Waterhouse v Bell* (1991) EOC ¶92-376; and *Harrison v Department of TAFE* (unreported, Anti Discrimination Board (NSW), 19 June 1978, No 3 of 1978).

83   Discussed in Janke, T, *Our Culture, Our Future* (AIATSIS, Canberra, 1997), pp 48-53 (also at <http://www. icip.lawnet.com.au>); and Cassidy, J, "Federal and State Land and Resource Use Management and Allocation Regimes" (unpublished, Deakin University, Victoria, 1995). Note, that proposals to amend the Commonwealth's *Aboriginal and Torres Strait Islander Cultural Heritage Act* 1984 are currently being considered by the government; it is unclear what part the recommendations of Justice Evatt's comprehensive review of the Act will play in these deliberations. Justice Evatt's final Report was presented to the responsible Minister, Senator Herron, in August 1996; its recommendations are discussed in (1997) 2(3) *Indigenous Law Reporter* 433.

84   See Mead, G, *A Royal Omission* (published by the author, PO Box 6042, Halifax St, SA, 1995); *Kartinyeri v Commonwealth* [1998] HCA 22: Gummow and Hayne JJ clearly would not countenance any restrictions on the competence of parliament to "limit the scope of a special law by a subsequent legislative determination that something less than the original measure was necessary" (at 850).

Cultural and intellectual property rights

Indigenous cultural and intellectual property takes on a wide variety of forms and includes "all expressions of the relationship between the people, their land [and water] and the other living beings and spirits which share the land [and water], and is the basis for maintaining social, economic and diplomatic relationships ... [its particular content] must be decided by the [individual indigenous group] themselves".[85] These rights are reflected strongly in the Draft Declaration.[86]

Indigenous Australian cultural and intellectual property can occur in many forms such as secret/sacred knowledge and information; scientific, environmental, and medical knowledge; "artefacts" including skeletal remains, and sacred and utilitarian objects; designs; dances; paintings; carvings; songs; and stories. The applicability of Australian legal categories to these varies.

The Indigenous common law which governs Indigenous Australian cultural and intellectual property can be very complex. Generally, this "property" is not freely available, and the laws define who may have access to it and their responsibility to control its use. Those responsible for Indigenous cultural and intellectual property can be subjected to severe punishment for their failure to observe these responsibilities strictly.

These interests can be included within the notion of "cultural rights" and so can gain protection in the ways discussed above. Janke identifies several other international instruments which may also be asserted to protect Indigenous cultural and intellectual property interests:[87] art 15(4) of the *Berne Convention for the Protection of Literary and Artistic Works* (unpublished folklore); arts 1-8, 22, and 27 of the *Trade-Related Aspects of Intellectual Property Rights Agreement;* the *UNESCO Convention on Cultural Property;* art 15(c) of the ICESCR; and art 23 of the ILO 169.

Indigenous cultural and intellectual property is specifically "protected" by cultural heritage legislation. However, to date, no provisions have been enacted within Australian intellectual property laws which deal specifically with Indigenous cultural and intellectual property. Nonetheless, some potential exists for the use of intellectual property and other laws to protect these interests,[88] such as legislation dealing with cultural heritage, museums, and racial vilification, ss 52 and 53 of the *Trade Practices Act* 1974 (Cth),[89] the tort of passing off, breach of confidence,[90] breach of contract, defamation and blasphemy.[91] Puri argues that the recognition of Indigenous land laws in *Mabo (No 2)* may be used by analogy to find the

---

85   Daes, E, *Study on the Protection of Cultural and Intellectual Property of Indigenous Peoples* (E/CN.4/Sub 2/1993/28, 28 July 1993), p 9.

86   Articles 12, 24, 26, 28-30.

87   Janke, above, n 83, at <http://www. icip.lawnet.com.au>, Information Sheet 2.

88   Janke, above, n 83, pp 54-58. See also Janke, T, "Don't Give Away Your Valuable Cultural Assets: Advice for Indigenous Peoples" (1998) 4(11) *Indigenous Law Bulletin* 8.

89   *Milpurrurru v Indofurn* (1994) 30 IPR 209.

90   *Foster v Mountford* (1977) 14 ALR 71; *Pitjantjatjara Council Inc and Peter Nguaningu v Lowe and Bender*, "Casenote" (1982) 4 *Aboriginal Law Bulletin* 11.

91   Miller, D, "Collective Ownership of Copyright in Spiritually-Sensitive Works: *Milpurrurru v Indofurn*" (1995) 6 *Australian Intellectual Property Journal* 206.

recognition of Indigenous cultural and intellectual property laws.[92] The Dambartung Aboriginal Corporation of Western Australia plans to challenge an agreement made by the Western Australian Government (Conservation and Land Management Department) with a United States group, to undertake research into conocuruone, a compound found in smokebush. Dambartung asserts that this agreement has failed to acknowledge Nyoongar knowledge or ownership of the smokebush and its medicinal qualities. This agreement potentially contravenes the native title rights of the Nyoongar people in relation to their knowledge and ownership of the smokebush plant.[93]

An examination of copyright law illustrates some of the difficulties that arise through the use of Australian laws to protect Indigenous Australian cultural and intellectual property rights. A significant issue is the focus of Australian laws on individual rights; most Indigenous Australian cultural and intellectual property rights are held communally. In *Yumbulul v Reserve Bank of Australia* (the 10 dollar note case),[94] the Federal Court found that communal rights were not protected by Australian copyright laws. Nonetheless, some recognition of communal rights has been made by the Federal Court in *Milpurrurru v Indofurn*,[95] in that it awarded damages to the claimants collectively, leaving them to distribute the damages themselves according to their Indigenous common law rights.[96]

Another difficulty arises in proving originality and authorship, as the work of an Indigenous Australian artist often draws on the wealth of their cultural heritage, including pre-existing language group designs and motifs. In *Yumbulul*, French J had no difficulty finding that originality was proven even though the work was derived from a pre-existing tradition. Similarly, in *Milpurrurru* the court found (on the facts) that there was sufficient scope for an individual Indigenous Australian artist to interpret pre-existing cultural expressions, to satisfy the requirement of originality. Golvan also argues that an equitable interest may arise in favour of the "traditional" owners of a design that is reproduced or reinterpreted in a later work.[97] Another aspect of this difficulty is that the copyright laws protect the expression of an idea, but not the *style* of expression. Therefore, the cross-hatch or rarkk style of painting used by artists from the Arnhem land regions gains no protection under Australian law.[98]

Finally, another significant issue arises as to whether copyright law can provide adequate compensation to Indigenous Australians for the loss suffered through the reproduction of their cultural and intellectual property. Australian copyright laws are

---

92   Puri, above, n 70, p 157-58.

93   Betti, L, "Test Case on Cultural Right to 'Cure'", *Western Australian*, 10 November 1997. See also, in respect of New Zealand, Waitangi Tribunal, October 1991, Claim No 262; Maori claim to recognition of rights over Indigenous knowledge of flora and fauna, and rights over the genetic resource contained therein.

94   (1991) 21 IPR 481.

95   Above, n 89.

96   Janke, above, n 83, p 43.

97   Golvan, C, "Aboriginal art and the Protection of Indigenous Cultural Rights" (1992) 2(56) *Aboriginal Law Bulletin* 5. See Hardie, M, "Casenotes: Bulun Bulun and Milpurrurru v R & T Textile" (1997) 3(90) *Aboriginal Law Bulletin* 18.

98   Janke, above, n 83, p 41.

directed at protecting commercial – rather than moral or cultural – interests. They provide no *secure* way of preventing reproduction of secret/sacred material, which would be deeply offensive to Indigenous common law.

However, in *Milpurrurru*, the plaintiffs argued that this type of injury should be recognised in the damages awarded to them, as they would be subjected to punishment under Indigenous common law for allowing the design to be reproduced. The Court acknowledged the validity of this submission, and awarded damages under s 115(4)(b) of the *Copyright Act* 1968 (Cth), for flagrant infringement of the plaintiff's copyright, to reflect the culturally based harm suffered by them.[99]

It remains to be seen whether other activities which are offensive to Indigenous common law, might also be compensable, for instance, the reproduction of a design in a demeaning or trivial fashion.[100] There may be further potential to argue that aggravated or exemplary damages (where they are available) should be awarded against defendants who commit acts offensive to Indigenous common law and/or who act with "contumelious disregard"[101] of Indigenous cultural and intellectual property rights.

Hunting, fishing and gathering rights

The Draft Declaration recognises the rights of indigenous peoples to their lands, territories and *resources*, including the enjoyment of their traditional economic activities (art 21), and the right to "own, develop, control and use ... the flora and fauna and other resources that they have traditionally owned or otherwise ... used" (art 26).

These rights are also arguably encapsulated in the cultural rights protected under the ICCPR and the ICESCR, and related documents. Indeed, the United Nations Human Rights Committee has observed that "culture manifests itself in many forms, including a particular way of life associated with the use of land resources, specially in the case of indigenous peoples. That right may include such traditional activities as fishing or hunting and the right to live in reserves protected by law".[102]

Before *Mabo (No 2),* Indigenous common law hunting, gathering and fishing rights were only recognised by the domestic legal system if legislation had been enacted which specifically gave this recognition.[103] Hunting, fishing and gathering rights are expressly recognised as native title rights within s 223 of the NTA subject, of course, to meeting the requirements related to proving native title.

This assertion of native title in the form of hunting, fishing and gathering rights and interests may also provide a defence to a prosecution under flora and fauna protection legislation, for the gathering of bush foods or medicines, hunting game, or fishing. This defence has been accepted by the Supreme Courts of both New

---

99   *Milpurrurru* (1994) 30 IPR 209 at 244-49.

100   See Puri, above, n 70, pp 134-37; and Orr, G, "Damages for Loss of Fulfilment in Indigenous Community Life" (1997) 4(6) *Indigenous Law Bulletin* 17.

101   See *Lamb v Cotogno* (1987) 164 CLR 1.

102   Human Rights Committee, above, n 73, pp 235-36.

103   For example, *Land Rights Act* 1983 (NSW).

South Wales in *Mason v Tritton*[104] (for the gathering of abalone) and Western Australia in *Derschaw v The Queen*[105] (for taking fish), in relation to native title rights over marine areas (submerged lands). Kirby P, in *Mason v Tritton*, clearly indicates that the defence would also apply to "dry lands".[106]

The defence was also recognised by a Queensland Magistrate, who dismissed charges laid under the State's fauna conservation laws, against Mr Murandoo Yanner for the taking of two salt-water crocodiles.[107] The Magistrate was not swayed by the prosecution's assertion that Mr Yanner had not used "traditional hunting methods". However, the Queensland Court of Appeal recently overturned this decision, finding that the fauna laws had extinguished Native Title.[108] Mr Yanner intends to appeal this decision in the High Court.[109]

The question of how far beyond the coastline that marine native title rights may be claimed is more problematic. The matter depends both on how far the common law can be said to extend beyond the low water mark of Australia's shores and on the manner in which sovereignty over these areas was acquired by the Commonwealth. Arguably the common law extends with full force up to 12 nautical miles (over which the Commonwealth exercises full sovereignty), and at least has some force to the nation's 200 nautical mile limit.[110] Even so, in relation to the second matter, Cullen argues that the process involved in acquiring rights offshore is legally different to that onshore, and so:

> Indigenous sea rights exist as matter of fact and their "origins" are not founded on any concept of English land law, or ... international law, as they depend entirely for their existence on observance by [I]ndigenous people of their traditional laws and customs [which] ... pre-date international or municipal law notions of sovereignty ... With such a factual basis, recognition by the common law need not necessarily be determined by the application of historical common law rules, although it might require consistency with existing Australian law.[111]

---

104 (1994) 34 NSWLR 572.

105 *Derschaw v The Queen* (1996) 90 A Crim R 9 (affirming Heenan J's judgment in *Sutton v Derschaw* (1995) 82 A Crim R 318). Both of these cases, as well as other international jurisprudence which support them, are discussed in Meyers, G, and others, *A Sea Change in Land Rights Law: The Extension of Native Title to Australia's Offshore Areas* (Australian Institute of Aboriginal and Torres Strait Islander Studies (AIATSIS), Canberra, 1996), pp 23-31. For international jurisprudence, see, in respect of New Zealand, *Te Weehi v Regional Fisheries Officer* [1986] 1 NZLR 680; and in respect of Canada, *R v Sparrow* [1990] 1 SCR 1075.

106 In *Mason v Tritton* (1994) 34 NSWLR 572 at 580, Kirby P found such a right could be found to exist in connection with the use, possession and occupation of submerged lands, in a manner different from, but consistent with the use, possession and occupation of dry lands.

107 Meade, A, "State challenges acquittal of activist who ate crocodile", *Weekend Australian*, 31 May - 1 June 1997.

108 *Eaton v Yanner* (unreported, CA (Qld), Fitzgerald P, McPherson and Moynihan JJ, 27 February 1998).

109 *The 7:30 Report*, ABC-TV, 12 March 1998.

110 This is discussed in detail in Meyers, above, n 105, at pp 34-36.

111 Meyers, above, n 105, p 40: The recognition of native title in offshore areas is discussed in detail in pp 33-52. See also Watson, J, above n 27.

A question remaining, then, is whether hunting, fishing and gathering rights can be asserted as native title rights over land, coastal and inland waterways where native title has been lawfully extinguished.

One way may be the use of the defence outlined in *Walden v Hensler*,[112] in which the defendant, Walden, pleaded an honest claim of right in relation to an offence under the *Fauna Conservation Act* 1974 (Qld) for the taking of a bush turkey. Walden argued that he honestly believed that he had a legal claim of right to take the bird, as he was exercising Indigenous common law hunting rights. The High Court held that this defence could be made out where the defendant had such an honest belief, and the defendant *also* believed that Australian law recognised the right claimed – it being immaterial whether the Indigenous common law actually is recognised within Australian law. Thus, if a defendant could establish the honesty of their *belief* that native title rights did exist over an area, this defence would be successful.

Alternatively, rather than reliance upon the NTA which links usufructuary rights to ownership of land, Löfgren suggests that the existence of usufructuary rights could be based upon a *sui generis* right[113] and/or an indigenous right which is a human right, guaranteed by international law.

Thus, usufructuary rights can be asserted by Indigenous Australian peoples on the basis of their distinct identity as indigenous peoples,[114] and/or on the basis of their cultural rights, and thus can influence the development of the common law.[115]

THE ADMINISTRATION OF CRIMINAL JUSTICE

The experience of Indigenous Australians within the criminal justice system presents an overwhelming range of issues, given their continuously alarming rates of arrest, detention and deaths in custody.[116] This section focuses on aspects of their experience which reflect the denial of Indigenous Australian cultural rights and the practice of discriminatory law enforcement processes. These are not exhaustive of the issues raised, but we believe, are fundamental to the problems experienced by Indigenous Australians within the administration of criminal justice.

Cultural rights

As noted above, in *Walker*, Mason CJ held that Indigenous criminal laws have been extinguished by the enactment of criminal legislation.[117] This is despite the continued practice of Indigenous criminal laws and their recognition within

---

112　(1987) 61 ALJR 646. See also, *R v Craigie* (unreported, Dist Ct (NSW), 1979) discussed in ALRC, No 31, above, n 7, paras 434-35.

113　*Delgamuukw* v *Queen in Right of British Columbia* (unreported, SC (Canada), Lamer CJ, La Forest, L'Hereux-Dube, Cory, McLachlin and Major JJ, 11 December 1997, No 23799).

114　Löfgren, above, n 15.

115　See *Mabo (No 2)* (1992) 175 CLR 1 at 42-43, per Brennan J.

116　RCADIC, above, n 2; Halstead, B, McDonald, D and Dalton, V, *Deaths in Custody* No 8 (Australian Institute of Criminology, Canberra, February 1995).

117　*Walker v NSW* (1994) 182 CLR 45 at 50.

sentencing decisions in several jurisdictions.[118] Mason CJ referred to the principle of equality before the law, finding that the existence of two different sets of laws would contradict this principle.[119] However, as discussed above in relation to Equality Rights, this formal reading of the notion of equality is out of kilter with international jurisprudence, and so the continued denial of the Indigenous criminal justice system contravenes the cultural rights of Indigenous Australians.

Further, the rejection of legal pluralism involving Indigenous common law ignores the pluralism already inherent within the Australian federation, which is comprised of three tiers of law making authority, each of which is supposed to complement the others. Indeed, Indigenous dispute resolution processes to deal with criminal matters are practised or are under consideration in several jurisdictions.[120]

Nonetheless, Indigenous criminal and other laws may provide defences to charges laid under Commonwealth, State or Territory laws.[121] As discussed in the previous section, the assertion of native title rights may, for instance, offer scope to defend some criminal matters.

However, the overall question remains: are cultural rights supported *within* the criminal justice system? We would suggest not and examine this in the context of language to illustrate the significance of cultural rights and practices within the fair administration of criminal justice.

Indigenous language is an aspect of the cultural rights protected under international human rights law.[122] These rights are reinforced within the administration of criminal justice by art 2 of the *Code of Conduct for Law Enforcement Officials*[123] which requires law enforcement officials to "respect and protect human dignity and maintain and uphold the human rights of all persons". Further, art 14 of the ICCPR, guarantees the right to be informed of charges in a language understood by the accused, and the right to an interpreter if (as in our context) a person cannot understand or does not speak English.

Within domestic laws, the interrogation of Indigenous Australians is governed to some degree by the principles set out in *R v Anunga*,[124] which are reflected in s 23H of the *Crimes Act* 1914 (Cth), and in various Police Standing Orders. Basically, the *Anunga* rules require police to provide an interpreter where an Indigenous Australian is not fluent in English and state that it is desirable that the person have a "prisoner's friend" present during the interrogation. These rules are aimed to ensure that communication between police and an accused person is

---

118 For example, *R v Walker* (unreported, SC (NT), Martin CJ, SCC No 46 of 1993).

119 (1994) 182 CLR 45 at 49-50.

120 Miller, B, "Crime Prevention and Socio-Legal Reform in Aboriginal Communities in Queensland" (1991) 2(49) *Aboriginal Law Bulletin* 10. Such schemes also exist in Aotearoa/New Zealand, and tribal and native courts have been operating in the Papua New Guinea, Canada and the United States for many years.

121 See, Blokland, J and Flynn, M, "Five Issues for the Criminal Law After Mabo", and Yeo, S, "The Recognition of Aboriginality by Australian Criminal Law", both in Bird, Martin and Nielsen, above, n 35.

122 ICCPR: arts 4(1), 26, 27; ICESCR: art 2(2); Draft Declaration.

123 GA Res, 17 December 1979.

124 (1976) 11 ALR 412. See also, RCADIC, above, n 2, Rec 99.

effective, as well as to remove the adversity Indigenous Australians encounter when subjected to police interrogation.

The significance of language may be most obvious in relation to those Indigenous Australians who retain their own language as their first language and who are not fluent in English. However, Indigenous Australians who are fluent in their usage of English can be misunderstood due to cultural differences in communication practices and differences in language usage. Linguist Diana Eades has documented many of the issues raised in legal proceedings by the use of "Aboriginal English" and Creoles (or krioles) by Indigenous Australians, as well as differences in English usage.[125]

For instance, in *R v Izumi*,[126] Ms Izumi was charged with attempted murder. During the police interview she was asked what her intention was when she used the weapon against the victim. She replied, "I wanted to kill him with that thing". At her trial, the admissibility of the record of interview was challenged on the basis of evidence from a linguist that Ms Izumi's use of the word "kill" was influenced by Aboriginal Creole. In Creole, the word "kill" has several meanings, including "kill dead" and merely "to harm". The police questioning Ms Izumi did not clarify which of these meanings she had intended during her interview. On this basis the trial judge excluded the record of interview, and subsequently a nolle prosequi was entered in relation to the charge of attempted murder.

Misunderstanding of cultural communications styles can also occur when body language is misread. For instance, some members of the judiciary have assumed that an Indigenous Australian who does not look them in the eye is untrustworthy or is lying.[127] Instead this behaviour by many Indigenous Australians is a sign of respect for an authority figure.

The importance of language and communication, and the relevance of cultural rights, is not confined to dealings with police and the courts, as *R v Kina*[128] illustrates. Ms Kina was convicted of murdering her de facto husband. Due to a lack of cultural awareness in communication styles and practices, her legal representatives did not obtain instructions from her which raised the potential of provocation and self-defence to the charge. On appeal to the Queensland Court of Appeal, a new trial was ordered on the basis that she had been denied adequate legal representation.

Thus, if language and non-verbal communications are not considered within their appropriate cultural context, it can lead to improper convictions. Such convictions could be challenged where there is a failure to provide an interpreter or a failure to consider an Indigenous Australian person's statements or testimony in the context of their cultural language usage. This would contravene the right to fair

---

125 Eades, D, *Aboriginal English and the Law: Communicating with Aboriginal Clients* (CLE Department of the Queensland Law Society, Brisbane, 1992); and Eades, D, (ed), *Language in Evidence: Issues Confronting Aboriginal and Multicultural Australia* (UNSW Press, Sydney, 1995).

126 Trezise, P, "Casenotes: *R v Jean Denise Izumi*" (1996) 3(79) *Aboriginal Law Bulletin* 17. The casenote also discusses the application of the *Anunga rules* to Ms Izumi's police interview.

127 Personal experience. See Cunneen, C, "Judicial Racism", in McKillop, S, (ed), *Aboriginal Justice Issues*, Proceedings of the Australian Institute of Criminology Conference, 23-25 June 1992 (Australian Institute of Criminology, Canberra, 1993).

128 Unreported, CA (Qld), 29 November 1993.

trial provided in art 14, raising potential for argument within domestic courts to require consistency with international legal principles, as well as a complaint under the First Optional Protocol.

Discrimination in the administration of criminal justice

Indigenous Australians feature in the criminal justice system in overwhelming numbers. The RCADIC documented the myriad of factors which contribute to their overrepresentation, and highlighted the historically poor relationship between the Indigenous Australian community and police as a significant contributing factor.[129]

Cunneen identifies the overpolicing of Indigenous Australian communities as leading to their high rates of arrest and detention for relatively minor public order offences, contributing to the rate of custodial deaths.[130] Its effects are also psychologically damaging to Indigenous Australian communities and Cunneen argues[131] that various actions by police against Indigenous Australians breach Australia's international obligations under the ICCPR (art 7) and the *Convention Against Torture & Other Cruel, Inhuman or Degrading Treatment or Punishment* (CAT),[132] as they amount to cruel, unusual punishment or to torture. They could also breach arts 2 and 5 of the *Code of Conduct for Law Enforcement Officials*.

The practices Cunneen identifies include: the illegal detentions of intoxicated persons, which endure longer than permitted by the relevant legislation; the failure to abide by various police regulations in the treatment of Indigenous Australian prisoners; raids which have, at best, questionable legal status;[133] the use of paramilitary forces and policing practices;[134] and ill treatment amounting to torture as defined in international law.

He describes the effects of these practices on Indigenous Australian peoples as equivalent to those suffered by refugees who have been subjected to torture.[135] This psychological damage is of particular significance to assess accurately compensation claims by those who experience such ill-treatment. These matters may also be highly relevant to Indigenous Australians charged with offences against police.[136]

In a similar vein, Barker argues that mandatory sentencing laws and practices (as currently exist in some Australian jurisdictions), particularly against young

---

129 RCADIC, above, n 2.

130 Cunneen, C, "Policing and Aboriginal Communities: Is the Concept of Over-Policing Useful?", in Cunneen, C, (ed), *Aboriginal Perspectives on Criminal Justice* (Sydney University Institute of Criminology, Sydney, 1992), p 31. See also Leicester, S, "Policing in Wiluna" (1995) 20(1) *Alternative Law Journal*; 3(72) *Aboriginal Law Bulletin* 16.

131 Cunneen, C, "Detention, Torture, Terror and the Australian State: Aboriginal People, Criminal Justice and Neocolonialism", in Bird, Martin and Nielsen, above, n 35.

132 GA Res, 10 December 1984.

133 Such as the police shooting of David Gundy: see Cunneen, above, n 130, pp 22-24.

134 See RCADIC, above, n 2, Rec 61.

135 Cunneen, above, n 131, pp 24-31, 33-36.

136 See, Yeo, above, n 121, pp 241-42, 248-49; and van Gelder, V, "Casenote: Factors in Sentencing Indigenous Women" (1996) 3(85) *Indigenous Law Bulletin* 27.

people, breach Indigenous Australian rights under the ICCPR and CERD.[137] He also argues that rights under the ICCPR may be breached where an Indigenous Australian person dies in custody.[138]

Ironically, the corollary to the over-policing of Indigenous Australian communities is the under-policing of complaints they make of offences committed against them.[139] Indigenous Australian women, in particular, are critical of the failure by police to respond to their complaints of sexual assault and other forms of violence.[140] Under-policing is a matter which can be properly subject to claims in tort for negligence or breach of statutory duty, complaints to the police ombudsman, and complaints of racial discrimination under the relevant commonwealth and state legislation. In international law complaints could be made for breaches of equality rights of the guarantee to equality before the law, in the ICCPR and CERD.

FAMILY AND KIN

A fundamental aspect of any society is the way in which the relationships between individuals and groups are organised. At international law, everyone has the right to found a family,[141] and the "family is the natural and fundamental group unit of society and is entitled to protection by society and the State".[142] Article 30 of the *Convention on the Rights of the Child* (CROC)[143] guarantees the right to children of ethnic, religious or linguistic minorities to enjoy, "in community with other members of his or her group, ... his or her own culture, to profess and practise his or her own religion, or to use his or her own language".

The Draft Declaration recognises "the right of indigenous families and communities to retain shared responsibility for the upbringing, training, education and well-being of their children" (Preamble), a full guarantee against genocide, ethnocide, or any other form of violence, "including the removal of indigenous children from their families and communities under any pretext" (art 6), and rights of indigenous peoples to retain, revive and to exercise their unique cultural and social

---

137　ICCPR: arts 2(1), 9(1), 10(3), 14(4), 24(1), 26; CERD: arts 5(a), 2(1)(c): Barker, above, n 4, p 41. See, in particular, *Crime (Serious and Repeat Offenders) Sentencing Act* 1992 (WA), *Juvenile Justice Act* 1983 (NT) (as amended), *Juvenile Justice Act* 1992 (Qld), and the *Children (Protection and Parental Responsibility) Act* 1997 (NSW). The human rights of young people within the criminal justice system are discussed in ALRC/HREOC, 1997, *Seen and Heard: Priority for Children in the Legal Process*, Report No 84 (AGPS, Canberra, 1997). For an account of the over-representation of young Indigenous Australians within the criminal justice system, see Garth, L and Cunneen, C, *Aboriginal Over-representation and Discretionary Decisions in the NSW Juvenile Justice System* (Juvenile Justice Advisory Council, Sydney, 1995).

138　Articles 2(1), 6(1), 7, 10(1), 10(2)(b), 10(3), 14(4), 24(1), 26, 27; Barker, above, n 4, p 42. See also the *Basic Principles for the Treatment of Prisoners*, GA Res, 14 December 1990.

139　Leicester, above, n 130, p 17.

140　Atkinson, J, "Violence Against Aboriginal Women: Restitution of Community Law – The Way Forward" (1990) 2(46) *Aboriginal Law Bulletin* 6.

141　UDHR art 16.

142　ICCPR art 23. See also ICESCR art 10 and *Convention on the Rights of the Child art 5*.

143　GA Res, 20 November 1989. See also the *Declaration of the Rights of the Child*, GA Res, 20 November 1959.

practices, which would include laws and practices concerned with family and kinship relations.

Thus, in the international forum, the unique features of indigenous family structures are emphasised as deserving of protection. However, within the domestic sphere, these structures gain little recognition. Indeed, as HREOC documents through its *Bringing them home* Report,[144] many of the "welfare" practices implemented in relation to Indigenous Australian children and families are contrary to Australia's international obligations under the Genocide Convention.[145]

Not surprisingly, perhaps, Indigenous Australians have shown a marked reluctance to use court processes, including the Family Court,[146] and prefer to use Indigenous common law to resolve family issues. Thus, Indigenous family issues may be of most relevance in custody or child welfare proceedings, particularly where only one parent is an Indigenous Australian. The focus of this discussion will, then, be on the issues related to Indigenous Australian children. To put this in an appropriate context, we will begin by briefly looking at the Indigenous Australian "family".

Customary marriage and the Indigenous Australian "family"

Indigenous common law defines marriage and family structures, and may be far more complex than that reflected within Australian customs and laws. Generally, Indigenous common law marriages may be legally recognised as de facto relationships.[147] Nonetheless, some legal rights and benefits may only be available to or more easily available to those in a "legal" marriage. For example, "traditional" marriages are only recognised within adoption legislation in Victoria, South Australia and the Northern Territory, as giving the biological father the right to be consulted on the adoption of an ex-nuptial child.[148] Thus, it is important to consider whether an Indigenous common law marriage can meet the defined requirements giving rise to the rights and benefits of those who are "married".

Where this is not the case, it would be valuable to consider the use of anti-discrimination laws to challenge action or policies which may discriminate (both directly or indirectly) on the basis of marital status. Alternatively, consideration should be given to complaints based on cultural rights (as discussed above), where Indigenous common law marriages are not recognised. In this instance a complaint of racial discrimination may also be relevant.

---

144 HREOC, above, n 2.

145 See *Kruger v Commonwealth* (1997) 71 ALJR 991 (Casenote: (1997) 4(6) *Indigenous Law Bulletin* 22). Current welfare practices are discussed below.

146 As it is irrelevant to their needs, or because of unfavourable experiences with courts: HREOC & ALRC, *Speaking for Ourselves: Children and the Legal Process*, Issues Paper 18 (AGPS, Canberra, 1996), para 52.

147 Compare the definition of de facto relationships with the description of customary marriages given in Sutton, P, "Aboriginal Customary Marriage – Determination and Definition" (1985) 1(12) *Aboriginal Law Bulletin* 13.

148 HREOC, above, n 2, Ch 22 "Adoption". See also, Wilkinson, D, "Marrying Law and Custom" (1995) 3(72) *Aboriginal Law Bulletin* 23/20(1) *Alternative Law Journal* 23.

The responsibilities of "extended" family members – such as, aunts, uncles, cousins and grandparents – in Indigenous Australian families, can be far more significant than those within the dominant "nuclear family" model. For instance, in the Tiwi family, primary responsibility for raising children lies with Tiwi women, but with several of the women related to the child – rather than *only* the biological mother. So, a Tiwi child immediately has several mothers, though the biological parent retains ultimate responsibility. Child rearing, then, is not exclusively the right *or* responsibility of the biological parents, and instead children are raised in large extended families.[149] These practices are reflected in art 5 of CROC, which requires nation states to recognise the "responsibilities, rights and duties of parents or ... members of the extended family or community as provided for by local custom".

A fundamental problem, then, arises for Indigenous Australian families in their use of the *Family Law Act* 1975 (Cth) (FLA), as its emphasis is upon parent-child relationships as understood within the "nuclear family". In terms of "parental responsibility", s 61C only recognises biological parents, and fails to recognise the child-rearing obligations of others.[150] Although, s 60D(3) of the Act discusses "relatives", there is no recognition within its definition of Indigenous common law kinship relations.[151] Thus, other family members recognised as "parents" by Indigenous common law may be excluded from having a "say" in the child's welfare by s 60B(2).[152]

Indigenous Australian family laws and structures arguably gain international recognition under the right to found a family, particularly when read alongside the cultural rights and religious rights (described above) of indigenous peoples. A failure to recognise these rights, or action which interferes with their exercise, may therefore breach international human rights, giving rise to a complaint under the ICCPR or CERD. At domestic level, all of the international instruments which recognise these rights have the potential to influence the development of the common law and government policy.

Growing up with culture – a right of Indigenous Australian children

Parental responsibility, residence and contact proceedings in the Family Court

Section 68F(2)(f) of the FLA specifically requires the Court to take into account "any need to maintain a connection with the lifestyle, culture and traditions of Aboriginal peoples or Torres Strait Islanders", in determining the "best interests of the child". This does not oblige the Court to prefer an Indigenous Australian parent in a dispute.

The Full Court of the Family Court has recognised the importance of culture *and* of the experiences of Indigenous Australian children in determining the "best interests of the child". In *In Marriage of B and R*, the Full Court acknowledged the

---

149 Davis, R and Dikstein, J, "It Just Doesn't Fit" (1997) 22(2) *Alternative Law Journal* 64.

150 HREOC, above, n 2, Ch 23 "Family Law: Kinship Obligations".

151 Davis and Dikstein, above, n 149.

152 Ibid.

significance of "Aboriginality" in determining the child's "best interests", by virtue of the right in art 30 of CROC, and acknowledged the importance of expert evidence related to the lived reality of Indigenous Australians stating that:[153]

> It is not just that [A]boriginal children should be encouraged to learn about their culture, and to take pride in it in the manner in which any other child might be so encouraged. … The struggles which [Aboriginal people] face in a predominantly white culture are … unique. Evidence which makes reference to these types of experiences and struggles travels well beyond any broad "right to know one's culture" assertion. It addresses the reality of Aboriginal experience [which is] relevant … to any consideration of the welfare of the child[.][154]

The Court also suggested that it would be expected that a separate representative should be appointed for every Indigenous Australian child involved in a parenting dispute, to ensure that all relevant issues are put before the court.[155] The weight properly to be attached by the court to "Aboriginality" can be supported by reference to the international instruments mentioned above. This position can only be strengthened by the adoption of the Draft Declaration.

Fostering and adoption

Generally speaking, the right of an Indigenous Australian child to grow up within its family, is respected unless there is some intervention in the family by State or federal authorities. However, such disturbances occur all too often in many Indigenous Australian families.[156] This intervention may result either in a child being fostered temporarily or, in some cases, may result in adoption.

The international legal principles related to the fostering and adoption of children are described in the *Declaration on Social and Legal Principles relating to the Protection and Welfare of Children, with Special Reference to Foster Placement and Adoption Nationally and Internationally*.[157] Generally, these principles place primacy on retaining the child in the care of their natural parent (art 2); if the child must be taken out of that care then they should be placed in the care of relatives of the child's parents, or another appropriate family (art 4). In placing a child in such care, then the best interests of the child are a paramount consideration. In relation to indigenous children, these principles should be read alongside the rights defined in

---

153 (1995) 19 Fam LR 594 at 601-06. The Full Court's judgment provides an extensive discussion of the "history" of cases before the Family Court concerned with the welfare of Aboriginal children in custody disputes (at 606-15); as well as relevant international jurisprudence: at 615-20. See also, Buti, T, Casenote: "Court Decides Child to Stay with Indigenous Mother" (1996) 3(86) *Indigenous Law Bulletin* 12: Buti documents the effects of forced removal, which is of relevance to the construction of compensation claims.

154 (1995) 19 Fam LR 594 at 602.

155 (1995) 19 Fam LR 594 at 624.

156 Indigenous children are over-represented in care and protection proceedings throughout Australia. "The NSW Department of Community Services acknowledges that the Department is considered to be an agency that takes away your kids": HREOC & ALRC, above, n 146, paras 7.51, 7.10. See also Payne, S, "Aboriginal Women and the Criminal Justice System" (1990) 2(46) *Aboriginal Law Bulletin* 9: Payne documents the effects of removal on children *and* their mothers.

157 GA Res, 3 December 1986.

art 30 of CROC, so that primacy is given to placing the child within its Indigenous Australian family, before *any* other options are considered.

This right has been given some recognition by Australian law, in the form of the Aboriginal Child Placement Principle (ACPP). Its practice is most relevant to State child welfare legislation.[158] Broadly, legislative recognition of the principle requires two things. First, *before* an Indigenous Australian child is placed in care outside its natural family, the relevant Aboriginal child care agency must be contacted.[159] Secondly, the order of priority for placement of the child should be:

- A member of the child's extended family;
- Other members of the child's Aboriginal community who have the correct relationship with the child in accordance with Aboriginal Customary Law;
- Other Aboriginal families living in close proximity;
- Other placement options.[160]

In relation to adoption, similar issues arise about the application of the ACPP. The ACPP is recognised within adoption legislation in only four jurisdictions, and within the relevant policy of the others.[161]

However, a significant difference exists in the Indigenous common law of Torres Strait Islanders and that of other Indigenous Australians. Torres Strait Islander law recognises customary adoption practices,[162] akin to legal adoptions within State and Territory systems. However, the concept of adoption is (generally) contrary to all other Indigenous common law.[163] The issue to be considered, then, is whether the adoption of an Indigenous Australian child is contrary to the relevant Indigenous common law – either because the practice is not recognised, or because the manner in which the adoption is effected is not consistent with cultural practices or the ACPP. If so, the child's cultural rights would be breached, on the basis of the arguments made above.

This could also constitute a forcible transfer of a child, contrary to the Genocide Convention. Indeed, it may also breach rights contained in the ICCPR,[164] giving rise to a potential complaint under the First Optional Protocol.

Generally, then, the human rights specific to Indigenous Australian children in relation to welfare practices and adoption are based on the ICCPR (cultural rights) and CROC. As these are both ratified treaties, significant weight can be given to these Conventions within domestic litigation both in relation to the legislative

---

158 *Children (Care and Protection) Act* 1987 (NSW); *Community Welfare Act* 1983 (NT); *Youth Court Act* 1993 (SA), *Young Offenders Act* 1993 (SA), *Children's Protection Act* 1993 (SA); *Children and Young Persons Act* 1989 (Vic). The other States and Territories recognise the principle in child welfare policy.

159 Except in New South Wales.

160 Wilkinson, D, "Aboriginal Child Placement Principle" (1994) 3(71) *Aboriginal Law Bulletin* 13 at 13.

161 *Adoption Act* 1993 (ACT); *Adoption of Children Act* 1994 (NT); *Adoption Act* 1988 (SA); *Adoption Act* 1984 (Vic).

162 Ban, P, "Slow Progress: the Legal Recognition of Torres Strait Islander Customary Adoption Practice" (1997) 4(7) *Indigenous Law Bulletin* 11; see *Casimel v Insurance Corporation of British Columbia* (1993) 106 DLR (4th) 720.

163 HREOC, above, n 2, Ch 22 "Adoption".

164 Articles 8, 9, 10, 12, 17, 18, 23, 24, 26, 27: Barker, above, n 4, p 42.

expressions of the ACPP and those expressions of it within government policy.[165] The exercise of these rights by Indigenous Australian children is central to their enjoyment of their cultural rights. Furthermore as the next generation of Indigenous Australians, these rights are also central to the continuation of Indigenous Australian culture.

CONCLUSION

Several significant issues could not be discussed within this chapter, which are also of great significance to the human rights of Indigenous Australian peoples. These include health,[166] housing and adequate standards of living, rights to social security, rights in employment, and the right to education. By not addressing these matters, we are not dismissing their significance to Indigenous Australian human rights. Instead, the issues we have chosen tend, in our view, to reflect matters that most conspicuously raise human rights issues and are most likely to arise in the context of legal practice. There are many excellent resources available to explore all of these issues further.[167]

This chapter, then, has really only begun a discussion of the many human rights applicable to Indigenous Australian peoples. Nonetheless, it illustrates the unique nature of the human rights claims of Indigenous Australian peoples and the central importance of their culture within those claims. The culture of Indigenous Australians includes their common law, their connection to their lands, their traditions, family and kin structures, their knowledge, artistic and other cultural expressions, and the control over and ability to pass on these distinctive features to their future generations.

International law has potential – both within the international and the domestic forums – to bolster the claims by Indigenous Australians to the recognition and protection of these singular features of their identity and tradition. "The eyes of the world are watching now"[168] and the power of that scrutiny – effected through international and domestic legal mechanisms, and/or through political pressure – must be pursued so as to effect human rights for Indigenous Australians.

---

165 *Minister of State for Immigration and Ethnic Affairs v Teoh* (1995) 183 CLR 273; on which see discussion in Ch 4 by McMillan and Williams in this volume.

166 See Barker, above, n 4, pp 41-42.

167 See in particular *Indigenous Law Bulletin* (formerly *Aboriginal Law Bulletin*), Published by the Aboriginal Law Centre, UNSW, 1985-; *Australian Indigenous Law Reporter*, Published by the Aboriginal Law Centre, UNSW, 1996- . McCorquodale, J, *Aborigines and the Law: A Digest* (Aboriginal Studies Press, Canberra, 1987). An extensive list of references is given in the bibliography of McRae, H, Nettheim, G and Beacroft, L, above, n 6. Websites: Australian Institute for Aboriginal and Torres Strait Islander Studies, Canberra, <http://www.aiatsis.gov.au/>; Council for Aboriginal Reconciliation, Reconciliation and Social Justice Library, <http://www.austlii. edu.au/rsjlibrary/>; Indigenous Peoples Centre for Documentation, Research and Information, <http:/www.docip.org>; Researching Indigenous Peoples Rights under international law, <http://www.law.uc.edu:81/Diana/ipr.html>; Aboriginal law and legislation online, <http://www. bloorstreet.com/ 300block/ablawleg.htm>.

168 From "Biko", by Peter Gabriel (Peter Gabriel Ltd, 1990).

6

CRIMINAL LAW AND HUMAN RIGHTS

Simon Bronitt* and Maree Ayers**

INTRODUCTION

This chapter will explore how international human rights law impacts on domestic criminal proceedings. The range of laws potentially affected, both directly and indirectly, by international human rights law is broad. Rather than address the human rights dimensions of discrete areas of the substantive criminal law, the topics selected for discussion in this chapter are those considered to have relevance and application to criminal matters *generally*; namely, the right to a fair trial (focusing specifically on the right to silence, the rules governing hearsay and prosecution disclosure), the judicial discretion to exclude evidence obtained by law enforcement misconduct and the role of administrative law in police and prosecution decision-making.

The aim of the chapter is to illustrate how human rights arguments based on international legal sources (including the cognate jurisprudence of the European Court of Human Rights and related common law jurisdictions) can broaden the repertoire of legal arguments available to both the defence and the prosecution. Since human rights law may be a novel jurisprudential terrain for many legal practitioners, our subsidiary aim is to provide an overview of the key sources of international and domestic law which impact upon human rights and the administration of criminal justice.

THE RIGHT TO FAIR TRIAL

Transnational perspectives

The *International Covenant on Civil and Political Rights*[1] (the ICCPR) contains a number of due process safeguards which have the potential to impact on domestic criminal practice. Article 14 guarantees the general right, in both criminal and civil proceedings, to a "fair and public hearing by a competent, independent and

---

*   I would like to thank Alison Smith for her research assistance and my colleagues, Fiona Wheeler, Robert McCorquodale and Peter Bailey, for their interest and assistance. I would also like to thank the Australian Institute of Criminology for supporting this research by hosting my sabbatical leave during 1997.

** This chapter does not represent the views of the Commonwealth Director of Public Prosecutions, in which office the author is a senior legal officer.

1   Aust TS 1980 No 23; 999 UNTS 171; New York, adopted 16 December 1966, entered into force 23 March 1976.

impartial tribunal established by law". Article 14(3) then specifically stipulates the following "minimum guarantees" for those accused of committing a criminal offence:

(a) To be informed promptly and in detail in a language which he understands of the nature and cause of the charge against him;

(b) To have adequate time and facilities for the preparation of his defence and to communicate with counsel of his own choosing;

(c) To be tried without undue delay;

(d) To be tried in his presence, and to defend himself in person or through legal assistance of his own choosing; to be informed, if he does not have legal assistance, of this right; and to have legal assistance assigned to him, in any case where the interests of justice so require, and without payment by him in any such case if he does not have sufficient means to pay for it;

(e) To examine, or have examined, the witnesses against him and to obtain the attendance and examination of witnesses on his behalf under the same conditions as witnesses against him;

(f) To have the free assistance of an interpreter if he cannot understand or speak the language used in court;

(g) Not to be compelled to testify against himself or to confess guilt.

The development of the "common law" right to a fair trial by the Australian courts over the last decade illustrates the increasing influence of international human rights law on domestic law. The idea of the fair trial as a distinct right protected by the common law first emerged in *Jago v District Court of New South Wales*.[2] In this case, the High Court considered whether undue pre-trial delay violated the accused's right to a fair trial resulting in a miscarriage of justice. Although the High Court made no reference to the ICCPR in support of this common law right, Kirby P in the New South Wales Court of Criminal Appeal below expressly referred to Australia's obligation under art 14(3)(c) to guarantee trial "without undue delay".[3]

Three years later, in *Dietrich v The Queen*,[4] the High Court reconsidered the right to fair trial in the context of an indigent accused who had been tried and convicted of a serious drug offence without legal representation. By contrast with *Jago*, the judgments in *Dietrich* are peppered with references to the fair trial guarantees in the ICCPR and the equivalent guarantees contained in the *European Convention on Human Rights* (ECHR) and the *Canadian Charter of Fundamental Rights and Freedoms*.[5] The majority held that, although there is no right to legal

---

2   (1989) 168 CLR 23.

3   *Jago v District Court of New South Wales* (1988) 12 NSWLR 558 at 569 per Kirby P.

4   (1992) 177 CLR 292.

5   See discussion of art 14 of the ICCPR in the following judgments in *Dietrich* (1992) 177 CLR 292: at 300, 305-07 per Mason CJ and McHugh J, at 337 per Deane J, at 351, 359-61 per Toohey J, and at 373 per Gaudron J. Although dissenting, Brennan J viewed the ICCPR as an expression of "contemporary values" and therefore was relevant in general terms to the development of the common law: at 321. His refusal to extend the right to a fair trial however was motivated by concern about the appropriate limits of judicial intervention in the law-making process. Dawson J, dissenting, also accepted that the common law was inconsistent with art 14(3)(d), but concluded that the ICCPR had no bearing on the development of the common law since the relevant case law was clear and unambiguous: at 347-49.

representation at public expense, compelling an indigent accused to face serious criminal charges without legal representation could result in an unfair trial. Although the terms of art 14(3)(d) provided limited assistance in shaping the common law right, the majority of the High Court noted that their "qualified approach" to legal representation followed the interpretation adopted by the European Court of Human Rights and the Supreme Court of Canada.[6]

In *Jago* and *Dietrich* the High Court significantly expanded the notion of the fair trial under the common law. Procedural fairness is no longer simply an aspirational value of the criminal justice system, rather it is a *legally enforceable right* which imposes upon the courts an obligation to stay legal proceedings which are unfair.[7] Indeed, the availability of a prophylactic remedy for procedural unfairness revolutionised priorities and policies of Legal Aid Commissions around Australia.[8] In addition to its practical impact, the decision in *Dietrich* signified a new "transnational approach" to legal adjudication. Binding obligations under international law, including those contained in the ICCPR, were now regarded as a legitimate influence on the judicial development of the common law.[9]

The notions of procedural fairness embodied in the right to a fair trial, and its American counterpart of "due process", have a much older pedigree than the ICCPR. While procedural fairness underlies many common law rules, such as the presumption of innocence and the right to silence, the High Court in *Jago* and *Dietrich* went one step further by identifying an umbrella concept, which, in the words of Mason CJ in *Jago*, underpinned "the *whole* course of the criminal process".[10] However, the precise limits of the fair trial concept remain illusive and there are indications that the present High Court is taking a narrower course, restricting the concept to the criminal trial only.[11] Judicial toleration of pre-trial unfairness is clearly undesirable. As Ashworth has observed, "since the court hearing is but one stage in the criminal process, and since most hearings involve a

---

6   (1992) 177 CLR 292 at 307-09 per Mason CJ and McHugh J.

7   The duty of the trial judge to grant a stay of proceedings to prevent an unfair trial was first recognised in *Barton v The Queen* (1980) 147 CLR 75 at 95-96; see also *Williams v Spautz* (1992) 107 ALR 635.

8   See Zdenkowski, G, "Defending the Indigent Accused in Serious Cases: A Legal Right to Counsel?" (1994) 18 *Criminal Law Journal* 135 and Garkawe, S, "Human Rights in the Administration of Justice" (1994) 1 *Australian Journal of Human Rights* 371. In Victoria, the effect of *Dietrich v The Queen* has been abrogated by statute, although the courts have been given the power to order Legal Aid to provide legal representation in cases where the accused is unable to receive a fair trial: see *Crimes Act* 1958 (Vic) s 360A.

9   See also *Mabo v Queensland (No 2)* (1992) 175 CLR 1. See further, Mason, A, "The Influence of International and Transnational Law on Australian Municipal Law" (1996) 7 *Public Law Review* 20. See also Ch 2 by Sir Anthony Mason in this volume. The House of Lords has held that, in cases of ambiguity, the English courts should presume that parliament intended to legislate in conformity with the European Convention on Human Rights: *R v Secretary of State of Home Office Department; ex p Brind* [1991] 1 All ER 720.

10   *Jago v District Court of New South Wales* (1989) 168 CLR 23 at 29 (emphasis added).

11   See *Fuller v Field* (1994) 62 SASR 112, where the Supreme Court of South Australia held that the absence of legal representation at the pre-trial committal stage did not prejudice the right to a fair trial. The High Court, agreeing with the Supreme Court, refused special leave to appeal: *Fuller and Cummings v DPP (Cth)* (1994) 68 ALJR 611. See generally, Mason, A, "Fair Trial" (1995) 19 *Criminal Law Journal* 7 at 9-10.

plea of guilty and not a trial, this notion of fairness should surely be extended to other decisions taken before a case comes to court".[12] Indeed, in England, the law governing abuse of process has been extended into the pre-trial phase. The House of Lords has recently confirmed that the courts may stay proceedings on the grounds of unfairness in cases of entrapment or where the accused's presence in the jurisdiction had been secured by unlawful abduction rather than by lawful extradition.[13]

The judicial power to grant a stay of proceedings in order to prevent an unfair trial is described as part of the inherent jurisdiction to prevent an abuse of process.[14] The description of this jurisdiction as "inherent" suggests that it is an autonomous concept which cannot be fettered or abrogated by parliament or the executive – it is for the judiciary, rather than the other organs of government, to determine the precise attributes of a fair trial and when its proceedings are being invoked for an improper purpose.[15] However, the prospect of a common law remedy for preventing an abuse of process fettering a clear contrary intention of parliament raises obvious implications for the doctrine of parliamentary supremacy. There are preliminary indications that the High Court will not sanction the use of the stay where the source of unfairness is derived from the operation of a validly enacted statute. In *Grills and PJE v R*,[16] the High Court dismissed the accused's application for special leave to appeal, endorsing the view of the Supreme Court of New South Wales that a court cannot stay a trial on the ground that a statute enacted by parliament caused unfairness to the accused. This novel restriction on the abuse of process doctrine is undoubtedly related to the dominance of Brennan CJ and his reluctance, evidenced in his earlier dissenting judgment in *Dietrich*, to sanction judicial interference in areas of the criminal justice system which are, in his view, properly the responsibility of parliament or the executive.[17]

---

12 Ashworth, A, "Concepts of Criminal Justice" [1979] *Criminal Law Review* 412 at 414, fn 6.

13 *R v Latif & Shahzad* [1996] 1 WLR 104 and *R v Horseferry Road Magistrates Court; ex p Bennett* [1994] 1 AC 42, respectively. See Mackarel, M and Gane, C, "Admitting Irregularly or Illegally Obtained Evidence From Abroad into Criminal Proceedings – A Common Law Approach" [1997] *Criminal Law Review* 720. In Australia, evidence of guilt procured by illegal or improper police is not an abuse of process per se, although such evidence may be excluded, at the discretion of the judge, on the grounds of public policy: *Ridgeway v The Queen* (1995) 129 ALR 41.

14 The abuse of process doctrine extends generally to proceedings which have been invoked for an improper purpose: see Paciocco, D, "The Stay of Proceedings as a Remedy in Criminal Cases: Abusing the Abuse of Process Concept" (1991) 15 *Criminal Law Journal* 315 and Weinberg, M, "Criminal Procedure and the Fair Trial Principle" in Finn, P (ed), *Essays on Law and Government* vol 2 (Law Book Co, Sydney, 1995).

15 "The courts cannot contemplate for a moment the transference to the Executive of the responsibility for seeing that the process of law is not abused": *Connelly v Director of Public Prosecution* [1964] AC 1254 per Lord Devlin; approved in *Jago v District Court of New South Wales* (1989) 168 CLR 23 at 29 per Mason CJ.

16 *Grills and PJE v R* (unreported, HCA, 9 September 1996). The litigation arose from a series of decisions in NSW where sexual assault proceedings had been stayed permanently on the ground that the "rape shield" law, which excluded evidence of the complainant's sexual history, infringed the accused's right to a fair trial: *R v Morgan* (1993) 30 NSWLR 543; *R v Bernthalr* (unreported, CCA (NSW), 17 December 1993); cf *R v PJE* (unreported, CCA (NSW), 9 October 1995). See "Editorial – Staying a Trial for Unfairness: The Constitutional Implications" (1994) 18 *Criminal Law Journal* 317.

17 *Dietrich v The Queen* (1992) 177 CLR 292 at 324-25.

The alternate conception of the abuse of process doctrine, namely that the inherent jurisdiction to prevent an unfair trial cannot be abrogated or fettered by statute, may be bolstered by implications drawn from the Commonwealth and State Constitutions which envisage a separation of judicial from legislative and executive powers.[18] Indeed, the clearest judicial statement on the potential conflict between the principles of legality and fairness was offered by Gaudron J in *Dietrich,* who suggested that the notion of fairness embodied in "due process" was autonomous from the requirement that a trial should be conducted according to law:

> [T]he law recognises that sometimes, despite the best efforts of all concerned, a trial may be unfair even though conducted strictly in accordance with law. Thus, the *overriding* qualification and universal criterion of fairness!.[19]

While this statement was made in the context of a discussion of the guarantee of due process implied from Ch III of the Constitution, it could be interpreted as having wider application to the common law governing abuse of process.[20]

Fair trial jurisprudence is in a nascent state of development in Australia and the extent to which it offers a remedy where the unfairness derives from laws enacted by parliament or the policies of the executive is yet to be determined. In *Dietrich,* the High Court acknowledged that the right to a fair trial is, by its nature, an evolving concept incapable of exhaustive definition.[21] Undoubtedly, in further elaborating the content of this right, legal practitioners and judges should draw upon the "minimum guarantees" laid down in art 14(3) and the rich jurisprudence and commentary which has developed around the ICCPR and its European and Canadian counterparts.[22] In the following section of this chapter we identify some domestic strategies for challenging those legal rules and practices which do not adequately respect the fair trial guarantees identified in the ICCPR.

The right to silence

Article 14(3)(g) of the ICCPR provides that the accused has the right "[n]ot to be compelled to testify against himself or to confess guilt". The ICCPR's inclusion of the accused's right to silence before and during the trial undoubtedly reflects the fundamental importance attached to the common law privilege against self-

---

18   Hope, J, "A Constitutional Right to A Fair Trial? Implications for the Reform of the Australian Criminal Justice System" (1996) 24 *Federal Law Review* 173 at 181-89 and Wheeler, F, "The Doctrine of Separation of Powers and Constitutionally Entrenched Due Process in Australia" (1997) 23(2) *Monash University Law Review* 248.

19   *Dietrich v The Queen* (1992) 177 CLR 292 at 362 per Gaudron J (emphasis added); see also at 326 per Deane J. These views were not endorsed by other members of the court and are strictly obiter; the applicant based his appeal on the common law, abandoning earlier arguments based on fair trial implications drawn from the *Constitution Act* 1975 (Vic).

20   Following *Kable v DPP (NSW)* (1996) 138 ALR 577, the scope of constitutional due process has been broadened to State as well as Federal courts. The High Court held that, to the extent that State courts are invested with Federal jurisdiction, they may not act in a manner incompatible with Ch III of the Constitution.

21   *Dietrich v The Queen* (1992) 177 CLR 292 at 300 per Mason CJ and McHugh J, at 353 per Toohey J.

22   Duggan, KP, "Reform of the Criminal Law with Fair Trial as the Guiding Star" (1995) 19 *Criminal Law Journal* 258 at 271.

incrimination, *nemo tenetur accusare seipsum* (no person is bound to accuse himself or herself). Although the privilege originated as a means of protecting suspects from torture and oppressive interrogation, it is now recognised as a basic human right protecting personal freedom and human dignity.[23] The characterisation of the privilege as a *human* right underlies the High Court's refusal to extend the protection to artificial legal persons such as corporations.[24]

The privilege against self-incrimination underlies a bundle of entitlements and immunities which apply both before and during the criminal trial. The "right to silence" provides that a person is not under a duty to answer questions or otherwise cooperate with the police or the prosecution during a criminal investigation and that, accordingly, the trial judge and the prosecution are not permitted to suggest that the accused's silence before trial can provide a basis for inferring consciousness of guilt or inferring that the defence raised at trial is a recent invention, or is otherwise suspect because the accused failed to mention it.[25] During the trial itself, most jurisdictions prohibit the prosecution from commenting on the accused's failure to give evidence and the trial judge from directing the jury that this failure to give evidence is because the accused was, or believed he or she was, guilty of the offence charged.[26] Although the privilege cannot be invoked where the accused has chosen to testify, it may nevertheless be invoked by other witnesses as a legitimate reason for refusing to answer a question during their examination.[27] In this respect, this protection afforded under the common law – that is, to persons other than the accused – is broader than that envisaged by the ICCPR.

Notwithstanding its purported fundamental legal status, the privilege against self-incrimination has been qualified or restricted both by statute and common law development.[28] To combat the problem of "trial by ambush", legislation has been enacted in most jurisdictions requiring pre-trial disclosure of alibi evidence. In these jurisdictions, the accused's failure to comply with these disclosure obligations may

---

23 The historical origins of the privilege and its human rights rationale are explored in *Environmental Protection Authority v Caltex* (1993) 178 CLR 477 at 497-500 per Mason CJ and Toohey J. See also dicta in *Controlled Consultants Pty Ltd v Commissioner for Corporate Affairs* (1985) 156 CLR 385 at 394-95 and *Pyneboard v TPC* (1983) 45 ALR 609 at 621-22, where Murphy J described the privilege as part of the "common law of human rights".

24 *Environmental Protection Authority v Caltex* (1993) 178 CLR 447.

25 *Petty v The Queen* (1991) 173 CLR 95 at 99. See also *Evidence Act* 1995 (NSW/Cth) s 89. See NSWLRC, Discussion Paper 41, *The Right to Silence* (1998), Ch 3.

26 *Evidence Act* 1995 (Cth/NSW) s 20.

27 In some jurisdictions, the witness (other than the accused) may be compelled to give evidence in the interest of justice. In such cases, a certificate is issued by the court which prevents that evidence being used against the witness in any subsequent proceeding: *Evidence Act* 1995(NSW/Cth) s 128.

28 The High Court in *Sorby v Commonwealth* (1983) 152 CLR 281 held that a Federal Act which abolished the privilege against self-incrimination in proceedings before a Royal Commission did not infringe Ch III of the Constitution. See further Wheeler, above, n 18. By contrast, the European Court of Human Rights in *Saunders v United Kingdom* (1996) 23 EHRR 313 held that it was a violation of art 6 to admit evidence during a criminal trial which had been obtained at an earlier administrative hearing during which the accused had been compelled by statute to answer questions and adduce evidence of a self-incriminatory nature.

be subject to adverse judicial comment.[29] Although it is stressed that "mere silence" cannot found an inference of guilt, non-disclosure of relevant material may be used to discredit defences subsequently raised at trial. Legislation in Victoria goes further, establishing a general regime of pre-trial disclosure applicable to both the defence and prosecution. Section 15(1) of the *Crimes (Criminal Trials) Act* 1993 (Vic) provides that either party may introduce evidence which was not disclosed by their opponent and which represents a departure from the case disclosed before trial. In these circumstances, under s 15(2), a departure may be subject to any comment that the judge or the party (with the leave of the court) thinks appropriate.

The elusive distinctions drawn between permissible and impermissible uses of the accused's silence during official questioning mirror those devised by the courts for determining the evidential significance of the accused's silence during the trial itself. The High Court in *Weissensteiner v The Queen*[30] recognised that failure to give evidence during the trial, while not constituting evidence of guilt, may have some probative bearing on evidence led by the prosecution in cases where the accused has not supported any hypothesis which is consistent with innocence from facts which are perceived to be within his or her knowledge. A broader qualification to the right to silence has been enacted by statute in the United Kingdom. The statute permits the tribunal of fact to draw adverse inferences from the accused's silence, both pre-trial and at trial, in specified circumstances.[31] In *Murray v United Kingdom*,[32] the European Court of Human Rights considered whether such statutory qualifications to the right to silence violated the right to a fair hearing protected by art 6 of the ECHR. The court affirmed that the right to silence, both at trial and pre-trial, lies at the heart of the notion of a fair hearing, but concluded that these provisions, which entitled the jury to draw "common sense" inferences from silence, did not violate art 6. As the court observed, the domestic statute prevented the jury from convicting *solely* on the basis of the accused's decision to remain silent.[33] The decision to uphold the domestic law was greatly influenced by the presence of these safeguards, although the precise delimitation between permissible and impermissible inferences from silence remains unclear.[34]

In Australia, by contrast, the statutory and common law qualifications to the right to silence may not adequately safeguard the interests of suspects. Unlike its English counterpart, the customary caution offered before official questioning does not advise suspects that their failure to answer questions in certain circumstances

---

29 See, for example, *Crimes Act* 1900 (NSW) s 405A and *Criminal Law Consolidation Act* 1935 (SA) s 285c. Where an alibi is not disclosed before trial, the trial judge may direct the jury that the silence of the accused pre-trial deprived the investigator of the opportunity of testing the alibi. However, the jury cannot draw such inferences from silence during police questioning in cases where the accused had first been cautioned of his or her right to remain silent: *King v R* (1986) 68 ALR 27 at 36 per the court.

30 (1993) 178 CLR 217.

31 *Criminal Justice and Public Order Act* 1994 (UK) ss 34-37.

32 (1996) 22 EHRR 29 (Case No 417/1994/488/570). The legislation challenged in this case had been enacted only for Northern Ireland, see *Criminal Evidence (Northern Ireland) Order* 1988 (UK). The *Criminal Justice and Public Order Act* 1994 (UK) is modelled on this statute.

33 Ibid, para 48.

34 See Dickson, B, "The Right to Silence and Legal Advice under the European Convention" (1996) 21 *European Law Review* 424.

(for example, failing to disclose an alibi during questioning) may result in adverse inferences being drawn against them in subsequent proceedings.[35] Moreover, suspects are more vulnerable to psychological pressure in Australia since the police in many jurisdictions are not required, as a matter of law, to tape record interviews or to facilitate access to legal representation during official questioning.[36] As result, the vulnerability and isolation felt by suspects under investigation may significantly undermine the forensic value and fairness of drawing adverse inferences from their decision to remain silent.[37]

The characterisation of the privilege against self-incrimination as a "rule of law" rather than merely as a testimonial immunity has justified its expansion into the pre-trial phase. Although this right to remain silent during official questioning is well established in Australia, there is limited authority on whether the privilege against self-incrimination limits the scope of summons, subpoenas and search warrants.[38] Indeed, it has been suggested that the law of privilege draws a distinction between physical and testimonial evidence; as the High Court observed, the privilege "has no application to the seizure of documents or their use for the purpose of incrimination provided that they can be proved by some independent means. The privilege is not a privilege against incrimination; it is a privilege against self-incrimination".[39] A similar view has been taken by the European Court of Human Rights in *Saunders v United Kingdom*,[40] which observed that the right not to incriminate oneself is "primarily concerned with respecting the will of an accused person to remain silent", and thus "did not extend to the use in criminal proceedings of material which may be obtained from the accused through the use of compulsory

---

35   Accordingly, the typical Australian caution has been described as a "misleading entrapment for the innocent accused who takes it on face value and does not provide an early explanation": Ligertwood, A, *Australian Evidence* (Butterworths, Sydney, 2nd ed, 1993), p 251. The New South Wales Police Commissioner's Instructions (1995), for example, advise that the following caution should be read to suspects: "I am going to ask you certain questions. You are not obliged to answer unless you wish to do so, but whatever you say may be used in evidence. Do you understand that?".

36   The rules governing interviewing and taping are contained in legislation in the ACT and Federal jurisdiction: *Crimes Act* 1914 (Cth) ss 23A-23W. By contrast, in New South Wales, the procedures governing official questioning are contained in administrative guidelines: see NSW Police Commissioner's Instructions (1995). To combat the dangers of verballing, the High Court has held that juries should be warned of the dangers of convicting the accused on the basis of an uncorroborated confession which is later disputed at trial: *McKinney v The Queen* (1991) 171 CLR 468; see also *Evidence Act* 1995 (Cth/NSW) s 165(1)(f).

37   The dangers of suspects making false confessions are explored in Gudjonsson, G, "Psychological Vulnerability: Suspects At Risk" in Morgan, D and Stephenson, G (eds), *Suspicion and Silence: The Right to Silence in Criminal Investigations* (Blackstone Press, London, 1994), p 91. See also Chaaya, M, "The Right to Silence Reignited: Vulnerable Suspects, Police Questioning and Law and Order in NSW" (1998) 22 *Criminal Law Journal* 82.

38   There is authority in Australia suggesting that a party to proceedings may object to the production of documents required under a subpoena on the grounds of self-incrimination: see *Commissioner for Railways v Small* (1938) 38 SR (NSW) 564; *Evans v Staunton* [1958] Qd R 96. By contrast, the US Supreme Court and the European Court of Justice have held that the privilege against self-incrimination does not entitle a person to refuse to hand over documents: *Braswell v US* 487 US 99 (1988) and *Orkem v European Commission* [1989] ECR 3283, respectively.

39   *Controlled Consultants Pty Ltd v Commissioner for Corporate Affairs* (1985) 156 CLR 385 at 393 per Gibbs CJ, Mason and Dawson JJ.

40   (1996) 23 EHRR 313.

powers but which has an existence independent of the will of the suspect such as, *inter alia*, documents acquired pursuant to a warrant, breath, blood and urine samples and bodily tissue for the purpose of DNA testing".[41] Significantly, the court left undecided the question whether the privilege is absolute or whether infringements of it may be justified in particular circumstances.[42]

Basing the protection afforded by the privilege on a distinction between physical and testimonial evidence is arbitrary and, ultimately, may be unworkable.[43] The preferable approach, consistent with its human rights rationale, is to consider the role that the privilege plays in ensuring a fair trial. The purpose of the privilege is not to disentitle the state from gathering incriminating evidence from the accused per se, but rather to ensure that a fair balance is maintained between the State and the individual. In drawing this balance, the primary question for the courts is whether the investigative methods employed have had the effect of *unfairly or improperly* depriving the suspect (or any other person) of the right not to furnish evidence of his or her own guilt.[44] In this regard particular attention should be paid to those cases where covert police operations unfairly or improperly deprive suspects of their right to remain silent.

The High Court has consistently held that the mere use of deception or trickery during an investigation is neither improper nor unfair.[45] Indeed, the trend towards covert policing is evident in recent cases where the police have equipped undercover officers or informers with listening devices for the specific purpose of recording incriminating statements from suspects for subsequent use at trial. In Queensland and England, the courts have been generally reluctant to exercise their discretion to exclude such evidence on the grounds of either unfairness or public policy.[46] However, the High Court in *R v Swaffield; Pavic v R* (1998) 151 ALR 98 recently held that confession evidence covertly recorded by undercover police or informers may be excluded in the discretion of the trial judge in some circumstances. Adopting the approach taken by the Supreme Court of Canada, the majority of the High Court focused on the extent to which the tactics used by the police caused unfairness to the accused; namely, whether the accused's freedom to choose to speak to the police (or state agent acting on behalf of the police, such as

---

41   (1996) 23 EHRR 313 at 338, para 69.

42   *Saunders v United Kingdom* (1996) 23 EHRR 313 at 340, para 74.

43   See the dissenting opinion of Judge Martens, joined by Judge Kuris: (1996) 23 EHRR 313 at 355, para 12.

44   The power of the court to set aside a subpoena on the grounds that it serves an impermissible purpose or compliance would be oppressive is an aspect of inherent jurisdiction to prevent an abuse of process: *Botany Bay Instrumentation & Control Pty Ltd v Stewart* [1984] 3 NSWLR 98 at 99-101 per Powell J.

45   *Ridgeway v The Queen* (1995) 129 ALR 41 at 53 per Mason CJ, Deane and Dawson JJ; *R v Swaffield; Pavic v R* (1998) 1515 ALR 98 at 114 per Brennan CJ.

46   *O'Neill* (1995) 81 A Crim R 458 (CCA (Qld)) per Dowsett and Pincus JJ, Fitzgerald P dissenting; *R v Davidson and Moyle; ex p Attorney-General* [1996] 2 Qd R 505; *Swaffield* (1996) 88 A Crim R 98; *Wackerow* (1997) 90 A Crim R 297; *Cadette* [1995] Crim LR 229 and *Parker* [1995] Crim LR 233. See Bronitt, S, "Contemporary Comment-Electronic Surveillance and Informers: Infringing the Rights to Silence and Privacy" (1996) 20 *Criminal Law Journal* 144.

an informer) had been improperly impugned.[47] To be excluded on the grounds of unfairness, the confession must have been elicited in clear breach of the suspect's right to choose whether or not to speak. Relevant factors to the exercise of the discretion include whether (i) the admissions were deliberately elicited in circumstances where the suspect had previously expressed a desire to remain silent; (ii) the conversation can be characterised as a "functional equivalent" to an interrogation; (iii) the police exploited any special characteristics of the relationship between the suspect and their agent.[48] In cases where the impropriety did not cause unfairness to the accused, the judges may nevertheless use their residual discretion to exclude this evidence on the grounds of public policy (see discussion below).[49]

By framing submissions on the privilege against self-incrimination in terms of potential human rights violations, the fundamental importance of the privilege as a safeguard to the accused is rendered explicit. Indeed, it is hoped that references to the emerging international jurisprudence on the privilege against self-incrimination may have a salutary effect on the level of protection offered to individuals both before and during the trial.

The rule against hearsay

The traditional reasons for not admitting hearsay into evidence are that a statement made "out of court" is not the best evidence and that, moreover, since the person making the statement is not available for cross-examination, it cannot be tested for its truthfulness or accuracy.[50] The High Court in recent times has adopted a flexible "common-sense" approach to determining whether a hearsay statement should be admitted as evidence based on whether the statement in the particular case is "sufficiently reliable and free from the risk of concoction to render it appropriate for consideration".[51] The *Evidence Act* 1995 (Cth/NSW) has endorsed this by allowing a hearsay statement into evidence if it was made in circumstances which make it highly probable that the statement is reliable.[52]

International human rights law provides a useful normative resource for further refining the present law governing hearsay. Indeed, the New South Wales Court of Criminal Appeal in *Astill*[53] considered the human rights rationale of the rule against

---

47 (1998) 151 ALR 98 at 127 per Toohey, Gummow and Gaudron JJ, referring to *Hebert* [1990] 2 SCR 151 (SC (Can)) and *Broyles* [1991] 3 SCR 595 (SC (Can)). See also *R v Brown* (1993) 105 DLR (4th) 199 (SC (Can)).

48 (1998) 151 ALR 98 at 128 per Toohey, Gummow and Gaudron JJ, at 142 per Kirby J. See also *Smith, Turner and Altinas* (1994) 75 A Crim R 327 (SC (SA)).

49 (1998) 151 ALR 98 at 127 per Toohey, Gummow and Gaudron JJ. Cf Brennan CJ (at 114) who confined the unfairness discretion narrowly to evidential unreliability and consequently relied upon the public policy discretion to determine whether evidence obtained by impugning the suspect's right to silence should be excluded. On the public policy discretion, see *Bunning v Cross* (1978) 141 CLR 54; *Evidence Act* 1995 (Cth/NSW) s 138.

50 *Teper v R* [1952] AC 480 at 486 per Lord Normand. See generally, Choo, A, *Hearsay and Confrontation in Criminal Trials* (Clarendon Press, Oxford, 1996).

51 See Mason CJ and Deane J in *Walton v The Queen* (1989) 166 CLR 283, see further Collis, B, "Will Hearsay Stand the Test of Time?" (1994) 68(4) *Law Institute Journal* 266 at 267; Palmer, A, "The Reliability-Based Approach to Hearsay" (1995) 17(4) *Sydney Law Review* 522.

52 See *Evidence Act* 1995 (Cth/NSW) s 65(2)(c) in relation to criminal proceedings.

53 (1992) 63 A Crim R 148.

hearsay in order to determine whether an out of court statement should be admitted into evidence. Kirby P held that reliability was neither the final nor the decisive factor in admitting hearsay evidence.[54] In his view, the obligations under the ICCPR were of particular significance, since art 14(3)(e) explicitly entitled the accused to "examine, or have examined, the witnesses against him and to obtain the attendance of witnesses on his behalf under the same conditions as witnesses against him". In holding that the contents of a series of telephone calls between two prosecution witnesses should be admitted into evidence despite their contents being hearsay, Kirby P stated that the contents of the telephone calls did not encroach upon the protection envisaged in art 14(3)(e) of the ICCPR. A strict reading of art 14(3)(e) would prohibit the prosecution from leading hearsay evidence since an accused is entitled to examine all prosecution witnesses.[55] However, art 14(3)(e) does not apply to hearsay evidence led by an accused and, in this respect, diverges from the common law which traditionally applies indiscriminately, excluding hearsay evidence which may be relevant either to the accused's guilt or innocence.[56] The express articulation of the fair trial rationale for the admission of hearsay evidence would encourage the courts to develop and apply consistent rulings about the admissibility and exclusion, which would be preferable to the "flexible" approach of expanding the scope of existing exceptions to the rule in an ad hoc fashion, or resorting to vague criteria for admissibility based simply on "common-sense" and the perceived reliability of the statement.

Prosecution disclosure

The ICCPR does not expressly impose an obligation on the prosecution to disclose material in its possession which is favourable to the accused. Article 14(3)(b), however, protects the right of the accused to "adequate time and facilities for the preparation of his defence". It has been suggested that the term "facilities" includes access to the documentation necessary for the defence.[57] In any event, the right to disclosure of the prosecution case (including documentary evidence), although not an express guarantee, is an important implication drawn from the right to a fair trial protected by art 14(1).[58] In Canada, the Supreme Court has held that the prosecution is under a duty of disclosure to the extent necessary to ensure the accused may make "full answer and defence".[59]

---

54   (1992) 63 A Crim R 148 at 158.

55   See Osborne, C, "Hearsay and the European Court of Human Rights" [1993] *Criminal Law Review* 255 at 261.

56   As the common law rule against hearsay admitted no discretion to the trial judge, hearsay evidence was excluded even where it bore directly on the innocence of the accused: see *Sparks v R* [1964] AC 964; *Myers v DPP* [1965] AC 1001.

57   Noor Muhammad, H, "Due Process of Law for the Persons Accused of Crime" in Henkin, L (ed), *The International Bill of Rights: the Covenant on Civil and Political Rights* (Columbia University Press, New York, 1981), p 152.

58   Ibid, p 146, noting its importance in maintaining the equality of the parties and the full opportunity of the accused to participate in the trial.

59   *Stinchcombe v The Queen* (1991) 68 CCC (3d) 1 at 9 (SC (Can)).

By comparison, the common law governing disclosure in Australia is relatively undeveloped.[60] The extent of prosecution disclosure required is determined by reference to the right of the accused not to be subjected to an unfair trial.[61] Accordingly, the obligation of disclosure on the prosecution has been restricted to the trial itself and does not extend to either the committal or pre-trial hearings.[62] Moreover, the prosecution is under no obligation to disclose (a) material which is irrelevant, or (b) material, which though relevant, is exempt from disclosure because of public interest immunity or an equivalent privilege created by statute.[63]

There is a danger that such non-disclosure may prejudice the right to a fair trial. Indeed, the Supreme Court of Canada has held that public interest immunity cannot attach to material which is relevant to the accused's defence.[64] The delicate balancing of competing public interests apparent in the adjudication of public interest immunity claims is impossible where disclosure of material is strictly prohibited by statute. For example, the blanket prohibitions contained in the *Telecommunications (Interception) Act* 1979 (Cth) (TI Act) significantly impair the right of the accused to obtain disclosure of material relevant to his or her defence.[65] Although such provisions hamper the defence, the judicial remedy of the stay would be difficult to invoke for the following reasons. First, the accused may simply be unaware that relevant material is being withheld. Secondly, the court may refuse to grant a stay since the source of the unfairness derives from the operation of a validly enacted statute (see discussion above). Thirdly, the stay would have to be granted on the basis of material gathered under a warrant which the court may be prohibited by statute from disclosing to either the accused or prosecution.[66] Clearly post-hoc

---

60   See Hunter, J and Cronin, K, *Evidence, Advocacy and Ethical Practice* (Butterworths, Sydney, 1995), p 199.

61   See *Lawless v The Queen* (1979) 142 CLR 659 and *R v Ward* [1993] 2 All ER 577.

62   *R v Saleam* (1989) 16 NSWLR 14; *Sobh* (1993) 65 A Crim R 466. The common law is supplemented in NSW by Supreme Court Standard Directions (25 March 1994) which require disclosure by the prosecution during a committal and an obligation on the defence to reply within a prescribed time. In Victoria, a case statement must be provided by the prosecution and the defence must reply to any propositions of law in that statement and indicate those upon which the defence proposed to rely: *Crimes (Criminal Trials) Act* 1993 (Vic) ss 8, 11. In England, a statutory scheme of disclosure has recently been enacted: see *Criminal Procedure and Investigations Act* 1996 (UK), see Commentary in [1997] *Criminal Law Review* 308. Each State and Territory, except the ACT, has statutory provisions relating to the service of briefs of evidence.

63   See *Evidence Act* 1995 (NSW/Cth) s 130. Under the common law, the police and prosecution may invoke public interest immunity to withhold the identity of informers: *Marks v Beyfus* (1890) 25 QBD 494 (CA (Eng)); *Attorney-General (NSW) v Stuart* (1994) 34 NSWLR 667 (CCA (NSW)).

64   *R v Seaboyer; R v Gayne* [1991] 2 SCR 577 at 607 per McLachlin J, speaking for the majority of the court. Under Australian law, the scope of public interest immunity is determined by weighing the desirability of maintaining the confidentiality of the material against the importance of the evidence to the defence and the criminal nature of the proceedings: *Alister v R* (1983) 50 ALR 41 at 44-46 per Gibbs CJ; see also *Evidence Act* 1995 s 130(5).

65   The Act provides that it is unlawful to intercept, disclose or admit evidence of an intercepted communications unless authorised by the Act: ss 7, 62, 74, 75, 76, 76A, 77, TI Act. Disclosure of unlawfully intercepted material cannot be disclosed to the defence under the TI Act, however the prohibition applies only to "persons" and does prevent disclosure to the court: *Green* (1996) 85 A Crim R 229, see also *R v Preston* [1993] 4 All ER 638.

66   This degree of adjudicative secrecy clearly undermines public confidence in the impartiality of the court and may, for this reason alone, justify the granting of a stay of proceedings to prevent an abuse of process. We are grateful to Fiona Wheeler for this insightful observation.

judicial remedies are inadequate in these circumstances and the preferable approach would be to remodel the privacy safeguards in the TI Act in a manner which better respect the right to a fair trial. This could be achieved by mandating the pre-trial disclosure to the accused of any intercepted material which will be adduced during the trial (as is required in Canada and the United States) and, furthermore, by allowing the disclosure of illegally intercepted material to parties to proceedings where it is necessary to do so in the "interests of justice".

In practice, the limited disclosure obligations under the common law are tempered by ethical and professional duties. To ameliorate the risk of injustice to the accused, prosecution guidelines have been adopted clarifying the disclosure of "unused" material to the defence.[67] However, the protection of fundamental human rights, such as the fair trial, should not rest on non-binding guidelines. While breach of these guidelines may result in professional or judicial reprimand, the trial judge cannot stay the proceedings unless the defence can establish that the unfairness likely to be caused by non-disclosure constitutes an abuse of process. The lack of certainty regarding pre-trial disclosure to the defence in Australia requires urgent attention. In the absence of legislative clarification, domestic courts, in further developing the common law, may usefully consider the international jurisprudence on the right to a fair trial and its implications for the duties of disclosure.

THE EXCLUSIONARY PRINCIPLE: LAW ENFORCEMENT MISCONDUCT AND HUMAN RIGHTS

Since the 1970s, the Australian courts have recognised that the function of the rules of evidence is not only to ensure fairness to the accused but also to maintain public confidence in the administration of criminal justice.[68] The High Court in *Bunning v Cross*[69] held that the discretion to exclude evidence on public policy grounds under the common law involves,

> no simple question of ensuring fairness to an accused but instead the weighing against each other of two competing requirements of public policy, thereby seeking to resolve the apparent conflict between the desirable goal of bringing to conviction the wrongdoer and the undesirable effect of curial approval, or even encouragement, being given to the unlawful conduct by those whose task it is to enforce the law.[70]

The primary purpose of exclusion is to maintain public confidence in administration of justice, particularly in relation to the judiciary and those officials who are entrusted with enforcing the law. The Australian Law Reform Commission (ALRC) identified further rationales for exclusion including the public interest in

---

67 Disclosure guidelines have been issued by the Directors of Public Prosecutions in the ACT, New South Wales, Queensland, Western Australia and the Northern Territory. The Commonwealth Director of Public Prosecutions proposes to issue similar guidelines in the near future.

68 In this respect, the Australian law diverges from the common law and statutory discretions in England where the discretion to exclude evidence obtained illegally or improperly is linked explicitly to the unfairness caused to the accused: see *Sang* [1980] 2 All ER 1222; *Police and Criminal Evidence Act* 1984 (UK) s 78; *Khan (Sultan)* [1996] 3 All ER 289.

69 (1978) 141 CLR 54.

70 (1978) 141 CLR 54 at 74 per Stephen and Aikin JJ.

disciplining police illegality or impropriety, deterring future illegality, protecting individual rights, ensuring fairness at trial, and encouraging other methods of police investigation.[71] The discretion is not limited to breaches of the law, but extends to all forms of official misconduct; thus breaches of the Police Commissioner's Instructions, or similar administrative guidelines, may be relevant to the exercise of the discretion. Although there is no authority directly on point, the concept of illegality and impropriety under this discretion is conceivably wide enough to encompass violations of the ICCPR.

In the Australian Capital Territory, New South Wales, and in courts exercising Federal jurisdiction, the *Bunning* discretion is now supplemented by s 138(1) of the *Evidence Act* 1995 (Cth/NSW). Most significantly, the section alters the onus of proof. The defence no longer has to prove that the law enforcement misconduct in obtaining the evidence justifies its exclusion. Instead, the section states that illegally or improperly obtained evidence is *not* to be admitted "unless the desirability of admitting the evidence outweighs the undesirability of admitting evidence that has been obtained in the way in which it has been obtained". In determining this issue, s 138(3) provides that the court *must* take into account the following factors:

(a) the probative value of the evidence; and

(b) the importance of the evidence in the proceeding; and

(c) the nature of the relevant offence, cause of action or defence and the nature of the subject-matter of the proceeding; and

(d) the gravity of the impropriety or contravention; and

(e) whether the impropriety or contravention was deliberate or reckless; and

(f) whether the impropriety or contravention was contrary to or inconsistent with a right of a person recognised by the International Covenant on Civil and Political Rights; and

(g) whether any other proceeding (whether or not in a court) has been or is likely to be taken in relation to the impropriety or contravention; and

(h) the difficulty (if any) of obtaining the evidence without impropriety or contravention of an Australian law.

The first reported decision on the operation of this section is a Supreme Court of the Australian Capital Territory ruling, delivered in the course of a trial, on the admissibility of evidence. In *Truong*,[72] Mr Boland, an acquaintance of the accused, reported to the police that the accused had confessed to his participation in a robbery which had occurred several years previously. The police provided Mr Boland with a listening device and directed him to re-initiate his conversation with the accused. During that conversation, which was recorded onto a tape by the police, the accused admitted his involvement in the offence. Although the use of the device by Mr Boland was permitted by statute, the recordings of the conversation by the police could only be done under a judicial warrant. A warrant had not been obtained in this case, as the police, relying on the wording of the statute and on legal advice from Director of Public Prosecutions, believed (wrongly) that a warrant was

---

71   ALRC, *Evidence*, Report No 26 (Interim), Vol 1 (1985), pp 529-32. Zuckerman has identified a number of theories underlying the exclusionary principle, such as the remedial or vindication theory, the deterrent theory and the legitimacy theory: Zuckerman, AS, *Principles of Criminal Evidence* (Clarendon, Oxford, 1989), pp 346-58.

72   (1996) 86 A Crim R 188.

not needed where the listening device was being used by an informer rather than a police officer.

The accused sought exclusion of this evidence under s 138 of the *Evidence Act 1995* (Cth). Although not required to do so by the Act, the judge supplied written reasons for his decision. Miles CJ noted that the section contained:

> a non-exclusive list of matters which must be taken into account, leaving it to the court to decide how much such matters are to be taken into and what weight is to be given to each. The subsection does not state whether the relative weight of any such matters favours admission or non-admission. It may be implied that the weight of some matters favour admission. For instance, if the probative value was high, that would tend to favour the admitting of the evidence. If the impropriety or contravention were deliberate that would tend to favour not admitting the evidence. On the other hand, it is far from clear whether the "importance" of the evidence favours admission or non admission. Behaviour contrary to the International Covenant on Civil and Political Rights would appear to favour non-admission.[73]

Section 138(3) of the *Evidence Act* 1995 (Cth/NSW) has imposed an obligation on judges and legal practitioners appearing before Federal, ACT and New South Wales courts to acquaint themselves with the provisions and jurisprudence of international human rights law. Although defence counsel did not specifically allege ICCPR violations in his submission, Miles CJ took judicial notice of the provisions of the Covenant. He concluded from his own reading of the ICCPR that no violation had occurred.[74] In his opinion, the prosecution had established that the desirability of admitting evidence (which was highly probative and related to a serious offence) outweighed the undesirability of admitting evidence obtained in these circumstances. Miles CJ was particularly influenced by the fact the police, acting in good faith, had no intention to contravene the law and had relied on mistaken legal advice from the DPP.

It is not surprising that a trial judge confronted by the ICCPR, and unaided by submissions from counsel, would overlook potential human rights violations. In the adversarial context of a criminal trial, the level of protection accorded by the ICCPR will depend foremost on the knowledge and competence of legal practitioners and trial judges in international human rights law.[75] A brief survey of this jurisprudence would have revealed a substantial body of law and commentary pertaining to the conduct of criminal investigations, including decisions on arbitrary search and seizure of evidence, electronic surveillance, the use of torture or inhuman and degrading treatment to obtain confessions and the right to silence.[76] Indeed, such a survey may have led the court in *Truong* to re-evaluate the significance of the ICCPR in this case. Arguably, the use of warrantless and unlawful participant surveillance at the instigation of the police constituted an arbitrary interference with

---

73   (1996) 86 A Crim R 188 at 195.

74   (1996) 86 A Crim R 188 at 195-96.

75   On which see Ch 14 by Eastman and Ronalds in this volume.

76   For an critical analysis of the law governing criminal investigation and the trial process from an international human rights perspective, see Ashworth, A, *Criminal Process – An Evaluative Study* (Clarendon Press, Oxford, 1994).

the right to privacy under art 17 of the ICCPR.[77] Moreover, the role of Mr Boland in conducting a "covert interview" of a suspect without appropriate safeguards may have infringed the fair trial guarantees in art 14 by unfairly depriving the suspect of his right to silence (see discussion above).

The decision in *Truong* alludes to some of the dangers of filtering human rights violations into an exclusionary framework based on judicial discretion. A significant drawback is that fundamental human rights *must* be weighed against other competing public interests such as the reliability or probative value of the evidence, the seriousness of the offence and the difficulty in obtaining the evidence by legitimate means. As Miles CJ perceptively observed above, basing the exclusionary principle on a discretion provides no indication of the relative weight to be attached to these competing public interests. Clearly, there is a danger that fundamental human rights will be subsumed within a discretionary framework which is heavily weighted towards the interests of crime control.[78]

The ALRC report on the law of evidence, upon which the *Evidence Act* 1995 (Cth/NSW) is based, sheds some light on intended operation of this discretion. The ALRC took the view that the factors relating to probative value, the importance of the evidence or the seriousness of the offence should favour the admission of the evidence. However, such an approach could be counterproductive, fostering "creative adaptation" within the law enforcement culture: the law may encourage officials to conduct themselves strategically, reserving misconduct for cases involving *serious* offences or where the evidence likely to be obtained would be highly probative of guilt.[79] Indeed, such an approach not only undermines the principle of legality, but it also effectively neutralises the disciplinary potential and deterrent effect of the exclusion. In *Bunning v Cross,* Stephen and Aickin JJ were cognisant of this danger:

> To treat cogency of evidence as a factor favouring admission, where the illegality in obtaining it has been either deliberate or reckless, may serve to foster the quite erroneous view that if such evidence be but damning enough that will of itself suffice to atone for the illegality involved in procuring it. For this reason, cogency should, generally, be allowed to play no part in the exercise of discretion where the illegality involved in procuring it is intentional or reckless.[80]

---

77   *Klass v Federal Republic of Germany* [1978] 2 EHRR 214 (ECHR Series A, No 28, 1978); *Malone v United Kingdom* [1984] 4 EHRR 330 (ECHR, Series A, No 82, 1984); *Kruslin v France* (1990) 12 EHRR 547 (ECHR, Series A, No 176B, 1990).

78   A study of unreported decisions after *Ridgeway*, suggests that the discretion to exclude evidence on the grounds of public policy does not restrict the use of entrapment by the police since in virtually every case, the courts have exercised the discretion in favour of admission of evidence rather than exclusion: see Bartlett, M, *Police Entrapment* (unpublished Research Unit Thesis, Australian National University, 1996).

79   For an overview of the research examining the operational rules and practices of the police see Reiner, Report, "Policing and the Police" in Maguire, M, Morgan, R and Reiner, R, (eds), *The Oxford Handbook of Criminology* (Clarendon, Oxford, 2nd ed, 1997), Ch 28. It is important not to overstate the effect of the due process and legality as constraints on police conduct. As one sociologist has suggested the legal and procedural rules governing criminal investigation, though often purporting to protect due process values, in reality often serve the interests of crime control: see McBarnet, D, *Conviction – Law, the State and the Construction of Justice* (Macmillan, London, 1981).

80   (1978) 141 CLR 54 at 79.

While the ALRC acknowledged the risk of these "unintended consequences", it rejected the idea that the discretion to exclude evidence on the grounds of impropriety should incorporate the above qualification: "The question for the judge is whether the balance of public interest favours admission – he (sic) should consider all factors on both sides of the equation".[81]

Although Australian courts have been prepared to assume an overtly disciplinary role in relation to law enforcement misconduct, that role is not pursued in isolation from other competing public policy objectives. The "trade off" between human rights and crime control objectives is highly likely in those cases where the misconduct caused no unfairness to the accused. As the ALRC observed, although unfairness is not specifically included in the proposed statutory discretion to exclude on the grounds of impropriety or illegality, "[t]he total scheme of rules of admissibility and exclusionary discretions should ensure fairness to the accused".[82]

A further difficulty with s 138 from a human rights perspective is the obligation on the court to consider "whether any other proceeding has been or is likely to be instituted with respect to the impropriety".[83] The prosecution may argue that the appropriate forum for determining human rights violations under the ICCPR is the United Nations Human Rights Committee. This is particularly relevant in Australia since individuals, as well as Contracting Parties, have the right to petition the Committee under the First Optional Protocol to the Covenant.[84] However, the *mere existence* of alternative proceedings for vindicating alleged human rights violations should not automatically favour the admission of evidence obtained in breach of the ICCPR. Adopting such an interpretation would significantly limit, if not eliminate, the role of domestic courts in protecting against human rights abuses. The domestic courts must acknowledge the many practical difficulties facing individuals who seek to institute proceedings before the international human rights tribunals; not only are such proceedings time-consuming and costly, but leave to petition is unlikely to be sought for alleged human rights violations committed during investigations of minor criminal matters.

In balancing the competing public policy interests under this discretion, the human rights protected by the ICCPR should be regarded by the courts as "higher-order laws", fundamental normative values which should be given paramount weight. While this approach falls short of mandatory exclusion of evidence obtained by violating the ICCPR, a properly weighted discretion would offer high levels of protection for human rights in Australia.[85] Whether human rights violations occurred in the investigation of serious or trivial offences, whether they were

---

81   ALRC, above, n 71, p 536.

82   ALRC, above, n 71, p 536. See *Truong* where Miles CJ notes that "The issue of unfairness in this respect is not entirely divorced from considerations to be made under s 138(1)": at 195.

83   *Evidence Act* 1995 (Cth/NSW) s 138(3)(g). Although the common law does not provide a remedy for breach of privacy, an accused who is subject to improper or illegal electronic surveillance by law enforcement officials may pursue the compensatory remedies provided under the *Privacy Act* 1988 (Cth) or the *Telecommunications (Interception) Act* 1979 (Cth) ss 107A(1)-107F.

84   Note that under the Optional Protocol, individuals have the right to petition the United Nations Human Rights Committee only in cases where they have exhausted their domestic legal remedies: see art 5.2(b), ICCPR. See further, Ch 14 by Eastman and Ronalds in this volume.

85   The arguments favouring mandatory exclusion are explored in Bronitt, above, n 46.

deliberate or inadvertent, whether they caused no unfairness to the accused, whether they were perpetrated outside of the jurisdiction, whether the accused is pursuing other remedies, domestic courts should be reluctant to condone human rights abuses. As Murphy J observed in *McInnis v The Queen*: "often courts cannot remedy denial of human rights which occurs outside of the judicial system, but there is no excuse for tolerating it within the system".[86]

LAW ENFORCEMENT DECISION-MAKING: ADMINISTRATIVE LAW AND HUMAN RIGHTS

Until recently, the scope for judicial review of decisions made by law enforcement officials has been quite restricted. The courts have been reluctant to exercise judicial review over decisions by the police or prosecutors made during the criminal investigation or prosecution. Judicial review has been limited to cases involving clear abuse of power, such as the complete failure to perform a legal duty or exercising power for improper purposes.[87] Pre-trial decisions which confer only "conditional authority", such as those relating to arrest, search and seizure of evidence, have been considered to be reviewable.[88] Indeed, with the rise of special statutory bodies with broad investigative powers to combat crime and corruption, such as the National Crime Authority, administrative law remedies have been successfully used to limit the scope and exercise of their investigative powers.[89]

Of particular significance to the themes raised in this chapter is the trend in administrative law toward the protection of individual rights, particularly those rights recognised under binding international treaties. In articulating the elements of procedural fairness, the High Court in *Teoh*[90] held that ratification of a treaty by the executive may ground a "legitimate expectation" that the rights therein will be respected during domestic decision-making and that the person affected by the decision will be provided with an opportunity to argue against any contrary course of action. As this protection is procedural rather than substantive, the High Court refused to impose an obligation on decision-makers to comply with binding international treaty obligations. The criticism of *Teoh* has been varied, including a concern, couched in language of separation of powers, that "[t]he creation of

---

86   (1979) 143 CLR 575 at 593.

87   See *R v Metropolitan Police Commissioner; ex p Blackburn* [1968] 2 WLR 893; *R v Metropolitan Police Commissioner; ex p Blackburn (No 3)* [1973] 2 WLR. 43. On the limited justiciability of selective policies of law enforcement, see *Wright v McQualter* (1970) 17 FLR 305.

88   Williams, DGT, "Criminal Law and Administrative Law: Problems of Procedure and Reasonableness" in Smith, P (ed), *Criminal Law: Essays in Honour of JC Smith* (Butterworths, London, 1987).

89   See further Allars, M, "Reputation, Power and Fairness: A Review of the Impact of Judicial Review upon Investigative Tribunals" (1996) 24(2) *Federal Law Review* 235. On the potential of administrative law to control decision-making in the criminal justice system, see Galligan, DJ, "Regulating Pre-Trial Decisions" in Lacey, N (ed), *Criminal Justice* (Oxford University Press, Oxford, 1994).

90   See *Minister for Immigration and Ethnic Affairs v Teoh* (1995) 183 CLR 273. The majority of the High Court held that provisions of international conventions or treaties which have been ratified by Australia (though not necessarily incorporated into domestic law) can be made relevant to the administrative decision-making process through the doctrine of "legitimate expectations".

domestic rights and responsibilities is the responsibility of parliament, not the executive in the conduct of international relations".[91] However, such criticism misconceives the nature of international law which does not address its obligations *solely* to the domestic legislature; in fact, it imposes enforceable obligations on all governmental organs including the judiciary and the executive.[92]

Due to the perceived generality of international law, *Teoh* has been further criticised for establishing a standard of invalidity in administrative decision-making which is "inappropriately vague and uncertain".[93] In the criminal justice context, some might argue that it is both impractical and unrealistic to expect police "on the street" or prosecutors to identify and apply, as relevant considerations, the provisions and jurisprudence of the ICCPR.[94] This accusation of vagueness and uncertainty presumes that international law, both in form and substance, universally consists of abstract and general principles. However, international law is not monolithic[95] and, while the accusation of uncertainty may be appropriately levelled at many treaty obligations, it is less persuasive in relation to those which protect individual rights. Indeed, international human rights instruments like the ICCPR create highly specific legal entitlements (such as the right to legal counsel and the right to an interpreter).[96] Many of these rights would be familiar to domestic lawyers. Moreover, these statements of rights have been examined, clarified and applied by courts or tribunals, for example, both the European Court of Human Rights and the United Nations Human Rights Committee deal with individual complaints about abuses of human rights and their views create binding obligations on the parties to those treaties. Surely such normative propositions offer as much predictability for administrative decision-making as the hallowed "Wednesbury" standard of unreasonableness under the common law.[97] Indeed, it may be the lack of knowledge and domestic competence in international human rights law, rather than its inherent uncertainty, which motivate these concerns.

Arguably, imposing an obligation on law enforcement officials to protect human rights would neither be unreasonable nor illegitimate in light of the increasing awareness that law enforcement officials play an important role in protecting human rights. At the international level, the expectation that law enforcement officials should respect and protect fundamental human rights is

---

91 McMillan, J, "Recent Themes in Judicial Review of Federal Executive Action" (1996) 24(2) *Federal Law Review* 347 at 355. For a contrary view, foreshadowing *Teoh* and the uses of international law in administrative decision-making, see Bayne, P, "Administrative Law, Human Rights and International Humanitarian Law" (1990) 64 *Australian Law Journal* 203, and Ch 4 by McMillan and Williams in this volume.

92 See, for example, ICCPR art 2(2), as clarified by the United Nations Human Rights Committee General Comment, Nos 2 and 3, 36 UN GAOR, Supp No 40 (a/36/40), annex VII.

93 McMillan, J, above, n 90, p 354, and Ch 4 by McMillan and Williams in this volume.

94 These concerns are reflected in the Joint Ministerial Declaration issued by the Federal Government in order to condemn and confine the effects of *Teoh*. See also *R v Chief Immigration Officer; ex p Bibi* [1976] 1 WLR 979 at 984-85 per Lord Denning MR.

95 See generally, Higgins, R, *Problems and Process: International Law and How We Use It* (Clarendon Press, Oxford, 1994).

96 ICCPR art 14(3), extracted above.

97 We are indebted to Robert McCorquodale for this provocative argument, and for providing many other helpful references in the preparation of this section.

expressly contained in the *United Nations Code of Conduct for Law Enforcement Officials*, art 2 of which provides:

> In the performance of their duty, law enforcement officials shall respect and protect human dignity and uphold the human rights of all persons.[98]

Although the Code of Conduct is a non-binding instrument, it serves as a useful reminder that the obligations contained in the ICCPR have particular relevance for law enforcement officials. Regrettably, although the Code was adopted over 15 years ago, there is little evidence of its implementation into Australian policing practice; it does not inform ethical debates on the future direction of policing in Australia or overseas.[99] Indeed, the recent developments in administrative law outlined above provide an opportunity for reinforcing the relevance of the ICCPR to domestic law enforcement – a form of legally mandated, human rights "consciousness raising" that compels law enforcement officials to consider the impact of their decisions on the human rights of all persons, especially those under investigation.[100]

CONCLUSION

This chapter provides a sketch of the potential role and impact of human rights on the criminal process. Our survey is necessarily incomplete and overlooks the use of the ICCPR as an interpretive tool in the construction of domestic statutes.[101] Human rights jurisprudence widens the range of legal argument, providing the legal community with normative standards which can be used to challenge and reshape domestic legal practice. International human rights law can no longer be regarded by legal practitioners as a strategy of last resort, available only in cases where domestic legal remedies have been exhausted.

Human rights provide a practical ethical discourse which operates as a constraint upon the administration of criminal justice. They also have a legitimating function. Jürgen Habermas has suggested that, in the age of modernity, legitimacy of law rests upon a system of fundamental rights and principles.[102] Fundamental rights and principles derive not only from *internal* legal sources, such as the Constitution, but also from *external* sources, such as international treaties and the

---

98   Adopted by the UN General Assembly on 17 December 1979.

99   See Kleinig, J, *The Ethics of Policing* (Cambridge University Press, Cambridge, 1996), which devotes only one paragraph to the UN Code, concluding that "in the member states it has never achieved the acceptance that was sought for it": p 237.

100   Kleinig, J, op cit, Ch 12.

101   See, for example, *Human Rights (Sexual Conduct) Act* 1995 (Cth) s 4, which was adopted to give effect to the United Nations Human Rights Committee ruling that Tasmanian homosexual offences violated the right to privacy protected by the ICCPR: *Toonen v Australia* Communication No 488/1992, UN Doc CCPR/C/50/D/488/1992, 4 April 1994. See further Bronitt, S, "The Right to Sexual Privacy, Sado-masochism and the Human Rights (Sexual Conduct) Act 1995 (Cth)" (1995) 2(1) *Australian Journal of Human Rights* 59. See also, Ch 2 by Sir Anthony Mason in this volume.

102   Habermas, J, *Between Facts and Norms: Contributions to a Discourse Theory on Law and Democracy* (MIT Press, Massachusetts, 1996); see also Bal, P, "Discourse Ethics and Human Rights in Criminal Procedure" in Deflem, M, (ed), *Habermas, Modernity and Law* (Sage, London, 1996), p 71.

jurisprudence from cognate domestic legal systems.[103] In the criminal justice context, Murphy J recognised the role of the ICCPR as a moral and legitimating force. Murphy J foreshadowed the fusion of international human rights and domestic law in series of judgments examining the privilege against self-incrimination, coining the phrase "the common law of human rights" to denote the broader role for the common law in the protection of individual rights.[104] Although the subsequent influence of Murphy's judgments continues to be debated, as this chapter demonstrates, his legacy of a "common law of human rights" is no longer merely aspirational – it is an integral part of domestic criminal practice.

---

103 Bal, op cit, p 77.

104 See Brown, D, "Lionel Murphy and the Criminal Law" and Bronitt, S, "Commentary" in Coper, M and Williams, G (eds), *Lionel Murphy –Influential Or Merely Prescient?* (Federation Press, Sydney, 1997).

7

IMMIGRATION LAW
AND HUMAN RIGHTS

Mary Crock and Penelope Mathew[*]

THE RHETORIC AND REALITY
OF IMMIGRATION CONTROL

The interface between human rights law and migration law is in some respects a matter of ancient usage and in others, a uniquely modern phenomenon. People have been travelling across state and geographical boundaries since time immemorial, requiring rules to be devised as to the ability of strangers to transgress upon "foreign" territory on temporary or permanent bases. As Nafziger points out,[1] it is only in recent times that states have begun to assert an absolute, sovereign right to exclude aliens from their land. The move towards immigration control appears to have been a by-product of the rise of the nation-states and technological improvements which have facilitated movement between states.

If the earliest theorists were prepared to recognise a right to freedom of movement between states,[2] modern publicists such as Nafziger who argue for such a right are very much in the minority.[3] What is interesting about his theory, however, is the distinction he draws between the theory and practice of immigration control. While most countries place restrictions on the grant of residence to foreigners, few, if any, place a complete ban on the admission or stay of aliens who come as tourists or for business related purposes. Countries that do not permit their nationals to sponsor foreigners as immediate family members are rare indeed.[4] In the heat of debates about migration to Australia, migration is often presented with images of

---

[*]   We wish to acknowledge our research assistants, Ms Deborah Siddoway and Ms Sam Brown and our partners Ron McCallum and Don Anton for their wise suggestions and comments.

1   See Nafziger, JAR, "The General Admission of Aliens Under International Law" (1983) 77 *American Journal of International Law* 804.

2   See above, n 1, pp 810-14, examining the works of Hugo Grotius, Francisco de Vitoria, Samuel Pufendorf. See also Nafziger's analysis of the work of E de Vattel.

3   As Nafziger acknowledges (above, n 1, p 805), many publicists have noted the discrepancy between theory and practice. See, for example, Borchard, E, *The Diplomatic Protection of Citizens Abroad; or the Law of International Claims* (Banks Law Publishing, New York, 1915); and Oda, M, "The Individual in International Law" in Sorensen, M, *Manual of Public International Law* (Macmillan, London, 1968), p 469.

4   For a comparative analysis of these issues in the American and European contexts, see Motomura, H, "The Family and Immigration: A Roadmap for the Ruritanian Lawmaker" (1995) 43 *American Journal of Comparative Law* 511; Gordon, C, "Family Sponsored Migration (1990) 4 *Georgetown Immigration Law Journal* 201; and Guendelsberger, J, "The Right to Family Reunification in French and US Immigration Law" (1988) 21 *Cornell International Law Journal* 1 at 41-43.

plane or boatloads of "strangers", of "new" Australians. The reality is quite different. The vast majority of the migrant intake in Australia is made up of people who come for temporary purposes or who have pre-established links with the country. They come in increasing numbers as spouses of Australians,[5] as sponsored employees or simply as tourists or foreign students. Although they appear to engender a disproportionate amount of public angst, it is only a tiny number who come "uninvited" as refugees or as fugitives from natural disasters, civil war or human rights violations.[6] The practical and conceptual impediments to a completely closed-door migration policy mandate the inclusion of migration in the mainstream of human rights discourse.

The positive obligations Australia has assumed as party to the chief international human rights instruments create basic standards that have helped to shape our laws and policies. In this chapter, we consider various aspects of the interplay between migration and human rights law. We begin by looking at the human rights aspects of one of the most basic determinants of our identity: nationality. The chapter continues with a discussion of whether there is a human right to migrate. In this context we examine the human rights norms most relevant to migration and refugee professionals, and the extent to which these have been incorporated into the domestic laws of Australia. The chapter looks then at how human rights discourse has and has not affected various aspects of migration and refugee law in Australia. We explore the human rights attaching to families and how these intersect with the migration program. There follows a treatment of the laws governing the grant of refugee status and the admission of other persons in need; and a discussion of human rights and the enforcement of migration laws. The chapter concludes by summarising the ways in which human rights laws has been a useful tool in migration and refugee cases in Australia.

Our conclusion is that in spite of the growth in importance of human rights law, control of migration to this country remains firmly fixed in the hands of the Australian government. At best, international law offers possibilities for external scrutiny of particular policies and practices, and provides a broader context for judicial interpretation of domestic laws. At worst, it is "soft law" that has no impact beyond the compromised arenas of politics and international relations. Nowhere is the gulf between ideals and realpolitik more apparent than in the domain of international human rights law. In an ideal world, human rights laws may work to down-size sovereignty to a responsible exercise of power that respects human dignity. Too often, the harsh reality is that the emergent jurisprudence has not altered greatly the traditional position that immigration control is a matter of domestic jurisdiction and that states have the power to exclude non-nationals from their territory.

---

5   On the trends in spousal migration to Australia, see Birrell, R, "Policy Implications of Recent Migration Patterns" (1995) 3(4) *People and Place* 32; and Birrell, Report, "The 1995-96 Migration Program" (1995) 3(2) *People and Place* 30.

6   The Department of Immigration and Multicultural Affairs, Fact Sheet, December 1997 states: "Some 2,719 people have arrived in Australia by small boat since November 1989, and 75 children have been subsequently born to those people in Australia making a total of 2,794 people. Of these, 2,046 have left Australia to return home or to travel to other countries, and 521 have gained permanent residence, mainly as refugees". These figures pale in comparison with the number of undocumented aliens who enter the United States each year, to take that country as an example.

HUMAN RIGHTS AND NATIONALITY

The difficulties facing migrants in enforcing their human rights reflect the extent to which aliens are quintessentially outsiders, seeking recognition or membership of a club where all the power is held internally. The problems extend even to the point of gaining the basic form of identity in our global community: a nationality. This traditional link between an individual and the state is bestowed by the state and is largely a matter of domestic jurisdiction rather than a matter governed by international law.

Article 15(1) of the *Universal Declaration of Human Rights* (UDHR) states that everyone has the right to a nationality. However, there is no correlative duty on any particular state to confer citizenship, nor is there any more than a very general attempt made to lay down rules concerning the principles by which nationality should be conferred. Broadly speaking, international law requires a link between an individual and the state in order for the state to exercise its power to confer nationality and to invoke the rights which flow from nationality such as the right of diplomatic protection.[7] The links typically relied on by states are birth of the individual on state territory or descent from a national of the state. Voluntary naturalisation is also accepted as a means of acquiring nationality. In this context, international law leaves states with broad discretions to determine the preconditions for the grant of citizenship.[8]

While there is no general customary international law requiring states to confer nationality on these or other bases, art 15(2) of the UDHR provides that no-one shall be arbitrarily deprived of his nationality or denied the right to change his nationality. This is accepted by many jurists as having attained the status of customary international law.[9] In addition, there are treaties which attempt to prevent and mitigate the problem of statelessness.[10] It is accepted that the norms of racial and sexual equality have had some impact on matters of nationality,[11] particularly in relation to what is considered an arbitrary deprivation of nationality.

---

7   See the *Nottebohm Case* (*Lichtenstein v Guatemala*) ICJ Rep 1955 4.

8   On this point, see Goodwin-Gill, G, *International Law and the Movement of Persons Between States* (Clarendon Press, Oxford, 1978).

9   Note, however, that art 15 was not fully translated into the ICCPR. The only reference in that instrument to a right to acquire nationality is in art 24(3) which protects the child's right to acquire a nationality.

10   See the *Convention relating to the Status of Stateless Persons* (1954) and the *Convention on the reduction of Statelessness* (1961).

11   Both the 1957 *Convention on the Nationality of Married Women* and art 9 of the *Convention on the Elimination of Discrimination Against Women* confirm that a woman cannot lose the nationality of her birth without her consent simply by marrying a man of a different nationality. Invidious discrimination concerning the benefits of nationality is also not permitted. In the Case of the East African Asians expelled from Uganda in 1971 by Idi Amin, the European Commission on Human Rights held that the refusal to admit persons holding British nationality to Britain amounted to degrading treatment within art 3 of the *European Convention on Human Rights: East African Asians v United Kingdom* [1973] 3 EHRR 76. The *Inter-American Court of Human Rights* held that proposed Costa Rican naturalisation provisions, which provided the opportunity for women but not men spouses of Costa Rican nationality to obtain Costa Rican nationality, offended the principle of equality enshrined in the American Convention on Human Rights: *Amendments to the Naturalization Provisions of the Constitution of Costa Rica (Advisory Opinion)*, January 19, 1984, No OC-4/84, reprinted in (1984) 5 *Human Rights Law Journal* 161. The principle of non-discrimination is probably accepted as having the status of customary international law and *jus cogens*.

Australian citizenship can be acquired by birth, descent, adoption or by grant.[12] However, Australia's citizenship laws no longer provide for the grant of citizenship as a birthright. Since 1986, children born in the country have been deemed to assume the immigration status of their parents, with citizenship following only in cases where at least one parent is either a citizen or a permanent resident.[13] Special provisions have been enacted to prevent persons from being stateless.[14] Nevertheless, the tenuous acceptance of migrants – even those who commit themselves by voluntarily acquiring Australian citizenship – is reflected in amendments to the *Australian Citizenship Act* in 1997. The present s 21 of that Act confers powers on the Minister for Immigration and Multicultural Affairs (the Minister) to revoke the citizenship of any person who gained either their citizenship or their permanent resident status by fraud or misrepresentation of any kind. In some respects the power relationship inherent in this provision sets the tone for those areas where migration law and the human rights of non-citizens come into conflict.

HUMAN RIGHTS INSTRUMENTS AND THE "RIGHT TO MIGRATE" AT INTERNATIONAL LAW

The primary international instruments for (general) migration lawyers and advocates are the UDHR and the *International Covenant on Civil and Political Rights* (ICCPR).[15] As well as containing provisions outlawing discrimination on grounds such as race, colour, sex, language, religion, political or other opinion, or national or social origin (art 2 and art 26), the ICCPR contains specific safeguards relevant to migrants. For example, arts 12 and 13 deal with freedom of movement within and expulsion from the territory of a state.[16] These provisions echo art 13 of the UDHR. The difficulty facing non-citizens is that the "rights" in these instruments are qualified. Nowhere is there recognised a "right" per se to migrate to another country.

Freedom of movement within a country is a right reserved for persons who are in the country lawfully. As a matter of customary international law, states were obliged to admit only their nationals. The UDHR protects the right to freedom of movement and residence *within* the borders of each state (art 13(1)) and the right of any person to leave any country and to return to their own country (art 13(2)). Article 12(4) of the ICCPR also refers to the right of any person to enter "his own country". This may include a country of nationality or a country of permanent residence. The right is a qualified one, however, insofar as art 12(4) merely proscribes *arbitrary* deprivation of the right to enter one's own country. Article 13

---

12 *Australian Citizenship Act* 1948 (Cth) Pt III ss 10-15.

13 Defined as a non-citizen whose presence in Australia is not subject to any limitation as to time. See *Australian Citizenship Act* 1948 (Cth) s 10. For a summary of the law governing Australian citizenship, see Jones, M et al, "Citizenship" in Burnett, R et al, *Australian Immigration Law* (Butterworths, Sydney, looseleaf), Vol 1, p 3021.

14 See *Australian Citizenship Act* s 23D.

15 On this topic, see O'Neill, N and Handley, R, *Retreat From Injustice: Human Rights in Australian Law* (Federation Press, Sydney, 1994), Ch 25.

16 See also Sieghart, P, *International Law of Human Rights* (Clarendon Press, Oxford, 1983), p 179.

also prohibits expulsion of persons lawfully within the country in the absence of some measure of due process.

In line with the prevailing theories on state sovereignty, Australia's migration laws provide that the only persons with an unfettered right to enter the country are Australian citizens. All non-citizens are required now to possess a visa, actual or deemed.[17] For those in possession of a visa, however, a right to enter follows upon "immigration clearance", the process for checking people upon their arrival in the country. For present purposes, the real questions arise at the point of applying for a visa. The human rights issues – and the obligations Australia has assumed – are reflected in the criteria used in determining the right to particular categories of visa. The two broad categories that we focus on in this chapter are those affecting the admission of family members and refugee/humanitarian cases.

A right to asylum?

The only provision of the UDHR which comes close to recognising a right of entry to state territory for non-nationals is art 14 which provides that every person has the right to seek and to enjoy in other countries asylum from persecution. However, there is no correlative duty on any state to grant asylum. The provision is accepted as conferring a mere right to seek asylum, and to enjoy asylum if and when it is granted. This provision was not included in the ICCPR.

In 1951, the international community adopted the *Convention relating to the Status of Refugees* (the Refugee Convention) as amended by the 1967 Protocol,[18] the Refugee Convention aims to protect persons who are outside their country of nationality (or habitual residence if stateless) as a result of a well-founded fear of persecution for reasons of race, religion, nationality, political opinion or membership of a particular social group. Again, this instrument does not refer to a right to asylum, nor a right of admission to third states. However, the cardinal obligation of the Convention is to protect refugees from return, in any manner, to places where life or liberty would be threatened. The practical requirements of non-refoulement have meant that applications for refugee status have served as a means of admission to state territory. In Australia, for example, a successful application for refugee status entitles a person to a protection visa.

Refugee status is not the same as citizenship or national protection. Rather, it is a temporary status pending a durable solution. There are three recognised durable solutions for refugees: voluntary repatriation to the country of origin, local integration in countries to which the refugee has first fled (known as countries of first asylum) or resettlement in a third country. Since states have some obligation to work towards finding durable solutions for refugees, permanent residence within state territory has usually been offered by Western states as it is the one durable solution firmly within a state's own jurisdiction. Pursuant to art 34 of the Convention, states are obliged to "facilitate" naturalisation. The case of refugees

---

17   See *Air Caledonie International v Commonwealth of Australia* (1988) 165 CLR 462 at 469; and s 166 of the *Migration Act* 1958 (Cth).

18   The Refugee Convention was adopted in Geneva on 28 July 1951 (see Aust TS 1954 No 5, 189 UNTS No 2545, at 137). The Protocol was signed on 31 January 1967, and ratified on 13 December 1973 (see Aust TS 1973 No 37, 606 UNTS No 8791, at 267).

from the former Yugoslavia has been something of an exception and is problematic. Such people have often been sheltered under the rubric of "temporary protection" as states have expressly sought to limit the duration and quality of their obligations. The only durable solution contemplated in this case has been "voluntary" repatriation.[19]

In addition to the Refugee Convention, art 3(1) of the *Convention Against Torture and other Cruel or Degrading Treatment or Punishment* (the Torture Convention) provides that a person shall not be returned to a place of torture. Similar obligations follow from provisions of the ICCPR. The Human Rights Committee, which supervises the ICCPR, has power to issue general comments in the context of its consideration of state reports on the domestic implementation of the instrument. In its general comment on the position of aliens under the ICCPR, the committee has confirmed that there is no right of entry under the Covenant. However, it added that considerations such as family unity or subjection to degrading treatment may bring the provisions of the ICCPR into play even in relation to entry.[20] These general comments may be viewed as an interpretative tool in relation to the ICCPR.

Other guarantees for non-citizens

Apart from the question of entry to, and expulsion from, a country, the ICCPR contains important guarantees for non-citizens. The rights in the Covenant apply to all persons within the territory and jurisdiction of the state without discrimination. Non-citizens have all the rights contained in the ICCPR unless expressly excluded as in art 25 concerning political participation, and the Human Rights Committee has expressed its opinion to this effect in its general comment on the position of aliens under the Covenant (referred to above). Some rights are relevant to the treatment of non-citizens in relation to their application for entry to or stay of deportation from a country. For example, the right to liberty contained in art 9 and the right to humane treatment of detainees set out in art 10 apply to aliens subject to exclusion and deportation procedures.

The incorporation of international human rights norms into Australia's domestic laws

The problem for advocates is that these provisions of international human rights laws – qualified as they are in the case of aspiring migrants – have not been enacted directly into Australian law. With regard to the ICCPR and the *International Covenant on Economic, Social and Cultural Rights* (ICESCR), only the former has been scheduled to the *Human Rights and Equal Opportunity Commission Act* 1986 (Cth) (HREOC Act). Moreover, although the *Convention on the Rights of the Child* (CROC) is one of the international instruments containing the rights and freedoms

---

19 Joly, D, "The Porous Dam: European Harmonisation on Asylum in the Nineties" (1994) 6 *International Journal of Refugee Law* 159 at 178; Luca, D, "Questioning Temporary Protection" (1994) 6 *International Journal of Refugee Law* 535 at 356.

20 See para 5 of General Comment 15/27, reproduced in Nowak, M, *UN Covenant on Civil and Political Rights: CCPR Commentary* (Engel Publisher, Strasbourg, 1993), p 861.

which define "human rights" for the purposes of the functions and powers of the Commission under the HREOC Act, it is not strictly scheduled – rather a declaration has been made with respect to it under s 47 of the Act. Clearly, these gestures are not sufficient to enact the content of those instruments into Australia's domestic law.[21]

While Australia has signed and ratified the Refugee Convention, it has chosen not to implement the terms of that instrument directly, other than to adopt as a standard the definition of refugee contained in art 1A of the instrument. The *Migration Act* 1958 merely refers to persons to whom Australia has protection obligations under the Refugee Convention and sets out the procedures for review of refugee status applications and, in recent years, the government has legislated specifically to exclude groups of applicants from access to these procedures altogether.[22] The Act was amended in 1991,[23] to interpose a certain distance between the UN standard and the decision made by either the Minister or the Refugee Review Tribunal (RRT). A protection visa is granted now where the Minister "is satisfied" that the applicant meets the Convention definition of refugee. The task of the courts in reviewing a refugee decision no longer involves a simple examination of whether an applicant meets the definition of refugee. Rather, the role of the judge is to determine whether there was any evidence upon which the decision maker could *be satisfied* that an applicant did or did not meet the definition of refugee.[24] The legislative framework is designed to give maximum autonomy to the RRT, standing as it does in the shoes of the original decision maker.

The Torture Convention is set out as a schedule to the *Crimes (Torture) Act* 1988 (Cth), an enactment that has extraterritorial but no internal operation. The decision not to enact this Convention into Australia's domestic laws was based on the notion that our domestic laws already offer sufficient protection from such gross abuse of human rights. One by-product of the omission, however, is that there is no enactment of the protection against refoulement or return to a country where a person is at risk of being tortured or subjected to cruel or inhumane treatment.[25] We discuss this issue further below.

Some aspects of other human rights treaties relevant to migrants have been enacted into legislation. For example, the *Racial Discrimination Act* 1975 (Cth), the first major piece of federal human rights legislation, is an almost complete enactment of the *Convention on the Elimination of All Forms of Racial*

---

21 Even so, the controversy surrounding the High Court's decision in *Minister for Immigration and Ethnic Affairs v Teoh* (1995) 183 CLR 273 has led to calls for Australia to renounce the CROC lest that instrument impose unwarranted burdens on administrators to comply with its terms. At time of writing, these calls had been resisted. However, the Senate Legal and Constitutional Legislation Committee had endorsed the "anti-Teoh" Administrative Decisions (Effect of International Instruments) Bill 1997 (Cth) which remains before Parliament. *Teoh's* case is discussed below at n 36 and accompanying text.

22 See below, n 104ff.

23 See s 22A of the Act of 1958-1991.

24 See *Minister for Immigration and Ethnic Affairs v Wu Shan Liang* (1996) 185 CLR 259.

25 See Taylor, S, "Australia's Implementation of its Non-Refoulement Obligations under the Convention Against Torture and Other Cruel, Inhuman or Degrading Treatment or Punishment and the International Covenant on Civil and Political Rights" (1994) 17 *University of New South Wales Law Journal* 432.

Discrimination (CERD). Even in this instance, the domestic Act did not incorporate art 4 of CERD which prohibits racial vilification and propaganda. Since 1995, the controversial *Racial Hatred Act* 1995 (Cth) has gone some way toward filling the gap. The Racial Discrimination Act was followed in 1984 by the *Sex Discrimination Act* 1984 (Cth), which partially enacts the *Convention on the Elimination of all Forms of Discrimination Against Women* (CEDAW). The *Sex Discrimination Act* contains no general prohibition on discrimination and a number of broad exemptions from its scope.

This failure to enact the specific terms of the various human rights treaties and conventions to which Australia is a party does not necessarily mean that Australia has failed to take international legal obligations seriously. In most respects Australia has worked to ensure that its laws are not in direct conflict with its international legal obligations.

MIGRATION AND THE HUMAN RIGHTS OF THE FAMILY

The central importance of family in any society is recognised in the UDHR. Article 16(1) affirms as a fundamental human right the right of (consenting) men and women of full age ... to marry and found a family. The instrument continues in para (3): "The family is the natural and fundamental group unit of society and is entitled to protection by society and the state". These provisions are repeated in art 23 of the ICCPR. Specific protections are afforded in these and other instruments to children who form a critical part of many family units. The child's right to protection without discrimination as to race, colour, sex, language, national or social origin, property or birth, is enshrined in art 25(2) of the UDHR and art 24 of the ICCPR, as well as being central to the CROC.[26]

These principles of international law underpin many aspects of Australia's domestic migration program. The coincidence may be serendipitous: recognising the rights of families is good domestic politics as those affected are often electors. Although the present government has reduced the place of families in the overall migration intake, family migrants remain by far the biggest component of the program. The 1997-98 planning levels allocate 32,000 of the 68,000 places in the non-humanitarian program to family migrants.[27]

Within the migration program preference is given to family members to a greater and lesser extent according to the various degrees of family relationship. Migrants in the economic categories are required to demonstrate that they possess skills or qualifications or other attributes that make them attractive as migrants. In contrast, visas are granted to the closest family members almost exclusively on the basis of the non-citizen's relationship with the Australian citizen or permanent

---

26   See also the *Declaration of the Rights of the Child* (1959).

27   Department of Immigration and Multicultural Affairs Fact Sheet 2: 1997-98 Migration Program planning levels (22 May 1997). Note that the 1995-96 family intake figures include the concessional family places. The 1997-98 figures place the new skilled Australian-linked places within the places in the skill stream.

resident acting as sponsor. Like other migrants, "preferential" family[28] are subject to health and character requirements, as well as certain "re-entry" criteria (see Schs 4 and 5 to the *Migration (1994) Regulations*). However, they stand apart in that discretions have been built in so as to allow for the waiver of the health and character tests in special circumstances.

Spouses, dependent children and aged parents also receive special treatment in other respects. The issue of visas in these classes is demand driven and cannot be suspended (see ss 85-91 of the *Migration Act* 1958 (Cth) (the Act). In addition, concessions are made so as to allow persons meeting the definition of close or preferential family to gain residence even if they are unlawful non-citizens.[29]

For its part, the Federal Court has shown a willingness in some cases to use international human rights norms as tools for the interpretation of Australia's domestic migration laws in relation to family migration. For example, in *Chen Wen Ying v Minister for Immigration and Ethnic Affairs*[30] Davies J considered the principles set out in the *Declaration of the Rights of the Child* (1959) in his interpretation of the phrase "special need relative". In the result the judge extended the phrase so as to allow the minor children of the non-citizen in question to sponsor their mother on grounds that their infancy rendered them her "special need relatives".[31] In his judgment, Davies J cited the comment of Brennan, Deane and Dawson JJ in *Chu Kheng Lim v Minister for Immigration, Local Government and Ethnic Affairs*:[32]

> We accept the proposition that the courts should, in a case of ambiguity, favour a construction of a Commonwealth statute which accords with the obligations of Australia under an international treaty.

Spouse and "interdependent" relationships

By world standards, Australia's migration laws regarding spousal relationships are liberal.[33] Persons in de facto relationships are treated in much the same way as partners in a legal marriage, with provisos made that de facto parties meet extra requirements concerning length of relationship and co-habitation. Provision is made also for the sponsoring of partners in homosexual or other relationships where a

---

28 This component comprises spouses and de facto partners, interdependent partners, dependent and adopted children, parents who meet the balance of family test and orphaned unmarried relatives. See also the Preferential relative (migrant) (class AY) visa, which includes visa cl 104 for aged dependent relatives; remaining relatives (as defined) and special need relatives. For a discussion of these categories, see Crock, M, *Migration and Refugee Law in Australia* (Federation Press, Sydney, 1998), Ch 5.

29 This right is a qualified one that depends on how the individual became an unlawful non-citizen and how long he or she has held that status. On this point see Crock, above, n 28, Ch 9.

30 (1994) 51 FCR 332.

31 The case arose because the woman could not be sponsored on spouse grounds by the father of her children. Note that a quite different approach was taken by the Full Federal Court to a case with similar facts in *Huang v Minister for Immigration and Ethnic Affairs* (unreported, Fed Ct FC, 29 November 1996).

32 (1992) 176 CLR 1 at 38.

33 This point can be made about a number of aspects of the family migration rules. Compare the analyses of the authors cited above, n 4.

requisite degree of "interdependence" can be demonstrated. Spouses and interdependent partners can be sponsored from abroad or from within Australia. Indeed, while certain pre-conditions have to be met, a partner's unlawful status in Australia is not a complete bar to that person's ability to gain residence on the basis of his or her relationship with an Australian citizen or permanent resident. Both Australian citizens and permanent residents are eligible to act as sponsors in relation to these visa subclasses.

The Federal Court has stressed that it is the simple fact of the relationship between the parties to a marriage that is critical to the person's entitlement to a spouse visa.[34] The government has moved to ensure that this aspect of the migration program is not abused by persons seeking to gain residence in Australia by means of a contrived or sham relationship with an Australian party. A foreign spouse is now placed on probation for two years before permanent residency is granted, and this requirement applies whether persons apply to migrate as a spouse from overseas or seek to change their status within the country. The two-year probation can be waived where partners have been married for more than five years, or where a marriage has lasted two years or more and a child has been born of the partnership. Permanent residence is granted also where the Australian sponsor dies inside the two-year waiting period or where the non-citizen partner is a victim of domestic violence.[35]

Other measures have been introduced to deal with perceived abuses of the spousal migration stream. These include initiatives to increase the scrutiny of spouse applications processed at overseas posts and policy requirements that women applicants in some centres view a video on domestic violence and the problems associated with men who have sponsored a series of foreign women as their wives: see Migration (1994) Regulations, reg 1.20.

Human rights, family rights and criminality

The interface between international law and the "right" to family unity under Australian immigration law became the subject of vigorous public debate in 1995 when the High Court handed down its ruling in *Minister for Immigration and Ethnic Affairs v Teoh*.[36] That case concerned a Malaysian citizen who was married to an Australian citizen and who had primary responsibility for the care and control of no less than seven Australian born children. Mr Teoh was seeking permanent residence on the basis of his marriage, but was denied a permit (now visa) and placed under a deportation order because he had been convicted of a criminal offence involving the importation of heroin. His case became a cause celebre when the High Court accepted arguments that Australia's ratification of the CROC created a legitimate expectation that the Minister would take into account the terms of art 3 of this

---

34 See *Dhillon v Minister for Immigration and Ethnic Affairs* (1989) 86 ALR 651 at 655-57. The case is discussed in Crock (1998) above, n 28, Ch 5.

35 See Migration (1994) Regulations: reg 1.03 (definition of long term spouse relationship); reg 1.15A (definition of spouse); sch 1, 1220A (spouse (provisional) (class UF); sch 1, 1129 (spouse (migrant) (class BC); sch 2, subcl 309 (spouse (provisional) visa); and sch 2, subcl 100 (spouse visa). Equivalent visas are provided for persons applying within Australia at sch 2, subcll 801 and 820.

36 (1995) 183 CLR 273. See further Ch 4, by McMillan and Williams, in this volume.

Convention when making a decision as to whether to order Mr Teoh's deportation. Article 3 provides that, in all actions concerning children, the best interests of the child shall be a primary consideration.

The majority of the High Court held that the doctrine of legitimate expectation created procedural rights, but did not mean that decision-makers may be compelled to apply the terms of the treaty. Such a ruling to compel, it was said, would contravene the well-accepted position that unincorporated treaties do not confer justiciable rights on individuals within Australia. However, where the administrative decision-maker does not take the terms of the treaty into account, procedural fairness requires that the subject of the decision be given a hearing on the issue.[37]

Teoh's case demonstrated the increasing relevance of international law as both a legal weapon and as an interpretative tool in the domestic legal context in Australia.[38] It also highlighted the significance of the various international instruments that impact on migration law. In practical terms, however, it has not altered the substance of many of the decisions made where the parent of Australian-born children is threatened with deportation or removal because of the criminal conduct or bad character of that parent.

Australian migration laws have always provided for the deportation of non-citizens convicted of serious crimes. The present Act contains three provisions for the deportation of such persons.[39] In addition, the Minister has special powers conferred by ss 501-502 of the Act to revoke the visa of non-citizens who are considered to be "not of good character". The deportation provisions of s 200 of the Act recognise the human rights or superior immigration status of persons who have gained permanent residence in the country. Permanent residents are only liable to deportation if they are convicted of a crime for which they are sentenced to at least 12 months in prison. Liability to deportation ceases if the permanent resident is not convicted of a crime within 10 years of gaining that status.[40] Permanent residents who are subject to a deportation order have a right to appeal to the Administrative Appeals Tribunal (AAT): see s 500 of the Migration Act 1958. They also have an unrestricted right to take their cases to the Federal Court on a question of law under s 44 of the *Administrative Appeals Tribunal Act* 1975 (Cth).

The ruling in *Teoh* appears to have heightened consciousness of the rights of those affected by the decision to deport a criminal permanent resident.[41] Interesting issues have arisen about the effect of measures taken by successive governments to

---

37   Ibid at 286-87 per Mason CJ and Deane J, and at 298 per Toohey J.

38   On the significance of the case, see Allars, M, "One Small Step for Legal Doctrine, One Giant Leap Towards Integrity in Government" (1995) 17 *Sydney Law Review* 204; and Mathew, P and Walker, K, "Case Note: *Minister for Immigration v Ah Hin Teoh*" (1995) 20 *Melbourne University Law Review* 236.

39   See ss 200-203 of the Act. These provisions deal with standard serious crimes where the offender is sentenced to 12 months or more in prison; crimes involving matters of national security ; and with the more exotic crimes such as treason and inciting sedition.

40   Note, however, the definition of 10 years permanent residence in s 204 of the Act.

41   See, for example, *Re Francis and Minister for Immigration and Ethnic Affairs* (1996) 42 ALR 555. See also *Department of Immigration and Multicultural Affairs v Ram* (1996) 41 ALD 517; and *Re "WAG" and Minister for Immigration and Multicultural Affairs* (1996) 44 ALD 663 – cases involving issues of character (s 501 exclusions), rather than criminal deportations.

negate the effect of the decision.[42] While the status of the decision may be uncertain, Federal Court judges have emerged as proponents of the continuing operation of the *Teoh* decision[43] against those inclined to dismiss it as a "jurisprudential artefact".[44] The recognition of a theoretical right to a hearing, however, has not been translated into more favourable outcomes for those fighting a deportation order. The number of criminal deportations has not decreased since the ruling in *Teoh*. A notable exception in this trend is the case of *Vaitaiki v Minister for Immigration and Multicultural Affairs*.[45] In that case, the Full Federal Court found close parallels between the *Teoh* case and the matter before it. Their Honours spent considerable time discussing the effect of the High Court's ruling and found ultimately that the AAT had erred in failing to give greater consideration to the rights of the Australian children affected by the decision to deport Mr Vaitaiki.

Teoh's case also seems to have increased awareness of other international legal obligations assumed by Australia and how these affect the exercise of statutory discretions in the domestic sphere. Apart from the consideration of the family of prospective deportees, review bodies have had to consider the interface between the power to deport criminal permanent residents and the obligation not to "refoule" a recognised refugee to a country where he or she faces persecution. The lapse into criminality may be an easy one – and in some cases understandable – for persons accustomed to living by their wits on the fringes of society, or who are left in Australia bereft of friends and family networks. In *Re Le Geng Jia and Minister for Immigration and Multicultural Affairs*,[46] the AAT took a compassionate approach to one individual seeking residence in Australia who was a fugitive from Tienanmen Square. Le was convicted of serious sex offences against his former lover who had stolen his savings of $11,000 to feed her gambling addiction and who had left him for another man.[47] This case represented an exception to the general rule: most convicted criminals fail in their bids to remain in the country, even if they have a claim for refugee status. In other cases,[48] the AAT and the Federal Court have

---

42   See the Joint Ministerial Statement of 10 May 1995; and the Administrative Decisions (Effect of International Instruments) Bill 1996.

43   See *Vaitaiki v Minister for Immigration and Multicultural Affairs* (unreported, Fed Ct, Beaumont J, 20 June 1997) and *Salameh v Minister for Immigration and Multicultural Affairs* (unreported, Fed Ct, Beaumont J, 23 June 1997).

44   See the comments of Deputy President McMahon in *Re Vaitaiki and the Minister for Immigration and Ethnic Affairs* (unreported, AAT, 2 November 1995). Compare the remarks of Deputy President Gerber in *Re Yad Ram and Department of Immigration and Ethnic Affairs* (unreported, AAT, 5 December 1995), who described the statement of 10 May 1995 as an "ukase" (an arbitrary edict of a Russian Tzar) and preferred the rock of the High Court as legal authority.

45   (1998) 150 ALR 608.

46   (1997) 42 ALD 700.

47   The case raised the ire of the Minister who intervened to ensure that Mr Le was removed from Australia by cancelling his visa in accordance with s 501 of the *Migration Act* 1958. The Minister's action has been challenged in the Federal Court.

48   See, for example, *Todea v Minister for Immigration and Ethnic Affairs* (1994) 2 AAR 470; *Bengescue v Minister for Immigration and Ethnic Affairs* (1994) 35 ALD 429 (extract); *Dhayakpa v Minister for Immigration and Ethnic Affairs* (unreported, Fed Ct, French J, 25 October 1995); and *Vabaza v Minister for Immigration and Multicultural Affairs* (unreported, Fed Ct, Goldberg J, 27 February 1997).

invoked the public interest/ national security exception to the non-refoulement obligation contained in the Refugee Convention.[49]

In 1997, the present Minister instituted an inquiry into the criminal deportation scheme by the Joint Standing Committee on Migration. The Committee is due to report in 1998, following which fresh legislative changes are expected. In its submission to the inquiry, the Department outlined a number of options for reform that would allow the government to take a tougher line against migrants who are perceived to abuse their privileges as members of the Australian community.[50] These include a suggestion that the Minister's power to deport be "codified" so as to mandate deportation in cases involving serious crimes or offences. It proposes that the Minister have a non-compellable power to make concessions in exceptional circumstances. The Department also proposed changes to speed up the deportation process. These include conferring on the Immigration Review Tribunal (IRT) the role of reviewing criminal deportation decisions; the appointment of a Special Immigration Commissioner to do this job; the abolition of merits review altogether; the exclusion of judicial review; and the return to the system in place before 1992. The last option is that the review authority resume a recommendatory function, with the final decision made by the Minister.[51] One of the most serious of the Department's recommendations, however, is the suggestion[52] that the 10-year limit on criminal deportations be removed so that immunity from removal should apply only to Australian citizens.

In the context of Australia's obligations under the ICCPR, it is interesting to note in the Department's submission[53] a reference to complaints made to the UN Human Rights Committee by two prospective deportees. They are claiming that their removal would result in their being sentenced to death in their countries of origin. The Department does not recommend directly that the government renounce its accession to the First Optional Protocol to the ICCPR. However, the submission makes veiled references to the potentially dire consequences should criminal deportees choose to use this mechanism to slow the removal process.

Even without knowing the outcome of the 1997 Inquiry into Criminal Deportation, it would appear that the present Minister has specific concerns about the current process and the role that he has to play in it. This much is evident in a Bill already before Parliament which would dramatically increase the Minister's powers to intervene in any cases involving non-citizens who are found to be "not of good character".[54] The suggestions put forward by the Department concerning the criminal deportation provisions have already solicited opposition from the AAT.[55]

---

49   See arts 32 and 33(2) of the Refugee Convention.

50   See submission of the Department of Immigration and Multicultural Affairs to the Joint Standing Committee on Migration's Inquiry into Criminal Deportation. Submission No 38, dated 14 August 1997, p 9.

51   Ibid, pp 12-14. Before 1992 the AAT's function was recommendatory only.

52   Ibid, pp 15-16.

53   Ibid, p 6.

54   See the Migration Legislation Amendment (Strengthening of Character and Conduct Provisions) Bill 1997 (Cth). This Bill was considered and approved by the Senate Legal and Constitutional Legislation Committee. At the time of writing it remains in the Senate.

55   See submission of the AAT to the Inquiry into Criminal Deportation, Submission No 23, dated 16 April 1997 and Supplementary Submission, November 1997.

Within the prevailing climate of anti-immigration sentiment, the politics of criminal deportation would seem to make the prospect of legislative changes almost inevitable. How the legislation emerges from this imbroglio over "unworthy" migrants remains to be seen.

HUMAN RIGHTS AND REFUGEES

The rights of refugees

The question of refugee status is governed at international law by the Refugee Convention[56] and its 1967 Protocol. The Protocol served to remove the temporal and geographic restrictions on the Convention definition of a refugee: originally, states were only obliged to protect refugees fleeing events occurring before 1951 and there was an option to limit states' obligations to cover only those refugees fleeing as a result of events that had occurred in Europe. The primary obligation towards refugees contained in the Refugee Convention is the obligation of non-refoulement, contained in art 33.

In addition to the Refugee Convention, the United Nations High Commissioner for Refugees (UNHCR) was established in 1950 to protect refugees. The UNHCR was created pursuant to a statute adopted by the General Assembly of the United Nations. The statute is distinct from the 1951 Convention, although states party to the Convention have a duty to co-operate with the UNHCR under art 35 of the Convention. The UNHCR is supervised by an "Executive Committee" (known as Excom) comprised of governmental delegates. Excom adopts "conclusions" regarding protection of refugees which, though not formally binding, are part of the "soft law" that may be used to interpret the Convention.[57]

As a party to both the Refugee Convention and the Protocol, Australia is required by art 33 of the Convention to protect refugees from return to a place of persecution. The Convention also sets out a number of other obligations to refugees, such as the right to work and the right of freedom of movement within the state, although these may be limited in their scope to refugees "lawfully present" or "lawfully staying" in the territory of the state and distinctions may be made between the rights of refugees and nationals. General human rights law may have had an impact in relation to such matters, however, since the ICCPR and ICESCR extend to all persons within state territory and jurisdiction, including non-citizens. In Australia, grant of refugee status usually leads to permanent residence status and, if the refugee desires, to citizenship. Thus the refugee is generally entitled to the same rights as other permanent residents and citizens of Australia. Consequently, the controversies in relation to refugees in Australia have arisen at the stage of determination of refugee status because of the risk of refoulement that a deficient procedure for determination of refugee status creates. With the exception of some areas relating to the treatment of unauthorised arrivals which have been the subject of controversy, the laws governing the grant of refugee status comply in most respects with Australia's international legal obligations.

---

56   See above, n 18.

57   See Sztucki, J, "The Conclusions on the International Protection of Refugees Adopted by the Executive Committee of the UNHCR Program" (1989) 1 *International Journal of Refugee Law* 285.

Determination of refugee status

The Refugee Convention does not specify procedures for determination of refugee status. States party to the instrument are free to adopt mechanisms most suited to their situation, provided always that determinations are carried out in good faith. It is accepted that as a matter of international law such procedures are merely declaratory, rather than constitutive, of refugee status. This means that a person is a refugee as soon as he or she meets the definition contained in the Refugee Convention, accruing all the rights attending refugee status.

Refugee status determination may be considered constitutive for the purposes of Australian domestic law, since rights and benefits under Australian law flow from the recognition of the person as a refugee. In *Chan's* case, the High Court held that determination of refugee status proceeded on the basis of the facts existing at the time of the determination, not only the facts existing when the refugee fled her country of origin.[58] However, the importance attached to the events that caused the refugee to flee and the consideration of whether there had been a fundamental change in the country of origin indicates that the asylum-seeker clearly was a refugee at the time he left: the task of Australian decision-makers was to confirm whether this was still the case.

In Australia, the Act provides that a protection visa (cl 866) may be granted to "persons to whom Australia has protection obligations under the Refugee Convention".[59] Applications for a protection visa are heard at first instance by an officer of the Department. Merits review is then available before a member of the Refugee Review Tribunal (RRT). Traditionally, judicial review has been available before the Federal Court, and matters may ultimately go before the High Court. However, in recent years, the jurisdiction of the Federal Court concerning refugee matters has been removed from the *Administrative Decisions (Judicial Review) Act 1977* (Cth) and a more limited capacity for review has been included within Pt 8 of the *Migration Act 1958*. In 1997, the Minister introduced a Bill that aims to replace these provisions with a privative clause, removing the jurisdiction of the Federal Court altogether in migration cases.[60] The original jurisdiction of the High Court under s 75 of the Constitution remains, however, as that cannot be removed without Constitutional amendment. At time of writing, the legislation was stalled in the Senate.

The determination of refugee status in Australia raises issues of international human rights law in two main contexts. First, there is the substantive question of how the definition of a refugee is interpreted: the standard is set by an international instrument. Second, there are procedural matters concerning the rights of persons seeking recognition as refugees before their status is determined. These include the right to liberty and freedom of movement; the right to legal advice; and the right to

---

58   *Chan v Minister for Immigration and Ethnic Affairs* (1989) 169 CLR 379 at 390 per Mason CJ, at 399 per Dawson J, at 408 per Toohey J, at 415 per Gaudron J, and at 431-45 per McHugh J.

59   See s 36(2) of the *Migration Act 1958* (Cth).

60   See Migration Legislation Amendment Bill (No 5) 1997 (Cth); and Media Release by Minister for Immigration and Ethnic Affairs, "Government to Limit Refugee and Immigration Litigation," MPS 32/97, 25 March 1997. The Bill is the subject of a report by the Joint Standing Committee on Migration, dated 28 October 1997.

access refugee determination procedures at all. Like a number of other refugee-receiving countries, Australia has gradually implemented strategies for "burden sharing". In practical terms this has provided mechanisms for preventing some asylum seekers from seeking protection in Australia where another country to which a person can be sent has been declared "safe".

Substantive issues: the definition of a refugee

The Refugee Convention definition of a refugee may be broken into several components, although care must be taken not to break the nexus between these components, particularly in Australia where the jurisprudence of the Federal and High Court has stressed the "common thread" tying together the elements of the definition:[61]

- A person seeking recognition as a refugee (an asylum-seeker) must be outside the country of origin and unable or unwilling to return.

- The person must fear persecution. Though persecution is not defined in either the Convention or the Protocol, it is generally accepted as meaning serious violations of human rights symptomatic of a failure in state protection.[62] The High court in *Chan's* case held that persecution involves some serious penalty or punishment.[63]

- Fear of persecution must be well founded. Both a subjective element of fear and an objective element of reasonableness are required. The test applied in Australia is that there must be a "real chance" of persecution.[64]

- The persecution must be linked to the state in the sense that the state is unwilling or unable to protect the asylum-seeker from persecution. Thus the human rights violations need not stem directly from the state. They may be the result of action by private individuals, but if the state fails to prevent or punish such action the requirement of a nexus to the state is satisfied.

- Finally, persecution must be related to one of the five grounds, which are known as "Convention grounds" or "Convention reasons". The leading Australian case concerning the nexus between the persecution feared and the five Convention grounds is *Applicant A v Minister for Immigration and Ethnic Affairs.*[65] McHugh J emphasised that the concept of persecution refers not only to the nature of the harm to the individual, but whether the harm was selective and discriminatory on the basis of one of the five Convention grounds.[66]

---

61 *Ram v Minister for Immigration and Ethnic Affairs* (1995) 130 ALR 314; *Applicant A v Minister for Immigration and Ethnic Affairs* (1997) 142 ALR 331 at 341 per Dawson J. On this case, see Mathew, P, "Case Note" (1997) 22 *Melbourne University Law Review* 277; and Crock, M, "Apart from Us or Part of Us: Immigrants' Rights, Public Opinion and the Rule of Law" (1998) 10 *International Journal of Refugee Law* (forthcoming).

62 Hathaway, J, *The Law of Refugee Status* (Butterworths, Toronto, 1991), pp 99ff.

63 *Chan v Minister for Immigration and Ethnic Affairs* (1989) 169 CLR 379 at 388 per Mason CJ.

64 *Chan* (1989) 169 CLR 379 at 389 per Mason CJ, at 398 per Dawson J, at 407 per Toohey J, and at 429 per McHugh J.

65 (1997) 142 ALR 331.

66 Ibid at 554 per McHugh J.

This case involved the difficult question of the meaning of the phrase "particular social group". The High Court found against the appellants by a majority of 3 to 2. The appellants were a Chinese couple fleeing forcible sterilisation[67] under the policy that families in China may have only one child. The court ruled that the pair were fleeing the enforcement of a generally applicable policy which did not single out any particular group for maltreatment, and therefore did not meet the definition of a refugee. The majority held that what was required for membership of a particular social group was some "unifying" element among members of the group.[68] Persecution must be feared on account of this unifying element rather than by virtue of individual conduct pursuant to a generally applicable law or policy.[69] The unifying element could not be fear of persecution pursuant to a generally applicable law or policy. McHugh J nominated several factors defining a social group, namely a common "characteristic, attribute, activity, belief, interest or goal".[70] Both Dawson and McHugh JJ acknowledged the importance of external perceptions of a particular characteristic perceived to define a group, as did Kirby J (who dissented in the result). It would appear that gender might be regarded by the High Court to operate as a unifying characteristic.

In addition to the "inclusive" components of the definition of a refugee, there are a number of exclusion and cessation clauses,[71] and an exception for refugees who pose a danger to the community of the country of refuge.[72] Space does not permit examination of them here.

Procedural issues: rights of asylum-seekers

In spite of the freedom given to states in the procedures they can adopt to determine refugee status, the Refugee Convention does provide some safeguards for asylum seekers. Article 31 of the Refugee Convention provides that illegal entrants shall not be subjected to any penalty on account of illegal entry and that only such restrictions on freedom of movement as are necessary shall be imposed. For its part the UNHCR has also issued recommendations through its Excom. Excom conclusion 8 sets out minimum standards of procedural fairness in relation to applications for refugee status.[73] Excom conclusion 44 provides guidelines on the circumstances in which such people can be held in detention.[74]

---

67 While women are generally more likely to be subjected to forcible sterilisation than men, the RRT accepted that the male partner in this case had a well-founded fear of sterilisation.

68 (1997) 142 ALR 331 at 341 per Dawson J, at 359 per McHugh J, and at 375-76 per Gummow J.

69 Ibid at 341 per Dawson J, at 358-59 per McHugh J, and at 376 per Gummow J.

70 See above, n 68.

71 See arts 1C-1F of the Refugee Convention.

72 See art 33(2) of the Refugee Convention.

73 Reproduced in Goodwin-Gill, G, *The Refugee in International Law* (Clarendon Press, Oxford, 1997), pp 472-73.

74 Reproduced in Goodwin-Gill, above, n 73, pp 491-92.

The ICCPR also protects asylum-seekers' rights. Article 9(1) of the ICCPR provides that no-one shall be subjected to arbitrary detention.[75] Where persons are detained, art 10 of the ICCPR requires them to be treated with humanity and with respect for the inherent dignity of the human person. Although formally non-binding since they are in the nature of resolutions or guidelines adopted by the UN, there are two further instruments which may be used in the interpretation of the standards contained in the ICCPR. The first is the Standard Minimum Rules for the Treatment of Prisoners,[76] which the third committee of the General Assembly of the UN recommended be taken into account in the interpretation of art 10 of the ICCPR. (The third Committee was involved in the drafting of the ICCPR.) The second instrument is the Body of Principles for the Protection of All Persons under Any Form of Detention or Imprisonment adopted by the UN General Assembly in 1988. In its general comment on art 10, the Human Rights Committee invited states to include in their periodical reports under art 40 of the ICCPR material concerning their implementation of the Body of Principles.[77] The UN Working Group on Arbitrary Detention has considered the status of the Body of Principles and has noted that most of its provisions are declaratory of pre-existing rights at customary international law.[78] The following provisions of the Body Principles are relevant here. Principle 13 provides that a state must provide the detainee with "information on and an explanation of his rights and how to avail himself of such rights". In other words, relying on the prisoner's ignorance of the law is not appropriate for the detaining authorities. Principle 15 guarantees that communication "with the outside world" shall not be denied for more than a matter of days. Principle 17 provides that a detainee shall be entitled to have the assistance of legal counsel. Principle 18 provides that a detained or imprisoned person shall be entitled to communicate and consult with his or her legal counsel.

As will be seen below, these instruments have been used in Australian litigation. Where parliament has legislated effectively to exclude consideration of these instruments, refugee advocates may turn to international fora in order to place pressure on government, although the impact of international scrutiny of the treatment of immigrants and refugees may be less potent than in other areas.

Detention

Like many other states, Australia distinguishes between "asylum-seekers," whose status has not been determined, and refugees. Within the category of asylum-seekers, the Act discriminates between people who have entered Australia with a valid visa and then apply for refugee status, even if they have become unlawful non-citizens in the interim, and those who arrive without visas and apply for entry at the

---

75   For an analysis see Mathew, P, "Sovereignty and the Right to Seek Asylum: the Case of Cambodian Asylum-Seekers in Australia" (1994) 15 *Australian Yearbook of International Law* 35, pp 87-99. See also Goodwin-Gill, above, n 8, pp 247-51.

76   Adopted 31 July 1957, ESC Res 663C (XXIV), 24 UNESCOR, Supp (No 1) at 11 (1957), extended 13 May 1977, ESC Res 2076 (LXIII), 62 UN ESCOR, Supp (No 1) at 35 (1977).

77   General Comment 21/44. Reproduced in Nowak, above, n 20, p 873.

78   Working Group on Arbitrary Detention, Deliberation 02, Report of the Working Group on Arbitrary Detention, UN Doc E/Cn.4/1993/24, p 9.

border. The universal visa requirement which has applied since 1994 means that, in theory, all unlawful non-citizens are subject to mandatory arrest, detention and removal.[79] However, boat people and other unauthorised arrivals are more restricted in their access to bridging visas which permit release into the community pending the determination of their application for entry. Bridging visas for unauthorised arrivals are limited to those who have applied for a refugee protection visa and who are over 75 years of age, spouses of Australian citizens, children, or former victims of trauma and torture.[80]

The government's argument in favour of mandatory detention of asylum-seekers rests on the distinction between asylum-seekers and refugees and the need to protect Australia from illegal entry. Refugees are entitled to stay in Australia, but status must be confirmed before permission to stay can be granted. The validity of these arguments was accepted by the High Court in *Chu Kheng Lim v Minister for Immigration and Ethnic Affairs*,[81] which involved legislative provisions for mandatory detention of boat people introduced in 1992. The court upheld most of the legislation on the basis that it appeared necessary and proportionate to the exercise of the Commonwealth's power to make a decision as to entry, exclusion or deportation.[82] The High Court found that it could not refer to relevant international legal standards, because the legislative scheme contained a provision which stated that the legislation overrode all laws other than the Constitution.[83]

One of the affected asylum-seekers in that case made a communication to the Human Rights Committee, alleging, among other things, a violation of art 9 of the ICCPR. In 1997, the Human Rights Committee delivered its "views" regarding the communication.[84] The Committee noted that of course it might be necessary to detain an illegal entrant initially for investigation or to deal with a person who would not co-operate with authorities.[85] However, it said that Australia had "not advanced any grounds particular to the author's case, which would justify his continued detention for a period of four years".[86] Thus the mandatory nature of the detention violated art 9(1) relating to arbitrary detention. The Committee also found a violation of art 9(4) regarding court review of detention. This was because Australian courts were limited to an examination of whether the asylum-seeker had been detained correctly according to the terms of the legislation, rather than according to whether detention was necessary and reasonable in all the circumstances of the case as required by art 9(1).[87] In addition, the Committee found that art 2(3) of the Covenant, which obliges states to provide an effective remedy for any human rights violation, had been breached.[88] It stated in its "opinion" that an

---

79   See ss 189 and 198 of the Act.

80   Generally, they must also demonstrate that adequate arrangements for their care during release have been made and that they will not abscond. See reg 2.20, as amended by SR 280 of 1994.

81   (1992) 176 CLR 1.

82   Ibid at 118 per Brennan, Deane and Dawson JJ, at 129 per Toohey J, and at 145 per McHugh J.

83   Section 54T (now s 186).

84   *A v Australia*, Communication No 560/1993, UN Doc, CCPR/C/59/560/1993 (30 April 1997).

85   Ibid, para 9.4.

86   Ibid, para 9.4.

87   Ibid, para 9.5.

88   Ibid, para 10.

effective remedy in this case should include adequate compensation for the length of detention to which the asylum-seeker was subjected.[89]

Disappointingly, the government has indicated its intention not to act on the views of the Committee. It has announced that it disagrees with the Committee's assessment that the asylum-seeker's detention was arbitrary or that there was inadequate provision for review of the lawfulness of detention. It rejects the Committee's views regarding violations and notes that the opinions expressed as to the adequacy of available remedies are not binding on Australia in any event. Thus it is argued that compensation is not payable. The government also takes the view that changes to the system of detention, particularly the introduction of bridging visas, mean that there are now safeguards against prolonged detention.[90]

The government's arguments in defence of its decision to reject the Committee's decision are the same arguments that it made before the Committee.[91] It is apparent that these arguments, which focussed on the necessity of preventing a group of people, namely "illegal entrants," from absconding, were not sufficient to justify four years in detention for one particular person, being the author of the communication to the Committee. The changes in the detention system, especially the introduction of bridging visas for the most vulnerable asylum-seekers is welcome, but they do not fully meet the Committee's concerns either. There is still no procedure justifying and permitting court review of the detention of each individual. In addition, while the Department of Immigration attempts to make its determination as to refugee status within six months, this is not required by legislation, and if the asylum-seeker has to appeal a decision to refuse refugee status, she will remain in detention. A proper response to the Committee's views would involve broadening the criteria for bridging visas to take account of individual circumstances as well as consideration of different mechanisms for immigration control, such as open detention centres which asylum-seekers can leave during the day.

The reliance on the non-binding status of the Committee's views is perhaps the most disappointing aspect of all. It is true that the Committee is not a court. However, as the body to which states have voluntarily given power to hear communications under the ICCPR, the Committee clearly has some sort of mandate to interpret this treaty. Thus the government cannot claim with authority that it is in compliance with its international obligations. Furthermore, the response in this case may not augur well for adequate governmental responses to other communications to the Committee concerning Australia. On the other hand, variables such as the immigration context, the involvement of Federal policies, or the political party in government could be the key reasons for the failure to address the Committee's concerns.

---

89   Ibid, para 11.

90   Joint News Release, Minister for Immigration and Multicultural Affairs and the Attorney-General, 17 December 1997.

91   See above, n 84 at paras 7.1, 7.2 and 7.3.

Procedural fairness: access to lawyers

The question of procedural fairness in immigration generally is made difficult by the proposition that immigration is a plenary power, therefore procedural fairness in relation to hearings concerning an alien's right to entry is whatever the legislature says it is. The evolving standards of natural justice now applied in most administrative proceedings in Australia have also been applied to immigration proceedings, although Migration Legislation (Amendment) Bill No 5 of 1997 may change the position before the Federal Court if it is passed.

Access to lawyers for unauthorised arrivals has been problematic for some time. Section 256 of the Act provides that legal assistance must be provided on *request*. Unlike persons who have entered Australia on a valid visa, unauthorised arrivals have no right to be informed of the possibility of applying for a visa.[92]

Given that refugee status determination may involve life and death considerations, the obligation of non-refoulement requires a high level of procedural fairness in order for a state to claim that it has fulfilled the obligation in good faith.[93] The Australian government appears to assume that unauthorised arrivals are not owed the minimum standards required by UNHCR until the asylum-seeker satisfies an officer from the Department of Immigration that she intends to apply for refugee status, or that she has a claim for refugee status. In practice, this may be viewed as a Departmental determination that the unauthorised arrival is an asylum-seeker who has a "manifestly unfounded claim"- a determination that UNHCR has consistently categorised as a substantive determination of refugee status which requires minimum standards of procedural fairness.[94] Certainly, Australia's compliance with the obligation of non-refoulement may be in jeopardy as matters are left to the unfettered and unreviewable discretion of immigration officials.

Australia's practice may also be challenged on the basis of general human rights law. At first blush, international law's primary concern for procedural fairness appears to relate to the sphere of criminal justice, rather than administrative proceedings. Article 14 of the ICCPR includes a long list of rights for an accused, including the right to free counsel in cases where the interests of justice require. Article 9(4) which provides for a speedy determination of the reasons for one's detention, applies to detention of any kind. It provides that anyone deprived of liberty by arrest or detention shall be entitled to take proceedings before a court, in order that the court may decide without delay on the lawfulness of her detention and order her release if the detention is not lawful. The Australian government has taken the position that art 9(4) is not at risk of violation because asylum-seekers *are* given access to a lawyer in order to challenge detention *upon request*.[95] The dispute is over whether detainees should be given access to advice as a matter of course. This is the norm envisaged by the Standard Minimum Rules for the Treatment of Prisoners, and the Body of Principles for the Protection of All Persons under Any

---

92   See ss 193-196 and 198 of the Act.

93   Good faith implementation of all treaties is required by art 26 of the *Vienna Convention on the Law of Treaties*. Done at Vienna May 23, 1969, 8 ILM 679 (1969).

94   Excom Conclusion 30 (XXXIV), para (e). Reproduced in Goodwin-Gill, above, n 73, p 486.

95   See the evidence of Mr Henry Burmester to Senate Legal and Constitutional Legislation Committee, 26 June 1996, p 157 of transcript of Committee hearings.

Form of Detention or Imprisonment which may be used to interpret art 9(4) and art 10 of the ICCPR. This issue was not determined in the hearing of the communication to the Human Rights Committee concerning Australia's detention policy, as the asylum-seeker had in fact been provided with access to lawyers.[96] However, the Committee was prepared to consider the question pursuant to art 9(4) and art 14 at the merits phase of the communication procedure (art 10 which provides for humane and non-degrading conditions in detention, was not invoked by the asylum-seeker in relation to this issue). This may indicate that the Committee favours the idea that automatic access to lawyers and information about legal rights are fundamental rights of all detainees.

The ICCPR standards were invoked in *Wu Yu Fang v Minister for Immigration and Ethnic Affairs*, when the Human Rights and Equal Opportunity Commission (HREOC) intervened in the case. The Full Federal Court held by a majority of 2 to 1 that the Act effectively denied the asylum-seekers procedural fairness. However, it denied relief on the ground that parliament had deliberately legislated to achieve the exclusion of the rules of procedural fairness.[97] In the minority, Carr J accepted that the legislation should be read as being compatible with standards of procedural fairness extant at international law and the common law, and he found that these standards had been violated.[98] Unfortunately, the government had retrospectively legislated to deny the asylum-seekers access to the refugee status determination procedures on the basis that they had been resettled in a third country. This meant that Carr J was limited to making a declaration that the relevant standards had been violated.[99]

The HREOC had also attempted to intervene by using its powers to deliver letters to detainees.[100] This provoked a hostile governmental reaction. The Commission's action was unsuccessfully challenged in court.[101] Migration Legislation Amendment Bill (No 2) 1996 sought to tighten the Act so that it was clear that the Department was under no duty to provide information about legal rights. It also proposed to remove the powers of the Commission and the Ombudsman to initiate contact with immigration detainees: the detainees would have to initiate contact. The Bill was dropped and the Commission pursued the matter no further when the detainees were granted access to independent advisers.

Burden-sharing?

Increasingly, states are moving to shift responsibility for refugees to other countries. It should be noted at the outset that "burden sharing" is different to a blanket exclusion of asylum-seekers from refugee status determinations and protection from refoulement. Such action is permitted only under the terms of the express exclusion

96   *A v Australia*, above, n 84, paras 9.6 and 9.7.

97   (1996) 135 ALR 583 at 628-35 per Nicholson CJ, Jenkinson J concurring.

98   Ibid at 602-06 (using the doctrine of legitimate expectation in relation to international legal standards of procedural fairness) and at 607-10 (in relation to Common Law standards of procedural fairness), per Carr J.

99   Ibid at 611-12.

100   *Human Rights and Equal Opportunity Act* 1986 (Cth) s 11(1)(f).

101   *HREOC v Secretary of the Department of Immigration* (unreported, Fed Ct, Lindgren J, 30 May 1996).

clauses contained in the Refugee Convention. (Note, however, that the content of the exclusion clauses may inform a decision to pass responsibility to another state.) Three principles have been used to attempt to transfer responsibility to other states, particularly among the countries of the European Union.[102] First, particular countries of origin may be designated as "safe," or a presumption may be raised that they are not persecutory and that claims emanating from such countries are "manifestly unfounded". Second, an asylum-seeker may be required to return to a so-called "country of first asylum" in which she has previously sojourned in order to have her claim for refugee status determined there. Third, states may refuse to permit the asylum-seeker to access the refugee status determination system on the basis that there is a "safe third country" in which the asylum-seeker has already gained protection.

In 1993, Amnesty International wrote a scathing critique of the operation of Britain's "safe third country" procedures, observing that the cost involved was exorbitant and that asylum-seekers were subjected to the phenomenon of "refugees in orbit" as they were "bounced" back and forth between Britain and the so-called "safe country".[103] This phenomenon is arguably a form of degrading treatment within art 7 of the ICCPR and art 1 of the Torture Convention in and of itself. Furthermore, in so far as it carries a risk of return to a place of persecution, it is not a good faith implementation of the non-refoulement obligations contained in art 33 of the Refugee Convention, or art 3 of the Torture Convention.

The idea of safe countries of origin is a particularly dangerous interpretation of the Refugee Convention which may, depending on how it is implemented, amount to a geographic reservation to the terms of art 33. No reservations are permitted to art 33. If designation as a safe third country operates only to raise a rebuttable presumption, it may be acceptable, but procedural safeguards become all-important.

The concept of safe countries of origin has not been adopted by Australia, so far. However, Australia has adopted the principles of country of first asylum and safe third country in relation to particular groups of asylum-seekers.[104] The notion of country of first asylum underlies ss 91A-91F of the Act which prevented or restricted the consideration of refugee claims by asylum-seekers who came to Australia from countries participating in the Comprehensive Plan of Action (CPA).[105] The CPA was an arrangement whereby countries in the South East Asian region agreed to give temporary refuge to Vietnamese asylum-seekers on condition that Western immigration-based countries would resettle those asylum-seekers found to be refugees.

---

102 See Goodwin-Gill's discussion of the Dublin and Schengen Agreements, above, n 73, p 332 ff.

103 Dunstan, "Playing Human Pinball: The Amnesty International United Kingdom Section Report on UK Home Office 'Safe Third Country' Practice" (1995) 7 *International Journal of Refugee Law* 606.

104 For a discussion of these measures, see Poynder, N, "Australia's Recent Implementation of the Refugee Convention and the Law of Accommodations under International Treaties: Have We Gone Too Far?" (1995) 2(1) *Australian Journal of Human Rights* 75; and Taylor, S, "Australia's Safe Third Country Provisions: Their Impact on Australia's Fulfillment of its Non-Refoulement Obligations" (1996) 15 *University of Tasmania Law Review* 196.

105 *Migration Legislation Amendment Act (No 4)* 1994 (inserting ss 91A-91F into the Act).

The principle of safe third country was first adopted by Australia in relation to asylum-seekers who had been resettled from Vietnam in China's Bei Hai region.[106] In addition, there has been judicial application of the safe third country principle in a case involving a person who had been recognised as a refugee in France.[107]

It is difficult to say whether it is desirable for the courts or for parliament to be making the assessment of these issues. An independent judiciary is capable of making a determination about the safety in the particular case of the asylum-seeker. In contrast, parliament is likely to enact legislation prescribing particular countries as safe, having the exclusion of unwanted asylum-seekers and foreign policy motives in mind. When making submissions to a court about the nature and extent of Australia's protection obligations, advocates should attempt to invoke international standards. These include the standards relevant to the phenomenon of refugees in orbit referred to earlier, and UNHCR guidelines which are examined below. Courts should bear in mind the fact that the executive has the power to enter into agreements for return of asylum-seekers to safe countries. (This will often be essential if the asylum-seeker is not a national of the safe country.) What should a court do if faced with the situation where the "safe" country now refuses to receive the asylum-seeker and the person's application for refugee status has been denied?

The idea of country of first asylum relies on the fact that while the Refugee Convention forbids refoulement, it does not expressly allocate responsibility for determination of refugee status to any particular state. There is no right of entry referred to in the Convention. As long as the asylum-seeker is not returned to the place of persecution, it may be argued that the asylum-seeker has no right to choose the country that will grant him or her refugee status. Where the asylum-seeker enters illegally, the refugee may be required to obtain admission into another country: Article 31.[108] The prohibition on expulsion to non-persecutory states contained in art 32 is reserved for those lawfully within the country, while the prohibition on penalties for illegal entry in art 31 is reserved for those coming *directly* from a place where they fear persecution. The travaux préparatoires to the Convention confirm that expulsion is not a prohibited penalty under art 31. Thus a prima facie case may be made for the legality of the concept of a country of first asylum.

The concept is necessarily limited, though. The state which seeks to return the asylum-seeker is still bound by the norm of non-refoulement. It must assure itself that the asylum-seeker will be accepted into the asserted country of first asylum, given a fair hearing and, if found to be a refugee, protection from refoulement.[109]

---

106 The preclusion of access to Australia's refugee status determination system by asylum-seekers from safe third countries was achieved by the same legislative amendments which adopted the principle of country of first asylum. See above, n 104. The amendments were then applied retrospectively to asylum-seekers fleeing from the Bei Hai region by *Migration Legislation Amendment Act (No 2) 1995*, which inserted s 91G into the Act.

107 *Minister for Immigration and Multicultural Affairs v Thiyagarajah* (1997) 151 ALR 685. On this point, see Crock, above, n 28 at 154-57.

108 Article 31(2) states that restrictions on freedom of movement shall only be applied until the "status is regularised or [the asylum-seekers] obtain admission into another country". Goodwin-Gill notes that this is the article in the Convention that comes closest to the question of admission. See Goodwin-Gill, above, n 73, p 152.

109 Stenberg, G, *Non-Expulsion and Non-Refoulement: The Prohibition Against Removal of Refugees with Special Reference to Articles 32 and 33 of the 1951 Convention relating to the Status of Refugees* (Lustus Forlag, Uppsala, 1989), pp 121-30; Hathaway, above, n 62, p 46.

Excom conclusion 15 stipulates that the question of the state responsible for examining a request for asylum should be answered by reference to a number of considerations. These include: the intentions of the asylum-seeker regarding the country in which she wishes to seek asylum;[110] the existence of a connection with the country of first asylum;[111] and an assessment of whether it "appears fair and reasonable" to require the asylum-seeker to request asylum from that state.[112] In addition, since states are only obliged to admit their nationals, return cannot be effected without the consent of the potential country of first asylum.[113] Such consent should be fleshed out in an agreement.[114]

Australia's application of the principle of country of first asylum to persons coming from countries participating in the CPA is controversial because of the criticisms of the procedures for determination of refugee status in countries that participated in the CPA.[115] Where parliament legislates specifically to achieve such a result, opportunities to utilise international legal standards may arise if the statute is ambiguous, or if the statute confers a discretion on decision-makers.

The notion of "safe third countries" is also considered by UNHCR to be limited in its scope, though permissible. Excom has stated that the "irregular" movement of refugees from safe third countries where a person has already been given protection is undesirable and that return of such asylum-seekers is permissible.[116] However, the relevant conclusion stipulates that protection in the country to which the asylum-seeker is to be returned must be consistent with "recognised basic human standards". It is also expressly recognised that there may be cases in which the asylum-seeker may justifiably claim a fear of persecution in the so-called safe third country.[117] It is stated that such cases should be given favourable consideration. Australia's treatment of China as a safe third country is of dubious legitimacy given the generally bad human rights record of that state.

A final way in which responsibility for asylum-seekers may be avoided is the invocation of the multiple nationality clause contained in the definition of a refugee. The definition of a refugee contained in art 1A(2) of the Refugee Convention refers to a person who is outside the "country of nationality," and subsequently states that "country of nationality" refers to all countries of which the person is a national. A person may be returned to a country of nationality that is not persecutory. These

110 Excom 15, para h iii. Reproduced in Goodwin-Gill, above, n 73, p 475.

111 Paragraph h iv.

112 Ibid.

113 Marx, R, "Non Refoulement, Access to Procedures, and Responsibility for Determining Refugee Claims" (1995) 7(3) International Journal of Refugee Law 383 at 395.

114 Excom, General Conclusion on International Protection, October 1993, para 19(k) of the Report of the 44th session. Reproduced in (1994) 6 International Journal of Refugee Law 123. See also UNHCR, "The Concept of Protection Elsewhere" (1995) 7(1) International Journal of Refugee Law 123; Goodwin-Gill, above, n 73, p 339.

115 For criticisms of the CPA determination procedures, see Lawyers Committee for Human Rights, Hong Kong's Refugee Status Review Board: Problems in Status Determination for Vietnamese Asylum-Seekers (1992); Hathaway, J, "Labelling the "Boat People": The Failure of the Human Rights Mandate of the Comprehensive Plan of Action for Indo-Chinese Refugees" (1993) 15 Human Rights Quarterly 686.

116 Excom 58, para f. Reproduced in Goodwin-Gill, above, n 73, p 497.

117 Paragraph g. See also Excom 15 (k).

provisions are not expressly incorporated into the Act, however the Act merely provides that a protection visa may be granted to persons to whom Australia has protection obligations under international law. Consequently, it would appear that it is open to decision-makers to consider the question of alternative sources of national protection, and they have done so in a number of instances including the situation of East Timorese.

A determination that there is another country of nationality will generally proceed by examination of the relevant domestic law. However, if protection is illusory, unavailable or ineffective, the asylum-seeker will be granted refugee status. The question of alternative, effective protection by a country of nationality has been most controversial in relation to East Timorese asylum-seekers in Australia. East Timorese are regarded by the Australian government as having Indonesian nationality as a result of Indonesia's illegal invasion of the territory of East Timor which Australia has effectively decided to over-look through its *de jure* recognition of Indonesian sovereignty over East Timor. Australia claims that East Timorese are also to be regarded as Portuguese nationals as a result of the fact that Portugal still regards itself as the administering power of the territory, as does the United Nations, and the terms of Portuguese law extend Portuguese nationality to East Timorese.[118]

Not surprisingly, Portugal has not been particularly co-operative with Australian efforts to ensure that the Timorese are deported to Portugal. Portugal has informed the Department of Immigration that it regards protection in Portugal as an *option* for East Timorese given the decolonisation context, rather than a claim to assimilate East Timorese as part of the Portuguese nation, and that it will not make arrangements regarding East Timorese deportees from Australia.[119] It appears also that the process of confirming an East Timorese asylum-seeker's right to Portuguese nationality is fairly bureaucratic and time-consuming. The asylum-seeker may need to be present in Portugal and aspirants can expect lengthy waiting periods when their rights to work and benefits are limited. The Full Federal Court in *Jong Kim Koe v Minister for Immigration and Multicultural Affairs*[120] accepted that the East Timorese applicants were Portuguese nationals as a matter of Portuguese law. However, it ruled that the question of whether Portuguese nationality was available and effective in fact had not been considered properly by the RRT. Three decisions by the RRT to grant refugee status following the Federal Court's decision[121] have been appealed by the government.

---

118 This position was made public when an advice from Chief General Counsel of the Australian Attorney-General's Department dated September 20, 1995, was supplied to the RRT. Copy on file with author Mathew, P.

119 File note by Mr L Bugden of 8 August 1995, cited in RRT decision V96/0476 (15 August 1996).

120 (1997) 143 ALR 695.

121 Decision N93/00512 (30 May 1997); Decision N93/00583 (2 June 1997); Decision V93/01124 (2 June 1997). the texts of these decisions are available at the Austlii website: <http://www.austlii.edu.au>. For a discussion of, and guide to, the electronic access to human rights material, see Ch 15 by Bliss and Roushan in this volume.

CONCLUSION

A number of points can be made about the many and diverse developments in migration and refugee law in recent years. At the most fundamental level, cases like *Chu Kheng Lim* and *Teoh* and the very phenomenon of litigious asylum seekers highlight the roles that international law in general and human rights law in particular, have come to play in Australia's domestic legal context. Many commentators have remarked on the steady internationalisation of Australian law. Nowhere is this more marked than in a field such as migration law where norms of international law are directly relevant in shaping, applying and interpreting the laws of the land.

A closer look at the jurisdiction, however, reveals a situation of paradox and contradiction that underscores the intensely political nature of migration and refugee decision-making. On the one hand, litigants are demonstrating a new familiarity with norms of international human rights law. People are actively seeking to use the tools available to them to agitate for the enforcement of their perceived rights. Arguments about human rights law have been advanced at every level of the federal system, including the AAT, the Federal Court and the High Court, and many of the arguments have been successful. On the other hand, there is still a measure of deference by review bodies to the older notion that nationality or citizenship is the ultimate determinant of an individual's "right to have rights". In a series of cases, the High Court has consistently refused to extend to non-citizens or "aliens" many of the rights that it has found by implication in the Constitution. While acknowledging that non-citizens are not "outlaws", the court has agreed that such persons can be detained for lengthy periods of time pending decisions relating to their entry or right to remain in the country.[122] It has declined to extend the implied Constitutional freedom of communication to protect the situation of lawyers wishing to advise non-citizens applying for entry to Australia.[123] On close scrutiny, other decisions may reveal a degree of judicial deference to politics or popular opinion, despite disclaimers to the contrary. The case of *Applicant A*[124] may be an example where both majority and minority were swayed by moral and political considerations. For instance, Gummow J appears to have been influenced in his interpretation of the terms "particular social group" by the desire of the framers of the Refugee Convention to safeguard immigration control. On the other hand Brennan CJ and Kirby J quite openly emphasise and use as foci of their judgments the human rights of the asylum-seekers.[125]

For its part, the executive is often strident in its insistence on the fundamental difference between citizens and non-citizens and the perceived need to keep a tight rein on immigration, and it has frequently amended the migration legislation to ensure this over the objections of human rights advocates. Little is done to educate Australians as to the benefits of migration or to attack the myths surrounding migration. If this were attempted, the humanity and common human experiences of

---

122 *Chu Kheng Lim* (1992) 176 CLR 1.

123 See *Cunliffe v Commonwealth* (1994) 182 CLR 272.

124 *Applicant A* (1997) 142 ALR 331.

125 On this case, see Crock, M, above, n 61.

migrants might be more readily recognised. Only then can we hope for greater respect for the rights of non-citizens, and a greater willingness to treat aspiring migrants and asylum-seekers in a manner that accords with international human rights standards.

8

FAMILY LAW AND HUMAN RIGHTS

Juliet Behrens and Phillip Tahmindjis

INTRODUCTION

It is only in recent times that human rights discourse has begun to influence "family law" disputes. Even today, the full potential of human rights arguments in the area remains unrealised. That potential is, however, enormous. This is particularly so given what has been identified as a very recent conceptual shift in family law. The period after the introduction of the *Family Law Act* 1975 (Cth) (FLA) has been portrayed as a move away from rights-based family law where divorce was a remedy for a wrong (breach of the marital "contract"), and entitlement to spousal maintenance (for example) was (at least in theory) a form of damages, to a focus on interests and welfare by reference to utility rather than entitlements.[1] However, it has been persuasively argued that we may now be moving towards a "third stage" of family law[2] and that there has been a move back to rights and rules based system with greater normative content in more recent years.[3] What that content should be continues to be contested, but it is at least possible that internationally recognised human rights will provide part of the content in this "third stage". Indeed there is evidence for this in the recent inclusion in the FLA of reference to particular children's rights.[4] Thus, a "conceptual shift" in family law seems to carry significant hope for the relevance of human rights arguments in family law disputes.

Despite this potential, it is important to recognise the somewhat tenuous relationship between human rights arguments and family law. In classical liberal philosophy the family has been constructed as the "private sphere" – as a place to be governed not by individualism and rights-based thinking, but by the values of *gemeinschaft* – loyalty, self-sacrifice, community. Of course, feminist commentators have noted that it is no coincidence that "the family" is the sphere in which much of women's and children's activity is concentrated, nor that this has traditionally been a place where men have considerable power. In addition, husbands and fathers *did* have legal rights (to custody of their legitimate children, for example, and to use

---

1   Parker, S, Parkinson, P and Behrens, J, *Australian Family Law In Context: Commentary and Materials* (Law Book Co, Sydney, 1994), p 99.

2   Parker, S, "The New Place of Conduct in Family Court Proceedings: Signs of Paradigm Lost", Paper presented to the Family Law Practitioners' Association Residential (July 1997, in authors' possession).

3   Dewar, J, "Reducing Discretion in Family Law" (1997) 11 *Australian Journal of Family Law* 309 at 312.

4   Ibid, p 316.

reasonable force to discipline their wives and children) which bolstered their power within families. Hence, the denial of individual claims within the family, on the basis of the inappropriateness of state intervention, allows male power to reign there and is a major contributor to women's and children's disadvantage.[5]

While the last several decades have seen increasing attention being paid to rights arguments in the context of claims by individual family members against another family member, evidence continues of a reluctance to give full meaning to rights where claims are made in this context. The discourse of family privacy continues to be reflected in public debates and implementation policies. For evidence of this, we have only to refer to the recent debate over Australia's ratification in 1990 of the United Nations *Convention on the Rights of the Child* (CROC),[6] and the strong adverse reaction within some parts of the community to the Convention based on the fact that it challenged notions of parental autonomy and family privacy.[7] Further, even as we detect a move towards the recognition of children's interests and rights in law, we see evidence of the retention of concepts of family privacy, at least in a context where the parents are in (perhaps superficial) agreement as to the treatment of the children. It continues to be the case that we are more willing to see state intervention to protect children's rights and interests where there is a dispute between the parents.[8]

This general background goes part of the way to explaining the tenuous relationship between human rights law and the family. The potential for human rights arguments to be used for progressive causes is also affected by the fact that international instruments allow states to define "family" for themselves. There is a significant and important symbiosis between international and national law in this respect; what the state says is "family" and "marriage" provides the content of the international obligation. As Ghandi and Macnamee have pointed out:

> To accept that whatever is defined within a state as a family will attract, without question, the protection of art 23 [of the *International Covenant on Civil and Political Rights* (ICCPR)], and that whatever falls outside of this definition will not, is to allow states to draw a boundary around the notion of the family and accept that human rights considerations have no place within the enclosed space.[9]

---

5   See Graycar, R and Morgan, J, *The Hidden Gender of Law* (Federation Press, Sydney, 1990); Naffine, N, *Law and the Sexes: Explorations in Feminist Jurisprudence* (Allen and Unwin, Sydney, 1990); Olsen, F, "The Family and the Market: A Study of Ideology and Legal Reform" (1983) 96 *Harvard Law Review* 1497.

6   (1989) Official records of the General Assembly A/RES/44/25, ratified by Australia on 17 December 1990.

7   See Alston, P, "Australia and the Convention", in Alston, P and Brennan, G (eds), *The UN Children's Convention and Australia* (Centre for International and Public Law, ANU, Canberra, 1991); Cass, B, "The Limits of the Public Private Dichotomy" in Alston, P, Parker, S and Seymour, J (eds), *Children, Rights and the Law* (Clarendon Press, Oxford, 1992), p 142.

8   As an example, under s 68F(3) of the FLA where the court is making consent orders it need not have regard to the list of best interests factors in s 68F(2). Similar provisions apply in respect of the registration of parenting plans (s 63E(3)). Note, however, s 65G under which there are special requirements in respect of the making of consent orders in favour of "non-parents".

9   Ghandi, PR and MacNamee, E, "The Family in the UK Law and the International Covenant on Civil and Political Rights 1966" (1991) 5 *International Journal of Law and the Family* 104 at 110.

Thus, there are significant limitations on the extent to which policies that, for example, exclude transgendered persons from marrying as a member of their desired sex or prevent gay and lesbian marriages, can be challenged as breaching international human rights norms. This issue is explored further below.

As a final introductory point we should note that in indicating the potential impacts of human rights arguments, we have focused largely on the traditional paradigm of "family law", but would urge practitioners to consider areas of activity beyond this. There is scope for practices of infertility treatment clinics, social security policies, taxation policies, immigration policies[10] and so on to be challenged for breaching the international human rights to, for example, the protection of the family unit.

WHAT ARE HUMAN RIGHTS AS THEY PERTAIN TO THE FAMILY?

There are several international human rights instruments which are binding on Australia and which contain provisions relevant to the family. Not all of them will have a significant impact on family law in Australia as traditionally defined. However, some international human rights instruments are potentially of great significance.

The seminal international human rights instrument is the *Universal Declaration of Human Rights* (UDHR).[11] While this is a resolution of the United Nations General Assembly, and therefore not binding as a treaty, it is generally regarded as being customary international law and therefore contains legal obligations. It provides in art 16:

(1) Men and women of full age, without any limitation due to race, nationality or religion, have the right to marry and found a family. They are entitled to equal rights as to marriage, during marriage and at its dissolution.

(2) Marriage shall be entered into only with the free and full consent of the intending spouses.

(3) The family is the natural and fundamental group unit of society and is entitled to protection by society and the State.

This is significant both for what it says and also for what it does not say. There is a right to marry. There is a right to found a family. There shall be no discrimination in the exercise of these rights other than that the parties be "of full age". Entry into marriage shall be without duress. The family is entitled to protection. There is also a right to equality during and after marriage. However, except indirectly, there is neither definition nor description of "the family", "marriage", "full age", "consent" or "protection", and the "natural and fundamental" nature of the family is left totally unexplained.

Article 16 is not unique in the UDHR for its ambiguity, which was necessary to obtain agreement on it. Indeed, the Declaration has been regarded as containing a

---

10 See, for example, *Minister for Immigration. Local Government and Ethnic Affairs v Teoh* (1995) 183 CLR 273.

11 3 UNGAOR 962 (1948), Res 217III ©.

"productive ambiguity"[12] which has enabled it to apply to "extended" as well as "nuclear" family forms and has laid the foundations for further developments in the light of new circumstances. However, this ambiguity has also implanted in it the seeds of further discrimination; questions are raised about the extent to which one-parent families, families created by in-vitro fertilisation and same-sex marriages enjoy the protection and support of the article.

Most importantly, however, is the fact that the ambiguity of these provisions means that in order for them to have meaning their operational context is crucial (there being no general right to equality in the UDHR). Thus, the meaning of "full age", "free consent", "marriage" and "family" will only become apparent in accordance with the accepted definitions of the concepts in any given jurisdiction, establishing a symbiotic relationship between the international norm and the domestic law.

The ICCPR[13] makes provision in art 23 in similar terms to art 16 of the UDHR. Thus, the limitations seen there also apply here, particularly with respect to the symbiotic relationship between the Covenant and the domestic understanding of the terms used. This has been conceded by the Human Rights Committee,[14] the body set up under art 28 to monitor compliance with the Covenant. The European Court of Human Rights, considering equivalent provisions in the *European Convention for the Protection of Human Rights and Fundamental Freedoms* (ECHR) 1950, has come to a similar conclusion.[15] However, the ICCPR does at least raise the possibility of mounting a challenge to the constricted paradigms seen above. Article 2 provides that parties will "ensure to all individuals ... the rights recognised in the present Covenant without distinction of any kind" and there is also a general equality provision providing equality before the law, the equal protection of the law, and for non-discrimination not limited by or to the other articles of the Covenant.[16] There is also a link made between the family and the right to privacy in art 17[17] which may entail both positive and negative results (see below). There are thus duties of forbearance as well as performance upon the state parties to this Covenant.

However, a further limitation in the ICCPR occurs in art 2(2) which provides that if action is necessary to comply with its provisions, this will be taken in accordance with the country's constitutional processes. In a federation like Australia, this can be a limitation on the obligation to "ensure" equal rights in areas normally falling under State jurisdiction, such as laws relating to de facto relationships and child welfare provisions.

---

12   McKeon, R, "Philosophy and History in the Development of Human Rights" in Kiefer, HE and Munitz, MK (eds), *Ethics and Social Justice* (State University of New York Press, Albany, 1968), pp 303-07.

13   (1966) UNTS Vol 999, p171, ratified by Australia on 13 August 1980.

14   General Comment 19(39), adopted at the 102nd meeting, 24 July 1990: UN Doc CCPR/C/21/Rev 1/Add 1-4. See also the Committee's decision in *Balaquer v Spain* (Communication No 417/1990) that the protection of children referred to in art 23 only applies to children of "formal" marriages.

15   The rights of gays or transgender people to marry lie outside the Convention: *Rees v United Kingdom* (1987) 9 EHRR 56; *Cossey v United Kingdom* (1991) 13 EHRR 622.

16   Article 26.

17   Article 17(1): "No one shall be subjected to arbitrary or unlawful interference with his privacy, family, home or correspondence ...".

The *International Covenant on Economic Social and Cultural Rights* (ICESCR)[18] is predicated upon progressive realisation of the rights it contains[19] rather than upon the creation of immediate obligations of implementation. Article 10 provides that "the widest possible protection and assistance should be accorded to the family, which is the natural and fundamental group unit of society" and that "special protection should be accorded to mothers during a reasonable period before and after childbirth. During such period working mothers should be accorded paid leave or leave with adequate social security benefits".

In addition to the comments already made above with respect to the very concept of family and its naturalness and fundamentality, there is a minor difference here in that even though free consent to marriage is part of the article, it is the family, rather than marriage, which is the concept around which the article revolves. This may lessen the heterosexist bias seen in the Articles discussed above. However, the obligation is to "protect" and "assist" the family and to give special protection to mothers and children on a *progressive* basis. Thus, although not all Australian working women receive paid maternity leave or necessarily receive social security benefits, this does not amount to a breach of this article.

Article 5(d)(iv) of the *Convention on the Elimination of All Forms of Racial Discrimination* (CERD)[20] provides that parties will "guarantee the right of everyone, without distinction as to race ..., to equality before the law ... [in] the right to marriage and choice of spouse". This does not allow merely for progressive implementation but clearly states an existing right which must be guaranteed. However, without a definition of marriage and, in the light of the symbiotic relationship between the international norm and domestic law mentioned above, the equality before the law guaranteed by this provision tends to be formal rather than substantive. For example, this provision means that Indigenous people cannot be prevented from marrying, but it does not necessarily provide them with a right to legal recognition of customary Aboriginal marriages. Locally based values with respect to marriage are to this extent unaffected by the Convention. The right is for Aborigines to enter a European-style marriage. The symbiosis in terms of definitions means that the Convention has difficulty giving voice to cultural diversity within countries in matters of marriage and related areas.

The *Convention on the Elimination of All Forms of Discrimination against Women* (CEDAW)[21] provides generally for equality of women with men (which may in itself be a drawback)[22] and in particular provides that marriage will not automatically change the nationality of a wife[23] and that a woman will have the

---

18   (1966) UNTS Vol 993, p 3, ratified by Australia on 10 December 1975.

19   Article 2.

20   (1965) UNTS Vol 660, p 195, ratified by Australia on 30 September 1975.

21   (1979) UNTS Vol 1249, p 13, ratified by Australia on 28 July 1983.

22   See Wright, S, "Human Rights and Women's Rights: An Analysis of the United Nations Convention on the Elimination of All Forms of Discrimination Against Women", in Mahoney, K and Mahoney, P (eds), *Human Rights in the Twenty-First Century: A Global Challenge* (Martinus Nijhoff, Dordrecht, 1993), pp 75-88. Wright argues that by providing for equality with men, there is an acceptance of the validity of a male standard which indirectly silences or subverts the value of specifically female experiences and results in provisions dealing with maternity or child care being classified as "special measures", pp 79-80.

23   Article 9(1).

same right as a man to enter into marriage, and the same rights and responsibilities during and after marriage, including the same parental responsibilities regardless of the marital status of their union.[24] In addition, a woman has the same rights as a man to decide the number and spacing of children, the same rights and responsibilities with respect to guardianship, wardship and adoption, the same personal rights (such as choosing a family name) and the same rights with respect to ownership and administration of property.[25] Also, the betrothal of a child shall have no legal effect.[26] The rights with respect to family planning and parental responsibilities mark a new approach in the international instruments to the concept of family. However, the equality being with men, these rights are automatically skewed towards those "male" rights already existing in the domestic legal system. Moreover, the obligation in art 16 is to take "all appropriate measures" and art 24 provides that parties will take measures "aimed at achieving the full realisation of the rights recognised in the present Convention". Implementation is thus to be progressive and a current shortfall does not necessarily amount to a breach.

The CROC provides that the child has the right to know and be cared for by his or her parents (art 7(1)), recognises that family relations are a part of the child's identity (art 8(1)) and provides that the child should not be separated from his or her parents except when determined by competent authorities subject to judicial review (art 9(1)). A child who is capable of forming his or her own views has the right to express them in all matters affecting him or her, and those views are to be given appropriate weight, particularly in judicial or administrative proceedings (art 12). The Convention also recognises the rights and duties of parents as the principal people who direct the child in the exercise of rights, considering the evolving capacity of the child (art 14(2)), and as the people who have the primary responsibility for the child's upbringing and development (art 18(1)). The overriding principle of the Convention is that in all actions concerning children, the best interests of the child shall be the primary consideration (art 3). These are obligations of result as well as obligations of means. However, the implementation of these rights shall be undertaken through "all *appropriate* legislative, administrative and other measures" and economic, social and cultural rights are to be implemented "to the maximum extent of [the State's] available resources" (art 4). Thus, the right of the child to preserve his or her identity through connections with family shall be preserved "as recognised by law" (art 8(1)). The child's right not to be separated from his or her parents pertains except when "in accordance with applicable law and procedures" (art 9(1)).

The *International Labour Organisation Convention No 156 (Workers with Family Responsibilities)*[27] provides that parties will make it an "aim of national policy" that workers with responsibilities for caring for a dependent child or other immediate family member will not be discriminated against in their employment (art 3). This will be done in accordance with "all measures compatible with national conditions and possibilities" (arts 4, 5 and 7). In particular, family responsibilities shall not, as such, constitute a valid reason for terminating employment (art 8).

---

24   Article 16(1)(a), (b), (c), (d).

25   Article 16(1)(e), (f), (g), (h).

26   Article 16(2)

27   (1981) Registration Number 22346.

These instruments are thus potentially of great significance to Australian family law and further ramifications of this are discussed below. Other provisions in these instruments can also be significant. Thus, for example, the question of violence is covered by the ICCPR[28] and the CROC[29] as well as a declaration;[30] the issue of mobility is addressed in ICCPR,[31] and questions of religion are dealt with in ICCPR[32] and CROC.[33] However, while this potential is great it should not be overstated. Some of the obligations are only of a progressive nature and while the vagueness of the terms may lead to a productive ambiguity, the symbiosis between the international norms and the domestic legal system with respect both to terms and mechanisms of enforcement means that the values explicit or implicit in the domestic system can predominate.

RELEVANT HUMAN RIGHTS CONCEPTS IN AUSTRALIAN LEGISLATION

Australian legislation dealing with family law already contains several concepts recognised in international human rights norms. For example, the *Marriage Act 1961* (Cth) provides that people may marry and prescribes requirements with respect to capacity and formalities. In 1991 this Act was amended to remove a difference in marriageable age which amounted to discrimination based on sex: the previous ages of 18 for males and 16 for females were amended to a common marriageable age of 18.[34] However, this improvement must now be considered in the light of the Children's Convention which posits a notion of *evolving* capacity. The Act also prescribes Australian marriage as being monogamous and hetero-sexual, although only by implication (in the solemnisation requirements).[35] Thus, in the light of the symbiotic relationship between the international and domestic norms mentioned above, there may be scope for the notion of marriage in Australia to expand into "non-traditional" areas, such as same-sex marriages, transgender marriages and to recognise Aboriginal customary marriages, but this result is by no means a foregone conclusion, particularly considering the constitutional issues involved in a federation.[36]

Similarly, the FLA provides, prima facie, for equal rights on the dissolution of marriage and for children's rights in what were formerly called custody decisions

---

28 Article 7: "No-one shall be subjected to ... cruel, inhuman or degrading treatment".

29 Article 37(a): "No child shall be subjected to cruel, inhuman or degrading treatment".

30 General Assembly Resolution 48/104 (20 December 1993) "Declaration on the Elimination of Violence Against Women" covers various forms of physical, sexual and psychological violence against women.

31 Article 12(1): "Everyone ... shall ... have the right to liberty of movement and freedom to choose his [sic] residence".

32 Article 18(1): "Everyone shall have the right to freedom of thought, conscience and religion".

33 Article 14(1): "States Parties shall respect the right of the child to freedom of thought, conscience and religion".

34 See *Sex Discrimination Amendment Act* 1991 (Cth) s 11.

35 Sections 45 and 46 provide that the celebrant should say words to the effect that marriage is the union of a man and a woman to the exclusion of all others.

36 See Dickey, A, *Family Law* (Law Book Co, Sydney, 3rd ed, 1997), Ch 2.

(now decisions about "parental responsibilities").[37] Changes with respect to the latter came into effect in 1996,[38] one of the stated aims of these reforms being to align this Act with Australia's human rights obligations to children.

A major domestic legal impact of the CROC has been on Pt VII of the FLA. This Part deals with children. In particular, where the Act used to provide that the "welfare" of the child was the paramount consideration in matters concerning the child, the amendments now mirror the wording of the Convention[39] and provide that the "best interests" of the child are the paramount consideration.[40] It remains to be seen whether this change will produce a line of argument in the cases substantially different from those cases interpreting the welfare of the child. This was not the intention of the amendments.[41] That they will have that effect seems unlikely as a statutory elaboration of the term remains in the Act[42] which is substantially in the same terms as the previous definition of welfare.[43] There are some changes to the list of relevant factors, however. First, it now makes specific reference to considerations of the child's background (including the need to maintain a connection with Aboriginal or Torres Strait Islander communities). Second, there is an added emphasis on the child's right to maintain personal relations and direct contact with both parents (both of which appear in the Convention).[44] Third, the statutory description of "best interests" includes a specific reference to family violence[45] which appears in the Convention with respect to violence against the child[46] but which in the Act now includes violence against other members of the family, which earlier cases had held not to be relevant to the child's welfare.[47] Indeed, the Act can be said to go beyond the Convention in being explicit in this regard. In addition, the best interests of the child are "the paramount consideration" in the Act whereas the Convention requires that they be "a primary consideration", the former having been interpreted as an overriding, if not sole, consideration.[48]

While the FLA provides that the best interests of the child shall be the paramount consideration in decisions about parenting orders,[49] location orders,[50] recovery orders[51] and orders relating to the welfare of the child,[52] there are other

---

37 FLA ss 61Aff.

38 *Family Law Reform Act* 1995 (Cth).

39 In art 3(1).

40 Section 65E.

41 See Chisholm, R, "Assessing the Impact of the Family Law Reform Act 1995" (1996) 10 *Australian Journal of Family Law* 183; *B and B* (1997) FLC ¶92-755 at 84,217.

42 Section 68F.

43 In s 64(1) of the former Act.

44 Articles 5(3), 8, 9, 18.

45 Section 68F(2)(i). See also the new s 43(ca) which includes "the need to ensure safety from family violence" as one of the principles to be applied with respect to the whole Act.

46 Article 19.

47 *Heidt and Heidt* (1976) FLC ¶90-077.

48 *In marriage of Kress and Kress* (1976) FLC ¶90-126.

49 Section 65E.

50 Section 67L.

51 Section 67V.

52 Section 67ZC(2).

decisions taken by the court (for example, decisions about injunctions under s 114 and decisions about enforcement) and other bodies (for example, legal aid commissions)[53] where it can be argued that the best interests of the child should be a primary consideration on the basis of CROC.

The influence of the Convention can particularly be seen with the introduction of express objects and principles into Pt VII.[54] These provide for the object of ensuring that children receive adequate and proper parenting (corresponding with arts 3(2), 5, 7 and 18 of the Convention) and for four underlying principles:

(a) children, including ex nuptial children, have the right to be cared for by both parents (corresponding with art 7(1));

(b) children have the right to regular contact with both parents and with others who are significant in their care, welfare or development (corresponding with art 9(3));

(c) parents share duties and responsibilities concerning the care, welfare and development of their children (corresponding generally with art 5);

(d) parents should agree about the future parenting of their children.

This last principle has no direct counterpart in the Convention. This may be explained by the fact that Pt VII of the Act is primarily focused on disputes about parenting whereas the Convention is of a more general standard-setting character. However, it illustrates a shift in the Act away from the notion of parental rights to parental duties and responsibilities. This can also be seen in principle (c) under which parents share these duties and responsibilities; and corresponds generally with art 5 of the Convention which provides that: "States Parties shall *respect* the responsibilities, rights and duties of parents ... to provide ... appropriate direction and guidance in the exercise *by the child* of [his or her] rights". The parental duties in the Convention thus serve as a check on the implementation by states of rules dealing with the rights of the child, the latter being the principal concern. In the Act, the emphasis is the other way around: parental duties are the main focus of the substance of Pt VII and the rights of the child provide the direction in which these are to be exercised.

Similarly, the "welfare" concept previously existing in other parts of the Act, such as in s 55A which prevented a decree nisi for the dissolution of a marriage becoming absolute unless proper arrangements had been made for the welfare of any children under 18, has been changed to "care, welfare and development", which better reflects the intent of the Convention. This is further emphasised by the fact that art 5 talks about the "rights" of parents, as well as of their duties and responsibilities. On the other hand, these responsibilities are expressed to continue beyond separation for both parties[55] so that, as Nygh has aptly remarked: "For good or ill, the notion of continuing parental responsibility will empower those who now languish as 'access parents'".[56] It has been argued, for example, that the "access"

---

53   *Heard v De Laine* (1996) FLC ¶92-675 where the Full Court of the Family Court held that it had no power to order a Legal Aid Commission to pay the costs of a child's representative.

54   Section 60B.

55   As a guiding principle of Pt VII expressed in s 60B(2)(a).

56   Nygh, PE, "The New Part VII – an Overview" (1996) 10 *Australian Journal of Family Law* 4 at 16.

parent (usually the father) might use this provision to manipulate or intimidate the mother.[57] It has also been argued that the child's "right" to contact with both parents might lead to relocation disputes when either parent, with or without the child, wants to move.[58] The answer to these questions may lie in the very notion of the child's "rights" under the Act: that they are not exactly the same as those in the Convention but, because of the symbiosis mentioned above, are more of the nature of primary positions. To this extent, it may be questioned whether this part of the legislation is really about children's' rights at all.

The reforms to the Act represent, on the one hand, a significant advance away from the notions of "custody" and "guardianship" being equated with power and control over children. However, many provisions of CROC remain to be fully implemented in Australian law. For example, art 7(1) provides that: "The child shall be registered immediately after birth and shall have the right from birth to a name, the right to acquire a nationality and, as far as possible, the right to know and be cared for by his or her parents". Australian law already provides for registration of births[59] but the provisions usually say nothing or are ambiguous about such things as how the registration form designates the baby's sex in circumstances of doubt or whether this can be changed on the form as a result of operative procedures on the child.[60] Similarly, Australian legislation also provides for the naming of children[61] but does not always allow for freedom of choice of name (for example, the child being given the hyphenated surnames of the mother and father).[62] There is the duty of the parents to *register* a name rather than the right of the child to a name other than that designated by legislation. Similarly, nationality is governed by legislation[63] with Australia providing Australian nationality for children born here but not recognising dual nationality, even if that might be in the child's best interests. The right to be cared for by parents is now enshrined in the FLA as a basic principle, but the right to *know* one's parents is not.[64]

The FLA continues the discretion to appoint a separate representative for a child, but now focuses this around the notion of the child's best interests as well as

---

57 See Behrens, J, "Shared Parenting: Possibilities ... and Realities" (1996) 21 *Alternative Law Journal* 213.

58 Chisholm, R, above, n 41, pp 182ff. See further the following section of this chapter.

59 *Registration of Births Deaths and Marriages Act* 1961 (WA); *Births Deaths and Marriages Registration Act* 1996 (SA); *Registration of Births Deaths and Marriages Act* 1980 (NT); *Registration of Births Deaths and Marriages Act* 1962 (Qld); *Births Deaths and Marriages Registration Act* 1995 (NSW); *Births Deaths and Marriages Registration Act* 1996 (Vic); *Registration of Births Deaths and Marriages Ordinance* 1963 (ACT); *Registration of Births Deaths and Marriages Act* 1895 (Tas).

60 An exception here is the *Transgender (Anti-Discrimination and Other Acts Amendment) Act* 1996 (NSW).

61 See the legislation referred to in n 59, above. The particular sections are: Western Australia: s 21A; South Australia: s 21; Northern Territory: s 17; Queensland: s 27A; New South Wales: s 21; Victoria: s 23; ACT: s 18; Tasmania: s 20.

62 Those which do allow such a choice are the sections referred to in the last footnote in South Australia, New South Wales, Victoria and the ACT.

63 *Australian Citizenship Act* 1948 (Cth)

64 See the Human Rights and Equal Opportunity Commission (HREOC), *Bringing Them Home: Report of the National Inquiry into the Separation of Aboriginal and Torres Strait Islander Children from their Families* (HREOC, Sydney, 1997).

his or her welfare.[65] This is emphasised by the fact that this provision is now located in the Division of the Act which specifically deals with the notion and meaning of the "best interests" principle. This then raises the question of the effect of the Convention on the current approach to separate representation. The Full Court in *Re K*[66] laid down guidelines based on the Convention for the criteria of appointment.[67] This is discussed in more detail below. The question that now arises in the light of the amendment of the Act to reflect the Convention is whether the appointment (or removal except for misconduct) of a separate representative is any longer discretionary or whether such a representative must be appointed in all cases involving children. Article 12(1) of the Convention states that children who are capable of forming their own views have the right to express them and they should be given due weight. Therefore, for very young children this aspect of separate representation will not be affected. For other children, however, the Convention states in art 12(2): "the child shall in particular be provided the opportunity to be heard in any judicial and administrative proceedings affecting the child, either directly, or through a representative ...". Australian courts have consistently refused to adopt an incorporationist approach rather than a transformationist approach to the question of the effect of international law on Australian law (see discussion below). This is so even if a Convention is adopted as a Schedule to an Act. Thus the use of terms and concepts in legislation may mirror an international Convention, but this does not incorporate that Convention into Australian law. The issue thus becomes the relationship between the separate representation section (s 68L) and the "best interests" section (s 68F). Section 68L(1) provides that separate representation may be ordered in any matter where the child's best interests or welfare are the paramount consideration or are relevant. There is thus a link to the factors the court must consider with respect to the child's best interests in s 68F, but this is only a preliminary question to indicate the circumstances where the "right" applies. Subsection (2) then proceeds to make the appointment of a representative in these circumstances discretionary. There are no indicators as to how this discretion is to be exercised and it is here that a judge may refer back to s 68F to aid in this interpretation. It therefore remains a matter of degree in each case and it is submitted that the amendments based on the Convention do not now give an overall right to separate representation in all cases.

The amended Act retains the principle that the wishes of a child should be given reasonable weight depending on such things as the age and maturity of the child as one of the factors to consider when ascertaining the child's best interests[68] and accords with the Convention in this regard.[69] The case law on this matter is discussed below.

The Act also now pays greatly increased attention to violence within the family[70] corresponding to the requirements of art 19 of the CROC as well as with

---

65 Section 68L.
66 (1994) FLC ¶92-461.
67 Ibid at 80,773-76.
68 Section 68F(2)(a).
69 Article 12.
70 See particularly Pt VII, Div 11 and s 43.

internationally recognised rights to protection from such violence. As yet there has been no reference to such rights in the case law. They would provide the basis, however, for bolstering arguments for injunctions under s 114.

Overall, the Australian legislation is, in its general concepts, consistent with Australia's international human rights obligations and there is no dissonance between the two. However, the symbiotic relationship between the two sets of norms allows domestic courts to put a particularly localised interpretation on those norms which has a potential to stymie the development of a Family Law which has a human rights focus rather than merely a human rights background.

The combined effect of the lack of conceptual dissonance and the functional symbiosis between the international and domestic norms has been such that opportunities to apply international human rights have frequently been lost as the relevance of the latter is not always obvious. Thus, for example, the applicability of federal anti-discrimination legislation which is directly based on human rights instruments is left often unused. Under the *Racial Discrimination Act* 1975 (Cth), the *Sex Discrimination Act* 1984 (Cth) and the *Disability Discrimination Act* 1992 (Cth) it is unlawful to discriminate on the bases of race, sex, pregnancy, marital status or disability in the administration of Commonwealth laws and programs.[71] This could apply to the Family Court and its officers, including its judicial officers. However, no mention of these provisions has been made in cases concerning the fairness of Family Court proceedings when one of the parties was unable to speak English;[72] where preconceptions about the roles of men and women in child care disputes have emerged;[73] where allegations of bias were made because of a relationship between a presiding judge and counsel appearing before her;[74] and when considering whether to take into account the cost of special services required by a person with a disability in a maintenance dispute.[75] This is a potentially rich but as yet untapped resource in Australian family law.

HUMAN RIGHTS APPLIED IN THE CASES

The impact of international human rights law on "family law"

While earlier chapters of this book have explored the general issue of the relevance of international human rights norms to the interpretation and application of domestic law, it is important for those working in family law to be aware of the decisions and dicta of the Family Court of Australia on this point. So far as that particular court is concerned, there is an increasing willingness amongst judges to accept the relevance of international law in general, and human rights documents in particular, to their decision-making, although the court has adopted a transformative, rather than an incorporationist approach. In *Murray v Director, Family Services, ACT*[76] (an

---

71   *Racial Discrimination Act* 1975 (Cth) ss 9 and 10; *Sex Discrimination Act* 1984 (Cth) ss 5-7D and 26; *Disability Discrimination Act* 1992 (Cth) ss 5-9 and 29.

72   *In marriage of Sajdak and Sajdak* (1993) FLC ¶92-348.

73   *McMillan v Jackson* (1995) FLC ¶92-610.

74   *In marriage of Kennedy and Cahill* (1995) FLC ¶92-605.

75   *In marriage of Davies and Davies* (1995) FLC ¶92-646.

76   (1993) FLC ¶92-416.

international child abduction case), Nicholson CJ and Fogarty J reviewed the law on the impact of international law on the interpretation of domestic law.[77] In referring to the impacts of international conventions which have not been implemented into domestic law, their honours expressed the view that, not only could the terms of the convention be resorted to for the purpose of resolving ambiguity in domestic primary or subordinate legislation but that: "such conventions may also be resorted to in order to fill lacunae in such legislation".[78] In referring to the CROC as such a Convention, their honours commented that: "As such it may well have a significant role to play in the interpretation of the FLA and in the common law relating to children".[79] This decision has been referred to in subsequent decisions of the Full Court.[80]

A number of relevant conventions have not been directly incorporated, but have been listed in the Schedule to the *Human Rights and Equal Opportunity Commission Act* 1986 (Cth) (HREOC Act). The significance of this is referred to in a number of cases in the Full Court. In *Re Marion*,[81] Nicholson CJ was of the view that the *Declaration on the Rights of Mentally Retarded Persons*, and other instruments incorporated into the Schedule to the HREOC Act, "have been recognised by the Parliament as a source of Australian domestic law by reason of this legislation".[82]

Most recently, the Full Court in *B and B (Family Law Reform Act 1995)*[83] (hereafter *B*) has reviewed the relevance of international human rights instruments in family law decision-making. In this case the court considered arguments expressed in human rights terms (these are considered below). On the general point of the relevance of international instruments, the court provides a useful overview of the decisions in the area. Specifically the court considered the impact of CROC, the ICCPR and CEDAW on decision-making about parental mobility under the FLA. So far as CROC is concerned, the court was of the clear view that it could refer to the whole of CROC in interpreting the legislation (although it found there were no enforceable rights of the child created under the Act).[84]

So far as the relevance of ICCPR and CEDAW were concerned, the court did not express a clear view but did say that:

---

77   Their honours reviewed the decision of Gummow J in *Minister for Foreign Affairs and Trade v Magno* (1992) 112 ALR 529; and the High Court cases of *Dietrich v R* (1992) 109 ALR 385 and *Mabo v Queensland (No 2)* (1992) 107 ALR 1.

78   (1993) FLC ¶92-416 at 80,257.

79   Ibid. Their honours ultimately concluded that there was no inconsistency between the CROC (namely – the "best interests of the child" dictate) and the Hague Convention on International Child Abduction but that "[e]ven if it could be said that there was an inconsistency between the Hague Convention and the UN Convention in this regard, the Hague Convention would prevail, insofar as it has been incorporated into Australian domestic law" (at 80,258).

80   See *H and W* (1995) FLC ¶92-598; and *N and S* (1996) FLC ¶92-655 per Fogarty J.

81   (1991) FLC ¶92-193.

82   Ibid at 78,303. In *Murray*, it was noted that "it may be this is still an open issue" at 80,256 per Nicholson CJ and Fogarty J.

83   (1997) FLC ¶92-755.

84   See the extensive reasons given at 84,226-29.

There can be little doubt that a general right of freedom of movement is a right recognised by Australian law, but in proceedings under Part VII it is a right that cannot prevail over what is considered to be in the best interests of the children in a particular case. The rights of women to live their lives free of discrimination would appear to be similarly recognised, and a doctrinaire approach to the question of relocation may, in practice in some cases, have the effect of discriminating against women ...[85]

Of particular importance for family law is the reference in the judgment to the relevance of conventions and treaties where a court has a discretion.[86]

As has been indicated, the Family Court has been at the forefront of recognition of the potential impacts of international law on the interpretation of domestic law. In addition, Chief Justice Nicholson of the Family Court has indicated in extra-curial forums the relevance of human rights arguments.[87]

Children's rights

Discussions of the case law on children's rights traditionally begin with the 1970 decision of Lord Denning MR in *Hewer v Bryant*,[88] where he recognised the concept that parental rights over children "yield to the child's right to make his own decisions when he reaches a sufficient understanding and intelligence".[89] The House of Lords adopted and applied this concept in its decision in *Gillick v West Norfolk and Wisbech Area Health Authority*,[90] where the court held that a doctor can lawfully prescribe contraceptives for a girl under the age of 16 (that being the relevant age in Britain for consenting to medical treatment) if, on the facts, the girl is sufficiently mature to make a judgment. In other words, prescribing contraceptives in such a case does not infringe the rights of the girl's parents to make decisions for her. Further, children acquire a right to make such decisions when they attain competency.

The principles in *Gillick* were given support in Australia by the High Court in *Secretary, Department of Health and Community Services and JWB and SMB (Marion's Case)*[91] and have also recently been referred to with approval by the Full Court of the Family Court in *B*.

Recent English authority suggests, however, that the parents' right to make decisions on behalf of the child does not fade away as the child develops capacity; in other words, that parents, the court and the child may make decisions until the child reaches the legal age of majority.[92] This may well not be the law in Australia.[93]

---

85   (1997) FLC ¶92-755 at 84,231.

86   See ibid at 84,224.

87   See Nicholson, A, "The Changing Concept of Family" (1997) 11 *Australian Journal of Family Law* 13.

88   [1970] 1 QB 357.

89   Ibid at 369.

90   [1986] 1 AC 112.

91   (1992) FLC ¶92-293.

92   See *Re R (A Minor)* [1991] 3 WLR 592; *Re W (A Minor)* [1993] 4 All ER 627; and Parker, Parkinson and Behrens, above n 1, pp 771-73.

93   See Parkinson, P, "Children's Rights and Doctors' Immunities: The Implications of the High Court's Decision in *Re Marion*" (1992) 6 *Australian Journal of Family Law* 101.

So far as the relevance of *Gillick* to FLA proceedings is concerned, the Full Court has recently referred to the potential clash of the best interests test and children's rights approaches:

> The "Gillick-competent" test is helpful by analogy. But where a court is concerned with the welfare of a child no question of "self-determination" by a mature child can arise. In the ultimate, whether by a statute or at common law, whilst the wishes of children are important and should be given real and not token weight the court is still required to determine the matter in the child's best interests and that may in some circumstances involve the rejection of the wishes of the child.[94]

Concepts of children's rights have, however, been specifically referred to in decision-making about the appointment of separate representatives, the relevance of children's wishes, and contact. We discuss these in turn.

The Full Court relied heavily on the CROC in making its important decision in *Re K*[95] in which it provided guidelines as to the circumstances in which separate representatives should be appointed by the court. The court stated that "[i]n developing these guidelines, we have had regard to the provisions of the United Nations Convention on the Rights of the Child and in particular to arts 9 and 12 thereof".[96] The court raised the possibility that the Convention requires that a child be separately represented in any custody or access proceeding (as these proceedings were then called). They also indicated that a response to this argument might be that "provided that a family report is obtained, or the views of the child are otherwise obtained (where it is practicable to do so) and his or her interests are otherwise protected before the court, this is sufficient compliance with the Convention".[97]

On the question of the relevance of children's wishes, the major statement is in *H and W*, where an appeal by the father against an award of custody to the mother was successful in part on the basis of a failure by the trial judge to give sufficient attention to the wishes of two children aged 8 and 7. In a lengthy and important judgment, Baker J referred specifically to CROC, to the terms of the FLA and to psychological literature. He stated that "[t]here appears to have been a tendency for adults to underestimate the wisdom of children and their ability to make sound choices about their future welfare".[98] Baker J concluded that:

> [A] child's wishes must not only be considered, but must be shown to have been considered, in the reasons for judgment of the Trial Judge. Furthermore, if the trial Judge decides to reject the wishes of a child, then clear and cogent reasons for such a rejection must be given particularly if, as in this case, the separate representative submits that the Court should give effect to such wishes.[99]

In cases where children are too young to express wishes, a children's rights approach might nonetheless have some impact. In particular, Eekelaar has argued that using a children's rights approach, the court should consider what wishes the

---

94   See *H and W* (1995) FLC ¶92-598 at 81,947 per Fogarty and Kay JJ.

95   (1994) FLC ¶92-461.

96   Ibid at 80,776.

97   Ibid.

98   *H and W* (1995) FLC ¶92-598 at 81,964.

99   Ibid at 81,967.

child *would have expressed* if he or she were old enough to do so.[100] There will, of course, be no clear answer to this question in most cases. It is possible, however, that bodies of empirical evidence could be used to influence outcomes. For example, the stories of "the Stolen Generations" reported in the Human Rights and Equal Opportunity Commission's (HREOC) *Bringing Them Home* Report make a persuasive case for Aboriginal children to be placed within Aboriginal homes.[101]

In *N and S* Fogarty J referred to art 9(3) of CROC, which provides that states must "respect the right of the child who is separated from one or both parents to maintain personal relations and direct contact with both parents on a regular basis, except if it is contrary to the child's best interests" in an appeal by the mother against an award of access to the father in the context of allegations of sexual abuse by the father of the child. In *N and S* Fogarty J (who was in dissent as to the substance of the appeal) concluded that a child's best interests remain the paramount consideration, and justified this in children's rights terms.[102]

Subsequently, in *B* the court came to the same conclusion (that best interests are paramount), but denied that the child's right to contact was a legally enforceable right. In a somewhat confusing explanation for this statement of the law, the court states that:

> [T]he unenforceability of these rights is fundamentally because of the inherent conflict between the child's best interests on the one side and self-determinism by the children on the other, again a background of age, maturity, vulnerability to pressures. It may also reflect the nature of the practical day-to-day relationship between parents and their children.[103]

In other words, the court seems to be stating that children do not have legally enforceable rights under the legislation, because the principle on which Pt VII is based is that the best interests of the child are paramount. An alternative approach would have been to adopt the approach of Baker J in *H and W* in recognising that the child's right to contact is enforceable where that contact is in the child's best interests, and to note that one of the child's rights is to have their best interests taken into account in decision-making. On the other hand, it is certainly arguable (as the Full Court seems to be suggesting in *B*) that a best interests approach is different from a children's rights approach.

One area where a children's rights argument has been attempted without success is in relation to attempts by a husband to prevent his wife from having an abortion. In *F and F*,[104] Lindenmayer J rejected an argument for jurisdiction based on the protection of a child's right to life. In the course of the argument counsel for the husband had referred to the ICCPR and the United Nations *Declaration of the*

---

100 Eekelaar, J, "The Importance of Thinking that Children Have Rights" in Alston, Parker and Seymour (eds), above n 7, p 221.

101 The "Aboriginal Child Placement Principle" (ACPP) is based on this central tenet of the placement of children within the indigenous community to which they belong. The ACPP operates at various levels in all State and Territory jurisdictions – that is, in the forms of statutory incorporation, as a regulation or as a policy guideline; for discussion and an outline of the standing of the ACPP in each jurisdiction, see Ch 5 by Neilson and Martin in this volume.

102 *N and S* (1996) FLC ¶92-655 at 82,708.

103 (1997) FLC ¶92-755 at 84,233.

104 (1989) FLC ¶92-031.

Rights of the Child. The judge was of the view that a foetus has no legal personality and "cannot have a right of its own until it is born and has a separate existence from its mother".[105] Thus it could not enforce in a court any rights it might or might not otherwise have. The husband's right to procreate did not extend to giving him a right to force his wife to continue with a pregnancy against her wishes (the parties had separated).

So far as applications for parenting orders are concerned, various provisions of CROC provide "hooks" on which to hang arguments for particular outcomes. For example, arts 7, 9 and 18(1) could well be used in arguments in favour of natural parents in contests with strangers in proceedings for parenting orders.[106] Article 18(1) could be used as an argument in favour of residence-residence orders and against the making of specific issues orders. Similarly, these provisions could be used to argue for the making orders requiring parentage testing, particularly given the evidence about children's need to know their biological origins.

Another difficult series of cases involve applications for parenting orders where one party is a member of an extreme religious sect (for example, the Plymouth Brethren). While several of the articles in CROC refer to the need to respect the freedom of religion of the child and parents, the tenor of the others (for example, art 29) may dictate against placement of children with sects which are not going to allow, for example, freedom to receive information and to get an education.

In cases involving abuse and neglect, reference can be made to arts 19 and 34, which refer to the need to protect children from abuse and neglect. The fact that those articles refer to all forms of physical or mental violence or abuse could be used in cases where the abuser has been violent towards his spouse but not directly towards his children.[107]

The Convention provisions strengthen arguments for tough enforcement of child maintenance obligations; for example, art 27 imposes on states parties an obligation to secure the recovery of maintenance for the child from the parents or other persons having the financial responsibility for the child. Tay and Farrugia have suggested that "it is arguable that the child support legislation does not comply with CROC, Art 27 by failing to cover all sole parent families, and by the Child Support Agency's inadequate enforcement of the payment of arrears".[108]

Other substantive areas of family law in respect of which there are relevant CROC provisions include adoption[109] and international child abduction.[110]

Equality

As has been indicated, anti-discrimination legislation[111] only applies to activities in certain areas. These are generally areas of "public" activity. However, as pointed

---

105 Ibid at 77,434.

106 In recent case law the idea that there is a presumption in favour of natural parents has been rejected: *Re Hodak* (1993) FLC ¶92-421 and *Rice and Miller* (1993) FLC ¶92-415.

107 In any case, this is now relevant under the FLA s 68F(2).

108 Tay, A and Farrugia, A, "Families and Education" in *Laws of Australia* (Law Book Co), 21.8, Human Rights, para [31].

109 Articles 7 and 21. On adoption and human rights see ibid, Ch 4.

110 Article 11. This issue has been discussed in detail above.

111 On which in general, see Ch 13 by Bailey and Devereux in this volume.

out above, it seems at least arguable that the Commonwealth legislation applies to decisions of the Family Court, and decisions made under the FLA. Although we have not been able to identify any decisions of the Family Court which refer to anti-discrimination legislation, there are an increasing number of references to rights to equality before the law and freedom from discrimination in decisions of the court.

The Full Court of the Family Court has recently explicitly embraced the concept of substantive equality in its decision making. The case of *B and R and the Separate Representative*[112] involved a custody/access dispute between a white Australian father and an Aboriginal mother about their two-year-old daughter. The trial judge granted the father custody and the mother access. During the trial the separate representative sought to file an affidavit by an expert who had written a report for the Victorian Aboriginal Child Care Agency on the placement of Aboriginal children with non-Aboriginal families. During the course of deciding whether to admit the evidence, exchanges took place between the trial judge and the separate representative about the relevance of it. During this exchange, the trial judge indicated that he saw the case as involving parents who were Australian citizens and that he could not see why this evidence should be given any particular weight or why a case involving an Aboriginal child should be treated any differently from a case involving a child with any other cultural background. The mother appealed on the basis of a failure to give sufficient attention to the child's aboriginality and the evidence brought about it. On appeal the Full Court embraced the substantive equality approach:

> To say that the doctrine of equality before the law requires that all people receive equal treatment is superficially correct. However, that is no more than the starting point of an examination of equality.
>
> Perhaps the principle is better expressed by saying that all people should be treated with equal respect. By recognising that this represents the essential content of the ideal of equality, one realises that equal justice is not always achieved through the identical treatment of individuals. In many cases, superficially identical treatment has a disparate impact on individuals; the same law or conduct may have the effect of respecting the essential humanity of certain persons, while ignoring or undermining that of others. Equality and discrimination cannot be measured at the superficial level ...
>
> What emerges once the concept of equality, or equal justice, is examined in any real sense, is the recognition that it cannot simply be equated with identical treatment. One cannot use what has become known as "formal equality" as the sole test of the presence of equality, or the absence of discrimination.
>
> In place of the former adherence to formal equality as the relevant criterion, the notion that equality in substance is achieved by treating individuals in a manner which recognises, and responds to, their relevant differences, has gained acceptance ...[113]

This approach has been followed by the Full Court in *In re CP*[114] where cultural differences *among* indigenous people were taken into account. This focus on substantive equality can be seen in other areas of decision-making of the Full Court, and has tended to combine with a sense of social realism, and taking judicial notice of the social contexts within which decision making takes place. In particular, in

---

112   (1995) FLC ¶92-636.

113   Ibid at 82,412-13.

114   (1997) FLC ¶92-741.

Best and Best[115] and *Mitchell and Mitchell,*[116] the court indicated a greater willingness to make decisions awarding spousal maintenance, in part on the basis of a recognition of the economic disadvantage women suffer on marriage breakdown. The rejection of a strict formal equality model is also evident in the decision in *P and P*[117] (referred to below under Rights of the Disabled).

Discrimination on the ground of sex is made unlawful in international conventions and in all Australian anti-discrimination legislation. The concept of discrimination incorporates not only direct discrimination but also indirect discrimination – that is, imposing an unreasonable criterion which persons of one sex find more difficult to comply with than persons of the other sex, thus producing less favourable treatment. Decisions under the FLA are potentially open to challenge for being discriminatory: for example, if judges in exercising their discretion about parenting orders pay more attention to factors which men more easily comply with than women, and which are producing unfavourable results for women, and which are unreasonable.[118] Of course, in this context a common response will be that the factors being applied, for example, the question of who was the primary caregiver, are relevant to the children's best interests, and therefore reasonable.

In *B* we had the first attempt to argue before the Family Court that an approach to the interpretation of legislation and the exercise of discretion could potentially breach the requirement of equality before the law. Counsel for the wife argued in this case that:

> [A]ny consideration of the best interests of children must include the parents' rights to freedom of movement pursuant to domestic law and as a human right recognised by the International Covenant on Civil and Political Rights (ICCPR), by Australia's obligations under the Convention on the Elimination of All Forms of Discrimination against Women (CEDAW) and under CROC, and which she submitted, were relevant to the interpretation of Part VII.[119]

The potentially discriminatory impacts of decisions on mobility were highlighted by counsel for the wife by reference to the following contextual factors, taken largely from the factum of the Women's Legal, Education and Action Fund to the Supreme Court in Canada in *Goertz v Gordon*:[120]

- the largely private nature of child care responsibility;
- the greater domestic child care responsibility borne by women, whether or not they are also in paid work;
- that such responsibility for children has socially defined women as secondary earners who are likely to limit their paid workforce participation for that reason;

---

115 (1993) FLC ¶92-418.

116 (1995) FLC ¶92-601.

117 (1995) FLC ¶92-376.

118 Annette Hasche has argued that a focus on economic factors and repartnering in decisions about parenting is discriminatory: see Hasche, A, "Sex Discrimination in Child Custody Determinations" (1989) 3 *Australian Journal of Family Law* 218.

119 (1997) FLC ¶92-755 at 84,190.

120 (1995) 85 WAC 156.

- this division of labour has exacerbated women's inequality in the paid workforce by contributing to systemic pay and employment inequality;

- upon separation, women are more likely to have custody of children of the relationship; and that

- single parent mothers are far more likely to live in poverty than mothers raising children with a male partner.[121]

While indicating that the best interests of the children are the paramount consideration in a particular case, the Full Court noted that:

> The rights of women to live their lives free of discrimination would appear to be similarly recognised, and a doctrinaire approach to the question of relocation may, in practice in some cases, have the effect of discriminating against women. (at 84,231)

Tay and Farrugia have provided some indications of areas of family law which may be amenable to challenge on the basis that they do not comply with international human rights norms providing for freedom from discrimination on the basis of sex or marital status.[122] In particular, they point to the fact that the property adjustment and spousal maintenance provisions of the FLA only apply to parties to a marriage, and that the absence of legislation for parties to de facto relationships in some jurisdictions, and the fact that where it exists it is interpreted in ways which are less favourable to women compared to the FLA, may provide the basis for a claim that the FLA discriminates against women in de facto relationships in violation of CEDAW.[123] They argue that this difference also has a discriminatory effect on children who are born outside of marriages, in that their financial position will be affected by the limits on the claims able to be made by their carers. This could be in breach of art 2 of CROC, which requires parties not to discriminate against children on the basis of the status or activities of the child's parents.

Tay and Farrugia argue further that interpretations of the FLA property provisions may involve discrimination against women in their failure to take sufficient account of superannuation entitlements, for example.[124]

Sexuality and transexuality

There is already an extensive case law and a considerable jurisprudence on the issue of custody claims by homosexual parents.[125] The general approach is that a parent's sexuality is irrelevant except to the extent that it affects parenting abilities or the

---

121 (1997) FLC ¶92-755 at 84,190.

122 See Tay and Farrugia, above, n 108, Ch 21.8.

123 There are, however, constitutional explanations behind the fact that Pt VIII of the FLA only applies to parties to a marriage.

124 Tay and Farrugia, above, n 108, paras [19]-[21].

125 *N and N* (1977) FLC ¶90-208; *Spry and Spry* (1977) FLC ¶90-271; *Cartwright and Cartwright* (1977) FLC ¶90-302; *L and L* (1983) FLC ¶91-353; *Doyle ·and Doyle* (1992) FLC ¶92-286; Otlowski, M, "*Doyle and Doyle*: Family Court Awards Custody to Homosexual Father" (1992) 11 *University of Tasmania Law Review* 261; Bateman, M, "Lesbians, Gays and Child Custody: An Australian Legal History" (1992) 1 *Australasian Gay & Lesbian Law Journal* 46; Bates, B, "Child Custody and the Homosexual Parent" (1992) 2 *Australasian Gay & Lesbian Law Journal* 1; Millbank, J, "Lesbian Mothers, Gay Fathers: Sameness and Difference" (1992) 2 *Australasian Gay & Lesbian Law Journal* 21.

welfare (now, best interests) of the child. Apart from the problem of the indeterminacy and value judgements necessary to make the latter decision, this approach in general accords with the intent of the CROC. Where problems may arise in the future is in the extent to which the rights of a homosexual parent to equality under other human rights instruments, such as ICCPR,[126] clash with the principle of the best interests of the child. It is submitted that, in general, the latter is likely to take precedence, but the value judgements on which this has been based in custody cases in the past (in particular with respect to parenting roles) will now have to stand a more rigorous equality test to be consistent with the international obligations, so that the arguments in such cases may henceforth shift ground to take this into account.

This can also be the case in matters not traditionally coming before the Family Court, such as child maintenance disputes where the litigants are former lesbian lovers[127] and the right to parenthood (by insemination) itself.[128] Also included must now be the issue of property disputes upon the breakdown of a same-sex relationship. With one exception,[129] de facto relationships legislation, including discrimination legislation, does not extend to same sex relationships in Australia.[130] As art 26 of the ICCPR specifically provides for equality before the law and to the equal protection of the law, it may only be a matter of time before the juridical focus in these cases shifts too, since the existence of remedies for heterosexual couples, but not for gay and lesbian couples, is discriminatory.

In Australia, marriage has been defined as strictly heterosexual and mono-gamous (at least in the serial sense).[131] Courts have refused to recognise a marriage of a male-to-female transsexual to a man,[132] including the European Court of Human Rights.[133] This has even extended to non-recognition of a marriage by a hermaphrodite to anyone at all (on the basis that such a person is neither male nor female for the purposes of Australian marriage law)[134] which is an undoubted breach of human rights. This situation is slowly changing. Same-sex partners with children have been held to be families for limited purposes, such as entitlement to concessional rates of health insurance.[135] It is similar with respect to transgender people.[136] However, the cases have only been successful to the extent that the same-

---

126 See *Toonen v Australia* CCPR/C/50/D/488/1992 where the Human Rights Committee held that references in the Covenant to equality on the basis of "sex" also included sexuality.

127 *W v G* (1996) 20 Fam LR 49. Interestingly, this case did not revolve around human rights but equitable principles such as promissory estoppel.

128 *JM v QFG* (1997) EOC ¶92-876. A lesbian was found to have been unlawfully discriminated against by a fertility clinic when it refused her access to an insemination program.

129 *Domestic Relationships Act* 1994 (ACT).

130 See Tahmindjis, P, "Anti-Discrimination Legislation", in Wilmott, L (ed), *De Facto Relationships Law* (Law Book Co, Sydney, 1996).

131 *Marriage Act* 1961 (Cth) s 46.

132 See *Corbett v Corbett (otherwise Ashley)* [1970] 2 All ER 33.

133 *Cossey v United Kingdom* EHRR Series A, No 184 (1990).

134 *In marriage of C and D* (1979) FLC ¶90-636.

135 *NIB Health Fund Ltd v Hope* (unreported, SC NSW, McInerny J, 15 November 1996).

136 In *Secretary, Department of Social Security v SRA* (1993) 118 ALR 467, a male to female transsexual was held to be a woman for the purposes of social security entitlements.

sex relationships have emulated heterosexist paradigms and to the extent that a surgically changed body is, as Andrew Sharpe has put it, legally intelligible.[137]

Dewar explains the effect of the qualification to the right to marry (that is, according to national laws). He argues that:

> The most plausible distinction is between restrictions on types of relationships (which are permitted) and restrictions excluding individuals or groups of individuals from marriage (which are not permitted, apart from those under age, a restriction for which Article 12 expressly provides). Thus, "national law" may legitimately ban bigamous and polygamous marriages, marriages within the prohibited degrees, or homosexual marriage, because these are restrictions on types of relationship (that is, who may marry whom); however, "national laws" preventing for example, racial minorities or individuals from marrying, being restrictions on who may marry, are in breach of Article 12.[138]

Dewar cites *Hamer v UK*[139] in which it was held that a prisoner's right to marry under art 12 was breached by the Home Office's refusal to make arrangements for his temporary release from prison, where he could not marry, so that he could marry elsewhere. In applying this case to the issue of transsexuals and the failure of national laws to recognise surgical reassignments, Dewar writes that:

> [A] (permissible) ban on a type of relationship may amount in effect to a (forbidden) ban on an individual or group of individuals for whom that type of relationship offers the only realistic route to matrimony. This is the case with transsexuals. As long as the law refuses to recognise the legal sex reassignment of transsexuals, it is clear that [the effect of the Corbett decision is to constitute] a ban not merely on homosexual relationships, but on transsexuals as a group – and is therefore a breach of Article 12.[140]

Racial equality

Decisions of the Family Court also have the potential to discriminate on the basis of race. Practices and processes of the court may take insufficient account of particular cultural factors (this is an area that is yet to be explored in the case law).[141] Decisions on parenting orders may take insufficient account of children's rights to "enjoy his or her culture, to profess and practise his or her own religion, or to use his or her own language".[142] Decisions about orders may be based on a failure to understand and value parenting traditions within particular cultures, or may apply stereotypical assumptions about cultural practices. Beyond this, as the Full Court has recently pointed out, decisions about Aboriginal and Torres Strait Islander children may fail to grasp the importance of the information which we now have

---

137 Sharpe, A, "Judicial Issues of Transsexuality: A Site for Political Contestation" (1996) 21 *Alternative Law Journal* 153.

138 Dewar, J, "Transsexualism and Marriage" (1986) 15 *Kingston Law Review* 58 at 65.

139 (1982) 4 EHRR 139.

140 Dewar, above n 138, p 66.

141 But see, for example, the argument by Tay and Farrugia that conduct of proceedings without proper provisions for translation and interpretation would be in possible breach of the ICCPR, arts 14, 23, 26, above n 108, Ch 21.8, para [15].

142 CROC, art 30. Early decisions of the Family Court have been criticised on this basis: see, for example, *Goudge* (1984) FLC ¶91-534.

about "the effects on Aboriginal children of being raised in a white environment, in which the lack of reinforcement of their identity contributed to severe confusions of that identity and profound experiences of alienation".[143]

It is only in the recent case of *B and R* that children's rights arguments have explicitly been introduced in a context of decisions about parenting where the children are Aboriginal but only one parent is.[144] The court in that case made reference to CROC in its decision that upheld an appeal by an Aboriginal mother partly on the basis that insufficient attention had been paid by the trial judge to issues of the children's aboriginality. However, beyond this reference to rights to cultural identity, the court also touches for the first time on issues of racial equality, as indicated above. In particular, it adopts a substantive equality approach.

Rights of people with disabilities

A major context in which human rights arguments have been made in Australia has been in relation to applications for orders about the sterilisation of intellectually handicapped minors. During the 1980s and early 1990s the Family Court made a series of decisions on this issue. These decisions culminated in a decision of the Full Court of the Family Court in *Re Marion*[145] that parents cannot consent to such procedures. In this decision Nicholson CJ in the major judgment referred to the issue of the common law rights applicable in the case. He referred to the right to bodily inviolability and the right to procreate, or the right to choose whether to procreate or not.[146] He found these rights to be recognised in the common law. They are obviously not specifically related to the situation of disabled persons. While finding it not necessary to rely on international instruments, he made the points referred to above about the relevance of the fact that instruments have been incorporated into the HREOC Act. Nicholson CJ then referred to relevant international provisions.[147]

On appeal from that case, in *Secretary, Department of Health and Community Services v JWB and SMB (Re Marion)*,[148] the High Court found that parents cannot give their consent to such a procedure, that court consent must be obtained, and that such a step should be one of "last resort". The HREOC intervened in the proceedings. The Commission argued a requirement for court consent to safeguard the rights of retarded and disabled persons recognised in international Conventions and Declarations. In the major judgment, Mason CJ, Dawson, Toohey and Gaudron JJ concurred with Nicholson CJ in recognising a common law right to bodily inviolability. However, they expressed doubt that there is a common law right to

---

143 *B v R and the Separate Representative* (1995) FLC ¶92-636 at 82,395-96. See also HREOC, above, n 64. See also, discussion in Ch 5 by Neilson and Martin in this volume.

144 There are other cases where issues of aboriginality have been linked to children's best interests; see, for example, *McL* (1991) FLC ¶92-238.

145 *Re Marion* (1991) FLC ¶92-193; on this case and the human rights issues it raises in the context of health law, see Ch 12 by Freckelton and Loff in this volume.

146 Ibid at 78,299.

147 Clauses 1 and 7 of the *Declaration on the Rights of Mentally Retarded Persons*.

148 (1992) FLC ¶92-293.

reproduce which is independent of the right to personal inviolability.[149] This is an arid approach to children's rights and contrasts with Canadian cases like *Re Eve*[150] where, on the basis of the *Canadian Charter of Rights and Freedoms*,[151] similar issues were held by the Supreme Court of Canada to revolve around the rights of the person with the disability.

An issue which remained open after *Re Marion* was the test to be applied in determining whether the court should grant consent or not. In *P and P*,[152] the Full Court considered a decision of the trial judge that "sterilisation should not be approved if it would not be contemplated in the case of an intellectually normal girl with similar epilepsy".[153] This had been the test suggested by HREOC, and it was argued that this was non-discriminatory in that it equates the intellectually handicapped person with the non intellectually handicapped. However, the Full Court rejected the application of what it called the "but for" test, stating that "it is both unrealistic and contrary to the intention of the majority judgment in Marion's case to deal with a particular aspect of the child's needs and capacities as though it existed in isolation from other needs and capacities". Further on the court stated that the "responsibility to assess the child's best interests is not furthered by compartmentalising one or more of her attributes and measuring the appropriateness of the proposed treatment against a hypothetical child".[154] The court went on to explain the decision in terms of discrimination theory, pointing out that "[n]ot all distinction is discrimination. One must look to the basis for differentiation and also whether the differentiation gives rise to detrimental treatment".[155]

The issue of discrimination in family law decision-making against parents who are disabled has not been the subject of any significant academic discussion. However, it has been noted that:

> Intellectually disabled parents seeking custody confront the common perception that they are children, rather than adults who suffer from a disability. There is, in fact, no available evidence to suggest a direct relationship between IQ and the adequacy of child care. Courts have similar difficulty with parents who manifest a psychiatric condition and with weighing the evidence presented concerning the mental health of the various parties.[156]

OVERVIEW AND CONCLUSIONS

In earlier parts of this chapter we outlined provisions in international instruments, domestic legislation and Australian case law which deal with human rights in a family law context. We sought to stress the potential for the use of these arguments, as well as to describe how they have been used in both legislation and case law. An

---

149   Ibid at 79,182.
150   (1986) 31 DLR (4th) 1.
151   Sections 7 and 15.
152   (1995) FLC ¶92-615.
153   Ibid at 82,147.
154   Ibid.
155   *Ibid* at 82,148.
156   Tay and Farrugia, above, n 108, para [22].

illustration of the width of application is the 1996 decision of the UN Human Rights Committee in *X v Australia*.[157] Although this complaint was found by the Committee to be inadmissible because of a failure to exhaust all local remedies, it involved a dispute over the custody of children (under the pre-reform FLA) where the Aboriginal father claimed that the Family Court had struck out evidence of the benefits for the children of contact with the father's extended Aboriginal family. He claimed in addition that the Family Court had no jurisdiction over Aboriginal people and their children and property, principally arguing that, by extension of the *Mabo* decision, traditional Aboriginal law and custom should apply. These claims were brought pursuant to the rights under the ICCPR to equality before courts and tribunals (art 14(1)), the right to adopt a belief of one's choice (art 18(1)), the right of the family to be protected (art 23), and the right of ethnic minorities to enjoy their own culture (art 27). The fact that the Committee found it unnecessary to comment on the substance of the complaint leaves these issues potentially open.

An awareness of human rights norms and the Family Court's interest in them is not only properly the object of study for legal scholars, it also opens up new avenues of argument for practitioners in the area. However, new sets of problems can also emerge. Thus, while the objects and principles introduced into the FLA with respect to children's rights[158] can be informed by CROC, the problem of a competition between competing rights arises, such as the balance that must be drawn between a child's rights and a parent's rights to movement or to remarry. In addition, as human rights are a part of international law, problems of a sophisticated nature with respect to the binding nature of the instruments in which those rights are located, and hence about the authoritative nature of the rights themselves, may arise. Human rights in Australian family law will raise both opportunities and challenges for legal scholars and practitioners alike.

---

157 Communication No 557/1993, UN Doc CCPR/C/57/D/557/1993 (1996).
158 Section 60B.

9

LABOUR LAW AND HUMAN RIGHTS

Therese MacDermott[*]

INTRODUCTION

Labour law is a neglected area in human rights discourse. Although a wide range of multilateral human rights instruments have an impact on Australian labour law and practice, few human rights texts deal in any detail with the question of what labour standards constitute universal human rights.[1] The International Labour Organisation (ILO) has identified seven of its Conventions as dealing with fundamental human rights, covering the issues of forced labour; freedom of association, the right to organise and the right to bargain collectively; non-discrimination; and minimum age protections.[2] However, it remains an open question what labour law issues may be regarded as falling within the broad rubric of human rights.

This chapter focuses on two specific categories of rights, dealing first with those associated with equality of treatment and non-discrimination. International human rights instruments have had a profound influence on the development of anti-discrimination legislation in Australia. A variety of multilateral human rights treaties to which Australia is a party creates a right not to be subject to unlawful discrimination. This right has been given expression in the form of general anti-discrimination legislation applicable to employment, the details of which will be examined below. The second principal application of human rights instruments in the context of labour law is in relation to a group of fundamental rights protected by various international instruments. Included in this category of rights is the right to freedom of association, the right to organise, the right to bargain collectively, and the right to strike. These rights derive from several sources, including the *International Covenant on Civil and Political Rights* (ICCPR), the *International*

---

*   I owe a particular debt of gratitude to Breen Creighton for his helpful and detailed comments on ILO standards. I would also like to thank Ron McCallum and Brian Opeskin for their comments, and Jacinda de Witts for research assistance.

1   On the definition of human rights in a legal context, see Ch 1 by Kinley in this volume, and generally, Steiner H and Alston P, *International Human Rights in Context* (Clarendon Press, Oxford, 1996), pp 166-328.

2   ILO, *The ILO, Standard Setting and Globalisation* International Labour Conference 85th Session 1997. See Hepple, B "New Approaches to International Labour Regulation" (1997) 26 *Industrial Law Journal* 353 at 359. The seven "core" ILO Conventions are the *Forced Labour Convention*, 1930 (No 29); *Abolition of Forced Labour Convention*, 1957 (No 105); *Freedom of Association and Protection of the Right to Organise Convention* 1948 (No 87); *Right to Organise and Collective Bargaining Convention*, 1949 (No 98); *Equal Remuneration Convention*, 1951 (No 100); *Discrimination (Employment and Occupation) Convention*, 1958 (No 111); *Minimum Age Convention*, 1973 (No 138).

Covenant on Economic Social and Cultural Rights (ICESCR) and ILO Conventions such as the *Freedom of Association and Protection of the Right to Organise Convention* 1948 (No 87), and the *Right to Organise and Collective Bargaining Convention* 1949 (No 98). The new reform agenda in Australian labour law that is directed to a reconfiguration of Australian industrial relations through a gradual dismantling of the collective apparatus of industrial regulation, brings some of these rights into question.

A number of preliminary points should be noted in considering the efficacy of implementing international instruments as a means of achieving human rights objectives in the labour law context. First, in some circumstances the response of Australia has been to limit its obligations under various instruments, including by reservations to some instruments.[3] Secondly, Australia is selective in the instruments it chooses to ratify so as to avoid certain obligations, such as the right to fully paid maternity leave.[4] Thirdly, the obligations pursuant to many international instruments tend to be expressed in very general terms. For example, the recognition of the "right to work" and the "right of everyone to the enjoyment of just and favourable conditions of work" in the ICESCR,[5] whilst admirable sentiments, are a very vague basis on which to construct substantive rights in labour law.[6] International instruments that express obligations in the form of "promotional standards" allow scope for the subordination of issues relevant to women and other groups that occupy a position of disadvantage in the labour market.[7] The scope for auto-interpretation gives states a very wide berth in terms of implementation. Similarly, micro-economic issues such as wage restraint or wage relativity may be given priority over the general obligations dictated by international instruments so as to restrict access to equality of employment opportunities. Finally, international instruments have been used to justify forms of "protective" legislation which have served to deny access to employment opportunities, particularly in their application to women.

One of the difficulties with examining human rights issues in the labour law context is that discrimination issues have been traditionally regarded as distinct from industrial issues. This separation has been achieved through the maintenance of statutory exemptions of awards and agreements from the application of anti-

---

3   For example, Australia maintains a reservation to the obligation to provide paid maternity leave for all women workers in art 11(2) of the *Convention on the Elimination of All forms of Discrimination against Women*.

4   See *Maternity Protection Convention* 1952 (No 103). Ratification was considered in 1992, but was rejected on the basis of widespread non-compliance at State and federal levels, the cost of such measures, and the lack of a European style social insurance scheme by which to implement it: See Commonwealth of Australia, *Women in Australia: Australia's Second Progress Report on Implementing the United Nations Convention on the Elimination of all forms of Discrimination Against Women* (AGPS, Canberra, 1992), p 126.

5   Articles 6 and 7. See also *Universal Declaration of Human Rights* 1948, arts 22 and 23.

6   Bailey, P, *Human Rights: Australia in an International Context* (Butterworths, Sydney, 1990), p 360.

7   Amato, T, "Symposium: Women at Work, Rights at Risk – Toward the Empowerment of Working Women" (1992) 17 *Yale Journal of International Law* 139; Compa, L, "International Labor Standards and Instruments of Recourse for Working Women" (1992) 17 *Yale Journal of International Law* 151.

discrimination legislation,[8] a position that has only recently been altered. Further, discrimination issues have generally been seen as the problems of individuals, and hence more appropriate to the "private" form of adjudication offered by the conciliation procedures of the anti-discrimination jurisdiction, rather than the collective industrial solutions sought by trade unions within "mainstream" labour law. However, the integration of labour law and anti-discrimination principles is an important developing theme in labour law discourse. While anti-discrimination law is a distinct form of legal regulation, it should also be acknowledged as an integral aspect of labour law regulation.

In terms of labour law legislation, the focus here is on the recently enacted *Workplace Relations Act* 1996 (Cth). This Act presents a new landscape for industrial relations in Australia. Its approach challenges some of the fundamental collective aspects that have underpinned conciliation and arbitration, and hence some of the collective rights recognised in international instruments. It is imbued with notions of choice and freedom of bargaining that consequently shapes the framework for bargaining, the role of industrial tribunals in overseeing bargaining processes and outcomes, and the participation of trade unions within the new industrial relations framework. Other than New South Wales, which persists with a collective approach, State systems are by and large reasonably aligned with the ideological stance underlying the new federal system.[9] The ILO Committee of Experts has expressed the view that various provisions of the *Workplace Relations Act* do not promote collective bargaining as required by the Convention, and has requested the federal government review and amend its legislation. Similar conclusions were reached on some provisions in State industrial legislation.[10]

THE PRINCIPLE OF NON-DISCRIMINATION

Australia's anti-discrimination laws are intended to give effect to a range of human rights treaties to which Australia is a party that enshrine the principle of non-discrimination. In the federal area, an incremental implementation of human rights principles has occurred, largely issue by issue. The introduction of the *Racial Discrimination Act* 1975 (Cth) was followed by the *Sex Discrimination Act* 1984 (Cth) and the *Disability Discrimination Act* 1992 (Cth). The *Human Rights and Equal Opportunity Commission Act* 1986 (Cth) is more extensive in the grounds it covers, but is hampered by the fact that the powers it confers are largely confined to conciliation and educational functions without the power to make any deter-minations. Each of these Acts implements relevant human rights instruments. State and Territory legislation has also exhibited an incremental progression as new

---

8 Thornton, M, "Discrimination law/Industrial law; are they compatible?" (1987) 59 *Australian Quarterly* 162.

9 The State systems themselves are a further source of potential breaches of international labour standards. For example, recent amendments to industrial legislation in Western Australia were subject to informal scrutiny by the ILO "regarding their compliance with the freedom of association Conventions: see "Workers' Rights Swamped by Richard Courts Third Wave" *Labour Lawyer* (1997) Vol 2(3), p 8.

10 Report of the ILO Committee of Experts 1998. See *Australian Industrial Law News*, Newsletter 3/1998, 25 March 1998.

grounds and exemptions are added over time. Although not constitutionally tied to the implementation of relevant human rights instruments, State anti-discrimination legalisation clearly reflects the principles espoused in such instruments. The existence of both federal and State/Territory legislation, with their own distinct grounds, areas and exemptions, operating in respect of the same discriminatory conduct, makes for a complex matrix of coverage and difficult choice of forum issues.

While the principal pieces of federal anti-discrimination legislation are specific to issues of race, sex (and the related grounds of martial status, pregnancy, potential pregnancy, and family responsibilities in limited circumstances) and disability, State and Territory legislation covers a much wider range of grounds. Coverage varies from jurisdiction to jurisdiction. Issues common to most jurisdictions include race, sex, martial status, pregnancy, disability, sexuality, age and status as a parent or carer. Anti-discrimination laws apply to all stages of the employment process, covering recruitment, advertising and selection procedures, who is offered employment and on what terms, access to training, promotion and other benefits, harassment, and termination of employment. Termination of employment in the anti-discrimination context also intersects with unfair dismissal provisions under labour law legislation at both State and federal levels, which space does not allow for discussion in this chapter.[11] Specific statutory exemptions may exclude certain forms of employment from the application of anti-discrimination laws. For example, anti-discrimination legislation in New South Wales does not apply to employment in a private household, where the number of employees does not exceed five, or employment by a private education authority.

Direct and indirect discrimination

The principle of non-discrimination takes a specific legal form in the Australian context. In essence the principle is reduced to two concepts; direct discrimination and indirect discrimination. Direct discrimination occurs where a person receives less favourable treatment in comparable circumstances because of a particular proscribed ground of discrimination, such as race. For example, an Aboriginal person who is refused employment because of his or her race has been subject to direct discrimination. No intention to discriminate is required.[12] The notion of direct discrimination is sometimes referred to as first generational equality, as it mandates an equality of treatment or formal equality, but does not purport to secure an equality of outcome.[13] Not all employment based discrimination presents itself in the neat form of direct discrimination. Often discrimination may take the form of an apparently neutral requirement or condition that has the effect of disadvantaging members of a particular group because of a shared characteristic, such as disability.

---

11   See Chapman, A, "Termination of Employment under the Workplace Relations Act 1996 (Cth)" (1997) 10 *Australian Journal of Labour Law* 89.

12   See *AIS v Banovic* (1989) EOC ¶92-271, *Waters v Public Transport Corporation* (1991) 103 ALR 513; *X v Dr McHugh* (1994) EOC ¶92-623.

13   See generally Hunter, R, *Indirect Discrimination in the Workplace* (Federation Press, Sydney, 1992), and Thornton, M, *The Liberal Promise: Anti-discrimination Legislation in Australia* (Oxford University Press, Melbourne, 1990).

This is the concept of indirect discrimination. In a legal form the concept of indirect discrimination has traditionally been reduced to four requirements:

(1) a requirement or condition;

(2) that is satisfied by a substantially higher proportion of persons not sharing the same characteristic as the complainant;

(3) the requirement or condition cannot be satisfied by the complainant; and

(4) the requirement or condition is not reasonable.[14]

Examples of employment practices that might fit into this category include requirements for employment or promotion such as a tertiary qualification, a fixed number of years experience, service in a remote country area, or attendance at a week long residential training course. It is arguable that some of these requirements may be more difficult for women to satisfy than for men. Ultimately if a disparate impact is shown the question is then whether the requirement can be justified as reasonable. Indirect discrimination was to have been the new frontier for challenging a variety of processes and practices. But the small number of cases that have raised the issue of indirect discrimination indicate that this has not eventuated.[15] The complexity of the High Court's interpretation of indirect discrimination has contributed to this problem.[16] The qualification of reasonableness also contributes to a state of uncertainty. These problems are exacerbated by the fact that employers often unquestioningly regard the status quo as not unreasonable. More recently there have been moves to simplify the definition of indirect discrimination. The *Sex Discrimination Act* has been amended to move away from the mathematical calculation of substantial proportional difference in compliance with a test that looks to whether a requirement, condition or practice has the *effect* of causing disadvantage, hence closer to the underlying principle rather than the established legal form.

It is necessary to acknowledge the shortcomings of Australian law and practice in satisfying the norm of non-discrimination. Anti-discrimination laws do not provide a right to be free from discrimination per se, but make certain discriminatory conduct that occurs in the context of certain designated public spheres of activity unlawful, subject to a range of exemptions.[17] The current state of anti-discrimination legislation in Australia is clearly a product of political compromise and is constrained by a tradition of liberal legalism.[18] The form of anti-discrimination regulation is principally reactive rather than proactive, relying on the lodging of individual complaints to initiate any inquiry into alleged discriminatory conduct,[19] and on the resolution of discrimination complaints by the "private"

---

14 See Naughton, R, "A Re-examination of Indirect Discrimination" in Naughton R (ed), *Workplace Disability and the Law* (Centre for Employment and Labour Relations Law, Melbourne, 1995), p 36.

15 Ibid, p 37.

16 See *AIS v Banovic* (1989) EOC ¶92-271; *Waters v Public Transport Corporation* (1991) 103 ALR 513.

17 See Thornton, M, "Public Private Dichotomy: Gendered and Discriminatory" (1991) 18 *Journal of Law and Society* 1.

18 Thornton, above, n 13.

19 Ibid; see also, Ch 13 by Bailey and Devereux in this volume.

process of conciliation. Moreover, the focus on substantiating a compliant of a specific ground or grounds of discrimination distorts the experience of discrimination in terms of identity and intersectionality.[20] A complaints-based model that is dependent on the concepts of direct and indirect discrimination is an inadequate formulation of the principle of non-discrimination, and constitutes an under-utilisation of the relevant human rights instruments. Systemic discrimination remains largely untouched by these processes. Further, little use is made of the potential pursuant to such instruments for affirmative action measures, with the only federal legislation limited to the area of sex, and constituting a very weak version of affirmative action.[21]

As it is impossible to cover all the employment issues dealt with by the principle of non-discrimination, I have chosen three specific discrimination issues to examine individually. First, I propose to examine the area of disability discrimination in the employment context. While public consciousness regarding sex and race discrimination seems more established, although not necessarily observed, disability discrimination is not as well entrenched. In addition, the federal *Disability Discrimination Act* has some innovative provisions that take it beyond the established model of anti-discrimination regulation and are worth examining. The remaining two issues relate to sex discrimination. In the employment context, complaints on the ground of sex are the most common type of complaint. I propose to examine two manifestations of sex discrimination in the employment context. First, discrimination in the form of sexual harassment, which I have framed as the right to work in a harassment free work environment. Secondly, discrimination in terms of remuneration, that is, the right to equal remuneration for work of equal value.

Disability discrimination

Before the enactment of the *Disability Discrimination Act* 1992 (Cth), the only federal anti-discrimination legislation covering disability issues was the *Human Rights and Equal Opportunity Commission Act*, although there has been a reasonably long history of State legislation in this area. However, State legislation had been plagued by definitional and interpretive difficulties that made unifying national legislation a priority.[22] The *Disability Discrimination Act* does not rely on a single human rights instrument, but on a variety of sources including the ICESCR and the *Discrimination in Employment and Occupation Convention* 1958 (ILO

---

20 Astor, H, "A Question of Identity: The Intersection of Race and other Grounds of Discrimination" Race Discrimination Commissioner (ed), *Racial Discrimination Act 1975: A Review* (AGPS, Canberra, 1995).

21 *Affirmative Action (Equal Employment Opportunities for Women) Act* 1986 (Cth). State Anti-discrimination legalisation may provide for the implementation of equal opportunity employment management plans that have a limited application to public employment: see *Anti-Discrimination Act* 1977 (NSW) Pt 9A.

22 See Astor, H, "Anti-discrimination Legislation and Physical Disability – the lessons of Experience" (1990) 64 *Australian Law Journal* 113; Tyler, M, "The Disability Discrimination Act 1992 – Genesis, Drafting and Prospects" (1993) 19 Melbourne *University Law Review* 211.

No 111).[23] The Act has a wide application because of its very broad definition of disability, which moves beyond the attempts under State legislation to categorise all disabilities in terms of a physical or intellectual impairment.[24] The definition includes a present disability, a past disability, a future disability and an imputed disability. The Act also covers discrimination against a person because of the disability of an associate of that person.

Although the federal *Disability Discrimination Act* in some respects conforms with the established model of anti-discrimination regulation in Australia, the Act does have some innovative provisions that take it beyond the strict direct/indirect discrimination model. The most important of these is the foreshadowed introduction of disability standards.[25] The rationale for disability standards is that they overcome some of the inadequacies of the traditional anti-discrimination model by providing legislative deadlines, some degree of certainty and benchmarks for equality.[26] An example of the potential application of standards is the regulation of the procedures to be adopted for pre-employment medical testing. Once introduced it will be unlawful to contravene a disability standard, and compliance with the standard will provide immunity to an anti-discrimination complaint.[27] Draft standards have been made available for public comment in a number of areas, including employment.

A second innovation of the *Disability Discrimination Act* is the notion of "reasonable accommodation". The Act imposes on employers a duty of reasonable accommodation, unless an employer can substantiate unjustifiable hardship. Reasonable accommodation might include making physical adjustments to the work environment, providing specialised equipment, or flexible work hours or leave arrangements. The process involves a consideration of whether the person with a disability can perform the inherent requirements of the job, or that the making of the necessary adjustments to enable the person to perform the inherent requirements of the job would impose an unjustifiable hardship. The question of what is an inherent requirement is intended to be answered objectively, rather than the subjective appraisal that occurred under previous State legislation. The concept of "inherent requirements of the job" must be construed narrowly so as not to undermine the protection provided by the Act. However, the emerging trend at the appellate level has been to give reasonably wide interpretation to the notion of inherent requirements.[28]

---

23 Other relevant instruments include the *Convention the Rights of the Child* 1989, the *Declaration of the Rights of Mentally Retarded Persons* 1971, and the *Declaration of the Rights of Disabled Persons* 1975.

24 *Disability Discrimination Act* 1992 (Cth) s 4. The definition also resolved any ambiguity as to whether HIV-AIDS related discrimination is covered by disability discrimination provisions.

25 Section 31. Disability standards may be formulated in relation to employment, education, accommodation, the provision of public transport services, and the administration of Commonwealth laws and programs.

26 See Disability Discrimination Commissioner, *Disability Standards under the Disability Discrimination Act Issues Paper*, prepared for the DDA Disability Standards Working group (Human Rights and Equal Opportunity Commission, 1993), p i.

27 Sections 32 and 34.

28 *Qantas Airways Ltd v Christie* (1998) 152 ALR 365, and *Commonwealth v Human Rights and Equal Opportunity Commission* (1998) 152 ALR 182.

As to the issue of "unjustifiable hardship," the Act sets out a range of circumstances that are relevant to this assessment including the nature of the benefit or detriment, the effect of the disability, and the financial circumstances and costs required of the person claiming unjustifiable hardship.[29] Again a careful balancing is required in this assessment to ensure that the objects of the Act are not defeated.[30]

The right to work in a harassment free environment

The general prohibitions on discrimination against women contained in human rights instruments such as the *Convention on the Elimination of all Forms of Discrimination Against Women* (CEDAW) also extend to sexual harassment, which accounts for a significant proportion of sex discrimination complaints in employment. Sexual harassment also brings into question health and safety in working conditions that is addressed in a number of human rights instruments.[31]

Sexual harassment is a significant and ongoing workplace problem. In the 1995-96 financial year, 48% of complaints lodged under the *Sex Discrimination Act* involved the issue of sexual harassment.[32] The individual complaints-based approach to the issue of harassment fostered through anti-discrimination regimes has helped to disguise the wider ramifications of sexual harassment, particularly in terms of labour market segmentation. Sexual harassment maintains occupational and industrial segregation by discouraging women from exposing themselves to the risks that working in a non-traditional area of employment poses, and consequently works against affirmative action programmes.[33] Sexual harassment is a mechanism that reinforces women's traditional and inferior role in the labour market and maintains patriarchal control in a workplace, particularly in circumstances where women are a numerical minority.[34]

Pursuant to anti-discrimination legislation sexual harassment can be specifically proscribed or treated as a form of sex discrimination. In many jurisdictions both forms of regulation apply concurrently. In considering whether particular conduct amounts to sex discrimination or breaches a specific statutory prohibition of sexual harassment, anti-discrimination tribunals have identified the specific benefit of employment denied to a person subject to harassment as being the denial of quiet enjoyment. This extends to freedom from physical intrusion, freedom from being harassed, freedom from being physically molested or approached in an unwelcome manner, and the freedom not to be required to work in an unsought sexually permeated environment. Although anti-discrimination legislation generally provides the means by which an individual can be found liable for his or her sexually harassing conduct, from a regulatory perspective the attribution of liability to the

---

29   Section 11.

30   See *Telstra Corporation Ltd v Scott* (1995) EOC ¶92-717; *McLean v Airlines of Tasmania Pty Ltd* (1997) EOC ¶92-862.

31   See ICESCR, art 7 which refers to the right to "safe and healthy working conditions" and CEDAW, art 11(f) which refers to the right to protection of health and safety in working conditions.

32   Human Rights and Equal Opportunity Commission *Annual Report* 1995-1996.

33   Hughes, P, "The Evolving Conceptual Framework of Sexual Harassment" (1993) *Canadian Labour and Employment Law Journal* 1 at 3.

34   See *Horne v Press Clough Joint Venture* (1994) EOC ¶92-591; *Hopper v Mount Isa Mines Ltd* (1997) EOC ¶92-879.

employer is the critical factor. Various deeming provisions of anti-discrimination legalisation attribute vicarious and ancillary liability to an employer in certain circumstances, in addition to the numerous ways in which personal liability on the part of an employer may arise.[35] More recently a further avenue of potential liability has been explored, that is, liability on the part of trade unions stemming from their complicity in the creation or maintenance of a discriminatory work environment as a consequence of sexual harassment in the workplace.[36]

While regulation by anti-discrimination legalisation usually comes to mind when the issue of sexually harassing conduct in the workplace arises, the obligations that apply under anti-discrimination legalisation in the employment context can be seen as one manifestation of the duty to provide a harassment-free work environment. Comparable obligations are identifiable within other regulatory frameworks applicable in the employment context. The right to a healthy and safe work environment has been described as a basic "democratic" right of all workers.[37] This right is given expression through the common law duty of an employer to take reasonable care of his or her employees, a duty that is essentially replicated in occupational health and safety legislation. The right to work in an environment free from sexual harassment can be regarded in analogous terms. The use that can be made of an employer's liability in tort for sexual harassment is illustrated by the case of *Barker v City of Hobart*.[38] In that case an employee who was subject to persistent sexual harassment over a considerable length of time by her co-workers, including conduct that amounted to sexual assault, brought proceedings against her former employer and co-workers involving a range of tort actions, including negligence, defamation, false imprisonment, assault and battery. As far as the employer's liability was concerned, the proceedings were based principally on the employer's failure to provide a safe place for the employee to work and its failure to supervise her workplace, in addition to its vicarious liability. The employee was successful in her action and was awarded $120,000 damages.

Sexual harassment is also an occupational hazard for women, which can be regulated within the framework of occupational health and safety legalisation. Although generally construed as a discrimination issue, sexual harassment is as much an industrial issue as any other workplace hazard. Sexual harassment has been described as "the quintessential occupational health and safety issue for women".[39] Other jurisdictions such as Canada, have increasingly come to identify sexual harassment as a health and safety problem.[40] Traditional occupational health and safety discourse in Australia has failed to follow this approach.

---

35   See *M v R Pty Ltd* (1988) EOC ¶92-229.

36   *Horne v Press Clough Joint Venture* (1994) EOC ¶92-591.

37   Creighton, WB, "Occupational Health and Safety and Industrial Democracy: Some Legal and Practical Considerations" (1984) *Work and People* 10.

38   *Barker v City of Hobart and Barratt, Gentile and Stacey* (unreported, SC Tas, No 1501 of 1990, 6 May 1993). See also, Browne, R, "Common Law Victory" (1993) 8 *Alternative Law Journal* 243.

39   Hunter, R, "Representing Gender in Legal Analysis: A Case-book Study in Labour Law" (1991) 18 *Melbourne University Law Review* 305 at 311.

40   Cornish, M and Lopez, S, "Changing the Workplace Culture Through Effective Harassment Remedies" (1993) *Canadian Labour and Employment Law Journal* 99; Schucher, K, "Achieving a Workplace free of Sexual harassment: The Employer's Obligations (1995) *Canadian Labour and Employment Law Journal* 171 at 178ff.

The right to equal remuneration for work of equal value

An entitlement to equal remuneration for work of equal value is clearly established in various human rights instruments. This right is recognised in the ILO Constitution and the *Universal Declaration of Human Rights* 1948 states that "everyone without discrimination, has the rights to equal pay for equal work".[41] The ICESCR refers to "remuneration which provides all workers, as a minimum with fair wages and equal remuneration for work of equal value *without distinction of any kind*".[42] These instruments establish a right to non-discrimination in remuneration per se and that is not limited to issues of sex discrimination. However, the implementation of the principle of equal remuneration has largely been confined to the right to equal remuneration for work of equal value without discrimination on the basis of sex. A number of international instruments have this narrower application. For example, the relevant ILO Convention is confined to ensuring the "application to all workers of the principle of equal remuneration for men and women workers for work of equal value".[43] Similarly, the *Convention on the Elimination of All forms of Discrimination Against Women* establishes a "right to equal remuneration, including benefits, and to equal treatment in respect of work of equal value, as well as equality of treatment in the evaluation of the quality of work".[44]

The history of wage fixation in Australia has been dominated by explicit discrimination through the concept of the "family wage".[45] Complementing this has been a well-established tradition of occupational and industrial segregation on the basis of sex. The demise in a formal sense of the notion of the male wage as underpinned by the family wage concept has not prevented its continued manifestation in other forms, such as the use of criteria of value that are inherently biased towards the male model of work,[46] and gendered associations of women's paid work with the unpaid work performed by women in the home. The issue of pay equity entered the federal industrial arena through the *Equal Pay Cases* of 1969 and 1972.[47] The subsequent ratification of the ILO's Equal Remuneration Convention in 1974 did not precipitate a change in the nature of the regulatory structure as reliance continued to be placed on the decisions of industrial tribunals to secure equal remuneration for work of equal value. Although acknowledging in principle the notion of equal pay for work of equal value, the major shortcoming of the industrial tribunal process has been its failure to establish effective mechanisms for implementing the principle so as to provide a systematic gender-neutral method of comparing female occupations with male occupations. The unwillingness of the Australian Conciliation and Arbitration Commission to embrace the principle of

---

41   Article 23(2).

42   Article 7.

43   *Equal Remuneration Convention*, 1951 (No 100) Art 2.

44   Article 11(1)(d).

45   *Ex p HV McKay* (1907) 2 CAR 1.

46   Burton, C, *The Promise and the Price: The struggle for equal opportunity in women's employment* (Allen and Unwin, Sydney, 1992), p 138.

47   (1969) 127 CAR 1142; (1972) 147 CAR 172.

comparable worth[48] left the process without an adequate guarantee that women's work would be appropriately valued.

In 1994 the introduction of the *Industrial Relations Reform Act* 1993 (Cth) heralded a new era in industrial relations. Various statutory entitlements prescribing minimum employment conditions were introduced to underpin the move towards a more decentralised system of bargaining and to ensure labour standards in Australia met our international obligations. One of these new statutory minimum entitlements was a new division dealing with equal remuneration for work of equal value. It empowers the Australian Industrial Relations Commission (AIRC) to make such orders as it thinks appropriate to ensure that, for employees covered by the orders, there will be equal remuneration for work of equal value. The division is stated to give effect, or further effect, to the anti-discrimination Conventions,[49] the Equal Remuneration Recommendation[50] and the Discrimination (Employment and Occupation) Recommendation.[51] The most apposite of these are the Equal Remuneration Convention and the associated Recommendation. The Equal Remuneration Convention imposes an obligation to promote, as far as is consistent with national mechanisms for determining rates of remuneration in the countries concerned, the application of the principle of equal remuneration for men and women workers for work of equal value.[52] The terminology of the Convention is very general and permits wide scope for national procedures in the application of the principles. It does not prescribe a change in the framework by which the principle of equal remuneration for work of equal value is pursued.

An equal remuneration order can only be made on the application of an employee, trade union or the federal Sex Discrimination Commissioner to the Australian Industrial Relations Commission.[53] If the AIRC is satisfied that there is available to the applicant, or the employees represented by it, an alternative remedy under Commonwealth, State or Territory law that will ensure equal remuneration for work of equal value for the employees concerned, then the Commission must refrain from considering or determining the matter.[54] A separate power to deal with equal remuneration for work of equal value is vested in the Commission, which does not purport to implement the relevant international conventions and recommendations, but derives its constitutional validity from the conciliation and arbitration power.[55]

---

48 *Private Hospitals' and Doctors' Nurses' (ACT) Award 1972* (1986) 300 CAR 185. See Innes, J, "Discrimination: the ACTU's Comparable Worth Case" (1986) 11 *Legal Services Bulletin* 86.

49 Defined by s 4 to include the Equal Remuneration Convention, the *Convention on the Elimination of All forms of discrimination Against Women*, the *Convention concerning Discrimination in respect of Employment and Occupation*, and arts 3 and 7 of the ICESCR.

50 Recommendation No 90, adopted by the general Conference of the ILO on 29 June 1951.

51 Recommendation No 111, adopted by the General Conference of the ILO on 25 June 1958.

52 See art 2.

53 Section 170BD.

54 Section 170BE.

55 Section 170BI.

These minimum entitlement provisions dealing with equal remuneration are important in a number of respects.[56] First, they utilise a wide definition of remuneration provided for in the Equal Remuneration Convention that has the potential to apply to a wide range of employment benefits (including discrimination in the provision of over-award payments, allowances, overtime and bonuses).[57] It has been in respect of this array of employment-related benefits that discriminatory practices have consistently been evident[58] and where existing processes have been least effective. Secondly, the provisions require the principle of comparable worth to be applied. To justify differential rates that appear to discriminate on the basis of sex, the Convention appears to require that any such differences be determined by objective job appraisal so as to ensure a rate of remuneration free from discrimination based on sex.[59] The ILO has itself acknowledged difficulties in the practical application of the notion of objective appraisal, but recognises that "when the value of different jobs has to be compared, there should exist appropriate machinery and procedures to ensure an evaluation free from discrimination based on sex".[60] Implicit in the notion of paying women and men in accordance with the value of the work they perform pursuant to the Convention is the adoption of some technique to measure and compare objectively the value of the work done.

Although these provisions were targeted for repeal, the *Workplace Relations Act* has retained the existing provisions dealing with equal remuneration.[61] However, little effective use of the provisions has been made to date. The single case to come before the Industrial Relations Commission faltered on the question of how to determine "equal value"; the case is, however, being relitigated.[62] Moreover, it is important to realise that the framework for bargaining is at least as important, if not more so, than a statutory avenue for redress. Nowhere in the Act is there an express requirement that the pay equity implications of an agreement be considered, nor are the parties required to verify compliance of their agreement with anti-discrimination legislation. For pay equity to be even a remote possibility, transparent processes regarding pay and other benefits must be in place. Instead we are going down a path of "private" individualised agreements with minimal scrutiny and minimal disclosure, discussed in detail below.

---

56 See MacDermott, T, "Equality of Opportunity in a Decentralised Industrial Relations System: The intersection of minimum labour standards and anti-discrimination legislation" in McCallum, R, McCarry, G and Ronfeldt, P (eds), *Employment Security* (Federation Press, Sydney, 1994).

57 See art 1.

58 Human Rights and Equal Opportunity Commission *Just Rewards* (AGPS, Canberra, 1992).

59 Article 3(3).

60 See ILO, Report of the Committee of Experts on the Application of Conventions and Recommendations (Geneva, 1986), para 21.

61 With only a minor modification relating to not pursuing alternative remedies concurrently with an application under this Division: s 170BHA.

62 See *Automotive, Food, Metals, Engineering, Printing and Kindred Industries Union v HPM Industries Pty Ltd* (1998) AILR ¶3-739.

FREEDOM OF ASSOCIATION

There is no shortage of international human rights instruments that validate the principle of freedom of association. The Philadelphia Declaration, adopted by the International Labour Organisation in 1944, sets out the aims and purposes of the ILO. It refers to freedom of association as a fundamental principle on which the organisation is based.[63] The ICCPR states that "everyone shall have the right to freedom of association with others, including the right to form and join trade unions for the protection of his [sic] interests".[64] The ICESCR also establishes the right to form trade unions and join trade unions of one's choice.[65] Both the ICCPR and the ICESCR preserve the rights guaranteed under the ILO's *Freedom of Association and Protection of the Right to Organise Convention* 1948 (No 87), the principal human rights instrument dealing with freedom of association.[66] This Convention enshrines the right to establish and to join organisations of one's own choosing.[67] The *Right to Organise and Collective Bargaining Convention* 1949 (No 98) works together with the Freedom of Association Convention to provide protection against anti-union discrimination in employment and to facilitate collective bargaining. Australia has ratified both these Conventions.[68] The obligation to respect freedom of association arises in any event by virtue of membership of the ILO.[69]

The principle of freedom of association is generally taken to establish positive rights, such as the right to organise collectively to form trade unions and to participate in the activities of a trade union of one's choice.[70] Freedom of association arguably has a collective aspect to it. Some argue that it can only be exercised collectively.[71] However, more recently the principle has taken on a negative connotation, that is, preserving the right not to participate in trade union activities.[72] There are dangers in this approach to freedom of association. Von Prondyznski states that:

> If one adopts an individualistic view [of freedom of association], the main beneficiaries within industrial relations are non-unionists, individual dissidents within unions and

---

63   Article 1(b). The *Universal Declaration of Human Rights*, 1948 states that "everyone has the right to freedom of assembly and association": art 20(1). Article 23(4) also states that "everyone has the right to form and to join trade unions for the protection of his [sic] interests".

64   Article 22.

65   Article 8.

66   Creighton, WB, "Industrial Regulation and Australia's International Obligations" in McCallum, R and Ronfeldt, P (eds), *A New province for Legalism: Legal Issues and the Deregulation of Industrial Regulation* (ACIRRT Monograph No 9, 1993), p 104; Bailey, above, n 6, p 363.

67   Article 2.

68   The date of entry into force in Australia for both Conventions is 28 February 1974.

69   Creighton, WB and Stewart, A, *Labour Law: An Introduction* (Federation Press, Sydney, 2nd ed, 1994), p 107.

70   O'Neill, N and Handley, R, *Retreat from Injustice* (Federation Press, Sydney, 1994), p 220.

71   von Prondzynski, F, *Freedom of Association and Industrial Relations: A Comparative Study* (Mansell Publishing Ltd, London, 1987), p 84; Bailey, above, n 6, p 363.

72   A stated object of the *Workplace Relations Act* is "ensuring freedom of association, including the right of employees and employers to join an organisation or association of their choice, or not to join an organisation or association": s 3(f).

certain employers. The main causalities are trade-union strength, effectiveness and efficiency, and the stability of bargaining relationship.[73]

It is not clear whether the relevant international instruments *require* protection of the negative right to dissociate, although they may permit it. As Breen Creighton has argued "those aspects of Pt XA [of the *Workplace Relations Act*] which purport to protect the right not to belong to a trade union are not inconsistent with Australia's international obligations, *but nor are they impelled by them*".[74]

Freedom of association under the Workplace Relations Act

Part XA of the *Workplace Relations Act* deals specifically with freedom of association. The regime established purports to operate nationwide, so as to oust union security or preference provisions under any State scheme.[75] Under the new regime, no adverse action can be taken against an employee or independent contractor because of their involvement or non involvement with an industrial organisation or industrial action, or for other associated reasons.[76] Similar prohibitions apply to adverse action taken or threatened by industrial associations against employees, independent contractors, employers or members.[77] It is also unlawful for an employer to refuse to employ a person because she or he is not a union member, or does not propose to become a union member.[78] The Act purports to abolish the power of the AIRC to grant preference to union members,[79] although a decision of the full bench of the AIRC found that it had the power to certify agreements that contain preference clauses despite the freedom of association provisions in the Act.[80] The *Workplace Relations and other Legislation Amendment Act* 1997 attempts to reverse this decision by preventing certification of an agreement that includes any preference provisions that are inconsistent with the freedom of association provisions and by vesting the power in the Commission to vary any agreement to remove objectionable provisions that in any way directly or indirectly breach the freedom of association provisions.[81] Contraventions of Pt XA are dealt with upon application, including by the Employment Advocate, by the Federal Court which has wide remedial powers including the power to grant injunctive relief. In any proceedings, actions are taken to have been carried out for a

---

73   von Prondzynski , above n 71, p 232.

74   See Creighton, WB, "The Workplace Relations Act in International Perspective" (1997) 10 *Australian Journal of Labour Law* 31; see also Bailey, above, n 6, pp 363-66.

75   See Naughton, R, "Sailing into Uncharted Seas: The Role of Unions Under the Workplace Relations Act 1996 (Cth)" (1997) 10 *Australian Journal of Labour Law* 112 at 131.

76   Section 298L sets out the prohibited reasons. Anti-discrimination legalisation may also deal with discrimination on the grounds of political belief, opinion, conviction or activity, industrial activity or trade union activity.

77   Sections 298P-298S.

78   Section 298K(1)(d).

79   Section 122 is repealed. On preference generally, see Weeks, P, *Trade Union Security Law: A Study of Preference and Compulsory Unionism* (Federation Press, Sydney, 1995).

80   *CEPU v Woodside Heating and Airconditioning Pty Ltd* (1997) 74 IR 10.

81   Sections 170LU(2A), 298Z.

prohibited reason, unless proved otherwise.[82] While prohibition on victimisation of union members is not new, the emphasis on the rights of non-members is. Previously the protection of non-union members and independent contractors has been largely confined to conscientious objection provisions. The conscientious objection certification process has been retained under the Workplace Relations Act, although this seems unnecessary given the abolition of any preference for union members.[83]

The provisions of the Workplace Relations Act dealing with freedom of association came under intense scrutiny in the protracted waterfront dispute involving the Patrick stevedoring group and the Maritime Union of Australia (MUA). Proceedings were commenced in the Federal Court alleging breaches of the freedom of association provisions of the Act, together with other common law claims. The substance of the claims was that a restructure of the corporate arrangements within the Patrick group in September 1997 that split the functions of employing workers and operating the stevedoring business, together with other transactions, were undertaken to facilitate the dismissal of its workforce and that these were done for a particular reason – namely, the union membership of the workforce.

In an application to the Federal Court for interim injunctive relief to prevent the dismissal of its members, the MUA was successful in establishing that there was an arguable case of breach of the freedom of association provisions and of conspiracy, and that the balance of convenience favoured the retention of the workforce until these issues were determined at trial.[84] In so deciding, North J gave particular weight to the right of individuals to return to work, rather than simply to be compensated for their possible loss. Subsequent appeals from this decision were unsuccessful in challenging the jurisdiction of the Federal Court to grant such interim relief.[85] However, the High Court did vary the orders made to prevent any interference with the discretion of the administrators of the companies in question to decide whether, if trading were resumed, it would be feasible to retain the whole workforce.[86]

THE RIGHT TO ORGANISE

The general provisions of various international instruments dealing with freedom of association also support the right to organise. In addition, art 11 of ILO Convention No 87 specifically provides that:

> [E]ach Member of the International Labour Organisation for which this Convention is in force undertakes to take all necessary and appropriate measures to ensure that workers and employers may exercise freely the right to organise.

---

82   Section 298v.

83   Section 267. See Naughton, above, n 75, p 131.

84   *Maritime Union of Australia v Patrick Stevedores No 1 Pty Ltd* (1998) 79 IR 281.

85   *Patrick Stevedores Operation No 2 Pty Ltd v Maritime Union of Australia* (1998) 79 IR 305.

86   *Patrick Stevedores Operation No 2 Pty Ltd v Maritime Union of Australia* (1998) 153 ALR 643.

Historically, Australian trade unions have had a reasonably secure position because of their pivotal role in conciliation and arbitration. In exchange for a guaranteed voice in conciliation and arbitration, trade unions have been subject to substantial legislative regulation, dealing with issues such as registration, corporate status and financial accountability. By and large this regulation has not been seen as impinging on the right to organise. A notable exception is the compliant that was made by the Confederation of Australian Industry to the ILO's Committee on Freedom of Association in 1992 concerning the minimum membership requirement under the old *Industrial Relations Act* 1988 (Cth), which were found to breach Australia's obligations as far as choice of union is concerned.[87] However, we have entered a new era for unions, with an emphasis on choice regarding union representation and "healthy" competition between unions. The current level of intrusion into the internal affairs of trade unions and restrictions on choice of union mandated by the *Workplace Relations Act* possibly fall foul of ILO Conventions 87 and 98.[88] The pivotal role of unions in achieving bargaining outcomes is also seriously challenged under the Act. The role of unions in the bargaining process is being shaped as an agency arrangement, rather than as the guardian of the industrial interests of all workers, whether union members or not. The bargaining arrangements are discussed in detail below in the context of the right to bargain collectively. Moreover, Australian law and practice has never given full recognition to the right to strike which is a tool of collective labour organisation,[89] and is also discussed separately below.

The reforming zeal of the federal government has been particularly focused on the role of trade unions within the new framework of industrial relations established by the *Workplace Relations Act*, although full effect has not been given to its vision given the political compromise necessary to have the legislation passed. The Act directs its attention to reframing the trade union movement by various measures designed to facilitate the creation of small enterprise-based unions. The Workplace Relations Bill originally sought to remove the requirement for registration that an organisation of employees be capable of engaging in an industrial dispute, reduce the minimum membership from 100 to 20, do away with the requirement that an organisation be industry based, and abolish the "conveniently belong" rule. The Bill also sought to provide for the creation of autonomous enterprise branches of registered unions. The ultimate form of the provisions of the Act dealing with trade unions is a watered down version of the original proposal. The minimum membership requirement is 50 rather than 20. The capacity to engage in an industrial dispute is still required, except in the case of an enterprise association.[90]

---

87 Case No 1559, CFA, 281st Report 1992, paras 326-64; 284th Report, 1992, paras 200-63; See Creighton and Stewart, above, n 69, p 48.

88 See, for example, the investigation of financial affairs of trade union provided for in ss 280A and 280B of the *Workplace Relations Act* which may be in breach of ILO art 3: See Naughton, above, n 75, p 127.

89 O'Neill and Handley, above, n 70, p 229.

90 Section 188(1)(c). Where capacity to engage in an industrial dispute is no longer a requirement for registration the question arises whether the registration of such an association can be supported constitutionally as incidental to the conciliation and arbitration of industrial disputes: *Jumbunna Coal Mine, No Liability v Victorian Coal Mining Association* (1908) 6 CLR 309.

The "conveniently belong" rule has not been abolished, but modified to require that a union opposing the registration of another organisation must show that those employees sought to be covered could conveniently belong to its organisation *and* would be more effectively represented by it.

The government has abandoned the controversial proposal for autonomous enterprise branches of unions, but has allowed for the registration of enterprise associations. The establishment of an enterprise association requires evidence that a majority of persons eligible to be members of the association support its registration, and that the association is free from the control and influence of the employer. The association must satisfy the conveniently belong and no effective representation test, but this can be overcome by appropriate undertakings being given to avoid demarcation disputes that might otherwise arise. Although enterprise unionism is often presented as a more participatory process operating at the "grass roots" level, the reality is that it is highly unlikely that enterprise associations will have the resources and skills to represent their constituents adequately within the new framework of industrial relations.

Despite the possible increase in the number of trade unions that these processes may bring about, there are only limited circumstances in which the AIRC can order exclusive rights of representation in settlement of a demarcation dispute. These relate to actual or potentially harmful effects on the employer's operations.[91] In a similar vein, the Act establishes a process of disamalgamation to reverse the growth of large unions in the 1990s. An application may be made to the Federal Court for a ballot to be conducted to decide on the withdrawal of a constituent part. Strangely, the process does not provide for the participation of all members of the amalgamated organisation, only a vote by members of the constituent part seeking withdrawal. If more than 50% of the formal votes cast in a ballot are in favour of withdrawal, the court must facilitate the withdrawal of the constituent part from the amalgamated organisation and its registration as an organisation in its own right. Consequential orders regarding the apportionment of assets and liabilities can also be made. The process can take a constituent part beyond its pre-amalgamation formation.

Trade union rights of entry

The right to organise set out in art 11 of the *Freedom of Association and Protection of the Right to Organise Convention* (No 87) has been interpreted as including a right of access to workplaces for workers' representatives.[92] Rights of access to the workplace are also provided in the ILO's *Workers' Representatives Convention* 1971 (No 135). In the Australian context, the right has often been given force by statute or by award provisions.

The *Workplace Relations Act* involves considerable changes to union rights of entry. As envisaged in the original Bill, rights of entry were to be subject to a

---

91   Section 118A(1B). It is questionable whether s 118A itself may be inconsistent with art 2 of ILO Convention No 87.

92   See 234th Report, Case no 1221, para 114, International Labour Office Official Bulletin, vol LXVII, 1984, series B, no 2. See Shaw, JW and Walton, CG, "A Union's Right of Entry to the Workplace (1994) 36 *Journal of Industrial Relations* 546.

written invitation by relevant employees. Such an arrangement may have breached the relevant ILO Conventions, as an undue restriction on the ability of trade union representatives to communicate with non-members. In relation to Convention 135, the Committee on Freedom of Association has stated that:

> Governments should guarantee access of trade union representatives to workplaces, with due respect for the rights of property and management, so that trade unions can communicate with workers, in order to apprise them of the potential advantages of unionisation.[93]

The compromise arrangement that now appears in the Act is the establishment of a new permit system.[94] Where there are members employed at the workplace in question a union official can enter to investigate breaches of the Act, an award, an order of the AIRC, or a certified agreement to which the union is a party. There is no right of entry to check compliance with an Australian Workplace Agreement. Entry is subject to 24 hours notice being given to the employer. Entry for the purposes of discussion with employees is permitted where there are present at the workplace union members or persons eligible for membership and there is a relevant award binding on the trade union. Awards or other orders providing for rights of entry are now unenforceable, except where the AIRC has exercised its powers of conciliation and arbitration to prevent or settle a dispute about the operation of the new statutory scheme.[95] The compromised nature of the new regime, plus the ability to negotiate by agreement rights of entry above this minimum, probably mean the provisions are not in breach of the relevant Conventions.

A traditional weakness of the conciliation and arbitration system has been enforcement. The system has relied instead on the policing function carried out by trade unions to ensure compliance with awards and agreements. The new framework of bargaining seeks to cut unions out of the process whenever possible. If employees are to be armed to negotiate on their own behalf, then communication with trade unions regarding workers rights and obligations will be of increasing importance.

THE RIGHT TO BARGAIN COLLECTIVELY

Article 4 of the ILO *Right to Organise and Collective Bargaining Convention*, 1949 (No 98) states that:

> [M]easures appropriate to national conditions shall be taken, where necessary, to encourage and promote the full development and utilisation of machinery for voluntary negotiation between employers or employers' organisations, with a view to the regulation of terms and conditions of employment by means of collective bargaining.

Australia has not ratified the *Collective Bargaining Convention* 1981 (No 154) that also requires States to promote collective bargaining.[96]

---

93 See 284th Report, Case No 1523, para 195.

94 Sections 285Aff. See Naughton, above, n 75, pp 122-24.

95 Sections 127AA and 285G.

96 Article III of the *Philadelphia Declaration* refers to the recognition of the right to collective bargaining.

Historically the centralised system of award regulation has dominated industrial relations in Australia, although a certain amount of bargaining outside the formal system was always tolerated. Award regulation through arbitrated outcomes was traditionally on an industry-wide or occupational basis. However, the regulation of bargaining in Australia has changed markedly over the past 10 years. Numerous mechanisms now exist under industrial relations legislation for industrial parties to reach agreement themselves, and to have their agreements given a formal status through certification or approval processes. This move to institutionalise various forms of bargaining has also redefined the relevant bargaining unit. There has been a distinct downward thrust to bargaining arrangements, which has gradually minimised the collective input. The move to enterprise level bargaining has the effect of limiting the collective strength of employees to the employment unit.[97] But bargaining arrangements have moved beyond the enterprise level to individualised bargaining, in a way that bears little resemblance to collective bargaining. At the same time new bargaining arrangements limit trade union involvement in the process that has implications for collective bargaining. Before the *Workplace Relations Act*, a number of attempts to introduce individual contracts for workers were found to be inconsistent with the Australian system of collective industrial regulation.[98] However, the new bargaining arrangements established by the *Workplace Relations Act* weaken this position.

In this section, various bargaining regimes will be examined, with particular reference to those established at the federal level. These provisions bring into question Australia's compliance with art 4. In analogous circumstances the ILO Committee on Freedom of Association, in considering provisions of the *Employment Contracts Act* 1991 (NZ), was of the view that "the provisions did not encourage or promote collective bargaining".[99] The Australian Council of Trade Unions (ACTU) has sought advise from the ILO as to whether the new individualised bargaining regime is in breach of ILO Convention 98. The ILO Committee of Experts has expressed the view that the primacy given to individual rather than collective bargaining through the new bargaining arrangements does not promote collective bargaining under the Convention. In addition, the emphasis on single business agreements rather than multiple business agreements may infringe the right of workers to choose the level of bargaining in which they participate.[100]

Bargaining in the federal system

Rather than simplifying the bargaining process, the *Workplace Relations Act* increases the different forms of industrial agreements that can apply at a workplace level. Various types of certified agreements are available, in addition to the new

---

97   See Wedderburn, KW, "The New Policies in Industrial Relations Law" in Fosh, P and Littler C (eds), *Industrial Relations and the Law in the 1980s: Issues and Future Trends* (Gower Publishing Co, Aldershot, 1985), p 43.

98   *Re Aluminium Industries (Camalco Bell Bay Companies) Award 1993* (1994) 56 IR 403; *Australian Manufacturing Union v Alcoa of Australia Ltd* (1996) 63 IR 138.

99   292nd Report of the Committee on Freedom of Association, para 741(e). See Creighton, above, n 74, p 48.

100 See above n 10.

Australian Workplace Agreements ("AWAs"). Two avenues for non-unionised bargaining are available under the Act. This new framework for bargaining purports to overcome the frustration with the perceived "intermeddling" of unions and the AIRC in the preceding regime of non-unionised bargaining. For employees who are not able to access the new bargaining arrangements, the award system is the safety-net underpinning the various bargaining regimes. The ability of the award system to operate effectively as a safety-net has been compromised in recent legislative developments introduced by the *Workplace Relations Act* which restrict the powers of the AIRC in respect of making and varying awards to certain specified "allowable award matters".[101]

Australian Workplace Agreements

In an ideological sense, the new Australian Workplace Agreements are the centre-piece of the federal legislation, although some commentators have argued that the complexity of the scheme may have an impact on its actual use.[102] AWAs are individual agreements that may be entered into by an employer with an individual employee or a group of employees, but must in any event be signed individually by employees. Involvement on the part of trade unions and the AIRC in the negotiation and approval of such agreements is greatly restricted. This move to individual agreements questions the very foundation of collective labour relations. It is premised on notions of choice and equality of bargaining power that are a myth for a significant percentage of the workforce. This new form of workplace agreement does not rely on the labour power as its constitutional source, but on a number of other heads of constitutional power, including the corporations power, the territories power and the trade and commerce power.

The content requirement for an AWA is minimal; a non-discrimination clause and a dispute resolution clause.[103] The agreement must be in writing and its maximum duration is three years. Bargaining agents may be appointed in writing in relation to the making of an AWA, which could include a trade union. The Act requires the lodging of AWAs for approval by the Employment Advocate, although this was not part of the original proposed scheme, which provided no vetting mechanism. This approval process requires the Employment Advocate to apply a no-disadvantage test.[104] Only where, on balance, the approval or certification of an agreement leads to a reduction in the *overall* terms and conditions of those employees, judged against the relevant or designated award and other relevant laws, is the no-disadvantage test not satisfied.[105]

---

101 Section 89A.

102 See McCallum R "Australian Workplace Agreement – An Analysis" (1997) 10 *Australian Journal of Labour Law* 50 at 51.

103 Section 170VG.

104 Section 170VPB.

105 See *Tweed Valley Fruit Processors Pty Ltd v Ross* (1996) 137 ALR 70; *Enterprise Flexibility Test Case, May 1995* (1995) 59 IR 430. Where there is no applicable award the Employment Advocate is to designate an appropriate award to establish the benchmark for the no disadvantage test. The application of the no-disadvantage test is modified in relation to persons with disabilities employed in accordance with a supported wage scheme, persons undertaking approved traineeships, and persons undertaking apprenticeships.

The Employment Advocate must be satisfied that the AWA meets the additional approval requirements of s 170VPA of the *Workplace Relations Act*. These include the minimum content requirements, that the employee had the opportunity 14 days before signing the agreement to consider its contents,[106] an explanation of the effects of the agreement was provided to the employee before signing, together with an information sheet from the Employment Advocate setting out the available assistance from it and from bargaining agents. The Employment Advocate must also be satisfied that there is genuine agreement on the part of an employee. An employer is also required to declare that all employees doing the same kind of work have been offered an AWA on the same terms. Where the Employment Advocate is in some doubt on the issue of no-disadvantage, the Agreement must be referred to the AIRC. A protocol for referrals of AWAs by the Employment Advocate to the AIRC is being developed by the President of the AIRC.[107] The AIRC must apply the no-disadvantage test, although the AIRC must approve the agreement notwithstanding that the no-disadvantage test is not satisfied if the agreement is not contrary to the public interest.[108] If the AIRC proposes to inquire into a matter any proceedings must be conducted in private. The Act makes clear that there is no right of third party intervention in the approval of AWAs, allowing no scope whatsoever for trade union participation in the process other than in the role of appointed bargaining agents.

Certified agreements

While AWAs are a mechanism for individual agreements, certified agreements provide for collective arrangements. Certified agreements in a number of different forms have been available in Australia since 1988. The *Workplace Relations Act* makes available various types of certified agreements, including a non-unionised stream entered into directly between an employer and employees. A range of constitutional heads of power in addition to the labour power are used to facilitate these agreements. The legislative arrangements for certified agreements under the *Workplace Relations Act* retain approval by the Commission under the no-disadvantage test. There are various grounds on which the Commission must refuse to certify an agreement, including discrimination and breach of the freedom of association provisions. Information and consultation requirements also apply.

Because certified agreements retain a collective aspect, Australian labour law has not as yet reached a point of total decollectivisation. But there are a number of important issues at stake. First is the role of trade unions. Before the *Workplace Relations Act*, although non-union agreements were available, trade unions were allowed a voice in the certification process. The *Workplace Relations Act*, as is apparent for the AWA arrangements, tries to move the position of unions much closer to that of an agency arrangement, rather than the traditional role of an interest in the terms and conditions of all workers, whether union members or not. For a

---

106   Reduced to 5 days in the case of single business agreements as they apply to new employees.

107   Section 170VPE. The terms of the protocol must have the concurrence of the Employment Advocate.

108   Section 170VPG. An example is given as to where this might arise, such as a business in short term crisis or an attempted revival of a business.

trade union to have a right to participate in certification proceedings where the agreement is made directly between an employer and employees, the union must have been authorised by a member to represent her or him and to meet and confer with the employer. The union is a party in its own right in certification proceedings where the agreement is made directly between the employer and the union.[109]

Secondly, various safeguards apply regarding consultation and information in relation to bargaining for certified agreements. The introduction of this type of protective measure, both under the *Workplace Relations Act* and the preceding enterprise bargaining arrangements, is premised on the assumption that decentralisation will operate to the disadvantage of certain segments of the labour market. Little will be achieved by legislation prescribing a range of statutory requirements for informed consultation with women and other disadvantaged groups in the absence of avenues for genuine participation and representation. To ensure that these voices are heard, and the diversity of their experience acknowledged, attention must be directed to the mechanism for consultation and information, and their adequacy critically appraised.[110] Considerations of equity cannot be simply written into the bargaining process with the expectation of a significant change in outcome. Few cases under the preceding enterprise bargaining regimes gave substance to these requirements.

Raising discrimination issues in the bargaining context

Although in theory all industrial awards and agreements should be made in accordance with obligations under anti-discrimination legislation, many awards and agreements still retain discriminatory provisions. Therefore it is important to institute both proactive and reactive mechanisms to prevent and eliminate discrimination within the bargaining context. The traditional exemption of awards and agreements from anti-discrimination legislation has contributed to this problem. While the exemption has been removed under a number of anti-discrimination statutes, it remains problematic in the *Sex Discrimination Act*. Under a compromise arrangement in 1992, the exemption under the *Sex Discrimination Act* was modified so that all federal awards and certified agreements made or varied after 13 January 1993 are now subject to a review process. This enables the Sex Discrimination Commissioner to refer a complaint that an award or agreement is discriminatory to the Australian Industrial Relations Commission.[111] Australian Workplace Agreements are not exempt under the *Sex Discrimination Act*. Therefore the process of referring complaints does not apply. The principal avenue for redress where an AWA is discriminatory appears to be an individual complaint to an anti-discrimination tribunal. The shortcomings of a complaints-based system include the burden on individuals in identifying the systemic nature of the discrimination involved, and the willingness of individuals to take action against their employer. These problems are likely to be magnified in the new industrial relations environment of

---

109 Section 43(2).

110 Owens R "Law and Feminism in the New Industrial Relations" in Hunt, I and Provis, C (eds), *The New Industrial Relations in Australia* (Federation Press, Sydney, 1995), p 51.

111 *Sex Discrimination Act* s 50A; *Workplace Relations Act* s 113(2A).

individualised bargaining. A discrimination clause is part of the minimum content requirements of an AWA, although the terms of the standard discrimination clause are very general and its contractual enforcement presents difficulties. Moreover, the inclusion of a clause that merely makes a general commitment to discrimination issues does not contribute proactively to the elimination of discrimination. Although a discrimination clause is a minimum requirement, the approval process for AWAs does not specifically stipulate an agreement will not be approved if it is discriminatory. As far as certified agreements are concerned the AIRC must refuse to certify an agreement if it is discriminatory on a wide range of grounds.[112]

THE RIGHT TO STRIKE

Australian law and practice does not comply with the obligations implicit in a range of international instruments that protect the right to strike.[113] Although the relevant ILO Conventions do not explicitly refer to the right to strike, the right arises by "necessary implication" and by virtue of Australia's membership of the ILO.[114] The ICESCR explicitly refers to the right to strike, although subject to it being "exercised in conformity with the laws of the particular country".[115] Australia's non-compliance arises from a lack of any substantive immunity from the common law for industrial action, combined with the boycott provisions of the *Trade Practices Act* 1974 (Cth).[116] In addition no protection has traditionally applied to individual strikers whose industrial action has generally been regarded as being in breach of contract. The ILO has had occasion to consider whether law and practice in this area complies with Australia's obligations with respect to the right to strike. On the whole the views expressed have been unfavourable. Of particular concern has been the fact that the cumulative effect of the plethora of sanctions available "could be to deprive workers of the capacity to lawfully take strike action to promote and defend their economic and social interests".[117]

The classic justification of a right to strike is that the nature of collective bargaining necessitates the collective withdrawal of labour as a social and economic sanction in support of a bargaining position adopted.[118] In the Australian context,

---

112 Section 170LU(5).

113 See Creighton, above, n 74, pp 43-46.

114 Ibid, p 35.

115 Article 8(1)(d). In *Victoria v Commonwealth* (1996) 138 ALR 129 various provisions of the *Industrial Relations Reform Act* 1993 (Cth) dealing with a limited right to strike were found by the High Court to be appropriate and adapted to implementing the obligations under art 8 of the Covenant.

116 See Ewing, K, "The Right to Strike in Australia" (1989) 2 *Australian Journal of Labour Law* 18; Creighton, WB, "Enforcement in the Federal Industrial Relations System: an Australian Paradox" (1991) 4 *Australian Journal of Labour Law* 197.

117 277th Report of the ILO Committee on Freedom of Association, Geneva, 1991, paras 151-246; ILO, Committee of Experts on the Application of Conventions and recommendations, Freedom of Association and Collective Bargaining (Geneva, 1994), paras 136-51. See also Creighton, above, n 74, pp 43-46; McEvoy, KP and Owens, RJ, "On a Wing and a prayer: The Pilots' Dispute in an International Context" (1993) 6 *Australian Journal of Labour Law* 1 at 25-29.

118 von Prondzynski, above, n 71, p 103; Kahn-Freund, O and Hepple, B, *Law Against Strikes* (Fabian Society, London, 1972), p 101.

the existence of a system of compulsory conciliation and arbitration has historically guaranteed participation for trade unions in, and the benefits of, conciliation and arbitration. Hence it was argued that there had been a trading away of the right to strike by trade unions in exchange for a guaranteed role in conciliation and arbitration.[119] While the centralised system of conciliation and arbitration was un-questioningly accepted as the appropriate structure for industrial relations in Australia, this argument may have held some sway. However, the partial dismantling of this system heralds a new era both in terms of trade union participation in bargaining, access to tribunals and resort to industrial action.

The most significant change in the regulation of industrial action came with the *Industrial Relations Reform Act* amendments.[120] Included in these amendments were a limited right to strike during the negotiation of a certified agreement, a limited immunity from common law actions, the prohibition of dismissal or other adverse conduct against an employee who engages or proposes to engage in industrial action, and repeal of the s 312 offence of inducing breach of an award. The amending legislation also moved the boycott provisions out of the *Trade Practices Act* to the *Industrial Relations Act*, with some modifications.

The provisions granting protection to individuals against dismissal for engaging in industrial action were stated "to give effect, in certain respects, to Australia's international obligations to provide for a right to strike". Even at this stage the protection for the right to strike was regarded as flawed.[121] First, they applied only to bargaining with respect to certified agreements and not to non-union agreements. Secondly, even where this protection was granted, the statutory requirements were tortuous. Thirdly, the general immunity from common law actions for industrial action only took the form of a 72 hour cooling off period.[122] Finally, the wording of the protection granted to individuals by s 334A with respect to industrial action expressly referred to industrial action undertaken or proposed, but was unclear in its application to current industrial action. As the *Workplace Relations Act* diminishes these limited protections, the inescapable conclusion must be that Australia's non-compliance is significantly exacerbated by the new legislative regime.[123]

Industrial action under the Workplace Relations Act

Although the immunity from common law actions, such as it is, was to have been repealed by the *Workplace Relations Act*, it has been retained in a slightly modified form that denies a cooling-off period for action taken in breach of a direction of the AIRC. Other statutory protections for industrial action have also been rewritten, which confirms Australia's continuing non-compliance with its international

---

119 See Higgins, HB, "A New Province for Law and Order" (1915) 29 *Harvard Law Review* 13; McCarry, G, "Amicable Agreements, Equitable Awards and industrial Disorder" (1991) 13 *Sydney Law Review* 299 at 299-300.

120 See McCarry, G, "Sanctions and Industrial Action: the Impact of the Industrial Relations Reform Act" (1994) 7 *Australian Journal of Labour Law* 198.

121 Ibid.

122 Section 166A, unless the conduct otherwise qualified for the protection granted to bargaining with respect to certified agreements.

123 See Creighton, above, n 74, p 44.

obligations regarding the right to strike. Industrial action during the currency of a certified agreement or an AWA is prohibited. However, industrial action may be taken for the purpose of compelling or inducing a party to make an AWA. Immunity for such action is conditional upon advanced notice being given. Similarly, for the purpose of negotiating a certified agreement a bargaining period may be initiated by written notice.[124] A notice requirement for industrial action is not in breach of ILO standards provided it is reasonable. During that bargaining period duly authorised industrial action may be taken directly against the employer for the purpose of supporting claims made in respect of the agreement or responding to a lockout by an employer. Subject to meeting certain statutory requirements, this industrial action is given immunity as protected action.[125]

The Act dilutes the protection introduced by the *Industrial Relations Reform Act* against dismissal or other adverse action taken against an employee who engages in industrial action. While the protection granted by the *Reform Act* applied generally to industrial action taken by employees, the *Workplace Relations Act* has rewritten this protection so that it only applies to industrial action that is protected action for the purposes of negotiating an AWA or certified agreement. Moreover, the Act makes clear that refusing to pay for non-performance of work during a period of protected action does not come within the protection granted by the Act. Allowance is also made for a protected right on the part of an employer to lock-out employees, which includes the right to refuse to pay employees for the period of the lockout.[126] In addition, the demand, payment or acceptance of strike pay is prohibited and subject to a penalty.[127] Finally, the AIRC is vested with considerable power to make orders directing an end to industrial action that is not protected by the Act, with injunctive powers vested in the Federal Court to enforce compliance.[128]

As far as the application of boycott provisions to industrial action is concerned, the *Workplace Relations Act* returns the regulation of secondary boycotts to the *Trade Practices Act* 1974 (Cth), reversing its transfer to the industrial arena by the *Industrial Relations Reform Act*. There is no longer any cooling off period before an action can be commenced, nor is there a requirement that a certification of failed conciliation be obtained. These repealed measures had been introduced in 1994 to enhance the likelihood of resolving disputes by conciliation, and in recognition of Australia's international obligations regarding the right to strike. In their place the *Workplace Relations Act* now provides that the Federal Court is to consider in proceedings before it whether the application could have proceeded first by way of conciliation. Although the AIRC retains the power to settle boycott disputes by conciliation, where proceedings are pending before the Federal Court to which the Australian Competition and Consumer Commission (ACCC) is a party, the AIRC is not empowered to settle the dispute without the written consent of the ACCC.

---

124 Section 170MI.
125 Sections 170ML(2) and 170MT.
126 Section 170ML(3).
127 Sections 187AA, 187AB, 187AC and 187AD.
128 Section 127.

Much of the concern surrounding secondary boycott provisions has centred on their application not simply to secondary conduct, but to industrial action generally, including primary boycotts. The expansive interpretation given by the courts to s 45D of the *Trade Practices Act*, and the correspondingly narrow interpretation of the defence provision, has facilitated the broad reach of the provisions.[129] The new formulation of the provisions introduced by the *Industrial Relations Reform Act* sought to limit the legislation to what were considered boycotts with an authentic secondary aspect, not involving the industrial interests of the persons engaging in the conduct in question. Although the explanatory memorandum accompanying the Bill claims that the legislation is intended to apply only to genuine secondary boycotts, the *Workplace Relations Act* provisions do apply to some primary boycott situations.

Modelling the new provisions on the old formulation of s 45D has the potential to catch primary conduct once again. The proscribed purpose aspect of these new provisions is established if the conduct is engaged in for purposes that include that purpose. The new defence provision (s 45DD) has also returned to the more restrictive test of "dominant purpose", rather than the more generous test of "ultimate purpose". In addition, some sections on their face clearly apply to primary action. For example s 45DB prohibits two persons acting in concert where the purpose and effect, or likely effect, of the conduct is to prevent or substantially hinder a third person from engaging in trade or commerce involving the movement of goods between Australia and places outside Australia. The Act does protect conduct the dominant purpose of which relates to environmental protection or consumer protection where the conduct does not itself involve industrial action. The restrictions on State or Territory legislation attempting to deal with boycott conduct is repealed to facilitate complimentary State legislation, and the exemption granted for "peaceful picketing" in s 162A has been removed. Given Australia's non-compliance with international instruments under other regimes dealing with boycott conduct, the return to a harsher regime compounds that non-compliance.[130]

CONCLUSION

International standards provide a complex network of human rights relating to labour law. Australia has been an active participant in the establishment of ILO Conventions, and in the adoption of general human rights instruments at least since the Whitlam era. Australian law relies to a considerable extent on international instruments and the rights that they incorporate. This has been particularly evident in relation to anti-discrimination laws, although considerable scope remains for fuller domestic implementation. The framework of the most recent federal government changes to labour law is one that presents a new challenge for international human rights standards. There is a discordance between the tenor of

---

129 See *Tillmanns Butcheries v Australasian Meat Industries Employees Union* (1979) 27 ALR 267; *Mudginberri Station v Australasian Meat Industries Employees Union* (1985) 61 ALR 280; *Australasian Meat Industries Employees Union v Meat & Allied Trades Federation of Australia* (1991) 32 FCR 318; *Devenish v Jewel Food Stores* (1991) 172 CLR 32.

130 See Creighton, above, n 74, p 46.

these changes and the collectivist values that underpin a number of ILO Conventions and international instruments regarding freedom of association and related rights. The extent of incompatibility between these two approaches will no doubt be tested over time. Other issues may also emerge as important human rights issues in the Australian context. Rights in relation to termination of employment, although perhaps more aptly described as a social justice rather than a human rights issue, have taken on an increased significance in Australian labour law. In addition, the extent to which home-based work arrangements that are prevalent in certain industries may breach child labour standards remains an issue. Thus, while Australian labour law grapples with the influence of international standards in a number of areas of human rights, human rights principles established in international forums are likely to remain a focus of Australian labour law.

10

ENVIRONMENTAL LAW
AND HUMAN RIGHTS

Nicholas Brunton

INTRODUCTION

The natural systems of the earth – the atmosphere, hydrosphere (oceans and freshwater), cryosphere (frozen water), lithosphere (rocks and soils), and biosphere – continually exchange matter and energy across space and time. Humans affect these natural systems by diverting energy and matter (resources) from natural cycles to specifically human uses, as well as introducing waste energy and matter into the environment.[1]

This process has resulted in a disturbing level of environmental malaise. The deteriorating health of the planet's ecosystems is well documented in the regular reports of the World Resources Institute, the Worldwatch Institute, the United Nations Environment Programme (UNEP) and the World Bank.[2] These reports highlight problems of soil erosion, climate change, loss of native vegetation, destruction of stratospheric ozone, pollution and toxification of groundwater, rivers and marine waters, depletion of forest cover, increasing desertification and the collapse of critical life support systems in the developing world. The evidence from the relevant reports suggests that the measures taken to date are far from reversing the documented trends. The observations of the World Commission on Environment and Development in 1987 remain as relevant today:

> When the century began, neither human numbers nor technology had the power to radically alter planetary systems. As the century closes, not only do vastly increased human numbers and their activities have that power, but major, unintended changes are occurring in the atmosphere, in soils, in waters, among plants and animals and in the relationships among all of these. The rate of change is outstripping the ability of scientific disciplines and our current capacities to assess and advise. It is frustrating the attempts of political and economic institutions, which evolved in a different, more fragmented world, to adapt and cope.[3]

---

1   Aplin, G, Mitchell, P, Cleugh, H, Pitman, A, and Rich, D, *Global Environmental Crises: An Australian Perspective* (Oxford University Press, Oxford, 1995), p 3.

2   United Nations Environment Programme, *Global Environment Outlook* (United Nations Environment Programme, London, 1997); World Resources Institute, 1995, *World Resources 1994-95* (Oxford University Press, Oxford, 1995); Worldwatch Institute, *State of the World 1996* (Earthscan, London, 1996); World Bank, *The World Bank and the Environment: Annual Report* (World Bank, Washington, 1993).

3   World Commission on Environment and Development, *Our Common Future* (Oxford University Press, Melbourne, Aust ed, 1987), p 22.

The deterioration in the quality of the global environment in the past three decades has led to unprecedented calls for its protection. Environmental movements seeking to protect the environment have based their claims on a number of philosophical, political, legal and even moral foundations.[4] This chapter is concerned with the view that people have a human right to live in a "clean" or "healthy" environment and the extent to which this right is expressed in Australian law. It commences with a brief overview of the conceptual and practical issues relating to human rights and environmental protection before detailing the extent to which this right is incorporated into Australian pollution law. It concludes with a summary of emerging trends in this area.

HUMAN RIGHTS AND ENVIRONMENTAL PROTECTION – CONCEPTUAL ISSUES

Given that human beings are fundamentally dependent on clean air and water and uncontaminated food, there are many similarities between claims for a right to a clean environment and the broader agenda of human rights. The interrelationship can arise in a number of ways. On the one hand, an institutional, legal and political order that permits environmental degradation is one that is more likely to a breakdown in the human rights to life, health and livelihood. The communities of Nigeria's Ogoniland recently protested against the exploitation of the natural resources of their region by the oil industry only to incur the wrath of the Nigerian military dictatorship and suffer significant violations of their human rights. As Simpson and Jackson note, the execution of Ken Saro-Wiwa and other leaders of the Ogoni people vividly illustrate the relationship between environmental protection and fundamental human rights.[5]

Conversely, ensuring the protection of civil and political human rights is more likely to ensure appropriate environmental safeguards. The recent history of environmental politics in Australia clearly shows that being free to articulate dissent in the press and through lawful demonstrations can be a powerful tool to achieve environmental protection.[6] Another example has been the introduction of freedom of information legislation which provides a vital avenue for the community to understand and object to government decision-making in all areas, including the environment.[7]

---

4   See, for example, Irvine, S and Ponton, A, *A Green Manifesto* (Macdonald Optima, London, 1988); Conroy C and Litvinoff, M, *The Greening of Aid* (Earthscan Publications, London, 1988); Seager, J, *Earth Follies: Coming to Feminist Terms with the Global Environmental Crisis* (Routledge, New York, 1993); Trainer, T, *Towards a Sustainable Economy* (Envirobook and Jon Carpenter Publishing, Sydney, 1996); Schumacher, EF, *Small is Beautiful* (Abacus, London, 1974); Plumwood, V, *Feminism and the Mastery of Nature* (Routledge, New York, 1993); Brown-Weiss, E, *In Fairness to Future Generations: International Property Law, Common Patrimony and Inter-generational Equity* (United Nations University, Japan and Transnational Publishers, New York, 1989).

5   Simpson, T and Jackson, V, "Human Rights and the Environment" (1997) 14(4) *Environmental Planning and Law Journal* 268 at 269. See also Clymonds, J, "The Human Right to a Healthy Environment: An International Legal Perspective" (1992) 37 *New York Law School Review* 586.

6   See generally Walker, K (ed), *Australian Environmental Policy* (New South Wales University Press, Sydney, 1992).

7   See Ch 4 by McMillan and Williams in this volume. For a discussion of the issue in the context of European law and human rights, see Weber, S, "Environmental Information and the European Convention on Human Rights" (1991) 12 *Human Rights Law Journal* 177.

The deterioration of the global environment over recent decades has focused attention on the linkages necessary to achieve environmental protection, alleviate poverty and attain development aspirations of each nation. At both international and national levels, the principle of sustainable development has evolved to become the central policy framework for achieving these goals. This principle, discussed in more detail below, has come to mean development which "meets the needs and aspirations of the present without compromising the ability to meet those of the future".[8] This broad ambit of the principle incorporates human rights concerns by acknowledging the interests of the current disadvantaged and the interests of future generations. The principle has been widely adopted in international environmental law and forms the basis of many conventions and other international instruments.[9] Associated with the evolution of sustainable development is the growing recognition that people ought to have a substantive right to a clean environment. Although consensus on this issue at the global level remains elusive, a growing number of instruments[10] and national constitutions[11] include a right to a clean environment among their guarantees.

Article 66 of the Portuguese Constitution, for example, states that "everyone shall have the right to a healthy and ecologically balanced environment and the duty to defend it". In some countries judicial interpretation of certain constitutional guarantees has seen environmental protection gain a constitutional status. The Constitution of the Republic of South Africa goes even further. In addition to providing a right to an environment that is not harmful to health or well being, art 24 provides that everyone has a right to have the environment protected, for the benefit of present and future generations, by legislative and other measures that prevent pollution and degradation, promote conservation and ensure ecologically sustainable development.

While these developments point to the similarities between the right to a satisfactory environment and human rights, there is also tension between the two. On a conceptual level, many see the anthropocentric nature of human rights as particularly problematic. Is the protection of the environment for the benefit of humans only, or does it recognise the intrinsic and inherent value of other species and the environment in general? The latter view, often called the ecocentric

---

8   World Commission on Environment and Development, above, n 3, p 81.

9   The Indian Supreme Court has held that art 21 of the Indian Constitution which provides for a fundamental right to life includes a right to environmental protection: see *LK Koolwal v State of Rajastan* (1988) AIR Raj 2; *Madhavi v Tilakan* (1988) 2 Ker LT 730; *Kinkri Devi v State of Himachal Pradesh* (1988) AIR HP 4; and *T Damodar Rao v Special Officer, Municipal Corporation of Hyderadad* (1987) AIR AP 171.

10   See art 24 of the *Convention on the Rights of the Child* 1989 (1989) 28 ILM 1448; art 11 of the *Additional Protocol to the American Convention on Human Rights in the Area of Economic, Social and Cultural Rights* 1989 (1989) 28 ILM 156; art 24 of the *African Charter of Human and Peoples Rights* 1982 (1982) 21 ILM 58.

11   Kiss has identified some 44 national Constitutions as well as some 20 State Constitutions containing provisions relating to protection of the environment: Kiss, A, "Environment et Development ou Environment et survie" (1991) 118 *Journal Du Droit International* 263 at 266-67.

approach,[12] occasionally clashes with human rights and its focus on the protection of individuals. In situations where the threat to the environment is significant, the ecocentric approach requires human needs to be subservient to the needs of ecosystems. For example, the question of whether marginalised indigenous groups should be able to hunt and kill endangered species (such as the Artic Innuit hunting seals and their pups) is highly controversial and has deeply divided international environmental organisations.

Other major issues concern the mechanisms for change. Some consider a substantive human right to a clean, healthy or decent environment as a major problem as it entrenches the dominance of human concerns despite the evidence that humans have been responsible for the harm in the first place.[13] Others see procedural rights as more useful because they can incorporate the interests of non-humans into the (human) legal process.[14] Another problem relates to the definition of a substantive right in qualitative terms, such as "clean", "healthy" or "viable". This is always going to give rise to uncertainty and ambiguity, both legal and scientific. Boyle suggests that this problem may even undermine the very notion of human rights.[15] An example of the definitional problem arose in the Canadian province of Ontario. That province proclaimed an Act called the *Environmental Bill of Rights* on 15 February 1994. It was proposed initially that the Act include a substantive right to a "healthy and sustainable environment". However, extensive debate over nature and effect of such a substantive right resulted in its deletion from the final instrument adopted. The resultant *Environmental Bill of Rights* focuses on granting significant procedural rights to the citizens of Ontario to participate in decisions which affect the environment.[16]

---

12   For some of the most significant works in this area, see Leopold, A, *A Sand County Almanac*, reprinted in (Oxford University Press, Oxford, 1949, reprinted 1968); Carson, R, *Silent Spring* (Houghton Mifflin, Boston, 1962); Naess, A, "The Shallow and the Deep, Long Range Ecology Movement. A Summary" (1973) 16 *Inquiry* 95; Muir, J, *The Wilderness World of John Muir* (Houghton Mifflin, Boston, 1976); Bookchin, M, *Social Ecology* (Black Rose Books, Montreal, 1980); Sax, J, *Mountains Without Handrails: Reflections on the National Parks* (University of Michigan Press, Chicago, 1980); Clark, S, *The Moral Status of Animals* (Clarendon Press, Oxford, 1977); Singer, P, *Animal Liberation* (Basic Books, New York, 1975); Regan, T, *The Case for Animal Rights* (University of Chicago Press, Chicago, 1983); Tribe, LH, "Ways Not to Think About Plastic Trees: New Foundations for Environmental Law" (1974) 83 *Yale Law Journal* 1315.

13   Redwell, C, "Life, the Universe and Everything: A Critique of Anthropocentric Rights", in Boyle, AE and Anderson, MR (eds), *Human Rights Approaches to Environmental Protection* (Clarendon Press, Oxford, 1996), pp 71-88. See also, generally, Shelton, D, "Human Rights, Environmental Rights, and the Right to Environment" (1991) 28 *Stanford Journal of International Law* 105, and Clymonds, above, n 3.

14   See generally Cameron, J and Mackenzie, R, "Access to Justice and Procedural Rights in International Institutions" in Boyle and Anderson, above, pp 129-52, and Douglas-Scott, S, "Environmental Rights in the European Union – Participatory Democracy or Democratic Deficit?", in Boyle and Anderson, above, pp 109-28. For a recent Australian example of the protection of endangered species through procedural mechanisms, see *Threatened Species Conservation Act* 1995 (NSW).

15   Boyle, AE, "The Role of International Human Rights Law in the Protection of the Environment", in Boyle and Anderson, above, n 13, p 50.

16   See Walker, S, "The Ontario Environmental Bill of Rights" in Deimann, S and Dyssli, B (eds), *Environmental Rights: Law, Litigation and Access to Justice* (Cameron May, London, 1995), pp 20-32.

Notwithstanding these issues, it is becoming increasingly clear that the international community is moving towards a recognition of the interrelationship between environmental protection and human rights. This is reflected in the emergence of the broad concept of sustainable development and its incorporation into international and domestic law.

HUMAN RIGHTS AND SUSTAINABLE DEVELOPMENT

The call for a new approach to the environment is part of the growing acceptance that development must be ecologically sustainable in the long term if humans are going to have a long-term future on the planet. The concept of sustainable development is now one of central importance in international environmental law and the concept and its principles are increasing being included in conventions, declarations and action programs.[17] Sustainable development has a long, if unrecognised, history. O'Riordan traces its lineage to the Greek vision of "Gaia", the Goddess of the Earth.[18] According to the principles of Gaia, provincial governors in ancient Greece were rewarded and punished according to the state of the land in their province. Signs of erosion or other environmental damage led to admonishment or even exile, while healthy looking land was strongly approved.[19]

This century, sustainable development has gained widespread acceptance following the publication of the report *Our Common Future* in 1987 by the World Commission on Environment and Development.[20] The Commission was established by the United Nations in 1983 to formulate an agenda for change to protect the environment. After a three-year review of the state of the global environment, the Commission found that "failures to manage the environment and to sustain development threaten to overwhelm all countries".[21] It called for all nations, rich and poor, to commit themselves to sustainable development so that nations could "meet the needs and aspirations of the present without compromising the ability to meet those of the future".[22] Central to sustainable development is the call for a new paradigm of decision making which integrates both environmental and economic policy, not just to protect the environment, "but also to protect and promote development".[23] *Our Common Future* and subsequent reports developed certain principles to guide governments towards achieving sustainable development. These

---

17 See, for example, *Convention for the Protection of the Marine Environment of the North-East Atlantic* 1993, *Washington Declaration of Protection of the Marine Environment from Land-Based Activities; Rio Declaration on Environment and Development; The Convention on Biological Diversity 1992; United Nations Framework Convention on Climate Change 1992.*

18 See O'Riordan, T, "The Politics of Sustainability", in Turner, RK, (ed), *Sustainable Environmental Economics and Management: Principles and Practice* (Belhaven Press, London, 1993), pp 44-45.

19 Ibid.

20 World Commission on Environment and Development, above, n 3, p 81.

21 Ibid.

22 Ibid, p 84.

23 Ibid, p 81.

include the precautionary principle,[24] intergenerational and intragenerational equity (discussed below) and the protection of biodiversity.

The integration of the environment with issues of development was the focus for the subsequent United Nations Conference on Environment and Development (UNCED) held in Rio de Janeiro in 1992.[25] This conference, and the establishment of a permanent United Nations Commission on Sustainable Development, cemented sustainability as the central framework for global action programs on the environment.

INTERGENERATIONAL AND INTRAGENERATIONAL EQUITY

A crucial feature of sustainable development is that it recognises that the environment cannot be divorced from human rights in general. This is reflected in the principles which have been developed to guide its implementation. These principles include a commitment to intergenerational and intragenerational equity. Intergenerational equity requires the present generation to ensure that the health, diversity and productivity of the environment is maintained or enhanced for the benefit of future generations.[26] It can be seen as aimed towards protecting the human rights of future generations. Yet in this principle lies a paradox. Because we cannot survey the views of future generations, there is debate as to what exactly the present generation should bequeath.[27] If the environment is broadly defined, ought not the social and cultural environment be preserved for future generations as much as biological diversity and ecological integrity? If so, does this not require that the same or enhanced economic environment be passed on as well? How are all these broadly defined aspects of the environment to be measured?

If one accepts that future generations deserve an environment equal to the one we currently enjoy, there can be no ethical objection to promoting intragenerational equity. Intragenerational equity seeks to achieve equity within each generation. It thus focuses on the uneven rates of development in the northern and southern hemispheres. As it is ethically untenable that the developing world should live at lower levels of development so that the developed world can continue their current consumptive patterns, the concept requires countries like Australia to reduce their

---

24 In Australia, the precautionary principle has come to mean that "where there are threats of serious or irreversible environmental damage, lack of full scientific certainty should not be used as a reason for postponing measures to prevent environmental degradation", see Commonwealth of Australia, *National Strategy for Ecologically Sustainable Development* (AGPS, Canberra, 1992), p 8.

25 The major documents and conventions arising from the United Nations Conference on Environment and Development are reprinted in Johnson, S, (ed), *The Earth Summit: The United Nations Conference on Environment and Development (UNCED)* (Graham & Trotman, London, 1993).

26 See Commonwealth of Australia, *Intergovernmental Agreement on the Environment* (AGPS, Canberra, 1992), p 14. For a broad discussion of the implications of this concept see Young, MD, *For Our Children's Children: Some Practical Implications of Intergenerational Equity, the Precautionary Principle, Maintenance of Natural Capital, and the Discount Rate* (AMNRS Programme Division for Wildlife and Ecology, CSIRO, 1993), Working Document 93/5.

27 Diesendorf, M, "Principles of Ecological Sustainability" in Diesendorf M and Hamilton C (eds), *Human Ecology, Human Economy* (Allen and Unwin, Sydney, 1997), p 76. See also Brown-Weiss, above, n 4.

consumption of non-renewable resources and the emission of wastes. This is seen as a necessary and vital process to enable the developing world to move beyond the vicious cycle of poverty and achieve sustainable development.

On both international and national levels, intragenerational equity requires measures far broader than those relating to environmental protection. However, as they are linked by the same ethical duty, environment protection cannot be divorced from a wider human rights project.

AUSTRALIAN PERSPECTIVES ON ENVIRONMENTAL PROTECTION AND HUMAN RIGHTS

Having provided a background to the relationship between environmental protection and human rights, the remainder of this chapter examines the extent to which Australian pollution law provides its citizens with a right to a clean environment. From the outset it should be noted that the Australian governments readily embraced the concept of sustainable development as a policy principle following the UNCED conference in 1992 and thus, at least in theory, recognised the interrelationship of environmental protection and human rights. The concept of (ecologically)[28] sustainable development was accepted by all of the Australian jurisdictions in a landmark agreement, the Intergovernmental Agreement on the Environment, signed in May 1992.[29] That Agreement was followed by the National Strategy for Ecologically Sustainable Development to which, in theory, each government is committed.[30]

Since 1992, the concept of sustainable development has gradually become incorporated into Australian environmental legislation, both in form and in substance. Across the nine Australian jurisdictions, there are now over 180 statutes principally relating to environmental and planning matters with an additional 140 statutes which partially, or indirectly, deal with such matters. The more recent statutes often reflect and state certain values and principles in their "objects clauses".[31] These values and beliefs have included notions of sustainability, precaution, equity, and the desirability of public participation[32] in resource management, land-use planning and environmental protection. For example, the objects of

---

28   The prefix ecologically was adopted to ensure that sustainability did not refer, as some suggested, to sustainable economic development.

29   *Intergovernmental Agreement on the Environment*, above, n 26.

30   See *National Strategy*, above, n 24.

31   See, for example, *Environment Protection Act* 1993 (SA) s 10; *Land Use Planning and Approvals Act* 1993 (Tas) Sch 1; *Queensland Heritage Act* 1992 (Qld) s 3; *Threatened Species Conservation Act* 1995 (NSW) s 3.

32   The term "public participation" is employed in a number of differing contexts with slightly different meanings. Some commentators draw a distinction between "public" and "community participation". The term "community participation" generally denotes input from non-commercial, non-professional and non-political type interested parties whereas the term "public participation" refers to input from commercial, professional, political as well as other interested groups. The term "public participation" is used in the present chapter in the sense of including both of these meanings; see further, Brown, V, "Community Consultation as Dispute Resolution: Them or Us, Weak or Strong, Conservative or Creative" (proceedings of Defending the Environment Conference, Adelaide, 1995).

the *Protection of the Environment Operations Act* 1997 (NSW) include "to provide increased opportunities for public involvement and participation in environment protection" and "to ensure the community has access to relevant and meaningful information about pollution".[33]

In substance, many statutes incorporate features and mechanisms which, while not expressly providing a substantive right to a clean environment, do provide significant procedural and other rights to the community. These mechanisms have their origin in planning law, which has for many years involved the public in land-use planning and in government decision-making. For example, broad rights to participate in land-use planning and development control were introduced in New South Wales with the *Environmental Planning and Assessment Act* 1979. In Victoria, public participation has been a feature of planning law since the 1960s, although recently there have been changes which have significantly narrowed these procedural rights.[34] By and large, these mechanisms have played a significant role in providing access to justice.

As the right to a clean environment is focused on pollution and contamination,[35] the next section examines the extent to which the right to a clean environment is embodied in Australian pollution law. The purpose of this review is to highlight some of the more novel features of the legislation and illustrate how pollution law has embodied many concepts relevant to human rights. It will show that unlike most other areas of law, the statutes recognise the inherently political, as opposed to purely scientific, technical or economic, aspects of environmental policy. This will be shown by an overview of various aspects of pollution law including administration, policy formulation, rights to information, rights to participate in decision making, merit appeals, and enforcement.

ADMINISTRATION OF POLLUTION LEGISLATION IN AUSTRALIA

Public participation in the administration of pollution legislation is a recent development. As noted above, many jurisdictions expressly provide that an object of the legislation is, among others, to include the public in its administration. In Queensland and South Australia, the relevant legislation goes further providing that the legislation must be administered in consultation with the public.[36] In both States, the legislation requires those conferred with functions or powers to perform their

---

33   See s 3(b) and (c). See also *Environment Protection Act* 1997 (ACT) s 3(1)(f); *Land Use Planning and Approvals Act* 1993 (Tas) cl 1(c) Sch 1; *Environmental Planning and Assessment Act* 1979 (NSW) s 5(c); *Environmental Protection Act* 1994 (Qld) s 4(4)(b) and (5)(b); *Coastal Management Act* 1994 (Vic) s 4(e); *Environment Protection Act* 1993 (SA) s 10(b)(ix).

34   Raff, M. "The Curtailment of Public Participation in Planning in Victoria" (1995) 12 *Environmental Planning Law Journal* 73.

35   Scientists often make a distinction between the two concepts. Pollutants are materials that otherwise would not be present in the environment in that particular form. Scientists often argue that they are not a problem until they reach certain concentrations, and then they become contaminants. Others reject the distinction.

36   *Environment Protection Act* 1993 (SA) s 10(1)(ix); *Environmental Protection Act* 1994 (Qld) ss 4(4) and 6.

functions or exercise their powers in a way that best achieves the objectives of the legislation.[37] Section 6 of the *Environmental Protection Act* 1994 (Qld), for example, specifically requires administrative authorities to consult with Aborigines and Torres Strait Islanders under Aboriginal tradition and island custom.

Another important avenue of participation for the public is through membership of various advisory committees and councils established under the legislation. The provisions often expressly require representatives from non-government environmental organisations devoted to environmental protection to be on such committees.[38] More often than not, the role of these committees is advisory only, although some have specific functions to perform.[39]

POLICY FORMULATION

In addition to general obligations to include the public in the administration of the legislation, pollution law grants significant rights for public input into policy formulation. This is a unique feature of environmental law. Unlike other policy areas, such as immigration, social security, and health, environmental law expressly encourages the public to contribute to the development of important policy matters. Often the policy position is cemented into binding subordinate instruments. For example, in all jurisdictions except the Northern Territory, the legislation provides that the public has the right to make submissions on the making of environment protection policies ("EPPs").[40] These policies typically establish the desired background environmental standards, establish mechanisms to achieve those standards and provide a benchmark for the administration of the legislation and the granting of licences and approvals. The role of the public in developing such policies is vital, for they are used for the making of important decisions on whether a person may discharge pollution and so can dramatically affect quality of life for those living nearby. These provisions, therefore, can be seen as an expression of the human right to have adequate standards of living and the continuous improvements in living conditions.[41]

Across the jurisdictions, there is no standard approach for public participation in policy formulation. In Victoria, for new EPPs the Environment Protection Authority (EPA) must prepare and advertise a policy impact assessment report and comments must be sought from the public.[42] In Queensland, there is a right to make

---

37 *Environmental Protection Act* 1994 (Qld) s 5; *Environment Protection Act* 1993 (SA) s 10(2).

38 See, for example, the Environment Protection Advisory Forum established under Div 2 of the *Environment Protection Act* 1993 (SA) and the State and three regional community consultation forums established under s 24 of the *Protection of the Environment Administration Act* (1991) (NSW). Each of these bodies must include representatives of non-government organisations devoted to environment protection

39 See ss 26-28 which establish the Environmental Education Committee.

40 *Environment Protection Act* 1970 (Vic) s 16; *Environmental Protection Act* 1986 (WA) s 27; *State Policies and Projects Act* 1993 (Tas) s 8; *Environmental Protection Act* 1994 (Qld) ss 26 and 28; *Environment Protection Act* 1993 (SA) s 28; *Environment Protection Act* 1997 (ACT) s 25; *Protection of the Environment Operations Act* 1997 (NSW) s 17.

41 See *Universal Declaration on Human Rights* 1948 (UDHR) art 25; *International Covenant on Economic, Social and Cultural Rights* 1976 (ICESCR) art 11.

42 See *Environment Protection Act* 1970 (Vic) ss 18A-18D.

a submission on what an EPP should contain before it is formulated[43] and a right to make submissions of amendments to EPPs provided the amendments are not trivial.[44] In South Australia, the EPA, except where the Minister has determined otherwise, must hold a public hearing in which interested persons may be heard in relation to the draft EPP and any submissions made.[45]

RIGHTS TO INFORMATION

Fundamental to the protection of human rights to health, both at home and in the work place,[46] is information about the environment in which a person lives and works. Information is also vital to allow persons to obtain legal redress through the courts for breaches of the legislation.[47] Without knowledge, or without the means to gain knowledge, communities are powerless to protect the environment and redress environmental harm.

Pollution law has dramatically improved the nature and quality of information available to the public concerning such matters. In the following section, the various provisions in pollution law statutes relating to providing information to the public are discussed. In addition to these provisions, there are of course various statutory rights to information held by government.[48] However, a discussion of these is beyond the scope of this chapter.

In Queensland, South Australia, New South Wales, the Australian Capital Territory and Tasmania various information held by the relevant authorities[49] must be kept in a register and be made publicly available.[50] The legislation differs in the types of documents required to be kept in the register. Generally the information includes copies of licences, works approvals (including their conditions), details of environmental reports, results of monitoring programs, details of environmental management programs and environmental protection orders, clean up orders, lists of authorised officers, details of pollution incidents and civil and criminal enforcement action and other prescribed information. In each jurisdiction, the register must be kept open for inspection by the public who are permitted to take extracts from the register or, on payment of the appropriate fee, given a copy of the register or a part of it.

---

43   *Environmental Protection Act* 1994 (Qld) s 26.

44   Ibid, s 32.

45   *Environment Protection Act* 1993 (SA) s 28(6)(d).

46   In respect of human rights to a safe workplace, see ICESCR art 7(b).

47   See UDHR art 8.

48   See *Freedom of Information Act* 1989 (NSW); *Freedom of Information Act* 1982 (Cth).

49   In South Australia and New South Wales, the relevant authority is each States' Environment Protection Authority. In Queensland the records must be kept by either the Department of Environment or the relevant local council. In Tasmania, the register must be kept by the Board of Environmental Management and Pollution Control and in the ACT it must be kept by the Environment Management Authority.

50   *Environment Protection Act* 1993 (SA) s 109; *Environmental Protection Act* 1994 (Qld) ss 213-214; *Environmental Management and Pollution Control Act* 1994 (Tas) s 22; *Protection of the Environment Operations Act* 1997 (NSW) ss 308-309; *Environment Protection Act* 1997 (ACT) ss 19-20.

In Queensland, recent amendments to the *Environmental Protection Act* 1994 (Qld) require a Environmental Management Register to be kept which records contaminated land which is considered to be "low-risk". High-risk sites are recorded in a separate Contaminated Land Register. In New South Wales, a similar approach is adopted under the *Contaminated Land Management Act* 1997 (NSW) where a register of sites which have been subject to an investigation or remediation order must be kept by the New South Wales EPA. In the other jurisdictions, no formal register of contaminated land is required to be kept by the legislation, although a non-statutory register does exist in Victoria.

In Queensland, New South Wales and Tasmania state of the environment reports must be prepared by the relevant authorities which must contain the information prescribed by the relevant legislation.[51]

RIGHTS TO PARTICIPATE IN DECISIONS

Decisions concerning the natural and built environment can fundamentally affect peoples lives. Factories, roads, mines and major earthworks are just some of the matters which can seriously affect residential amenity, increase exposure to chemicals and other risks, and destroy aesthetic qualities of the environment. A law which recognises that citizens have a right to take part in the conduct of public affairs without unreasonable restrictions and to have equitable access to public service is an important expression of certain fundamental civil rights.[52] Pollution law recognises such rights by providing the means to participate in important decisions which affect the environment. The following reviews concerns the rights to participate on decisions to grant government approvals to pollute the environment. A failure to comply with such provisions is, in all jurisdictions, subject to judicial review.[53]

Approvals, permits and licences

In South Australia, Queensland, Victoria and the Australian Capital Territory any person has the right to make submissions on applications for proposals to discharge pollution to the environment. The typical model is to require industry to first obtain approval to install or modify polluting equipment (often called a works approval). It is at this stage that the legislation usually gives the public an opportunity to be either directly notified or through advertising to peruse the application and to make written

---

51   *Environmental Protection Act* 1994 (Qld) s 218; *State Policies and Projects Act* 1993 (Tas) s 29; *Protection of the Environment Administration Act* 1991 (NSW) s 10.

52   See *International Covenant on Civil and Political Rights* 1966 (ICCPR) art 25. See also UDHR art 21.

53   Access to judicial review, is of course, vital to remedy any violations of those rights provided by law, see UDHR art 8; ICCPR art 2(3).

submissions.[54] After such equipment is installed or modified, the legislation allows the applicant to obtain a licence for its operation.

In Tasmania and New South Wales, approvals for pollution discharges are integrated with planning approvals. In Tasmania, for those activities which are permissible with consent by the local council approval under the *Land Use Planning and Approvals Act* 1993 (level 2 activities), the applications must be notified, copies must be available for public inspection and the public may make submissions.[55] Projects of State significance are assessed by the Sustainable Development Advisory Council and the public has a right to make submissions to the Council on the draft integrated assessment report.[56] For both types of development, the relevant decision maker must further the objects of the Resource Management and Planning System of Tasmania which is included in the form of a schedule to the relevant legislation. In New South Wales, most activities which require a licence to discharge are what is called "designated development" under the *Environmental Planning and Assessment Act* 1979 (NSW). Such development requires a detailed environmental impact statement, is subject to special notification and advertising requirements, and the public has a period to make submissions on the application. The consent authority must provide a copy of the development application to the New South Wales EPA which, if it considers a licence should be granted, must provide draft conditions to the consent authority within 30 days.

In South Australia, Western Australia and the Australian Capital Territory, the respective agencies must have regard to public submissions made in relation to a works approval or licence,[57] although this is not the case in Queensland.[58] In Queensland, the right of the public to participate depends on the type of activity. For activities requiring a licence, applications must be advertised, copies of the application must be available for inspection and the public has a right to make submissions.[59] If a person made a submission they must be notified in writing if a licence is granted.[60] In relation to licence applications, the administering authority may invite applicants for a licence and those who made submissions to a conference to help it decide the application. The conference may be notified to the public in writing by the administering authority or, where it is not practical to do so, through

---

54 *Environment Protection Act* 1993 (SA) s 39(1); *Environment Protection Act* 1997 (ACT) s 48; *Environmental Protection Act* 1994 s 42; *Environment Protection Act* 1970 (Vic) s 19B(3)(b)(iv). In South Australia, Western Australia and Victoria the legislation provides for the granting of works approvals which are the equivalent of pollution control approvals under the *Pollution Control Act* 1970 (NSW). In Queensland, the *Environmental Protection Act* 1994 (Qld) only provides for licences (for level 1 environmentally relevant activities) and approvals (for level 2 environmentally relevant activities). In Tasmania, the planning and environmental processes are integrated with permits and are issued by local councils for level 2 activities under the *Land Use Planning and Approvals Act* 1993 (Tas) and level 1 activities are assessed by the Sustainable Development Advisory Council under the *State Policies and Projects Act* 1993 (Tas).

55 *Land Use Planning and Approvals Act* 1993 (Tas) s 57.

56 *State Policies and Projects Act* 1993 (Tas) s 23.

57 *Environment Protection Act* 1993 (SA) s 47(1)(h); *Environment Protection Act* 1986 (WA) s 54(3); *Environment Protection Act* 1997 (ACT) s 49(1).

58 *Environmental Protection Act* 1994 (Qld) s 45.

59 Ibid, s 42.

60 Ibid, s 45(1)(d).

publishing a notice in a newspaper. Independent persons may be appointed by the administering authority to mediate the conference.

Submissions in relation to other matters

In Queensland the public has a right to make submissions to draft environmental management programs[61] submitted by the proponent of an activity for approval by the relevant authority. Such draft environmental management programs must be advertised and the notice must invite submissions from the public and state the day by which submissions may be made to the administering authority. Similarly, the administering authorities may invite the public to a conference to assist it to decide whether or not to approve the program.[62] Similar notification provisions to those discussed above apply.

APPEALS

The ability to have decisions to licence pollution by regulatory authorities subject to merits review is vital to ensure a meaningful procedural right to a clean environment. This is because there is evidence that public authorities can be captured by polluters, or provide inappropriate approvals or issue approvals with inadequate conditions. The pressure of possibly having a court review decisions on their merits requires government authorities to consider carefully their statutory duties and functions.

All jurisdictions, except South Australia and the Northern Territory, provide the public with a right to appeal the granting of a licence to pollute. In New South Wales and Tasmania, the right to appeal is in relation to the grant of planning approval or development consent by the consent authority, rather than in relation to the grant of a licence. Because of the central importance of these rights, a brief outline is appropriate.

Queensland

In Queensland, those who made submissions on licence applications, applications to amend a licence, or on proposed environmental management plans may apply to the administering authority for a internal review by the administrative authority of what was called an "original decision".[63] Original decisions are set out in Sch 1 to the Act and include, among others, the grant of a licence, the imposition of conditions on a licence, the amendment of a licence and the approval of a draft environmental management program.

The application for an internal review must be dealt with by a person who did not decide the original decision and who is no less senior than that person.[64] The internal review decision must be notified to relevant persons and include the reasons

---

61   Ibid, s 85.
62   Ibid, s 87.
63   Ibid, s 202.
64   Ibid, s 202(7).

for the decision and inform the persons of their right to appeal against the decision. This internal review process does not apply when the original decision was made by the elected members of the local government itself or the chief executive officer of the local government personally.[65]

Those who seek an internal review but are dissatisfied with the result may appeal the matter to the Planning and Environment Court. If the matter is one where the review decision provisions do not apply (that is, a decision made by an elected council or a council's CEO) those who made submissions on the original applications may appeal against the original decision directly to the Planning and Environment Court.

Australian Capital Territory

Section 135 of the *Environment Protection Act* 1997 (ACT) provides that an "eligible person" may make an application to the Administrative Appeals Tribunal for review of a decision of the Environment Management Authority to, among other things, grant or vary an environmental authorisation. Section 135(5) provides that an "eligible person" includes any person whose interests are affected by the decision.

Section 135 of the Act allows eligible persons also to seek a review of a decision of the Minister, where the Minister has decided to use his powers under s 92(2)(b) of the Act. That section allows the Minister to notify the Environment Management Authority that a decision to be made under the Act is not to be made by the Authority but by the Minister.

Victoria

A person who is aggrieved by the decision of the EPA to grant a works approval (or a licence where a works approval was not obtained), or to amend a licence or remove the suspension of a licence, may appeal to the Victorian Administrative Appeals Tribunal.[66]

Western Australia

The public only has a right of appeal to the Minister in relation to conditions attached to a works approval or licence, not the grant of the works approval or licence.[67] The Minister must consult with the CEO of the EPA and may request a report in relation to the appeal, or may require the CEO of the EPA to consider the appeal and to consult with the appellant and any other appropriate person. Alternatively, the Minister may appoint an appeals committee to consider the appeal and report to the Minister.[68] After receiving any such report(s) in relation to the

---

65   Ibid, s 202(12).

66   *Environment Protection Act* 1970 (Vic) s 33B.

67   *Environmental Protection Act* 1986 (WA) s 102(3).

68   Ibid, s 106.

appeal, the Minister may allow or dismiss the appeal and the decision is final and without appeal.[69]

There is also a right of appeal to the Minister in relation to matters subject to the environmental impact assessment procedures under Pt IV of the *Environmental Protection Act* 1986 (WA).[70]

Tasmania

If a person made a representation in relation to an application for a discretionary planning permit (which may be granted in respect of polluting activities), then that person has the right to the Resource Management and Planning Appeal Tribunal.[71]

New South Wales

Those who lodged a written objection to a proposed designated development may appeal to the Land and Environment Court against the grant of development consent by the consent authority.[72] If development consent is granted and no appeal is made, then there is no opportunity to appeal the subsequent grant of a licence by the New South Wales EPA for the same activity. For activities which do not fall within the category of designated development (which is more or less replicated in the Schedule to the *Protection of the Environment Operations Act* 1997 (NSW)), and which is likely to cause water pollution, a licence is also required. However, there is no right to appeal against the granting of a licence by the EPA in this instance.

ENFORCEMENT

The enforcement of pollution law is seen by the public as fundamentally important. In most jurisdictions, apart from New South Wales and Victoria, the use of civil or criminal proceedings to enforce the legislation is very rare. This has led to calls to provide the public with an opportunity to bring proceedings to ensure compliance. Thus in some jurisdictions, the law expressly provides for civil enforcement in addition to judicial review proceedings. It is becoming increasingly common for the legislation to grant standing to any person to bring civil proceedings, regardless of whether their personal interests are affected.[73] The New South Wales legislation goes even further by providing the public with a right to bring criminal proceedings (these provisions are discussed below). Pollution law can therefore be seen as embodying the principles required by art 8 of the *Universal Declaration of Human Rights* (UDHR).

More recently, there has been a trend to make it easier for regulatory authorities to bring prosecutions. The legislation typically allows authorised officers to enter

---

69 Ibid, *s* 107.

70 Ibid, *s* 100.

71 *Land Use Planning and Approvals Act* 1993 (Tas) s 61(5).

72 *Environmental Planning and Assessment Act* 1979 (NSW) s 98.

73 See also *Environmental Planning and Assessment Act* 1979 (NSW) s 123; *Heritage Act* 1997 (NSW) s 153; *National Parks and Wildlife Act* 1974 (NSW) s 176A; *Wilderness Act* 1987 (NSW) s 27; *Local Government Act* 1993 (NSW) s 674.

premises, conduct searches, seize documents, take samples, and so forth. In some jurisdictions, these powers are regularly used. To environmental lawyers it was no surprise that it was the use of these powers which led to the High Court decision of *Environment Protection Authority v Caltex*[74] which determined that corporations cannot claim the privilege against self-incrimination.

Paradoxically, these provisions have intruded into other fundamental human rights. For example, the New South Wales *Protection of the Environment Operations Act* 1997 (NSW) incorporates a provision abrogating the fundamental human right to remain silent as provided by art 14(3)(g) of the *International Covenant of Civil and Political Rights* 1966 (ICCPR). Section 203(1) provides:

> [A]n authorised officer may require a person whom the authorised officer suspects on reasonable grounds to have knowledge of matters in respect of which information is reasonably required for the purposes of this Act to answer questions in relation to those matters.

To fail to answer questions is a criminal offence for which there is a maximum penalty of $11,000. The Act also provides the EPA with a broad power to issue a notice requiring the provision of information. Moreover, s 212 provides that it is not a defence to refuse to answer questions or provide information on the ground that it may incriminate that person or make that person liable to a penalty. However, s 212(3) provides that any answer given by a natural person, or information provided by that person, is not admissible in evidence against the person in criminal proceedings if:

- the person objected at the time on the ground that it might incriminate the person; or
- the person was warned on that occasion that the person may object to furnishing the information or giving the answer on the ground that it might incriminate the person.

This defence presupposes that those subjected to an interview understand the nature of the warning and the law of self-incrimination. Given that environmental offences typically arise in factories whose employees often have low education levels, this assumption is presumptuous. In any event, having been informed on certain facts, the EPA can simply use other investigative powers to collect evidence and prosecute the individual who was forced to answer questions.

The extent to which the regulatory authorities use civil and criminal proceedings to enforce environmental legislation varies considerably across the jurisdictions. New South Wales and Victoria have for many years adopted a fairly rigorous approach to non-compliance and regularly bring criminal proceedings. On the other hand, other jurisdictions very rarely prosecute offenders, some almost not at all. For example, it has been suggested that the low rates of prosecution by the Queensland Department of Environment and the Environmental Compliance Unit of the Department of Mines and Energy are evidence that they have been "captured" by industry and mining interests.[75] For many years it has been argued that there is

---

74   (1993) 178 CLR 477.

75   See Briody, M and Prenzler, T, "The Enforcement of Environmental Protection Laws Queensland: A Case of Regulatory Capture?" (1998) 15(1) *Environmental Planning Law Journal* 54.

no justification for preventing the public from bringing civil and criminal proceedings to enforce legislation for the public benefit.[76] This is especially important where the regulatory authorities are not performing that role. Accordingly, many jurisdictions now provide opportunities for the public to enforce the legislation. The regimes vary and can be summarised as follows.

New South Wales

Section 252 of the *Protection of the Environment Operations Act* 1997 (NSW) allows the public to institute proceedings in the Land and Environment Court to restrain or remedy a breach of the that Act or the regulations under that Act. Such proceedings may be brought whether or not any right of the person has been or may be infringed by the breach or as a consequence of the breach. The former *Environmental Offences and Penalties Act* 1989 (NSW) imposed a condition on the exercise of these rights by requiring the applicant to obtain leave of the Land and Environment Court. Such restrictions have now been removed.

Section 253 of the *Protection of the Environment Operations Act* 1997 (NSW) also provides a general right to bring proceedings to restrain or remedy a breach of any other Act or statutory rule under any other Act, if the breach (or threatened or apprehended breach) is causing or is likely to cause harm to the environment. Again such proceedings may be brought regardless of whether the rights of the applicant have been breached. In both types of actions, the court has a general power to make such orders to restrain or remedy the breach as it sees fit.

Tasmania

The public may bring civil proceedings where a person contravenes or fails to comply with the *Land Use Planning and Approvals Act* 1993 (Tas) (including contraventions of permits issued in respect of pollution) if they have, in the opinion of the Tribunal, a proper interest in the subject matter of the appeal.[77]

South Australia

The public may bring civil proceedings in the Environment, Resources and Development Court for an order to:

(a) restrain or remedy a breach of the Act;

(b) rectify any resulting environmental damage;

(c) pay damages for injury, loss or damage to property as a result of a contravention of the Act;

(d) pay exemplary damages;

(e) enforce the provisions of an environment performance agreement.[78]

---

76 See Stein, P, "A Specialist Environmental Court: An Australian Experience", in Robinson D and Dunkely J, *Public Interest Perspectives in Environmental Law* (Wiley Chancery, London, 1995), pp 255-74.

77 *Land Use Planning and Approvals Act* 1993 (Tas) s 64.

78 *Environment Protection Act* 1993 (SA) s 104.

Those who can bring these proceedings include those whose interests are affected by the subject matter of the application and any other person with the leave of the court.[79] The court may only grant leave for any person if the proceedings will not be an abuse of process, there is a real or significant likelihood that the requirements for the making of an order would be satisfied and it is in the public interest that the proceedings be brought.[80]

Queensland

The public may bring civil proceedings in the Planning and Environment Court for orders to restrain or remedy an offence against the Act.[81] Those who may bring such proceedings include:

(a) those whose interests are affected by the subject matter of the proceeding; and
(b) someone else with the lead of the court even though they do not have a proprietary, material, financial or special interest in the subject matter of the proceeding.

There are hurdles to overcome in order for the court to grant leave to a person to bring civil proceedings. The court must be satisfied that:

(a) environmental harm has been or is likely to be caused; and
(b) the proceedings are not an abuse of process of the court;
(c) there is a real or significant likelihood that the requirements of making an order would be satisfied;
(d) it is in the public interest that proceedings should be brought;
(e) written notice has been given to the Minister, administering authority requesting proceedings be brought and such proceedings have not been brought;
(f) the person is able adequately to represent the public interest in the conduct of the proceedings;
(a) the court may grant leave to bring proceedings subject to conditions including conditions requiring security for the payment of costs and conditions requiring undertakings for damages.[82]

Australian Capital Territory

Section 127 of the *Environment Protection Act* 1997 (ACT) provides that any person may, with the leave of the Supreme Court, make an application for an order under s 128. Section 128 allows the court to make certain orders, where it is satisfied that the respondent has or is contravening, or there is a significant likelihood that the respondent will contravene, an environmental authorisation, an environment protection order or a provision of the Act. The court can make interim

---

79   *Environment Protection Act* 1993 (SA) s 104(7)(b) and (c).
80   Ibid. *s* 104(8).
81   *Environmental Protection Act* 1994 (Qld) s 194.
82   Ibid, s 194(2).

and final orders including ordering the respondent to remedy the contravention, to restrain from continuing to commit the contravention, and to restrain from committing the threatened or anticipated contravention. In addition, the court can make other orders as it sees fit.

Victoria/Western Australia

The public has no right to bring civil or criminal proceedings to enforce either the *Environment Protection Act* 1970 (Vic) or the *Environmental Protection Act* 1986 (WA).

COSTS IN PUBLIC INTEREST LITIGATION

It is one thing to provide open standing provisions to allow the public to enforce legislation designed to protect the environment, it is another to see them used. Without rules and procedures that remove traditional hurdles to the public interest plaintiff, the efficacy of open standing provisions will be reduced. In New South Wales, for example, the Land and Environment Court has developed a doctrine of not awarding costs against the unsuccessful public interest plaintiff in certain circumstances.[83] The merits of the doctrine were outlined by Stein J in *Oshlack v Richmond River Shire Council*:[84]

> In summary I find the litigation to be properly characterised as public interest litigation. The basis of the challenge was arguable, raising serious and significant issues resulting in important interpretation of new provisions relating to the protection of endangered fauna. The application concerned a publicly notorious site amidst a continuing controversy. Mr Oshlack had nothing to gain from the litigation other than the worthy motive of seeking to uphold environmental law and the preservation of endangered fauna. Important issues relevant to the ambit and future administration of subject development consent were determined including the developer's acceptance of the need for a fauna impact study for stage 2. These issues have implications for the Council, the developer and the public.

However, after Stein J refused to award costs in favour of the successful respondent, the respondent appealed to the Court of Appeal arguing that, in the exercise of his judicial discretion, Stein J had taken irrelevant matters into account.[85] The Court of Appeal allowed the appeal and awarded costs in favour of the successful respondent council. It argued, unanimously, that it had to follow High Court's decision in *Latoudis v Casey*[86] despite the fact that that case concerned costs in criminal proceedings.

---

83   The decisions include *F Hannan Pty Ltd v Electricity Commission (NSW) (No 3)* (1985) 66 LGRA 306; *Prineas v Forestry Commission for New South Wales* (1983) 49 LGRA 402; *Cambell v Minister for Environmental Planning* (unreported, Land and Environment Ct, Cripps J, No 40061 of 1987); *Nettheim v Minister for Planning and Local Government* (unreported, Land and Environment Ct, Cripps J, No 40139 of 1988); *Rundle v Tweed Shire Council (No 2)* (1989) LGRA 21; *Liverpool City Council v Roads and Traffic Authority (No 2)* (1992) 75 LGRA 210.

84   (1993) 82 LGERA 222 at 246.

85   *Richmond River Shire Council v Oshlack* (1996) 91 LGERA 99.

86   (1990) 170 CLR 534.

But, recently the High Court reversed (by a 3/2 majority) this decision of the Court of Appeal.[87] Brennan CJ and McHugh J (both dissenting) followed the decision in *Latoudis*. It was no surprise that McHugh J did so as his was the leading judgment in that case and his decision was followed by all three judges of the Court of Appeal. Gaudron and Gummow JJ on the other hand, held that the true issue is not whether the case involved "public interest litigation". Rather, they considered that the question was whether the subject-matter, the scope and purpose of s 69 of the *Land and Environment Court Act* 1979 (which grants to the court the discretion to award costs) was such that Stein J's reasons were irrelevant to the exercise of the discretion conferred by that section.[88] They held that s 69 should not to be so interpreted. If it was, they considered that the principle would be hardened into rules of law. If this was the outcome, the discretion conferred by s 69 would become irrelevant. Their Honours held that the decision in *Latoudis* was not determinative of the question of costs in this case, as this case dealt with civil rather than criminal litigation.

Kirby J, in a separate judgment, also distinguished the decision in *Latoudis* arguing that it in no way was authority for a general rule governing the exercise of all unqualified statutory cost discretions. He took a broader view of the objects, scope and purpose of the legislation, particularly the broad standing provided by s 123 of the *Environmental Planning and Assessment Act* 1979. His Honour noted the importance that Parliament had placed upon giving individuals the right to enforce environmental law and the importance of ensuring the awarding of costs does not frustrate that right:

> The proper approach to the exercise of a statutory discretion may be illuminated by the particular language in which it is expressed and the purpose for which it has been provided. ... Given that statutory context and the clear purpose of Parliament to permit, and even encourage, individuals and groups to exercise functions in the enforcement of environmental law before the Land and Environment Court, a rigid application of the compensatory principle in costs orders would be completely impermissible. It would discourage, frustrate or even prevent the achievement of Parliament's particular purposes.[89]

The importance of the High Court's decision in *Oshlack* lies in the fact that it lifts a potentially very substantial practical barrier to those who seek to have enforced environmental rights or duties in law that are likely to benefit others as much, if not more, than themselves. It is indeed appropiate given the inclusive nature of environmental protection, that such litigants not be effectively blocked from seeking enforcement in the face of the certainty of costs being awarded against them should their argument, in the end, not succeed.

EMERGING TRENDS

The provisions discussed in this chapter are mostly of recent origin and reflect a new maturity in environmental law. The statutes now incorporate a range of more

---

87   See *Oshlack v Richmond River Council* [1998] HCA 11, 25 February 1998.

88   Ibid at 31.

89   Ibid at 5.

sophisticated regulatory techniques tools that give regulatory authorities the capacity to deal with complex and problematic pollution issues. Of the new initiatives, one of most significant is the formalisation of opportunities for the community to contribute to policy and administration and to empower those who wish to protect and improve their environment. In this respect, the legislation gives effect to principle 10 of the Rio Declaration on Environment and Development which provides that:

> Environmental issues are best handled with the participation of all concerned citizens, at the relevant level. At the national level, each individual shall have appropriate access to information concerning the environment that is held by public authorities, including information on hazardous material and activities in their communities, and the opportunity to participate in decision-making processes, States shall facilitate and encourage public awareness and participation by making information widely available. Effective access to judicial and administrative proceedings, including redress and remedy, shall be provided.

While the Australian statutes do not provide a substantive right to a clean environment, most of the statutes do adopt various values and normative positions. In practice, these provisions amount to a right to participate in decisions which affect the environment and to take action to protect it. In many respects, these rights allow communities access to justice in a way that a substantive right, hampered by definitional issues, could not. With environmental quality degrading so quickly, resolving practical problems is often more productive than pious points of principle.

While some of these provisions are novel, many follow trends developing elsewhere. For example, both Federal and State laws in the United States have provided for civil enforcement for many years, and a significant body of public interest civil enforcement case law has developed.[90] Douglas-Scott has examined the evolution of environmental law in the European Union finding the emergence of three specific rights: the right to information, the right to participation and rights to obtain legal redress.[91]

By providing such valuable rights to participate in policy design and implementation, environmental law has been important in ensuring the protection of certain human rights. Within the broad rubric of environmental law, pollution law in particular, offers considerable protection of the human right to health both at home and in the workplace. It also ensures valuable rights to civil enforcement and judicial review if these human rights, as well as other legal rights, are infringed. In addition, environmental laws have been fundamentally important in developing a jurisprudence which expressly incorporates public participation, and which removes traditional hurdles of litigation by liberalising rules of standing and the discretion to award costs.

The evolution of these rights in pollution law has no doubt been prompted by the alarming deterioration in some aspects of the Australian environment.

---

90 See, for example, Frye R, "Citizens' Enforcement of the US Clean Water Act", in Thomas, P (ed), *Water Pollution Law and Liability* (Proceedings of Committee F International Bar Association Residential Seminar on International Environmental Law, Graham & Trotman, London, 1992), pp 183-96. See also Robbins, D, "Public Interest Environmental Litigation in the United States", in Robinson and Dunkley, above, n 76, pp 3-38.

91 Douglas-Scott, above, n 14, pp 109-28.

Governments have attempted to negotiate the competing interests of bureaucratic resistance, industry pressure and public demand by developing the various procedural rights and mechanisms. This process has not been without debate and, in some jurisdictions such as Victoria, there has been a recent reversal of some important procedural rights.[92]

The development of these rights provides a wider and more meaningful avenue to participate in the democratic process[93] and provides access to justice in a way that standard domestic regulation or tort law cannot. In particular, the Australian developments in this area recognise that it is important for environmental groups to have the right to take action on behalf of their members.[94] This can be seen as part of a wider international trend towards providing non-governmental organisations with various rights in the various international environmental regimes. This, it has been argued, has assisted in the effectiveness of these regimes by calling to account holders of public power in their national courts for failing to fulfil commitments made at the international level, and by directly representing sectoral or special interests at the international level.[95]

The rights described in this chapter are far from ideal, restricted unnecessarily in some jurisdictions, and nor are they by themselves adequate. The evidence of recent assessments of the state of the Australian environment suggests that to ensure a future healthy environment, the rights of the public need to be further entrenched into political and legal discourse, policy-making and legislation. In this respect, necessarily, environmental protection has much in common with the wider project of developing appropriate human rights.

---

92 See Cristoff, P, "Degreening Government in the Garden State: Environment Policy under the Kennett Government" (1998) 15(1) *Environmental Planning Law Journal* 10.

93 See generally Pateman, C, *Participation and Democratic Theory* (Cambridge University Press, Cambridge, 1970); Birch, A, *The Concepts and Theories of Modern Democracy* (Routledge, New York, 1993).

94 For example, s 252(5) of the *Protection of the Environment Operations Act* 1997 (NSW) provides that "[a]ny person on whose behalf proceedings are brought is entitled to contribute to or provide for the payment of the legal costs and expenses incurred by the person bringing the proceedings".

95 Cameron and Mackenzie, above, n 14, p 152.

11

INFORMATION TECHNOLOGY LAW AND HUMAN RIGHTS

Christopher Arup and Greg Tucker

WHICH HUMAN RIGHTS?

The responsibility for this chapter requires us to juggle several dynamic relationships. The first is the relationship between human rights and our particular field, that of information technology. Today, information technology is broadly conceived to be a combination of computing and communications media. The technology promises access to greatly enhanced means of producing, distributing and using information of various kinds. In this way, it can be seen that the technology carries much positive potential for the advancement of human rights. But it can also be seen to give rise to certain dangers for human rights, dangers that come with the capture of its powers, particularly by strong states or large private organisations. So we suggest that the relationship between information technology and human rights proves to be a complex and contingent one. For example, respect for the right of privacy might necessitate controls being placed on certain uses of the technology, yet that same respect could actually encourage more people to take up the technology, and the technology may in part provide the means to ensure that respect. The complexity of the relationship between information technology and human rights is compounded by its newness. As such, the relationship is far from fully developed or understood. Our treatment in this chapter of its legal framework and regulation is therefore necessarily more conceptual and speculative than is the case with the form of other chapters in this book.

Our discussion also requires us to appraise within this context the relationship between different rights. If information technology seems to epitomise innovation and change, it presents us with legal and human rights issues which are perhaps not so novel. It is not possible here to provide a comprehensive analysis of all these issues, in particular or general form; in these respects, we defer to the work of others and especially the other contributors to this volume. These issues start of course with an identification and definition of the rights which are relevant to this realm of social interaction.[1] They progress to the problems of implementation of such rights, and not the least the balancing, even the reconciliation where possible, of the various rights which are engaged, where they might tend to clash.[2] In this chapter, we see the rights most directly engaged by information technology as the rights to

---

1   See Ch 1 by Kinley in this volume.
2   Ibid.

privacy, property, freedom of speech, education and development. Without hoping to resolve the issues, we identify challenges that will be encountered in balancing and reconciling these rights. The clash between freedom of speech and privacy is most readily appreciated but other clashes can arise, such as a clash between property and freedom of speech or education and development, depending in part on how the rights are fashioned.

Definition of human rights and indeed the actual effects of rights depend on the different contexts in which they are situated. The context for our discussion of human rights cannot be just technological. The relationship between information technology and human rights depend on economic, political and cultural context too. In particular, the context shapes the role of the state, a role which is vital to the realisation of basic human rights.[3] To appreciate this, van Hoof[4] suggests we think in terms of the obligations which would need to be applied if rights were to be made effective. Support for human rights commonly begins with the kind of rights that require respect from government: those which oblige the state not to encroach itself on the freedom of individuals. In the liberal tradition, van Hoof is suggesting that the rights and freedoms requiring respect by the state itself are often the first to be recognised and accepted; they enjoy lexical priority and legal enforceability. As we move away from these kinds of rights, less legal support seems to be forthcoming and, if claims to rights clash, the later rights are likely to give way to the former. But it is worth noting that civil and political rights can also necessitate positive action on the part of the state, to protect them from violations by others with the private power to encroach upon them. Property rights demand this intervention, so too, rights to freedom of speech and privacy. For example, to be implemented effectively, the right to privacy may need to include the right to find out that information is held by others and to have that information deleted or corrected.[5]

However, some human rights, namely social and cultural rights, seem to demand more again of the state if they are to be effective. Such rights can only be ensured by the state actively creating in society the conditions necessary to bring about their realisation. Indeed, they may require promotion in a more programmatic way by the state. Such programs rely on the resources of the state, which it must in turn enlist from those who command private resources. A common critique of the social rights is that they lack the specificity as well as the support needed to operationalise them as truly enforceable legal rights.[6] Rights to education and development also fall into this category, but so too does the right to freedom of

---

3   Bailey, P, *Human Rights: Australia in an International Context* (Butterworths, Sydney, 1990), p 12.

4   Van Hoof, G, "The Legal Nature of Economic, Social and Cultural Rights: A Rebuttal of Some Traditional Views", in Alston, P, and Tomasevski, K (eds), *A Right to Food* (Martinus Nijhoff, Utrecht, 1984), p105.

5   For example, both the *Privacy Act* 1988 (Cth) (Pt III, especially s 14 (Information Privacy Principle 7)), and the *Freedom of Information Act* 1982 (Cth) (s 48) provide such rights of access and correction. See further, Australian Law Reform Commission (ALRC) and Administrative Review Council (ARC), *Open Government: A Review of the Federal Freedom of Information Act 1982*, ALRC Report No 77/ARC Report No 40 (1995), Chs 4, 5 and 12; and, for a discussion of the importance of such access to official information to the protection and promotion of human rights through administrative law, Ch 4 by McMillan and Williams in this volume.

6   Steiner, H and Alston, P, *International Human Rights in Context: Law, Politics, Morals* (Clarendon Press, Oxford, 1996), p 269.

speech if it is defined as the freedom to seek, receive and impart information and ideas through any media and regardless of frontiers.[7] Such a right depends upon capacities as well as liberties; so implementation depends, for instance, on universal service and non-discriminatory access obligations being applied to core communications carriers.[8]

Our context highlights this issue. Information technology has provided authoritarian states with capacity to monitor, contain and discipline their subjects but information technology and the human rights associated with it have also done much to undermine their hold.[9] Today, this struggle continues. But the formative context increasingly favours a limited role for the state. In many countries, we see a retraction and privatisation of government's role in the provision of information technologies through schools, libraries, telecommunications, publishing and broadcasting. So a basic problematic becomes the implementation of rights that would seem to run counter to the free play of market forces.[10] Correspondingly, rights are more likely to attract institutional support if they can be linked with the commercial benefits which flow from the marketplace. Sometimes this means that the human rights take on a commercial flavour, for instance, intellectual property or freedom of speech assume more of the character of economic or industrial than moral or cultural rights. In other instances, putative human rights give way to the claims of commercial rights; thus, personal privacy has had to coexist with the information gathering and dealing activities of media and finance industries.

Information technology itself presents huge obstacles to the effective regulation of certain rights. While some components of the technology have assumed a large scale and fixed position –for example, main-frame computers, satellite transponders or telephone wires – minaturisation and diffusion have placed capacity within the reach of many people. The clearest consequence is the enormous difficulty regulators face trying to prevent commercial enterprises, informal networks and domestic households from receiving, copying and disseminating unauthorised information.

An added complication today is the globalisation of such practices. If governments are persuaded of the need to implement certain human rights, the information technology challenges directly their regulatory competence to do so. The technology enables information to be transmitted privately along routes that circumvent the national territories on which legal jurisdictions have been based. This enabling enhances certain liberties, but it also makes transgressions of rights harder for the national authorities to control. Domestically, locals develop orientations and affinities which cut across national lines and the state finds its authority to define national interest or public morality challenged. If governments try to extend their regulatory reach, they come into conflict with the laws of other

---

7   International Covenant on Civil and Political Rights (ICCPR) art 19.

8   See discussion under "Access to the technology" below.

9   See generally, Metzl, J, "Information Technology and Human Rights" (1997) 18 *Human Rights Quarterly* 705.

10   Alston, P, "International Law and the Human Right to Food", in Alston and Tomasevski, above, n 4, p 54.

countries which reflect differing economic, political or cultural perspectives.[11] They also run up against the norms of free trade. International regulatory cooperation and multilateral standard setting may be needed if rights are to be realised in such a situation.

With those brief remarks about context, the first part of the chapter proceeds to focus on the right to own property which is among the rights enumerated in the *Universal Declaration of Human Rights* (UDHR).[12] We shall try to characterise this right and then relate it to other rights which seem germane to this realm, including the rights to freedom of speech, education and development. The second part of the chapter takes, as its starting point, the right to privacy and engages the same process. The analysis cannot expect to be comprehensive and the emphasis is on rights which have, or potentially have, domestic legal enforceability.

STATE SUPPORT FOR
INTELLECTUAL PROPERTY RIGHTS

In the realm of information technology, the key kind of property is intellectual property. Rights to this manner of property are invoked to capture the value of both information and technology, not just of traditional literary and artistic works but other expressive subject-matter such as records and films, indeed to all manner of utilitarian media such as computer programs and data bases. Where the right to physical property is now a widely accepted right, controversy can still surround the right to appropriate such intangibles as ideas, observations, techniques and images.

The discussion often starts with a suggestion that the subject-matter of intellectual property has tendencies to be (what economists would call) a public good. In contrast to physical property, we can think of an idea being shared by as many people as possible without any destruction of the resource itself.[13] But producers say they need to be able to control access if they are to obtain a return on the often sizeable investment they have made in its production. The milieu of the new technology undermines private self-help strategies to control access, whether they be technical, economic or cultural strategies, as much as it does government attempts to impose controls.[14] Producers seek legally enforceable rights from the state as a protection from other individuals who, without their authorisation, make hard or electronic copies of the information, or simply gain entry to the technology in order to display, view, browse and network the information it contains. The most relevant category of legal rights has been that of copyright and its neighbouring or related rights, though other categories of intellectual property such as patents and confidential information have also been enlisted to this cause.[15]

---

11 Arup, C, *Capturing the Value of Australian Online Content: Mapping the Regulatory Domain* (La Trobe University Online Media Project, School of Media Studies, Melbourne, 1997).

12 Article 17.

13 The nature of intellectual property is discussed throughout Boyle, J, *Shamans, Software and Spleens: Law and the Construction of the Information Society* (Harvard University Press, Cambridge, Mass, 1996).

14 Arup, C, *Innovation, Policy and Law* (Cambridge University Press, Cambridge, 1993).

15 McKeough, J and Stewart, A, *Intellectual Property Law in Australia* (Butterworths, Sydney, 2nd ed, 1997), Ch 9.

Any market in intangibles must work within a very strong framework of legal rules. The state is asked to commit both its symbolic and material resources to ensuring the conditions in which claims to property can be realised.[16] Legislative, judicial and administrative infrastructure must be provided to meet the task of identifying appropriable subject-matter and settling individual entitlements to it. This recognition of rights is at times backed up with coercive powers. Lately, the authors of international intellectual property instruments have understood this point well and made it an essential component of the relevant protection stipulations that states provide effective mechanisms for the civil enforcement of such rights. Two important instruments for our purposes, the 1994 Agreement on Trade-Related Intellectual Property Rights (TRIPs) from the World Trade Organisation (WTO)[17] and the 1996 Copyright Treaty from the World Intellectual Property Organization (WIPO),[18] do so.

These instruments are shaping the future of the law in Australia. In the Uruguay round, Australia supported the formation of the TRIPs agreement and, in becoming a member of the WTO, adopted its provisions. The Australian Government has since enacted amendments to the relevant local legislation, the *Copyright Act* 1968 (Cth), in order to ensure that it meets the requirements of TRIPs.[19] Australia has long been a party to the Berne Convention for the Protection of Literary and Artistic Works 1886 (the Berne Convention). Australia participated actively in the Diplomatic Conference and supported the text of the WIPO Copyright Treaty. The Commonwealth government is expected to become a signatory soon and has issued a discussion paper in which it proposes to implement requirements of the Treaty.[20]

---

16 Bailey, above, n 3, p 12.

17 The TRIPs agreement is part of a package of agreements concluded within the Uruguay Round of the General Agreement on Tariffs and Trade (GATT). Adoption of the agreement is a condition of membership of the GATT's successor, the WTO. The text of the TRIPs agreement is contained in WTO, *Legal Documents Embodying the Results of the Uruguay Round of Multilateral Trade Negotiations* (The Legal Texts, WTO, Geneva, 1994). It is also available on-line at the WTO's web site, address: <http://www.unicc.org/wto>. For analysis of the agreement, see Blakeney, M, *Trade Related Aspects of Intellectual Property Rights: A Concise Guide to the TRIPs Agreement* (Sweet and Maxwell, London, 1996). The enforcement obligations are elaborated at length in arts 41-61.

18 The Diplomatic Conference convened by the WIPO concluded two Treaties in December 1996, the Copyright Treaty (which deals with works) and the Performances and Phonograms Treaty. The Treaties can be regarded as supplements to the established Berne Convention; those who sign the Treaties must also be prepared to adopt the Berne Convention. The texts of the Treaties are available from the WIPO's web site, address <http://www.wipo.org>. For analysis of the Treaties, see Cresswell, C, "Copyright Protection Enters the Digital Age: the New WIPO Treaties on Copyright & on Performances & Sound Recordings" (1997) 15 *Copyright Reporter* 4. In contrast to the TRIPs agreement, the enforcement obligation is stated in general terms; see art 14 of the Copyright Treaty.

19 *Copyright (World Trade Organisation Amendments) Act* 1994 (Cth).

20 Attorney-General and Minister for Communications and the Arts, *Copyright Reform and the Digital Agenda* (Discussion Paper, Attorney-General's Department, Canberra, 1997). The paper builds on earlier work in this area, including the report of the Copyright Convergence Group, *Highways to Change: Copyright in the New Communications Environment* (AGPS, Canberra, 1994); and the draft amendments circulated by the Minister for Justice, *Copyright Act Amendments: Proposed Provisions Implementing Government Decisions for Reform: Exposure Draft and Commentary* (Attorney-General's Department, Canberra, 1996). In respect of consideration of changes to performers' rights, see Attorney-General and Minister for Communications and the Arts, *Performers' Intellectual Property Rights: Scope of Extended Rights for Performers under the Copyright Act 1968* (Discussion Paper, Attorney-General's Department, Canberra, 1997).

We have more to say about these international instruments and their local implementation below.

It is worth noting that the protection packages extend to requirements that nation states commit the resources of their criminal law to the realisation of such rights, especially at the border where unauthorised copies are imported or exported. Thus, for example, customs officials have become involved in policing copyright laws.[21] The disembodied transmission of information technology, which transcends the physical borders of countries, has resulted in further international obligations, this time to criminalise devices that enable people to intercept satellite signals, crack encryption codes or enter computer banks.[22] Such offences which regulate directly dealings in the technology are designed not only to protect intellectual property, they may for instance be concerned to safeguard privacy. Offences relating to eavesdropping on telephone conversations provide one example, monitoring electronic transactions another.

Implementation of a right to intellectual property can also demand that the state call on the resources of private parties. A contemporary debate concerns the appropriate level of responsibility which "third persons", specifically those who provide the means to post or convey the intellectual property content, ought to carry for policing violations – for protecting or ensuring the right. Content producers wish to make such intermediaries responsible because it is unrealistic to police the domestic end users. Their responsibility is framed in terms of third party liability for authorising or contributing to an infringement by another person. The strictness of such liability became a major point of contention during the WIPO diplomatic conference to settle copyright on the digital environment.[23] At the Conference, a strong lobby against the extension to the digital technology of the rights afforded by copyright, such as rights of reproduction and communication, came from the telecommunications carriers and commercial internet access providers. Public access providers such as libraries were also concerned about liability. In addition, computer hardware manufacturers were opposed to the criminalisation of circumvention devices.[24] We can expect these players to be active in Australia too

---

21   So see *Copyright Act* 1968 (Cth) Pt V Div 7.

22   Both the Copyright Treaty (art 11) and the Performances and Phonograms Treaty (art 18) require contracting parties to provide adequate legal protection and effective legal remedies against the circumvention of effective technological measures that are used to in connection with the exercise of the rights of copyright. The Government proposes to enact appropriate offences, see Attorney-General and Minister for Communications and the Arts, *Copyright Reform and the Digital Agenda*, above, n 20, p 35.

23   The Copyright Treaty chose to leave the definition of liability to national legislation, though the agreed statements concerning the Treaty declared that "it is understood that the mere provision of physical facilities for enabling or making a communication does not of itself amount to communication within the meaning of the Treaty or the Berne Convention" (communication to the public is one of the exclusive rights conferred on the copyright holder under art 8 of the Treaty.). In Australia, the Commonwealth Government's 1997 *Copyright Reform and the Digital Agenda* Discussion Paper (above, n 20), foreshadows leaving the issue of liability to the general case law. But it does invite comment on a proposal to create a specific legislative exemption for internet service providers who provide warning notices to their subscribers; ibid, p 30.

24   For reports of the proceedings of the Conference, see the November and December 1996 issues of the World Intellectual Property Report; see also the commentary by Cresswell, above, n 18, p 4 (Cresswell was head of the Australian delegation to the Conference).

when the time comes to make decisions on how to implement the requirements of the Copyright and the Performances and Phonograms Treaties.[25]

INTELLECTUAL PROPERTY RIGHTS AS HUMAN RIGHTS

In the European tradition, which provided the foundation for international intellectual property, such rights are associated with the idea of an individual author. But of course today many works are taken up by others, often corporate entities, then reworked and transformed into other media. The so-called multimedia forms involve the manipulation, adaptation and recombination of bits drawn from all manner of existing works. To guard against the most disrespectful of these practices, authors may be accorded rights of attribution and integrity (so-called "moral rights"), including the right to object to the derogatory treatment of their work, even after they have assigned their work in the marketplace. Article 27(2) of the UDHR recognises this interest by declaring a person's "right to protection of the moral and material interests resulting from any scientific, literary or artistic production of which he is the author".

Moral rights are already embodied in the long-standing copyright instrument, the Berne Convention.[26] They were not however to be incorporated in the TRIPs agreement. Countries such as the United States and Australia which have favoured a more economic or industrial view of copyright than the Europeans and others, have preferred not to protect moral rights. However, Australia is now introducing a version of such rights into the *Copyright Act.*[27]

Notwithstanding the issue of moral rights, much of the subject-matter of contemporary intellectual property cannot be identified with the persona of the individual author and so cannot call upon what is perhaps the core rationale for many human rights. Intellectual property rights commonly end up being held by a corporation and, in the international context, they are thus likely to become the trade-related rights of corporate world citizens. Does this recognition of the collective nature of intellectual property rights then offer support to other groups, such as Indigenous communities? Where other strategies have failed, Indigenous groups may look to intellectual property as a means to protect their culture from misappropriation. Yet, intellectual property rights present such groups with a dilemma: while they offer a kind of protection, they also introduce these cultural artifacts into the value system of the marketplace, dividing communities and selling

---

25 There is also resistance among television broadcasters, film producers and record producers to the extension of rights to performers such as musicians and actors. Both in the international instruments and in the Australian legislation, performers rights have fallen short of the copyright and related rights afforded to others.

26 Article 6bis.

27 See Copyright Amendment Bill 1997 Sch 1. For background see Minister for Communications and the arts and Minister for Justice, *Proposed Moral Rights Legislation for Copyright Creators* (Discussion Paper, Department of Communications and the Arts, Canberra, 1994); and also, Paras, K, "Is Australia on the Road to Formally Recognizing Moral Rights, or is this one International Obligation which will never be Formally Implemented?" (1997) 2 *Media and arts Law Review* 16.

their heritage.[28] In Australia where the question is germane, sensitively handled cases, such as *Milpurrurru v Indofurn Pty Ltd*,[29] have highlighted such a quandary.

As intellectual property moves away from an association with natural persons, it seeks more of an instrumental or utilitarian justification.[30] Often, from a modernist Western perspective, it is to be judged according to the contribution it can make to such socially worthwhile activities as the production and dissemination of works, and progress in science and the arts. Thus, its contribution to social goals such as communication, education and development comes directly into consideration, among the other goals we suggested initially can be cast in terms of human rights.

THE SCOPE OF THE RIGHT
TO FREEDOM OF SPEECH

In relating other rights to intellectual property rights, we begin with the right of freedom of speech, loosely equating it with expression or communication. The *International Covenant on Civil and Political Rights* (ICCPR) states in art 19 that everyone has the right to freedom of opinion and expression. This right is primarily supported by its association with the development or fulfilment of the individual, including the opportunity which it might provide for the individual to participate in social life. At the same time, it is argued, a contribution is made to the health of society overall, particularly to its conduct along democratic lines.

Within van Hoof's typology, the right to freedom of speech is most likely to be asserted against the encroachments of the state itself, say through the imposition of censorship. Censorship of information technology is a human rights issue, as governments seek to control access to information, emanating for instance from outside the country, on a variety of political, social or cultural grounds. In Western societies, the censorship debate often centres on pornography. In the United States, the Supreme Court has recently ruled that legislation limiting the availability of pornography on the Internet is contrary to the first amendment.[31] Locally, where the constitutional position is not so explicit, the Australian Broadcasting Authority has nonetheless favoured self-regulation.[32]

---

28   Ziff, B and Rao, P (eds), *Borrowed Power: Essays on Cultural Appropriation* (Rutgers University Press, New Brunswick, 1997), p 8.

29   (1994) 130 ALR 659. For further discussion, see Ch 5 by Neilson and Martin in this volume. See also, Minister for Communications and the arts and Minister for Justice, *Stopping the Rip-Offs – Intellectual Property Protection for Aboriginal and Torres Strait Islander Peoples* (Department of Communications and the Arts, Canberra, 1994) and O'Brien, C, "Protecting Secret-Sacred Designs – Indigenous Culture and Intellectual Property Law" (1997) 2 *Media and arts Law Review* 57. Note now the case concerning the Aboriginal flag, *Thomas v Brown* (unreported, Fed Ct, Sheppard J, 9 April 1997).

30   Drahos, P, *A Philosophy of Intellectual Property* (Dartmouth, Aldershot, 1996), Ch 9.

31   *Reno v American Civil Liberties Union* 138 L Ed 2d 849 (1997). The court saw the *Communications Decency Act* as a content-based, blanket restriction on speech which could not be considered as reasonable regulation with regard to time, place or manner of speech. See Vick, D, "The Internet and the First Amendment" (1998) 60 *Modern Law Review* 414.

32   Australian Broadcasting Authority, *Investigation into the Content of On-Line Services* (AGPS, Canberra, 1996).

The ICCPR concedes that the right should be subject to restrictions necessary for respect of the rights or reputations of others.[33] The right to privacy can provide such a justification; so too, the right to a fair trial[34] might justify controls being placed on the freedoms and powers of the new audio-visual media.[35] But the intersection of two rights claims creates a balancing problem: when should the impact on the other right be considered to outweigh the encroachment on free speech. In Australia, a poignant case concerned the argument that legislative controls on political advertising were needed to temper the electoral advantages obtained by wealthier citizens.[36]

The ICCPR also concedes that the right might be qualified if the protection of national security or public order, or public health or morals, is at stake.[37] In the cold war climate which prevailed post-war, international organisations such as UNESCO were caught up in a fierce political struggle over the scope to be given to "free flows of information".[38] A few countries, such as the Peoples Republic of China, are trying to maintain government restrictions on flows, but today the clash is just as likely to result when free trade claims to market access meet with defences of local cultural integrity.

With the broad shift to a post-industrial society, which places emphasis on knowledges and images, much speech assumes an economic complexion. Where grounds such as national security or public morals are invoked to restrict the flow of speech, free traders are inclined to allege that the motive is the protection of local industry from foreign competition. This is perhaps too simple an interpretation. Countries such as Singapore and Malaysia seek to control exposure to what they see as contaminating cultures by confining such on-line communications to special corridors and sectors.[39] Western countries (such as France, Canada, and Australia itself[40]) have also imposed controls, such as limits on the foreign ownership of communications media, restrictions on the employment of foreign personnel, and quotas on the broadcasting of foreign products, in an attempt to safeguard national cultural values.

---

33   Article 19(3)(a).

34   ICCPR art 14.

35   Walker, C, "Fundamental Rights, Fair Trials and the New Audio-Visual Sector" (1996) 59 *Modern Law Review* 517.

36   *Australian Capital Television v Commonwealth* (1992) 177 CLR 106. The court found that the legislation was trumped by a constitutional right to freedom of political speech. See further, Ch 3 by Gageler and Glass in this volume.

37   Article 19(3)(b).

38   Alleyne, M, *International Power and International Communication* (St Martin's Press, New York, 1995), p 41.

39   See, for instance, the report in (1996) 124 *Communications Update* 15.

40   For example, *Broadcasting Services Act* 1992 (Cth) s 122; see further Australian Broadcasting Authority, *Australian Content on Pay TV*, Report to the Minister for Communications and the arts (Australian Broadcast Authority, Sydney, 1997). These defences are now under pressure from free trade agreements; see in particular the WTO General Agreement on Trade in Services and the negotiations surrounding the Organisation for Economic Co-operation and Development's (OECD) draft Multilateral Agreement on Investment (MAI). The Australian-New Zealand Closer Economic Relations Trade Agreement has been the source of a legal challenge to the Australian content standard, see *Australian Broadcasting Authority v Project Blue Sky* (1996) 141 ALR 397; the challenge was upheld by the High Court: [1998] HCA 28 (18 April 1998).

INTELLECTUAL PROPERTY
AND FREEDOM OF SPEECH

A right to intellectual property will intersect with a right to freedom of speech. On the one hand, intellectual property may stimulate communication. The property right is meant to give producers the security they need to release their information; they can rely upon a legal means to regulate those who are not prepared voluntarily to respect their conditions of access. In particular, they have a basis on which to obtain a recompense for the investment they have made in the production of that information. In the case of published works, the greatest threat to the investor is the making of multiple copies and intellectual property becomes a means to obtain a fee from the copiers. Indeed, in some instances, the state has gone further and provided the scheme to fix and collect those fees.[41]

Nevertheless, intellectual property has been employed on occasions to control speech.[42] Thus, the British Government sought to invoke a claim to confidential information in the *Spycatcher* case[43] and in the case of *Commonwealth v John Fairfax*,[44] the Australian Government asserted copyright as a way of suppressing a newspaper article about the conduct of foreign affairs. It should be understood that, in such cases, the government is appealing to national security as the justification for the suppression and that intellectual property law is being employed as a means to that end. Perhaps the more interesting contemporary case involves the efforts of private interests to suppress commentary on their affairs, there is an overlap with privacy here, especially in respect of protection against breach of confidences;[45] defamation laws have also been used in certain jurisdictions.[46] The conventional state/citizen or public/private divide has tended to discount the importance of free speech in commercial affairs, yet society may benefit from counter-balances to the speech power of private corporations.[47]

Copyright law is said to protect the expression of an idea but not the idea itself from being copied. From within copyright law, this idea/expression distinction might provide an opening for freedom of speech. The idea underlying a communication can be engaged, just so long as the particular way in which it has been expressed is not reproduced. However, copyright does limit freedom of speech in those situations in which the commentator wishes to reproduce the expression

---

41 The *Copyright Act* 1968 (Cth) provides for the collective administration of licences, including the services of a Copyright Tribunal.

42 See the examples provided throughout Drahos, P, "Decentring Communication: The Dark Side of Intellectual Property", in Campbell, T and Sadurski, W (eds), *Freedom of Communication* (Dartmouth, Aldershot, 1994).

43 *Attorney-General (UK) v Guardian Newspapers (No 2)* [1988] 3 WLR 776. But the House of Lords would not grant an injunction to restrain further publication.

44 (1980) 147 CLR 39.

45 See, for example, *Warne v Genex Corporation Pty Ltd* (1996) 35 IPR 284.

46 The *cause célèbre* is the McDonalds defamation case in the United Kingdom; see Vidal, J, *McLibel: Burger Culture on Trial* (Macmillan, London, 1997). For a discussion related to Australia, see Richardson, M, "Freedom of Political Opinion and Intellectual Property Law in Australia" (1997) 19 *European Intellectual Property Review* 631.

47 MacMillan Patfield, F, "Towards a Reconciliation of Free Speech and Copyright" (1996) *Yearbook of Media and Entertainment Law* 199 at 206.

itself; maybe the commentator wishes to hold it up to scrutiny in a critical or satirical manner, and one of the most interesting issues recently has concerned the freedom to parody popular political and commercial figures.[48]

In that situation, the commentator must look instead to any exception made in the law to infringement of copyright, such as the exception commonly made for "fair dealing". The concept of fair dealing ranges over a number of specific allowances which are concerned with the purpose and the extent of the dealing with the copyrighted work or other subject-matter. The *Copyright Act* contains fair dealing exceptions for such purposes as research or study, criticism or review, and reporting news.[49]

The use of intellectual property to suppress speech is the most extreme and unusual instance of a clash with freedom of speech. When we consult art 19 of the ICCPR on freedom of opinion and expression, we begin to see that the implications of the right to property may be more extensive. Embracing the freedom to seek and receive as well as impart information, it represents the interests of the consumers as well as the speakers of information. The consumer may just as much disapprove of the controls which governments place on content such as censorship. But the consumer may be interested in information for more practical purposes; we have said that, increasingly, information is treated as an economic and social resource. It is possible for intellectual property to obstruct the realisation of such a right if it is not suitably qualified. On this basis, the freedom complements rights to education and economic and social development. This connection is apparent if we cross-reference art 27 of the ICCPR which provides that "everyone has the right freely to participate in the cultural life of the community, to enjoy the arts and to share in scientific advancement and its benefits". Indeed, such freedom of speech may be one of the specific ways a broad aspirational goal like economic and social development can be translated into law.

THE RIGHT TO CONTROL COMMUNICATION TO THE PUBLIC

The flashpoint for these concerns is the extension of copyright, out from its core right of reproduction, to rights of distribution such as a right to control communication to the public. Spurred by international developments, this extension has been foreshadowed for Australia. But before identifying the new law, we should consider what the information technology places at stake here.

When works were fixed in a material form, and their reproduction could be controlled, producers were usually prepared to publish them. But it followed that the information contained in these works became available to anyone who was prepared to pay the price of a hard copy (such as a book or a disk); it was available too to those to whom the copy was subsequently circulated. The technology of reprography has

---

48 For example, it is understood that Pauline Hanson is to pursue litigation over the ABC's Triple J compilation of the song "Backdoor Man".

49 See ss 41-43. Note that the provisions are part of the Copyright Law Review Committee's (CLRC) simplification reference; see CLRC, *Simplification of the Fair Dealing Provisions of the Copyright Act 1968*, Issues Paper (AGPS, Canberra, 1997). The Committee is yet to report on its reference.

already of course become an enormous problem for content producers and publishers, it is a major reason why third party liability is in issue, but the on-line media further enhance the opportunities for users to access the material, in some situations obviating the need entirely to obtain a hard copy. At the same time, this technology can enable a superior service to be provided – a service of location, authentication, selection, and presentation of information – which greatly enhances its accessibility and utility. Commercial providers would like to charge users for access to these valuable on-line information services, whether they retain copies or not, or maybe to charge suppliers for the service of delivering such an audience.

Arguably, on-line communication involves at certain points the reproduction of the works But to avoid a difficult legal issue, and especially to ensure that the activities of the intermediaries are encompassed, the rights of the holder need to be extended beyond reproduction. So the focus for copyright law turns to the right to control access to a service transmitted on-line; for some it becomes criminalisation of the theft of a service. However, it is the critics' contention that should such control be established, freedom of communication will be threatened. The underlying ideas and knowledges will be just as inaccessible as their particular forms of expression, for those people who cannot meet the entry or visitation charges.[50] The result will be a new resource inequity based on exclusive access to information services.[51]

The TRIPs agreement did not address the question of copyright in the digital on-line environment. However, the new WIPO Copyright Treaty is most notable for requiring those countries which become contracting parties to provide an exclusive right "to authorise any communication to the public by wire or wireless means, including the making available to the public of works in such a way that members of the public may access these works from a place or at a time individually chosen by them".[52] The right is recognition of the interests of the owners of copyright in works.[53] Even before the advent of the new Treaty, the Australian Government had drafted amendments to the copyright legislation to institute a broadly based, technology neutral right of transmission to the public.[54] The right was to protect works and other subject-matter including films, sound recordings and broadcasts. Now the government foreshadows both a transmission right and a right of making available to the public.[55]

---

50   Van Caenegem, W, "Copyright, Communications and New Technologies" (1995) 23 *Federal Law Review* 322 at 325.

51   See generally, Mosco, V, and Wasko, J (eds), *The Political Economy of Information* (University of Wisconsin Press, Madison, 1988).

52   Article 8.

53   A second Treaty, the Performances and Phonograms Treaty, splits the right of making available from the right of communication, making the first an exclusive right and the second a right to equitable remuneration; see above, n 18 and accompanying text.

54   Minister for Justice, above, n 20.

55   A right of making available is an additional right because it catches those who, rather than send material, place it where members of the public can access it individually, for example in a server. It remains to determine when the material is communicated or made available "to the public". The Commonwealth government's *Copyright Reform and the Digital Agenda* Discussion Paper proposes to leave this concept to the case law, above n 20, p 26. In this regard, the High Court decision, in *Telstra Corporation v Australasian Performing Rights Association* (1997) 146 ALR 649, will be a key source.

The extension of copyright to these new rights leads us on to the question whether the familiar exceptions such as fair dealing and other limitations on copyright should be made available. The suppliers of on-line services say that such allowances, especially for browsing on-line, would strike at the very way the services are to be exploited.[56] Furthermore, the technology will be able to provide its own means to meter and charge for such small uses. But schools, libraries and other public access institutions have already expressed concern about the impact of unmitigated rights over access, especially if the on-line media were to become the main source of information.[57]

Article 9(2) of the Berne Convention concedes space for certain limitations and exceptions to be made to the right to reproduce a work. The parties to the Convention may do so in "certain special cases", provided that their legislation neither conflicts with a normal exploitation of the work or unreasonably prejudices the legitimate interests of the author. Professor Ricketson[58] observes that art 9(2) was agreed at a time when the facilities of the new technology were not available; the paradigm case would have been a researcher taking notes by hand. Today, as well as conceding fair dealing, some countries have facilitated schemes for the non-voluntary licensing of various kinds of intellectual property, subject in some instances to the payment of equitable remuneration. For example, in Australia, non-voluntary licensing is extended to educational institutions to allow them to make multiple copies of works for distribution to their students.[59] Such a scheme enables the copyright holder to collect a fee but, as some of us know from experience, the bounds of the licences are exceeded in practice and it is doubtful in any case whether art 9(2) accommodates such large scale copying. It might be worth noting that, after the Convention's protection for copyright was strengthened at Stockholm, a conference in Paris added a schedule to the Convention that established a (limited) set of circumstances in which *developing* counties are entitled to license the local reproduction of works for purposes of systematic instructional activities.

The TRIPs agreement embraced the Berne Convention's art 9(2) provision and in fact extended it to each of the rights which it attached to copyright and not just the right of reproduction.[60] The WIPO Copyright Treaty has also done so,[61] the agreed statements concerning the Treaty indicating that countries can "carry forward and appropriately extend into the digital environment limitations and exceptions in their national laws which have been considered acceptable under the Berne

---

56 Australian Copyright Council, *Fair Dealing in the Digital Age, Bulletin* (No 92) (Australian Copyright Council, Sydney, 1996).

57 Mason, A, "Reading the Future" (1996) 9 *Australian Intellectual Property Law Bulletin* 133 at 134.

58 Ricketson, S, *The Berne Convention for the Protection of Literary and Artistic Works 1886-1986* (Kluwer, Deventer, 1987), p 486.

59 *Copyright Act* 1968 (Cth) Pts VA and VB. Allowance is further made for copying of works in libraries. See Copyright Law Review Committee, 1997 Issues Papers: *Copying by Libraries and Archives*; *Educational Copying*; and *Copying for the Disabled* (AGPS, Canberra, 1997).

60 Article 13.

61 Article 10.

Convention". Similarly, they may devise new exceptions and limitations appropriate to this environment.[62]

ACCESS TO THE TECHNOLOGY

In the past, many governments have furthered the rights to freedom of expression and opinion, education and development by providing individuals with the means to receive information. They have used public instrumentalities to cross-subsidise indigent users in schools and households. Such programmatic support was recognition of the fact that often the real barrier to entry has not been the cost of the information but the technology itself. Once again, in the context of a neo-liberal emphasis on the market as the way to meet people's needs, specifically in the wake of the privatisation of public media channels, another mechanism might be needed to guarantee universal service. If the concept of a common carrier loses its purchase, private distributors may need to contribute a levy to a community fund or to provide facilities in public places.[63] Achievement of this goal will not be made any easier by the fact that universal service needs now to expand beyond the standard telephone line or public television broadcast to take in enhanced services such as data transmission and internet access.[64]

In an era when government controlled the channels or media of communication, freedom of speech also demanded that government provide access so that unpopular and critical views could be aired. Now in a world where content and carriage of communications are largely in private hands, the realisation of a right to freedom of speech becomes a question whether government should have a positive obligation to ensure that the private sector does not restrict access to the means by which that information can be conveniently imparted. If the right to expression (and, arguably, the right to education and development) depend on the means to send information as well as receive it, then enablement includes safeguards by government that independent producers are not denied access by those who obtain control over "essential facilities" of distribution.[65]

The optimists anticipate that the technology will provide its own solution to this problem.[66] With so much carrying capacity and so many alternative routes becoming available, no one will have an incentive to tie up the facilities in order to

---

62   The Australian government's *Copyright Reform and the Digital Agenda* Discussion Paper proposes that the Act be amended to provide for exceptions in relation to temporary or incidental copies made in the course of the technical process of transmitting copyright material. It invites comment on whether the fair dealing provisions in the Act should apply to the new rights proposed in the paper. It doubts whether the licensing arrangements for libraries should extend to the digital environment; see above, n 20, p 33.

63   Locally, see *Telecommunications Act* 1997 (Cth) Pt 7 Div 6.

64   Australian Standard Telephone Service Review, *Report to the Minister for Communications and the Arts* (Department of Communications and the Arts, Canberra, 1996). The *Telecommunications Act* 1997 (Cth) incorporates standard telephone services, pay phones and prescribed carriage services within its universal service regime and foreshadows an inquiry into whether digital data capability should be included: see Pt 7 of the Act.

65   Arup, above, n 11, Pt 4.

66   See generally, Gilder, G, *Life After Television, The Coming Transformation of Media and American Life* (Norton, New York, 1994).

favour their own services. Others are not so sanguine.[67] In the past, governments have relied on industry-specific regulation of various kinds to ensure pluralism in the media, especially to provide a space for local and less powerful voices. We might now have to look to a body of law not traditionally connected with human rights – competition law – to realise such a right.

Already, competition law is assuming an international complexion through the access rights afforded to service suppliers by the Annex on Telecommunications contained in the WTO's General Agreement on Trade in Services.[68] At its Singapore meeting late 1996, the WTO established a working party to report on the question of competition law generally.[69] In Australia, codes of reasonable and non-discriminatory access are supplementing the use of general proscriptions, for example of misuse of market power.[70] But the head of the responsible regulatory authority, the Australian Competition and Consumer Commission (ACCC), has warned that competition law has an essentially economic focus; its brief does not run to promotion of such social goals as media diversity. Equally so, the norms of the free trade frame of reference are limited in their ambitions. Broader international codes of conduct may be required to take the place of the national legislation which is disappearing.[71]

PRIVACY AND INFORMATION TECHNOLOGY

At the heart of the relationship between the right to privacy and information technology is the potential conflict over the free flow of personal information. Should the transfer of personal data be unrestricted? In this way, the right to privacy presents similar issues to intellectual property rights, though of course the reasons for wishing to control the flow can be different. The issues do not present a new polemic; rather the increasing reliance and value placed on information technology, in conjunction with powerful communications systems, has exacerbated the problem and brought it into sharp relief.

The use of information technology may deprive individuals of the sense that their privacy is being diminished or threatened. It reduces personal information to one common form (bits and bites) which can be matched with other data or transferred to undisclosed third parties for whatever use. Individuals may have no knowledge that this is taking place; the process is not necessarily transparent or in the public eye. In this way, use of the technology may heighten the individual's loss

---

67   See generally, Rheingold, H, 1993, *The Virtual Community: Homesteading on the Electronic Frontier*, Addison-Wellesley, New York.

68   WTO, 1994, above, n 17.

69   Declaration of the Ministerial Meeting of the WTO, clause 20. The text is available from the WTO web site, above, n 17.

70   In respect of telecommunications, see now *Trade Practices Amendment (Telecommunications) Act 1997* (Cth); for an earlier decision, invoking the general proscriptions, see *Pont Data v ASX Operations* (1990) ATPR ¶41-1007. Generally see Wyburn, M, "Copyright, Databases & Misuse of Market Power" (1997) 15(1) *Copyright Reporter* 46.

71   Preston, P, "Competition in Telecommunications Infrastructure: Implications for Peripheral Regions and Small Countries in Europe" (1995) 19 *Telecommunications Policy* 253.

of control over personal information. In some cases, this loss of control may engender a broad distrust of the medium.

At the same time, lack of precision characterises the use of the term privacy and hinders its realisation as a legally enforceable right. Privacy has much to do with the goals of personal autonomy and self-determination, goals that are frequently the rationale for human rights. Its breach has been associated with a wide range of activities, including telephone tapping, body cavity searches, computer hacking, mapping human genes, and electronic tracking of vehicles. Legislative protections may however adopt a narrower focus. In Australia, the *Privacy Act* 1988 (Cth) does not define privacy. Instead, it focuses on the protection of personal information and provides something of a complementary regulatory scheme to that of the freedom of information legislative regimes in the Commonwealth and all States and Territories, except the Northern Territory.[72] In this way the legislation avoids the establishment of the broad human right of privacy. Attention is drawn to the information itself rather than the interests of the individual.

Leaving aside its linguistic and definitional shortcomings, privacy may be translated into the following operational domains, physical, spatial, surveillance, communication and information privacy.[73] Information and surveillance privacy are the categories of most relevance and concern to the technology under consideration here. As we shall see below, much work has been undertaken internationally in an attempt both to recognise interests in information and surveillance privacy and to reconcile them with other interests, including the demand for the free flow of information. In this chapter, the concern is largely with the collection, storage and use of personal information about identified (or identifiable) individuals.

The international perspective

International recognition of the right to privacy, in its modern manifestation, grew out of the widespread revulsion with the atrocities of the second world war. Privacy became recognised as a right worthy of respect in the UDHR and subsequently the ICCPR. In these instruments the right to privacy is left undefined. The ICCPR, for example, states: "No one shall be subjected to arbitrary or unlawful interference with his privacy, family, home or correspondence, nor to unlawful attacks on his honour and reputation".[74] Thus stated, the right is clearly not absolute and may be qualified, not least when it conflicts with other rights.

As computer and communication technology has become global, business and government have shared concerns that privacy regulation might become a non-tariff barrier to trade – where that trade involved the transfer of personal data. Such regulation might prohibit personal data from being transferred to or from countries which lack the requisite privacy protection. These concerns precipitated the Organisation for Economic Cooperation and Development (OECD), a think tank for the governments of developed countries, to issue appropriate guidelines – namely,

---

72   See further Ch 4 by McMillan and Williams in this volume.

73   See Australian Privacy Charter Group, *Australian Privacy Charter* (School of Law, University of New South Wales, Sydney, 1994).

74   Article 17.

the *Guidelines on the Protection of Privacy and Transborder Flows of Personal Data*.[75] Through the coordination of national approaches, they attempted to strike a balance between the economic imperatives of free trade and the need to respect a fundamental human right. Although the Guidelines themselves are only abstract and indicative principles, they have already formed the basis of many of the data protection laws around the world. Australia is of course a member of the OECD.

In parallel with the OECD development, an increasing number of European countries have ratified the Council of Europe's *Convention for the Protection of Individuals with Regard to Automatic Processing of Personal Data* (1981)[76] and enacted data protection laws. In such countries, the emphasis has now shifted from defining privacy to protecting it. The development of the European Community into the European Union (EU) and a single market, free, by 1992, from non-tariff barriers, was to engender a more prescriptive approach to the issue of privacy protection. In order to ensure that privacy was not a barrier to trade within the member states, a detailed directive, a binding legal document, was created to provide a model for the regime which was to be instituted in all states of the EU.[77] The Directive takes full effect from October 1998.

The passage of the 1995 Directive is of significance to countries outside of the Union. It dictates in what circumstances personal information may be sent to countries beyond the EU member states. Essentially, it requires that personal data should only be transferred from an EU country to another country if there is "adequate" protection for personal data in that recipient country.[78] While the concept of adequacy is not defined, some indication of the requisite level of protection is provided. All circumstances surrounding the data transfer are taken into account in the assessment of the adequacy of the safeguards including any legislative and non-legislative measures. For example, the sensitivity of the data to be transferred would be considered.

At the same time, the Directive involves a series of specific derogations from the adequacy requirement.[79] These derogations include, to use the language of the Directive: where the data subject has "unambiguously consented" to the transfer; where the transfer is necessary for the performance of a contract between the data subject and the controller of the data or the performance of pre-contractual measures in response to the data subject's request; where the transfer is necessary in the interest of the data subject to conclude a contract between a third party and the controller of the data; where the transfer is necessary or legally required on public interest grounds or is necessary in order to exercise or defend a legal claim; where the transfer is necessary to protect the "vital interests" of the data subject; and, finally, certain transfers from public registers are also sanctioned.

As a trader with Europe, the interpretation of these derogations may prove of some importance to Australia should it not have adequate data privacy laws in place

---

75   OECD, 1980, Paris.

76   Convention no 18/1981, Strasbourg.

77   Directive 95/46EC with regard to the processing of personal data and on the free movement of such data, Brussels, 1995.

78   Ibid, art 25.

79   Ibid, art 26.

by the time the Directive is fully operative. In addition, the enactment of sweeping privacy legislation by a major trading partner, New Zealand,[80] has added further pressure to enact similar legislation in Australia.

It has long been regarded as a *sine qua non* of the establishment of the "information highway" that privacy interests must be protected. Without this, the construction of networks upon which future commerce and social advancements has been based, may be misconceived. Consumers may be unwilling to use this medium, instead continuing to prefer to use the traditional means of communication for conducting business. Central to the success of the information highway is the notion of trust or confidence in the medium. The architects and proponents of the information highway need to promote a trustworthy vehicle which is seen to take account of the privacy and security interests of those who wish to use it. Their challenge is to strike the appropriate balance where the several interests clash: the interests in the free flow of information, privacy, national security and law enforcement.

In the process, mere laws and other forms of regulation will not be sufficient; there will need to be extensive efforts to ensure public awareness of the issues backed by appropriate education. Furthermore, the global nature of these transfers suggests that common international standards are desirable to provide a basis for orderly transfers. The EU Directive may be the harbinger of this development. Some consideration is also being given to the development of an information privacy standard through the International Standards Organisation (ISO).[81]

The Australian position

Even though Australia is a signatory to the ICCPR, this of course does not automatically import the relevant rights into Australian law; they must be enacted locally. Accordingly, in the absence of such legislation, they are of persuasive value, perhaps morally binding, but they lack the force of law.[82]

There is no right to privacy at common law in Australia though various courts have considered this matter.[83] Instead, those seeking protection from intrusion into their private lives must seek to rely upon contract or tort law. For example the common law has implied a contractual duty of secrecy in the bank/customer relationship.[84]

The *Privacy Act* 1988 (Cth) promises much but delivers only limited protection, its 11 privacy principles only applying to federal government agencies.[85] The scope

---

80   *Privacy Act* 1993 (NZ).

81   The ISO has set up an ad hoc advisory group to determine whether it should develop international standards on the protection of personal information; see the ISO's web site address <http://www.iso.ch>

82   See Ch 2 by Sir Anthony Mason and Ch 14 by Eastman and Ronalds in this volume.

83   *Victoria Park Racing and Recreation Grounds Co. Ltd v Taylor* (1937) 58 CLR 479 per Evatt J; *Tucker v News Media Ownership Ltd* [1986] 2 NZLR 716; and *T v Attorney-General* [1988] 5 NZFLR 357 at 378 per Ellis J. Generally, see Seipp, D, "English Judicial Recognition of a Right to Privacy" (1983) 3 *Oxford Journal of Legal Studies* 325.

84   See *Tournier v National Provincial and Union Bank of England Ltd* [1924] 1 KB 461; *Robertson v Canadian Imperial Bank of Commerce* [1995] 1 All ER 824.

85   Section 14.

of the legislation is further reduced where government corporatises or privatises aspects of its empire, for example, in the area of telecommunications. The Act also regulates the tax file numbers system and the use of personal information in the consumer credit industry. At State level there is very general legislation. In New South Wales, there is a *Privacy Committee Act* 1975 and in South Australia an administration order.[86] The other States have seen only fitful proposals to develop meaningful privacy legislation; to date nothing has emerged.

The Commonwealth Government has rejected the need for comprehensive privacy legislation, thereby resisting for the time being the European and New Zealand approaches discussed above. Instead it has been proposed, through the Office of the Privacy Commissioner, that a mosaic of voluntary codes of conduct be set in place across the private sector in Australia.[87] The scheme envisages that the private sector develop codes of conduct in consultation with the Privacy Commissioner. It is intended that the codes adhere to a common set of privacy principles proposed by the Commissioner.

Nevertheless, this proposal has the capacity to enshrine existing inconsistencies in the approach to privacy protection across Australia. Already, there are a significant number of industry codes of conduct or guidelines and codes drafted by individual companies, such as the Australian Direct Marketing Association and the Telstra Corporation. In 1994, the bank sector, through the Australian Bankers Association, codified its privacy regime in the *Banking Industry Code of Conduct*.[88] Perhaps the document prepared by a public interest group, the *Australian Privacy Charter*, will still set a benchmark for the regulation of privacy in Australia.[89] It is also unclear how the codes will be enforced, whether, for example, through existing industry dispute resolution bodies or through a newly created, independent body. The credibility of the system relies upon an effective dispute resolution body.

Of greater concern still is whether this proposal meets international benchmarks. In particular, it becomes an issue whether it comes to terms with the notion of adequacy required of third countries by the EU Directive. Should it fail to do so, then any company in Australia wishing to make use of personal data from an EU member country, may have to commit to contractual privacy obligations in order to permit the data to be transferred to it. This approach will be cumbersome and ad hoc.

In Victoria, the Data Protection Advisory Council completed its recommendations for privacy legislation for the public sector in 1996. These recommendations are currently being reviewed as part of a legislative package of electronic commerce reforms which include the use of digital signatures. The New South Wales Government has had legislative reform of privacy laws on its agenda for some time, however, a privacy bill is yet to be debated.

---

86 Cabinet Administration Instruction, No 1 of 1989; re-issued 30 July 1992.

87 See Privacy Commissioner, *Information Privacy in Australia: A National Scheme for Fair Information Practices in the Private Sector* (Human Rights and Equal Opportunity Commission, Sydney, 1997).

88 See Pt IIIA of the *Privacy Act* 1988 (Cth).

89 See above, n 73.

In short, Australia lacks a comprehensive privacy regime, placing it in a precarious position with some of our trading partners once the European general data protection directive is implemented. The extent to which it will affect trade between Europe and other countries remains to be seen. However, it leaves Australia's commitment to the human right in some doubt. In the context of the development of electronic commerce, this lack of meaningful protection may deter Australians from the use of the new global technological infrastructure. In this unregulated environment, the consumer may not be aware who is controlling the personal information which is collected on the network almost inevitably with international reach. It is difficult to see how the privacy laws or regulations of any one country can be isolated in such an environment; it is naturally a supra-national issue.

SURVEILLANCE AND TECHNOLOGY

Surveillance technology provides enormous advantages for society as it can monitor remotely, yet precisely, what is taking place. The benefit is observable, for instance, in the use of surveillance cameras in the workplace for safety and discipline reasons and through the use of satellite tracking systems to determine the exact position of ships, aircraft and road transport vehicles. Consideration should also be given to the nature of the information collected by surveillance, together with its use and disclosure to others, and the potential for breach of privacy.[90] Surveillance cameras are commonplace and have become a low cost, reliable device for policing and security activities, particularly in traffic surveillance, shopping malls and secured areas, such as banks.[91]

Outside of the federal public sector, these practices remain unregulated, provided that the surveillance equipment has been placed in position on the relevant legal authority and does not involve any trespass or a breach of contract. They go beyond the listening devices legislation at the State level. Thus, in general, personal data which is collected lawfully through surveillance activities, may be stored, used and disclosed. In many cases the data is collected without the knowledge or consent of the person subject to surveillance, with obvious privacy implications for these people. It has been a contention that activities like these require justification, so that it is demonstrated how the benefits outweigh the diminution to privacy.[92]

Again, viable regulation is complicated by jurisdictional conflicts where the information is collected remotely. For example, the movements of individuals can be traced through the signals emitted from a mobile phone. Where movements are being tracked internationally via satellite, complex issues arise as to which law (if any) applies to the protection of the personal information collected.

---

90   Flaherty, D, *Protecting Privacy in Surveillance Societies* (University of North Carolina Press, Chapel Hill, 1989), p 380.

91   See generally, Privacy Committee of New South Wales, *Invisible Eyes: Report on Video Surveillance in the Workplace*, Report No 67 (Privacy Committee of New South Wales, Sydney, 1995).

92   Australian Privacy Charter Group, above, n 73.

SECURITY, TECHNOLOGY AND PRIVACY

A number of mechanisms are available to protect privacy. The technology employed to collect, store and analyse personal data, itself may incorporate software so as to ensure that privacy protection is maximised. The use of encryption, or codes, has become an important tool in the construction of the information highway. This mechanism permits users to transfer information freely over the network to others knowing that, even if the message is intercepted, it cannot be understood unless the interceptor has the key to unscramble the code. Encryption algorithms are becoming increasingly sophisticated and difficult to crack. However, encryption should be regarded as a complementary tool and no substitute for the privacy measures already discussed. Nonetheless, it necessitates some consideration here, because the same tool, when used in another manner, may erode privacy.

Central to the relationship between privacy and encryption is the issue of control. The party which has control of the key to the encryption algorithm is in a strong position, assuming that third parties are unable to discover or crack the code easily. If the key is not held by the parties to the communication but by a third party, then it is this party who must be trusted not to use the key improperly or to disclose the decoded information to unauthorised parties. Conversely, where only the parties to the communication have access to the key, then it becomes a potent privacy or confidentiality tool. The control of the key by government has been central to the "Clipper Chip" debate in the United States where government has argued that its control, subject to safeguards, is necessary for public order and law enforcement purposes such as the ability to follow the money trail.[93] Such an issue cannot be far off in Australia; already the Australian Taxation Office has mounted a major project of research into solutions to the tax compliance hazards of electronic commerce.

A further enhancement of encryption provides the ultimate privacy safeguard. The development of digital signatures provides the recipient of a *signed* electronic communication, with the confidence that the message is from the party who has, on the face of it, sent it. As such, it is a security measure that ensures the integrity of the communication. However, the development of blind digital signatures promotes privacy protection by permitting communications to be anonymous at the same time as the recipient can be confident that the message is unconditionally verifiable.[94] No personal information need be transferred. The most obvious application for blind digital signatures is in payment systems. A financial institution is able to provide a payment system for its customers which allows them to make payments to merchants who are, in turn, reimbursed by the financial institution, without the institution being able to identify which customer has spent the electronic money.[95] This system then may be closely aligned with cash payments. It is a good paradigm for a privacy protective system in that it eradicates the need to collect or transfer any personal information at all.

---

93   Mitchell, W, *City of Bits: Space, Place and the Infobahn* (MIT Press, Cambridge, Mass, 1995), p 124.

94   Chaum, D, "Achieving Electronic Privacy" (1992) (August) *Scientific American* 76 at 78.

95   See generally, Tyree, A, *Digital Cash* (Butterworths, Sydney, 1997), Chs 2 and 3.

Encryption then sits awkwardly between the use of technology and privacy protection. It has both the potential to ensure privacy or to erode it; the outcome is determined by the person who has control of the keys to the electronic coding tool. The OECD has played a leading role in mediating these relationships through the development of the *Guidelines for the Security of Information Systems* in 1992 and the *Guidelines on Cryptography Policy* in 1997. These two sets of guidelines are interconnected; coding information has obvious security benefits. Neither set of guidelines is binding, but they will be of considerable influence as a model for the national and international solutions to the tensions which are being crafted.

The *Guidelines for the Security of Information Systems* provide a framework for the protection of people who rely on information systems from the damage that may result from failures of availability, confidentiality and integrity. Australia adopted these Guidelines in 1992.[96] The Cryptography Guidelines deal with a more specific area – an internationally agreed approach to the use of encryption. The OECD's news release[97] states that the Guidelines: "are intended to promote the use of cryptography, to develop electronic commerce through a variety of commercial applications, to bolster user confidence in networks, and to provide for data security and privacy protection". Australia adopted these Guidelines in 1996.[98]

The Cryptography Guidelines seek the appropriate balance between the use of cryptography for national security and law enforcement objectives, on the one hand, and its legitimate use as a means to secure electronic commerce and maintain confidentiality and privacy, on the other. Respect for the security of information and the privacy of individuals figures strongly in the guidelines. The creators and developers of electronic commerce appreciate that due weight must be given to these matters, if, as we have noted, people are not to be deterred from using the new infrastructure. But, even if governments implement these policies, considerable trust will be demanded of the participants. It will not be immediately apparent to them whether their rights have been respected or not; the workings of the powerful new communication technology are opaque to the average person. For example, they may not be aware that much data relating to electronic transactions finds its way offshore and is stored, used or disclosed there.

The OECD guidelines recognise the commercial importance of cryptography to the advancement of electronic commerce. In the process, they acknowledge the need for respect for privacy and even anonymous communications. But, as Alston suggested was likely,[99] they entrust the development of this aspect to the practices of the marketplace. Australia's approach follows suit. In Australia, there is no restriction on the importation or use of cryptographic products. There are restrictions on the export of cryptographic or encryption products but these restrictions are imposed for national security and defence reasons rather than privacy reasons.[100]

---

96   Australia accepted the Guidelines at a meeting of the Council of the OECD in Paris on 26 November 1992. Australia is a member of the OECD.

97   OECD, Paris, 27 March 1997.

98   They were adopted by the Commonwealth Government on 27 March 1997 as a Recommendation of the Council of the OECD. See generally, Kirby, M, "OECD Cryptography Guidelines in Context" (1996) 3 *Privacy Law and Policy Reporter* 121.

99   Alston, above, n 4.

100 See item 43 of Sch 13 to the *Customs (Prohibited Exports) Regulations* 1958 (Cth).

In relation to cryptography, privacy protection has gained an unlikely ally in the business lobby. Both individuals and corporations have good reason to resist government attempts to insist that it play a central role in the regulation of encryption, extending to control, directly or indirectly, over the keys used to encrypt information within the jurisdiction. Corporations and companies are suspicious of this role, not only because of the possible bureaucratic mistakes or abuses, but also because government has become, in many fields, a competitor with the private sector as it corporatises its operations. Making secret electronic messages accessible to government, through its control over the encryption key, may be placing sensitive information in the hands of competitors. Clearly, business would favour mechanisms that ensure confidentiality of communications and that do not provide government with special access. In a similar vein, privacy advocates argue that cryptography provides a means of protecting personal information and should not be placed under the control of government.

OTHER HUMAN RIGHTS

Communication technologies have laid the foundation for an information infrastructure which has the potential to provide a level of surveillance not previously available. Other human rights may be brought under the umbrella of privacy, almost inadvertently, as privacy is seen to have a broader scope. One should not too readily support this extension, for privacy is only one of several fundamental rights that could be affected. For example, the use of intelligent transport systems to track motor vehicles for toll collection and possibly law enforcement purposes, could be seen as having an adverse impact on the freedom of movement[101] and possibly the freedom to associate,[102] as well as privacy.

In addition, the technology may provide impetus for new rights to be formulated. A right of anonymity has been raised as a result of the apprehension that communication technology will be able to collect and divulge all things to all people. This right has been mooted as an inalienable right to communicate anonymously, for example, in certain financial transactions.[103] It has also been suggested that there should be a right not to know in some circumstances, for example, where disclosure of a genetic abnormality may not be in the best interests of the patient. No legislation in these areas has been proposed to date.

CONCLUSION

Respect for human rights is not anathema to technological progress. It has been seen that, in some circumstances technology can support human rights such as privacy, the right to property and freedom of expression. Indeed, human rights should not be regarded as inconsistent with technological advancements, rather they should be approached as one fundamental consideration in their creation and implementation.

---

101   ICCPR art 12.

102   ICCPR art 22.

103   Australian Privacy Charter Group, above, n 73.

Where conflicts arise, creative solutions aside, some balancing between the free use of the technology and the various rights is desirable. Where the balance with human rights is not struck then some adverse reaction to the use of the technology can be expected.

A common theme running through this chapter is the appropriate manner in which to address the human rights issues. There are already international conventions and guidelines in many cases. Sometimes these have found their way into Australian law, on other occasions no substantive law exists and less formal regulatory processes have been adopted such as codes of conduct. In many cases the technology has become global yet regulation remains fragmented, with international bodies and national governments each adopting different approaches. Australia displays the same ambivalence as other countries. This attitude has not been so much the experience with internationally standardised intellectual property laws, where Australia is very supportive, but in terms of domestic regulation, it is still the case with freedom of expression and privacy protection. Such an outcome tends to give weight to the view that the human rights which are commercially compatible are more readily developed and consolidated.

The supra-national nature of the technologies available now, as well as the international reach of their developers and users, present challenges for governments. There is more pressure than ever to have a coordinated international approach to many of the human rights issues, however with the main aim being to ensure they do not become a non-tariff trade barrier. In such a context, these regulatory standards are likely to be driven by the perspectives and interests of the private sector. National governments and social objectives are in some danger of being disengaged, or at least distanced, from the process. Legal systems evolve over many years typically within a single locality; the challenge is, over a relatively short period and over a range of countries and cultures, to establish sets of rules for the intersection of information technology and human rights that are workable at both domestic and international levels.

12

HEALTH LAW
AND HUMAN RIGHTS

Ian Freckelton and Bebe Loff

INTRODUCTION

Health rights postulate values that mediate the boundaries between patients and health care practitioners. The assertion of such rights necessarily embraces the contention that fundamental principles of human rights – entitlement to dignity, non-discrimination, confidentiality and equitable distribution of resources – are relevant to the provision of health care and to the allocation of priority in the distribution of limited health resources.[1] It can legitimately be said that a collection of human rights, such as respect for autonomy, consent, truth-telling, confidentiality, personhood and persons, human dignity and justice permeates almost all scenarios that involve the intervention of health laws into the relationship between health professionals and their patients.[2] However, it has been pointed out by a number of commentators, including Kennedy and Grubb, that legal obligations in relation to provision of health care services for a long time have not been sufficiently emphasised and recognised.[3] The only partial exception to this proposition lies in the series of cases, in especially England and New Zealand, which have dealt with the circumstances in which life support for those in a permanent vegetative state or suffering from Guillain-Barré Syndrome should be able to be terminated. These decisions have tended to articulate relevant principles in a more organised and human rights-oriented manner than has occurred elsewhere in the course of medico-legal judgments. They have stressed matters such as the dignity of the patient and

---

1   Leary, V, "The Right to Health in International Human Rights Law" (1995) 1 *Health and Human Rights* 25 at 27.

2   Kennedy, I and Grubb, A, *Medical Law: Text and Materials* (Butterworths, London, 2nd ed, 1994), p 4; see also Kennedy, I, "Patients, Doctors and Human Rights" in Blackburn, R and Taylor, J (eds), *Human Rights for the 1990s: Legal, Political and Ethical Issues* (Mansell Publishing, London, 1991), p 84.

3   Ibid, p 52.

the inutility of the provision of futile treatment. They have also taken account of the impact of continuing ineffective treatment upon patients' relatives.[4]

Otto has usefully argued that:

> Perhaps the most important outcome of conceiving health as a human right is that it makes human rights principles applicable to health standards and practices. A human rights framework provides new tools for challenging and reimagining the utilitarian and technical approaches to health that have been preferred by WHO and the conservative professional medical community.[5]

While there is merit in principle for the analysis of health law in terms of human rights, such a vehicle for analysis historically has been subject to real limitations. In the context of medico-legal litigation initiated in Australia, it has been comparatively rare for principles of international law and even the instruments to which Australia is a signatory to impact upon the rulings of courts and tribunals. Moreover, the complex and competing principles which are relevant to health law decisions in the forensic arena for the most part have been ill-articulated and frequently not the subject of clear delineation in reported decisions. However, a number of charters of health rights and responsibilities on the part especially of government have started to enter Australian law. This has been part of the movement toward involvement of consumers in the formulation of health policy and of the creation of health complaints mechanisms. While the justiciability of such statements of rights remains to be finally determined by the courts, in principle, such charters may enable creative actions to enforce provision not only of services but services of the standard mandated within the charters.

Applying the broad approach of Kennedy and Grubb, whereby the notion of health rights is construed liberally, this chapter examines a range of areas of medical practice in which rights could be thought to arise for patients, and may be susceptible of enforcement via legal means. Given space limitations, it deals with a series of important issues that have come before the courts but does not address controversies relating to euthanasia and abortion in any detail. While these areas were highly controversial in Australia in 1997 and 1998, the law is clear in relation to the illegality of deliberately assisting another person to kill themselves and in

---

4   See, in particular, the analysis of fundamental principles by the House of Lords in *Airedale NHS Trust v Bland* [1993] 2 WLR 316, in terms of sanctity of life and discussion of art 2 of the *European Convention for the Protection of Human Rights and Fundamental Freedoms* and art 6 of the *International Covenant of Civil and Political Rights* (ICCPR); the principle of self-determination; respect for the dignity of the patient; the operation of the doctrine of necessity; and the notion of the benefit able to be derived from the provision of medical treatment. See further Freckelton, I, "Withdrawal of Life Support: the Persistent Vegetative State Conundrum" (1993) 1 *Journal of Law and Medicine* 35; Kerridge, I, Mitchell, K and McPhee, J, "Defining Medical Futility in Ethics, Law and Clinical Practice: An Exercise in Futility?" (1997) 4 *Journal of Law and Medicine* 235; Gillett, G, Goddard, L and Webb, M, "The Case of Mr L: A Legal and Ethical Response to the Court-Sanctioned Withdrawal of Life-Support" (1995) 3 *Journal of Law and Medicine* 49; Peart, N and Gillett, G, "Re G: A Life Worth Living? (1998) 5 *Journal of Law and Medicine* 239; McLean, S, "Letting Die or Assisting Death: How Should the Law Respond to the Patient in a Persistent Vegetative State?" in Petersen, K (ed), *Intersections: Women on Law, Medicine and Technology* (Dartmouth, Aldershot, 1997).

5   Otto, D, "Linking Health and Human Rights: A Critical Legal Perspective" (1995) 1(3) *Health and Human Rights* 273 at 276.

relation to the unlawfulness of committing homicide, even if the victim consents.[6] In relation to abortion, important debates in Western Australia resulted in the *Acts Amendment (Abortion) Act* 1998 (WA), which provides that abortion is now available for adult women who consent to the procedure. However, elsewhere in Australia the common law remains as uncertain as it did in the 1960s.[7]

The chapter examines the role of public law in the context of the regulation and protection of people's rights, and the contribution made by international human rights instruments and local guidelines implementing obligations created by Australia's becoming signatory to such instruments to Australian citizens' rights to the provision of health care. It analyses an aspect of the *Toonen* decision[8] in which the Human Rights Committee accepted and applied arguments relating to Australian domestic law, including health law, framed in terms of international human rights law. Then it examines a range of important areas of Australian medical law, where individual patients have asserted their need for redress or assistance from courts, including consent to treatment, sterilisation, reproductive rights and the entitlement of patients to gain access to their medical records. The chapter concludes with an analysis of the significant "legal" steps forward in relation to the rights of the mentally ill to be accorded due process but highlights the fact that the clampdown on available resources and the emphasis on deinstitutionalisation have resulted in many patients who need treatment failing to receive what is required for them to return to reasonable health. However, it suggests means by which those with mental illnesses may be able to use legislative responses to Australia's international obligations to enforce their rights to particular kinds of health service provision. Wherever possible, the chapter examines rights issues in terms of patients' "rights" to "self-determination", information about risks, freedom to reproduce, rights to dignity and rights to information held about them.

PUBLIC HEALTH AND HUMAN RIGHTS

The discipline of public health focuses upon the health of populations rather than clinical treatment of individuals. It is a given to public health practitioners that a critical determinant of health status is socio-economic status.[9] However, because there seems to be no workable alternative, health policy and programmes continue to operate within a biomedical framework. This model tends to promote consideration of illness in individuals and a response to a series of individual problems, rather than focusing upon systemic factors of causation. Mann, who has been a leader in the development of thinking in the area of health and human rights, has argued that the difficulty for public health in

---

6   See, in particular, the discussion by Mendelson, D, "The Northern Territory's Euthanasia Legislation in Historical Perspective" (1995) 3 *Journal of Law and Medicine* 136.

7   See, for example, Stuhmcke, A, "The Legal Regulation of Fetal Tissue Transplantation" (1996) 4 *Journal of Law and Medicine* 131; Eburn, M, "The Status of the Living Fetus"(1997) 4 *Journal of Law and Medicine* 373.

8   *Toonen v Australia*, Human Rights Committee, CCPR/C/50/D/ 488/1992; views of the Committee adopted on 31 March 1994, delivered on 4 April 1994.

9   See, for instance, Reynolds, C, *Public Health Law in Australia* (Federation Press, Sydney, 1995).

addressing the indisputably predominant social determinants of health status is exacerbated by the lack of a coherent conceptual framework for analysing societal factors that are relevant to health; the social class approach, while useful is clearly insufficient. Public health action based on social class is simply accusatory and it raises, but cannot answer, the question: "what must be done?"[10]

In this sense, "poverty" as a root cause of ill health (though clearly not the only cause) is both evident and paralysing to further thought and action. Also, without a consistent approach or vocabulary, we cannot identify the societal factors common to different health problems (cancer, heart disease, injuries, infectious diseases) and to different countries. Finally since the way in which a problem is defined determines in part what is done about it, it is significant that the prevailing public health paradigm is unclear about the nature and direction of societal change that is needed to promote health.

This school of thought argues that health policies and programmes may be enhanced by placing them in a human rights framework. Instead of imagining the unwell person as *the other*, as commonly happens in the context of infectious disease, the aim is to maximise the individual's human rights in so far as this is consistent with good science. A good example of this approach is the Australian National Strategy on HIV.[11] The legal component of this Strategy promoted the protection of privacy, informed consent, graded coercive powers ranging from minor restrictions to detention and rights of review and appeal when restrictions are imposed. Harm minimisation approaches in the context of drug usage have also been informed by consideration of human rights. The creation of laws supporting needle exchange schemes is also, in part, a recognition of a right to health. Similar comments could be made about the supply of condoms in prisons.

Comparatively rarely under current Australian law have individual litigants been able to utilise international human rights instruments to enable them to assert their own rights. An exception is to be seen in *Toonen v Australia*[12] where health policy issues were the subject of attempts at lobby-induced change at the behest of two men who asserted health rights to practice their sexuality as they wished. In December 1991 the United Nations Human Rights Committee, received a petition from Nicholas Toonen, an activist for homosexual rights in Tasmania. He sought to challenge ss 122(a) and (c) and 123 of the Tasmanian *Criminal Code* that criminalised sexual contact between gay men in private on the basis of their functioning in a discriminatory way. Ultimately the decision of the Human Rights Committee was based upon the right to privacy under art 17 of the ICCPR and what it characterised as an arbitrary infringement of this right.

However, in the course of argument before the Committee health issues were raised both in favour of and against the criminalisation of homosexual activity. Amongst the arguments proffered, Tasmania stated that, although laws criminalising homosexual activity might constitute an arbitrary interference with privacy, they

---

10   Mann, J, "Health and Human Rights" (1996) 312 *British Medical Journal* 924.

11   See for example Watchirs, H "HIV/AIDS and the Law: The Need for Reform in Australia" (1993) 1 *Journal of Law and Medicine* 9.

12   Above, n 8; see further, Joseph, S "Gay Rights under the ICCPR – Commentary on *Toonen v Australia*" (1994) 13 *University of Tasmania Law Review* 393; and Ch 14 by Eastman and Ronalds in this volume.

should be retained in order to protect public health and prevent the spread of HIV/AIDS in that jurisdiction. This argument was opposed by the federal government which contended before the Committee that such laws impede public health programmes by driving people underground. Further, it pointed out that the position of the Tasmanian government ran counter to the National HIV/AIDS Strategy.

The Committee found that criminalisation of homosexual activity was not a "reasonable means or proportionate measure" to prevent or limit the spread of HIV.[13] The Committee noted further that there was no evidence which demonstrated that criminalising homosexuality was effective in limiting the spread of HIV. The Committee did not accept the argument that this matter was a moral concern and thus a domestic matter. The *Toonen* decision highlights an opportunity, albeit a comparatively rare one, for health rights arguments to be invoked under the framework of the ICCPR to facilitate the achievement of health, in the broad sense of the concept, by individuals otherwise deleteriously affected by legislative impediments to their health.

Not surprisingly, though, individual case decisions on occasions have achieved the opposite result. The interpretation by the courts of important public health initiatives is not always consistent with the effective provision of needed services. For instance, in *Atyeo v Aboriginal Lands Trust*[14] Templeman J of the Western Australian Supreme Court found public health legislation relating to the provision of adequate sewerage facilities and sanitation not to be binding upon the Crown for the advantage of Aborigines. Section 99 of the *Health Act* 1911 (WA) prohibits a person from erecting, rebuilding, maintaining or using any house without providing it with sanitary conveniences and with bathroom, laundry and cooking facilities in accordance with the by-laws of the local authority. It allows a local authority to require a landlord to provide and install apparatus for the treatment of sewerage. The plaintiff, who was the Principal Environmental Health Officer for a shire in Western Australia sought a declaration that the Aboriginal Lands Trust was bound to comply with such a notice "because of his concern about the lack of toilet and ablution facilities" at an Aboriginal reserve. Templeman J found that the purpose of the legislation in preventing disease was not determinative and that the Crown, and therefore the Trust, was not bound by it. Thus, the purpose of the public health legislation was thwarted. The case was ultimately decided on the basis of the black letter issue of whether certain kinds of legislation should be taken to bind the Crown, but its resolution, and the manner of its resolution, in which health rights issues ended up becoming secondary considerations, have important, if depressing, ramifications.

In addition, some developments in the area of public health law are inconsistent with a rights based approach such as proposals for the criminalisation of the intentional spread of serious disease with a maximum penalty of life imprisonment. The risk thereby created is that fewer HIV positive persons will submit to testing and so more people will be put at risk of the transmission of the disease.[15] However, the health and human rights framework is gaining support amongst the

---

13   Above, n 8, paras 8.4-5.

14   (1996) 93 LGERA 57.

15   In relation to regulation of the passage of HIV to women see S Hardy, "Regulating the Conduct of HIV-positive Women" (1998) 6 *Journal of Law and Medicine* (forthcoming).

international community.[16] It may be that the move toward the development of a "therapeutic jurisprudence", which explores ways in which, consistent with the principles of justice, the knowledge, theories and insights of the health and related disciplines can help shape the development of the law,[17] has the potential to facilitate the evolution of health law in a direction which is consistent with an integrated rights framework. By its focus upon the development of law in a way which promotes health, such a jurisprudence carries the promise of influencing law-making by legislatures as well as the interpretation of laws in cases such as *Atyeo* to the advantage of those whose health such legislation is designed to enhance.

INTERNATIONAL LAW AND THE RIGHT TO HEALTH

In international law there are many references to the "right to health" but few to specific rights in relation to particular kinds of treatment, to what constitutes "adequate treatment", or to the remedies available for persons adversely affected by the treatment that they do receive. A right to health is not only located in the *Universal Declaration of Human Rights* (UDHR) and the *International Covenant on Economic Social and Cultural Rights* (ICESCR). References to a right to health may be found in the preamble to the Constitution of the World Health Organisation (WHO), art 24(1) of the *Convention on the Rights to the Child* (CROC), art 5(e)(iv) of the *Convention on the Elimination of All Forms of Racial Discrimination* (CERD) and art 11(1)(f) of the Convention on the Elimination of All Forms of Discrimination Against Women (CEDAW).

The basic reference, art 12 of the ICESCR, provides that:

(1) The State Parties to the present Covenant recognise the right of everyone to the enjoyment of the highest attainable standard of physical and mental health.

(2) The steps to be taken by the State Parties to the present Covenant to achieve the full realisation of this right shall include those necessary for:

    (a) The provision for the reduction of the stillbirth-rate and of infant mortality and for the healthy development of the child;

    (b) The improvement of all aspects of environmental and industrial hygiene;

    (c) The prevention, treatment and control of epidemic, endemic, occupational and other diseases;

    (d) The creation of conditions which would assure to all medical service and medical attention in the event of sickness.

This right is limited in the help which it extends for the framing of health legislation. For a start, the meaning of the article is not all that clear, although there has been an

---

16   See, for example, the *International Guidelines on HIV/AIDS and Human Rights* published by the United Nations (New York and Geneva, 1998) and the UNAIDS Guide to the United Nations Human Rights Machinery for AIDS Service Organisations, People Living with HIV/AIDS, and Others Working in the Area of HIV/AIDS and Human Rights (UNAIDS, 1997).

17   See, for example, Magner, ES, "Therapeutic Jurisprudence: A New American (?) School of Thought" (1998) 5(2) *Psychiatry, Psychology and Law* (forthcoming); Winick, B, "The Jurisprudence of Therapeutic Jurisprudence" in Wexler, DB and Winick, BJ (eds), *Law in a Therapeutic Key: Developments in Therapeutic Jurisprudence* (Carolina Academic Press, Durham, Nth Carolina, 1996).

ongoing, albeit not very successful, international process aimed at its clarification. The Committee created to monitor the implementation of the Covenant sought to issue a General Comment on Article 12 to provide a better standard against which to measure States' compliance. International health experts debating the possible content of such a General Comment struggled with the knowledge that health status is generally determined by social and economic factors. They concluded:

> By over-emphasising the correlations between health and other factors, the impression may appear that any health specific effort is doomed to fail in the absence of general socio economic reforms. A next step would be that the State may feel justified to suspend its health promotion and health care programs until better times come. Given the fact that the "healthy and wealthy" hardly ever depend on State interventions in the field of health, the implications of such a State withdrawal would disproportionately affect the poor and vulnerable groups in society. The consequence of such a decision would be that the gap between rich and poor and between healthy and less fortunate would dramatically increase.[18]

The right to health has been the subject of considerable controversy concerning whether it is a meaningful or enforceable right.[19] It has been suggested that if health is defined as "a state of complete physical, mental and social well-being" then it must be extremely difficult to implement and unlikely to be justiciable.[20] Defining human well-being is far from a straightforward exercise and it has been observed that public health and human rights have actually been used at times as powerful tools for maintaining the status quo and reinforcing hierarchies of power based on race, gender and class.[21]

However, Gostin and Lazzarini have suggested that the right to health may be defined as "the duty of the state, within the limits of its available resources, to ensure the conditions necessary for the health of individuals and populations".[22] This definition only requires the state to act within its capabilities to achieve as good a standard of health as it can and recognises that while government may do a great deal to improve population health there are also many factors beyond the power of the state.[23]

Two important recent cases – in South Africa and New Zealand – have tested the right of patients to treatment.[24] It is significant that both did so by using the mechanism of arguing that entrenched objectives of the provision of health care had not been met. It will be argued below that this is a mechanism likely to be more frequently availed of by litigants in the future, advocacy services and legal aid resources permitting.

18　See Hendriks, A "The Right to Health" (1994) 1(2) *European Journal of Health Law* 187 at 195.

19　See, for instance, Bell, S, "Rationing the Right to Health" (1998) 6(1) *Journal of Law and Medicine* 83.

20　Gostin, LO and Lazzarini, Z, "Human Rights and Public Health in the AIDS Pandemic" (Oxford University Press, Oxford, 1997), pp 28-29.

21　See, for example, Freedman, L, "Reflections on Emerging Frameworks of Health and Human Rights" (1995) 1(4) *Health and Human Rights* 315.

22　Gostin and Lazzarini, above, n 20, p 29.

23　However, note that the term employed in art 12 of the ICESCR is for the "highest attainable standard" of health to be striven for by the state.

24　For a useful discussion, see Bell, above, n 19.

In *Soobramoney v Minister of Health (Kwazulu-Natal)*,[25] a patient with renal failure sought to be reinstated on dialysis treatment by reliance on a provision in the South African Constitution which provided that all citizens had the right to health care services, subject to the availability of necessary resources, and that no-one could be refused emergency treatment. The court, while it conceded that the preservation of human life was of paramount importance, held that treatment for end-stage renal failure did not constitute emergency treatment and that acceptance of the patient's argument would have the effect of undermining the values which the provision in the constitution sought to protect by an unwarranted conflation of emergency and non-emergency treatment.

Similarly, in New Zealand a number of decisions in the courts were generated by the refusal of access by the Northland Regional Health Authority to an end-stage renal failure programme for an elderly man with renal failure. The patient initially challenged the decision on the ground that the Authority was not fulfilling the duty it owed him under the *Health and Disability Services Act* 1993 (NZ), maintaining that the Authority was in breach of its obligation to provide the best health care and support to those needing health services and had failed its obligation to exhibit a sense of social responsibility and to provide its services in accordance with the ethical standards to be expected to providers of health and disability services. Thus the claim was one of treatment based upon application of the values statutorily mandated of health care providers. However, Salmon J of the New Zealand High Court applied the reasoning of Lord Donaldson MR in *Re J (A Minor)*,[26] holding that the obligations spelled out in the legislation were not absolute but subject to the exercise of clinical judgment. Balcombe J went even further, emphasising "the absolute undesirability of the court making an order which may have the effect of compelling a doctor or health authority to make available scarce resources … without knowing whether or not there are other patients to whom these resources might more advantageously be devoted". The court declined to interfere with the Authority's decision, holding that the clinicians had relied properly on the Authority's guidelines in relation to the allocation of resources in a principled manner and without any reviewable administrative deficiency. The Court of Appeal upheld the High Court's decision.[27]

As already noted, of greater assistance in conceptualising health in terms of rights are the notions of rights to life, liberty and security of the person; the right to be free of arbitrary interference with one's privacy; the right to benefit from scientific advances; the right to seek, receive and impart information and ideas; and the right to found a family. Merely the enunciation of such a series of rights illustrates the indivisibility and interdependency of fundamental human entitlements. In this regard Leary has noted that a consequence of "embracing a human rights paradigm is the assumption that universal health standards, which are legally cognisable and enforceable, can be identified. That is, health is constructed as a legal entitlement rather than a privilege, commodity or result of altruism".[28]

---

25   CCT 32/97, 27 November 1997.

26   [1992] 3 WLR 507.

27   *Shortland v Northland Health* (unreported, CA NZ, 10 November 1997, CA 230/97).

28   Ibid at 276.

Nevertheless, it must be conceded that the statements of rights to health which emanate from international documents are frequently not immediately helpful in arguing cases locally. In areas where well-established precedent exists, such as in the area of medical malpractice, it is unlikely that submissions constructed in a rights framework will be accepted by an Australian court. Greater scope exists where the boundaries of current law are challenged and international human rights law may then become a useful resource. In addition, increasing scope exists for human rights discourse and analysis to influence the development of new statutory regulation of health care processes.

AUSTRALIAN MEDICAL LAW

There is no specific right to "treatment" or to "good treatment" in Australia. However, the common law has entitled persons to sue if they have been harmed in the course of treatment. The law that has built up around medical malpractice, largely framed in terms of the law of tort (negligence, nuisance, and trespass to the person) goes some way toward enabling litigants to assert rights in respect of their bodies. The notion of a person's right to autonomy of decision-making and thus the right to make decisions about accepting or refusing medical treatment on the basis of adequate information to make such decisions are central.

In the following discussion we concur with other writers in locating their deliberations concerning autonomy and consent in the right of the patient to security of the person.[29] Gostin and Lazzarini, for instance, suggest that to realise the right to personal security:

> Individuals must remain free to voluntarily accept or refuse physical intrusions, even when the purpose is benign. The doctrine of voluntary consent to medical testing, treatment, or research, which much of the international community endorses, may be seen as arising from the right to security of the person.[30]

Only when competent persons make uncoerced choices, based on full information, can they truly exercise their right to security of the person. Security of the person, then, requires "information, competency, and a voluntary assent to intervention absent undue influence, duress, or coercion".[31] Other options for classification of rights within the provision of health care are the right to self-determination or remotely, the right to privacy, but in terms of Australian jurisprudence the right of a person not to be the subject of medical intervention, save in certain circumstances, can most usefully be termed not as a function of decision-making but as a right to bodily integrity, save when that is waived by the person's own decision.

---

29 ICCPR art 17. Privacy is central in medical law and the right to privacy as understood in international law is relevant to this element. However, it is distinct from consent. Self-determination as a principle may apply both to populations and, especially in the medical law context, to individuals. For a useful discussion, see Jones, M and Marks, LA, "Female and Disabled: A Human Rights Perspective on Demand Medicine" in Petersen, above, n 4.

30 Gostin and Lazzarini, above, n 20, pp 14-15.

31 Ibid, p 15.

Consent to treatment

The most significant Australian case in relation to patients' rights to sound treatment and to decide upon medical treatment is the High Court decision of *Rogers v Whitaker*.[32] The defendant ophthalmic surgeon, Rogers, conducted surgery on the injured and sightless right eye of the plaintiff, Mrs Whitaker. This resulted in a condition known as sympathetic ophthalmia and consequential loss of sight in the respondent's left eye, leaving her almost totally blind. Evidence was given that the chance of this occurring was one in approximately 14,000 cases and that the condition did not always result in loss of vision.

The ground upon which the case was argued was that the surgeon had been negligent in failing to warn his patient of the risk of sympathetic ophthalmia. The trial judge concluded that such a warning was necessary in light of the respondent's desire for this information, she having particularly expressed concern about the conduct of the operation and her capacity to continue to enjoy vision.

The traditional view applied by the English courts was that derived from the case of *Bolam v Friern Hospital Management Committee*.[33] This was relied upon by the surgeon when he suggested that the standard of care required of him was no more than that of the ordinary skilled person exercising and professing to have a special skill. In this instance there was a body of reputable medical practitioners who would not have warned the patient of the risk of sympathetic ophthalmia, so it was said that the surgeon had behaved in accordance with the standard required.

This test had been applied by the English courts to diagnosis, treatment and the provision of information. Such a test is professionally-oriented, rather than oriented toward the wishes and needs of the patient. In *Sidaway v Bethlem Royal Hospital Governors*,[34] Lord Scarman, in a dissenting judgment, stated that it was a matter of law whether or not a doctor has provided a patient with sufficient information. The relevant standard, he held, was not a matter able to be determined solely by reference to current accepted practice. In arriving at this position, Lord Scarman referred to the Canadian decision of *Reibl v Hughes*[35] and, in doing so, recognised that the significant determining factor in the information to be imparted was individual autonomy, that is the patient's right to decide what will happen with respect to medical treatment.

In *Rogers v Whitaker*[36] the majority in the High Court held that:

---

32   (1992) 175 CLR 479.

33   [1957] 1 WLR 582.

34   [1985] 1 All ER 643.

35   (1980) 114 DLR (3d) 1.

36   See also the discussion in *Anasson v Koziol* (unreported, SC ACT, 20 December 1996) at 13, where Miles CJ commented that, "it might be observed that it seems that the *Bolam* principle is not as rigid as Australian lawyers have sought to express it in order to reject it. With respect to their Lordships, they might have been surprised to learn that they had delegated the duty of the courts to the medical profession (*F v R* (1983) 33 SASR at 193), let alone handed over their responsibilities to a section of the community with an interest in the outcome (*Reibl v Hughes* (1980) 114 DLR at 13). Some might regard *Bolam* as a case decided on its facts. It was not considered important enough to be published in the authorised reports".

[I]n the field of non-disclosure of risk and the provision of advice and information, the Bolam principle has been discarded and instead the Courts have adopted ... the principle that, while evidence of acceptable medical practice is a useful guide for the courts, it is for the courts to adjudicate on what is the appropriate standard of care after giving weight to the "paramount consideration that a person is entitled to make decisions about his own life".[37]

They resisted characterising the obligations of the medical practitioner as a matter of "the patient's right of self-determination", seeing this as pertinent to cases where there may be doubt as to whether a person has agreed to a treatment or procedure generally. They suggested that concepts like self determination or informed consent were applicable to actions in trespass or battery, but not in negligence. However, the effect of the decision is to forge a connection between a patient's right to self-determination in terms of consent or refusal to treatment, a self-determination founded in the provision of information which enables the making of a considered decision about medical intervention.

While the court dealt with the case as one located within the framework of negligence law, the requirement imposed upon medical practitioners by the decision is broadly consistent with a rights framework and the right to security of the person in particular. The court held that:

> The law should recognize that a doctor has a duty to warn a patient of a material risk inherent in the proposed treatment; a risk is material if, in the circumstances of the particular case, a reasonable person in the patient's position, if warned of the risk, would be likely to attach significance to it or if the medical practitioner is or should reasonably be aware that the particular patient, if warned of the risk, would be likely to attach significance to it.[38]

The decision needs to be seen within context. It has not ushered into Australia the doctrine of the oft-used and somewhat amorphous phrase "informed consent". In fact, the court observed that there was nothing to be gained by reiterating expressions used in United States authorities such as "the patient's right of self-determination" or even "informed consent",[39] pointing out that the term "is apt to mislead as it suggests a test of the validity of the patient's consent and that, moreover, consent is relevant to actions framed in trespass, not in negligence".[40]

The decision has been responsible for a major shift away from an environment of medical paternalism toward a recognition of patient autonomy in that the patient's views and desires are now preferred to what the doctor might paternalistically and without proper consultation consider to be in the patient's best interests.[41] However, the High Court decision has left many questions unresolved in relation to doctor-patient interaction. Included among the uncertain factors in the aftermath of *Rogers*

---

37 (1992) 175 CLR 479 at 487.

38 Ibid at 490.

39 Ibid at 490.

40 *Breen v Williams* (1996) 138 ALR 259 at 298 per Gummow J.

41 Note though the comment of Dawson and Toohey JJ in *Breen v Williams* at 278 that *Rogers v Whitaker* had nothing to say about medical paternalism save, perhaps, to the extent that it decides that it is for the court, not medical opinion, to determine whether the required standard of care has been observed.

v Whitaker is the variable of the extent to which a doctor must take steps to acquaint him or herself with the personal circumstances of a patient so as to provide information responsive to idiosyncratic aspects of the patient's circumstances and wishes. Another fundamental question, that has troubled medical practitioners, is the extent to which remote risks, but of a kind which would prompt anxiety in patients, need to be drawn to their attention. If risks as remote as one in 14,000 need to be the subject of warning, where does the obligation cease? And how can it be discharged – for instance, by the provision of written information or video tapes descriptive of the procedure.

To what extent does communication through such media need to be supplemented by one-to-one doctor-patient interaction?

The difficulties inherent in the case of *Chappel v Hart*[42] are illustrative of the uncertainties that exist in relation to the entitlements of patients in the post-*Rogers v Whitaker* era. The plaintiff sued her ear, nose and throat surgeon for failing to warn her of the dangers of a procedure which he advised her to undergo. She expressed concern about side-effects but was not advised of a significant complication of the operation that was ultimately undertaken. Notwithstanding the surgeon's exercise of due care and skill, her oesophagus was perforated and she developed an infection which damaged her laryngeal nerve, resulting in paralysis of her right vocal chord. The difficult aspect of the case was that she would have undertaken the operation even if properly advised of the risks. No negligence in the conduct of the procedure was asserted.

The New South Wales Court of Appeal found that had the patient been advised of the risks, she would have postponed the operation and had a more experienced surgeon carry it out. However, the evidence was equivocal about whether this would have reduced in any way the risks of the complications which ultimately afflicted the patient.[43] Mahoney JA, with whom Handley JA agreed, framed the duty to advise thus:

> The doctor is responsible for the damage by reason of the failure to warn of the existence of the possibility of damage only when, in the circumstances, he has a duty to give a warning of it. ... [W]here, as here, it is accepted that there was a duty to warn, then the failure to warn may properly be held to be the cause of the damage when the risk eventuates.[44]

Thus, the right to bodily integrity was very generously construed by the court and the burden placed squarely upon the medical practitioner's shoulders to ensure that adequate information was provided to the patient, the penalty for failure to do so being liability for any damage thereafter ensuing from the procedure undertaken by the patient in the absence of such information.

---

42 Unreported, CA NSW, 24 December 1996. See further Freckelton, I "Medical Malpractice Litigation" in Freckelton, I and Petersen, K (ed), *Controversies in Health Law* (Federation Press, Sydney, 1998) (forthcoming).

43 For a discussion of the case, see Mendelson, D, "The Breach of the Medical Duty to Warn and Causation" (1998) 5(4) *Journal of Law and Medicine* 312.

44 At the time of writing, an appeal had been argued before the High Court and the decision was reserved.

Sterilisation

If human rights are to have any role in medical law, it should be in the protection of the most vulnerable in our community. A case that demonstrates the influence of a human rights approach to a difficult health care issue is *Secretary, Department of Health and Community Services v JWB and SMB (Marion's Case)*,[45] which involved an application for the sterilisation of a young intellectually disabled girl with severe deafness, epilepsy, "behavioural problems" and an ataxic gait. Her parents sought an order authorising the performance of a hysterectomy and a bilateral oophorectomy. The hysterectomy was sought to prevent pregnancy and menstruation and their psychological and behavioural consequences. The oophorectomy was proposed to stabilise the hormone fluxes, helping to eliminate consequential stress and behavioural responses. The term "sterilisation" was used as a shorthand reference to these procedures.

The issue before the High Court was whether such a sterilisation could be performed, and if so whether it could be done with the provision of parental consent or only in accordance with an order of the Family Court. Basic human rights, the concept of "best interests of the child" and the ability to distinguish therapeutic from non-therapeutic treatments or procedures were discussed in the course of the decision-making process by the Family Court and then, on appeal, by the High Court. The High Court addressed the power of parents to consent to medical treatment on behalf of a child, the capacity of a child to consent and the specific issue of sterilisation. The decision of the majority, comprising Mason CJ and Dawson, Toohey and Gaudron JJ, was that except where sterilisation is an incidental result of surgery performed to cure a disease or to correct a malfunction, the decision to sterilise a minor falls outside the ordinary scope of parental powers and thus the powers and duties of a guardian. They found that the task of the Family Court when approached in its parens patriae jurisdiction to authorise the sterilisation of a child is to determine what is in the child's "best interests". They remitted the task of formulating guidelines for determining what is in such a child's best interests to the Family Court.

The majority summarised the reasons given in previous cases for considering the authorisation of sterilisation to be beyond parental power: "first, the concept of a fundamental right to procreate; secondly, in some cases, a similarly fundamental right to bodily inviolability or its equivalent; thirdly, the gravity of the procedure and its ethical, social and personal consequences".[46] They found court authorisation to be a necessary safeguard for sterilisation which is not the "by-product of surgery appropriately carried out to treat some malfunction or disease". Sterilisation was characterised as irreversible surgery carrying a significant risk of error which in turn could bring grave social and psychological consequences. Children with an intellectual disability were recognised as falling into a particularly vulnerable category of the community.

---

45   (1992) 175 CLR 218. For discussion of this case in the context of family law and human rights, see Ch 8 by Behrens and Tahmindjis in this volume.

46   Ibid at 249.

The majority endorsed the well-known formulation of the principle of inviolability articulated by Cardozo J in *Schloendorff v Society of New York Hospital*:[47] "Every human being of adult years and sound mind has a right to determine what shall be done with his own body; and a surgeon who performs an operation without his patient's consent commits an assault."

The majority judges in the High Court based their conclusion upon what they termed "a fundamental right to personal inviolability existing in the common law", a right which they said underscored the principles of assault, both criminal and civil, as well as upon the practical exigencies accompanying this kind of decision. They emphasised, though, that their conclusion did not "rely on a finding which underpins many of the judgments discussed; namely, that there exists in common law a fundamental right to reproduce which is independent of the right to personal inviolability".[48]

The High Court's decision in *Marion's Case* is the most prominent example of a judicial decision in Australia which has canvassed in detail and with sophistication the conflicting human rights issues in a medical law context. However, the decision also included powerful dissents by Brennan, Deane and Wilson JJ.

The Human Rights and Equal Opportunity Commission was permitted standing to appear before the High Court.[49] It argued that an invasive surgical procedure such as a sterilisation of a young woman who is unable to provide her own consent should only be undertaken with the authorisation of a court. It successfully contended that this requirement is consistent with the exercise of the parens patriae or statutory welfare jurisdiction of the Family Court and "as such is sufficient safeguard of the rights of the mentally retarded and disabled persons recognised in the international Conventions and Declarations incorporated in schedules to the *Human Rights and Equal Opportunity Commission Act*".[50]

Brennan J, in dissent, though, rejected the Commission's approach. He sought to identify the "basic principles of our legal system" since there were no cases of binding authority. He looked to what in the law governs physical integrity and noted that:

> Blackstone declared the right to personal security to be an absolute, or individual, right vested in each person by "the immutable laws of nature".[51] Blackstone's reason for the rule which forbids any form of molestation, namely, that "every man's person [is] sacred", points to the value which underlines and informs the law: each person has a unique dignity which the law respects and which it will protect.[52]

He pointed out that "human dignity"[53] is a value common to Australian municipal law and to international instruments relating to human rights:

---

47   105 NE 92 (NY 1914), referred to at 234. Schloendorff was determined independently of the United States Bill of Rights considerations.

48   Ibid at 253-54.

49   See Ch 14 by Eastman and Ronalds in this volume.

50   (1992) 175 CLR 218 at 231.

51   Ibid (*Blackstone's Commentaries on the Laws of England*, vol 1, pp 124, 129; vol 3, p 119).

52   Ibid at 266.

53   Ibid, "[t]he inherent dignity of all members of the human family is commonly proclaimed in the preambles to international instruments relating to human rights": at 266.

The law will protect the hale and hearty and the dignity of the weak and lame; of the frail baby and the frail aged; of the intellectually able and the intellectually disabled. ... Human dignity requires that the whole personality be respected: the right to physical integrity is a condition of human dignity but the gravity of any invasion of physical integrity depends on its effect not only on the body but also upon the mind and self perception.[54]

In considering what is to be incorporated within the term, "physical integrity", he included the psychological impact of a physical interference and the impact upon that person's human dignity, a notion well known in human rights dialogue.

Brennan J noted the idea of third party authorisation, or substituted consent, but dismissed it as a "semantic legerdemain" and the antithesis of consent, thus unreliable. However, he found utility in the distinction between "therapeutic" and "non-therapeutic", a distinction by contrast that the majority found to be imprecise. He defined treatment as being therapeutic when administered "for the chief purpose of preventing, removing or ameliorating a cosmetic deformity, a pathological condition or a psychiatric disorder, provided the treatment is appropriate for and proportionate to the purpose for which it is administered".[55] His Honour accepted that the intellectually disabled should have the same rights as others "to the maximum degree of feasibility", as proposed under the Declaration of the Rights of Mentally Retarded Persons. He held that to accord in full measure the human dignity "that is the due of every intellectually disabled girl", her right to

retain her capacity to bear a child cannot be made contingent on her imposing no further burdens, causing no more anxiety or creating no further demands. If the law were to adopt a policy of permitting sterilisation in order to avoid the imposition of burdens, the causing of anxiety and then the creating of demands, the human rights which foster and protect human dignity in the powerless would lie in the gift of those who are empowered and the law would fail in its function of protecting the weak.[56]

He expressed himself loathe to endorse a "best interests" approach on the basis of its failure to offer a hierarchy of values,

which might guide the exercise of a discretionary power to authorise sterilisation, much less any general legal principle which might direct the difficult decisions to be made in this area by parents, guardians, the medical profession and courts ... the best interests approach depends upon the value system of the decision maker. Absent any rule or guideline, that approach simply creates an unexaminable discretion in the repository of the power.[57]

Because of the majority decision of the High Court, the matter was remitted to the Family Court for articulation of criteria on the basis of which a decision could be made as to whether Marion should or should not be sterilised.[58] On remittal

---

54 Ibid at 266.

55 Ibid at 269.

56 Ibid at 276.

57 Ibid at 270-01. Brennan J accepted the need for guidelines lest the law fail the person in respect of whom the order for sterilisation is sought. He held that a non-therapeutic sterilisation could only be justifiable if its purpose was of greater value than physical integrity. He added that financial security, for example, was not "to be preferred over the equal protection of the law of the human rights of every member of the community": at 275.

58 *Re Marion (No 2)* (1994) FLC ¶92-448.

Nicholson CJ constructed the series of guidelines called for in the High Court[59] and approved her sterilisation as a step of last resort in order to minimise the potential to her of further neurological damage and in particular to stem the effects of seizures to which she was subject.

The decisions in the cases relating to Marion represent a high point in the analysis of basic and complex principles of health law in terms of rights asserted in international instruments and articulated in human rights discourse. The powerful dissent of Brennan J highlights the difficult balancing exercise when the rights of the intellectually disabled to autonomy and bodily integrity have to be placed in the scales against what objectively speaking is in the best health interests of a person unable to make their own decisions.

Reproductive rights

Article 10(2) of the ICESCR requires that "[s]pecial attention be accorded to mothers during a reasonable period before and after childbirth". Article 12, the right to health, requires reduction of the stillbirth rate and of infant mortality. Gender equity is a significant part of achieving reproductive rights and this, of course has its reflection in the CEDAW. In particular art 12 of that Convention states:

1. States Parties shall take all appropriate measures to eliminate discrimination against women in the field of health care in order to ensure, on a basis of equality of men and women, access to health care services, including those related to family planning.

2. Notwithstanding the provisions of paragraph 1 of this article States Parties shall ensure to women appropriate services in connection with pregnancy, confinement and the post-natal period, granting free services where necessary, as well as adequate nutrition during pregnancy and lactation.

Reproductive rights are a recent concept:

One of the cornerstones of the concept of reproductive rights is the right of access to family planning. This idea has been fundamental to definitions of reproductive rights from the beginning, appearing repeatedly in population and human rights documents as the right to have the "information and means" to decide freely and responsibly the number and spacing of children. Without such access, reproductive rights have, practically speaking, no real meaning.[60]

---

59   The relevant factors which went to determining whether sterilisation was in an intellectually disabled girl's best interests were held to be:
    (i)   the condition which required the procedure or treatment;
    (ii)   the nature of the procedure or treatment proposed;
    (iii)   the reasons for which it was proposed that the procedure or treatment be carried out;
    (iv)   the alternative courses of treatment that are available in relation to the condition;
    (v)   the desirability and effect of authorising the procedure or treatment proposed rather than the available alternatives;
    (vi)   the physical effects upon the person and the psychological and social implications for the person of authorising or not authorising the proposed procedure or treatment;
    (vii)   the nature and degree of risk to the person of authorising or not authorising the proposed procedure or treatment; and
    (viii) the views, if any, expressed by the person's guardians; anybody entitled to custody of the person; anybody responsible for the person's daily care and control; and of the person themself.
    See also In the Matter of P and P (1995) FLC ¶92-615; Re Jane (1989) FLC ¶92-007.
60   "Reproductive Rights and Reproductive Health: A Concise Report" (United Nations, New York, 1996).

The International Conference on Population and Development held in Cairo in 1994 defined reproductive rights as embracing:

> certain human rights recognised in national and international legal and human rights documents: the right of couples and individuals to decide freely and responsibly the number and spacing of their children, and to have the information and means to do so; the right to attain the highest standard of sexual and reproductive health; the right to make decisions free of discrimination, coercion or violence.[61]

Expressed in this manner, reproductive rights relate to much more than the entitlement to personal inviolability. They encompass positive rights articulated more fully at the Fourth World Conference on Women in Beijing 1995.[62] Reproductive rights might include the freedom to have a safe and satisfying sexual life, the ability to have a safe pregnancy and childbirth, the ability to control one's own fertility, access to gender-sensitive initiatives to deal with sexually transmitted diseases and to information about reproductive health and access to safe abortions. They might also be said to include the right to be free from unwanted sexual interference which is an aspect of the right to bodily integrity.

The right to reproduce was not accepted as a right independent of personal inviolability by the majority in *Marion's Case* which held that:

> If the so-called right to reproduce comprises a right not to be prevented from being biologically capable of reproducing, that is a right to bodily integrity. The same applies, though in a different way, to a woman's "right to reproduce". Again, if the right is, in fact, a right to do with one's person what one chooses, it is saying no more than there is a right to bodily integrity. Furthermore, it is impossible to spell out all the implications which may flow from saying that there is a right to reproduce, expressed in absolute terms and independent from a right to personal inviolability. We think it is important, in terms of the judgment, to make it quite clear that it is inviolability that is protected, not more.[63]

The majority classified the right to reproduce as a limited and indistinct right. It is apparent, therefore, that the approach of the majority of the High Court in *Marion's Case* is one that significantly circumscribes the extent of women's reproductive rights within Australian medical law. What this means in practice is that the range of issues regarded as coming into play in assessing whether or not there is an interference with a woman's reproductive capacity is far more limited than has been proposed by recent international forums on the subject.

Patient access to medical records

The matter of the rights of patients to medical records generated on their behalf has been a troubled and controversial one in Australia and internationally during the 1990s. It is an aspect of the privacy of the doctor-patient relationship, arguably comprehending the entitlement of the patient to know what it is that has been generated by her or his medical advisers in the course of consultations and tests

---

61   "Action for the 21st Century: Reproductive Health and Rights for All" (Family Care International, New York, 1994), p 10.

62   *Report of the 4th World Conference on Women, United Nations* (Beijing, September 1995), pp 4-15. See also Ch IV of the Report, Part C, paras 89-111.

63   (1992) 175 CLR 218 at 254.

conducted in order to provide advice or to facilitate decisions related to intervention or non-intervention. At an international level, it is significant that art 10 of the European Draft Convention on Human Rights and Medicine prescribes that "everyone is entitled to know any information collected about his or her health". This is stated to be subject to the qualification that "in exceptional cases" restrictions may be placed on the exercise of such rights to information, where restriction would be in the interest of the patient.[64]

However, to a significant degree the issue is a limited one in Australia in light of the applicability of freedom of information legislation to records generated by public health facilities and the availability of records under prelitigation discovery, discovery and subpoena. In addition, 1997 legislation in the Australian Capital Territory has given patients significant rights to their records. However, the reasoning engaged in by the High Court in determining that patients have no common law right to their health records is of real moment for the construction of Australian health law and for understanding the nature of the doctor-patient relationship in this country.[65]

In 1996 the High Court determined the issue authoritatively, holding in *Breen v Williams*[66] that patients hold no proprietary right or interest in the information contained in a doctor's medical records. Such records were determined to be the property of the doctor, enabling medical practitioners to refuse patients access to such records. As a matter of contract and fiduciary law, the High Court repudiated the contention that patients are entitled to inspect their records on demand.[67]

However, Brennan CJ held that in certain circumstances information with respect to a patient's history, condition or treatment which is obtained by a doctor in the course of giving advice or treatment must be disclosed to a patient on request. He found such circumstances to arise where refusal to make the disclosure might prejudice the general health of the patient, whether the request is reasonable, having regard to all the circumstances, and where reasonable recompense for the service of disclosure is tendered or assured by the patient.[68]

Dawson and Toohey JJ held that the contractual obligation of the doctor was to use reasonable care and skill in treating and advising the patient. They rejected the assertion that an incident of such duties was the provision of access to the patient's medical records. Gaudron and McHugh JJ held that a doctor does not impliedly promise to act in the best interests of the patient and found that the primary duty owed by the medical practitioner was to exercise reasonable care and skill. While they accepted that there is a tortious duty on the part of doctors to exercise reasonable care toward patients, they repudiated the implication of a general

---

64 See Ch III of the Council of Europe's Draft Convention on Human Rights and Medicine, reproduced in (1997) 1(1) *International Journal of Human Rights* 115.

65 *Health Records (Privacy and Access) Act* 1997 (ACT). See also the position in England (s 3 of the Access *to Health Records Act* 1900) and New Zealand (*Health Information Privacy Code* 1994 (NZ); *Health Act* 1956 (NZ); *Privacy Act* 1993 (NZ)); see McSherry, B, "Access to Medical Records: What Legislation Must Take into Account" (1997) 4 *Journal of Law and Medicine* 211; Blomberg, C, "Medical Records" in Freckelton and Peterson, above n 42.

66 (1996) 138 ALR 259.

67 For a provocative analysis of the case, see Olbourne, N "Patients' Access to Doctors' Records" (1998) 6(2) *Journal of Law and Medicine* (forthcoming).

68 Ibid, at 263.

contractual duty of care and held that the uncertainty of "best interests" as an obligation further militated against the general implication of such a term.

The court had been pressed by the applicant for access to the records to follow Canadian case law[69] and to find a general relationship of fiduciary and beneficiary to exist between doctor and patient. However, the court did not accept such a characterisation, preferring to maintain the traditional English and Australian approach to fiduciary law and to find that aspects of the relationship are fiduciary and will be protected by equity where a doctor, for instance, exercises undue influence over a patient to their financial detriment.

The High Court's decision in *Breen v Williams* confirms the obligations of medical practitioners to take reasonable care in the provision of treatment and advice to patients where the failure to do so could result in a foreseeable risk of harm to their patients. However, it circumscribes significantly the extent of doctors' contractual duties to their patients. Most significantly, it has declined to characterise the relationship between medical practitioners and their patients as fundamentally fiduciary in the sense of its being a relation of unequals and "trust-like". The privacy interest of patients to know what has been generated about them in terms of notes and medical records is for the most part unenforceable save where statute intervenes to provide such a right.

Rights of the mentally ill

The area of law probably most archetypally associated with the emergence of the legal protection of human rights in respect of health is that of mental health law. The past 30 years in Australia, as in other parts of the western world, have seen the emergence of substantial regulation of the circumstances in which the mentally ill can be involuntarily detained. The focus of the human rights lobby, which has been highly influential, has been to limit the autonomy of doctors to make decisions about the best interests of their psychiatric patients without being accountable and adhering to prescribed due processes, drafted to prevent the abuse or deprivation of liberty without just therapeutic cause. The past 30 years have seen the prescription of the processes of commitment by psychiatrists and the establishment of monitoring bodies, both review boards and tribunals, whose task it is to evaluate whether criteria for detention of those identified as mentally ill have been met. In addition, there has been increasing regulation of techniques of restraint and seclusion of those with mental illnesses who are housed within psychiatric institutions. Legislation has also stipulated in many jurisdictions when and how certain kinds of particularly intrusive treatment such as psychosurgery and electro-convulsive therapy can be administered.[70] To this extent, it can accurately be said that under mental health law,

---

69   See, in particular, *McInerney v MacDonald* (1992) 93 DLR (4th) 415.

70   See Wilson, B, "Psychosurgery: Ethical and Legal Issues" (1996) 4 *Journal of Law and Medicine* 21; Wilson, B and Freckelton, I, "Electroconvulsive Therapy: Ethical and Legal Issues" (1999) 6 *Journal of Law and Medicine* (forthcoming); Brookbanks, W, "Electro-convulsive Therapy and the Mental Health (Compulsory Assessment and Treatment) Act 1992 (NZ)" (1994) 1 *Journal of Law and Medicine* 184.

patients have been accorded statutory human rights to a degree unparalleled in other areas of medicine.[71]

The more prescriptive medical environment that exists in relation to mental health law has generated a more sophisticated debate in some respects about consumers' health rights. In 1992 the Commonwealth Government in its *National Mental Health Policy* endorsed the United Nations Principles for the Protection of Persons with Mental Illness. Such a step seemed to promise much for the rights of those with mental illness to better treatment and facilities. Shortly afterwards, though, the Burdekin Report[72] in 1993 exposed an often-forgotten aspect of health rights – the fact that if adequate facilities for the provision of treatment are not available, this itself constitutes a serious impediment to a patient's potential to become well. Amongst many criticisms, the Burdekin Report made adverse findings in relation to the legislation in a number of Australian jurisdictions for having failed to ensure that the rights and freedoms of people with mental illness had been adequately protected.

Changes to legislation have taken place in most jurisdictions to implement the National Policy and to meet some of the criticisms levelled in the Burdekin Report.[73] However, while greater specificity now exists in a number of jurisdictions in relation to the definition of mental illness, uncertainty remains about the difficult overlap between personality disorders and mental illness. Moreover, a number of commentators have accurately observed that the mentally ill have relatively few rights in relation to treatment which will meaningfully address their health when they are discharged from compulsory detention and returned to the community. Zifcak, for instance, has conceded that civil libertarian approaches to mental health law reform, while they have improved a number of the procedures for commitment of the mentally ill and ensconced due process in procedures for challenge to commitment decisions, have achieved relatively little in improving community care facilities, staffing levels, conditions, standards of conduct and treatment regimes.[74] He has argued that mental health law now occupies a new space, influenced by the phenomena of deinstitutionalisation, mainstreaming of acute mental health services, the major provision of psychiatric services now being in the community, the decrease in funding of health services generally by governments, the role of managerialism in the delivery of health services and the requirement for efficiency as a primary factor in health service delivery.[75]

The Burdekin Report lambasted State and Territory governments for the quality of the follow-up available to persons discharged from psychiatric hospitals and pointed out the levels of homelessness among those recently involuntarily detained

---

71   See Appelbaum, PS, *Almost a Revolution: Mental Health Law and the Limits of Change* (Oxford University Press, New York, 1994).

72   Human Rights and Equal Opportunity Commission, *Report of the National Inquiry into the Human Rights of People with Mental Illness* (AGPS, Canberra, 1993).

73   See, for instance, *Mental Health (Amendment) Act* 1995 (Vic).

74   Zifcak, S, "The United Nations Principles for the Protection of People with Mental Illness: Applications and Limitations" (1996) 3(1) *Psychiatry, Psychology and Law* 1 at 5; compare Delaney, S, "The United Nations Principles for the Protection of People With Mental Illness and Victorian Law" (1992) 18 *Melbourne University Law Review* 565.

75   Zifcak, S, "Towards 2000: Rights, Responsibilities and Process in the Reform of Mental health Law" (1997) 4 *Australian Journal of Human Rights* 51 at 56-57.

for mental illness. It also castigated the quality of boarding houses frequently resorted to by those with mental illness, the lack of support for families living with the mentally ill and the degree of poverty and discrimination against those with mental illnesses.

Little since the Burdekin Report has changed save that the process of deinstitutionalisation has hastened. While patients who are involuntarily detained now possess a number of enshrined rights that regulate the circumstances of their detention, increasing numbers of still psychotic patients are discharged under pressure for hospital beds. Problems continue to exist with the coverage of disability discrimination legislation.[76] No appreciable increase in resources has been allocated for the escalating numbers of significantly symptomatic patients cared for within the community. In such circumstances, there is a real limit upon the extent to which it can be said that those with mental illness have rights to treatment and, in particular, to adequate treatment. A real issue within mental health law, as increasingly it is within the wider area of health law, is how patients can insist, with the assistance of the law, upon being provided with the treatment that they need for the alleviation of their pain and suffering.

Few cases in relation to the rights of the mentally ill reach the courts other than those in the criminal area in relation to insanity or unfitness to stand trial. A rare exception was *In the Matter of XY*[77] where the Victorian Court of Appeal was required to determine whether an involuntary patient should be regarded as having been properly detained in a psychiatric hospital against his will and thus whether the Victorian Mental Health Review Board had jurisdiction to review his detention. The decision analysed what constituted due process for a person to be involuntarily detained and then found that if a person was in fact admitted and detained as an involuntary patient, even if technically wrongly so detained, they should not be disadvantaged by a technical illegality if they are in need of care and treatment. The court found that even if the person had not been properly detained, they should still enjoy the advantage of their status being reviewed by the Mental Health Review Board. No recourse was overtly had by the Supreme Court to human rights principles or to international human rights instruments but the decision takes its place as a precedent supporting the right of persons detained to be accorded the right to have the propriety of their continued detention reviewed by an administrative review body, notwithstanding the possibility that their initial decision may have been wrongly determined.

However, legislation in a number of jurisdictions has latterly enunciated principles of treatment and care to which psychiatric patients are said to be entitled and objectives have been legislatively enshrined for the government health departments that have the responsibility for providing such treatment and care. For instance, s 6 of the *Mental Health Act* 1990 (NSW) states that the objectives of the New South Wales Health Department are to establish, develop, promote, assist and encourage mental health services which:

---

76   See Australian Law Reform Commission, *Making Rights Count: Services for People with a Disability*, Report No 79 (AGPS, Canberra, 1996).

77   (1992) 2 MHRBD 501 (decided 6 March 1992 by the Victorian Court of Appeal). See also *Murray v Director-General, Health and Community Services Victoria* (unreported, SC Vic, 23 June 1995) per Eames J.

(a) develop, as far as practicable, standards and conditions of care and treatment for persons who are mentally ill or mentally disordered which are in all possible respects at least as beneficial as those provided for persons suffering from other forms of illness, and

(b) take into account the various religious, cultural and language needs of those persons, and

(c) are comprehensive and accessible, and

(d) permit appropriate intervention at an early stage of mental illness, and

(e) support the patient in the community and liaise with other providers of community services.[78]

Similarly, s 4(1) sets out the objects of the Act in relation to the care, control and treatment of persons who are mentally ill and mentally disordered and s 4(2) stipulates that it is the intention of the New South Wales Parliament that every function, discretion and jurisdiction imposed by the *Mental Health Act* be performed or exercised so that:

(a) persons who are mentally ill or mentally disordered receive the best possible care and treatment in the least restrictive environment enabling the care and treatment to be effectively given, and

(b) in providing for the care and treatment of persons who are mentally ill or mentally disordered any restriction on the liberty of patients and other persons who are mentally disordered and any interference with their rights, dignity and self-respect are kept to a minimum in the circumstances.

In Victoria, the *Mental Health (Amendment) Act* 1995 introduced an even more extensive enshrinement of principles for the provision of services to those with mental illnesses. It listed a series of objectives for Victoria's mental health legislation, included amongst which are objects such as "to provide for the care, treatment and protection of mentally ill people who do not and cannot consent to that care, treatment and protection",[79] "to protect the rights of people with a mental disorder"[80] and to ensure that "people with a mental disorder are informed of and make use of the provisions of this Act".[81] In addition, guidelines are listed for the interpretation of the legislation. These articulate values against which the legislation itself, the actions of the Department of Human Services and the behaviour of services providers and those reviewing their decisions can be measured. Important examples are that "people with a mental disorder are given the best possible care and treatment appropriate to their needs in the least possible restrictive environment and least possible intrusive manner consistent with the effective giving of that care and treatment",[82] and that "in providing for the care and treatment of people with a mental disorder and the protection of members of the public any restriction upon the liberty of patients and other people with a mental disorder and any interference with their rights, privacy, dignity and self-respect are kept to the minimum necessary in the circumstances".[83]

---

78 See also *Mental Health Act* 1996 (WA) s 5.

79 *Mental Health Act* 1986 (Vic) s 4(1)(a).

80 Ibid s 4(1)(c).

81 Ibid s 4(1)(e).

82 Ibid s 4(2)(a).

83 Ibid s 4(2)(b).

The legislation also states that it is the intention of the Victorian Parliament that a series of principles be given effect to with respect to the provision of treatment and care to people with a mental disorder. Included amongst these are that:

- "people with a mental disorder should be provided with timely and high quality treatment and care in accordance with professionally accepted standards";[84]
- "wherever possible, people with a mental disorder should be treated in the community";[85]
- the provision of treatment and care should be "designed to assist people with a mental disorder to, wherever possible, live, work and participate in the community";[86]
- "the provision of treatment and care for people with a mental disorder should promote and assist self-reliance";[87]
- "people with a mental disorder should be provided with appropriate and comprehensive information about their mental disorder, proposed and alternative treatments, including medication, and services available to meet their needs;[88]
- "when receiving treatment and care the age-related, gender-related, religious, cultural, language and other special needs of people with a mental disorder should be taken into consideration";[89]
- "treatment and care should be provided by appropriately qualified people and within a multi-disciplinary framework";[90] and
- "every effort that is reasonably practicable should be made to involve a person with a mental disorder in the development of an ongoing treatment plan".[91]

The significant issue from a legal point of view that arises from the existence of these provisions has not as yet been tested in the courts. What the enunciation of these principles makes possible is challenge to decisions and the provision of care on the basis that they are not in accordance with the principles set out in the legislation. For instance, where the provision of care has failed to take into account the right of a person to care that is in accordance with professionally accepted standards because of fiscal restraints, an avenue for litigation is available. Where the provision of treatment has not been fashioned so as to assist a person with a mental disorder to work or return to work, this again may open up a means of redress. Similarly, if persons are treated at a place that is convenient to the treaters but against the patient's wishes, or is significantly geographically removed from the residence of their relatives, this may afford a means of challenge where previously none existed. While these provisions are new and as yet untested, they have the potential to enable a substantial number of court challenges in respect of the compliance by service providers with the intentions of Parliament as articulated in the codified principles for the treatment and care of those with mental disorders.

---

84   Ibid s 6A(a).
85   Ibid s 6A(b).
86   Ibid s 6A(c).
87   Ibid s 6A(d).
88   Ibid s 6A(e).
89   Ibid s 6A(g).
90   Ibid s 6A(i).
91   Ibid s 6A(j).

CONCLUSIONS

Relatively few rights exist under contemporary Australian law to assist those disadvantaged by illness. For those who are mentally ill or intellectually disabled, support and advocacy services are so inadequate, and the availability of legal aid is now so limited, that those few rights which they might loosely be said to possess cannot any longer be said to be meaningfully accessible.

Australia is a signatory to a number of relevant international human rights instruments, but the utility of these in directly affording protection to patients or in providing to them a means of enforcing a civil remedy against those who have impoverished their health is minimal. Those rights that do exist in respect of health have been little and narrowly articulated by Australian jurisprudence. By and large, there has been acknowledgment that patients are entitled not to be subjected to treatment that affects their bodily integrity without their having provided their consent and having been advised of the risks and options in respect of the treatment. However, even with respect to so fundamental an entitlement, enforceable principally under the civil law, it has not been the subject of coherent and principled analysis within a rights discourse. Interpretation of the right has been limited to argument for the most part about whether provision of information in the context of a particular case has been adequate and whether an individual plaintiff can be said to have provided consent to treatment. This is not particularly surprising as rights for those adversely affected by medical procedures by and large exist under the civil law and only to the extent that economically quantifiable damages are available as a result of negligence, breach of implied terms of the therapeutic contract, by reason of nuisance, breach of fiduciary duty or assault to the person.

However, means for patients to assert rights not only to treatment but to treatment that accords with the principles underlying the international human rights instruments to which Australia is signatory have been created by the enactment of guidelines and objects clauses within legislation binding those supplying health care services, especially in the public sector.[92] The advent of such provisions at least in principle is creating a way in which individual grievances about the practices and priorities within the public health care system in Australia may become actionable using human rights principles. Such legislation has for the first time provided a bridge between human rights discourse and the forensically enforceable provision of health care.

---

92 See Laufer, S, "A Code of Health Rights and Responsibilities: the Adequacy of Existing Recognition and Protection" (1994) 1 *Journal of Law and Medicine* 168 who instanced a range of statutory examples of the enunciation of such principles in Queensland: see, for example, *Health Services Act* 1991 (Qld) s 3.18(2)(a); *Disability Services Act* 1992 (Qld); *Medicare Agreements Act* 1992 (Cth); *Health Rights Commission Act* 1991(Qld) ss 37ff; *Health Act* 1958 (Vic) s 119. However, it needs to be acknowledged that the attempt in *Shortland v Northland Health* (unreported, CA NZ, 10 November 1997, CA 230/97) to utilise guidelines for the provision of health care by way of an administrative law challenge was unsuccessful: see above.

Part Three

Human Rights and Legal Practice and Procedure

13

THE OPERATION OF ANTI-DISCRIMINATION LAWS IN AUSTRALIA

Peter Bailey and Annemarie Devereux

Although the principle of non-discrimination has been deeply embedded in international law since at least the signing of the United Nations Charter in 1945,[1] Australian law addressing issues of discrimination dates from the mid-1970s and has continued to develop in Federal, State and Territory jurisdictions. The basic structure for addressing discriminatory practices has remained consistent. If an individual suffers discrimination on a prescribed ground or attribute in a prescribed area of activity, that individual has a right to lodge a complaint with a specialist body. Within the legislative schemes, primary reliance is placed upon conciliation as the means for resolving complaints, though there is provision for first instance and appellate adjudicatory mechanisms. Although some attempts have been made to address underlying structural problems leading to discrimination through the facilitation of indirect discrimination complaints and representative actions, the focus of anti-discrimination law remains the aggrieved individual complainant. This chapter focuses upon the operation of anti-discrimination complaint handling in Australia, examining the relevant legal frameworks, outcomes and parties' experiences, as well as teasing out some of the more vexed legal issues which have arisen. Given the growing trend towards formalism in anti-discrimination complaint handling processes and the fiscal constraints on most specialist bodies,[2] it is vital that legal practitioners are in a position to appropriately inform and support parties involved in discrimination complaints.

In order to appreciate the aims of anti-discrimination legislation, Part A of this chapter provides a brief overview of the international developments regarding non-discrimination and equality, setting the background for the emergence of Australian anti-discrimination legislation. Part B turns to the specific Federal, State and Territory legislation, noting the broad contours of the substantive discrimination legislation and outlining the procedures established under such legislation. Parts C, D and E examine the tripartite stages of complaint handling – conciliation, first instance tribunal hearings and secondary superior court proceedings. Part F addresses several legal issues that are currently of special interest in the mounting of

---

1   Article 1(3) of the United Nations Charter proclaimed one of the purposes of the United Nations to be promoting and encouraging respect for human rights and for fundamental freedoms for all without distinction as to race, language or religion. The specific incorporation of non-discrimination in international law is discussed in Part A of this chapter.

2   Note for instance the decision of the Federal Government to reduce the funding of the Human Rights and Equal Opportunity Commission (HREOC) by 40%: HREOC News Release, 13 May 1997.

cases of discrimination, or that are in the process of resolution by the courts and tribunals, namely, the definition of indirect discrimination, the concept of reasonableness, the role of natural justice in complaint handling and evidentiary requirements related to proceedings in tribunals and courts. In recognition of the fact that there are alternate means of redress for aggrieved individuals, particularly those whose complaint arises in the context of an employment relationship, Part G notes the parallel operation of other legal avenues.

Two caveats are relevant as to the analysis offered in this chapter. First, the chapter does not purport to examine in any detail anti-discrimination law itself. Specialist services and numerous articles and commentaries are available for those wishing to pursue the scope of particular aspects of discrimination law.[3] Secondly, evaluating the operation of discrimination complaint handling is inherently difficult because of the confidentiality prescripts which surround the process of conciliation, the limited reporting of tribunal determinations and the small number of cases which are the subject of formal adjudication. Fortunately, several recent studies undertaken at the Federal,[4] New South Wales[5] and Western Australia[6] levels provide some insight into the otherwise veiled operation of anti-discrimination bodies. Whilst all of these studies involve various methodological limitations,[7] they offer invaluable reflections of at least some parties' experiences with complaint handling procedures.

---

3   In this context, particularly good surveys of the legislation are to be found in Ch 17, O'Neill, N and Handley, R, *Retreat from Injustice: Human Rights in Australian Law* (Federation Press, Sydney, 1994), *Halsbury's Laws of Australia*, Section on Anti-Discrimination and Equality; Ronalds, C, *Principles of Affirmative Action and Anti-Discrimination Legislation* (AGPS, Canberra, 1988).

4   Devereux, A, "Human Rights by Agreement? A Case Study of the Human Rights and Equal Opportunity Commission's Use of Conciliation" (1996) 7 *Australian Dispute Resolution Journal* 280 ("Devereux study"). This study examines the conciliation files from approximately 40 cases dealing with Federal Respondents under the *Sex Discrimination Act* 1984, *Racial Discrimination Act* 1975 and *Human Rights and Equal Opportunity Commission Act* 1986, finalised during the 1989-90 financial year period. The HREOC itself commissioned a more extensive study of its complaint handling processes, however the results of the study have not been made public.

5   New South Wales Law Reform Commission, *Discrimination Complaints-Handling: a Study* (Research Report 8, 1997) ("NSW study"). This study, carried out by Keys Young conducted, inter alia, a postal survey of complainants and respondents whose cases were handled and finalised through conciliation or referred to the Equal Opportunity Tribunal during the financial year ending in June 1995. Response rates to the survey were in the 45-60% range. Complainants who were in the "no further contact" category after their initial lodgement of complaint were also contacted, though the response rate was somewhat lower (30%).

6   Report of the Steering Committee into Processes under the Western Australian Equal Opportunity Act 1984, *Investigation and Conciliation* (1994) ("WA study"). This Report used data collected from a random telephone survey of 196 complainants and respondents whose files were finalised in the 1991/2-1992/3 financial year, an examination of 225 Equal Opportunity Commission complaint files (representing 10% of files from 1985-93), ministerial submissions and interviews with Commission staff.

7   The Devereux study is limited because of its reliance on written documents and the small number of cases examined. The NSW study is limited because of its reliance purely on the subjective experiences of complainants and respondents and because the format of the questionnaire was largely multiple-choice, such that full data on parties experiences was not necessarily obtained, whilst the WA study focussed on a narrow set of queries in relation to the process.

A. INTERNATIONAL FRAMEWORK

Australia's anti-discrimination legislation draws heavily upon the non-discrimination principle embodied in international human rights law. With the signing of the United Nations Charter, countries including Australia committed to the promotion and respect of human rights and fundamental freedoms without distinction as to race, sex, language, or religion. With the development of what has been termed the "International Bill of Rights", the *Universal Declaration of Human Rights* (UDHR) the *International Covenant on Civil and Political Rights* (ICCPR), and the *International Covenant on Economic, Social and Cultural Rights* (ICESCR), and specialist Conventions dealing with racial and sex discrimination, the principle of non-discrimination and its accompanying obligation to provide remedies for discriminatory behaviour have become an entrenched feature of international law, even potentially a feature of customary international law.

TREATY NON-DISCRIMINATION OBLIGATIONS

The primary articulation of Australia's obligation in relation to non-discrimination is to be found in the international covenants dealing with human rights: the ICCPR, the ICESCR, the *Convention on the Elimination of all Forms of Racial Discrimination* (CERD) and the *Convention on the Elimination of all Forms of Discrimination against Women* (CEDAW).[8] Whilst included in the United Nations Charter and the UDHR, it was not until the ratification of the specialist international Conventions that Australia undertook binding, precise obligations with respect to non-discrimination. Article 2(1) of the ICCPR states the basic obligation thus:

> Each State Party to the present Covenant undertakes to respect and to ensure to all individuals within its territory and subject to its jurisdiction the rights recognised in the present covenant, without distinction of any kind such as race, colour, sex, language, religion, political or other opinion, national or social origin, property, birth or other status.

A similar formulation appears in art 2(3) of the ICESCR. Individual clauses refer to the equal rights of men and women (ICCPR art 3) and the equality of all persons before the law (ICCPR art 26). Even in times of national emergency, when derogation from many rights is considered acceptable, the ICCPR provides that discriminatory measures are not permissible (art 4.1). More specific application of the non-discrimination principle is to be found within CERD and CEDAW.

"Discrimination" is left undefined in the ICCPR and ICESCR, but is elucidated in the specialist Conventions. Under art 2 of the CERD, for instance, racial discrimination is explained as:

> any distinction, exclusion, restriction, or preference based on race, colour, descent, or national or ethnic origin which has the purpose or effect of nullifying or impairing the recognition, enjoyment or exercise, on an equal footing, of human rights and fundamental freedoms in the political, economic, social, cultural or any other field of public life.

---

8   For the full text of these Conventions, see Brownlie, I (ed), *Basic Documents in International Law* (Clarendon Press, Oxford, 4th ed, 1995).

The United Nations Human Rights Committee has accepted the applicability of this elaboration to the ICCPR and ICESCR, whilst emphasising that discrimination does not mean all distinctions, but only those not based on reasonable grounds.[9] Clearly non-discrimination is not synonymous with equality. The non-discrimination principle is the more limited concept – applying only in respect of particular grounds and selected activities.

However, the way in which the non-discrimination principle has been framed in international documents does offer scope for adopting an expansive interpretation of discrimination. First, in referring to "distinctions of any kind such as ...", the implication is that the listed grounds are not exclusive, but that the non-discrimination principle encompasses at least distinctions based on analogous grounds.[10] Secondly, by prohibiting discrimination on the basis of "other status", the non-discrimination principle embraces an undefined, potentially broad category of impugned discrimination. In considering art 26's use of similar language, the Human Rights Committee, for instance, has accepted coverage of a range of distinctions such as that between being a student at a private, rather than a public school, members of the military and civilians, natural and fostered children and minority versus majority cultural groups.[11] Thirdly, in recent debates concerning equality and non-discrimination, there has been an emphasis on the need for substantive rather than formal measures of equality, such that positive measures of protection may need to be taken to ensure relevant differences are taken into account and that all persons enjoy non-discriminatory treatment.[12]

Customary international law and non-discrimination

Various commentators and judges have suggested that the non-discrimination principle is a principle of customary international law. Judge Ammoun, in his separate Opinion in the *Namibia* Case for instance, stated:

> One right which must certainly be considered a pre-existing binding customary norm which the Universal Declaration of Human Rights codified is the right to equality which by common consent has ever since the remotest times been deemed inherent in human nature.[13]

---

9   Human Rights Committee, (1989), General Comment No 18: Non-Discrimination, HRI/GEN/1/25.

10   Seighart, P, *The International Law of Human Rights* (Clarendon Press, Oxford, 1983), p 75; BG Ramcharan, "Equality and Non-Discrimination" in Henkin, L (ed), *The International Bill of Rights: The Covenant on Civil and Political Rights* (Columbia University Press, New York, 1981).

11   *Blom v Sweden*, Comm No 191/1985, A/43/40 (1988); *RTZ v The Netherlands*, Comm No 245/1987; *Vuolanne v Finland*, Doc A/44/40, 249, p 256; See Bayefsky, A, "The Principle of Equality or Non-discrimination in International Law" (1990) 11 *Human Rights Law Journal* 1 at 8.

12   For a discussion of the implications of the substantive versus formal distinction for sex discrimination, see Hunt, P, *Reclaiming Social Rights: International and Comparative Perspectives* (Dartmouth, Aldershot, 1996), pp 91-97. This debate has surfaced most recently in Australia in the context of the *Native Title Act* 1993 amendments and the *Racial Discrimination Act* 1975.

13   *Namibia Case* (1971) ICJ Rep, 16. See too the judgment of the International Court of Justice in the *Barcelona Traction, Light and Power Company Limited Case (Belgium v Spain) Second Phase*, (1970) ICJ Rep, 3 at 34.

Comments limited to the status of the prohibition of racial discrimination were made in the *South West Africa* and *Namibia* cases[14] and have been included in the United States Restatement (Third) Foreign Relations Law.[15] Academics including Strossen, Parker, Neylon and Chen have affirmed the centrality of the non-discrimination norm as part of customary international law and even suggested that it is a non-derogable form of customary international law, *jus cogens*.[16] Ultimate resolution of the status of the non-discrimination principle in customary international law is not of immediate importance in Australia given that Australia is a party to the major international human rights conventions. However, the likelihood that at least part of the non-discrimination principle is embodied in customary international law would be relevant should Australia seek to denounce its ratification of the international covenants.[17]

Treaty obligation to provide remedies

Accompanying what might be termed the "substantive" obligation of non-discrimination is the State's responsibility to ensure that individuals are able to seek redress/remedies. Under art 2 of the ICCPR, for example, States are obliged to take necessary steps to provide an effective remedy, and to ensure that affected individuals have their rights determined by a competent judicial, administrative or legislative authority who are able to enforce such remedies.

B. DOMESTIC LEGISLATIVE FRAMEWORK

Even before Australia ratified the ICCPR in 1980, there were moves to enact anti-discrimination laws in several Australian States.[18] By 1997 all jurisdictions (Commonwealth, States and Territories) had enacted anti-discrimination legislation,[19] though the scope of the legislation, particularly in terms of impugned

---

14 See for instance Justice Tanaka's dissenting opinion in the *South West Africa (Second Phase)* [1966] ICJ Rep 6 at 284; *Namibia* [1971] ICJ Rep 31 at 51; see also *Koowarta v Bjelke-Petersen* (1982) 153 CLR 168 at 218-20.

15 Restatement, Third, of the Foreign Relations Law of the United States, s 702 states that: "A state violates international law if, as a matter of state policy, it practices, encourages, or condones ... systematic racial discrimination, or ... a consistent pattern of gross violations of internationally recognized human rights".

16 See Strossen, N, "Recent US and International Judicial Protection of Individual Rights: A Comparative Legal Process Analysis and Proposed Synthesis" (1990) 41 *Hastings Law Journal* 805 at 816-17; Parker, K and Neylon, LB, "Jus Cogens: Compelling the Law of Human Rights" (1989) 12 *Hastings International and Comparative Law Review* 411 at 441-42; and Chen, L, *An Introduction to Contemporary International Law: A Policy Oriented Perspective* (Yale University Press, New Haven, 1989), pp 367-68.

17 On further potential use of customary international law, see Ch 14 by Eastman and Ronalds in this volume.

18 The earliest piece of discrimination legislation was the South Australian *Prohibition of Discrimination Act* 1966. The Commonwealth passed the *Racial Discrimination Act* 1975 in 1975, and New South Wales and Victoria enacted discrimination legislation in the late 1970s.

19 At the Commonwealth level, there is the *Human Rights and Equal Opportunity Commission Act* 1986 (HREOC Act); the *Racial Discrimination Act* 1975 (RDA); the *Sex Discrimination Act* 1984 (SDA) and the *Disability Discrimination Act* 1992 (DDA). At the State and Territory level, there is: *Discrimination Act* 1991 (ACT); *Anti-Discrimination Act* 1992 (NT); *Anti-Discrimination Act* 1977 (NSW); *Equal Opportunity Act* 1995 (Vic); *Equal Opportunity Act* 1984 (SA); *Equal Opportunity Act* 1984 (SA); *Anti-Discrimination Act* 1991 (Qld); *Sex Discrimination Act* 1994 (Tas).

grounds and application to the public or private sectors varies considerably between the jurisdictions. Nonetheless, in each jurisdiction, in order to pursue a discrimination complaint, it is necessary to demonstrate:

(1) distinctive treatment;

(2) based on a specific grounds or attributes ("grounds") identified in the legislation as being prohibited bases of distinction;

(3) that the distinctive treatment related to an area of activity covered by the legislation; and that

(4) there is no general or specific exemption or exceptions provided for in the legislative schemes applicable to the situation.

Whilst the language of unlawfulness employed in discrimination legislation might suggest that discrimination law is based on a "public law" view of discrimination such that officers of the Crown would be responsible for prosecution of infringements, discrimination complaint handling processes fit within a "private law" view of human rights. Unlawful discrimination is not a crime,[20] nor is it civilly actionable. Instead, it can be the subject of complaint through administrative channels and can result in the award of damages under the relevant statutes.

Coverage of legislation

As stated above, the grounds of discrimination and areas of activity covered under discrimination legislation vary as between jurisdictions. The table on p 298 highlights the coverage of grounds in each jurisdiction, noting some of the most significant exceptions and exemptions:

Areas of activity

Most legislation covers the basic areas of employment and recruitment, goods and services, access to premises, accommodation, education, sport and clubs. Correlation between grounds and areas of activity, however, is not universal. In Queensland, for instance, breastfeeding discrimination is limited to application to the provision of goods and services. Under the HREOC Act, International Labour Organisation (ILO)-ground related discrimination relates only to employment. Distinctions are made in some jurisdictions between private and public sector bodies. In New South Wales, for instance, age discrimination is only unlawful as it relates to compulsory retirement in the public sector and in the general areas with respect to the private sector, whilst the Federal SDA does not apply to the State public service (see below). At the Federal level, there are some distinctions between coverage in relation to Federal and State bodies. Federal, State and Territory legislation incorporate specific and general exemptions for particular activities

---

20　Only one attempt was made in the first Racial Discrimination Bill 1973 to include criminal sanctions for discriminatory deprivation of rights. However, this proposal met with intense opposition, such that with the exception of discriminatory advertising, the only criminal sanctions in anti-discrimination legislation today relate to what might be termed "incidental matters" such as procedural non-compliance and victimisation of persons complaining of discrimination and the more recent introduction in some jurisdictions of serious vilification.

GROUNDS OF DISCRIMINATION UNDER DISCRIMINATION LEGISLATION

Ground	ACT	NT	NSW	VIC	SA	WA	Qld	Tas	Cth
Sex, Marital Status, Pregnancy	*	*	*	*	*	*	*	*	*
Race	*	*	*	*	*	*	*		*
National Origin	*	*	*	*	*	*	*		
Sexuality[a]	*	*	*	*	*	*	*		*
Disability	*	*	*	*	*	*	*		*
Age	*	*	* (limited)[b]	*	*	*	*		*
Religious Belief/Activity	*	*		*		*	*		*
Political Belief/Activity	*	*		*		*	*		*
Association	*	*		*			*		*
Employer Association / Trade Union	*	*				*	*		*
Criminal Record		*				*	*		
Family Resp / Parenthood	*	*		*		* (limited)[c]	*	*	*
Breast-feeding		*					* (limited)[d]		
Carer	*			*					*

a   Whilst the term "sexuality" is used in the Northern Territory, in the ACT and South Australia the reference is to "heterosexuality, homosexuality, bisexuality, and transsexuality", in Queensland and Victoria to "lawful sexual activity", and in New South Wales to "homosexuality".

b   In New South Wales, age discrimination is limited to coverage of compulsory retirement in the public sector and the six major areas for the private sector.

c   In Western Australia, discrimination on the basis of family responsibility is limited to the areas of employment and education.

d   In Queensland breastfeeding discrimination is limited to the provision of goods and services.

including, inter alia, "genuine occupational qualifications", residential care of children, religious institutions, including educational bodies, voluntary bodies, combat duties, and acts done under statutory authority. Exemptions may be applicable on a temporary or permanent basis.

Application of Commonwealth statutes in the States

Each of the Federal anti-discrimination Acts applies in the States, at least to the private sector within the State[21] though the RDA, SDA and the DDA provide that if a State or Territory law covers the same issues, the State or Territory law shall continue to operate and will not be rendered invalid under s 109 of the Commonwealth Constitution. By virtue of this express reference, the Commonwealth legislation negates any implication which might otherwise arise that the Commonwealth legislation is intended to "cover the field" so as to invalidate State legislation on the same topic.[22] A State/Territory law may go beyond the scope of Commonwealth legislation provided that it remains in keeping with the spirit of the international conventions. It may also remain silent on a topic and not provide a parallel State/Territory remedy. If, however, it attempts to make lawful something made unlawful in the Federal legislation, it will be invalid and will not be saved by virtue of the express reference in the Commonwealth legislation to State systems.

Choice of forums

Under the Federal legislation, a complainant who lodges a complaint under State or Territory legislation is excluded from proceeding under the Federal system. There is nothing which specifically excludes complaints lodged under the Federal Act from being lodged under the State Act, though it is possible that the complaint may be rejected on another available basis such as that the complaint is frivolous or vexatious. It may be, however, that the choice of forum is of greater importance at the theoretical rather than practical level. In several States, the Commonwealth and States have entered co-operative arrangements under which the State handles federal

---

21 The SDA does not apply to State public sector employment. There are also indications that the implied constitutional limitation on the Federal Government in relation to not impairing the integrity of the States may partially restrict the application of all powers of the discrimination legislation to the State public sector: see for instance the High Court's reading down of the Commonwealth's industrial relations provisions concerning discrimination in *Victoria v Commonwealth* (1995) 187 CLR 416 at 532, 497-505.

22 Such a provision was included in the RDA in 1983 and subsequently included in later discrimination legislation because of the problem with arose in *Viskauskas v Niland* (1983) 153 CLR 280. In *Viskauskas*, the High Court held that the RDA was intended to cover the field of racial discrimination, such that the racial discrimination provisions of the *Anti-Discrimination Act* 1977 (NSW), whilst consistent in their operations with the Federal Act, were invalid. When Commonwealth legislation purported to correct retrospectively the problem by an amendment stating that there was no intention to invalidate consistent State legislation, the High Court held that the Commonwealth was not able retrospectively to avoid the operation of s 109: *University of Wollongong v Metwally* (1984) 158 CLR 447. There have been some suggestions that should State legislation be "rights-conferring" or beneficial to individuals, the court will tend to adopt an interpretation of the legislation, such that no inconsistency arises.

complaints in its jurisdictions,[23] such that the practical significance of lodgment is somewhat lessened. However, for those States whose bodies carry out their operations separately from the Commonwealth, some care needs to be exercised in ensuring the most advantageous forum is chosen. Relevant considerations may include the location of proceedings, any limitations on possible remedies, time limitations, and the enforceability of determinations.

Framework of complaint handling processes

The basic process of complaint handling at the State, Territory and Federal levels consists of investigation and (if appropriate) conciliation, followed by a hearing by a specialist body and court processes. The catalyst for the commencement of the process is the lodgement with a specialist anti-discrimination Commissioner or, at the State level, with a specialist anti-discrimination body, of a written complaint by an aggrieved individual.[24] After its lodgment, the complaint is subject to initial investigation by the Commissioner to determine whether the complaint appears to be within the jurisdiction of the Commissioner and whether it raises a prima facie issue of discrimination. If so satisfied, the Commissioner is in general obliged to undertake conciliation.[25] If the conciliation is unsuccessful or the complaint is considered unsuitable for conciliation at the outset,[26] the complaint may be referred to a public hearing at the specialist tribunals/Commissions.[27] Provision is then made for the complaint to be appealed to (or heard by, in the case of federal complaints) superior courts.[28]

---

23   In Victoria, South Australia and Western Australia, co-operative arrangements mean that in general the State Equal Opportunity Commissions receive and handle discrimination complaints under federal legislation. The South Australian and Western Australian Commissions do not handle complaints under the DDA or complaints of racial hatred.

24   In some jurisdictions, the anti-discrimination body/Commissioner may itself institute an inquiry.

25   Even where a complaint appears to be within jurisdiction, it may be rejected on specific grounds. Under the Federal legislation, for instance, these grounds include where the Commissioner is satisfied the act is not unlawful, where more than 12 months after the act has elapsed or where the complaint is viewed as frivolous, vexatious, misconceived or lacking in substance: see RDA s 24(2); SDA s 52(2); DDA s 71(2). The complaint may also be rejected where it is apparent that a more appropriate remedy is otherwise available. Rejection of a complaint is reviewable in most cases.

26   No statutory guidance is provided as to when conciliation will be by-passed, though in the authors' view appropriate circumstances might include where one party is obviously intransigent, where there are significant power imbalances between the party including where there is an alleged pattern of violence and oppression. The Australian Law Reform Commission (ALRC) has suggested that "recidivist respondents" should be denied the opportunity for a private settling of their case, whilst noting that automatic referral might punish the complainant: ALRC, *Equality Before the Law: Justice for Women*, ALRC Report No 69, Vol 1 (AGPS, Sydney, 1994), p 86.

27   The Minister also has the power to refer a matter directly for hearing. At the Federal level, see SDA s 58; RDA s 25; DDA s 76.

28   For the distinction in enforcement powers between State and Territory tribunals and HREOC, see n 85 below.

Who may lodge a complaint?

The complainant must be a person "aggrieved" in the sense of having a "special interest" in the subject matter of the complaint. In the words of the Federal Court in *Cameron v HREOC*, the complainant must be:

> likely to gain some advantage other than the satisfaction of righting a wrong, upholding a principle or winning a context, if his [her] action succeeds or to suffer some disadvantage other than a sense of grievance or a debt for costs, if his [her] action fails.[29]

Representative complaints may be brought under the Federal legislation and some State legislation. Under the Federal scheme, the provisions governing when representative complaints will be accepted and the modified procedural rules to be applied are to be found in Pt IVA of the *Federal Court of Australia Act* 1976. Whilst all State laws provide for multiple complaints to be lodged, Victoria, South Australia and the Northern Territory do not include a mechanism to permit representative actions. State tribunals, however, have the power to join together complaints should it appear that the complaints raise similar issues of fact or law.[30] Unfortunately, whilst representative complaints have the potential to raise wider issues underlying discriminatory practices, particularly in the area of indirect discrimination, there have been very few instances of representative complaints in Australian jurisdictions.[31]

Against whom should the complaint be brought?

Selection of the correct respondent party is one of the difficulties facing many complainants. In cases where the difficulty lies with nominating the correct corporate identity, anti-discrimination bodies have shown complainants considerable latitude in allowing them to amend their complaints.[32] The more difficult question, however, relates to the choice of whether to pursue a complaint against the individual perpetrator of discrimination or in conjunction with his/her supervisor and employer. Clearly, where an employer has contributed to the discriminatory conduct in some fashion, overtly or covertly, he/she will be jointly liable for the discriminatory conduct. In cases where the discrimination has occurred without the knowledge or approval of the employer, and in fact in a fashion which is contrary to the directions of the employer, there is a need to ensure the employer comes within the circumstances of vicarious liability established in the legislation. Under all State/Territory legislation and under the Federal scheme, liability is cast also upon persons who cause, encourage or request another person to do an act which is unlawful under the legislation. To date, these provisions have not been relied upon extensively, though have been applied so as to cast liability onto a union which was found to have contributed by causing or failing to prevent sexual harassment against one of its members.[33]

---

29 (1993) 119 ALR 279 at 285.

30 *Najdovska v Australian Iron and Steel Pty Ltd* (1985) EOC ¶92-140.

31 See further, Ch 14 by Eastman and Ronalds in this volume.

32 *Re New South Wales Corporal Punishment* (1986) EOC ¶92-160; *R v Equal Opportunity Board; ex p Burns* (1984) EOC ¶92-112.

33 *Horne v Press Clough Joint Venture* (1994) EOC ¶92-556, ¶92-591 (EOT WA).

Anti-discrimination bodies reject a significant proportion of complaints on the basis that they do not appear to come within the jurisdiction of the body.[34] Whilst complainants have expressed frustration at and a lack of understanding of the reasons for such preliminary rejection,[35] the rate of rejections appears less remarkable when comparisons are made with international counterparts.[36] Anti-discrimination bodies must not reject complaints at this early stage without proper consideration of the matter. It is likely that scrutiny of "potential outside jurisdiction" cases has increased since the criticism of the Federal Sex Discrimination Commissioner's handling of a complaint in *Proudfoot*.[37] However, the decision of the New South Wales Equal Opportunity Tribunal that anti-discrimination bodies are not bound by natural justice when carrying out their investigation processes,[38] suggests that the scope for administrative challenge is not unduly large.

C. CONCILIATION

Given that the vast majority of cases which reach the conciliation stage of complaint handling are resolved during the conciliation process, its operation is of extreme interest to practitioners and commentators of anti-discrimination law.

Nature of conciliation

It is somewhat difficult to talk of a conciliation process per se since "conciliation" is an imprecise term, permitting a variety of applications. None of the human rights statutes provides a definition for "conciliation". Neither is there elucidation of the term in the legislative debates surrounding the anti-discrimination Acts, despite its being lauded as likely to produce positive and lasting solutions and an inexpensive and informal process.[39] The elusiveness of the term has also been noted in reviews of anti-discrimination bodies.[40]

---

34 According to the New South Wales Anti-Discrimination Board's *Annual Report 1995-6*, for instance, 16% of cases were considered to be outside jurisdiction and were declined: NSW study, above, n 5, p 4.

35 One third of complainants who were informed by the New South Wales Anti-Discrimination Board that it could not take their matters further agreed that they did not understand why the Anti-Discrimination Board could not do more to assist them: NSW study, above, n 5, p 32.

36 In 1995, the European Commission of Human Rights, for instance, regarded only approximately 30% of complaints submitted to it as admissible: Council of Europe, *Information Sheet No 36* (Strasbourg, 1995), p 47. One would expect the figures for the United Nations Human Rights Committee to be similarly low. One cannot rely too heavily on the comparison, however, given the need for international complaints to demonstrate an exhaustion of domestic remedies in addition to the substantive matter of discrimination.

37 (1991) 100 ALR 557. In *Proudfoot*, the Sex Discrimination Commissioner had noted on an internal memorandum that the complaint was "another example of a male wasting our time with trivia". The Commissioner's handling of the complaint was itself the basis of a sex discrimination complaint, though the complaint of sex discrimination was not upheld.

38 *Re New South Wales Corporal Punishments in Schools: Determination on preliminary matters* (1986) EOC ¶92-160; see further, discussion below at n 103 and accompanying text.

39 For an examination of the historical record concerning conciliation, see Devereux, A, *The Complaint Handling Procedures of the HREOC* ("Devereux thesis") (unpublished thesis, 1991), copy accessible at Australian National University, or with the authors, pp 5-8.

40 WA study, above, n 6, pp 3-4.

Criticisms of conciliation

Whilst to a large extent, those operating within anti-discrimination bodies have maintained their enthusiasm for conciliation as the primary mode of dispute resolution,[41] not all commentators have supported the continued reliance on conciliation. Particular attention has focussed upon the potential for conciliation to reinforce existing power imbalances[42] and its possible impeding effect on the development of a broader consciousness of the structural issues of discrimination.[43] Chapman has also noted that the emphasis on compromise in informal processes may work to disadvantage complainants and represent the acceptance by the complainant of a lesser form of justice than would be expected in a more formal setting.[44] The secrecy of the process, originally envisaged as a means of promoting frank discussions has also been subject to attack. Early critics decried the unfairness of a process akin to a Star Chamber,[45] whilst more recent critiques have suggested that privacy serves neither the individual nor the community interest. Parties, particularly complainants, are seen to be more vulnerable to undue manipulation by bureaucrats who favour rapid resolution[46] and complainants remain isolated, unaware of similar proceedings or outcomes.

Conciliation in practice

Perhaps surprisingly, the parties are brought together for a conference in only a minority of cases conciliated by anti-discrimination bodies. Instead, the majority of complaints are resolved through an exchange of letters alone. In Devereux's study of cases against federal respondents handled by the HREOC under the SDA, RDA and HREOC Act in the 1989-90 year period, for instance, only approximately one third of cases resolved during conciliation involved a conciliation conference.[47] In the remainder of cases, conciliation consisted in an exchange of letters between the HREOC and the parties to the dispute or the withdrawal of the complaint. Similarly, in the more recent study of the New South Wales Anti-Discrimination Board, 20% of complainants whose complaints were resolved during conciliation reported having attended a conciliation conference.[48] Although in some cases the reason for

---

41 See for instance, Long, J, "The RDA After 10 Years", *Address to the Australian Institute of International Affairs* (Canberra Branch, 27 November 1985), p 7; Pentony, P (ed), *Conciliation Under the Racial Discrimination Act 1975: A Study in Theory and Practice*, Human Rights Commission, Occasional Paper No 15 (AGPS, Canberra, 1986), p 105.

42 Kessel, K and Pruit, DG discussed by Thornton, M, "Equivocations of Conciliation: The Resolution of Discrimination Complaints in Australia" (1989) 52 *Modern Law Review* 733 at 743.

43 Scutt JA, "The Privatisation of Justice: Power Differentials, Inequality and the Palliative of Counselling and Mediation" in Mugford J, (ed), *Alternative Dispute Resolution Proceedings* (Australian Institute of Criminology, Canberra, 1996), p 195.

44 Chapman, M, "Notes for Conciliators on Handling Aboriginal Complaints or 'I'm still waiting for my beer'" (HREOC Internal Document, 1989), pp 6-7.

45 House of Representatives, *Hansard*, 8 April 1975, 1289 per Mr Killen.

46 Thornton, above, n 42, p 739.

47 Conciliation conferences were held in 6 of the seventeen conciliated cases. All of these conference cases involved employment: Devereux study, above, n 4, p 287.

48 NSW study, above, n 5, p 43.

not holding a conciliation conference may be "principled" in the sense of an individual assessment that a conference would inflame the situation, or would be inappropriate where there are significant power imbalances or residual antagonism,[49] the approach of anti-discrimination bodies appears to be to hold conferences only where they are regarded as absolutely necessary.

The approach of minimising the number of conferences contrasts, however, with the expectations of complainants. In the NSW study, for instance, whilst overall only 32% of complainants felt that they had been either very or fairly successful in achieving their objectives through conciliation,[50] the percentage rose to 49% amongst the subset whose complaints were the subject of a conciliation conference.[51] Respondents, on the other hand, were likely to have a more positive view of the Anti-Discrimination Board if they had not attended a conciliation conference.[52] Similarly, in the WA study, 75% of complainants and 69% of respondents indicated a preference for holding a conciliation conference soon after the complaint was lodged.[53]

Representation during conciliation process

Parties have no right to representation during conciliation. In practice, involvement of legal representatives appears to be discouraged. Rayner has expressed support for the use of advocates appearing on behalf of discrimination complainants given that the basis of the system is essentially adversarial in nature.[54] Critics of lawyers' participation in conciliation have claimed that lawyers tend to distort and formalise the process.[55] Taking into account the usual disparity of resources of complainants and respondents, permitting representation of parties at conciliation conferences as of course may serve to advantage those with sufficient resources to use sophisticated legal strategies in order to avoid effective conciliation. One would expect thus that representation as of course would tend to benefit respondents.

Existing data would tend to suggest that the conciliation process has not become the domain of lawyers. In Devereux's study, 47.5% of complainants and 25% of respondents had representation during the conciliation stage.[56] In the NSW study, only 19% of complainants reported having a lawyer present at the conciliation conference, with a higher proportion amongst male complainants than female complainants, and a higher proportion (approximately 25%) amongst persons of non-English speaking background.[57] Respondents, on the other hand reported a 30% rate of being accompanied by a lawyer at the conciliation conference.[58] The

---

49   HREOC, *HREOC Complaints Manual* (Internal Document, 1996), para 3.5.1, p 84.

50   NSW study, above, n 5, p 31.

51   Ibid.

52   NSW study, above, n 5, p 112.

53   WA study, above, n 6, p 33.

54   House of Representatives Standing Committee on Legal and Constitutional Affairs, *Sex Discrimination Legislation*, proceedings of seminar (AGPS, Canberra, 1990), per Rayner, M.

55   Scutt, above, n 43, p 191, 195; Thornton, above, n 42, p 746.

56   Devereux study, above, n 4, p 291

57   NSW study, above, n 5, p 43.

58   NSW study, above, n 5, p 62.

disparity between levels of representation of complainants and respondents in the two studies may not be surprising, but may have been influenced by the fact that Devereux's study was limited to cases involving Federal respondents. One might posit that complainants in such cases are more aware of the need to obtain legal representation, and that Federal agencies have sufficient legal resources "behind the scenes" so as not to require representation in all stages of the process. In any event, it is clear that neither a majority of complainants nor respondents have formal legal representation at the time of conciliation.

Outcomes from conciliation

Although there is only limited data from which to evaluate the outcome of conciliated cases,[59] it would appear that whilst non-monetary agreements are usually closely tailored to the circumstances (with the notable exception of recruitment cases), significant monetary settlements remain relatively rare. In Devereux's study, the outcomes reflected the need to change practices and provide the individual with an appropriate remedy. In immigration cases, for instance, applications were re-assessed, and administrative policies re-considered.[60] In employment cases, conciliation staff focused discussions on settlements rather than punitive damages.[61] Packages tended to involve an apology for any embarrassment caused, the placing of the complainant in a position so that s/he could apply for future positions/promotion and the institution of equal employment opportunity/sexual harassment training programs.[62] Annual Reports include references to sizeable compensation agreements, and more recent reports have cited more cases of the re-employment of individuals.[63] There seems to have been little headway, however, in the area of overcoming discrimination in recruitment processes. Although legislators originally envisaged that the process might foster future relations even in recruitment processes, no attempt seems to be made to force an employer to employ a person in circumstances where the recruitment process tainted with discrimination.[64]

The satisfaction expressed by anti-discrimination bodies in relation to their high resolution of cases is not necessarily shared by parties. A high proportion of complainants (33%) and respondents (17%) in the NSW study whose complaints were finalised during conciliation, for instance, characterised the outcome of their complaints as "no clear outcome".[65] Furthermore, all studies have shown a high

---

59   One of the difficulties with evaluating the outcomes of conciliated discrimination cases is the paucity of evidence with which to found conclusions. Annual Reports only include selective cases and existing studies relate to small numbers of cases. Whilst the ALRC called for the establishment of a register in which the outcomes of conciliated cases could be listed (with sufficient protection for individual's identities) in order to assist potential complainants, no such register has been established: see ALRC, above, n 26, p 83.

60   Devereux study, above, n 4, p 294

61   Ibid.

62   Ibid.

63   See for instance, *Human Rights and Equal Opportunity Commission Annual Report 1995-96* (AGPS, Canberra), p 92.

64   Ibid, p 295.

65   NSW study, ab, n 5, pp 39, 60.

level of complainant withdrawal at an early stage of the conciliation process. In the NSW study, the most common response amongst the "withdrawing" complainants[66] was that withdrawal was related to negative perceptions of the process, expressed variously as "no solution was appearing, taking too long, too hard, not enough support". Such data would indicate the need for increased support and education programmes for those making discrimination complaints.

D. HEARING BY SPECIALIST TRIBUNAL/COMMISSION

General framework

At the Federal level, unresolved complaints (with the exception of ILO 111 complaints)[67] are referred to an inquiry by the HREOC which is conducted by one or more of its members. The HREOC has wide powers with respect to determinations, though as an administrative body lacks the power to enforce its decisions.[68] State tribunals,[69] unimpeded by any separation of powers issues have the powers of a court[70] including the power to award monetary compensation if a complaint is substantiated.

---

66 Some 222 complainants – a group representing 52% of complainants who responded to the conciliation-focussed survey: NSW study, above, n 5, pp 32-34.

67 Note that ILO 111 complaints under the HREOC Act cannot be the subject of an inquiry. Instead, the Human Rights Commissioner may make a report to the Attorney-General for tabling in Parliament.

68 The constitutional limitations of the HREOC were confirmed by the High Court in *Brandy v Human Rights and Equal Opportunity Commission* (1995) 183 CLR 245. In holding invalid the provisions of the HREOC Act which provided for the lodgment of HREOC determinations in the Federal Court and their enforcement as Federal Court orders, the High Court referred to the separation of powers established under Ch III of the Commonwealth Constitution. By virtue of this, judicial power (including the power to issue binding determinations) could only be exercised by federal courts. Given that the HREOC is an administrative body, it could not be given such judicial powers. The Government's immediate response was to repeal the impugned provisions and replace them with a modified version of the original scheme – that is, hearing by HREOC, followed by a de novo hearing in the Federal Court. Some attempt was made to ameliorate the possible duplication of process as between the two hearings by providing that the court may receive as evidence the HREOC's determination, any document that was before the HREOC and a copy of the record of the inquiry: see SDA s 83A. As of the time of writing, the Government has introduced a Human Rights Legislation Amendment Bill 1997 to provide for unsuccessfully conciliated complaints to be referable directly to the Federal Court on the initiative of the parties. There is provision for Registrars to exercise many of the hearing powers in the Federal Court, though such delegation would appear to be constitutionally problematic: see Bailey, P, Submission No 2 to the Senate Legal and Constitutional Legislation Committee, dated 3 April 1997; Evidence 7 April 1997, 331-33.

69 In the Northern Territory, the Local Court is the designated tribunal. The Northern Territory Commissioner is also in the unusual position of being able to make an administrative determination after a failed conciliation procedure. In Victoria, and Queensland, the specialist tribunal is called the Anti-Discrimination Tribunal; in the ACT, the Discrimination Tribunal, and in the remaining States the title of the body is the Equal Opportunity Tribunal (EOT).

70 *Australian Postal Commission v Dao* (1986) 6 NSWLR 497.

Level of formality of processes

The complaint-based processes embodied in State and Federal legislation were consciously designed to be informal, accessible, and inexpensive. With the exception of the Northern Territory's adjudicative body, the "hearing bodies" under the State and Federal legislation are not bound to comply with the rules of evidence.[71] Evidence of what has occurred during the conciliation process is not admissible, however, and the Federal Court has been critical of the rare examples in which adjudicative bodies have commented upon the level of co-operation shown by parties in conciliation in their determinations.[72] Even with the movement away from HREOC hearings and towards Federal Court proceedings under the proposed changes to the HREOC Act, the intention to retain this level of informality remains. The Human Rights Legislation Amendment Bill 1997 thus provides that the "Court is not bound by technicalities or legal forms" subject to Ch III of the Constitution.[73] There is still some evidence that complainants find the hearing bodies' procedures difficult to follow, whilst respondents (particularly those represented during hearings) have complained that complainants' solicitors enjoy "undue flexibility" in framing and altering their claims, that there is insufficient filtering of vexatious complaints, and that the anti-discrimination tribunals are "unprofessional".[74]

Public nature of proceedings

In general the hearings of specialist tribunals are in public, though bodies have the power to order that the whole or part of a proceeding be in public and may prohibit the publication of evidence or facts such as the identities of the parties. In the Federal arena, for instance, this power to suppress the identities of the parties has been used to protect the identity of underage persons involved incidentally in a sex discrimination case, whilst more recently the power of suppression was used in Queensland in relation to a sexuality discrimination case. Suppression powers have also been widely used in relation to HIV discrimination cases in recognition of the significant stigma attached to HIV and AIDS. Many parties retain a preference for anonymity at all stages of the complaint handling process,[75] though increasingly courts seem to be stressing the competing interest of society in an open, transparent system of justice which may prevail over the individual's interest in privacy.[76]

Separation of hearing personnel from conciliation personnel

Although in most jurisdictions different personnel hear the discrimination complaint than are involved in the conciliation process,[77] there is some evidence of a

---

71 The ACT and Queensland legislation are silent on this point; other legislation is specific. In the Northern Territory, the rules of the Local Court apply.

72 See the comments of Heerey J in *AMC v Siddiqui* (1996) 137 ALR 653 at 672-73.

73 Clause 46PO.

74 NSW study, above, n 5, p 98.

75 Complainants in the NSW study expressed concern over the lack of anonymity at tribunal hearings: NSW study, above, n 5, p 88.

76 See, for example, comments in *DM v TD* (unreported, SC NSW, 4 February 1994, BC 9402267).

77 In the Northern Territory, the Commissioner may conduct a hearing, but only if she/he has not conducted the investigation of the complaint or taken part in the conciliation process.

continuing concern that the current structure fails to provide a neutral hearing body. This concern, for instance, was noted in relation to the WA study and seemed to be exacerbated by the fact that complainants along were eligible for statutory assistance from the Commissioner of the Anti-Discrimination Board in pursuing their complaint with the tribunal. Even though the Steering Committee found that complainants were not given advantageous access to Commission files (one of the fears of respondent's solicitors) the Committee noted the significant level of unease amongst respondents. At the Federal level, if the hearing processes move entirely from the HREOC to the Federal Court, there will be little room for arguments concerning structural bias in favour of complainants. Attempts appear to be underway in State systems to increase public perception of the separation of anti-discrimination boards and the anti-discrimination tribunals.

Experience of parties with first instance hearing bodies

Despite the fact that the hearing bodies operate in public, there has been little analysis of the fate of discrimination complaints in such bodies. One contributing factor may be the small number of cases which proceed through to such adjudication with the proportion of cases in which a body issues a determination even lower. Thus we await an indepth analysis of the functioning of State and Federal hearing bodies and a comparison of the methods of such bodies to the operation of generalist courts.[78]

The increasing emphasis on legal formalism within specialist tribunals, whilst to some extent unavoidable given the vulnerability of tribunal determinations to review by superior courts of law, appears to create difficulties for complainants attempting to establish complex discrimination complaints. As Thornton's interesting study of outcomes from State and Territory race-discrimination tribunal hearings demonstrates, the only cases in which complainants are consistently successful are the most direct, unequivocal acts of discrimination. In her assessment, unless the conduct is unequivocal, the burden of proof in the Tribunal setting is virtually insuperable for complainants. Thus in the area of employment in which the evidence is always a matter of controversy, complainants have been particularly unsuccessful. There has been some suggestion, however, that awards of damages are significantly lower than in comparable common law damages, leading to the ALRC's recommendation in its *Equality Before the Law* Report that decision makers use guidelines based on common law damages.[79]

Representation at tribunals

In the State tribunals, the parties do not have a right to representation, though the tribunal may give leave for parties to be so represented. In the HREOC, parties may

---

78 In some jurisdictions, the local court is the prescribed first instance hearing body – for example, in the Northern Territory and the ACT.

79 ALRC, above, n 26, p 88. Note, however, the operation of statutory limits on damages/ compensation in New South Wales and Western Australia. The CCH Discrimination Law Service provides a useful table of damages payments in reported cases: CCH *Equal Opportunity Law and Practice*, vol 1, Resolution of Disputes, Topic 89-960.

be represented by a solicitor or counsel only where the Commission has appointed counsel assisting the Commission, or where it gives leave for the parties to be so represented. In cases where one party is represented (in most circumstances, the respondent), it is not unusual for counsel assisting the Commission in effect to give assistance to the unrepresented complainant. During debates on the Racial Discrimination Bill and on the establishment of the HREOC, some parliamentarians decried the lack of a right to representation for those called before the HREOC, interpreting such as a significant threat to due process.[80] If the current Human Rights Legislation Amendment Bill is passed, parties will have a right to be represented by a barrister or a solicitor, or in fact another person, unless the court considers it inappropriate. In practice, higher levels of respondents than complainants employ representatives in tribunal hearings.[81]

Costs

Under most State legislation, there are specific provisions militating against an award of costs unless the proceedings were frivolous or there are special circumstances justifying an award of damages.[82] Under the Federal legislation, there is provision for the granting of financial assistance from the Attorney-General. The issue of costs continues to create significant resentment amongst both complainants and respondents – with some complainants critical of their inability to recoup costs even when they are the successful party,[83] and respondents equally virulent that costs orders should be used as a disincentive against complainants' pursuit of meritless actions.[84]

E. PROCEEDINGS IN COURTS

The courts stand in a different relationship to the primary hearing body, depending whether the jurisdiction of the HREOC or of the State tribunals is involved. At the Commonwealth level, the Federal Court is not an appellate forum as such, but hears matters de novo. In the States, an appeal lies from the hearing body to a court, in most instances the Supreme Court, on questions of law.[85]

---

80 See, for instance, House of Representatives, *Hansard*, 8 April 1975, 1289 per Mr Killen; House of Representatives, *Hansard*, 14 November 1985, 2747 per Mr Spender.

81 In the NSW study for instance, whilst some 56% of complainants had representatives in the EOT, the comparable figure for respondents was closer to 90%: NSW study, above, n 5, pp 83, 95.

82 Awarding of costs must be "reasonable" or there must be another justification. Under the Queensland legislation, there is no limitation on the awarding of costs.

83 NSW study, above, n 5, p 88.

84 Ibid, p 100.

85 In *Australian Postal Commission v Dao* (1986) 6 NSWLR 497, the NSW Court of Appeal held that the Equal Opportunity Tribunal of NSW has the status of a court, and this decision would appear to apply in all other State and Territory jurisdictions. In each case, the tribunal has power to enforce its decision. However, HREOC is not given power to enforce its determinations under Commonwealth anti-discrimination legislation, and seemingly could not be permitted to do so while it remains an administrative body, because of the separation of the judicial power: *Brandy v HREOC* (1995) 183 CLR 245.

It is difficult to assess the extent to which the tribunals (including HREOC) have promoted the purpose of eliminating discrimination by being more sympathetic to the broad purpose of the legislation than the courts. It is likely that they have drawn attention to issues that might have gone unnoticed had the initial hearing been in a court. Although one measure is the extent to which the courts' decisions have adversely affected the complainant by either directing a rehearing or by finding against the complainant, even here it is difficult to make a final assessment. The High Court, for example, disapproved the finding of the Supreme Court of Victoria in *Arumugam*[86] on the matter of intention, and in so doing upheld the original decision of the Equal Opportunity Board. Similarly, the Federal Court overturned the finding of the HREOC in *Sheiban*[87] in a way favourable to the complainants. At present the best one can venture is that the courts have in some way reversed decisions of tribunals in rather less than half of the cases that have come before them. That is probably a little lower proportion reversed than in the general appellate jurisdiction exercised by those courts. Accordingly, if one can make the general assumption that the tribunals have adopted purposive interpretations of the legislation, one could say that the courts have at least been reasonably sympathetic. While on the information currently available it is not possible to go beyond that to reach any fact-based conclusion about whether the courts would have been as sympathetic if they had not had the advantage of a prior tribunal hearing, it seems not unreasonable to assume that the tribunals have had a positive effect on the way in which the courts have interpreted the legislation.[88]

F. SOME CURRENT LEGAL ISSUES

In this section four legal issues that are currently of special interest in the mounting of cases of discrimination, or that are still in the process of resolution by the courts and tribunals, are briefly reviewed.

Indirect discrimination

Indirect discrimination, sometimes termed systemic or covert or effect-based discrimination, is in concept an integral part of discrimination, if discrimination is broadly defined to comprehend disadvantage caused to a person by rules that apply to her or him rather than by an act that is obviously based on the prohibited ground. But direct discrimination can occur as the result of rules, just as can indirect discrimination, and thus there is an overlap between the two. It is, for example, directly discriminatory to have a rule that only persons of a particular age or sex

---

86 *General Manager, Department of Health v Arumugam* (1987) EOC ¶92-195. The case in which the High Court indicated that intention is not necessary in committing an unlawful discriminatory act, whether directly or indirectly discriminatory, is *Australian Iron and Steel Pty Ltd v Banovic* (1989) 168 CLR 165.

87 *Hall v Sheiban* (1989) EOC ¶92-250.

88 Peter Bailey is currently analysing the nearly 1000 cases reported in the EOC series, and hopes during 1998 to be able to publish the resultant findings. Meanwhile, the best source is his earlier analysis, contained in Bailey, P, *Human Rights: Australia in an International Context* (Butterworths, Sydney, 1990), pp 223-24.

may apply for an ordinary clerical job. It is indirectly discriminatory if the rule is what is often described as "facially neutral", but is covertly discriminatory, as when an employer uses the normally fair rule that when there is a downturn in business, employees will be laid on in reverse order of appointment – "last on first off" as the practice is often termed. If the employer has in the past practised hiring on a basis that is discriminatory against women, and has just begun to redress the imbalance in workers by employing more women, then they will obviously be the first to be laid off, and the normally non-discriminatory rule will be found to be discriminatory.[89]

Ironically, British and Australian anti-discrimination legislation placed a definitional frame round indirect discrimination in their respective enactments in the late 1970s and early 1980s, because it was assumed the regular courts would not recognise the kind of discrimination identified by the United States Supreme Court in *Griggs v Duke Power Co*.[90] In that case, Title VII discrimination was found when a rule was adopted that only persons with matriculation standard education would be appointed to the powerhouse's workforce. The court found that such a rule was discriminatory on grounds of race, because only 12% of the relevant black population matriculated, compared with 34% for whites, and the powerhouse workforce had many jobs that required less than education to matriculation standards. In the British and Australian formulation, which is gradually being superseded in Australia, a person would discriminate if he or she imposed a condition or requirement on the aggrieved person:

- with which a substantially higher proportion of persons not of the same sex (or other proscribed status or attribute) could not comply; and
- which is not reasonable in the circumstances; and
- with which the aggrieved person does not or cannot comply.

This rule neatly encapsulates the finding of the Supreme Court in *Griggs*. It is, however, a tight kind of rule in that it has been found very difficult to apply in less clear circumstances.[91] Accordingly, more recent formulations of the concept of indirect discrimination have focused on the need for a requirement (whether purposive or not) that has the *effect* of unreasonably discriminating against a person or group of persons on the proscribed ground. The condition or requirement does not have to be formally expressed for it to bring into operation the legislative proscription,[92] although it will need to have some identifiable form.[93]

---

89   *Australian Iron and Steel Pty Ltd v Najdovska* (1985) EOC ¶92-140, (1986) EOC ¶92-176 (both in the Equal Opportunity Tribunal of New South Wales) and (1988) EOC ¶92-223 (New South Wales Court of Appeal). For the sequel in the High Court, see ns 91 and 92 below and accompanying text.

90   *Griggs v Duke Power Co* 401 US 424 (1971).

91   See, for example, the seven or eight formulations of the "pool" involved in the first requirement contained in *Australian Iron and Steel v Banovic*, the successor to *Najdovska* (which was heard in the Equal Opportunity Tribunal of New South Wales, the Supreme Court of New South Wales and then the High Court.

92   See *Waters v Public Transport Corporation* (1991) 173 CLR 349 and *Australian Iron and Steel Pty Ltd v Banovic* (1989) 168 CLR 165, (1989) EOC ¶92-340. In the latter, the informal rule of "last on first off" was held to be a "requirement" for purposes of the legislation.

93   *Waters v Rizkalla* (constituting the Equal Opportunity Board) (1990) EOC ¶92-282 at 77,854 (Cummins J, Supreme Court).

The least obscure of the new formulations is found in the *Discrimination Act* 1991 of the ACT. That legislation wraps up the two forms of discrimination (direct and indirect) in the one section by providing that discrimination occurs if a person, on the basis of a proscribed ground or attribute, treats another person unfavourably (direct discrimination) or imposes an unreasonable condition or requirement that has a similar effect (indirect).[94] The Federal Court aptly summed up the position relating to the nature of this condition or requirement when it observed that it must be one that is "fair in form and intention but discriminatory in impact and outcome".[95] Nevertheless, the simpler legislation has not yet led to agreement within the courts about how precisely the "unreasonableness" criterion should be applied, as discussed in the following section.

The criterion of unreasonableness

In all anti-discrimination legislation, the search for equality is the primary objective, and final resort is often had to the criterion of reasonableness or unreasonableness. The criterion has been included specifically in the legislation defining indirect discrimination (see above), in the provisions relating to discrimination on grounds of pregnancy, and in those relating to disability. In the latter, the term is usually "unjustifiable hardship", but this is in effect a synonym for unreasonable.

The concept of reasonableness was fully discussed in *Waters*,[96] the leading case on disability, where Mason CJ and Gaudron J in a minority judgment (on this point) noted that there are two views of the meaning of "reasonable in the circumstances". They preferred the "strict" view which, having in mind the purpose of anti-discrimination legislation, is that the reasonableness has to be measured by reference to the interests of the disadvantaged person or group. The "broad" view is that reasonableness is concerned with both the effect of the discriminatory conduct on the disadvantaged group and the cost to the discriminator of avoiding the conduct. In *Waters*, the discriminatory action complained of was withdrawal of conductors from trams on some services, and a requirement that passengers use "scratch" tickets for all journeys. On both counts, all judges found the conduct had disadvantaged the complainants, who suffered various forms of disability, with the majority judges also finding that the cost to the corporation of ceasing the discriminatory conduct was not excessive or "unreasonable" (Mason CJ and Gaudron J indicated that they would accept the majority view of unreasonableness).

The judgment of Dawson and Toohey JJ in *Waters* appears to have been the basis for the subsequent formulation in Commonwealth legislation of the interpretation to be given to the criterion of unreasonableness.[97] They suggested that reasonableness could be determined by reference to:

---

94   The formulation in the SDA is, since 1995, in similar but rather more complex terms.

95   *Secretary of the Department of Foreign Affairs and Trade v Styles* (1989) 88 ALR 621 at 627 per Bowen CJ, Gummow J.

96   *Waters v Public Transport Corporation* (1991) 173 CLR 349

97   See, for example, SDA s 7B and their Honours' judgment in *Waters* at (1991) 173 CLR 395.

- the nature and extent of the disadvantage (presumably to the complainant);
- the feasibility of overcoming or mitigating the disadvantage (presumably by the discriminator, but possibly — and in the authors' view desirably — in consultation about alternatives with the disadvantaged person or group); and
- whether the disadvantage (presumably to the complainant) is proportionate to the result sought by the person imposing the condition (the discriminator).[98]

The courts appear to have been relatively even-handed in their balancing of the interests of the disadvantaged persons against those of the provider of the employment or the service. In the area of employment, while it is not open for a tribunal to go as far as to redetermine the terms of an offending duty statement, the requirement the duty statement contains must still be "reasonable".[99]

Natural justice and procedural fairness

Two situations arise in which, during the course of the handling of a complaint, a question of natural justice or procedural fairness may arise. The first is when a complaint is lodged, and relates to the way it is handled within the office. The second is when it proceeds to conciliation.

In relation to the receipt of complaints, all the legislation requires that the complaint be made in writing, although in most cases an office will assist with this process, and in two jurisdictions is required to assist.[100] The legislation also imposes a time limitation on how long after the incident complained of a complaint can be made (usually 12 months, except in New South Wales and South Australia, where the period is six months, but with extension possible in the former). Nevertheless, it is not permissible for a complaint received out of time to be rejected out of hand: it will in many cases have to be considered having in mind the remedial and beneficial purposes of the legislation.[101]

The second situation, when a complaint proceeds to a formal conciliation process, has led to two apparently inconsistent decisions. In *Koppen*, the Federal Court held that the Commonwealth Commissioner for Community Relations was under an obligation to ensure that the person in charge of a conciliation under the racial discrimination legislation had to act in accordance with the principles of procedural fairness and must appear to be impartial.[102] The person convening the proceedings was Aboriginal, and during the compulsory conciliation conference indicated that she was aware from her own daughters that the particular nightclub bar did discriminate. Spender J said there was a chance the proceedings might end

---

98 The words in brackets (except the final bracket) are supplied by the authors by way of explication/commentary, the other words are drawn directly from the reasons for judgment.

99 *Bugden v State Rail Authority of New South Wales* (1991) EOC ¶92-360.

100 The obligation to assist is contained in the DDA s 69 and in the *Equal Opportunity Act 1995* (Vic) s 106.

101 So held by the Supreme Court of New South Wales in *McAuliffe v Puplick* (1996) EOC ¶92-900, and a New Zealand decision by the Complaints Review Tribunal added that whether the refusal to accept would constitute a denial of natural justice has also to be considered: *Proceedings Commissioner v McCulloch* (1996) EOC ¶92-818.

102 *Koppen v Commissioner of Community Relations* (1986) 11 FCR 360, (1986) EOC ¶92-173, especially at 76,670.

up in court if not settled, and that therefore the alleged harasser stood in jeopardy of legal action if the conciliation failed. On the other hand, in the *Corporal Punishment* case,[103] Mathews J, sitting as the Equal Opportunity Tribunal of New South Wales, held that the conciliation and investigatory processes were preliminaries and that it was inappropriate for there to be a requirement of natural justice or procedural fairness at that stage. It was up to the parties to try to reach a solution, and the process should be as flexible as practicable. It had as such no effect on legal rights.

The two cases may be distinguished on the basis that the Commonwealth's RDA required, as it then stood, that a certificate be issued by the Commissioner of Community Relations or the Human Rights Commission 1981 before a complainant could take the case to a court.[104] Alternatively, they could be distinguished on the basis of the decisions being challenged in each case – with *Koppen* focusing upon the issue of a certificate that conciliation had failed, and *Corporal Punishment* on the management of the conciliation process itself – whether conciliation could be effective. Nevertheless, *Koppen* is usually cited as authority for the general proposition that the conciliation process is subject to the requirements of procedural fairness. The Mathews decision in *Corporal Punishment* appears to be more soundly based in the realities of the conciliation process. The whole idea of the conciliation process is to achieve an agreement between the parties, and in all the legislation it is (properly, we consider) insulated from the tribunal process by provisions that nothing said or done during it can be brought as evidence in a tribunal or court. Conciliation is designed to be a flexible process, unencumbered by a concern with excessive legal formality. If one party is being intractable, the conciliator needs to have the capacity and flexibility to use a myriad of techniques to ensure that, as far as is possible, a genuine attempt at conciliation on fair and equal terms is facilitated.

At the same time, it would hardly be appropriate to leave the conciliation process entirely without some form of review. A mid course might be to start with the principle enunciated in *Corporal Punishment* but to add that there is an onus on the Commission to appoint a person as conciliator who is impartial and acceptable to both parties. What would then be reviewable would be the Commission's appointment rather than the detail of the conciliation proceedings themselves.

Evidentiary requirements

Except in the few cases where criminal provisions are included in the legislation, such as in relation to discriminatory advertising and to offences against those carrying out the provisions of the legislation, the evidentiary burden of proof is civil, namely on the balance of probabilities. It has been confirmed regularly that the rule in *Briginshaw* normally applies.[105] This means that the complainant must make out a

---

103 *Re New South Wales Corporal Punishment* (1986) EOC ¶92-160; *R v Equal Opportunity Board; ex p Burns* (1984) EOC ¶92-112.

104 RDA s 24(3).

105 *Briginshaw v Briginshaw* (1938) 60 CLR 336: see, for example, *Erbs v Overseas Corporation Pty Ltd* (1986) EOC ¶92-181; and in the Northern Territory and Tasmania this situation is at least partially confirmed by the anti-discrimination legislation. In the Commonwealth, Queensland and Western Australia the respondent is required to prove the reasonableness of the requirement in relation to indirect discrimination .

prima facie case of discrimination, after which the onus shifts to the respondent to show on the balance of probabilities that the discrimination did not occur. The same situation continues to apply as further points are brought forward by either side. However, motive is not relevant in anti-discrimination cases, a point that frequently arises when indirect discrimination is complained of.[106]

Most of the legislation provides that unlawful discrimination occurs even if it is not the sole or the main reason for the discriminatory action.[107] This means that a case can lead to a finding of unlawful discrimination if the complainant wishes to proceed with an action. The balance between a finding of unlawfulness and the injustice of full condemnation is found by determining that the damages or other remedy will not be large if the discriminatory element forms a relatively minor element in the particular case.

It is also important to note that all the tribunals are exempted from the necessity of applying the strict rules of evidence. Even though this is the formal situation, the exemption serves less to create a very free process in the tribunals than it does to avoid the ability to take and pursue excessively technical points about evidentiary rules. Because there is always an appeal on a point of law to a court, the tribunals tend to be careful to apply the main rules of evidence, while avoiding lengthy discussions on fine issues. This seems a useful position, and probably results in quicker hearings and a greater possibility of reasonably well informed parties being able to represent themselves.

G. ALTERNATIVE REDRESS

The grounds and areas covered in anti-discrimination legislation can in some cases overlap with other legal remedies.

Workplace remedies

Anti-discrimination legislation, under the description of "work", now covers a broad range of activities, some of which have been comprehended in the new workplace relations legislation.[108] Both areas may now cover, in addition to employees, contract workers and organisations registered under the workplace relations legislation. But the latter legislation may not extend to commission agents, partnerships or the activities of qualifying bodies.[109] Nevertheless, the Commonwealth's sex discrimination legislation now contains provisions that enable the Sex Discrimination Commissioner to intervene in a matter before the Industrial Relations Commission and also to bring before the Commission particular cases that have been brought to her attention.

---

106 See *Australian Iron and Steel Pty Ltd v Banovic* (1989) 168 CLR 165, and the similar approach adopted in *Birmingham City Council v Equal Opportunities Commission* [1989] AC 1155 and *Canadian National Railway v Canadian Human Rights Commission* [1987] 1 SCR 1114.

107 See, for example, SDA s 8.

108 See Ch 9 by MacDermott in this volume.

109 Qualifying bodies are charged with conferring, renewing or withdrawing authorisation or qualification needed for the practice of a profession or the carrying on of a trade.

The State legislation does not contain similar provisions, but the special complaints provisions in the Victorian legislation are noted below.

Actions in tort

It may be expected that as the general law absorbs the principles in discrimination law (perhaps hastened by the Commonwealth's move to vest powers to determine unconciliated cases in the Federal Court), other areas of law, particularly tort law, will increasingly begin to provide discrimination-based remedies. That would, in our view, be a highly desirable development. Now that all jurisdictions have legislated against discrimination, it seems wrong that only formal and not substantive equality is available through the mainline legal system. It may not be too much to hope that the courts will increasingly incorporate the principles of substantive equality embodied in anti-discrimination law in other areas of law under their control.

Indeed, the process has already started. It has occurred in two ways. The first is through bypassing the conciliation gateway to curial litigation provided in the anti-discrimination legislation. The second is through actions brought in tort for personal injury.

The main case which so far has bypassed the conciliation process is *Styles v Department of Foreign Affairs and Trade*.[110] The case was brought directly to the Federal Court. In it, Ms Styles claimed, pursuant to the *Administrative Decisions (Judicial Review) Act* 1977 (Cth), that she had been denied promotion by the Department pursuant to the *Public Service Act* 1922 (Cth), because of discrimination made unlawful by the SDA. She claimed that the discrimination arose partly from a failure to consider her application when a round of promotions was being considered, and partly because the procedures required by the Department's equal employment opportunity program were not followed. Sitting at first instance, Wilcox J found in favour of Ms Styles on the second ground, because appropriate selection procedures had not been determined. Indirect discrimination under the SDA was found, the decision to appoint a person other than Ms Styles was set aside, and the Department was ordered to reconsider according to law the question of the identity of the person to be appointed. On appeal, the Full Court by majority overruled the decision, based on a different interpretation of the indirect discrimination provisions.

There was no challenge to the basic justiciability of the case by the procedure adopted, so it stands as an alternative, albeit more expensive, to the more standard approach through the conciliation gateway.

The second case was one of assault, battery and false imprisonment brought in Hobart by Ms Barker, an apprentice with the Hobart City Council, against the Council and a number of fellow employees.[111] Over a period of several months the employees had, despite her resistance and complaint, subjected her to unwelcome sexual approaches and false imprisonment. Although there was at the time no State

---

110 (1988) EOC ¶92-239.

111 *Barker v City of Hobart and Barratt, Gentile and Stacey* (unreported, SC Tas, 6 May 1993, No 1501 of 1990).

anti-discrimination legislation operative in Tasmania, the Supreme Court awarded substantial damages.[112]

The reasons for judgment are not reported, but they focused largely on evidentiary matters including the admissibility of opinion evidence and of evidence relating to embarrassment as perceived by an onlooker. There was no questioning of the availability of a remedy in relation to the actions of the defendants, but equally no use of the Commonwealth legislation, which would have been available for much of what was claimed.

Increasingly, it may be expected, as observed earlier, that the courts will be willing to provide remedies in situations where clearly discriminatory conduct has occurred. Thus alternative process and remedies are likely to be more readily available as discrimination law and principles become more embodied in the general law.

Special complaints involving significant financial effects

A new possibility for an alternative source of remedy has emerged from the 1995 replacement in Victoria of the earlier equal opportunity legislation. Under Pt 7 Div 2 of the new *Equal Opportunity Act* 1995, provision is made for the referral to the Supreme Court of Victoria of "special complaints" without prior process within the machinery provided by the Act. A special complaint is defined as one "the resolution of which may have significant social, economic or financial effects on the community or a section of the community", or whose resolution "may establish important precedents in the interpretation of this Act".

It appears that an important part of the reason for introducing the new provisions is the difficulty the Victorian Government experienced in relation to the proposed closure of schools in Richmond and Broadmeadows, in both of which there were disadvantaged students, including in particular Aborigines in Broadmeadows.[113] It is disturbing that the Supreme Court appears to have been perceived to be a possibly less sympathetic forum for decision-making than was the Equal Opportunity Board in the long series of cases relating to the two schools, which the Board directed the government not to close. However, it cannot be assumed that the apparent expectation of the government will be fulfilled, particularly as the general courts become increasingly involved in the administration of anti-discrimination law. Indeed, it may be hoped that with their greater authority and their awareness of the importance of protecting individual and community rights over a much broader field than the equal opportunity tribunals cover, the move to vest the new jurisdiction in the Supreme Court may herald a further opportunity for the broadening of the impact of the move towards substantive equality.

So far, no other States have legislated in the Victorian mode, but if that occurs it will be further evidence of a gradual move to absorb substantive equality law into the general legal system.

---

112 Damages of $91,000 against the Council and further damages amounting to $29,000 against the three other defendants.

113 The main cases in the long saga are *Sinnapan v Victoria* (1994) EOC ¶92-498; *Victoria v Sinnapan*, (1995) EOC ¶92-663 and (1995) EOC ¶92-699.

CONCLUSION

Anti-discrimination and human rights bodies are clearly facing a variety of challenges – shrinking resources, increasing formalism and a need to grapple with some of the most complex legal issues in the discrimination field. Whilst at the individual complaints level such bodies seem to be providing an accessible form of dispute resolutions there remains a need to counter the structural underpinnings of discrimination through indirect discrimination complaints and education programmes. International law, from whence the central concept of discrimination has arisen, is enjoying a renewed prominence in shaping understandings of central concepts such as substantive equality and the appropriate targets of anti-discrimination law. Traditional court structures appear to be developing a range of remedies directed towards addressing discrimination in form and substance whilst integrating in the general law the pivotal notions of equality and non-discrimination.

14

USING HUMAN RIGHTS LAWS IN LITIGATION

A Practitioner's Perspective

Kate Eastman and Chris Ronalds

Human rights concern the inherent dignity of an individual to be treated fairly and equally. Human rights laws, in turn, prescribe the minimum standard of treatment that governments must accord to individuals and groups within their jurisdiction to ensure that their human rights are respected.

While human rights may be advanced through political action, the work of non-governmental organisations and education,[1] this chapter considers strategies for using human rights laws in litigation from the perspective of a practitioner. In particular, the chapter will focus on using international human rights instruments in Australian law. The chapter examines cases where human rights have been in issue and considers the potential uses of international human rights law in Australian litigation.[2] The final issue to be addressed is the availability of international human rights remedies such as the First Optional Protocol to the *International Covenant on Civil and Political Rights* (ICCPR).

This chapter is not intended to be a step-by-step guide to formulating an argument based on human rights principles in every matter. The objective of the chapter is to "kit out the tool box" so once armed with the appropriate tools, practitioners are then better equipped to build human rights arguments into litigation.

SOURCES OF HUMAN RIGHTS LAW

The starting point is to acquire a knowledge and familiarity with the sources of human rights law in Australian and international law. In the absence of a Bill of Rights,[3]

---

1   See Bailey, P, *Bringing Human Rights to Life* (Federation Press, Sydney, 1993) and Nettheim, G (ed), *Human Rights – The Australian Debate* (RLCP, Sydney, 1987), and Ch 1 by Kinley in this volume.

2   For the US perspective see Burke, K et al, "Application of International Human Rights Law in State and Federal Courts" (1983) 18 *Texas International Law Journal* 291; Lillich, R, "Invoking International Human Rights Law in Domestic Courts" (1985) 54 *University of Cincinnati Law Review* 367; and Franck, T and Fox, G (eds), *International Law Decisions and National Courts* (Transnational Publishers Inc, New York, 1996). For the UK perspective see Hunt, M, *Using Human Rights in English Courts* (Hart Publications, Oxford, 1997) and New Zealand, Mulgan, M, "Implementing International Human Rights Norms in the Domestic Context: The Role of a National Institution" (1993) 5 *Canterbury Law Review* 235.

3   Alston, P (ed), *Towards an Australian Bill of Rights* (Centre for International and Public Law and the Human Rights and Equal Opportunity Commission, Canberra, 1994), Nettheim, above, n 1, and Wilcox M, *An Australian Charter of Rights?* (Law Book Co, Sydney, 1993).

Australian human rights laws are found in the common law, legislation and the Constitution.[4] Much has been written about the inadequacy of the common law and the Constitution as both a source and protector of human rights.[5] Apart from Commonwealth, State and Territory anti-discrimination laws, statutory protection of human rights is also limited.

In contrast, international human rights laws guarantee a wide range of civil, political, social, economic and cultural rights. The relevant international human rights laws are those contained in treaties, declarations and customary international law.[6] While the former Chief Justice of Australia has acknowledged that international law has always been a source of Australian domestic law,[7] international human rights laws are not automatically part of Australian law. They have no legal effect upon the rights and duties of Australian citizens.[8] Likewise, Australian legislation, which is otherwise valid, cannot be held invalid on the ground that it is inconsistent with international law.[9]

APPLICATION OF INTERNATIONAL HUMAN RIGHTS LAWS TO AUSTRALIAN LAW

Accepting that international law has no direct effect in Australian law, what use may be made of international human rights laws? There are a number of ways international human rights principles have been used in Australian litigation. The four main areas are:

- statutory interpretation
- influencing the common law
- administrative law and decision-making
- constitutional interpretation and implications

---

4   O'Neill, N and Handley, R, *Retreat from Injustice* (Federation Press, Sydney, 1994), Chs 2-4, and Bailey, P, *Human Rights: Australia in an International Context* (Butterworths, Sydney, 1990), Ch 4; and Charlesworth, H, "The Australian Reluctance About Rights" in Alston, above, n 3, pp 21-40.

5   O'Neill, N, "A Never Ending Journey?" in Nettheim, above, n 1, pp 14-18. Unlike other jurisdictions, Australian courts have rejected the notion of "fundamental rights" in the common law (see decisions of Cook J in the New Zealand High Court – *Frazer v State Services Commission* [1984] 1 NZLR 116 at 121, *Taylor v New Zealand Poultry Board* [1984] 1 NZLR 394 at 398) opting for the supremacy of Parliament and the power of Parliament to make laws which may withdraw or impair fundamental rights. See *BLF v Minister for Industrial Relations* (1986) 7 NSWLR 372 at 401-06 and Kirby, M, "The Struggle for Simplicity – Lord Cooke and Fundamental Rights" (New Zealand Legal Research Foundation, 4-5 April 1997): see http://www.hcourt.gov.au/cooke.htm, and Kinley, D, "Constitutional Brokerage in Australia: Constitutions and the Doctrines of Parliamentary Supremacy and the Rule of Law" (1994) 22 *Federal Law Review* 194.

6   Department of Foreign Affairs, *Human Rights Manual* (AGPS, Canberra, 1993), Chs 2-3.

7   Sir Anthony Mason "International Law as a Source of Domestic Law" in Opeksin, B and Rothwell, D (eds), *International Law and Australian Federalism* (Melbourne University Press, Melbourne, 1997), p 210; see also, Ch 2 by Sir Anthony Mason in this volume.

8   *Chow Hung Ching v The King* (1948) 77 CLR 449 at 478; *Bradley v Commonwealth* (1973) 128 CLR 557 at 582; *Simsek v McPhee* (1982) 148 CLR 636 at 641; *Kioa v West* (1985) 159 CLR 550 at 570; *S & M Motor Repairs Pty Ltd v Caltex (Oil) Pty Ltd* (1988) 12 NSWLR 558 at 580-82; *Coe v Commonwealth* (1993) 68 ALJR 110; and *Lee v Darwin City Council* (unreported, SC NT, Thomas J, 28 July 1993) and see Mathew, P, "International Law and the Protection of Human Rights" (1995) 17 *Sydney Law Review* 177.

9   *Chu Kheng Lim v Minister for Immigration* (1992) 176 CLR 1 at 37-38, 52 and 74; *Horta v Commonwealth* (1994) 181 CLR 183; and *Schaik v Neuhaus* (unreported, SC ACT, Miles CJ, 15 April 1996).

Each of these areas will be considered. In all cases Australian courts take judicial notice of international law[10] so there is no requirement to prove international human rights law, other than where a party seeks to rely on a rule of customary international law.

Statutory interpretation

International human rights instruments may be used as an aid to the construction of Commonwealth, State and Territory enactments in the following way.[11] First, where an Australian statute incorporates or refers to a provision of an international human rights instrument, either in whole or in part, the statute must be given the same meaning as the international instrument.[12] Generally, if an Australian enactment incorporates a provision of an international instrument, that instrument may either be expressly included in the enactment[13] or scheduled or annexed to the relevant statute or regulation.[14] In circumstances, where the instrument is not scheduled to the relevant enactment, international human rights instruments may be found in a number of collected texts and treaty series.[15] The instruments are also available on a number of Internet sites.[16]

A recent example of interpreting an Australian statutory provision in accordance with its international meaning is the High Court's decision in *Applicant A v Minister of Immigration and Ethnic Affairs*[17] where Brennan CJ observed:

---

10   But note s 174(1) of the *Evidence Act* 1995 (Cth) which includes international law in the form of treaties as foreign law and applies the rules in relation to proof of foreign law.

11   For an overview of the principles, see Gummow J in *Minister for Foreign Affairs and Trade v Magno* (1992) 37 FCR 298 and note s 15AB(2)(d) of the *Acts Interpretation Act* 1901 (Cth) provides that where any treaty or other international agreement that is referred to in an enactment, the court may have regard to that treaty to confirm that the meaning of the provision is the ordinary meaning conveyed by the text of the provision taking into account its context in the Act and the purpose or object underlying the Act; or to determine the meaning of the provision when: (i) the provision is ambiguous or obscure; or (ii) the ordinary meaning conveyed by the text of the provision taking into account its context in the Act and the purpose or object underlying the Act leads to a result that is manifestly absurd or is unreasonable.

12   *De L v Director General, NSW Department of Community Services* (1996) 187 CLR 640.

13   For example: *Human Rights (Sexual Conduct) Act* 1994 (Cth); *Evidence Act* 1995 (Cth) s 138; *Privacy Act* 1988 (Cth); *Passports Amendment Act* 1984 (Cth) ss 9 and 10; and *Crimes (Torture) Act* 1988 (Cth) s 3(1)(b).

14   For example, *Racial Discrimination Act* 1975 (Cth); *Sex Discrimination Act* 1984 (Cth); *Human Rights and Equal Opportunity Commission Act* 1986 (Cth); and the *Family Law (Child Abduction Convention) Regulations*. See generally, Table: "Main International Human Rights Instruments Relevant to Australia" in p xxxii of this book.

15   Brownlie I, *Basic Documents on Human Rights* (Oxford University Press, Oxford, 3rd ed, 1992) and United Nations 1988, *A Compilation of International Instruments* UN Doc ST/HR/1/Rev.3.

16   For example, the Department of Foreign Affairs Treaty Data Base for treaties to which Australia is a party to is available through the Australian Legal Information Institute or the Australian Human Rights Information Centre at <www.austlii.edu.au>. The United Nations home page at <www.un.org>, has a complete list of treaties concluded by the UN, together with resolutions of UN organs. Specific international human rights sites include the UN High Commissioner for Human Rights home page at <www.unhchr.ch>, and the University of Minnesota Human Rights Library at <www.umn.edu/humanrts/>. For a fuller list of sites and commentary see Ch 15 by Bliss and Roushan in this volume.

17   (1997) 71 ALJR 381 at 383 per Brennan CJ, at 394-96 per McHugh J and at 419 per Kirby J.

If a statute transposes the text of a treaty or a provision of treaty into the statute so as to enact it as part of domestic law, the prima facie legislative intention is that the transposed text should bear the same meaning in the domestic statute as it bears in the treaty.[18]

In that case, the court examined the application of the Refugee Convention and the term "refugee" to Chinese nationals who sought asylum on the grounds that they would be persecuted if returned to China because they would be forcibly sterilised. The court held that the terms used in the *Migration Act* 1958 (Cth) derived from the Refugee Convention should be interpreted to give effect to its meaning in international law.

A further limb to this interpretative principle is where the parliament has incorporated only part of an international instrument. The courts may have regard to the balance of the instrument as an aid to its interpretation. In *De L v Director General, NSW Department of Community Services*[19] the issue concerned the *Family Law (Child Abduction Convention) Regulations* made pursuant to s 111B of the *Family Law Act* which only partially give effect to the terms of the *Hague Convention on the Civil Aspects of International Child Abduction*. In that case Kirby J said:

> The apparent purpose of the Regulations is to make provision of the kind permitted by s 111B of the Act. So far as is presently relevant (and subject to the complaint about variance) reg 16(3) follows quite closely the language of the Convention. It may therefore be inferred that it was intended by the rule maker that the words used in the Regulations should attract the same meaning as would be given by international law to the words of the Convention itself.[20]

Consistently with this approach, Australian courts will interpret the treaty provision in accordance with the international rules governing treaty interpretation, namely the *Vienna Convention on the Law of Treaties* 1969.[21] The Vienna Convention provides that:

Article 31 – General rule of interpretation

1. A treaty shall be interpreted in good faith in accordance with the ordinary meaning to be given to the terms of the treaty in their context and in the light of its object and purpose.

2. The context for the purpose of the interpretation of a treaty shall comprise, in addition to the text, including its preamble and annexes:

    (a)   any agreement relating to the treaty which was made between all the parties in connexion with the conclusion of the treaty;

    (b)   any instrument which was made by one or more parties in connexion with the conclusion of the treaty and accepted by the other parties as an instrument related to the treaty.

---

18   Ibid at 383.

19   (1996) 187 CLR 640.

20   Ibid at 675.

21   *De L v Director General* (1996) 187 CLR 640; *Victrawl Pty Ltd v Telstra Corp Ltd* (1995) 183 CLR 595 at 621-22; *Shipping Corp of India v Gamlen Chemical Co A/Asia Pty Ltd* (1980) 147 CLR 142 at 159. In *Mohazab v Dick Smith Electronics Pty Ltd (No 2)* (1996) 62 IR 200 at 204, the Full Industrial Relations Court relied on the general rules of treaty interpretation in arts 31 and 32 of the *Vienna Convention on the Laws of Treaties* when interpreting the term "termination of employment at the initiative of the employer".

3. There shall be taken into account, together with the context:

    (a) any subsequent agreement between the parties regarding the interpretation of the treaty or the application of its provisions;

    (b) any subsequent practice in the application of the treaty which establishes the agreement of the parties regarding its interpretation;

    (c) any relevant rules of international law applicable in the relations between the parties.

4. A special meaning shall be given to a term if it is established that the parties so intended.

Article 32 – Supplementary means of interpretation

Recourse may be had to supplementary means of interpretation, including the preparatory work of the treaty and the circumstances of its conclusion, in order to confirm the meaning resulting from the application of article 31, or to determine the meaning when the interpretation according to article 31:

    (a) leaves the meaning ambiguous or obscure; or

    (b) leads to a result which is manifestly absurd or unreasonable.

Merely construing the words may not provide the courts with sufficient guidance as to the meaning of the instruments. The language of international instruments is often vague and broad. The right and correlative obligations on a state may be expressed in aspirational terms. International instruments may lack the precision which the Australian courts are accustomed to in domestic legislation.

In construing the provisions of an international instrument, Australian courts give some weight to the decisions of specialist international tribunals, such as the International Court of Justice,[22] the International Labour Organisation (ILO)[23] and United Nations Human Rights Committee established under the ICCPR and the European Commission and Court of Human Rights operating under the European Convention on Human Rights (ECHR).[24]

Other aids to interpreting the scope and operation of international instruments include judicial decisions of other domestic courts which have considered similar issues and the preparatory working documents to the treaty (*travaux préparatoires*), historical, argumentative and other relevant background material to determine the meaning of

---

22   The High Court has referred to ICJ decisions in the following cases: *Koowarta v Bjelke-Petersen* (1982) 153 CLR 168 at 205 and 219; *Commonwealth v Tasmania* (1983) 158 CLR 1 at 222; *Gerhardy v Brown* (1985) 159 CLR 70 at 128 and 135; *Street v Queensland Bar Association* (1989) 168 CLR 461 at 487, 510-12, 571; *Polyukhovich v Commonwealth* (1991) 172 CLR 501 at 559; *Mabo v Queensland (No 2)* (1992) 175 CLR 1 at 40 and 181; and *Sykes v Cleary* (1992) 176 CLR 77.

23   *Qantas Airways Ltd v Christie* (1998) 152 ALR 365; *Christie v Qantas Airways Ltd* (1995) 65 IR 17 and on appeal (1996) 138 ALR 19 where the Industrial Relations Court of Australia referred to ILO Conventions together with ILO General Survey Reports in considering the application of ILO Conventions in Australian law.

24   *Dietrich v The Queen* (1992) 177 CLR 292 at 304-05; *Leask v Commonwealth* (1996) 187 CLR 579 at 615; and *Grollo v Palmer* (1995) 184 CLR 348 at 367-38.

international instruments.[25] In the area of refugee law, the courts have taken into account such material.[26]

In *Chan Yee Kin v Minister for Immigration*[27] the High Court was required to construe the meaning of "a well founded fear of persecution" in art 1A(2) of the Refugee Convention. The appellant argued that regard should be had to the United Nations High Commissioner for Refugees' *Handbook on Procedures and Criteria for Determining Refugee Status* (1979). He argued that the principles set out in the *Handbook* were declaratory of customary international law. Mason CJ rejected this submission and held:

> [W]ithout wishing to deny the usefulness of the admissibility of extrinsic material of this kind, in deciding questions as to the content of concepts of customary international law and as to the meaning of the provision in treaties, I regard the Handbook more as a practical guide for those who are required to determine whether or not a person is a refugee than as a document purporting to interpret the meaning of the relevant parts of the Convention.[28]

The second area where international law may be used to construe a statute is where a statute does not specifically incorporate or refer to an international human rights instrument. In these circumstances the courts have indicated that legislation should be construed to prevent breaches of fundamental human rights.[29] There is a presumption, albeit rebuttable, that the parliament intended to legislate in accordance with its international human rights obligations.[30] In this respect, it is accepted that statutes should be interpreted and applied as far as their language admits consistently with the provisions of an international instrument.[31] In accordance with this principle, any provision which may have the effect of limiting or restricting rights should be construed narrowly.[32]

International human rights laws can be used in this context for standard setting. The international rights may be used as a benchmark against which decisions or actions can

---

25   For different approaches, see Full Court of the Family Court in *In Marriage of Hanbury-Brown: Director-General of Community Services* (1997) 20 Fam LR 334; *Qantas Airlines Ltd v Christie* (1995) 65 IR 17; and *De L v Director General* (1996) 187 CLR 640.

26   *Minister for Immigration v Mayer* (1985) 157 CLR 290; *Somaghi v Minister for Immigration* (1991) 31 FCR 100; *Morato v Minister for Immigration* (1992) 39 FCR 401; *Chan v Minister for Immigration* (1989) 169 CLR 379; and *Gunaleela v Minister for Immigration* (1987) 15 FCR 543.

27   (1989) 169 CLR 379.

28   Ibid at 392; and see *Simsek v McPhee* (1982) 148 CLR 636; *Morato v Minister for Immigration, Local Government and Ethnic Affairs* (1992) 39 FCR 401 at 404, 413-15; and *Lek v Minister for Immigration, Local Government and Ethnic Affairs* (1993) 117 ALR 455 at 459.

29   *Re Bolton; ex p Beane* (1987) 162 CLR 514 at 523; *Coco v The Queen* (1994) 179 CLR 427 at 436-38; *Commissioner of Taxation (Cth) v Citibank Ltd* (1989) 20 FCR 403 at 433; *Taciak v Commissioner of the Australian Federal Police* (1995) 131 ALR 319 at 330-33; *Potter v Minahan* (1908) 7 CLR 277 at 304; and *Bropho v Western Australia* (1990) 171 CLR 1 at 17-18.

30   *Newcrest Mining (WA) Limited v Commonwealth* (1997) 147 ALR 42 at 147; *Dietrich v The Queen* (1992) 177 CLR 292, 306, 348-49; *Minister of State for Immigration and Ethnic Affairs v Teoh* (1995) 183 CLR 273 at 287, 301-02, 315; *Magno* (1992) 37 FCR 298 at 304; and *Kable v DPP* (1995) 36 NSWLR 374 at 395 per Clarke JA.

31   *Jumbunna Coal Mine NL v Victorian Coal Miners' Association* (1908) 6 CLR 309 at 363; *Polites v Commonwealth* (1945) 70 CLR 60 at 80-81; and *Minister of State for Immigration and Ethnic Affairs v Teoh* (1995) 183 CLR 273 at 287.

32   *Piper v Corrective Services* (1986) 6 NSWLR 352 at 361; *Brown v Members of Classification Review Board of the Office of Film and Literature* (1997) 145 ALR 464; and *DPP v Serratore* (1995) 38 NSWLR 137.

be assessed, as fair or appropriate. Justice Perry averted to international human rights instruments as the means for setting appropriate standards in *Walsh v Department of Social Security*.[33] In that case, Mr and Mrs Walsh pleaded guilty to breaches of the *Social Security Act* 1991 (Cth). Both were sentenced to a term of imprisonment and they appealed against the severity of the sentence on the grounds that the sentencing judge failed to take into account all the relevant factors in s 16A(2) of the *Crimes Act* 1914 (Cth) and in particular the impact of the sentences on the couple's three young children. In his judgment, Perry J noted that international human rights instruments emphasised the protection of the family unit. In relation to the application of these instruments, he said:

> [A]lthough such instruments do not form part of Australian law, they serve to underscore the importance of provisions such as s 16A(2)(p) of the *Crimes Act* which, where possible should be construed and applied consistently with them.[34]

He varied the sentences and Mrs Walsh was not imprisoned.

The third relevant principle of statutory interpretation is that where an Australian statute has the objective and purpose of protecting human rights, the courts have indicated that human rights legislation should be construed broadly to give effect to the objectives of the legislation.[35] In doing so, international instruments may be used to identify the objectives. This interpretative approach is often applied in discrimination proceedings.[36] In *Waters v Public Transport Corporation*, for example, Mason CJ and Gaudron J observed:

> However, the principle that requires that the particular provisions of the Act must be read in the light of the statutory objects is of particular significance in the case of legislation which protects or enforces human rights. In construing such legislation the courts have a special responsibility to take account of and give effect to the statutory purpose.[37]

Some caution must be exercised in applying these principles of interpretation when examining the impact of any exceptions on the substantive provisions of the law.[38]

The fourth relevant principle is that international human rights instruments may be used where provisions of statutes or regulations are ambiguous or unclear.[39] Human rights instruments may also be resorted to in order to fill lacunae in legislation.[40]

33　(1996) 67 SASR 143.

34　Ibid at 147.

35　*Human Rights and Equal Opportunity Commission v Secretary of Department of Immigration and Multicultural Affairs* (1996) 137 ALR 207 at 216; *IW v City of Perth* (1997) 146 ALR 696 at 710 per Dawson and Gaudron JJ, referring to and adopting *Waters v Public Transport Corporation* (1991) 173 CLR 349 per Mason CJ and Gaudron J at 359 (with whom Deane J agreed) and also per Brennan J at 372, per Dawson and Toohey JJ at 394 and per McHugh J at 406-07.

36　*Australian Medical Council v Wilson* (1996) 137 ALR 653 at 655.

37　*Waters* (1991) 173 CLR 349 at 359.

38　*Qantas Airways Ltd v Christie* (1998) 152 ALR 365, McHugh J at 385 takes a narrower view than Kirby J (in dissent) at 42 on the approach to be taken and see also *Commonwealth v Human Rights and Equal Opportunity Commission and X* (unreported, Fed Ct FC, 13 January 1998), per Burchett J.

39　*Chu Kheng Lim v Minister for Immigration* (1992) 176 CLR 1 at 38. In *Murray v Director, Family Services, ACT* (1993) FLC ¶92-416, the Family Court considered the *Hague Convention on the Civil Aspects of International Child Abduction* in which the court was required to consider argument about the relationship between the Hague Convention, which had been given domestic effect by the Child Abduction Regulations and CROC. It had been argued that the Hague Convention was inconsistent with, and should be read as subject to CROC which succeeded it.

40　See *Young v Registrar, Court of Appeal (No 3)* (1993) 32 NSWLR 262 at 274 and the New Zealand Court of Appeal decision of *Tavita v Minister for Immigration* [1994] NZLR 97.

The Full Bench of the Family Court in decision of *B v B*[41] relied on human rights instruments to construe recent amendments to the *Family Law Act* 1975 (Cth). The court addressed the meaning of the "best interests" of the child in relation to parenting orders. The proceedings raised a number of competing interests and rights – the rights of two young children to have contact with both parents, the responsibility and interests of a father to be involved in his children's upbringing and the rights of the mother to travel and choose her residence. The court devoted part of its judgment to considering the relevance of international human rights instruments, noting:

> the status of international treaties and conventions and the way in which they operate in relation to family law has been the subject of increasing attention.

In that case, the Commonwealth Attorney-General, himself intervened in the proceedings to argue that the *Family Law Reform Act* 1995 (Cth) should be interpreted without regard to the *Convention on the Rights of the Child* (CROC). The court considered CROC and its predecessors – the UN *Declaration of the Rights of the Child* 1959 and the Declaration of Geneva adopted by the League of Nations in 1924. The court also referred to the Australian Government's report under CROC and concluded that against such a backdrop, the CROC was relevant matter for the court to have regard to.

In addition to these recognised interpretative principles, an area, which is likely to be of increasing importance, is where an Australian statute refers to provisions of international human rights law as a relevant matter for a court to take into account in exercising a statutory discretion. To date, few judges have used international human rights instruments in such a way. Some examples are where judges have considered international human rights law in considering whether the elements of an offence have been made out,[42] bail applications,[43] and in sentencing decisions be it pursuant to an enactment or in the common law. In *R v Hollingshed and Rodgers*,[44] the accused men pleaded guilty to offences of burglary and robbery. They were each sentenced to six years imprisonment. They appealed against the severity of the sentence and argued that their imprisonment would breach arts 2(3), 7 and 10(3) of the ICCPR. Miles CJ, noting that the submission was novel, devoted some time in his judgment to the application of the ICCPR and the United Nations Standard Minimum Rules for the Treatment of Prisoners to sentencing decisions. In concluding that ICCPR was relevant, he said:

> In *McKellar v Smith*, I suggested that Australian Courts might take judicial notice of the ICCPR, the Declaration on the Rights of the Child and other international instruments which contain provisions and establish standards relevant to exercising discretion to exclude evidence of a confession of a juvenile obtained unfairly. I see no reason not to adopt the same sort of approach in the sentencing process, where discretionary factors to be taken into account are numerous and conflicting.[45]

---

41 *B v B* (1997) 21 Fam LR 676.

42 *Schaik v Neuhaus* (unreported, SC ACT, Miles CJ, 15 April 1996); *Sillery v R* (1981) 180 CLR 353 at 361-62 per Murphy J; *R v Phillips and Pringle* [1973] 1 NSWLR 175.

43 *DPP v Serratore* (1995) 38 NSWLR 137.

44 (1993) 112 FLR 109.

45 Ibid at 115.

If international human rights laws are used in the exercise of judicial discretion, this will require the courts to do more than merely interpret the words of the statute. The courts will have to consider the content and nature of any relevant human right and how the application of a statutory provision may impact upon the rights of the person affected. The uniform Australian evidence laws specifically refer to the ICCPR and use rights based language in its operation. Section 138 of the *Evidence Act* 1995 (Cth) grants a court a discretion to exclude improperly or illegally obtained evidence.[46] The section provides:

(1) Evidence that was obtained:

    (a)   improperly or in contravention of an Australian law; or

    (b)   in consequence of an impropriety or of a contravention of an Australian law; is not to be admitted unless the desirability of admitting the evidence outweighs the undesirability of admitting evidence that has been obtained in the way in which the evidence was obtained. ...

(3) Without limiting the matters that the court may take into account under subsection (1), it is to take into account: ...

    (f)   whether the impropriety or contravention was contrary to or inconsistent with a right of a person recognised by the International Covenant on Civil and Political Rights ...

The section does not restrict the range of rights in the ICCPR which a court may consider, so evidence may be excluded if it was obtained in breach of a person's privacy, in a discriminatory manner or in circumstances where a person was treated in a cruel, inhuman or degrading manner.[47] The application of this provision will require a judge to apprise him or herself of a range of substance and procedural human rights contained in the ICCPR.

Common law

The extent to which the common law protects human rights is indeterminate. However, courts are prepared to have a regard to international human rights law in determining the nature and extent of the common law's protection of rights.[48]

In *J v Lieschke*,[49] Deane J relied on the Universal Declaration of Human Rights in holding that:

those rights and authority have been properly recognised as fundamental (see, eg, *Universal Declaration of Human Rights*, Arts 12, 16, 25(2) and 26(3)) ... They have deep roots in the common law. In the absence of an unmistakable legislative intent to the contrary, they cannot properly be modified or extinguished by the exercise of administrative or judicial powers otherwise than in accordance with the basic requirements of natural justice.

---

46   *R v Truong* (1996) 86 A Crim R 188.

47   See also s 83 of the *Evidence Act* 1995 (Cth) which excludes admissions influenced by violence and certain other conduct. That section uses language consistent with art 7 of the ICCPR in referring to violent, oppressive, inhuman or degrading conduct, whether towards the person who made the admission or towards another person.

48   Kirby, M, "Human Rights – Emerging International Minimum Standards" speech delivered to the Australian Society of Labor Lawyers, 14th Annual National Conference (Melbourne, 23 May 1992); and "The Role of the Judge in Advancing Human Rights by Reference to International Norms" (1988) 62 *Australian Law Journal* 514.

49   (1987) 162 CLR 447 at 463.

The first area where international human rights law may touch upon the common law is in identifying rights in the common law. Recently, in *R v Swaffield; Pavic v The Queen*,[50] Kirby J said:

> In judging whether a right is fundamental, regard might be had to any relevant constitutional or statutory provisions and to the common law. ... It is also helpful, in considering fundamental rights, to take cognisance of international statements of such rights, appearing in instruments to which Australia is a party, particularly where breach of such rights give rise to procedures of individual complaint.
>
> These provisions reflect notions with which Australian law is generally compatible. To the fullest extent possible, save where statute or established common law authority is clearly inconsistent with such rights, the common law in Australia, when it is being developed or re-expressed, should be formulated in a way that is compatible with such international and universal jurisprudence.

Brennan J in *Mabo (No 2)* explains a second means whereby international human rights law may touch upon the common law. He observed that international instruments provide a legitimate and important influence upon the common law:

> In discharging its duty to declare the common law of Australia, this Court is not free to adopt rules that accord with contemporary notions of justice and human rights if their adoption would fracture the skeleton of principle which gives the body of our law its shape and internal consistency. ...
>
> The expectations of the international community accord in this respect with the contemporary values of the Australian people. The opening up of international remedies to individuals pursuant to Australia's accession to the Optional Protocol to the International Covenant on Civil and Political Rights brings to bear on the common law the powerful influence of the Covenant and the international standards it imports. The common law does not necessarily conform to international law, but international law is a legitimate and important influence on the development of the common law, especially when international law declares the existence of universal human rights.[51]

Both Brennan J in *Mabo (No 2)* and Kirby J in *Swaffield* indicate that international human rights law may also be used to revisit the common law where that law may offend human rights. This is the third area where international human rights law is relevant to the operation of the common law. Both judges recognise the need for Australian law to be consistent with international law. In this respect, Australian courts cannot ignore international developments and international human rights standards.

In the 1970s Murphy J advocated revisiting unjust common law rules by reference to international instruments. In a dissenting judgment in *Dugan v Mirror Newspapers Ltd*,[52] he considered an application for special leave to appeal to the High Court to challenge the common law rule that a person convicted of a felony was considered to be civilly dead. In revisiting the common law rule, he referred to the UDHR, ICCPR, the ECHR and decisions of the European Court of Human Rights. Having regard to these instruments, he said the rule offended the rule of law and due process and did not accord with modern standards in Australia. He observed:

---

50   (1998) 151 ALR 98 at 136-37.

51   *Mabo v Queensland (No 2)* (1992) 175 CLR 1 at 42.

52   (1978) 142 CLR 583.

There is thus an overwhelming weight of opinion against the doctrine that a convicted person should, while under sentence, be without redress for a personal wrong whether the wrong occurs before, during or after imprisonment. It is unjust that such a person injured in, for example, an ordinary road or factory accident cannot sue. Although the doctrine treats the person as dead if he seeks to be a plaintiff, it treats him as alive when he is a defendant. The doctrine is anachronistic and beset with problems ...[53]

Like statutory interpretation, one of the main areas where international law has been used in the common law is as a device to determine the scope of a rule where the common law is unclear.[54] This reflects the increasing use of the Bangalore Principles[55] developed in February 1988 in Bangalore, India by a group of lawyers and judges from common law jurisdictions within the Commonwealth.[56]

International instruments may be used by a court as a guide to ascertaining the law.[57] In *Dietrich*, Mason CJ and McHugh J referred to a "common sense approach" of having regard to international obligations to resolve uncertainty or ambiguity in judge made law.[58] In *Dietrich*, the appellant was charged with drug offences and committed for trial. His application for legal aid was rejected. He was unrepresented at the trial and his application for an adjournment was rejected. Following a lengthy trial, he was convicted. The issue to be determined by the High Court, on appeal, was whether an accused person charged with a serious crime who cannot afford counsel has the right to be provided with counsel at public expense.

The court held that there was no right to provided with counsel at public expense but acknowledged the importance of being tried fairly and the role that legal representatives play in ensuring that an accused person receives a fair trial. The court held that the right to a fair trial was a fundamental element of the Australian criminal justice system, but noted that the right had not been defined in the Australian context. Some members of the court referred to relevant provisions of international human rights instruments where the right to fair trial is broadly defined and they accepted that the right, as it existed in Australian law, accorded with these international principles. In this respect, the court was assisted by relevant international human rights principles and it accepted that the international principles influenced the development of the common law and the procedural guarantees associated with the right to a fair trial.[59]

The use of international human rights laws has probably had the greatest impact on issues concerning fair trial and the operation of the criminal justice system. Justice Kirby, as the then President of the New South Wales Court of Appeal, often referred to international human rights instruments in appeals touching upon the right to a fair

---

53 Ibid at 608-09.

54 *Ballina Shire Council v Ringland* (1994) 33 NSWLR 680.

55 Reproduced in (1988) 14 *Commonwealth Law Bulletin* 1196.

56 Kirby, M, "The Growing Rapprochement Between International Law and National Law" in Sturgess, G and Anghie, A (eds), *Visions of the Legal Order in the 21st Century — Essays to Honour His Excellency Judge CJ Weeramantry*, at http://www.hcourt.gov.au/weeram.htm.

57 *Dietrich v The Queen* (1992) 177 CLR 292 at 360 and see Garkawe, S, "Human Rights and the Administration of Justice: *Dietrich v The Queen*" (1994) 1 *Australian Journal of Human Rights* 371.

58 *Dietrich* (1992) 177 CLR 292 at 392-93.

59 *Barton v The Queen* (1980) 147 CLR 74 at 96; *R v Catalano* (1992) 107 FLR 31 and, in relation to treatment of those in detention, *R v Shrestha* (1991) 173 CLR 48.

trial[60] in matters concerning the right to an interpreter,[61] bias,[62] costs[63] and the right to a speedy trial.[64]

A further area where international human rights law may impact upon the development of the common law is in the exercise of judicial discretion. The Family Court in *B v B* expressed the view that international human rights instruments, particularly those dealing with children, may assist exercising its discretion in determining the best interests of a child.[65] The principles, which apply to the exercise of statutory discretions, which have been discussed earlier in this chapter, are equally applicable to the exercise of discretion in the common law.

The final area where international human rights law may impact upon the common law is in the relationship between customary international law and the common law. In England, customary international law was considered to be automatically part of the common law without the need for any enabling legislation. Over time, the English courts limited the wide ranging application of customary international law in the common law, but in Australia, there is little judicial consideration is the relationship between customary international law and the common law.

Reference to and use of customary international law in Australian courts is meagre compared to the use of treaties. There are only a few references to customary international law in Commonwealth enactments[66] and there has been no judicial pronouncement as to the place of customary international law in the common law of Australia. Australia has neither expressly followed nor rejected the approach adopted by the English courts, that customary international law automatically forms part of the common law.[67] Elizabeth Evatt has said:

> [C]ustomary rules and particularly principles of human rights, such as the principle of genocide and so on, are part of customary international law. As such, they would be accepted as part of the common law. Naturally as such, they can be overruled by legislation, as any part of the common law can. But we should not think of international

---

60 For a commentary on the decisions, see Kirby, M, "The Australian use of International Human Rights Norms: From Bangalore to Balliol – A View From the Antipodes" (1993) 16(2) *University of New South Wales Law Journal* 363 – and see *Herron v McGregor* (1986) 7 NSWLR 246; *S & M Motor Repairs Pty Ltd v Caltex Oil (Aust) Pty Ltd* (1988) 12 NSWLR 558; *Smith v The Queen* (1991) 23 NSWLR 1; *Gill v Walton* (1991) 25 NSWLR 190; *DDP v Saxon* (1992) 28 NSWLR 263; *Australian National Industries Ltd v Spedley Securities Ltd (in liq)* (1992) 26 NSWLR 411; *R v Astill* (1992) 63 A Crim R 148; and *Carroll v Mijovich* (1992) 58 A Crim R 243.

61 *Gradidge v Grace Bros Pty Limited* (1988) 93 FLR 414.

62 *Daemar v Industrial Commission of New South Wales* (1988) 12 NSWLR 45.

63 *Cachia v Hanes* (1991) 23 NSWLR 304.

64 *Jago v District Court of New South Wales* (1988) 12 NSWLR 558.

65 (1997) 21 Fam LR 676 and see also Miles J in *McKellar v Smith* (1982) 2 NSWLR 950 at 962.

66 For example, the *Industrial Relations Reform Act* 1993 (Cth) s 170PA(1)(e) – see *Victoria v Commonwealth* (1996) 187 CLR 416 at 546.

67 Higgins, R, "The Relationship Between International and Regional Human Rights Norms and Domestic Law" (1992) 18 *Commonwealth Law Bulletin* 1268; Shearer, I, "The Implications of Non-Treaty Law Making: Customary International Law and its Implications" in Alston, P and Chiam, M (eds), 1995, *Treaty Making and Australia: Globalisation v Sovereignty* (Federation Press, Sydney, 1995); and Shearer, I, "The Relationship Between International and Domestic Law", in Opeksin and Rothwell (eds), above, n 7; see also *Koowarta v Bjelke-Petersen* (1982) 153 CLR 168 at 224-55.

law as being an entirely separate thing from the law of Australia. Some parts of it we would recognise.[68]

In practice, the courts have not been receptive to arguments about customary international human rights law. This may be because customary international law is often difficult to identify and prove, particularly where the rules of customary international law are not codified.[69]

Customary international law is relevant to any discussion about the use of international human rights law in Australian law because of the status of declarations such as the UDHR and the prohibition against racial discrimination. As a declaration alone, the UDHR is not binding as a matter of international law, but is now accepted as codifying international law and therefore is binding as a matter of customary international law.[70] If customary international law is part of the common law, it is arguable that the rights contained in the UDHR are part of the common law to the extent that they have not been modified by any statutory provision. This means that the rights contained in the UDHR could potentially found a cause of action based on a breach of human rights.

To date, the courts have not been receptive to such an argument. In *Re Jane*[71] the Human Rights and Equal Opportunity Commission intervened in the proceedings to argue that norms of customary international law were also applicable to the rights provided for in international treaties.[72] Nicholson CJ summarised the Commission's submissions:

> [The Commission] submits that Australian courts will treat customary international law as incorporated into the domestic law of Australia so far as it is not inconsistent with any applicable statute law or with any binding precedent. ... The Commission further submits that in order to ascertain the nature of customary international law, the courts will have regard to international treaties and conventions, authoritative texts, the Charter of the United Nations, Declarations of the General Assembly and other international developments which show that a particular subject has become a legal subject of international concern.[73]

---

68 Report of the Senate Legal and Constitutional References Committee, *Trick or Treaty? Commonwealth Power to Make and Implement Treaties* (AGPS, Canberra, November 1995), pp 37-38. Sir Anthony Mason appears to be ambivalent about the place of customary international law. In an extra-curial speech, he has said that some rules of customary international law would be accepted by Australian courts and others may be not – see "The Relationship between International law and National Law and it Application in National Court" Address delivered to the International Law Association 64th Conference in 1990, referred to and discussed at p 4 of a report of the Australian Branch of the International Law Association, Committee of International Law in Municipal Courts, unpublished. See further, Ch 2 by Sir Anthony Mason in this volume.

69 *Polyukhovich v Commonwealth* (1991) 172 CLR 501.

70 See Lillich above, n 2, pp 378-79, and Burke, above, n 2, p 305, together with the Vienna Declaration and Programme for Action, adopted by the UN GA on 12 July 1993 UN Doc A/CONF, 157/23. For consideration by Australian courts see Brennan J in *Polyukhovich* (1991) 172 CLR 501 at 574.

71 (1989) 85 ALR 409.

72 Pursuant to s 11(1)(o) of the *Human Rights and Equal Opportunity Commission Act* 1986 (Cth), the Commission may, with the leave of the court, intervene in proceedings where is there is a human right in issue. Under the provisions of the Human Rights Legislation Amendment Bill (No 2) 1998, it is proposed that this right to intervene will be removed and be replaced by one in which leave of the Commonwealth Attorney-General must be granted before leave may be sought from the court; see the second reading speech of the Attorney-General, Mr Williams in HReps, Debates, 8 April 1998, p 1982.

73 (1989) 85 ALR 409 at 423.

He responded to these submissions by saying, "I am extremely doubtful as to whether these propositions represent the law in Australia".[74]

Notwithstanding the Family Court's decision in *Re Jane*, there may be opportunities to argue that customary international human rights laws, as declared in instruments such as the UDHR, have direct effect as part of the common law of Australia[75] particularly where the relevant right accords with rights existing in the common law.

Administrative law[76]

Substantive as well as procedural human rights may be affected by the making of administrative decisions.

Given the nature of the activities of modern governments, substantive economic and social rights are particularly likely to be affected. For example, since 1990 amendments to the social security and migration laws have removed the capacity for illegal immigrants, applicants for refugee status and migrants in their first three years of residency to be granted any social security payments, including special benefit which was designed originally to provide a wide "safety net".[77]

In one unusual special benefit case, the Administrative Appeals Tribunal held that children aged three and one were qualified to receive special benefit as they had no other means of support. Their mother was not qualified to receive any income support as she was not a permanent resident of Australia and their father's whereabouts were unknown. One factor considered by O'Connor J was "that although not binding in domestic law, Australia's international obligations do have some relevance to domestic law. To deny the respondents the special benefit would be in conflict with arts 26 and 27 of CROC (the right to benefit from social security and the right to an adequate standard of living)".[78]

It can also be argued that both the rights under the *International Covenant on Economic, Social and Cultural Rights* (ICESCR) to an income (art 7) and the related right to income protection and access to a source of financial support where a person is unable to earn an income (art 9) have been compromised as a consequence of decisions taken by the Commonwealth Government to regulate and restrict access to pensions and benefits payable under the *Social Security Act* 1991 (Cth).

The question of the extent to which procedural rights enshrined in administrative law provide protection against infringements of international human rights law is controversial. The High Court has held that ratification of international instruments gives rise to a legitimate expectation. As a matter of procedural fairness, if an administrative decision-maker proposes to act inconsistently with the terms of a relevant treaty, he or she will give notice to the person who will be affected by the decision, so

---

74   Though his Honour has modified his view in later judgments; see *Re Marion* (1994) FLC ¶92-448.

75   *Horta v Commonwealth* (1994) 181 CLR 183.

76   For further analysis, see Ch 4 by McMillan and Williams in this volume.

77   *Re Farah and Secretary, Department of Social Security* (1992) 65 SSR 910; now see *Social Security Act* 1991 (Cth) s 729(f).

78   *Re Secretary, Department of Social Security and Underwood* (1991) 25 ALD 343 at 348; applied in *Re Secretary, Department of Social Security and Kumar* (1992) 65 SSR 911.

that that person may make submissions or otherwise argue that the decision-maker should act in accordance with the terms of the instrument.

In *Minister for Immigration v Teoh*,[79] the Minister for Immigration failed in this respect to act in accordance with the terms of CROC and treat the best interests of the child as a primary consideration when determining the father's immigration application. His failure meant that the father-applicant was denied procedural fairness as he had not been given an opportunity to present a case against a decision, which did not meet his legitimate expectation for the matter to be considered.

The Labor Government's reaction to the *Teoh* decision was to introduce a Bill into Parliament which would have removed the capacity for any person to have any form of legitimate expectation from the ratification by the Australian Government of any international convention. This would have created the curious position whereby Australia was making one statement at an international level and an entirely different statement at a domestic level. In due course, a Bill was introduced to reverse the effect of *Teoh* but it lapsed when the 1996 election was announced. The new Howard government announced that it would not proceed with the Bill but in February 1997 a Joint Statement by the Australian Minister for Foreign Affairs and the Federal Attorney-General announced that legislation will, after all, be introduced into the Australian Parliament to reverse the effect of *Teoh*.

While the *Teoh* decision focused on Commonwealth decision-makers, some States were also concerned at the effect of the decision on actions taken by officers of State governments. Indeed, South Australia enacted legislation to ensure that such a treaty would not have the force of domestic law.[80]

Constitutional interpretation and implications

The Australia Constitution contained few specific human rights protections. The founding fathers considered it unnecessary to include a Bill of Rights in the Constitution believing that the common law would protect rights. Even in the absence of a Bill of Rights, the Constitution does contain both express and implied guarantees of civil and political rights and the operation of other provisions in the Constitution impact on the human rights of those within the jurisdiction of Australia.[81] In the recent decisions concerning implied Constitutional guarantees, the High Court has referred to international instruments in its discussion of the nature and scope of such rights or more properly described, restrictions on the Commonwealth's powers.[82]

---

79   (1995) 183 CLR 273 and see further, *Vaitaiki v Minister for Immigration and Ethnic Affairs* (1998) 150 ALR 608; see also, Ch 4 by McMillan and Williams in this volume.

80   *Administrative Decisions (Effect of International Instruments) Act* 1995 (SA).

81   *Adelaide Company of Jehovah's Witnesses v Commonwealth* (1943) 67 CLR 116 and see Bailey above, n 4, pp 79-105 and O'Neill and Handley, above, n 4, pp 44-74.

82   See *Davis v Commonwealth* (1988) 166 CLR 79; *Australian Capital Television Pty Ltd v Commonwealth* (1992) 177 CLR 106 at 140; *Nationwide News Pty Ltd v Wills* (1992) 177 CLR 1 at 48; *Theophanous v Herald & Weekly Times Ltd* (1994) 184 CLR 104; *Stephens v West Australian Newspapers* (1994) 182 CLR 211; *Langer v Commonwealth* (1996) 186 CLR 302; *Muldowney v South Australia* (1996) 186 CLR 352; *Levy v Victoria* (1997) 146 ALR 248; *Lange v Australian Broadcasting Corporation* (1997) 145 ALR 96; and for implied guarantees of equality, see *Street v Queensland Bar Association* (1989) 168 CLR 461 at 487, 510-12, 571; and *Leeth v Commonwealth* (1992) 174 CLR 455 per Toohey and Deane JJ. For further discussion, see Ch 3 by Gageler and Glass in this volume.

Human rights issues have also arisen in the application of s 109 of the Constitution where State laws are inconsistent with Commonwealth laws which give effect to international human rights instruments.[83]

International human rights laws may also be used in interpreting the Constitution, although it must be recognised that the scope for use of such instruments in limited. In a recent decision concerning the operation of the territories power (s 122) and the acquisitions power (s 51(xxiii)), Kirby J said:

> Where the Constitution is ambiguous, this Court should adopt that meaning which conforms to the principles of fundamental rights rather than an interpretation which would involve a departure from such rights.[84]

He further stated that the Constitution "should not be interpreted so as to condone an unnecessary withdrawal of the protection of [fundamental and universal] rights. At least it should not be so interpreted unless the text is intractable and the deprivation of such rights is completely clear".[85]

Gaudron J was somewhat stronger in *Kruger v Commonwealth* where she said that s 122 should not be interpreted so as to permit laws authorising gross violations of human rights and dignity contrary to established principles of common law.[86] Although her Honour's comments are limited to the exercise of power under s 122, it is arguable that such a principle should apply to all constitutional powers.

STRATEGIC USE OF HUMAN RIGHTS LAW

Having identified how international human rights laws may be used in Australian courts, the next step is to consider when to use international human rights law and their strategic application in Australian litigation. Arguments based on relevant human rights principles are applicable to all types of proceedings and in all courts. While the High Court and some appellate courts are receptive to submissions based on international human rights law, the task is to introduce human rights considerations at the trial level in all courts.[87] Where judges and practitioners are unfamiliar with the workings of international law, it is incumbent on the practitioner to lay carefully the foundation for an argument based on international human rights law. It is necessary to identify the source of international human rights, provide copies of relevant instruments and explain both their relevance and application to the proceedings in question.

---

83   *Koowarta v Bjelke-Petersen* (1982) 153 CLR 168; *Viskauskas v Niland* (1983) 153 CLR 280; *University of Wollongong v Metwally* (1984) 158 CLR 447; *Australian Postal Commission v Dao* (1987) 70 ALR 449; and in the Federal Court *Aldridge v Booth* (1988) 80 ALR 1.

84   *Newcrest Mining (WA) Ltd v Commonwealth* (1997) 147 ALR 42 at 147. See further, his Honour's reiteration and extension of this reasoning in *Kartinyeri v Commonwealth* (1998) 152 ALR 540 at 598-600.

85   *Newcrest Mining* (1997) 147 ALR 42 at 147.

86   (1997) 146 ALR 126 at 190.

87   In the Federal Court of Australia, the Industrial Relations Court of Australia and the Family Court of Australia it is increasingly common for the parties and judges to refer to international law in their decisions: see, for example, *Christie v Qantas Airways Ltd* (1995) 65 IR 17 and on appeal (1996) 138 ALR 19 . In the Federal Court, see *Friends of Hinchinbrook Society Inc v Minister for Environment* (1996) 69 FCR 1 at 11.

Creativity comes into play in identifying the human rights in issue, its application to Australian law and bridging the international and domestic legal divide. Human rights cases are not limited to facts which are obviously human rights based. The principles developed in application of human rights laws may be applicable to a range of matters as human rights issues touch upon a range of cases which raise procedural and substantive issues. International human rights principles may be used as a guide to determine how to balance competing rights or assess restrictions and limitations of rights.[88]

International human rights law in an Australian context

One of the objectives of using international human rights principles in Australian litigation is give those principles practical and effective operation in Australian law. Australian courts are more receptive to claims that can clearly link a right expressed in an international human rights instruments into some form of claim that is recognised in Australian law and where such a claim can be constructed, that there is an appropriate Australian legal remedy for the claim based on international law. Where a common law right exists but its nature and scope is unclear, international instruments may be used to refine and in some cases strengthen the common law protection.

In *Brown v Members of Classification Review Board of Office of Film and Literature*,[89] the applicants contended that the members of the Classification Review Board of the Office of Film and Literature erred in applying the National Classification Code by failing to have regard to their common law right to freedom of speech and expression. They sought judicial review of the Board's decision to refuse classification of a La Trobe University Students' Representative Council's monthly journal *Rabelais*. The particular edition included an article entitled "The Art of Shoplifting".

Merkel J accepted that the common law recognised a right of freedom of speech and expression.[90] In his decision, he considered the development of the right of free speech together with the permissible restrictions on the right. In doing so, he specifically referred to art 19 of the ICCPR, art 10 of the ECHR and decisions of the US and Canadian courts, to determine the nature of the right and importantly, the limitations on the right.[91]

While the application for review was dismissed, international human rights principles were relied upon by the court in determining the appropriate standards of decision-making and the types of matters which should be take into account where a decision may impact upon human rights.[92]

Where Australian law does not provide rights as expressed in international law, care must be taken in using international instruments to found a cause of action where it is claimed that such rights have been breached. The difficulties in this regard are

---

88　*Leask v Commonwealth* (1996) 187 CLR 579 at 583, 595 and 615; and *Chu Kheng Lim v Minister for Immigration* (1992) 174 CLR 455.

89　(1997) 145 ALR 464.

90　Ibid at 474.

91　Ibid at 471-74.

92　This line of reasoning was upheld on appeal in *Brown v Members of Classification Review Board of the Office of Film and Literature* (1998) 154 ALR 67.

illustrated in *Re Limbo*,[93] *Linden v Commonwealth (No 2)*,[94] *Coe v Commonwealth*[95] and *Thorpe v Commonwealth*.[96] In *Re Limbo*, Brennan J emphasised the importance of founding an appropriate cause of action with reference to recognised legal principle. In that case, Citizen Limbo sought a declaration that the Commonwealth's acts and omissions constituted genocide and breached international law. He said:

> [W]hen one comes to a court of law it is always necessary to ensure that lofty aspirations are not mistaken for the rules of law which courts are capable and fitted to enforce.[97]

In *Linden v Commonwealth (No 2)*, Mr Linden (formerly Citizen Limbo) sought declarations from the High Court of a similar nature as the questions submitted at the same time to the International Court of Justice for an Advisory Opinion concerning the illegality of the threat or use of nuclear weapons. His claim was struck out.

Likewise in *Coe v Commonwealth* the plaintiff, suing on behalf of the Wiradjuri people, sought a declaration that the Wiradjuri people were the owners of land in southern New South Wales. In the statement of claim, she alleged that the Commonwealth had engaged in acts of genocide and crimes against humanity which were contrary to the Genocide Convention and customary international law. The matter came before Mason CJ in August 1993, on the application of the Commonwealth to strike out the plaintiff's statement of claim. His Honour dealt with this aspect of the claim by stating:

> [A]n international convention to which Australia is a party does not give rise to rights under Australian municipal law in the absence of legislation carrying the Convention into effect. No such legislation has been enacted and, in any of the events the Convention post-dates most of the acts complained of. However, the plaintiff submits that municipal courts could have jurisdiction to try crimes against international law on the footing that the common law recognises international law as part of the common law. But, even if one accepted the propositions from which the plaintiff contends, the problem which confronts the plaintiff is to show how the acts pleaded in paragraphs 9-10 generate an entitlement to damages or compensation.[98]

It is important to note that Mason CJ did not reject the claim because it was based on customary international law, rather he said that the plaintiff would not be entitled to damages vis-a-vis the named respondent. He went on to say:

> [I]f it can be assumed that the Wiradjuri have a claim ... for reparations cognisable in Australian municipal courts for wrongs done to them in breach of customary international law, that claim does not extend to the wrongs done to which the second defendant was not a party.[99]

---

93   (1989) 64 ALJR 241.

94   (1996) 70 ALJR 541.

95   (1993) 68 ALJR 110.

96   (1997) 71 ALJR 767.

97   (1989) 64 ALJR 241 at 242.

98   (1994) 68 ALJR 110 at 116.

99   Ibid.

When to employ a human rights argument?

Where a practitioner encounters a case that raises numerous human rights issues, it might be difficult to determine whether to raise all the human rights at issue or whether to focus on one or two specific violations. A shopping list of human rights violations may evoke the sympathy of some judges, but there may be a strategic advantage on focusing on the strongest rights argument, rather than all arguments based on a number of rights.

In other instances, the human rights issues may be litigated without overt reference to international human rights principles and still achieve a result with protects internationally recognised human rights. The recent decisions of *Kruger v Commonwealth* and *Kable v Director of Public Prosecutions (NSW)* illustrate the differing approaches to using human rights principles in constitutional cases. Both exemplify how international human rights principles may be used to impact upon the common law, the legislative capacity of the parliament and the role of Constitution.

The *Kable* case concerned the validity of the *Community Protection Act* 1994 (NSW). The Act provided for the preventative detention of Gregory Kable, who had been convicted of manslaughter of his wife in August 1990. He was to be released in 1994. Before his release, the New South Wales Parliament enacted the *Community Protection Act* to keep Kable in detention because of concerns to the safety of others which arose after Kable had sent threatening letters to members of his wife's family. The Act applied only to Kable.

The proceedings in the New South Wales Supreme Court of Appeal challenged the validity of the Act and one of the grounds was that the Act involved "a gross infringement of human rights and the basic principles of criminal law".[100] The Supreme Court expressed its concern that the Act "infringed a fundamental safeguard of democratic rights of individuals in the community"[101] but upheld the validity of the Act on the ground that on the balance of probabilities Kable was more likely than not to commit a serious act of violence and it was appropriate that the community be protected by his ongoing detention.

The decision was reversed on appeal to the High Court.[102] In the High Court, Kable did not argue that the Act was invalid because it infringed Kable's human rights. Rather, the appeal focused on the compatibility of the Act with the exercise of judicial power in Ch III of the Commonwealth Constitution. The High Court held that the operation of the Act was incompatible with the integrity, independence and impartiality of the NSW Supreme Court exercising judicial power under Ch III. While human rights issues where not specifically raised in the High Court proceedings, the result was one which was consistent with international human rights principles.[103]

In *Kruger*[104] the plaintiffs argued that the *Aboriginals Ordinance* (NT) of 1918-1957 was unconstitutional. The plaintiffs sought declaratory relief and damages from

---

100 *Kable v Director of Public Prosecutions* (1995) 36 NSWLR 374 at 375. However, the court did not specifically refer to any international human rights in its judgment.

101 Ibid at 395.

102 (1997) 189 CLR 51.

103 See also *PJE v The Queen* (1996) 70 ALJR 905 refusing special leave from a decision of the NSW Court of Appeal.

104 (1997) 146 ALR 126.

the Commonwealth for loss suffered by the eight Aboriginal people removed from their communities as children under the Ordinance. In the statement of claim, the plaintiff challenged the validity of the Ordinance on a number novel and innovative submissions based on international human rights treaties and international customary law concerning genocide, although the grounds were cast as constitutional rights or guarantees. These included:

- implied right of freedom from and/or immunity from removal and subsequent detention without due process of law;
- implied right or guarantee of equality;
- implied right or guarantee of freedom of movement and association;
- implied freedom from or immunity against genocide; and
- freedom of religion in s 116 of the Constitution.

Each of the grounds raised novel arguments and built upon earlier cases concerning implied guarantees. Arguably any one of these grounds may have been sufficient to give rise to the proceedings. The application failed and the majority of the court rejected each of the grounds in turn.[105]

With the advantage of the judgments and the benefit of hindsight, one might speculate whether an incremental rather than broad range approach exemplified by *Kable* might have attracted one or more of the judges on isolated issues. At the same time, the expense of High Court litigation may well necessitate raising all the relevant grounds when the opportunity arises. This raises two further issues to be considered by practitioners in using human rights – that is the use of representative proceedings and interveners.

Representative or group proceedings

Where proceedings involve allegations of a pattern of violations or a systematic failure to protect the rights of a group of individuals, there may be some benefits in using representative proceedings or class actions. Representative proceedings have been used successfully in consumers' rights,[106] discrimination,[107] and environmental protection[108] cases.

Shortly after the representative proceedings provisions were enacted in Pt IVA of the *Federal Court of Australia Act* 1976 (Cth), a number of proceedings were commenced as representative proceedings on behalf of boat groups of asylum seekers.[109] Their claims were brought under the *Administrative Decisions (Judicial Review) Act* 1977 (Cth) in an attempt to highlight systemic defects in decisions concerns

---

105 See, in particular, at 158 per Dawson J.

106 *Qantas Airways Ltd v Cameron* (1996) 66 FCR 246.

107 *Australian Iron & Steel v Banovic* 168 CLR 165 and *Scott v Telstra Corporation Ltd* (1995) EOC ¶92-717.

108 See Ch 10 by Brunton in this volume.

109 See the series of decisions concerning *Wu Shan Liang v Minister for Immigration and Ethnic Affairs* (1994) 48 FCR 294, (1994) 51 FCR 232, (1995) 57 FCR 432 and (1996) 185 CLR 259. Other representative proceedings included *Mok v Minister for Immigration and Ethnic Affairs* (1994) 55 FCR 375; *Lek v Minister for Immigration and Ethnic Affairs* (1993) 45 FCR 100; *Guo Wei Rong v Minister for Immigration and Ethnic Affairs* (1996) 135 ALR 421.

refugee decisions. This approach enabled a number of asylum seekers to access the courts in circumstances where the costs for individual applicants would have been prohibitive. The use of a representative proceeding also enabled the parties to raise systemic human rights issues which affected asylum seekers generally in the manner in which their claims for asylum were being determined.

Human rights interveners and amicus curiae

In some cases, it may be appropriate for an intervener or amicus curiae to raise relevant human rights arguments, rather than one of the parties. As a general rule, courts have a discretion to allow non-parties to be heard if the intervener wishes to maintain some particular right, power or immunity in which they are concerned,[110] provided that the interveners has an interest which is a substantial interest, a legal interest or one which is known and protected by the law.[111] An intervener may be able to assist the court in fully informing it of human rights principles which may or ought to take into account in reaching its decision.[112]

In relation to human rights issues, the Family Court makes provision for a separate representative to participate in family law proceedings on behalf of the child.[113] While the role of the separate representative differs from that of a true intervener, the separate representative may bring to the court's attention issues concerning the rights of a child.

The Human Rights and Equal Opportunity Commission has a statutory function to seek the leave of the court to intervene in proceedings which raise human rights issues or issues concerning equal opportunity in employment.[114] The Commission has intervened in a number of High Court,[115] Federal Court,[116] and Family Court proceedings[117] making written and/or oral submissions on relevant human rights issues. Sometimes the parties do not raise the human rights issues or the Commission's submissions may support an outcome advocated by one of the parties.

In addition to interveners with a specific statutory function, human rights NGOs and public interest organisations such as the Public Interest Advocacy Centre, may also provide an invaluable role in proceedings as an intervener or amicus curiae bringing human rights issues to the court's attention.

---

110 *Australian Railways Union v Victorian Railways Commission* (1930) 44 CLR 319 at 331.

111 *R v Ludeke; ex p Customs Officers' Association of Australia* (1985) 155 CLR 513 at 522.

112 *United States Tobacco Co v Minister of Consumer Affairs* (1988) 20 FCR 520 at 534.

113 *F & M1 & M2* (1994) 18 Fam LR 221.

114 *Human Rights and Equal Opportunity Commission Act* 1986 (Cth) ss 11(1)(o) and 31(j). But note the proposed changes to this right, above, n 72.

115 Some of the proceedings include: *Kartinyeri v Commonwealth* (1998) 152 ALR 540; *Qantas Airways v Christie* (1998) 152 ALR 365; *Croome v Tasmania* (1996) 71 ALJR 430; *Teoh* (1995) 183 CLR 273; *Secretary, Department of Health and Community Services v JWB and SMB* (1992) 175 CLR 218; *ZP v PS* (1994) 181 CLR 639; and *P v P* (1994) 181 CLR 583.

116 *Wu Yu Fang v Minister for Immigration* (1996) 135 ALR 583; *Langer v Australian Electoral Commission (No 2)* (1996) 59 FCR 450, (1996) 59 FCR 463; and *Aldridge v Booth* (1988) 80 ALR 1.

117 *Re Michael (No2)* (1994) FLC ¶92-486; *In re A Teenager* (1988) 13 Fam LR 85; *Re Jane* (1988) 12 Fam LR 662; *In Re Marion (No 2)* (1994) FLC ¶92-448, *B v B* (1997) 21 Fam LR 676.

INTERNATIONAL HUMAN RIGHTS REMEDIES

In the event that there are no Australian legal remedies available or an Australian remedy is ineffective, there is the option of accessing an international human rights remedy by lodging a complaint with one of the specialist international human rights committees. There are three main UN committees: the Human Rights Committee, established under the First Optional Protocol to the ICCPR, the CERD Committee established under the *Convention on the Elimination of All Forms of Racial Discrimination* (CERD) and the Torture Committee established under the *Convention Against Torture* (CAT). Of these three Committees, the Human Rights Committee deals with the greatest number of communications.

When Australia ratified the First Optional Protocol to the ICCPR on 25 December 1991 it recognised the competence of the Human Rights Committee to receive and consider communications from individuals subject to Australia's jurisdiction who claim to be victims of violations of the rights set out in the ICCPR and who can demonstrate that he or she has exhausted all local remedies, to the extent that those remedies are both effective and available.[118]

The difficulty with establishing that the complainant or "author" has exhausted all local remedies in respect of the ICCPR rights alleged infringed is that the ICCPR is not a part of Australian law and there are no general remedies available for an individual alleging a breach of human rights. However, the lack of local remedy for the alleged violation of a substantive right may itself also is a violation of the ICCPR. In *Dietrich*, Mason CJ and McHugh J observed that:

> On one view, it may seem curious that the Executive Government has seen fit to expose Australia to the potential censure that the rights enshrined in the ICCPR are incorporated into domestic law.[119]

To date there have been two significant decisions of Human Rights Committee concerning Australia and breaches of the ICCPR. In both matters, the complainants resorted to international remedies because Australian law did not provide them redress for the breaches of human rights. In *Toonen v Australia*[120] the Human Rights Committee found that the ss 122(a), (c) and 123 of the Tasmanian *Criminal Code* which criminalised various forms of sexual conduct between homosexual men in private was an interference with Toonen's right to privacy as expressed on art 17 of the ICCPR. Following the Committee's decision, the Federal Parliament enacted the *Human Rights (Sexual Conduct) Act* 1994 (Cth) providing that sexual conduct involving consenting

---

118 For a more detailed discussion about lodging a communication and accessing these committees, see Chinkin, C, "Using the Optional Protocol: The Practical Issues" (1993) 3 (64) *Aboriginal Law Bulletin* 6; Eastman, K, "International Human Rights Remedies" Ch 15.3, *Lawyers Practice Manual (NSW)* (Law Book Co, Sydney); Charlesworth, H, "Australia's Accession to the First Optional Protocol to the International Covenant on Civil and Political Rights" (1991) 18 *Melbourne University Law Review* 428 and Löfgren, N, "Complaint Procedures under Article 22 of the Convention Against Torture and Other Cruel Inhuman or Degrading Treatment of Punishment" (1994) 1 *Australian Journal of Human Rights* 400.

119 (1992) 177 CLR 292 at 305.

120 CCPR/C/50/D/488/1992, views the Committee adopted on 31 March 1994 and delivered on 4 April 1994.

adults was not to be subjected to any arbitrary interference with privacy.[121] Toonen relied on this Act to initiate High Court proceedings arguing that the Tasmanian Criminal Code was inconsistent with the Act and pursuant to s 109 of the Constitution was invalid.[122] The provisions of the Code were eventually repealed.

The second matter concerned a communication lodged by "A", a Cambodian citizen who came to Australia and sought asylum. Under the *Migration Act* 1958 (Cth) he was been detained by the Commonwealth over four years while his application for refugee status was processed. Following proceedings in the High Court,[123] "A" lodged a communication to the Human Rights Committee in June 1993. He claimed that he was arbitrarily detained within the meaning of art 9(1) of the ICCPR and the circumstances of his detention breached art 9 generally.

The Committee held that Australia breached arts 9(1) and 9(4) of the ICCPR and that pursuant to its obligations under art 2(3) Australia should provide an effective remedy to "A" to redress the breach.[124] The Committee recommended compensation. Unlike *Toonen*, the Commonwealth has taken no specific action to provide a remedy to "A" or to amend the relevant laws or policies which gave rise to the breach.

Practitioners in pursuing human rights remedies should not overlook the use of international human rights. However, recourse to international remedies will not result in a speedy resolution of a complaint and, as the case of "A" illustrates, does not guarantee that a complainant will receive an effective remedy in the domestic jurisdiction.

CONCLUSION

Advocacy of human rights requires creativity, courage and patience. In the absence of an Australian Bill of Rights and the courts' reluctance to use international law, some consider the opportunities for using human rights in Australian courts to be limited. In a strict sense, this may be so. However, where human rights are in issue there are many avenues open to practitioners to pursue and develop an appreciation of human rights in Australian law.

The conduct of cases which ventilate human rights issues arise in two different ways. The first is where an individual is involved in a factual situation which coincidentally gives rise to a broader issue or which tangentially crosses a matter that is considered within the international community as an appropriate matter for international concern and action. The second is where an individual or group of individuals set about creating litigation to demonstrate a particular point or to establish a principle which will have broader implications. Standing limitations can impose

---

121 Morgan, W, "The Human Rights (Sexual Conduct) Bill 1994" (1994) 1 *Australian Journal of Human Rights* 409; Joseph, S, "Gay rights under the ICCPR – commentary on *Toonen v Australia*" (1994) 13 *University of Tasmania Law Review* 392.

122 *Croome v Tasmania* (1996) 71 ALJR 430.

123 *Chu Kheng Lim v Minister for Immigration, Local Government and Ethnic Affairs* (1992) 176 CLR 1.

124 CCPR/C/59/560/1993 views adopted by the Committee on 3 April 1997. See Poynder, N, "A Milestone for Asylum Seekers" (1997) 4(1) *Australian Journal of Human Rights* 155.

barriers which can be insurmountable and so deny access to the courts to those with broader interests.[125]

Both types of cases can be difficult to pursue as at some points the judicial system can be unreceptive or unsympathetic to broader issues forming the basis of argument and then decision. The path, what is more, can be strewn with the detritus of previously failed attempts or with narrow or blinkered constructions which endeavour to keep out any arguments put on a broader plane and which try to bring in standards of international human rights and fundamental freedoms. Perseverance and patience may be needed to complete the case, as may appeals and fresh litigation.

As access to legal aid diminishes around Australia[126] and the costs of litigating become more prohibitive, the capacity of the legal system to permit an individual to pursue litigation which at least in part raises more lofty themes than an average case may become even more limited. It will be the role of human rights practitioners to make sure that the door within the Australian legal system remains ajar and if possible is prised opened further for the new century.

---

125 *North Coast Environment Council Inc v Minister for Resources* (1995) 127 ALR 617; *Tasmanian Conservation Trust Inc v Minister for Resources* (1995) 127 ALR 580.

126 *Attorney General (NSW) v Milat* (1995) 37 NSWLR 370.

15

HUMAN RIGHTS RESEARCH AND ELECTRONIC RESOURCES[*]

Michael Bliss and Shahyar Roushan

INTRODUCTION

As the reader inevitably will find, this chapter is different to the other chapters in this book. The primary focus of this chapter is to provide the reader with a concise guide to human rights materials available through electronic resources. Nevertheless, the authors feel that it is necessary, at the outset, to provide some theoretical justification for the use of electronic resources in human rights research. Of particular import are the global changes which are affecting and changing the way lawyers practice.

GLOBAL FORCES AND THE ROLE OF LEGAL PROFESSIONALS

As society continues to become increasingly global, legal professionals, educators, and students must face the challenges that this global society has created. These new challenges manifest themselves through a growing dependency of legal processes within the borders of nation-states on processes taking place outside these borders.[1] The interdependency of legal processes[2] requires a greater awareness on the part of legal academics and professionals of the way in which law is taught and practised.

Today, lawyers, as a status group, play a much more important role than they have previously. This is attributed in large part to the globalisation processes and the increasingly complex and interdependent nature of contemporary societies.[3] Using sovereignty as an example to demonstrate the significant changes that have occurred in terms of interdependence in the legal realm, Czarnota and Veitch observe that nation-states are no longer in possession of full sovereignty in the way it was conceived in the political and legal tradition from Bodin to Dicey. The constant and increasing pressure upon sovereignty in its state form from both

---

*   The web site addresses cited in this chapter are correct at the time of the book going to press (ie mid-September 1998). As anyone familiar with the Internet is frustratingly aware, web site addresses (or URLs) are prone to change.

[The authors and editor wish to express their gratitude to Julia Grix for editing the web site addresses.]

1   Czarnota, A and Veitch, S, "Globalisation and Challenges for Legal Education" (1996) 14 *Journal of Professional Legal Education* 159

2   See generally, "Symposium on Globalization" (1996) 46 *Journal of Legal Education* 311.

3   Czarnota and Veitch, above, n 1, p 160.

external and internal forces, has made it extremely difficult, if not impossible, to talk of the sovereignty of the nation-state as the ultimate source of all national law.[4]

> The impact of new types of supranational legal systems and their effect on national law, have led to a uniformisation and harmonisation of different national legal systems. At the same time, however, there is also a process of impact of standards within nation-state legal systems on supranational law and through it, in turn, on other national legal systems.[5]

In addition, the emergence of many new global issues, such as economic development, trade, banking, environment, communications, migration and human rights, have contributed to a transition from a hierarchic international system, with the sovereign independent state at the head, to a non-hierarchic system composed of networks of states, non-state actors and individuals.[6] The emergence of the new interdependent legal system has also highlighted the fact that we can no longer sharply differentiate international law from national law. Today, there is an increasing acceptance of issues formerly regarded as within "domestic jurisdiction" as issues that raise international concern, such as the growing awareness of the importance of environmental protection and the management of natural resources; and the growing transnational human rights consciousness.[7]

In this new global system, legal professionals, particularly lawyers and judges, play the role of the engine of the expansion of law outside the borders of nation-state and contribute to the deepening of the processes of integration.[8] At the same time, as the nation-state becomes increasingly enmeshed in the web of international and supranational legal structures there is a clear need for lawyers to be familiar not only with the operation of international law, but also with the techniques and substantive frameworks and material of other jurisdictions.[9] Lawyers need to be exposed to and to participate in a deeper investigation of the constitutive role played by law in general, and the role that external processes play in the formation of social and political expectations within national borders.[10]

The impact and operation of global processes is evident in Australia as in other parts of the world. It is possible to point to well documented examples of how legal and other developments occurring outside Australia and exposure to international

---

4   Ibid, p 162.

5   Ibid, pp 162-63.

6   Brown Weiss, E, "The Emerging International Legal System: Non-Hierarchic Networks" in Hiscox, D and Le Bouthilier, Y (eds), *Globalism and Regionalism: Options for the 21st Century* (Proceedings of the Twenty Fourth Annual Conference of the Canadian Council on International Law, Ottawa, 1995), p 65; and "The New International Legal System", in Jasentuliyana, N (ed), *Perspectives on International Law* (Kluwer Law International, London, 1995), pp 65-66.

7   Brown Weiss, above, n 6.

8   Ibid.

9   To take one example from Czarnota and Veitch, lawyers play a significant role in social, political and economic transformations in emerging new legal systems (for example, South Africa and former communist parts of the world), through careful designing of legal institutions and constitutions. "Here law plays the constitutive role for a new type of social relations. Founding a whole new series of political and social expectations requires structures whose mainspring lies in institutionalising legal safeguards, from elementary civil rights to market freedoms. In this scenario, the construction of the new social world is done by the legal profession": above, n 1, p 163.

10   Czarnota and Veitch, above, n 1, p 164.

pressures affect the functioning of domestic law,[11] and this impact is perhaps most clear in the area of human rights law.[12]

It is a moot point whether the heightened transnational human rights consciousness which has developed throughout the latter part of this century is a product of the widening acceptance of the notion of the universality of human rights or merely a growing awareness that such claims (and counter-claims) are made of human rights.[13] In either case, the cross-border dimension of human rights has made it necessary for all lawyers to become aware of international developments and, indeed, developments in other jurisdictions.

In the area of human rights law, practitioners around the world are working with the same international instruments, or with domestic legislation which is modelled on (or was a precursor to) those instruments. Human rights lawyers gain significant guidance not only from the decisions and writings in international and regional bodies in the human rights field, but also from the case law and writings of other domestic jurisdictions. It is not an overstatement to say that lawyers might be viewed as wholly inadequately serving their clients in human rights matters unless they are aware that there are international and inter-jurisdictional arguments that can be raised in Australian courts, and where domestic remedies are unavailable or are not forthcoming, that there may be remedies available from international institutions or mechanisms.[14]

THE USE OF INFORMATION TECHNOLOGY[15]

For lawyers in the emerging global legal system, the necessity of keeping abreast of rapid developments means having greater access to updated materials and information as well as new tools of legal research and practice. This seemingly arduous quest for new and updated information has been aided dramatically in recent years by communication and technological advances. Today, the use of technology is as fundamental to a rapid change in the modern law as the

---

11 See Mason, A, "International Law as a Source of Domestic Law" in Opeksin, B and Rothwell, D (eds), *International Law and Australian Federalism* (Melbourne University Press, Melbourne, 1997); and Wilson, R, "The Domestic Impact of International Human Rights Law" (1992) 24 *Australian Journal of Forensic Sciences* 57 at 63.

12 Australian courts have been receptive to the use of the domestic law of other countries in this area: see *Mabo v Queensland (No 2)* (1992) 107 ALR 1 per Brennan J at 29; *Dietrich v The Queen* (1992) 67 ALJR 1 per Toohey J at 37. See also *Somaghi v MILGEA* (1991) 102 ALR 339. However, the courts have also been careful to ensure that reliance is not made on such case law where that would be contrary to Australian case authority: see *A v MIEA* (1997) 142 ALR 331 at 384 per Kirby J. See also Mason, A. "The Influence of International and Transnational Law on Australian Municipal Law" (1996) 7 *Public Law Review* 20; Kirby, M, "The International Impact of Human Rights Law" (1992) 24 *Australian Journal of Forensic Sciences* 65; Wilson, above, n 11, and Ch 2 by Sir Anthony Mason in this volume.

13 For discussion of the universality point, see Ch 1 by Kinley in this volume.

14 See Brownlie, for instance, who states that: "[i]n general, the subject of human rights needs more attention from competent lawyers with a grounding in general international law": Brownlie, I, "International Law in the Context of the Changing World Order", in Jasentuliyana (ed), above, n 6, p 58.

15 For an analysis of the legal efforts to regulate the burgeoning development of information technology in the context of human rights protection, see Ch 11 by Arup and Tucker in this volume.

combination of the first written legal codes and the printing press.[16] The availability of new forms of technology means that "the law libraries of the world are open 24 hours a day for electronic research from the lawyer's desk".[17] The change from paper reports, journals and looseleaf services updated, at best, on a monthly basis, to electronic databases has been swift and reasonably comprehensive; and news and information are provided and updated on a speedy and regular basis. Electronic resources, such as the Internet, CD ROM technology, and e-mail are, therefore, having a major impact on the way lawyers practice. For the human rights lawyer in particular these technologies have a great deal to offer.

THE RESOURCES

While the Internet as the most recent and public advance in information provision, remains the focus of this chapter, it is necessary to outline briefly some of the other electronic databases not freely available on the Internet which may be of interest to the human rights practitioner, as well as scholars and students.

ELECTRONIC DATABASES

While a number of these are on-line,[18] and the information is accessed using the tools used to access the Internet, access is by subscription only. For others the information is provided on CD-ROM, and regularly updated.

The following are some of the more common electronic databases used in human rights research:

Australian Public Affairs Information Service (APAIS)

APAIS is produced by the National Library of Australia and is a bibliographical database that indexes and abstracts articles from published and unpublished materials.[19] Source documents include a wide range of periodicals, newspapers, scholarly journals, conference papers and books. This is an excellent place to search for articles on human rights law from an Australian perspective. Most law libraries will have this available to users.

---

16 Cooper Ramo, Report, "Executive Forward" to Burgess Allison, G, *The Lawyer's Guide to the Internet* (American Bar Association, Chicago, 1995), p xi. See also Brown Weiss, above n 6, p 69, who observes that information technology is critical to the new international legal system not only because new technologies empower groups other than states to participate in developing and implementing international law, but also because advances in communications technology have made the process governance and the development and implementation of international law much more transparent.

17 McGregor-Lowndes, M and Davidson, A, *The Internet for Lawyers* (Law Book Co, Sydney, 1997), p 1.

18 Used by accessing a database on a remote computer through a modem.

19 Note that only the titles and authors of articles are indexed; the full text of articles is not available.

Attorney-General's Information Service (AGIS)

AGIS is produced by the AGIS Section of the Lionel Murphy Library, Attorney-General's Department, Canberra, and is a bibliographical database that indexes abstracts from published materials on all aspects of law. Source documents include over 120 Australian, New Zealand and Pacific law journals, and selected articles from major law journals from the United States, Canada and the United Kingdom. Like APAIS, most law libraries will have this available to users.

Butterworths

The Butterworths Research Library is provided on CD ROM, and incorporates Halsbury's Laws of Australia, Australian Current Law, Australian Legal Words and Phrases and Federal Statutes Annotations. Legislation and case law may be searched on this CD ROM. The Halsbury's section also has a specific heading on Human Rights – this is identical to the hard copy version available in most law libraries, and useful for an overview of human rights law in Australia.

LEXIS/NEXIS

This is an international, subscription based collection of online legal and news information. It can be accessed through a specific modem line, or via the Internet. It is a very good tool to use to find more obscure information, particularly information from other countries. However subscriptions are expensive.[20]

We can now turn to the main focus of the chapter – namely, available human rights resources on the Internet. What follows is a concise guide to web sites containing legal information on human rights, general human rights web sites, newsgroups and mailing lists.

THE INTERNET

Much more than a passing trend, the Internet has become an important tool in most lawyers' practices. In fact it has already been suggested that a practitioner's duty of "due diligence" includes, or will soon include, a duty to conduct searches of relevant sites on the Internet to ensure that the most relevant and up to date information has been accessed.

This chapter is not intended to provide an introduction to the use of the Internet; there is insufficient space, and a number of useful guides to the Internet for lawyers already exist.[21] Rather this is an overview of some of the more useful Internet resources for practitioner and other individuals with an interest in human rights. Those readers who are already Internet-aware will be able to access the information described, and those who have not yet taken the step will hopefully be inspired to do so after learning what is available.

---

20 See Dayal, S, *Laying Down the Law Online* (Butterworths, Sydney, 1996), Ch 6 for a good introductory guide to the materials available on LEXIS/NEXIS, search techniques and an assessment of the strengths and weaknesses of the database.

21 Ibid; see also McGregor-Lowndes and Davidson, above, n 17.

The Internet has been described as a "limitless virtual library", and this means that, with the necessary technology, material may be accessed by anyone anywhere. Many practitioners and scholars have found that the Internet has truly revolutionised their research, enabling them to access quickly and easily material which was previously difficult, if not impossible, to find in paper form. This is especially true in respect of those areas that have a significant international dimension. Human rights laws are a quintessential example of such an area.

The volume of human rights information on the Internet has increased dramatically in recent years. Today one can find information on almost every aspect of human rights through a countless number of web sites. The Internet not only greatly improves access to human rights materials, it provides those materials in a more useful format. Materials in electronic form enable searching by free text search facilities, which makes finding relevant information far easier.[22]

This chapter attempts to provide the reader with a concise guide to where and how to find relevant material, rather than a "survey of good sites".[23] The following is a list of Internet sites which can assist the reader in finding international legal instruments, including treaties and conventions; decisions by international and regional tribunals; national legislation and case law; reports on human rights violations in specific countries; and information on specific issues, such as children's rights, indigenous issues and women's rights.

Finding international instruments

- ### *The University of Minnesota's Human Rights Library*
  <http://www1.umn.edu/humanrts/>

This site is perhaps the most useful site in matters of international human rights law. It holds full copies of major human rights instruments, such as the *Universal Declaration of Human Rights* (UDHR), the *International Covenant on Civil and Political Rights* (ICCPR), the *International Covenant on Economic, Social and Cultural Rights* (ICESCR), the *Convention on the Elimination of all Forms of Racial Discrimination* (CERD), the *Convention on the Elimination of All Forms of Discrimination against Women* (CEDAW), the *Convention on the Rights of the Child* (CROC); and may be searched by subject matter. This site also contains information on ratification of each instrument and the UN document citation. This is also a good place to browse if unsure whether there is in fact an international

---

22　There are two issues that a researcher using the Internet should be aware of: (i) unlike hard copy materials, anyone can publish information on the Internet. While the materials set out in this chapter are generally from established, authoritative sources, not all information which appears relevant is guaranteed to be accurate or reliable; and (ii) despite the vast amount of information available on the Internet, it does not mean that all information is available on the Internet. It is therefore important to view the Internet not as the only field of research or the sole source of information.

23　A "site" is similar to a particular library or collection of resources on the World Wide Web (WWW) – the network of computer databases which make up the most useful component of what is referred to as the Internet. These have addresses (called Uniform Resource Locators, or URLs), which are used to access the material. Many sites have "links" to other sites which provide relevant information. Note that URLs sometimes change – if this is the case, a site can usually be found by searching for it by name using a general search engine.

instrument dealing with a particular topic. The University of Minnesota site is part of **Project Diana**, a project undertaken by a consortium of academic institutions to create an international archive of human rights legal documents. For a guide to other **Project Diana sites**, see: **<http://diana.law.yale.edu/diana/main/dianasites. shtml>**.

- *The Fletcher School of Law and Diplomacy's Multilaterals Project at Tufts University:*

 <http://www.tufts.edu/departments/fletcher/multi/>

This site also contains a very useful collection of international human rights instruments. This site, however, is not as comprehensive as the University of Minnesota's collection.

- *The Australian Treaty Database:*

 <http://www.austlii.edu.au/au/other/dfat/>

This site is compiled by the Department of Foreign Affairs and Trade and contains full text copies of all international instruments to which Australia is a party, and details of Australia's signature and ratification of each instrument. This is the most reliable on-line source of information on Australia's international obligations, and includes the Australian Treaty Series reference for each document.

- *The United Nations Treaty Collection:*

 <http://www.un.org/Depts/Treaty/>

This United Nations site contains the texts of over 30,000 bilateral and multilateral treaties in their authentic language(s), along with a translation into English and French, as appropriate. Although the site is free, it is registration based and apart from the above, it contains information on the status of all the Multilateral Treaties deposited with the Secretary-General.

Finding United Nations Resolutions

- *The United Nations Site:*

 <http://www.un.org/>

The United Nations site provides full copies of resolutions of the United Nations General Assembly and Security Council. For example, using the search facility provided at the site and entering the terms "violence" and "women", finds the full text of the United Nations *Declaration on the Elimination of Violence Against Women*.[24]

- *United Nations High Commissioner for Human Rights:*

 <http://www.unhchr.ch/>[25]

This site contains resolutions concerning human rights made by other UN bodies, such as the Economic and Social Council, the Commission on Human Rights and Sub-Commission on Protection of Minorities and Prevention of Discrimination.

---

24   United Nations General Assembly Resolution 48/104, 48 UN GAOR Supp (No 49) at 217, UN Doc A/48/49 (1993), passed 20 December 1993.

25   This site is discussed further below.

- *The University of Minnesota's Human Rights Library:*
  <http://www1.umn.edu/humanrts/resolutions/res.html>

The Library contains a comprehensive collection of General Assembly and Security Council resolutions. This site is also equipped by search facilities. The Library also contains resolutions and reports of the United Nations Commission on Human Rights: **<http://www1.umn.edu/humanrts/commission/commission.htm>**.

Finding decisions, reports and other materials of international human rights bodies

There are a number of international bodies charged with the task of overseeing the implementation of international human rights instruments, and ruling on alleged violations of provisions of those instruments. These include the Human Rights Committee which, under the First Optional Protocol to the ICCPR, has jurisdiction to consider communications from persons individuals aiming to be victims of violations of any of the rights contained in the Covenant. Complaints may only be brought against those States which are parties to the Protocol.

Other treaty monitoring bodies include the Committee on the Rights of the Child, which oversees the CROC,[26] the Committee against Torture, which oversees the Convention against Torture and Other Cruel, Inhuman or Degrading Treatment or Punishment (CAT),[27] the Committee on the Elimination of Racial Discrimination, which oversees the CERD,[28] the Committee on the Elimination of Discrimination Against Women, which oversees the CEDAW,[29] and the Committee on Economic, Social and Cultural Rights which oversees the ICESCR.[30]

A number of the monitoring bodies listed above have the power to adjudicate complaints brought by individuals of contravention of the corresponding treaties by States. Some of these bodies have created a substantial jurisprudence on the meaning of the treaties which they oversee, and these decisions may be of use to practitioners, scholars and students in the human rights field.

Until very recently, it was extremely difficult to find copies of decisions of organs of the international human rights system. Through the Internet this material is now easily accessible.

- *Human Rights Committee (HRC):*
  <http://www1.umn.edu/humanrts/hrcommittee/hrc-page.html>

This site contains a list of material from that Committee, including general comments adopted by the HRC; HRC Comments on Country Reports; decisions and views of the HRC; HRC's Annual Reports; rules of Procedure of the Committee; guidelines regarding the form and contents of periodic reports from States Parties, HRC's Programme of Work; and a search facility for locating specific Committee documents.

---

26   Entered into force on 2 September 1990.
27   Entered into force on 26 June 1987.
28   Entered into force on 4 January 1969.
29   Entered into force on 3 September 1981.
30   Entered into force on 3 January 1976.

- *The Australian Human Rights Information Centre (AHRIC):*
  <http://www.austlii.edu.au/ahric/>

This site also provides such information under the headings "UN Human Rights Committee Decisions and Views", "Treaty Bodies" and "Charter Bodies". It provides a link to **Guide to the Optional Protocol <http://www.austlii.edu.au/ ahric/Secondary/booklet/index.html>**. This is an extremely useful resource for those seeking information on taking a matter to the Human Rights Committee under the First Optional Protocol to the ICCPR.

Reports and decisions of some of the other major international bodies can be located by visiting the following sites:

- *Committee Against Torture:*
  <http://www1.umn.edu/humanrts/cat/cat-page.html>

- *Committee on the Elimination of Racial Discrimination:*
  <http://www1.umn.edu/humanrts/country/cerd-page.html>

- *Committee on the Rights of the Child:*
  <http://www1.umn.edu/humanrts/crc/crc-page.html>

- *Committee on Economic, Social and Cultural Rights:*
  <http://www1.umn.edu/humanrts/esc/esc-country.htm>

- *International Labour Organization (ILO):*
  <http://www.ilo.org/>

This site provides the full texts of all ILO Conventions and Reports of the Committee of Experts. In addition to making available information about the ILO in general, the site also has a specific section entitled: ILO Standards and Human Rights. This section contains two very useful databases: one on international labour standards (ILOLEX) and the other on national labour laws (NATLEX). It also contains a monthly bulletin of recent labour legislation at both national and international levels (*Legislative Information*).

Finding other information from UN human rights bodies

- *United Nations High Commissioner for Human Rights (UNCHR):*
  <http://www.unhchr.ch/>

The office of the UNCHR was established in 1993 after the Vienna Conference on Human Rights. The Commissioner's mandate is to oversee and coordinate the human rights work and functions of the different UN institutions and offices.[31]

This site offers information on the United Nations Human Rights Program, the activities of the various United Nations human rights bodies, information of international human rights conferences and meetings, and a summary of the latest developments in the international human rights field. Also available are reports of

---

31   UN GA Res 48/141 (1993)

some of the various UN rapporteurs on human rights, such as the UN Rapporteur on the Former Yugoslavia, and the UN Rapporteur on Religious Intolerance. The collection at this site is by no means comprehensive, but definitely worth visiting.

- **United Nations High Commissioner for Refugees (UNHCR):**
  <http://www.unhcr.ch/>

This site provides a great deal of material on refugee issues.[32] Information available includes resolutions of the Executive Committee of UNHCR, information on the human rights situation in a wide range of countries, and summaries of selected domestic legislation and case law concerning refugee issues from a number of countries. This is a valuable resource for those with an interest in refugee issues.

Finding legal information from other jurisdictions

Although human rights are intended to apply universally, the process of making those rights a reality in domestic law, and protecting and enforcing those rights in individual cases, obviously differs significantly from country to country, and region to region. Unlike Australia, many countries have expressly enshrined certain rights in constitutional instruments,[33] or passed a statutory instrument which comprehensively articulates those rights.[34]

Europe

There are two legal regimes of relevance to human rights in Europe. The first regime centers on the *European Convention on Human Rights* (ECHR) which was established under the auspices of the Council of Europe, and is the predominant source of regional legal obligations in the human rights area imposed on States in Europe. Increasingly however, human rights issues are also being addressed by and through the law of the European Union.

The European Convention on Human Rights

The ECHR,[35] which broadly speaking protects rights first spelt out in the *Universal Declaration of Human Rights*, came into force in 1953. The European Convention is overseen by the European Court of Human Rights and the European Commission of Human Rights. Decisions of these bodies may provide useful guidance on the substance of aspects of international human rights law to the Australian legal practitioners. A copy of the Convention and its Protocols is accessible at the European Court of Human Rights site: **<http://www.dhcour.coe.fr/default.htm>**

---

32   This material is also provided in CD ROM form, known as RefWorld. The CD ROM version is updated regularly and is usually more up to date than the online version.

33   Canada and the United States are obvious examples.

34   New Zealand's *Bill of Rights Act* 1990 is one example. See Joseph, P, "The New Zealand Bill of Rights" (1996) 7 *Public Law Review* 162.

35   On which, see generally Harris, DJ, O'Boyle, M and Warbrick, C, *Law of the European Convention on Human Rights* (Butterworths, London, 1995).

Decisions of the European Court of Human Rights

- **European Court of Human Rights:**
  <http://www.dhcour.coe.fr/eng/Judgments.htm>

This site lists all judgments of the European Court of Human Rights, and provides access to the full text versions of recent judgments. It also provides general background information on the Court.

- **European Commission of Human Rights:**
  <http://www.dhcommhr.coe.fr/>

A full list of all decisions of the European Commission of Human Rights and the full texts of recent decisions are provided at this site. It must be noted that with the entry into force of Protocol No 11 to the ECHR on 1 November 1998, the Commission will be abolished as part of a radical reform of the Convention machinery. The present Commission and Court will be replaced by a single, permanent European Court of Human Rights.

It would appear that this site will, for the time being at least, remain in existence allowing continued access to the enormous and influential body of Commission jurisprudence.

European Union

As stated above, the European Union (EU), as established by the Treaty on European Union (TEU) 1993, expressly recognised the human rights provisions of the ECHR. Furthermore, the principal judicial organ of the European Community legal order (which constitutes the core of the EU), the European Court of Justice, has addressed human rights matters in a number of recent decisions, and commentators have stated that "the principle of protection of fundamental rights has [now] been firmly established by the case law of the European Court of Justice".[36]

- **The European Court of Justice:**
  <http://europa.eu.int/cj/en/index.htm>.

This site contains full text versions of decisions of the Court since mid 1997.

European Union material, including decisions of the European Court of Justice is also available, for a fee, at the **CELEX** site **<http://europa.eu.int/celex/>**. Some European Union legislation, decisions and other material, however, should be freely available at **<http://europ.eu.int>** before the end of 1998. The above materials can also be accessed through **LEXIS/NEXIS**, in the European Union section of the International Law library.[37]

---

36 Betten, L and MacDevitt, D, *The Protection of Fundamental Social Rights in the European Union* (Kluwer Law International, London, 1996).

37 As stated above, see Dayal, above n 20, Ch 6 for a good introductory guide to the materials available on LEXIS/NEXIS, search techniques and an assessment of the strengths and weaknesses of the database

Americas

- **Inter-American Court of Human Rights:**
  <http://www1.umn.edu/humanrts/iachr/iachr.html>

The Inter-American Court of Human Rights was established in 1979 and is an autonomous judicial institution whose purpose is the application and interpretation of the *American Convention on Human Rights*. The site provides vital information on the Court, including general information about the Court; basic documents relevant to the Court; the text of the *American Convention on Human Rights*; Statute of the Court; rules of procedure of the Court; case-law and advisory opinions and resolutions (procedural aspects). For jurisprudence of the Inter-American Commission on Human Rights see:

  <http://www1.umn.edu/humanrts/cases/commissn.htm>

Finding materials on specific countries

Canada

Canadian domestic law has been greatly influenced by the *Canadian Charter of Rights and Freedoms* 1982 and the *Canadian Bill of Rights* 1960.[38] These documents contain expressions of human rights in many ways similar to those enshrined in international human rights instruments. Decisions of Canadian courts concerning the Charter of Rights and Freedoms in particular may be of interest to practitioners and scholars in the human rights field in Australia.

- **Canadian Legal Resources on WWW:**
  <http://www.mbnet.mb.ca/~psim/can_law.html>.

This is the first place to look for Canadian legal material. The site provides a comprehensive index thorough which the visitor can access a comprehensive range of information, including Canadian legislation, Canadian case law, information on human rights and civil rights associations and institutes, Government, Law Reform Commissions and newsletters.

Another definitive source for Canadian law and justice information on the Internet is **Access to Justice Network (ACJNet): <http://www.acjnet.org/>**. This site is also highly recommended by the authors for research into Canadian jurisprudence.

- **Charter of Rights Decisions by the Supreme Court of Canada:**
  <http://canada.justice.gc.ca/Publications/CCDL/index_en.html>

This site contains a collection of decisions of the Canadian Supreme Court on the Canadian Charter of Rights collated by the Department of Justice. All **Supreme Court of Canada** decisions since 1989 can be located at a web site maintained by the University of Montreal: **<http://www.droit.umontreal.ca/doc/csc-scc/en/>**

---

38   See Berlin, ML and Pentney, WF, *Human Rights and Freedoms in Canada: Case Notes and Materials* (Butterworths, Toronto, 1987), paras 2-10 – 2-16

Decisions of the **Federal Court of Canada** are also available at:

<http://www.fja-cmf.gc.ca/en/cf/decisions.html>

United States

The United States *Bill of Rights*,[39] as part of the Constitution, is placed at the centre of the jurisprudence of the United States Supreme Court. While there are clear differences in Australian and United States concepts and interpretations of rights,[40] some US precedent can be of significant use to Australian lawyers.[41]

- *The MetaIndex for US Legal Research:*
  <http://gsulaw.gsu.edu/metaindex/>

This site includes links to most of the searchable legal sites in the US and is a good starting point for searches for US material. Decisions of the Federal Courts of Appeals (the Circuit Courts) are also available in full text.

- *The American Civil Liberties Union (ACLU):*
  <http://www.aclu.org/>

The ACLU has taken many cases on *Bill of Rights* issues to the courts, particularly in relation to alleged violations of free speech. The site contains an enormous amount of information about such cases, as well as the *Bill of Rights* generally.

- *FindLaw's Supreme Court Database:*
  <http://www.findlaw.com/casecode/supreme.html>

This site contains full texts of all US Supreme Court decisions since 1893. By using the search facility provided and entering the term "flag burning", for example, the decision of *United States v Eichman* 496 US 310 (1990) is retrieved, where the court held that a Texas statute which aimed to criminalise the desecration of the flag was unconstitutional, being contrary to the First Amendment right to freedom of expression.

Copies of US Federal and State legislation are available at the **US House of Representatives Internet Law Library** <http://law.house.gov/>.

South Africa

- *Centre for Applied Legal Studies, Wits University:*
  <http://www.law.wits.ac.za/>

This is the principal South African site in relation to legal and human rights matters and materials. The site contains full text versions of decisions of the Constitutional

---

39 The *Bill of Rights* is accessible through the US House of Representatives Internet Law Library <http://www1.pls.com:8001.his.1.htm>. This site has copies of US laws at Federal and State level. See also <gopher://ucsbuxa.ucsb.edu:3001/11/.stacks/.historical>.

40 Rich, W, "Converging Constitutions" (1993) 21 *Federal Law Review* 203.

41 For example, in the "free speech cases", *Australian Capital Television Pty Ltd v Commonwealth* (1992) 177 CLR 106 and *Nationwide News Pty Limited v Wills* (1992) 177 CLR 1, the High Court made extensive reference to US jurisprudence. See further, Ch 2 by Sir Anthony Mason, and Ch 3 by Gageler and Glass, in this volume.

Court, including those relating to the new South African Bill of Rights 1996, the Land Claims Court of South Africa and the Labour Courts of South Africa, and material from the South African Law Reform Commission. This is also linked to the South African Government Index **<http://www.polity.org.za/gnuindex.html>** which has full text versions of most national legislation since 1993, including the new Constitution as signed into law on 10 December 1996 .

United Kingdom

- *New UK Official Publications Online – Main Index:*
  <http://www.official-documents.co.uk/menu/uk.htm>

There is a notable lack of legal sites for the UK which are human rights specific though this is bound to change with the passage of the *Human Right Act* 1998. However, through the above site, a researcher can access full text versions of Acts of Parliament, judgments of the House of Lords and publications of and information about the Lord Chancellor's Department. A researcher can also access general legal materials by visiting the following sites:

- *UK Government Functional Index – Law:*
  <http://www.open.gov.uk/index/filaw.htm>

This site provides general information on law and legal services in England and Wales. Statutes, regulations, Hansard, official publications and parliamentary papers may also be located at **House of Commons – Publications on the Net: <http://www.parliament.the-stationary-office.co.uk/pa/cm/cmpubns.htm>** and **Her Majesty's Stationery Office: http://www.hmso.gov.uk/.**

Other countries

The constitutions and laws of many other countries are also available on the Internet. The following sites provide country-specific information :

- *The United States House of Representatives Internet Law Library:*
  <http://law.house.gov/>

This has an extensive collection of documents for a large number of countries, compiled under the heading "laws of other countries".

- *ForInt Law:*
  <http://lawlib.wuacc.edu/forint/forintmain.html>

This site is hosted by the Washburn University Law School in the US, and provides access to a wide range of legal material from many countries. It is categorised under country and subject.

The above mentioned sites may be of particular use to those practitioners preparing cases for refugee applicants and seeking relevant legal and other materials from their client's country of origin.

Finding general human rights information and materials from international NGOs

- *Derechos:*
    <http://www.derechos.org/>

Derechos is a major human rights site, and a good place to start for those interested in human rights internationally. It contains information on human rights situations around the world, and many useful links to other human rights organisations worldwide.

- *University of Minnesota's Human Rights Library:*
    <http://www1.umn.edu/humanrts/>

As noted earlier, this site has a comprehensive collection of links to local, national, regional and international non-government organisations.

- *Human Rights Internet (HRI):*
    <http://www.hri.ca/>

HRI is an NGO dedicated to the exchange of information within the worldwide. HRI's primary role is to serve as a documentation centre for the information needs of international scholars, human rights activists and lawyers. The HRI web site contains information on a range of human rights issues including children's rights and international criminal law.

- *International Law and Human Rights site at the University of Maastricht:*
    <http://doddel.cs.unimaas.nl/>

This site contains a comprehensive list of links to human rights NGOs, as well as many useful links to international organisations and international human rights instruments (including rules of procedure for some of the United Nations human rights bodies).

- *Amnesty International:*
    <http://www.amnesty.org/>

This site has information on Amnesty's activities and campaigns, and copies of their news releases and country reports. The Australian section of Amnesty International is accessible at **<http://www.amnesty.org.au/>**.

- *Human Rights Watch:*
    <http://www.hrw.org/>

The site has background information on the organisation, regional activities, copies of reports and updates on campaigns.

AUSTRALIAN MATERIALS ON HUMAN RIGHTS

Australia is leading the world in ensuring that domestic and international legal materials are freely available on the Internet.[42] All legal practitioners using the

---

42   Sinclair, J, "The Internet Comes of Age" (1996) 31(8) *Australian Lawyer* 18 at 19.

Internet will be aware of the AUSTLII and Foundation Law sites, and all those not yet using the Internet should commence doing so immediately if only to be able to access these resources.

- *AUSTLII:*
  <http://www.austlii.edu.au/>

This site provides the full texts of all Commonwealth legislation and some State legislation, and decisions (reported and unreported) of the principal Australian superior courts (Commonwealth and State) and most tribunals. A substantial volume of useful secondary legal material is also accessible.

- *Foundation Law:*
  <http://www.fl.asn.au/>

This the site established by the Law Foundation of NSW. The Law Foundation has provided considerable support to AUSTLII, and has "added value" to the primary materials on AUSTLII by organising them into practice collections.

It is not an overstatement to say that both these resources are revolutionising legal practice in Australia. The resources are useful for any area of legal practice, not least where human rights issues are raised or might be raised.

Finding legislation

- *Human Rights and Discrimination Practice Collection provided by FOUNDATION LAW:*
  <http://www1.fl.asn.au/practice/hr.html>

This site is probably the best place to start if Commonwealth or New South Wales "human rights" legislation is sought . The Commonwealth legislation listed includes the *Disability Discrimination Act* 1992, *Human Rights (Sexual Conduct) Act* 1994, *Human Rights and Equal Opportunity Commission Act* 1986, *Privacy Act* 1988, *Racial Discrimination Act* 1975, and the *Sex Discrimination Act* 1984.

- *AUSTLII:*
  <http://www.austlii.edu.au/>

As noted above, AUSTLII provides full text of all Commonwealth legislation and the legislation of most States. The SINO search engine provided by AUSTLII can be used to find legislation on a particular topic.

The noteup function[43] on the AUSTLII site allows the user to establish whether a particular section of a piece of legislation has been considered in case law. When viewing s 6 of the *Sex Discrimination Act* 1984 (Cth), which relates to discrimination on the basis of marital status, use of the note up function establishes that the section was considered by the High Court in a number of decisions including *Victoria v Commonwealth* (1997) 187 CLR 416.

---

43   Used by clicking on the "noteup" button on the button bar at the top of the screen.

Finding case law

- *AUSTLII:*
  <http://www.austlii.edu.au/>

AUSTLII provides full text of the decisions of an extensive, but not completely comprehensive, range of courts and tribunals. Both reported and unreported court decisions are available.

Commonwealth case law includes High Court decisions since 1947, Federal Court decisions since 1977, decisions of the Human Rights and Equal Opportunity Commission, the Commonwealth Administrative Appeals Tribunal and the Refugee Review Tribunal. State case law includes some decisions of the Supreme Courts of New South Wales, Tasmania, Northern Territory and South Australia. This material is often available on the day of judgment or decision.

All case law can be searched using the SINO search engine on the site. By taking the option to "search all AUSTLII databases"[44] and entering key words and terms, the search engine finds the decisions in which the key words or terms have been used.

Finding secondary materials on human rights in Australia

- *The Commonwealth Parliament:*
  <http://www.aph.gov.au/>

This site provides a list of Commonwealth government departments with links to their web-sites. Through this page it is also possible to access the latest press releases from the office of the Minister for Immigration and Multicultural Affairs,[45] search recent copies of Hansard for references to sex discrimination laws,[46] find out details of the terms of reference of the most recent study of the House of Representatives Committee on Legal and Constitutional Affairs,[47] or read a report of the Australian Law Reform Commission.[48] This requires a little patience and a strong clicking finger to search through the index of resources.

- *Human Rights and Equal Opportunity Commission (HREOC):*
  <http://www.austlii.edu.au/hreoc>

The HREOC site is an extremely useful one for the practitioner and student. Information on the area of work of each of the Commissioners as well as a list, and in some cases the full texts, of the Commission's publications are available at this site. A full text version of the *Bringing them home* Report of the National Inquiry into the Separation of Aboriginal and Torres Strait Islander Children from their families is also available: **<http://www.austlii.edu.au/au/special/rsjproject/ rsjlibrary/hreoc/stolen/>**

---

44 Note that by using AUSTLII's SINO search engine in this way all AUSTLII databases are used, and so both case law and legislation containing the term is retrieved.
45 <http://www1.immi.gov.au/minrel/index98.htm>
46 <http://www1.aph.gov.au/>
47 <http://www1.aph.gov.au/house/committe/laca/index.htm>
48 <http://uniserve.edu.au/alrc/ALRCReports.html>

- **Refugee Review Tribunal (RRT):**
  <http://www.austlii.edu.au/au/other/rrt/>

The site contains all the Tribunal's decisions (over 10,000) in full and the visitor is aided by a search facility.[49] Copies of the Tribunal's monthly Decisions Bulletin, which provides summaries of some Tribunal decisions and all significant court decisions on refugee determination, information on making an application to the Tribunal and the Tribunal's rules and procedures. are also available at this site.

- **Council for Aboriginal Reconciliation:**
  <http://www.austlii.edu.au/car/>

This site contains a Reconciliation and Social Justice Library with useful material on the human rights of Aboriginal and Torres Strait Islander people and the reconciliation process. Material made available includes the *Report of the Royal Commission into Aboriginal Deaths in Custody*: **<http://www.austlii.edu. au/au/rsjproject/rsjlibrary/rciadic/>**.

- **The Australian Human Rights Information Centre:**
  <http://www.austlii.edu.au/ahric/>

This site which is based at the University of New South Wales is a very useful resource for any human rights lawyer. The site is a good place to follow current developments, whether domestic or international, that affect human rights law in Australia. In addition, copies of the monthly publication, the *Human Rights Defender*, are available, as well as information on the *Australian Journal of Human Rights*.

OTHER RESOURCES

Although this chapter has looked at a range of material available on the Internet, it has thus far considered only sites on the World Wide Web – the more passive side of the Internet. The Internet also has another dimension – as a tool of active communication. This can be done through one to one communication by e-mail or through group communication; newsgroups and mailing lists. A newsgroup deals with one issue, and participants post messages concerning that topic to a central computer file for access by anyone.[50] These are not monitored, and so there is no control on the content posted. Many people do not bother with newsgroups as they are not as user-friendly as other methods of obtaining information and electronic communication.

We would, however, like to mention briefly two useful other resources: mailing lists and electronic news subscriptions.

---

49 The RRT is the only refugee determination body in the world to have put all its decisions on the Internet.

50 McGregor-Lowndes and Davidson, above n 17, p 9.

Mailing lists

A mailing list (or listserv) distributes messages to a group of people who have subscribed to that list. These are often monitored, and can be an invaluable source of information for the interested lawyer. A member of a list may ask a question of the whole list; another member will often provide an answer.

Many practitioners, academics, activists and students are finding lists a useful tool in their work. A question can be sent to a relevant list, and invariably someone will come up with an answer. Often a debate will be generated on the topic raised. A member of a list may send out a message such as: "I am looking for a 1993 decision of the Human Rights and Equal Opportunity Commission dealing with unfair dismissal of a pregnant employee from a Queensland University. Can anyone help?"; someone usually will. Obviously lists work most effectively when list members assist each other and share information freely. The rise of legal lists not only provides a useful tool for practitioners in many areas of law: they may also be a basis for the formation of a true "legal community".

- **<http://www.lib.uchicago.edu/~llou/lawlists/international.html>**

Maintained by Lyonette Louis-Jaques, Foreign and International Law Librarian at the University of Chicago Law School, is probably one of the best collections of law related lists.

- *INT-LAW*

This is a very active list for discussion of all sorts of international law issues, although its main focus is as a forum for discussion on accessing materials. International human rights law is a major focus of discussion. To join the list, send an e-mail message to: **majordomo@listhost.ciesin.orgHYPERLINK** with the text of the message: "subscribe INT-LAW [your name]".[51]

- *Asylum law*

This is another useful list for those with an interest in refugee law, and can be joined by sending an e-mail message to: **asylum-l@ufsia.ac.be** with message stating: "subscribe-l".

- *First Class Law:*
    <http://www.fl.asn.au/discussion/welcome.html#public>

This is a discussion group facility set up by the Law Foundation of New South Wales. There is a list on human rights issues.

- *Derechos Human Rights Mailing Lists:*
    <http://www.derechos.org/human-rights/maj-lists.html>

This is another useful mailing list.

News

There are countless number of news resources on line. These include magazines, journals, newspapers, radio programs, newsletters and many more. Listing all the

---

51 Note – do not type in the quotation marks for any of these messages.

human rights news providers on line is beyond the scope of this chapter. However, the following is a brief list of the most regular and easy to access human rights news and information.

- **Amnesty International**

A researcher or activist can send an e-mail message to: **majordomo@io.org** with the text of the message: "subscribe amnestyL" to receive news and press releases regularly from Amnesty International.

- **Human Rights Watch**

Human Rights Watch also provides news and press releases regularly for its subscribers. To subscribe, send an e-mail message to: **majordomo@igc.apc.org** with the text of the message: "subscribe hrwnews".

CONCLUSION

The Internet and other electronic databases and resources have made a vast body of information available and accessible for those with an interest in human rights law. This constitutes a great resource for lawyers and others to use in human rights advocacy and/or education.

It is true that the reach of human rights may yet be short of being universal in practice, no matter what is the theory.[52] However one of the traditional impediments to such universality – namely, the accessibility of human rights jurisprudence to lawyers for use in legal practice, law reform or policy making – is far less of an obstacle today. New opportunities are now open to all involved in the law. As a result, it is clear that arguments based on human rights law will be employed more frequently by our law-makers and in our courts, and the jurisprudence will develop accordingly. Lawyers will be both agents and subjects of these changes.

---

52   See, further, Ch 1 by Kinley in this volume.

INDEX

Aboriginal
see also Land rights
Aboriginal Protection Board, 42
children, rights of, 116-119, 191
criminal justice, 110ff
Anunga rules, 111-112
cultural rights, 110-113
discrimination in, 113-114
indigenous law extinguished, 96-97,
110
sentencing, 113
cultural and intellectual property rights,
106-108
held communally, 107
Australian copyright law, and, 107-
108
custody, deaths in, 114
customary marriage, 115-116
equality rights, 100-103, 197
hunting, fishing and gathering rights, 108-
110
Indigenous common law, 93-97, 106
international community and, 119
land rights, *see* Land rights
self-determination, right to, 98
sui generis rights, 95-96
Administrative law
see also Environmental law; Criminal law;
Privacy
executive discretions, 71-78
government information, access to, 67-69,
71, 230
human rights principles and, 88-90
individual rights, 70
legitimate expectation, 82-88, 151
natural justice, doctrine of, 82-83, 327
power of administrative government, 63
right to administrative justice, 9, 63-70
right to judicial review, 64, 66-67, 71ff,
137-140, 332-334
Affirmative action, 100
Anti-discrimination law, 8, 27, 45, 185-186,
194
see also Affirmative action; Labour law
actions in tort, 316
conciliation processes, 302-306
court proceedings, 309-310, 325
forum, choice of, 299
direct discrimination, 197-199
disability discrimination, 199-201
domestic law, 196-197, 296-302, 318
complainant, 301
hearings, 306-309
indirect discrimination, 197-199, 310, 318
international instruments, 294-296, 318
natural justice, 313-314

racial discrimination, 196-197, 294
sexual discrimination, 196-198, 201, 294,
311
workplace agreements and, 215-216
sexual harassment, 201-202, 301
unreasonableness, criterion of, 312-313
Asian value system, 5
Assembly, freedom of, 51
Association, freedom of, 51
see also Labour law
Asylum seekers, *see* Refugees and asylum
seekers
Australia
see also Constitution; International instruments
Bill of Rights, 27, 29, 47, 63, 88, 319, 341
international law and, 9, 26, 30, 43, 46, 48,
75, 83-88, 320, 328, 341-342
sources of human rights law, 27-31, 48
Australian Law Reform Commission, 54
Bangalore Principles, 329
Canada, 1, 8, 26, 45, 96, 99, 121, 130-132,
202, 224
Charter of Rights, 11, 45
Indigenous Indians, 103-104
China, 26
Censorship, *see* Information technology;
Speech and expression
Children, 63, 172
domestic law, 176-180
immigrants and refugees, as, 150-151
rights of, 174-175, 182-185, 279
Common law and human rights, 2ff, 45-46, 69,
327-332
see also International instruments
domestic law, 176-180
fair trial, right to, 45, 54-56, 120-124, 251
High Court, development by, 46
international law and, 48, 329
legal representation, right to, 45, 48
Constitution, Australian
acquisition of property 33-34, 52, 100-101
assembly, freedom of, 51
association, freedom of, 51, 338
conciliation and arbitration power, 204
discrimination against residents of States,
protection against, 35, 52-53, 59
due process rights, 54-56
express provisions, 36
external affairs power, 28, 29
freedom of communication on matters of
government and politics, 37-41, 49-
51, 59, 69
freedom of interstate trade, 34, 57
freedom of movement, 57, 59
freedom of religion, 34, 49, 59, 338

Constitution, Australia (*cont*)
  fundamental rights, doctrine of, 43
  human rights protections, 27ff, 47ff, 78-82
  implied human rights guarantees, 29, 36-43, 48, 338
  implied right of equality, 53
  judicial power, exercise of, 29, 31, 47-48
  race power, 44, 101-103
  responsible government, doctrine of, 48, 50
  rule of law, 31, 48, 67
  separation of powers, 28, 29, 31, 48
  States, reference of power by, 56
  Territories, 57-58
  trial by jury, 33, 56, 58
  voting rights, 32, 51
Constitutions, States
  criminal law and, 56
  limitations, 47, 62
Convention on the Elimination of All Forms of Discrimination Against Women (CEDAW) *see* United Nations
Convention on the Rights of the Child, *see* United Nations
Corporations, 11, 12
Copyright, *see* Information technology
Counsel, right to, *see* Trial
Criminal law
  see also Police; Prisoners; Trial
  Aboriginals and, *see* Aboriginals
  evidence
    exclusion of unlawfully obtained, 128
    exclusion on public policy grounds, 132-136
  immigration and, 150-154
  international instruments, 329
  judicial review and, 137-140
  legal representation, right to, 45, 48
    due process rights, 54-56
  punishments, cruel and unusual, 55
Defamation
  common law at, 40, 50
  defences, 39-41
  freedom of speech, impact on, 50
  implied freedom of communication, 37-41
  malice, 41
  qualified privilege, 40-41
Disabilities, 75-76, 191-192, 199-201, 279-281, 290, 312
  rights of mentally ill, 285-289
Discrimination, *see* Anti-discrimination law
Elections, *see* Voting rights
Employment, *see* Labour law
Environmental law
  administration of pollution laws, 228-229
  appeals, 233-235
  domestic law, 227-228, 241-242
  enforcement of, 235-239
    costs awards, 239-240
  environmental protection, 221-224, 240
  public participation, 229, 231-233

substantive rights, 224, 230
sustainable development, concept of, 225-227
Equal opportunity, *see* Anti-discrimination law
Europe, 163, 249, 251
  European Convention on Human Rights (ECHR), 12-13, 64, 67, 74, 121, 126
  European Court of Human Rights, 11, 120, 122, 127, 138, 328
Expression, freedom of, *see* Speech and expression
Family law
  see also Children; Disabilities
  domestic law, 172, 175, 192-193
  history, 169-171
  international instruments, 171-174, 180-182, 192-193
  racial equality, 190
  right to found a family, 171
  right to marry, 171, 173, 175
  sexuality, 188-190
  substantive equality, 186-188
Feminism, 6, 169
  see also Women
Government, *see* Administrative law
Health law
  see also Disability
  consent to treatment, 276-279
  domestic law, 275
  international instruments, 272-275, 290
  medical records, access to, 283-285
  public health, 269-271
    HIV/AIDS, 270-271
  reproductive rights, 282-285
  sterilisation, 279-282
High Court
  see also Constitution
  consent to treatment, 276-279
  domestic law, 275
  international instruments, 272-275, 290
  medical records, access to, 283-285
  original jurisdiction, 60, 66-67
  procedures in constitutional litigation, 60-62
  reproductive rights, 282-283
  sterilisation, 279-282
Homosexuality, 188-190, 270
Hong Kong, 26
Human Rights
  see also Constitution; International instruments; Judiciary; Rights
  definition of, 2ff
  duties and, 7-8
  group rights, 10-11, 16, 338-339
  human dignity, 280-281
  legal dimension of, 2ff
  moral right as, 4
  proportionality, 59-60
  substantive, 8-12
  universality of, 4-7

Human Rights and Equal Opportunity Commission, 27, 184, 331, 339
  see also Anti-discrimination law
  enforcement of anti-discrimination laws, 27
Immigration
  see also Refugees and asylum seekers
  criminality, 150-154
  disability, 75-76
  domestic law, 146-148
  family migration, 148-154
  international instruments, 144-146, 167-168
  nationality, right to, 143-144
Implied guarantees, see Constitution, Australian
India, 45
Individual rights, see Administrative law
Industrial Relations Commission, 37, 49
Information technology
  see also Privacy
  censorship, 250
  development of rights, 243-246, 265-266
  freedom of speech, right to, 252
  government controls on, 256-257
  intellectual property rights, 246-250
  right to reproduce, 253-257
International Court of Justice, 12
International Convention for the Elimination of All Forms of Racial Discrimination (CERD), see United Nations
International Covenant on Civil and Political Rights (ICCPR), see United Nations
International Covenant on Economic, Social and Cultural Rights (ICESCR), see United Nations
International instruments, 8, 30, 345
  see also Aboriginals, Common law, Human rights; United Nations
  administrative law and, 332-334
  application in domestic litigation, 334-339
  common law, 327-332
  domestic law and, 8, 319-320
  remedies, 340-341, 345
  statutory interpretation and, 321-326
  treaty interpretations, 322-323
International Labour Organisation (ILO), 97, 100, 106, 194, 203, 205-206, 208-212, 216, 218-220
International law
  see also Australia
  domestic law and, 330-332
  criminal justice and, 139-140, 329
  indigenous peoples and, 97
  rights jurisprudence, role of, 46
Interpreter, right to, 55
  Aboriginals, 111-112
Ireland, 45
Judiciary
  see also Constitution
  development of human rights and, 26ff

international jurisprudence obligations, 134
judicial activism, 55
judicial discretion, 330
judicial independence, 56
"margin of appreciation", 13, 59
Labour law
  see also Trade unions
  domestic industrial action, 217-219
  employment, 8
  freedom of association, 194, 208-210
  international instruments, 194, 219-220
  non-discrimination, 195-196, 315
    see also Anti-discrimination law
  right to bargain collectively, 194-195, 211-216
  right to equal remuneration, 203-205
  right to organise, 194, 208-210
  right to strike, 194, 216-217
  wage fixation, 203
  Workplace Agreements, 211-216
Land rights
  common law, at, 29
  customary international law and, 336
  international obligations, 100-103
  Northern Territory legislation, 105
  procedural fairness, 102
  race power, 101
  regional agreements, 99-100
  South Australian legislation, 44
Law
  see also Human rights
  enforcement of, see Legal sanction
  international law and, 30
  judicial interpretation and, 3, 20-22
  legislative statement, 3, 18-20
  social context and, 3, 24-25
Legal aid, 342
Legal equality, doctrine of, 42
Legal positivism, 17
Legal representation, right to, 45, 48, 329
  due process rights, 54-56
Legal sanction, 3, 22-24
Libel, see Defamation
Malaysia, 251
Marriage, see Family law
Medical law, see Health law
Meetings, see Assembly, freedom of
Moral rights, see Human rights
Natural justice, see Administrative law
Natural law theory, 5
New Zealand, 8, 26, 27, 74-75, 212, 267, 273-74
Nigeria, 222
Parliament
  presumption to legislate according to international obligations, 324
Police
  arrest, powers of 137
  bail, 55
  confessional evidence, 128
  investigations, 54, 136-137

Press, freedom of, *see* Speech and expression
Prisoners, *see* Criminal law
Privacy, right of
    common law, 251
    statute, by, 68-69, 78
    information technology and, 257-262
    security and technology, 263-265
    surveillance and technology, 262
Procedural rights, *see* Administrative law
Protest, right of, *see* Assembly, freedom of
Racial discrimination, *see* Anti-discrimination
Refugees and asylum seekers
    Australian procedures, 161
    Convention on the Status of Refugees, 44,
        154-155, 157, 163, 165, 322
    detention, 158-160
    determination of status, 155, 161
    international standards, 155, 163
    persecution, fear of, 156
    principle of safe third country, 162-166
    right to asylum, 145-146
    right to procedural fairness, 161-162
    rights of, 154, 157-158
    temporary protection, 159, 163
    United Nations Commissioner for
        Refugees, 154
Religion, *see* Constitution
Remedies, *see* International instruments
Research
    electronic, 345-347
    internet, use of in, 347ff
    lawyers and, 343-345
Rights, 4, 6, 9, 15-16
    see also Australia, Constitution, Human
        rights
    breach afford individual complaint, 328
    civil and political, 9
    economic, social and cultural, 9-10, 67
    justice and, 17
    legal entities, 11
    limitation of, grounds for, 13
    procedural rights, *see* Administrative law
Rule of law, 6, 31, 48, 67
Sex discrimination, *see* Anti-discrimination
    law
Singapore, 251
Speech and expression, freedom of
    see also Censorship; Contempt of court;
        Defamation; Information technology
    freedom of expression, 67, 250-252, 335
    historical background, 50
Spycatcher case, 69, 252
South Africa, 9-11, 273
States, Australian, *see* Constitutions, States
Statutory interpretation, *see* Administrative
    law

Strikes, *see* Labour law
Trade unions, 11, 12, 206-212
    see also Labour law
    minimum membership requirement, 209
    right of entry, 210-211
Trial of accused
    see also Criminal law
    confessions, admission of, 128
    fairness of, 128-129, 132, 136
    hearsay evidence, 129-130
    interpreter, right to, 55
    jury, by, 33, 56, 58
    presumption of innocence, 126
    privilege against self-incrimination, 127-
        129
    prosecution disclosure, 130-132
    right to fair trial, 45, 54-56, 120-124, 251,
        329
    right to silence, 124-129
    right to speedy trial, 55, 330
United Kingdom, 26, 74-75, 126, 163, 267,
    311
United Nations
    Convention on the Elimination of All
        Forms of Discrimination Against
        Women (CEDAW), 13, 173, 201,
        272, 282, 294
    Convention for the Elimination of All
        Forms of Racial Discrimination
        (CERD), 13, 27, 28, 100-102, 104,
        114, 173, 272, 294, 340
    Convention on the Rights of the Child
        (CROC), 30, 114, 116, 170, 174-179,
        183-185, 189, 191, 272, 326
    Convention on the Status of Refugees, 44,
        154-155, 157, 163
    International Covenant on Civil and
        Political Rights (ICCPR), 12, 13, 27,
        28, 45, 98, 102-103, 105, 108, 113-
        114, 118, 120-121, 124, 130, 134,
        136, 139, 144-6, 158, 159, 163, 170,
        172, 175, 184, 187, 189, 194, 206,
        236, 250-251, 272, 282, 294, 296,
        319, 326-328, 340
    International Covenant on Economic,
        Social and Cultural Rights (ICESCR),
        12, 98, 103, 108, 146, 173, 195, 199,
        206, 216, 294
United States, 8, 11, 26, 45, 249, 277, 311
Voting rights, *see* Constitution
Women
    see also Labour law
    gendered disparities, 6-7
    marriage, equal status, 173-174
    right to equal remuneration, 203-205
    sexual harassment, 201-202